TAKING Haiti

TAKING Haiti

Military Occupation and the Culture
of U.S. Imperialism, 1915–1940

MARY A. RENDA

The University of North Carolina Press

Chapel Hill & London

© 2001

The University of North Carolina Press

All rights reserved

Set in New Baskerville and Franklin Gothic

by Keystone Typesetting, Inc.

Manufactured in the United States of America

The paper in this book meets the guidelines for permanence and
durability of the Committee on Production Guidelines for Book Longevity
of the Council on Library Resources.

Library of Congress Cataloging-in-Publication Data

Renda, Mary A.

Taking Haiti : military occupation and the culture of U.S. imperialism,

1915–1940 / Mary A. Renda.

p. cm.

Includes bibliographical references (p.   ) and index.

ISBN 0-8078-2628-6 (cloth: alk. paper)

ISBN 0-8078-4938-3 (pbk.: alk. paper)

1. Haiti — History — American occupation, 1915–1934. 2. Haiti —
History — 1934–1986. 3. United States — Armed Forces — Haiti
— History. 4. Haiti — Relations — United States. 5. United States —
Relations — Haiti. I. Title.

F1927.R56 2001

972.94'05 — dc21   00-048926

05   04   03   02   01   5   4   3   2   1

To my parents,

Lucy P. Avenoso Renda

and

Rosario J. Renda

CONTENTS

Acknowledgments *xi*

Note on Usage *xvii*

Prologue *3*

Chapter 1. Introduction *10*

PART I. OCCUPATION

Chapter 2. Haiti and the Marines *39*

Chapter 3. Paternalism *89*

Chapter 4. Moral Breakdown *131*

PART II. AFTERMATH

Chapter 5. Haiti's Appeal *185*

Chapter 6. Mapping Memory and Desire *229*

Chapter 7. Race, Revolution, and National Identity *261*

Conclusion *301*

Notes *309*

Bibliography *365*

Index *391*

FIGURES AND MAPS

FIGURES

1. "The Missionary," a cartoon by Private Paul Woyshner *14*

2. Dartiguenave, center, and his cabinet, flanked by marines *32*

3. Portrait of Homer L. Overley, 1920 *40*

4. Homer L. Overley and fellow marines pose in the field *41*

5. Postcard sent home from Haiti by F. W. Schmidt *57*

6. Marines in barracks, Port-au-Prince *68*

7. Marines at leisure in Haiti *71*

8. Marine with Haitian woman *87*

9. Smedley Butler with his family *102*

10. "A Civilian before Military training and after" *121*

11. Caco leader: Valerius Pierre *152*

12. Unidentified Caco leader *153*

13. Marines with prisoner *157*

14. Faustin Wirkus with Haitian man *168*

15. Faustin Wirkus with Haitian woman *169*

16. Herman Hanneken and William Button *172*

17. The body of Charlemagne Péralte *174*

18. Charles Gilpin as the Emperor Jones *199*

19. Aaron Douglas, Untitled. Illustration for *The Emperor Jones* *201*

20. Aaron Douglas, *Forest Fear*. Illustration for *The Emperor Jones* *202*

21. Puppet production of *The Emperor Jones* *208*

22. Captain John Houston Craige posing with drums *214*

23. Mahlon Blaine's cover for *Black Majesty* *218*

24. Colombian Line, "Cruise the West Indies" *219*

25. Scenic wallpaper, "A Visit to King Christophe" *220*

26. Scenic wallpaper, panels 5–8 *221*

27. U.S. Marine Corps Travel Series, *Citadel of Christophe* *222*

28. Arthur B. Jacques's portrait of "a typical country woman" *235*

29. Jacob Lawrence, "The General," Toussaint L'Ouverture series *279*

30. Augusta Savage, *La Citadelle — Freedom* *280*

MAPS

1. Distances to Haiti *2*

2. Haiti *38*

3. The remapping of Haiti *139*

FIGURES AND MAPS

ACKNOWLEDGMENTS

My first thanks go to those I do not know, but whose work has made mine possible for I am indebted to a vast array of working people. I feel a special gratitude to those who keep Mount Holyoke College running from day to day and to those at Yale University who walked off their jobs in solidarity with graduate student employees when I was a graduate student there. But I also wish to acknowledge the men and women who wired my computer, crafted my reading table, cut and sewed my clothes, picked the fruit I ate at lunch, layered my sandwiches with lettuce and tomato, cleaned the offices and libraries in which I worked on this book, and handled the acid that powered the batteries that set my microcassette tapes spinning.

Happily, I can thank by name at least some of the many people who assisted me directly. Holly Sharac typed my first tape-recorded prose, bailed me out of a fix or two while I was focused on writing, and helped me in a thousand other ways over the past five years. Ellen Carey assembled meticulous footnotes out of my rough scratches in no time flat. Calyn Arnold put together my bibliography, brought me piles of obscure books, and saved me from innumerable errors. Pat Serio, Dawn Larder, Rhea Cabin, and Florence Thomas also smoothed my way, at different times, through their labors. Ivy Tillman's spirit and humor kept me from falling into the depths of computer-novice despair. Ivy, Aimé DeGrenier, Cynthia Legare, and a host of smart and patient folks at the Mount Holyoke College computer help desk walked me through many simple and some treacherous operations, helped me rescue lost sections of the manuscript—and at least once the entire manuscript. They are my e-heroes.

I could not have done this work without the help of many skilled and generous librarians and archivists. Special thanks to the circulation, reference, and interlibrary loan staffs at the Mount Holyoke College Library, the Frost Library at Amherst College, and Yale's Sterling Memorial Library; to J. Michael Miller, Amy Cantin, Frederick J. Graboske, and Leo J. Dougherty III, at the Marine Corps Historical Center; and to Barry Zerby at the National Archives. For their gracious assistance in my search for illustrations, I would like to thank Opal Baker, Eileen Johnson, Tritobia Benjamin, and Kevin Morrow.

Material and practical assistance of various kinds made this book possible. Thanks to the American Historical Association, Yale University, and the Woodrow Wilson Foundation, for financial assistance for the dissertation phase of this work. Faculty fellowships and research grants from Amherst College and Mount Holyoke College enabled me to follow up on a broad range of research leads in Haiti and in the United States. A year's leave from teaching allowed me to immerse myself in this project in a way that was essential for the development of my analysis. For helpful advice and assistance when my hands could no longer type, I thank Jeremy King, Gail Hornstein, Peter Berek, Megan Kerr, and especially Michael Hussin. For his encouragement over many years, I thank Lewis Bateman. For their guidance through the publishing process, I thank Alison Waldenberg, Ron Maner, David Perry, Kate Torrey, Pam Upton, and especially Mark Simpson-Vos. Thanks to all the folks at UNC Press, and thanks to Brian MacDonald for his careful attention to the details.

It gives me great pleasure to thank my teachers, mentors, and advisers. David Brion Davis showed enthusiasm for this project and offered valuable guidance from the outset. Hazel Carby, Nancy Cott, and David Brion Davis read the dissertation from which the book grew, and their readings helped me make the book much stronger. Emelia da Costa read Caribbean history with me and gave me the gift of conversation when I was first defining the project. I have also had the good fortune, at various stages of my own education, to work with and learn from William Cronon, David Montgomery, John Demos, Joan Scott, Elizabeth Weed, Mary Jo Buhle, and the late William McLoughlin. What I learned from each of them helped me fashion my approach to history. I was also inspired by a group of very talented public high school history teachers, including Robert Geise and Linda Rosenthal.

As a student of Haiti and of Haitian Creole I have had the privilege of working with another very talented set of teachers. Marc Prou, Lionel Hogu, Yvon Lamour, Lunine Pierre-Jerome, Lyonel Primé, and Renote Jean François offered their enormous talent and inspiration as teachers of Creole at the Haitian Creole Summer Institute at the University of Massachusetts, Boston, in 1996. For showing me the beauty and complexity of Creole, and enabling me to understand Haiti in ways that would have otherwise been lost to me, I am most grateful to them. Mèsi anpil anpil. Thanks also to Madame Josette Rameau and her daughter, who opened their home to me and patiently conversed with me in a language I was only beginning to learn. Thanks to Elizabeth McAlister for generously sharing her considerable knowledge with me.

For over ten years, the Haitian Studies Association has been an invaluable resource for me as I have carried out my research and worked through my ideas, first for the dissertation and then for the book. I am most grateful to Marc Prou, Leslie Desmangles, Carol Berotte Joseph, Gerdes Fleurant, Carol F. Coates, Alix Cantave, and other members of the HSA board and staff over the years, both for their work on the annual conferences and for their conversations with me about various aspects of Haitian history and culture. Thanks also to LeGrace Benson for her encouragement and for bringing to my attention the paintings of Philomé Obin. I am grateful also to the many conference participants who shared their work and their lives and from whom I learned more than I can say.

Many people welcomed me and assisted me while I was in Haiti. Warm thanks to Father Romel Eustache, who invited me to Hinche, hosted me while I was there, and introduced me to many generous men and women in town. Thanks also to Father Yves LaPierre and other residents at the rectory in Hinche who shared their home with me for a time. I wish to express my heartfelt respect for Roger Gaillard, Suzy Castor, and Father William Smart, and to thank them for taking time to talk with me about Haitian history. I am deeply grateful to everyone who was willing to speak with me about the occupation of 1915–34. Tcharly Pierre served as my guide the first time I was in Haiti. He assisted me in Port-au-Prince and traveled with me to Cap Haïtien and Hinche. He also taught me a great deal. For his intelligent assistance, caring, and generosity, I thank him. Thanks also to Richard Morse for his material support for my work in Port-au-Prince.

I have had the opportunity to present parts of this book and earlier versions of my argument in various settings. I am grateful to Marie-Denise Shelton for bringing me to the conference, Haiti: Voices/Images/Reflections, at the Claremont Colleges in 1993. Thanks also to Kristin Hoganson, Paul Kramer, Yukiko Hanawa, and all those who organized conference panels and works-in-progress talks, and invited me to give papers at various stages of this work. The American Studies Association, the Organization of American Historians, the Five College Women's Studies Research Center, and the Five College Social History Research Seminar have provided important contexts for working through my ideas. Thanks to the many people who asked thoughtful questions and made helpful comments in these settings. In particular, thanks to Peter Filene for his formal comments on one paper, and to Lisa Brawley for asking the right question at the right time. For sharing their research with me, I thank Judith Jackson Fossett and Jennie Smith.

It has been my great pleasure and privilege to live and work in the Pioneer Valley with such a rich community of committed scholars. The Department of Women's and Gender Studies at Amherst College provided an intellectually exciting atmosphere, and in that context the book took important new turns. Thanks to Amrita Basu, Margaret Hunt, and to all my WAGS colleagues. I had the great good fortune to team teach with Kristen Bumiller; for her friendship and for her keen mind, I feel happily indebted. Michèle Barale pushed me to explore the queer dimensions of my topic; I thank her for this excellent advice. I am grateful to Frank Couvares and other members of the History Department at Amherst. A five-college women's reading group was a boon for me when I first arrived. Thanks to Judith Frank, Amy Kaplan, Elizabeth Young, Nina Gerassi-Navarro, Karen Sanchez-Eppler, Brenda Bright, and Kathy Peiss for good conversation, then and since. Thanks to Five Colleges, Inc., and to the University of Massachusetts for various other opportunities to meet, converse, and work with other five-college colleagues.

At Mount Holyoke College, my colleagues in history, women's studies, and American studies have encouraged and supported me in crucial ways. I am indebted to Elizabeth Young and Eugenia Herbert for their careful and very helpful readings of significant portions of the book. I was fortunate also to have the opportunity to circulate Chapter 3 to my colleagues in American studies; their generous and thoughtful reception spurred on my writing at a critical time. I am grateful to Joe Ellis for his consistent interest in my work and for passing along one after another helpful reference, article, book, idea. Conversations with Amy Kaplan, Holly Hanson, Nina Gerassi-Navarro, Karen Barad, Rupal Oza, and many others helped me formulate and refine many of the ideas expressed in this book. Much appreciation to Daniel Czitrom for his generous encouragement and wise counsel. And thanks to all my colleagues in the History Department for being willing to engage in challenging conversations about what "history" is and how we approach it. Thanks also to the various visiting faculty members and Five College Minority Fellows from whom I have had the opportunity to learn over the past five years.

For their friendship and assistance at various stages of this work, I wish to thank Serene Jones, Leslie Frane, Adrienne Donald, Jill Lepore, Robert Riger, Susan Johnson, Reeve Huston, Barbara Savage, Lisa Cartwright, Nancy Schnog, and Calyn Arnold. For holding me in their loving embrace, sometimes over long distances and many years, and even when I was working too hard to make it to a big event, I wish to thank my wonderfully large "family of origin" and my "family" of friends — too numerous to name. Bob and Iris Leopold have also cheered me on and provided practical assistance in various ways. Tracy Washington, Amy Vernon-Jones, Anna May Seaver, Charles Tebbets, Nancy Robertson, Dan Simpson, Anita Simansky, Barbara Love, and many others have contributed significantly to whatever success I may have. Michelle Stephens, Preston Smith, and Harold Garrett-Goodyear have buoyed my spirits and made me hopeful by sharing in work that is close to my heart. Jane Levey contributed to my work on this project both intellectually and personally over many years. Her death in April 1999 was a difficult blow. But her life, right to its end, helped sustain me.

For physical, emotional, and moral support, especially in the (long) final stretch, I am deeply grateful to Becca Leopold, Carol Cohen, Judith Frank, Elizabeth Garland, and Holly Hanson. Eunice Torres, Debo Powers, Russ Vernon-Jones, Zoe Perry, Jeannette Armentano, Eileen Nemzer, Peter Elbow, and Jennie Sheeks also sustained me through the most arduous phases of the work and at the same time helped me revel in my love of writing. Chief reveler Lisa Drake heard just about every word of this book over the phone — and many more that I eventually had the wherewithal to delete. Somewhere along the line, she made a decision to back me up on this project, and I am enormously grateful for the many ways that decision materialized. Lynn Yanis and John Maher provided all manner of loving assistance. From substantive research to spur-of-the-moment library runs, from computer bailouts to hot dinners, they enabled me to maintain my stride. Loving thanks to this fabulous crew for keeping me afloat.

I wish to express my deep appreciation to Gail Bederman and Emily Rosenberg, who read the manuscript in its entirety at a relatively rough stage. This book would not be nearly as good were it not for their thoughtful and probing comments on the manuscript in progress. They were able to envision what I was reaching for, and if I have attained it in some measure, they must surely take some credit. Dennis Showalter also generously read and commented on the manuscript, for which I thank him. For readings of various chapters and offering important advice and criticism, I thank Regina Kunzel, Kathy Peiss, Judith Frank, Serene Jones, Peter Szabo, and Lynn Yanis. I am grateful for their friendship as well as for their feedback. I don't know how to thank Amy Kaplan, for she has been my most steady intellectual companion. A keen reader and a caring friend, she read every chapter at least once. I am grateful to her for all that work, but also for knowing when to hold back advice, and when to lay criticism on the line. Of course, I take complete responsibility for any errors.

Closest to home, words fail me. My appreciation for all that Becca Leopold has contributed to this work — as a fellow historian and a steady companion — seems frankly inexpressible. Thank you, Becca, and not least for the wisdom in your wisecracks. And finally, I dedicate this book to my parents, with love and deepest gratitude for all they have taught me and done for me. They have a long history of fighting to make things right in the world, and they are still at it, to my great good fortune and the world's.

NOTE ON USAGE

I use the term "U.S. American" to acknowledge that the United States constitutes part but not all of America and to address the problem posed by the word "American" for students of the Americas. Not only in the United States, but also in some parts of Latin America, the word is used to designate people and things in, of, or from the United States. Yet, Latin Americans rightly call attention to the imperialism embodied in this gesture of nomenclature. These matters are especially pointed in this book because the ambiguities associated with the term "American" and with the name "America" are part of the story being recounted here. The slippage between various uses of these terms turns out to have had political efficacy for various people in, of, or from the United States.

One response to this challenge has been to use the term "North American" in lieu of American. Yet, this too seems problematic in its erasure of the rest of North America, whether that is seen to include Canada alone or Mexico as well. I have chosen to intersperse the two terms "American" and "U.S. American," using the latter especially where clarity calls for the more precise designation. At other points it seems important to use the historically "appropriate" term in order to capture the ambiguities that were at work both in its casual use and in its strategic deployment. For contrasting views of this long-standing controversy, see Arciniegas, *El continente de siete colores* and Bemis, " 'America' and 'Americans.' "

TAKING Haiti

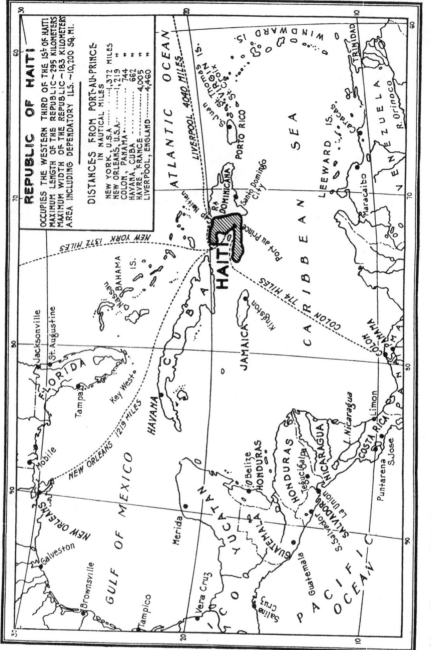

Map 1. Distances to Haiti. From Harold Palmer Davis, Black Democracy (1928). A promoter of Haiti's integration into the international economy, Davis shows on this map the distances from Port-au-Prince to Liverpool, New York, New Orleans, and the Panama Canal.

PROLOGUE

"Join the Marines and See the World" screamed the enlistment posters in
Wilkes-Barre. Within the space of ten days one young man from the collieries of
Pennsylvania was "seeing the world," not as a mere soldier, a bayonet in a force of a
thousand or one-hundred thousand bayonets by which fighting forces are
numbered — but as an arbiter of life and death.

FAUSTIN WIRKUS

Now and then the people of the United States should be reminded that they are
no longer merely citizens of a republic but also citizens of an empire which reaches
out from its native continent to include various isthmuses and islands far away
from New York or Chicago or San Francisco, from Iowa or Oregon. And at the
same time they should be reminded that ancient human moods and ideas have by
no means been subdued throughout the American empire to the modern, rational,
scientific temper which is supposed to administer the government and influence
the customs of the people.

CARL VAN DOREN

How does a man imagine himself when he is about to pull a trigger? As an
arbiter of life and death? As an agent acting on behalf of a rational state? If
he is a white man, setting his sights on a black man, what image of himself
does he conjure as the muscles in his hand tighten? If he is a man in
uniform, pointing his gun at a bandit, what training drills, what adventure
stories, what fragments of selfhood come before his mind's eye as his target
comes into focus? If it is 1918, and he is a private or a sergeant in the United
States Marine Corps — routing out rebels from the Haitian hills rather than
Germans from the fields of France — who does he think he is?

For Faustin Wirkus, as for other American men carrying out the United
States military occupation of Haiti between 1915 and 1934, such subjective
questions presented themselves even as they were elided in the strategic
calculations of military leaders. Hero? Cowboy? Outlaw? Outcast? For each
man a distinctive concentration of memories, experiences, images, fragments of culture — conscious and unconscious — coalesced to form a self, a
white man, an American, a soldier. Those responsible for the deployment of

troops could only hope that the military training they had provided would be sufficient to bring these selves, these soldiers, into line with the official goals and strategies of the occupation. On the ground, each "bayonet" would have to work out for himself his relation to the nation he was sent to represent, the empire he was on hand to build, and the people whose shores he had breached.

A private when he entered the Marine Corps in 1917, a sergeant when he laid down his arms, Faustin Wirkus was one of a few dozen U.S. marines who left a record of his musings on such matters. First, Wirkus told his story to a journalist named William Seabrook. And a story it was, as if straight from Conrad: an ordinary boy from the collieries of Pennsylvania joins the Marines, lands in the tropics, and ends up being crowned king of a Voodoo island. Seabrook made a pretty penny on the story, surrounding it with his own fanciful account of Haitian religious practices and beliefs in his popular travel narrative, *The Magic Island*.[1] A few years later, perhaps seeing the possibility of his own pot of gold, Wirkus engaged another journalist, Taney Dudley, to produce his own account, which he called *The White King of La Gonave*.[2]

Like Wirkus, a handful of marines wrote memoirs of their experiences during the occupation. Some were unmistakably sensationalized, such as Captain John Houston Craige's two books about Haiti, *Black Bagdad* and *Cannibal Cousins*.[3] Military leaders such as generals Smedley Butler and Chesty Puller featured Haiti in their published memoirs, often striking a similarly sensational note.[4] Other marines, like Corporal Homer Overley of Yeoman, Indiana, and Lieutenant Adolph Miller, of Germantown, Pennsylvania, produced more personal reflections, either on site or after returning home.[5] Yet others, who may have had no introspective intentions at all, revealed themselves in company diaries and other official records.[6] Taken together, these accounts provide clues about the subjective experience of the occupation for the men who carried it out. They help us understand how U.S. American culture operated in occupied Haiti. In particular, they illustrate the cultural processes that shaped the violence of imperialism.

Read side by side with these other accounts, Faustin Wirkus's own memoir provides a rich record of the discourses that shaped U.S. imperialism in Haiti. Yet, the story of Faustin Wirkus, "the white king of La Gonave," must also be read in relation to other popular accounts of Haiti and Haitian culture published during and after the occupation. This juxtaposition yields additional insights. It tells us not only about the uses of U.S. American culture in Haiti but also about the uses of Haiti in the United States. It helps us understand how, once the empire was established, other U.S. Americans came to imagine themselves in relation to it. For, once the violence of imperialism had done its work, the literature of empire would invite others to such imaginings. The story of Faustin Wirkus, especially as it was popularized by William Seabrook's *The Magic Island*, became one significant vehicle by which that invitation was issued.

Quite literally, in fact, William Seabrook invited his readers to write to Wirkus on La Gonave. He included in his book a mailing address for the Marine Corps sergeant, who was then serving as a lieutenant in the recently formed Haitian constabulary or Gendarmerie.[7] Among those who responded to the invitation were twenty-eight schoolboys from York, Pennsylvania, whose teacher, sensing room for identification between her young charges and this Pennsylvania boy turned king, had read to them portions of the book. "I am a Pennsylvanian the same as you," wrote William Dize, a ninth grader.[8] Gordon Haverstock also sorted out his connections to the lieutenant: "I don't live so far away from Pittston [and] . . . I belong to the Boy Scouts."[9] Donald Pifer seemed to draw on popular images of Africa and made his racial identification explicit, as he tried to imagine what it would be like to be in Wirkus's shoes: "I would like to know how you like it down there as king. Are there many wild animals there? I think that you would get very lonesome down there without any white people to talk to but I guess you are used to that by this time."[10] And Paul Redman evinced ethnological curiosity with his inquiry: "Please tell us about some of the native customs what they eat and how they live. Do they seem to be making any progress and what is their chief export?"[11]

In these letters, Helen Miller's students, all boys in the industrial class at the Hannah Penn Junior High School, left a partial but intriguing record of their engagement with the story of Faustin Wirkus in Haiti. Undoubtedly, they were compelled to write their letters as a required assignment for their English class with Miss Miller, but they fulfilled that requirement in their own ways. Many identified with Wirkus as Pennsylvanians and as working-class boys. Some drew connections between the institution that structured his life, the Marine Corps, and the institutions of their own daily lives, from school and football to the Boy Scouts and the drum and bugle corps.[12] Many showed their excitement over the opportunity to write to Wirkus, as William Dize did: "I never thought I would get the honor to write to a king."[13] A few, like Dwight Fonny, hinted at the loneliness they imagined he felt: "I guess it seems like a dream to receive a letter from a United States school boy."[14]

Helen Miller's young students were not alone in their enthusiastic response to *The Magic Island*. Popular reviewers heaped praise on the book, and even an academic reviewer, who questioned the rigor of Seabrook's approach, promoted the narrative as "exceptionally entertaining."[15] Selected by the Literary Guild to serve as its featured book for January 1929, Seabrook's fanciful account lit up the imagination of diverse readers in the United States. It inspired some to write their own fanciful tales of Voodoo magic and encouraged others to transfer such tales to radio and film. For adult readers, filmgoers, and radio audiences, as for Helen Miller's students, the book and its spin-offs introduced fascinating images of a mysterious culture located curiously within the bounds of American empire. They reminded U.S. citizens that they were part of an empire vast enough to encompass "ancient human moods."

Carl Van Doren, a professor of literature at Columbia University and a member of the Literary Guild's editorial board, thus praised *The Magic Island* as a significant work "in the literature of the American empire."[16] In a sense, Van Doren was interested in what Benedict Anderson has called the imagined political community of the nation.[17] He knew that literature had a crucial role to play in fostering shared mental images of the national community with which citizens identified themselves. He knew, too, that the nature of that national community had shifted. At the turn of the century U.S. political leaders had furiously debated empire and its implications for the nation; in 1929, Van Doren suggested, empire was no longer a matter for debate, but rather a simple fact and a point of pride.[18] Empire was synonymous with American greatness; it was to be unambiguously embraced. Literature now had to do its part.

Van Doren was not particularly interested in how the empire came to be. It simply was. Citizenship, the consciousness and imagination of the citizen, had merely to catch up with the facts. Yet, Van Doren's approach elided the relations of power that brought the empire into being and that sustained it. As I have suggested, and as the memoirs of men like Faustin Wirkus confirm, the relations of power underlying empire included the violence of imperialism and the cultural processes that enabled that violence. Moreover, the very act of cultural criticism and cultural production in which Van Doren engaged as a member of the Literary Guild's editorial board was part of the matrix of power relations that underwrote the empire. Through the vehicle of the Literary Guild, Van Doren called for the cultivation of an imperial consciousness, a consciousness that would support the international relations of power that constituted American greatness.

When we look closely at Van Doren's cultural intervention on behalf of imperial citizenship, we begin to see how his writing helped to produce the idea of empire even as it erased the very process of empire building. The machinery of ideological production within Van Doren's discourse was a series of dichotomies — historical, geographical, and cultural — that established a clear framework for understanding U.S. imperialism. These dichotomies enabled Van Doren to craft the nation, the citizen, and the empire in such a way as to reaffirm U.S. innocence in the matter of imperial violence. They also affirmed the unitary origin of the republic and the consistency of American culture over time, even as the imagined community of the nation came to encompass the empire. We have already glimpsed the first of these dichotomies, which I have labeled historical — that between republic and empire. For Van Doren, the people of the United States once were "merely citizens of a republic," but no more, and the new empire was wholly distinct from what had come before.

Yet, the people of the United States were never "merely citizens of a republic." On the contrary, the republic itself was, from the first, constructed out of empire insofar as colonial settlement and Indian wars established its very foundation.[19] Moreover, proponents of westward "expansion" championed imperialism in the nineteenth century before a host of negative connotations accrued to that term. Van Doren's neat opposition between republic and empire erased all traces of empire building from the long process by which the boundaries of the nation were drawn and redrawn as the scope of federal power encompassed more and more of the North American continent. It may be worth highlighting the most glaring chronological inconsistency in Van Doren's historical opposition between the republic of old and the newly dawning empire. Oklahoma, New Mexico, and Arizona, which presumably Van Doren considered "merely" part of the republic, were all admitted to statehood in the twentieth century, after the United States began to secure overseas possessions. Meanwhile, Hawaii, Guam, the Philippines, Panama, Puerto Rico, Haiti, the Virgin Islands, and other tropical acquisitions and protectorates constituted, for Van Doren, a new and wholly distinct empire. The question of future statehood for Hawaii or Puerto Rico was conveniently inconceivable within the framework of this dichotomy.[20]

Second, then, Van Doren's characterization of American empire created a neat geographical opposition between the nation on its native continent and the empire overseas and "far away." That some of those islands were not so very far at all from Florida and Louisiana did not disturb his tidy opposition. Van Doren's markers for the nation on its native continent were, of course, all northern cities and states. Might he have sought to keep conveniently out of view the troubling ambiguities of the South, with its proximity to the Caribbean, and with its legacy of slavery, and of the Southwest, with its Mexican origins and cultural influence? Yet, here was a geographical sleight of hand, for elsewhere Van Doren invoked Haiti's nearness to Florida: "only six hundred miles from the Florida coast," he wrote, Seabrook had arrived at "what to his readers may well seem one of the remotest corners of the world."[21] Indeed, it was the very paradox of a place so near and yet so remote that seemed so deliciously intriguing. For Van Doren, Haiti could be "only six hundred miles from the Florida coast" and yet "far away" from "America," which somehow seemed to reside peculiarly in the North. Thus, Van Doren used North and South to address the ambiguity of imperial holdings. If they were both near and far, certainly they were far from what defined the nation. In these ways, Van Doren bolstered the fiction of national self-consistency while heralding the expansion of U.S. influence and greatness.

Finally, Van Doren asserted a cultural dichotomy between "the modern, rational, scientific temper" of the United States and the "ancient human moods and ideas which have by no means been subdued" in Haiti and other parts of the empire. The cultural dichotomy was crucial for Van Doren's assertion of the significance of citizenship in an empire, as an attentive schoolboy might well have recognized. "I am a citizen of the Hannah Penn Junior High School," wrote Adam Wertz to Faustin Wirkus, knowing, undoubtedly, that citizenship conferred rights and privileges and came with duties and obligations.[22] Van Doren's citizens of empire could not, then, encompass all the inhabitants of the empire, with its recently broadened boundaries. Citizens of empire were those whose customs showed a modern, rational temper, an ability to meet the obligations of citizenship, which in turn made them worthy of the rights and privileges conferred by the nation. Thus, if the sites of empire were nearby, they remained safely in the realm of the other, barred from admission to the union by the obvious fact of their primitive temper. The empire could grow. The nation was safely intact.

A careful reading of Van Doren's discourse on imperial citizenship reveals some of the ways that empire troubles the nation. Specifically, when the circumference of national control encompasses imperial holdings, and when that fact is acknowledged, questions about national identity and citizenship are likely to emerge. This was certainly the case at the turn of the century when U.S. leaders debated whether the Constitution should follow the flag to such places as Puerto Rico and the Philippines. As a question of political representation and civil rights, the U.S. Congress resolved this question, at least to its own satisfaction, in the Jones Act of 1917 and other legislative measures. As a question of subjective identity and cultural affinity, however, it would have to be worked out repeatedly in such cultural arenas

PROLOGUE

as the Literary Guild and in the individual lives of citizens like William Dize and Faustin Wirkus. Nor would all U.S. Americans answer these questions the same way. While Van Doren relied in part on regional points of reference to resolve the contradictions of empire, others turned to the tropes of gender, race, and sexuality to arrive at somewhat similar ends. Yet others found themselves in very different places, far indeed from the imperial consciousness Van Doren prescribed.

My opening question, How does a man imagine himself when he is about to pull a trigger? thus turns out to have a corollary: How do self-described "Americans" imagine themselves when they read about the remotest corners of the world? More specifically, who did U.S. American men think they were in Haiti, and how did the people of the United States imagine themselves when they read about their nation's occupation there? These are questions about subjective experience and identity that, I would argue, can only be answered historically. They require an investigation of the operation of culture in the first U.S. occupation of Haiti and its aftermath in the United States. The fruits of that investigation, presented in the pages of this book, suggest something of the cultural and material dynamic of empire building. Culture, embedded in individual experience, gives rise to physical violence and other material practices. Acts of violence, in turn, underwrite the further elaboration of imperial culture. In other words, this book argues not only that empire requires stories as well as guns, as Edward Said and others have shown, but also that there is a more intimate relationship than we have generally acknowledged between stories and guns in the making of American empire.[23]

1
INTRODUCTION

The United States invaded Haiti in July 1915 and subsequently held the second oldest independent nation in the Western Hemisphere under military occupation for nineteen years. While in Haiti, marines installed a puppet president, dissolved the legislature at gunpoint, denied freedom of speech, and forced a new constitution on the Caribbean nation — one more favorable to foreign investment. With the help of the marines, U.S. officials seized the customshouses, took control of Haitian finances, and imposed their own standards of efficiency on the administration of Haitian debt.[1] Meanwhile, marines waged war against insurgents (called Cacos) who for several years maintained an armed resistance in the countryside, and imposed a brutal system of forced labor that engendered even more fierce Haitian resistance. By official U.S. estimates, more than 3,000 Haitians were killed during this period; a more thorough accounting reveals that the death toll may have reached 11,500.[2] The occupation also reorganized and strengthened the Haitian military. Now called the Gendarmerie, the new military organization was officered by marines and molded in the image of the Marine Corps.[3]

An occupation is, in one sense, a temporary arm of the state created to carry out a series of specific tasks. In this case, those tasks were to bring about political stability in Haiti, to secure U.S. control over Haiti with regard to U.S. strategic interests in the Caribbean, and to integrate Haiti more effectively into the international capitalist economy. Of course, supporters of the occupation, and those responsible for it, proposed that these goals would also bring about specific gains for Haiti. They pointed, for example, to the work of the Navy Medical Corps and to the construction of roads, bridges, buildings, and telephone systems under the marines' supervision.[4] With these changes, U.S. policy makers indeed sought to create an infrastructure to serve as the foundation for economic development and modernization. They also professed the hope that on this basis a new Haitian democracy would flourish.

On the ground, cross-cultural dynamics complicated Washington's script for the occupation. Some members of the Haitian elite initially cooperated with the U.S. military, even viewing their presence as potentially helpful, but other Haitians, long suspicious of foreign powers and of government in general, were less eager to play their parts. Many Haitians adopted a watchful stance in relation to the invading *blan* (or *blancs*, as foreigners were called), some engaging in varied forms of everyday resistance, while the Cacos, initially representing a small but significant sector of the population, mounted their armed rebellion. In time, the unabashed racism of many Marine Corps officers and enlisted men, and the outright brutality of the forced labor system implemented to carry out building projects, galvanized the population in opposition to the U.S. presence.[5] Far from laying the groundwork for the hoped-for advent of democracy, material improvements in transportation and communication served to increase the efficiency of the occupation as a police state, with marines and gendarmes in command of every district of the country.[6]

This extended breach of Haitian sovereignty constitutes an infamous but crucial chapter in Haitian history. In contrast, as an exercise of military power and imperial will, the occupation has earned little more than a footnote in standard accounts of U.S. history. On one level, the relative weight given to the occupation in these national historical narratives seems to reflect objective imbalances of size, power, and influence between the two nations. At first glance, it appears that the occupation had an obvious and far-reaching impact on Haiti, but little discernible effect on the United States. Whereas a relatively small number of marines fought, labored, and made themselves at home in Haiti beginning in 1915, much larger numbers of U.S. troops soon fought and died at Belleau Wood, Verdun, and Meuse-Argonne. In 1919, the year a few marines turned the tide against the Cacos by capturing and killing the rebel leader, Charlemagne Péralte, news was breaking elsewhere. Woodrow Wilson forged the League of Nations at Versailles, over 4 million U.S. workers went on strike, race riots racked the nation, and the U.S. Senate finally approved woman suffrage.[7] In the 1920s, while in Haiti officers played polo and enlisted men baseball; stateside, business leaders pioneered the modern corporation, and mass media emerged as a new force in U.S. American culture. In short, it seems that the real stuff of U.S. history during those years was taking shape within U.S. borders and in Europe, not in a small Caribbean nation. How, then, should the first occupation of Haiti by the United States figure in the larger picture of U.S. history?

This book contends that the military occupation of Haiti that began in 1915 was no sideshow. It was one of several important arenas in which the United States was remade through overseas imperial ventures in the first third of the twentieth century. The transformations of imperialism were also effected in Puerto Rico, Cuba, Nicaragua, China, the Philippines, and dozens of other places around the globe.[8] Foreign interventions and territorial seizures overlapped in time and personnel and built on one another to refine the techniques of imperial control and influence. Taken together, they formed a solid overseas foundation for new cultural departures in the United States. Each intervention also had its own particular character and thus contributed uniquely to the remaking of U.S. America. Like others who were the focus of U.S. imperial efforts, Haitians interacted with U.S. citizens and institutions in a manner that grew out of their own indigenous history and culture, thus contributing in unexpected ways to the matrix of an emerging U.S. imperial culture.[9]

My opening sketch of the occupation presents a stripped-down version of events in Haiti between 1915 and 1934. In its brevity, it inevitably distorts a much more complex historical record. The picture of gunboat diplomacy drawn in those first few paragraphs conveys little, for example, about how U.S. marines and sailors understood their role in Haiti and says nothing about how their involvement in the occupation changed them. Neither does it tell about the train of U.S. Americans—congressmen, businessmen, bankers, bureaucrats, diplomats, journalists, artists, activists, anthropologists, and missionaries—who traipsed through Haiti during and just after the occupation, for good and ill. When we begin to look at who went to Haiti, how they interacted with Haitians, and how they wrote and talked about what they saw and heard, a new picture of the occupation, and of American culture, comes into view.

My account of the occupation will center, then, on the marines who implemented U.S. policy. The intervention that began in 1915 was a coordinated attempt to transform Haiti, and marines were a crucial part of the machinery established to carry out this task. Yet, unlike Gatling guns and heavy artillery, marines themselves were men who brought with them their own ideas, desires, fears, and ambitions. They could not simply be placed in Haiti; they had to be conscripted into the project of carrying out U.S. rule. To be sure, the fundamental military value of obedience to the chain of command—necessary for the creation of efficient fighting forces—also helped to keep enlisted men and junior officers in line. Still, the exigencies of operating in a foreign land required marines, at various ranks, to exercise judgment as well as to follow orders. How, then, did the occupation position

U.S. American men in Haiti, and how did they, in turn, negotiate their relationship to the nation they were sent to occupy? How did they respond to the forces that attempted to fix them in a particular relation to Haiti?

Paternalist discourse was one of the primary cultural mechanisms by which the occupation conscripted men into the project of carrying out U.S. rule. The traces of paternalism can be found in evidence left by marines of varied ranks and experiences. Private Paul Woyshner expressed its importance in a cartoon for the *Marines Magazine*, in which a marine wags his finger at a recalcitrant Haiti, admonishing "Listen, Son!" (Figure 1).[10] Sergeant Faustin Wirkus emphasized it in his detailed memoir of Haiti, in which he described the strain of "being father and big brother to . . . our Haitian friends."[11] Yet, the role of paternalism in the cultural conscription of marines in Haiti is perhaps most vividly illustrated by the testimony of General Smedley Butler before a special Senate committee investigating the occupation in 1921 and 1922. A key player in the opening years of the occupation, Butler claimed, "We were all embued [*sic*] with the fact that we were the trustees of a huge estate that belonged to minors. That was the viewpoint I personally took, that the Haitians were our wards and that we were endeavoring to make for them a rich and productive property, to be turned over to them at such a time as our government saw fit."[12] These examples show some of the ways that paternalist discourse infused marines' accounts of their work in Haiti. They also suggest the possibility that paternalism helped to shape their understanding and experience of the occupation they were sent to carry out.[13]

Yet what conclusions may be drawn from the prevalence of paternalist images in marines' self-representations? Surely, the Marine Corps as an institution and marines as individuals would have wanted to show themselves in the best light. Can we take such self-representations seriously as a basis for historical analysis? U.S. historians have generally answered this question in one of several ways. One tradition has seen interventionist paternalism as a genuine reality. Historians writing in this tradition point to the social and material improvements marines attempted to bring to Haiti: hospitals, roads, bridges, public buildings, telecommunications, and so forth. Violence was part of the picture, they readily admit, but should not dominate our perception of what was intended to be a constructive enterprise, undertaken by U.S. Americans who were, in one historian's words, "determined to implant a sense of community in the tropics."[14] Another tradition has emphasized the violence of U.S. rule and has pointed to economic or strategic motives. In this version, paternalism was little more than a transparent veneer of rhetoric. Historians must see through such rhetoric, it is

Figure 1. "The Missionary," a cartoon by Private Paul Woyshner, published in the Marines Magazine, *April 1917. Courtesy of History and Museums Division, U.S. Marine Corps, Washington, D.C.*

supposed, to get at the truth of violence and imperialism in U.S.-occupied Haiti.[15] At least one historian has taken a middle course, identifying paternalism as a mitigating factor in a largely coercive and racist intervention.[16]

Treating paternalism as an obvious good, a mitigating factor, or a transparent veneer to be "seen through," historians have failed to notice its importance and complexity as an element of U.S. foreign policy. Paternalism was not merely a justification laid on after the fact in order to pretty up American wrongdoing. It was, instead, a whole constellation of meanings, images, ideas, and values that helped to shape and direct U.S. relations with former European colonial possessions. Paternalism was an assertion of authority, superiority, and control expressed in the metaphor of a father's relationship with his children. It was a form of domination, a relation of power, masked as benevolent by its reference to paternal care and guidance, but structured equally by norms of paternal authority and discipline.[17] In this sense, paternalism should not be seen in opposition to violence, but rather as one among several cultural vehicles for it.

The implementation of U.S. foreign policy in Haiti depended on such cultural vehicles as thoroughly as it depended on the USS *Washington* and *Tennessee*.[18] Paternalism, we might say, was the cultural flagship of the United States in Haiti. It served practical military purposes, including, but not limited to, announcing the identity of the invading force. As such, it must be understood as thoroughly as any military technology. To that end, we must turn our attention to the cultural terms and categories out of which paternalism was constructed and through which it functioned.

Most obviously, age, class, and race provided the building blocks of paternalism. From the eighteenth century to the early twentieth, the valence of these terms shifted as the discourse of paternalism developed in relation to changing family structures, emerging class formations, and novel racial ideologies. The institutional origins of paternalism in the United States included, for example, the master craftsman's workshop, in which an established artisan apprenticed boys and younger men to the ways of his trade.[19] Yet the slave plantation and the Indian reservation were perhaps its most significant institutional crucibles.[20] In those contexts, age came to function as a metaphor and mechanism for racial subordination. Later, white, native-born men in business and government figured themselves as fathers to a racialized immigrant work force.[21] Finally, as paternalism moved overseas its racial and class codes were further elaborated.

In crucial but perhaps less obvious ways, paternalism was also structured by gender and sexuality. Just as the father was (and remains) a gendered figure, so paternalism invoked gendered meanings associated with men, women, and families to naturalize and normalize the authority it asserted. It constructed male and female bodies and positioned men and women in particular ways. Moreover, paternalism constructed a given social space in terms of racialized (and class-specific) codes of masculinity and femininity. U.S. American workingmen, for example, rejected turn-of-the-century industrial paternalism as a patronizing denial of manhood.[22] Paternalism invoked sexual discourses on various levels as well. In relation to Haiti, it mobilized a variant we might call the discourse of paternity, which explicitly linked legitimacy, heritage, and identity to norms of female sexuality.

Smedley Butler's characterization of Haitians as wards of the United States provides one among many possible entry points into the complex web of meanings embedded in U.S. paternalism toward Haiti. Butler's use of the term "wards" called on a Progressive Era social narrative of children — orphaned by parental death, abandonment, or neglect — who must be taken under the formal guardianship of the state. Butler's phrasing was not new, nor was he the last to characterize Haiti as an orphan nation.[23] Indeed, over the course of the occupation paternalist discourse constructed Haiti as a nation orphaned by parental neglect, sometimes figuring France as the father who abandoned Haiti and Africa as the single mother incapable of raising her illegitimate child alone. Wilhelm F. Jordan, an evangelical missionary who labored in Haiti in the early 1920s, extended Butler's progressive social narrative along these lines, figuring Haiti as a wayward girl. Jordan invoked norms of female sexuality to emphasize the absence of proper discipline and the importance of the U.S. presence in Haiti. He wrote, "after the withdrawal of the French, left entirely to herself, Haiti started on the road to ruin, resting only occasionally from a mad orgy of civil wars, revolutionary uprisings, assassinations, and murders, until recently stopped by the occupation of the country by Uncle Sam's marines."[24] For Jordan, Haiti's history was a story of demise, inevitable for young girls "on the road to ruin" due to the absence of proper domestic influences. Casting social and political upheaval as "a mad orgy of civil wars," Jordan conflated political unrest with sexual impropriety, encoding both in a vague but suggestive image of illegitimacy.

These examples indicate some of the complexity of paternalism as the reigning discourse of the occupation. The cultural framework that positioned U.S. American men as would-be father figures in Haiti carried diverse implications for the ongoing negotiation of race, class, gender, and sexuality. Those and other cultural categories became the threads out of which paternalist discourse wove its story of American care and guidance and of Haiti's dire need for a stern disciplinary hand. Adding further to this complexity, the discourse of paternalism was internally contradictory. To cite an example of special importance, paternalism's narrative seemed on one level to establish clear boundaries between Haiti and America (one nation in need, the other ready to answer that need), while on another level it blurred those boundaries (two nations connected by a family relation, if only an adoptive one). U.S. American men grappled variously with paternalism's sometimes troubling, sometimes convenient inconsistencies.

The relationship between the dominant discourse of paternalism and the perspectives and actions of individual marines was further complicated by the perhaps obvious fact that paternalism was not the only discourse operating in the social space of the occupation. Other forms of racism and racial awareness competed for marines' attention, as did other narratives of gender and sexuality. Other accounts of U.S. power and its goals were available to marines, as were other discourses on Haiti and the Haitian people. Indeed, coming face to face with Haitians on Haitian soil would force U.S. American men to confront countless unexpected cultural realities. Haitian historical discourses, for example, embedded in architecture and in social practices as well as in printed volumes, held out alternative interpretations of Haiti's relation to the United States. Ultimately, Haiti offered marines (and others) a rich, new set of cultural resources that became the basis for articulating new ways of understanding race, gender, and Americanness. A full account of the interaction between Haitians and U.S. Americans, Haitian culture and U.S. culture, is beyond the scope of this book, but Haiti's impact on marines' sense of their role in the occupation must complicate any simple reading of the cultural frameworks U.S. Americans brought to Haiti.

Clearly then, to say that paternalism was the reigning discourse of the occupation is not to say that it can account for the full range of U.S. marines' utterances and actions. Indeed, the process by which discourses shape human actors, a process I call cultural conscription, can be profound, but it can never be seamless. In Haiti, both the internal contradictions of the dominant discourse and the crowded discursive terrain on which it operated challenged the hold paternalism could have on individual marines. For these and other reasons, marines did not respond with one voice to its imperatives. Determining how they did respond to the discourses that attempted to conscript them, and how, in particular, they negotiated the challenges of paternalism, shaping the discourse even as it shaped them, constitutes one of the central problems of this book.

Such an analysis of the marines' experience in Haiti contributes to our understanding of the occupation in several important ways. It helps us see that the cultural dimensions of the occupation were not limited to a set of attitudes that shaped policy makers' perspectives or to a set of lies that justified violence after the fact. The operation of culture was integral to the military, political, and economic project of the occupation insofar as the success of that project depended on the successful cultural conscription of the troops sent to carry it out. An analysis of the occupation that begins with the experience of the marines, and not with the experience of Haitians, cannot pretend to offer any kind of comprehensive account of U.S. imperialism in Haiti. But understanding the ways that marines were culturally conscripted, and the ways they resisted such conscription, will help us understand what happened in Haiti between 1915 and 1934 and what U.S. American culture had to do with that.

An analysis of the way marines negotiated the cultural minefield of the occupation also helps us understand the impact of the occupation on U.S. American culture. This is so because the marines in Haiti were engaged in a conversation with the nation at large about the occupation and about the U.S. role in the world. Marines contributed in unique ways to this national conversation. In Haiti, they hosted and guided visiting journalists, travel writers, missionaries, and other visitors; back in the States, many talked and some wrote about their experiences, on occasion encouraging others to find out more about "the Black Republic."[25] A few marines, like Faustin Wirkus, penned sensational memoirs about their Haitian tours of duty, and one, A. J. Burks, became a best-selling pulp fiction author.[26]

Yet the marines were not the occupation's only interlocutors, and paternalism was not only directed at men in uniform. It was equally a mechanism for conscripting other U.S. Americans — and, for that matter, Haitians — into the project of establishing U.S. empire. Moreover, marines were not the only ones to answer the call of paternalism in their own ways. Outside the armed services, African Americans and European Americans, men and women, popular writers and missionaries, supporters and critics of U.S. foreign policy weighed in with their own interpretations of Haiti and of the U.S. presence there. Like the marines, these commentators and cultural producers accepted some aspects of paternalist discourse and rejected others, sometimes forging new versions of Americanness in the process. Their goal was not necessarily to comment on the occupation per se, but their creative contributions to U.S. American culture began with one or more of the cultural shards deposited by it.

While some of those shards were deposited by marines, others also introduced Haiti and the occupation into American culture. Writing in support of the occupation, some journalists made plain that the invasion was a necessary response to the violence of the Haitian mob that was said to have butchered President Vilbrun Guillaume Sam and paraded his head about Port-au-Prince on a staff.[27] Adhering to the paternalist narrative, they stressed the uncivilized nature of Haitian political processes to date and portrayed the military occupation as a moral imperative. In the first five years of the occupation, few critical voices challenged their accounts; Jane Addams and the Women's Peace Party, W. E. B. Du Bois of the *Crisis*, and Lovett Fort-Whiteman of the *Messenger* were among the very few exceptions that proved the rule of acquiescence to the wisdom of paternalism.[28]

In 1920 the occupation's critics emerged in force, and with them came new levels of attention to Haiti. That year, James Weldon Johnson, poet, novelist, and field secretary of the National Association for the Advancement of Colored People (NAACP), visited Haiti and wrote a scathing critique of the occupation for the *Nation*. In "Self-Determining Haiti," Johnson also attempted to focus American attention on the dignity of the Haitian peasant, the cultural achievement of the educated Haitian, and, most of all, the grandeur of Haitian history and heritage.[29] Johnson later boasted that, through his writings and personal contacts, he had encouraged "a new literary interest in Haiti."[30] Indeed, his connection to Haiti contributed to the work of Eugene O'Neill, John Vandercook, William Seabrook, Langston Hughes, Mercer Cook, and others.[31] While some writers continued to denigrate Haiti's African origins and to peddle damning lies about Haitian religion, others began to suspect that Haiti's Africanness held elements of cultural wealth lacking in their own pale industrial civilization.

Ironically, writers in both traditions created Haiti as an exotic object of desire within American culture. Between the early 1920s and the late 1930s, U.S. Americans featured Haiti in stage plays, radio dramas, short stories, songs, novels, travel books, paintings, sculpture, dance, and even on wallpaper.[32] Popular magazines presented Haiti in stories on subjects ranging from politics to homemaking.[33] In 1929 William Seabrook's sensational travel narrative, *The Magic Island*, became a Literary Guild selection and a national best seller. In the next decade and half, Ethel Merman sang "Katie Went to Haiti," Edna Taft wrote *A Puritan in Voodoo Land*, Orson Welles's popular radio show, *The Shadow*, featured Haitian characters and settings, and Hollywood served up films like *White Zombie* and *I Walked with a Zombie*.[34] In 1934 a short story by Agnes Tait in the *New Yorker* began this way: "Suddenly I had to go to Haiti. You know how those decisions come to you: a few words heard at a party, a line or two in a book, or a picture in a steamship company folder, and all at once you realize that you have to go to Haiti."[35] Among those who "had to go to Haiti," or at least had to write about it, were a number of prominent African American artists and intellectuals. In the 1920s and 1930s, Arthur Schomburg, Langston Hughes, Arna Bontemps, Katherine Dunham, Jacob Lawrence, Zora Neale Hurston, and others mined the riches of Haitian culture and history for their work.

The impact of the occupation on the United States must be understood, then, with reference to the rich and varied cultural engagement it precipitated. U.S. Americans who presided over, visited, or read about Haiti found opportunities to reimagine their own nation and their own lives as they appeared to be reflected by and refracted through Haitian history and culture. To comprehend the occupation as an integral part of U.S. history, we must understand how it engaged these varied audiences, how it attempted to position them, and, to the extent we can discern it from the available evidence, how they negotiated the cultural landscape it helped bring into view.

To understand how the occupation engaged U.S. Americans — indeed, to understand how *the occupation* did anything — it may be useful to clarify the various senses in which we use this term. Most obviously, the occupation of 1915–34 was an event in the history of Haiti and in the history of U.S. foreign policy. Often, when we refer to "the occupation," we are referring, in a general way, to this event in all its complexity. At other times, we are referring to an action, a diplomatic and military endeavor undertaken by certain branches of the U.S. government — the State Department, the armed services. In a similar vein, the term may refer to the policy of the U.S. government in Haiti. Yet again, the occupation was also an institution, a power structure. In this sense, we use the term to refer to an arm of the U.S. government, a temporary state apparatus created for specific purposes. To some contemporaries, the power of the occupation seemed to be vested in the person of a particular military officer or diplomatic official, such as High Commissioner John Russell in the early 1920s. We, too, may at times seem to conflate the occupation with an individual or a group of individuals acting in its name, but we must also remember that the occupation as a political structure was more than the sum of its participants. Finally, while the occupation was an event, an action, a policy, and a structure, it was also an encounter and a process. Its effects arose in part from the fact that it entailed the meeting of two cultures within one geographical space. In this sense, "the occupation" refers to a process that could never be controlled by any one party, by any one man or group of men, not even by the men with authority over the men with guns.

This book is primarily concerned with understanding the occupation as an event in the cultural history of the United States, broadly conceived. To untangle the threads connecting the occupation and U.S. American culture, it will be helpful to begin with a few questions about the occupation as a structure of power. We need to know, for example, how this arm of the U.S. government, operating abroad, benefited from, relied upon, and, at times, actively made use of cultural resources to mobilize personnel and to foster imperial culture more broadly within the population. How did the occupation as an institution attempt to position U.S. Americans, in and out of the armed services, in relation to Haiti? How did the state benefit from cultural processes that were set in motion by official actions, but that took shape most likely beyond official control?

The occupation — that temporary arm of the state — sought to engage Americans as passive participants in and supporters of U.S. empire. Through paternalist representations of its work in Haiti, the United States encouraged not only marines but others as well to see themselves as benefactors helping out a needy, if recalcitrant, child. It also encouraged U.S. citizens to see Haiti as falling within the proper circle of American concern and action. Popular narratives that sensationalized Haiti and positioned readers as voyeurs in an exotic land made that move all the more appealing. In this sense, sensational narratives reinforced official discourses and strengthened their ability to conscript ordinary citizens into the logic of empire. Together, popular and official discourses invited U.S. Americans to adopt an imperial perspective and fueled public fascination with Haiti as one means to that end.

To a great extent, moreover, the attempt to foster imperial consciousness met with success. Popular culture brought images of Haiti, Cuba, Mexico, Polynesia, China, Africa, Arabia, and yet other parts of the world within the circumference of U.S. Americans' imperial imaginations. The very fact that in December 1941 most people in the United States could so readily accept the identification of Pearl Harbor as part of "America" indicates the widespread embrace of empire among citizens of the United States, whether or not they used the word "empire" to name it. As Carl Van Doren predicted in 1929, narratives about Haiti and Haitian culture took their place in the literature of empire that helped to produce that reality.

Between 1915 and 1940, Americans redefined the boundaries of their national community in part through their discussions of Haiti. Yet, if paternalist discourse succeeded in conscripting many Americans into the logic of empire, the implications of paternalism also troubled the nation and its assumption of self-consistency. For, as my discussion of Carl Van Doren's call to imperial consciousness illustrates, broadening the circle of American control and influence complicated questions of national identity. Could American culture continue to seem wholly separate from, and unaffected by, the foreign even as American empire came to encompass the foreign itself? The problem of empire would be how to ingest a territory, or another nation in the case of Haiti, without allowing it to become too obviously a part of the nation or the national culture. Exoticism provided at least one solution: incorporate the foreign into American culture, while at the same time inscribing its marginality and otherness. American exoticism toward Haiti thus contributed to an imperial culture organized, in part, around resolving the tension between nation and empire.

The implications of paternalism troubled the nation in other ways as well. Just as marines in Haiti sometimes put paternalism to their own uses, so other U.S. Americans did the same. With regard to race, the results of this cultural process were remarkably varied. Turning paternalist discourses to their own ends, African Americans would challenge the whiteness of American identity and demand rights and respect with new force. For many white Americans, popular paternalist discourses on Haiti would undercut the hostility and distancing of the more virulent forms of racism, while at the same time new types of racism would emerge and be strengthened. With regard to gender, masculinity and femininity would come to be freighted with the burden of signifying American greatness and power. In the process, hegemonic gender relations would be strengthened. At the same time, a handful of women artists, writers, and activists would challenge the status quo in part through their use of and response to paternalist discourse. With regard to sexuality, the discourse of exoticism, so essential to resolving the tension between nation and empire, contributed to the reshaping of sexual norms and representations. In short, as the discourse of paternalism called into play a whole variety of meanings and values surrounding race, gender, sexuality, and national identity, it opened up the possibility that those meanings and values could be reinvigorated, reconfigured, or, for that matter, challenged wholesale. For all its success, then, paternalist discourse yielded unexpected outcomes.

CULTURE AND HISTORY

Of course, the U.S. occupation of Haiti was not simply a cultural event. It cannot be explained solely in terms of discourses, cultural frameworks, or the individual experiences of the men sent to carry it out. It was also a matter of strategy, politics, economics, and policy. It had to do with the institutional growth and development of the U.S. government, particularly in terms of military structures and international relations. It had to do with the strategic needs of an emerging international economy. At various turns, it was shaped by the political ambitions of U.S. policy makers. These contexts should not be forgotten as we interrogate the cultural dynamics of this foreign military intervention. The burden of my argument surrounds the cultural processes set in motion by the U.S. invasion in 1915. Yet those cultural processes were never wholly distinct from economics, politics, and military practice.

What, then, shall we mean by the word "culture"? If culture is implicated in the realms of economics, politics, and military practice, indeed in all social relationships and institutions, can it have any specificity at all? If a military campaign report is as fully "cultural" as an opera or a novel, what is the special significance of aesthetic forms, if there is any, in the realm of culture? Shall we embrace a broad and inclusive "anthropological" definition of culture that refers to the texture of daily life or, more precisely, "the 'complex whole' of any individual society's material and ideational system"?[36]

We can complicate this older anthropological sense of the word by emphasizing the nature of culture as process. There can be no bounded "whole," no single "system," where cultural patterns of meaning are constituted and reconstituted over time. Anthropologists and cultural theorists have addressed this point by highlighting margins and borders as especially significant for the study of culture.[37] Culture in the borderlands, argues one, provides an apt metaphor for the process of culture in general, a process involving translation and fertilization across differences of identity, experience, and understanding, either within a single community or in a geographical space where two or more communities overlap.[38] The older concept of culture as "an autonomous internally coherent universe" minimizes the significance of such differences, renders "border zones" incomprehensible, and leaves insufficient room for the historian's concern with change over time.[39]

The concept of discourse also opens up possibilities for a more fully historical analysis of culture as process. Historian Joan Scott has defined the term "discourse" as a historically specific "structure of statements, terms, categories, and beliefs" generated within a particular social and institutional context.[40] This definition emphasizes the institutional relations of power that undergird processes of signification — that is, the production of meaning — in particular contexts. Ideas are not free-floating entities; they are produced within and in relation to specific structures of power. By focusing on institutionally grounded discourses we come to appreciate what one literary critic calls the "uneven development" of ideologies — and,

I would add, culture—over time.[41] The Christian missionary movement within and across particular churches, for example, developed certain versions of paternalism; in contrast, the U.S. Navy developed others. There was necessarily some overlap and some disjunction between these two powerful institutional contexts in which interventionist paternalism was elaborated. For this reason, the discourse of paternalism could not have developed in an even way across time and space.[42]

We must, therefore, examine local relations of power to illuminate larger historical trends. The career of paternalism arose, not out of some singular, overarching plan to subjugate Haiti, but rather, in one instance, out of the professionalizing aspirations of naval officers competing for funding and recognition within a military bureaucracy, and in another, out of the particular needs and aspirations of churchgoing citizens.[43] In a similar vein, Michel Foucault emphasized what he called "the infinitesimal mechanisms" of power that "have their own history, their own trajectory," but are then co-opted to serve the ends of the state or become embedded in a more general process of domination.[44] Thus, to say that the process of culture involves relations of power is not to say that culture is determined in any kind of top-down manner. Historians must examine the local, the particular, the context-specific processes that contribute to the larger phenomenon we recognize as culture.

The concept of discourse must be clarified in one further respect. For too often the term has been understood to imply an erasure of the significance of the material world. Yet, it is the very materiality of discourses and their effects that must be taken into account if we are to understand the full significance of terms such as discourse and culture.[45] The categories of meaning that constitute discourses give shape and form to human bodies, the physical environment, and the material resources and tools wielded by human actors. Military training, for example, functioned as a discursive regime that shaped the bodies of marines and sailors and invested them with particular meanings in the context of the U.S. imperial program and in the context of the world war. Uniforms and guns, in turn, bore meaning in relation to those transformed bodies and as extensions of them. As we shall see, such discourses could be deadly.[46]

Culture may be understood, then, to refer to the processes of signification through which people—consciously and unconsciously, intentionally and unintentionally—structure both social relationships and the material world. Collectively, people engage in the ongoing production of meaning, and in so doing they give shape and form to social relationships, institutions, and material practice. In turn, culture shapes the individual. Indeed, as I have suggested, through discourses culture scripts and conscripts individuals.

My preliminary, working definition of culture as process thus emphasizes the fluid and dynamic quality of social meanings, and the potentially shifting contours and boundaries of any "single" culture. My premise is that cultures are continually constituted and reconstituted through relations of power, that they are neither monolithic nor static. A national culture then, and in this case the culture of the United States, may be viewed as a contested terrain on which people identifying themselves as Americans formulate, dispute, and reformulate structures of meaning and power associated with various forms of difference such as gender, class, race, and nation.

This is not to deny the tenacity of certain structures of meaning and power, but rather to emphasize the error of a dangerously misleading synecdoche: that of taking the thought of one group (or individual) as indicative of a national culture in general.[47] For this inquiry into the dynamics of American culture on contact with Haiti, then, I juxtapose the variety of U.S. discourses on Haiti as articulated by African Americans and white Americans, by men and women, by military and nonmilitary figures, by architects of the occupation as well as by those who protested it, by scholars, popular writers, artists, and so on. Within each of these groups (and in the spaces between and beyond them), I emphasize distinctive particularities as well as the expression of common ground.[48]

In the course of my research, I have viewed group identities not as fixed sociobiological categories, but as culturally and historically constructed phenomena, fashioned and refashioned in particular contexts. Rather than seeing various authors as fully formed "Americans" or "Haitians," "African Americans" or "white people," "men" or "women," whose identities were always stable and unproblematic, I ask how such identities were both consolidated and unsettled in the specific historical and cultural context of the U.S. occupation of Haiti, and its aftermath in Haiti and in the United States.[49]

"Culture," according to my working definition so far, is a noun that names a process. Culture is the doing of something — specifically, the making of meanings and thereby the structuring of human relationships and so forth. Yet, it will be objected that I cannot so easily dismiss the fact of culture as an object. As some voices from the culture wars have insisted, there is indeed something called "American culture," and if we don't know what it is, certainly we should. If, indeed, culture refers to an object, and not just a process, as surely it does for so many people, then what is the nature of this object, this thing? Is it one thing? Over time? To different people? Certainly not. Yet, if it changes and if it is different to different people, it still appears, doggedly, to be fixed, objectively unified, even monolithic, and this persistent appearance of fixedness must be addressed.

Here, it may help to turn back to the unevenness with which ideologies develop. In this light, we may consider culture the sum total — at any given moment — of a collection of overlapping but not coincident discourses and fragments of discourses.[50] These discourses (and discursive fragments) are produced, engaged, and negotiated by a community of sorts, an overlapping but not coincident collection of groups and individuals who understand themselves to be connected to one another by their membership in the community and who use the name of that community to describe themselves. There is always some movement and flux in the sum total of these discourses, but there is also always some overlap, generally in such a manner as to overdetermine certain ideas, meanings, and images.

These overlapping discourses operate on unconscious as well as conscious levels, and from them emerge the flotsam and jetsam of our emotional lives as well as the fragments that get worked over and rearticulated through our unconscious mental processes. This definition of culture, then, necessarily encompasses the realms of the emotional, the unconscious, and the irrational as well as the realm of ideas and consciousness. This complex context gives rise to individuality, always in historically specific ways. Historian Carlo Ginzburg, in his portrait of a sixteenth-century miller named Menocchio, insists that his subject's "distinctiveness had very definite limits." He explains, "as with language, culture offers to the individual a horizon of latent possibilities — a flexible and invisible cage in which he can exercise his own conditional liberty. With rare clarity and understanding, Menocchio articulated the language that history put at his disposal."[51] Ginzburg's phrase, "the language that history put at his disposal," strikes me as an excellent way to describe culture in its relation to the individual.[52]

If culture is the sum total of a collection of overlapping but not coincident discourses, then the sum total of the discourses available to any given individual constitutes the "language that history put[s] at his [or her] disposal," or, in other words, his or her "horizon of latent possibilities." In this sense, there is no single, fixed, monolithic body of ideas, meanings, or images that can be described as *the* culture of a particular nation or group. But there are, within a given community, sets of ideas, meanings, and images that are overdetermined given the particular combination of overlapping discourses that seem to fix them in place, and given the weight of overlapping institutional power that supports their continued operation.[53]

INTRODUCTION

Examining the relationship between culture and the individual, between culture and consciousness, enables us to consider the process of cultural change in some detail. Cultural theorist Raymond Williams pointed in this direction with his concept of "structures of feeling," which he used to refer to "affective elements of consciousness and relationships."[54] Anthropologists have begun to explore the implications of Williams's concept in ways that are important for our understanding of the complex reverberations of the U.S. occupation of Haiti in the United States. One explains, referring directly to Williams's work, "structures of feeling . . . are just emerging, still implicit, and not yet fully articulate . . . [they are] in transition between being experienced as private and becoming recognized as social."[55] In a similar vein, another important anthropological study identifies "a realm of partial recognition and inchoate awareness, of ambiguous perception [and] . . . creative tension" that lies "between the conscious and the unconscious."[56]

Individuals positioned differently within a given social formation will experience discourses and ideologies — and indeed culture — in their own ways. In turn, the creative tensions and emerging structures of feeling to which their differing experiences give rise necessarily lead to novel and divergent articulations of an only partially shared "culture." A complex event, like the first U.S. occupation of Haiti from 1915 to 1934, will necessarily engage national cultures on multiple levels, through the diverse articulations of differently positioned participants and interlocutors. Those diverse articulations will manifest themselves variously in quotidian cultural forms, such as bank ledgers and military field reports, as well as in aesthetic texts, such as paintings and plays.

This framework for understanding cultural change thus helps us see the relationship between the anthropological and the aesthetic senses of the word "culture." It also suggests a methodology that brings together diverse objects of historical analysis that have generally been treated as distinct and unrelated. The everyday traces of subjective experience and the notable achievements of artistic production may take their places, side by side, in an analysis of the cultural dimensions of a military occupation.

This study therefore considers sources that promise to shed light on the various aspects of culture in play during and after the occupation of Haiti for U.S. Americans in Haiti and in the United States. Diaries, letters, photographs, memoirs, poems, songs, short stories, and essays, but also congressional testimony, reports, and memoranda, all help us understand the texture of daily life and subjective perception for marines and other Americans who participated in and/or observed the occupation. Field campaign reports, intelligence reports, official correspondence, military recruitment and training materials, and other official sources also serve as crucial cultural texts offering insight into the always intertwined institutional structures and cultural processes that shaped both the marines and the occupation. Taken together, these diverse sources reveal not only the dominant, multiply articulated discourses and ideologies that U.S. Americans recognized consciously at the time, but also structures of feeling that were only just emerging, about which marines and others may have had only an "inchoate awareness."

If we turn to the cultural aftermath of the occupation in the United States—that second crop of effects, not always recognized as such, that military action reaps at home—other sorts of sources provide a wealth of evidence. Often untapped by historians, fiction, drama, painting, film, travel writing, and ethnology, as well as self-consciously political writing, all serve to illuminate the ways that diverse members of the U.S. national community responded to the occupation and to the discourse of paternalism mobilized on its behalf. As U.S. Americans reckoned with the implications of the occupation, they brought forth—consciously and unconsciously—a new discursive terrain, which would, in turn, make possible new iterations of Americanness and new configurations of race, class, gender, and sexuality. As with the experiences of the marines themselves, so with the artists, writers, and activists who engaged discourses about Haiti during and after the occupation, structures of feeling and forms of inchoate awareness come to light through close textual readings.[57] These readings may seem to take us far from the usual concerns of U.S. foreign policy and foreign relations. Yet such explorations of the complex cultural responses called forth by U.S. imperialism are crucial for understanding the full range of effects wrought by the occupation.[58] They help us grasp the horizon of latent possibilities that would be available to the next generation of self-described Americans who would continue to shape and respond to U.S. foreign policies and U.S. relations with Haiti.

This approach to culture, and to the history of the U.S. occupation of Haiti, thus reveals a story not usually told by diplomatic historians. Through the dominant discourse of paternalism, the U.S. occupation of Haiti attempted to conscript U.S. Americans and Haitians in the service of U.S. imperialism. The unevenness of its success in this endeavor was attributable to the internal contradictions of that dominant discourse, the complexity of the discursive terrain in which the occupation attempted to operate, and the creative agency of those targeted for conscription, both in Haiti and in the United States. Even as it attempted to write Haitians and U.S. Americans, whites and blacks, men and women into a paternalist master narrative, the occupation itself created openings for those who would resist such conscription. The creative processes of conscription and resistance that emerged in and through the occupation gave rise to new subjective formations and, as such, enabled both the extension of U.S. imperialism and challenges to domestic relations of power, including racism. Through this complex set of (subjective and discursive) processes — that is, through culture — national, racial, gender, and sexual meanings and identities were unsettled and consolidated in new ways.

A BRIEF NARRATIVE OF U.S. INTERVENTION
AND OCCUPATION IN HAITI

U.S. involvement with Haiti began long before the marines landed in July 1915. Attempts to influence Haiti may even be dated back to the revolutionary period. The United States remained officially neutral toward Toussaint L'Ouverture's revolutionary government (1800–1802), but American merchants contributed to the success of the Haitian Revolution by supplying arms to the rebels.[59] U.S. president Thomas Jefferson may have supported this arms trade; certainly he welcomed the defeat of Napoleon's army in Haiti. But the threat to slavery in the U.S. South represented by a thriving, independent nation of former slaves, combined with the exigencies of U.S. relations with France, led him, in 1806, to approve the prohibition of trade between the United States and Haiti.[60] Although trade resumed, the perception of Haiti as a threat to the well-being of the slave South continued, and as a result the United States withheld formal recognition from the new republic until the South seceded.

Meanwhile Haiti loomed large in the imagination of U.S. Americans on both sides of the debate over slavery: proof that people of African heritage could govern themselves, on one side; proof that they could not, on the other.[61] And whereas slavery's defenders kept their nation at a formal distance from the nation that was their nightmare, African Americans forged links with Haiti, sometimes aided by Port-au-Prince and even Washington.[62] In the 1820s thousands of African Americans emigrated to Haiti, answering invitations tendered by Haiti's leaders to avail themselves of land and political liberty in a black republic.[63] In 1859 Haiti again sought to augment its population by attracting immigration from the North; that year, Haitian president Fabre Geffrard engaged James Redpath, an American citizen, as an agent to bring people of African heritage to Haiti from Canada and the United States. A few years later, President Lincoln supported the profit-making colonization scheme of a private citizen named Bernard Kock. Also during the 1860s the African American missionary Theodore Holly promoted emigration to Haiti.[64]

In 1862, with southern voices absent from Congress, the United States extended formal recognition to Haiti for the first time. U.S. secretary of state William H. Seward then began to pursue the expansion of U.S. influence and control in Haiti.[65] He initiated, for example, talks over the possibility of U.S. use of a Haitian deepwater port at Mole St. Nicholas.[66] By 1869 the United States was represented by an African American minister to Haiti, Ebenezer Bassett, who would be followed by others, including John Mercer Langston and, in 1889, the distinguished Frederick Douglass.[67] Meanwhile, in the late nineteenth century, U.S. investors began to extend their activities to Haiti in a significant way, and the U.S. government moved toward more serious attempts to broker protection for them in the midst of increasing Haitian political instability.

By the turn of the century, U.S. marines had landed on Haitian soil eight times "to protect American lives and property."[68] In 1901 the U.S. Navy stepped up its presence in the Caribbean, designating an entire squadron within its North Atlantic Fleet for that specific purpose.[69] On numerous occasions in the next fourteen years, U.S. gunboats—the *Topeka*, the *Chester*, the *Machias*, the *Montana*, and many others—would find themselves in Haitian waters precisely at the moment when U.S. influence could be brought to bear on Haitian affairs.[70] As U.S. capitalists made important inroads in Haiti, most notably through railroads and banking, instances of "gunboat diplomacy" would become more and more frequent. By 1910 the United States had achieved a position of dominance over other great powers in Haitian affairs, although German interests still constituted another important presence.[71] By 1913 President Wilson and his advisers were searching for a way to translate that position into definitive control. Attributing the instability of the Haitian government to political immaturity on the part of Haitians, Wilson attempted to secure that control at various points during 1914 and 1915, culminating in the decision to land marines and sailors on July 28, 1915.[72]

During the first nine months of the occupation, through April 1916, Admiral William B. Caperton oversaw the early stages of the U.S. assertion of control over Haitian government functions. Caperton's forces immediately set about disarming Port-au-Prince and arresting Caco revolutionaries, while Caperton and his immediate assistants, notably Captain Edward Beach, set about finding a cooperative client president to be duly "elected" as soon as possible. Caperton and Beach dismissed the heir apparent to the presidency, Dr. Rosalvo Bobo,[73] and settled on Philippe Sudre Dartiguenave who, Caperton observed, "realizes that Haiti must agree to any terms laid down by the United States."[74] The admiral succeeded in preventing the Haitian Congress from electing Bobo and reported to his naval superiors that he believed he could control that body.[75] The revolutionary committee in Port-au-Prince, which had heretofore been attempting to cooperate with Caperton, apparently perceived the same situation, to their dismay. To still his hand, on August 11 the committee moved to dissolve the Congress to prevent the election of a client president, but Caperton held all the cards. "I have dissolved the revolutionary committee and informed them that they have no further authority in Port-au-Prince and would be considered public enemies of the United States if they attempted to give any further orders or to menace U.S. policies," he reported directly to President Wilson.[76]

The next day, the Haitian Congress elected Philippe Sudre Dartiguenave president of the Republic of Haiti (Figure 2). Fresh from his inauguration, Dartiguenave was presented with an American-authored treaty, ready for his signature.[77] As Caperton began to press for ratification, Robert Lansing, the new U.S. secretary of state, reflected on the situation in a letter to Wilson, "I confess that this method of negotiations, with our Marines policing the Haitian capital, is high handed. It does not meet my sense of a nation's sovereign rights and is more or less an exercise of force and an invasion of Haitian independence. From a practical standpoint, however, I cannot but feel that it is the only thing to do if we intend to cure the anarchy and disorder which prevails in that Republic."[78] Prior to securing Dartiguenave's signature on the treaty, Caperton moved forward with the occupation. He took control of the customshouses, detailed a regiment of marines, under newly arrived Colonel Littleton W. T. Waller, to fight a war against the Cacos in the North, and, on September 3, 1915, consolidated his own authority by declaring martial law. With the application of considerable pressure, Dartiguenave signed the treaty on September 16, the Haitian Congress approved it on November 11, and the formal ratification came in May, 1916. In December 1915 Smedley Butler was detailed to establish the Gendarmerie. Despite Washington's decision to grant formal recognition to Dartiguenave's government once the new president had approved and signed the treaty, Admiral Caperton's martial law continued alongside Dartiguenave's nominally constitutional government. Caperton departed in April 1916 with relative quiet in the countryside and U.S. military control reasonably well established in the capital.

From the time of Caperton's departure through the assassination of Charlemagne Péralte and the adoption of a new Haitian Constitution in late

Figure 2. President Philippe Sudre Dartiguenave, center, and his cabinet, flanked by marines. National Archives.

1918, the occupation went through a period of consolidation. Caperton left Waller in command of the occupation and Butler in charge of the Gendarmerie. With Waller's marines providing protection for the new government in Port-au-Prince, U.S. treaty officials pressed for a new constitution, one that would be consistent with American goals for the occupation. Overturning Haiti's constitutional prohibition on foreign land ownership was both a primary goal of the United States and one of the most notable obstacles treaty officials faced.

Meanwhile, Butler built his fledgling military force with an officer corps made up of U.S. marines. Gendarmerie units, posted to each district and subdistrict around the country, sought to ensure the stability necessary for a resumption of economic productivity across the republic. Yet, the process of establishing control ignited the opposition. In 1917 Butler turned to forced labor to carry out a massive road-building project intended to link disparate communities and thus facilitate military and police operations. The Gendarmerie oversaw the establishment of this forced labor system, based nominally on a long-defunct corvée law requiring peasants to work on the roads or pay a road-building tax.[79] The Cacos' war against the occupation, ground down by the superior force of the marines while Caperton was still in command, now found new sources of strength in a population inflamed by the insults and the assaults sustained through the corvée. Under the leadership of Charlemagne Péralte and Benoit Batraville, and fueled by the impact of the corvée, the Cacos gained momentum and forced the marines to wage war for control of the population they had come to "assist."

With the assassination of Charlemagne Péralte in November 1918, the Marines turned a corner in the war against the Cacos. Yet, by this time, the occupation was under assault on a different front. A series of investigations, culminating in a full-scale U.S. Senate inquiry, put the occupation under the political microscope and threatened to bring down the occupying state apparatus that Caperton, Waller, and Butler had worked so hard to build. This period, from late 1918 to early 1922, can be characterized as the phase during which the U.S. regime faltered but did not fall. The Cacos pressed on in the countryside under Batraville, nationalist editors flouted occupation censorship in various Haitian newspapers, and others organized against the occupation with the help of African American allies in the NAACP. Most troubling to the international reputation of the United States, representatives of the organized opposition turned up at Versailles in 1919 to press the issue with Wilson while he was championing the rights of small nations in that context. Bad press for the occupation began in the United States when African American missionaries returned with stories of atrocities, but Haiti really caught the public's attention when it became an issue in the 1920 presidential election. There were official attempts to tone down the violence of the war against the Cacos at various points during this phase of the occupation, but the worst abuses continued under a particularly intransigent group of American officers in the north of Haiti. A series of investigations led to nothing. Once elected, Harding continued the occupation. The Senate established a select committee to undertake a formal investigation of the occupations of Haiti and the Dominican Republic. But once the stir surrounding the 1920 election had died down, the occupation was reorganized under a high commissioner, in effect consolidating U.S. colonial rule.

A period of relative tranquillity followed, from 1922 to 1929, with the occupying state apparatus consolidated under High Commissioner John Russell. Louis Borno replaced Dartiguenave as client president in 1922 and was reelected for another four years in 1926.[80] Borno's reelection sparked protests, but dissent remained largely below the surface during this phase of Pax Americana. The military resistance of the Cacos had been broken, and press censorship became the rule, so that Haitians who continued to protest the occupation landed in jail for their trouble.[81]

But in the fall of 1929 a phase of renewed protests began. Economic troubles linked to a depressed coffee market, combined with the occupation's imposition of harsher tax policies, brought antioccupation sentiments to a head.[82] A decision to change the scholarship policy for students at the agricultural college run by the Service Technique, the technical assistance arm of the occupation, provided the spark for a series of student strikes. In response to the threat of a general strike — which seemed poised to include not only students, workers, politicians, and businessmen, but also possibly the Gendarmerie itself — Borno announced that he would not seek another term as president of the republic. This pleased the occupation's critics but did not still them; customs employees in Port-au-Prince were the first to join the students in what quickly became a nationwide general strike. Relatively small detachments of marines faced thousands of Haitians demonstrating against the occupation and its client government in cities and towns around the country. On December 6, 1929, in one such confrontation, in Aux Cayes on the southern coast of Haiti, marines opened fire on a crowd of 1,500, killing 12 and wounding 23.

The Cayes massacre led to international condemnation of the occupation, thus forcing the U.S. president to act. Hoover appointed a commission headed by W. Cameron Forbes to review the general situation in Haiti, and another, headed by Robert Russa Moton of Tuskegee Institute, to review the education system. Members of the Forbes Commission could not fail to notice "the intense feeling" that existed "practically everywhere against the American occupation."[83] As one member noted, "the state of the public mind is such that unless measures are taken to meet their demands for a legislature that can elect a president in the near future, . . . grave public disorder will arise."[84] Within a few months, Haiti did have a new president. Stenio Vincent was elected in November 1930 in legislative elections, after a brief provisional government under Eugene Roy (May–November 1930).[85] The Forbes Commission, moreover, recommended the withdrawal of U.S. forces, and the long process of negotiating the terms of that withdrawal began. Four years later, on August 15, 1934, the long-awaited *désoccupation* came to pass, as the last U.S. marines departed. Direct U.S. supervision of Haiti's economy continued through 1942.

TAKING HAITI

The remainder of this account of the relationship between military intervention in Haiti and cultural change in the United States is divided into two parts and six chapters. Part I, entitled "Occupation," addresses the cultural dimensions of the nineteen-year U.S. military presence in Haiti; Part II, entitled "Aftermath," considers the impact of that military presence on the transformation of U.S. American culture between 1920 and 1940. Thus, the two parts are not consecutive, but overlapping. U.S. Americans articulated race, gender, and national identity in new ways, in the wake of U.S. intervention in Haiti, well before the last marines withdrew in 1934. Those articulations, in turn, shaped the course of events in Haiti in various ways.

My examination of the occupation itself is divided into three chapters. Chapter 2 introduces the reader to the marines and to the nation they invaded. What factors shaped the marines' consciousness as they arrived in Haiti in 1915 and after? How did marines perceive Haiti, and how did their subjective experience inform their conduct there? What histories, in turn, shaped the land they patrolled and inspired the men and women they sought to subdue? Chapter 3 examines the ideological machinery of the occupation. Specifically, it considers the precise nature of U.S. paternalism toward Haiti, in its various iterations, and shows how that paternalism facilitated the establishment of the occupying state formation. Chapter 4 explores the connections between paternalism and violence in the war against the Cacos and in the routine conduct of the occupation. My argument is that paternalism did not mitigate against violence but rather reinforced and extended it. The legends passed down by marines who served in Haiti and the stories they told one another provide important clues for our understanding of paternalism and violence in marines' negotiations of national, racial, and gender identity in Haiti.

If Part I assesses the uses of U.S. American culture in Haiti, Part II is concerned with the uses of Haiti in U.S. American culture. Thus, the second part of the book turns our attention to the discourses that emerged out of the occupation, that is, the national conversation initiated by the U.S. military presence in Haiti. In the aftermath of occupation, U.S. Americans set about "taking Haiti" in important new ways. Chapter 5 considers the appeal of Haiti in the United States as politics and popular culture turned their attention to "the black nation" in new ways beginning in 1920. It explores the tensions between political critique and cultural commodification in James Weldon Johnson's essays and Eugene O'Neill's play, *The Emperor Jones*, as well as in popular U.S. discourses on Haiti in the 1920s and 1930s. Chapter 6 examines the cultivation of imperial consciousness through travel literature and pulp fiction in the 1920s and 1930s. It focuses on the role of sexuality in travel accounts and traces the cultural construction of psychological interiority through such discourses. African American writers' and artists' interventions into racial politics in the United States through the vehicle of cultural production related to Haiti and the Haitian Revolution form the basis of Chapter 7, culminating in a discussion of Zora Neale Hurston's creative response to paternalist discourses in *Tell My Horse*.

The U.S. encounter with Haiti between 1915 and 1940 altered both Haiti and the United States. In more profound and immediate respects, this encounter transformed Haiti, though not necessarily in the ways intended by U.S. policy makers. By crushing Haitian peasant rebellion and by creating the mechanisms for strongly centralized government control in Port-au-Prince, the occupation eliminated the very safeguards against entrenched despotism that Haiti, for all its problems, had always successfully maintained. In doing so, U.S. Americans helped to lay the groundwork for two Duvalier dictatorships and a series of post-Duvalier military regimes.[86]

The impact of the occupation of Haiti on the United States, the subject of the present study, was less complete but nonetheless profoundly significant. This impact must be understood in the larger context of U.S. imperialist actions around the globe. The occupation of Haiti was one instance of this extraordinary transformation of the U.S. role in the world, and in U.S. Americans' beliefs about themselves as Americans.

At the same time, the 1915–34 occupation of Haiti facilitated the domestic renegotiation of racial and gender issues in ways that other interventions did not. Haiti's proximity to the United States may have had something to do with this, as well as the fact that the occupation lasted a long nineteen years. Yet, the major distinction seems to have been the U.S. American perception of Haiti as a distinctly black nation. This difference, this perception of Haiti as an "American Africa" just off the southern coast of the United States, positioned the Caribbean nation as a significant figure in contestations over U.S. American national identity between 1915 and 1940.

OCCUPATION

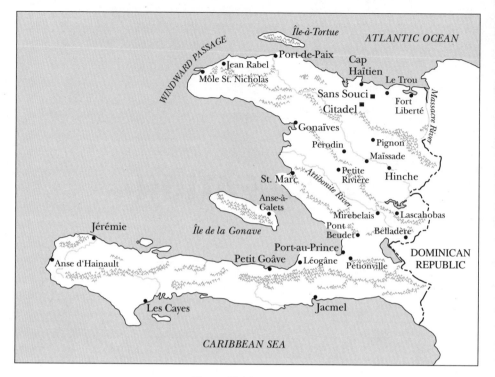

Map 2. Haiti

HAITI AND THE MARINES

MAKING SENSE OF THE OCCUPATION

Corporal Homer Overley didn't know what to think. He'd left a small, rural town in Illinois to join the Marines and, by 1920, had landed in Port-au-Prince with his new buddies in the Fifty-seventh Company. From their main post in the capital, Overley and his fellow recruits patrolled the hills around Mirebelais and Lascahobas, from Bon Repos, just north of the capital, to Belladère in the East, a stone's throw from the Dominican border. The main strength of the Cacos' military opposition had been sapped, but the war continued in fits, and the marines of the Fifty-seventh Company, searching out the remaining rebels, worried about "loosing" their heads in the hills.[1] Hungry, thirsty, and carrying a heavy pack over long, rough, rocky trails — as he later recalled — Overley sometimes cursed and sometimes kept his thoughts to himself.[2]

Nineteen years old and a private when he arrived in Haiti, the young Overley was quick to learn Creole and, before long, prided himself on his ability to communicate directly with Haitians.[3] Perhaps this contributed to his promotion to the status of a noncommissioned officer. Even so, as a corporal his allegiance was still clear; he was an enlisted man with all the resentment and apprehension toward officers that came along with that station.[4] And if learning Creole helped him learn a little more about the people whose nation he patrolled, it did nothing to help him understand the men above him. Orders didn't come with explanations. The average marine was left to wonder, and it seems that's just what Homer Overley did.[5]

He wondered about the Haitian workers he observed as he patrolled the Haitian American Sugar Company grounds near Port-au-Prince.[6] He wondered about the wealthy Americans and Europeans who owned HASCO.[7] He wondered about the fate of marines captured by the rebels; he'd heard

*Figure 3. Portrait of Homer L. Overley, 1920. Marine Corps
Research Center Archives, Quantico, Virginia.*

Figure 4. Homer L. Overley and fellow marines pose in the field. Overley is on the left. Marine Corps Research Center Archives, Quantico, Virginia.

stories enough to fuel his imagination on that question.[8] He wondered why it always seemed to be the officers who got the credit, when it was the men themselves who braved the odds and fired the decisive shots.[9] He wondered, one day as he approached a large group of Haitians with only four other marines on hand, whether they were Cacos or rioters who might overpower his small patrol.[10] He had orders not to speak to any natives, but he spoke to the group's leader, the local chief of section.[11] He had orders — or so he said — "to shoot all Cacos and Voodoes [*sic*]," but he didn't shoot, though he learned they were on their way to a dance in honor of their priestess.[12] Perhaps he wondered what went on at such dances; almost certainly he wondered what this "Voodoe" was, and what it had to do with the rebellion.

Other marines had more troubling encounters with the mysteries of this foreign culture in this land they had invaded. In the thick of the war against the Cacos, marines could find themselves disoriented, not only by unfamiliar terrain or insufficient rations, but also by the unnerving sounds of drums and conch horns coming from near and far. One marine described the experience of coming on a Caco camp: "We passed the outpost with no resistance but after passing them about 150 Cacos fell in behind us armed with rifles, machetes, and sharp pointed sticks, keeping up an incessant blowing of conch horns and beating of drums . . . at the second outpost . . . a much larger force . . . fell in rear of us also keeping up the conch horn music which will never be forgotten by the men as it was the weirdest of sounds under the circumstances any of us had ever heard."[13] We don't know whether Haitians — seeing the effect of the conch on marines in the field — ever purposely used "the incessant blowing of conch horns and beating of drums" to unsettle marines on patrol. Nor do we know whether Marine Corps officers realized the precise uses of the conch in battle. We do know, however, that officers in the field recognized that the conch posed a threat, at the very least, because it shook the confidence of their men. Hence Captain Chandler Campbell's promise, in the fall of 1915, to burn the houses and destroy the crops of the Cacos "if they blow anymore conches."[14]

What to make of the conches, the drums, the worshipers going to honor their priestess? What to make of commanding officers, demanding duty, silent fellow recruits? What to make of poor Haitians, wealthy Americans, French priests, and Germans? What to make of one's own role in such a complex situation? Some years later, with the benefit of hindsight and perhaps an anti-imperialist tract or two, ex-corporal Homer Overley reflected on his service in Haiti. "We who served in [the] Marines received little credit," he wrote; we "tried to keep Esprit du Corps high to cover for service which was often disillusioning," so disillusioning, in fact, "that we sometimes wondered just what was right or wrong" and "what it was all about."[15]

The State Department and the U.S. Navy certainly hoped to keep marines straight on the question of what it was all about. The official story of paternal guidance offered to a child-nation in need was intended in part to clarify questions of right and wrong. Yet the marines were operating in a complex cultural context, shaped not only by their government's rhetoric and propaganda, but also by the realities of Haitian history and culture that surrounded them. The encounter between Haiti and the marines that was initiated by the invasion of 1915 continued each time a patrol found a Caco camp or met a group of peasants going to a dance. The cultural baggage these young men brought with them to Haiti — from their upbringing, their training, their previous tours of duty, and their camaraderie en route — all this helped to shape what they saw and heard when they encountered Haitians and what sense they made of the occupation they were carrying out. Just as significant were the cultural and historical discourses that shaped the world the marines invaded. Before turning to the marines, let us first ask, Whose shores had they breached?

LANDSCAPES INSCRIBED WITH HISTORY

As marines patrolled the streets of Port-au-Prince and Cap Haïtien, as they made their way through the Haitian countryside, they encountered the traces of slavery, of independence, and of struggle. In a sense, every conch announced the living history of Haiti and Haitian resistance to domination. Every drum sounded a beat that echoed more than a century of political independence and cultural autonomy. To what extent marines and other Americans could decipher the history implicit in the sights and sounds that surrounded them is a question we must take up in time. But first, let us consider the cultural and historical terrain the marines trod in Haiti.

In the center of Port-au-Prince, in front of the Palace, which was built under the supervision of the marines, and across from the Champs de Mars, the fields on which those same marines conducted daily drills and exercises, now stands a statue, known as "neg maron." It is a towering representation of a maroon — an escaped slave — blowing a conch shell.[16] The statue shows the rippled muscles of a powerful man sounding a call to revolution. It invokes a proud history of Haiti, one that goes back to the connections between maroons and slaves, and their common bond in the New World religion of Vodou. In part on the strength of that religion, men and women who labored in Saint Domingue's cane fields under the brutal yoke of French slavery came together with those who had fled the plantations to plan and carry out the only successful slave revolution in the Atlantic world. In the summer of 1791, in the woods of northern Haiti, the sound of the conch horn was heard, and slaves and ex-slaves gathered for secret Vodou services that nurtured the will to rebel. It is said that on August 14, 1791, one such service took place, led by a priestess, whose name we do not know, and a priest named Boukman. The assembled took an oath, known as the Oath of Bois Caiman, to revolt in solidarity with one another.[17] A week later, the slaves of Saint Domingue's northern plains rose in unison against their masters.

The statue of neg maron did not greet the marines who entered Port-au-Prince between 1915 and 1934; it came later. Yet the proud history embodied in that statue was embodied earlier in the conch itself and in its use by Caco rebels and ordinary peasants. The conch or *lanbi* is sounded to link people across great distances, for example, to communicate across the field of battle.[18] It is used to call people together for a work gang, to call people in from the fields for a meal, and to signal the end of the workday. It is used, as we have seen, to announce the start of the Vodou service, just as it was used in Bois Caiman in 1791. Thus, the symbolism of the conch is powerful for a people who have drawn the strength to gain and maintain their independence from the power of their religion. (Conch meat, moreover, is said to make a man virile.) For all these reasons, a conch horn could function as a literal artifact of a proud history, passed down from father to son, again and again, linking a family across the generations, quite possibly from the Revolution down to the present.[19]

Conch shells were scattered across the landscape of Haiti during the occupation.[20] Whereas for Haitians they signified a revolutionary heritage, a connection to fearsome ancestors who took matters into their own hands, for U.S. Americans they could seem mere decorative appurtenances or, as we have seen, they could stimulate fear. Even after the definitive success of the military campaign against the Cacos, conch shells could be associated with danger. They turned up, for example, in the campaign against malaria and other mosquito-borne diseases carried on by the Service d'Hygiène, or Public Health Service, in the early 1920s. Lieutenant Commander Eaton of the U.S. Navy, serving as acting sanitary engineer, admonished marines to do their part for public health in Haiti by looking in their own yards for "those pink and white conch shells around the rose garden" and emptying them of water at least once each week. Lest his audience dismiss his plea as trivial, Eaton warned: "The prosperity of whole states, of whole countries[,] has been blighted[,] and the power of strong armies has withered and vanished[,] because of disease."[21] His warning may well have reminded marines and sailors in Haiti of what they had undoubtedly heard about the demise of the French in revolutionary Saint Domingue; reluctant to attribute military success to an army of black ex-slaves, some writers credited the mosquito with the defeat of Napoleon's army.[22] Vigilant marines could avoid the same fate by taking action in their own yards.

Pumpkins were scattered across the landscape of Haiti, too, at least at certain times of the year. And while they may have seemed a familiar sight to marines raised with Halloween traditions, like conch shells they resonated with the strains of Haiti's revolutionary heritage. Haitians raised — and still raise — pumpkins to make Soup Joumou. In some households, it is served every Sunday; in others it is reserved for even more special occasions. Certainly it is served at the feast celebrated on January 1, Haitian Independence Day — marking the triumph of the Revolution as declared by General

Jean Jacques Dessalines on January 1, 1804. The slaves of eighteenth-century Saint Domingue served their masters Soup Joumou every January 1 for the New Year's feast but were themselves denied the taste of pumpkin soup.[23] One tradition is that Haitians eat pumpkin soup on Independence Day to remind themselves that they are fully human — despite the lies of slavery.[24] Another recalls the history of slave resistance carried on by women who added poison to the Soup Joumou they served to their masters.[25]

From conches and pumpkins to flags and fortresses, a thousand details filled the marine's field of vision with the signs of a living history that was — and is — powerfully embodied in Haitian culture. Small material artifacts, imposing architectural structures, small gestures exchanged in greeting between Haitians, and the rhythmic sounds of sacred instruments all spoke to the significance of history and of ancestors in the daily life and culture of Haitians. *Dèsalin mwen monte'm* (the spirit of Dessalines is upon me) a marine may well have heard a Haitian utter in anger; the phrase captured the continued presence of the Revolution in the emotional lexicon of Haitian culture.[26]

A full appreciation of the importance of historical memory in Haiti would require a subtle understanding of the spiritual world of Haitian religion and its diverse cultural manifestations, secular as well as sacred. Haitians who participate in the sacred forms of that spiritual world describe their religious practice as *sèvi lwa* (serving the spirits).[27] For outsiders, the word "Vodou," derived from the Dahomean word for "spirit" or "deity," names the religion as well as the cultural context that surrounds and emanates from it.[28] Vodou has its roots in the religious traditions of West and Central Africa brought to the French colony of Saint Domingue by men and women forced into slavery in the seventeenth and eighteenth centuries. A syncretic religion and a creole cultural form, it was forged out of those traditions in combination with aspects of Amerindian sacred traditions and Catholicism in the New World context of Saint Domingue, and later Haiti.[29]

At the heart of Vodou is the process by which men and women (known as *sèvitè* in Creole, *serviteurs* in French) serve the spirits. That process includes, but is not limited to, the ceremonies in which a *manbo* (priestess) or *houngan* (priest) prepares the way for a spirit to enter the human scene through possession. When this takes place, the spirit is said to "mount" the devotee, just as a rider mounts a horse. Arriving in this way, the various spirits (*lwa/loa*) remind the assembled of their obligations and of their history. To cite one example, anthropologist Karen McCarthy Brown explains that the spirit known as Azaka or Papa Zaka, who is a humble and illiterate peasant farmer, "functions to remind devotees of their roots, of their need for family (a group that includes the ancestors and spirits), and of their connection to the land."[30]

The Haitians who greeted marines in 1915 and after were thus engaged in remembering and retelling their history as a people who had freed themselves from slavery and who had forged a nation and a way of life on their own ancestral terms. Yet marines and other U.S. Americans arrived wearing blindfolds fashioned from the discursive traditions of European and U.S. racism and so — most often — failed to see what was before them. They railed against the ignorance of the country people — so much superstition standing in the way of progress.[31] They confiscated drums and saved them as exotic souvenirs of a mysterious, primitive land, without ever knowing the richness of Haitian religious traditions.[32] They named their animals after revolutionary heroes like Toussaint L'Ouverture, while dismissing Haiti as "a classic example of the Negro not being able to govern himself well."[33]

Had they ventured into a bookshop or library in Port-au-Prince (and perhaps some did, though they did not leave a record of it), they would have found evidence of a long and textured tradition of Haitian historical writing that might have illuminated the significance of some of what they saw around them. The tradition began in 1804 with pamphlet writers who defended the Haitian Revolution against defamation by the defeated French. Historian Gordon K. Lewis describes these early pamphleteers as "proud, educated Haitians, theoreticians of a new black American Republicanism."[34] They called for military preparedness to protect the new nation, praised the laws and institutions of Haiti as bastions of freedom, and heralded the arrival of black civilization in a world dominated by slaveholding nations. Following the early pamphleteers, the baron De Vastey, a leading intellectual and political adviser to Haiti's King Henri Christophe, continued the defense of the Revolution, as did subsequent generations of noted Haitian historians including Thomas Madiou, Alexis Beaubrun Ardouin, Joseph Saint Remy, and others.[35]

A BRIEF NARRATIVE OF HAITI, 1791–1915

The revolution that lived — and lives — on in Haitian historical memory began in the course of the French Revolution when, on the night of August 22, 1791, the black slaves of Saint Domingue's northern plains torched the cane fields and set upon their masters with whatever weapons they had at their disposal.[36] For over twelve years, men and women who began the

46   OCCUPATION

Revolution as slaves fought with and against the Spanish, the English, and the French to secure their freedom and, eventually, their national independence.[37] Approximately 500,000 in number when the Revolution began, slaves far outnumbered both white slave owners and free, property-owning people of color, known as *affranchis*.[38] By 1793 slavery was abolished and Toussaint L'Ouverture had emerged as the leader of the blacks. The affranchis fought for control of the Revolution in a struggle that lasted to the end of the century and ended with power firmly in Toussaint's hands.

By mid-1800 Toussaint L'Ouverture established his own power so thoroughly that, while he did not formally break with Napoleon, there was no question as to who was in charge.[39] "The Black Consul" established a new government for Saint Domingue, complete with new laws, new taxes, a new currency, and, having ousted French officials from all administrative posts, new appointees of his own choosing.[40] Toussaint opened trade with Britain and the United States, encouraged French plantation owners to remain in Saint Domingue, and did what he could to return the former slaves to plantation labor.[41] The agricultural prosperity that had made Saint Domingue the crown jewel of the French empire would henceforth, he believed, secure the freedom of his people.[42] When the newly freed men and women of Saint Domingue resisted his entreaties and set about establishing themselves as independent farmers, Toussaint placed the plantations under military authority and promulgated a series of labor laws designed to restore the plantation system as the paramount mode of production in Saint Domingue.[43]

Other revolutionary leaders had other plans for Saint Domingue. Jean Jacques Dessalines and Henri Christophe, for example, disagreed with their leader's decision to rely on French planters to maintain Saint Domingue's prosperity. Like Toussaint, they sought to maintain an export-oriented economy based on plantation agriculture, but they were determined to remove the threat, represented by the continued presence of the French on the island, of a return to slavery.[44] With the arrest and deportation of Toussaint by French general LeClerc in June 1802, Dessalines and Christophe took the reins of the Revolution. Under the leadership of Dessalines, the revolutionary army finally succeeded in defeating the French army and ousting French plantation owners. With the founding of the Republic of Haiti in 1804 came a prohibition on foreign land ownership and the flight or massacre of most whites still remaining in Haiti.[45]

From the founding of the nation in 1804 to its occupation by the United States 111 years later, Haitians struggled to establish viable communities at local and national levels and to maintain the security of their freedom and independence. To appreciate the difficulty of these struggles, we must view them in the dual context of internal social divisions and international hostility and domination.

The most significant social division within the new nation was that between revolutionary leaders, with their visions of plantation-based prosperity, and the majority of former slaves, for whom "freedom" meant, above all, freedom from the brutalities associated with sugarcane cultivation.[46] At the time of the Revolution, sugar had been the most profitable crop and the most widespread form of cultivation in Saint Domingue, covering the colony's rich plains. Coffee plantations, on the other hand, had predominated in mountainous areas. Following the Revolution, Haitian workers sought an end to the plantation system and the assurance that they would never return to the backbreaking work of sugar cultivation or to the indignities of cane field overseers. As a result, many ex-slaves abandoned the estates, which were almost all in the hands of the state by 1806, and turned to the practice of squatting on vacant lands.[47] They cultivated subsistence crops and picked and marketed coffee beans from existing bushes according to local needs.[48] Those ex-slaves who were able to secure title to plots of land by virtue of their military service followed similar economic patterns. In this way, squatters and landowning ex-slaves established subsistence agriculture as their primary mode of existence while also making possible a limited export economy.[49]

Haiti's emerging political class did not respond to this trend with one voice. Indeed, following the assassination of Dessalines in 1806, the former revolutionary generals Alexandre Pétion and Henri Christophe established separate states based on divergent models of political leadership and economic development. This political division of Haiti also drew on ancillary social divisions within the new nation (e.g., between mulatto and black, between *ancien libres* and *nouveau libres*).[50] Civil war ensued for the next fourteen years. Pétion, sharing power with allied political elites through the institution of a strong Senate, effectively hastened the breakup of plantations by distributing significant parcels of land to army officers and also by making such parcels available by sale.[51] Christophe, operating within a more authoritarian system — which would be transformed into a monarchy by the constitution of 1811 — did more to maintain the plantation system, with strict military supervision over the labor process.[52]

With the death of Christophe and the reunification of the country under Jean-Pierre Boyer in 1820, the basic character of Haitian land and labor patterns seemed to be clearly established in spite of elite attempts to reinstitute the plantation system.[53] Boyer's Rural Code of 1826 represented a last systematic attempt to attach laborers to plantations as a way to revitalize the plantation system and thus strengthen the export economy. Its complete failure marked the successful creation of the Haitian peasantry.[54] The majority of Haitians now lived on relatively small plots of land, which they tilled either as squatters, as renters, or, in fewer cases, as titleholders. Men cultivated crops, if and when they were not serving in the army, while women worked the land and also marketed crops. Production was oriented, first and foremost, toward subsistence, but peasant families also produced for local and international markets. Women's roles in marketing thus encompassed both the sale of surplus food in local markets and the sale of export crops, such as coffee, to *spéculateurs*, who would in turn sell them to seaport merchants. These *spéculateurs* were also women, as were a whole range of midlevel entrepreneurs, known as *madam sara*, who bought and sold a variety of goods, and whose commerce constituted the primary trade networks between countryside and city.[55]

Relations between rural peasants and urban elites, including those who ran the government in Port-au-Prince, took shape in the context of ongoing elite struggles for control over economic production and ongoing peasant resistance to domination. Boyer, for example, persisted in the effort to revive large-scale cultivation; to this end, he attempted to attract black workers from the United States. President Fabre Nicolas Geffrard did likewise between 1859 and 1861, but neither effort shifted the dominant trend of small-holding subsistence-oriented production. Meanwhile, urban elites found other mechanisms to extract profit from peasants, leading to intermittent protest and revolt. Rebellions flared up in response to unfair land distribution, tax increases, the exploitation of rural producers by seaport merchants, and various manifestations of despotic government control. In some cases, populist figures rose to national office on the strength of the support they received as champions of peasant causes.[56] The most significant rebellions began in 1806 under the leadership of Goman in the South; in 1843 under Salomon, then under Acaau, also in the South; in 1865 under Salnave in the Artibonite Valley; in 1867 in the North; and again in 1911 in the North under Charlemagne Péralte.[57] Throughout the nineteenth century, national leaders were thus forced to take account of peasants' demands as they pursued the creation of a viable economy.

In 1920 Joseph Lanoue and Constant Vieux, the antioccupation editors of *Le Courrier Haïtien*, summed up this history of peasant struggle against those who held the reins of state power from one generation to the next. "Our poor and feeble country," they wrote, having "shaken off the yoke of the masters by one of the most beautiful episodes in the history of nations," went on to struggle against a succession of rulers who became, in effect, "new masters with whom it was always necessary to reckon," notwithstanding the fact that they consistently placed "themselves under the banner of our patriotic revolutions." "In the last resort," they concluded, "the result was always disastrously the same: he whom we raised to power was and could be only a new exemplar of him whom we had driven out."[58]

Yet, while most nineteenth-century Haitian political leaders did not share the social and economic goals of the peasantry, neither did they seek merely to subjugate their countrymen.[59] Drawn largely from among the elite descendants of Saint Domingue's free people of color and from the upper ranks of the military, these men embraced the economic and political models current in the Atlantic community. They sought paths of national development consonant with those models: the control of wealth by an educated merchant elite was one cornerstone of their vision. They were, without question, insensitive to the hardships of those from whose labor they sought to profit; they shared this insensitivity with their counterparts abroad. Yet they faced obstacles their foreign counterparts did not face. For Haitian leaders worked to integrate their nation into international networks of trade and credit on viable, if not highly profitable, terms in the face of international hostility as well as determined peasant resistance.[60]

Haitians experienced international hostility in several forms, including, most notably, political isolation and the threat of a French attempt to retake the island nation. Economic disadvantages related to the absence of diplomatic representation with trading partners and to the withholding of missionary assistance by the Vatican also raised problems for Haiti.[61] Haiti's political isolation resulted, most directly, from its nonrecognition by France in the wake of Dessalines's ouster of French planters from the new nation. As we have seen, U.S. president Thomas Jefferson considered his nation's relations with Napoleon when he decided to sever diplomatic relations with Haiti and impose an embargo in 1806, despite the significance of the West Indian trade to American merchants.[62] The new Latin American nations, in turn, acted out of concern for their relations with the United States when they snubbed Haiti at the first Pan-American talks in Panama in 1825. Other nations also refused to recognize Haiti until France agreed to do so. As a nation of freed slaves in a world dominated by slaveholding nations, Haiti effectively held pariah status.

If there was little Haitian leaders could do about their diplomatic isolation, the same could not be said about the military threat posed by France. Thus, to protect Haiti against French invasion, Dessalines initiated and Christophe presided over the building of a massive fortress known as the

Citadel, an architectural feat that would engender contradictory emotions in Haitians. Countless workers lost their lives in the course of its construction, carried out with compulsory labor under strict military direction. At the same time, the sheer enormity of its mass stood as a statement of Haitian will, independence, and defiance in the face of international racism. In the official discourse of Christophe's court, liberty was not an individual value to be enjoyed by peasants who would do as they please, but rather a collective status to be enjoyed by the nation as a whole and to be protected by strict military discipline.[63]

Haiti finally secured French recognition, and the promise of peaceful intercourse with France, in 1825, less than a decade after the completion of the Citadel. It came at a cost of 150 million francs, in the form of an indemnity to be paid to the former planters of Saint Domingue.[64] As Haitian leaders turned their attention to this new economic hurdle, they faced a host of problems including the insufficiency of their exports and a scarcity of credit. It was in this context that Boyer attempted to impose the Rural Code that failed so miserably.[65] Forced to accept French assistance to pay their former masters, Haitians found themselves operating under French domination for the next half century. Thus, the indemnity crippled an already troubled Haitian economy. And as the nineteenth century wore on, government corruption and factional struggles exacerbated the problem, with political aspirants attempting to use foreign powers to further their own career goals and economic interests.[66] The context of forced dependency thus framed the dissolution of Haitian independence, while internal social and political divisions hastened the process.

Economic instability, peasant revolts, factional elite coups, and government corruption increasingly provided the practical basis for foreign domination in Haiti. France maintained control through the manipulation of the indemnity and later the debt that replaced it; Britain exerted control in the guise of protecting British citizens and their property; German merchants financed revolutions and penetrated the Haitian economy, circumventing the prohibition on foreign property ownership through intermarriage with Haitian women; and, with increasing rapidity after the turn of the century, Americans became entrenched in Haitian economic affairs. Throughout the century, Haitian political leaders debated the relative benefits and dangers of using foreign capital to finance Haitian development and increasingly allowed for its introduction, laying the grounds for future interventions.

Among the most important economic and political developments leading up to the U.S. occupation were those events marking increased foreign investment in Haiti. In 1871 President Salomon presided over the founding of the Banque Nationale, in which France received a controlling interest, and saw to the legal revisions that would allow foreign companies limited land-ownership rights in Haiti. Under the presidency of Simon Sam, from 1896 to 1902, German involvement in Haitian affairs increased significantly. In 1908 President Antoine Simon signed the McDonald contract, giving extensive rights to an American company to build a railroad in Haiti. One Haitian commentator has identified 1910 as the crucial year of transition from French to American predominance in the Haitian economy; in that year, the United States secured control of the Banque Nationale.[67] The Caco rebellion of 1911 expressed peasant discontent with the economic domination manifested in the McDonald contract, brought Simon's presidency to an end, provided the muscle for a succession of other presidents, and continued long enough to meet the U.S. Marines in 1915.

Meanwhile, despite the mounting difficulty of maintaining economic and political control in Haiti, members of the Haitian elite continued to draw a profound sense of dignity and self-respect from the highly cultured community they had developed in Port-au-Prince — and abroad. Classical education, sometimes in Paris, artistic and literary achievements, and professional training in law and medicine set elite Haitians apart from the indignities peddled by sensationalist foreign writers. Although Europeans and Americans drew portraits of Haiti as a land of cannibalism and "Voodoo" licentiousness, elite Haitians challenged such base characterizations with a profound sense of pride in their own cultural achievements. At times, they even turned the discourse of civilization back on the whites who fashioned it. Thus, with the emergence of the Pan-African movement around the turn of the century, some educated Haitians spoke out against European colonialism, urging Africans, in one case, to "chase the savage and criminal oppressor from their territory." Indeed, the history of Haiti could provide the model: "Are there," Haitians asked from Paris, "no descendants of Toussaint and Dessalines in Africa?"[68]

Thus, Haitians — peasants and elites alike — invoked the names of their revolutionary heroes as they negotiated their respective present-day struggles. In sacred practices, oral traditions, material culture, and written narratives, they told and retold the history of the Revolution, and of the nation it birthed, as a way of understanding and confronting the challenges they faced. Whether a given narrator emphasized the heroism of Ogé and Chavannes, free men of color who challenged French domination several years before Boukman emerged as a leader of slaves and maroons, or that of Dessalines and Christophe, finally driving out the French and founding the nation, his or her particular version of Haitian history spoke of the present as well as the past.

Likewise, during the occupation of 1915–34, Haitians continued to retell their history with new lessons for the future. Jean Price-Mars, for example, a leading statesman and intellectual just returned from France, gave a series of lectures in Port-au-Prince in 1917 urging educated Haitians to embrace their connections to working people. Price-Mars put a new spin on the memory of Toussaint L'Ouverture. He was still the "immortal statesman" who had led Haitians to freedom, but he had too readily adopted the oppressive practices of the French toward the former slaves, setting a bad precedent for Haiti's future heads of state. As Magdaline W. Shannon has pointed out, Price-Mars drew a historical link between slave masters, Toussaint with his ill-gotten labor laws, nineteenth-century Haitian elites, and the U.S. military, which now sought to impose its will through the corvée.[69] For Price-Mars, as for so many others, the revolutionary past and its heroes could help Haiti get its bearings in the present.

By July 1915, more than ever, Haitians needed to get their bearings. Their nation was strife-torn and battle-scarred. With the elites' economic control collapsing under the combined weight of foreign and peasant pressure, and with the peasants primed to resist further economic domination, American marines landed.

AMERICAN MARINES

The marines who landed in Haiti in 1915 and after needed to get their bearings, too. Coming ashore on unfamiliar territory, making their way through a country with signs and sounds they could neither read nor heed, they had to keep their wits about them. One way to do that was to remember who they were: U.S. marines, American men, doing an errand for their nation.

Indeed, the marines who occupied Haiti were all American, and yet this small statement harbors a much more complex history than we might think at first glance. For each marine had a distinct relationship to the United States and to his own Americanness. To our knowledge, none of the marines were African American, unless there were men who passed as white when they joined the Marine Corps and managed to keep their secrets well thereafter. But among the thousands of "white" U.S. marines who served in Haiti between 1915 and 1934 were men with a wide range of ethnic, regional, and cultural backgrounds. Some were immigrants, some native-born, some farm boys, some streetwise urban toughs. Some were Minnesota lads who had never met a black man, some Carolina youths used to the ring of "Sir" and "Ma'am," some fresh recruits, some seasoned leathernecks. Each one confronted his whiteness and his Americanness in some new way when he encountered Haiti.

Southern white men's identification with America was, to begin with, crosscut in complicated ways by race and history in the first decades of the twentieth century.[70] As they disembarked in Haiti, southern marines could claim the president of their nation as one of their own, for Woodrow Wilson, though his father had been a northerner, was born in Virginia, and passed his childhood in Georgia and South Carolina.[71] On the other hand, the South's relation to the nation remained a live question for many sons and daughters of the Confederacy. The war with Spain had done much to re-unite North and South, and the national embrace of empire and evolutionary theory helped to strengthen a shared racial nationalism.[72] Yet northern publishers still printed textbook histories that read like so many lies to a loyal white southerner, who had heard stories of an altogether different nature at his grandfather's knee.[73] Growing up in Virginia, Archer Vandegrift was one such southerner, inspired by family stories and nearby Civil War battlefields. Thinking back to his childhood in the 1890s, he later commented, "In those years we lived rather close to the Civil War."[74]

Citizenship was racialized for southern white men, as it was for their fellow marines from the North; to be "American" was, implicitly, to be white. Yet, for southern white men, the connection between whiteness and citizenship had been forged in the context of relative interracial proximity and even intimacy. Historically, African Americans and whites shared the same geographic and physical spaces in the South but inhabited them according to strictly hierarchical notions of "place." Interracial contact was possible because, as Glenda Gilmore has pointed out, it was regulated by a precise caste system "in which skin color, class, and gender dictated the pattern of every daily interaction."[75] While an emerging regime of terror increasingly enforced this caste system in the decades leading up to the occupation, a persistent southern tradition of paternalism styled the South's relative inter-racial intimacy in familial terms, erasing the very relations of power that had constituted slavery. As one "Georgia daughter" explained in a 1912 lecture, "we have now living amongst us some who lived during the old plantation days—some who can now tell us from their own experiences what that institution of slavery was, and what it meant to them and to the negroes under their control. In those days we never thought of calling them slaves.

That is a word that crept in with the abolition crusade. They were our people, our negroes, part of our very homes."[76] In a strikingly similar vein, one marine from Fairfax County, Virginia, recalled with affection his "Mammy Page" and " 'Aunt' Sara Tyler, who had been a slave."[77] Claiming African Americans as "our people," white southerners shaped by paternalism felt that they knew all they needed to know about what life was like for "the negroes under their control." Thus, proximity, in and of itself, did not threaten the racial caste system or the exclusivity of citizenship.[78]

On the other hand, African Americans who claimed equality and citizenship did threaten the racial caste system, and that threat, combined with the challenges posed by economic dislocation, led white southerners to fashion the more unabashedly violent racial protocol of the late nineteenth and early twentieth centuries. Indeed, U.S. marines shipped off from a South shaped fundamentally by a regime of racial violence.[79] Violence, of course, had always been part of the system; within the framework of paternalism it had been couched as discipline. Following emancipation, white violence intensified as former slave owners sought to maintain a modified system of domination over African Americans, but, in time, some southern elites turned instead to the possibility of maintaining white supremacy through a paternalist accommodation with African American leaders. The seeming accommodation broke down as African American men asserted themselves as a political force. In the early decades of the twentieth century, self-styled "New White Men" rejected their fathers' paternalism and embraced the myth of rapacious black male sexuality to justify a reign of terror against African Americans.[80] As we shall see in Chapter 4, some marines brought with them to Haiti the tradition of tying black men to trees.

For white southerners, the special significance of race — with its affective component — could lead to special challenges in Haiti. According to Haitian oral tradition passed down from the days of the occupation, more than one marine flew into a rage when addressed by a native Haitian using an ordinary Creole phrase for hailing a stranger; for, no doubt, *neg*, which means simply, harmlessly, "guy," struck an especially painful chord in white southern ears.[81] In a slightly different vein, one wonders what it must have been like for a man from the hills of Tennessee to hear his fellow marines denigrate and condescend to Haitian peasants because the latter were barefoot. "The shoeless class," Smedley Butler called them.[82] Yet, a backwoods boy might have been shoeless for most of his own life before joining the military, as had A. D. Chaffin. In 1929, Chaffin wrote to fellow Tennesseean Robert Barker, who had been decorated for his service in Haiti, that as "a native of Jackson County, Tennessee," he "never wore shoes until seventeen years of age" and for years to come suffered "untold agony in submitting to such a convention."[83] Thus, whether wealthy or poor, whether of tidewater or mountain origins, whether close to traditions of plantation paternalism or to backwoods white ways of life, southern men experienced various forms of dissonance in their relation to America, forms of dissonance that could turn shrill in the unexpected circumstances of the Haitian occupation.

Meanwhile, young men from the North and Midwest had their own kinds of complicated relationships to U.S. national identity.[84] Homer Overley's Yeoman, Indiana, for example, and Faustin Wirkus's Pittston, Pennsylvania, marked them as particular kinds of Americans. As we shall see, when Jack Craige felt unsteady in the face of Haiti's radical otherness, he turned to his own heritage as a Pennsylvanian to get his bearings.[85] Whether they took their Americanness for granted or felt some dissonance in relation to it, northern and midwestern men experienced national identity in relation to local and regional ties. "Place" was as important to them as to southern marines, although they may have defined it differently.

Thus, northern and midwestern boys, like their southern brothers-in-arms, had the opportunity to experience their nation in new ways when they were thrown together with their fellow Americans from near and far. F. W. Schmidt, for example, sent home a picture of himself with a group of "boys" serving with him in Haiti (Figure 5). He carefully labeled almost every figure in the photograph: "Boy from Vineland, New Jersey," "Boy from Detroit," "Boy from Boston," and "Boy from Louisville, Kentucky" — the only southerner in the shot.[86] There were three from Detroit, as it happened, two from Philadelphia, one from Pittsburgh, two from Long Island, including Schmidt himself, and, finally, one "Boy from nowhere, a good for nothing bum." We are left to wonder what dishonor led to that ignominious label. Did the boy hail from some town so small or so far away from an urban center that, by a Long Island boy's lights, it did not even deserve a name? Or had the boy done something to bring on his messmates' derision, so that Schmidt refused to dignify him with a place, a name for home? Quite possibly he was one of the thousands of young working-class men who became transient workers, traveling between city and countryside, in search of meager wages as agricultural laborers, lumberjacks, construction workers, ice cutters, and the like.[87] In any case, the insult was clear enough in contrast to the honor Schmidt accorded the others. A "bum" had no "place." Local identities, signifying rootedness and status, mattered.

Quite apart from the regional mix of their company or platoon, young men from the North and Midwest had the opportunity to experience regional differences within their nation when they landed at Norfolk, Vir-

*Figure 5. Postcard sent home from Haiti by F. W. Schmidt, with his list of the
marines' hometowns. Schmidt, who called one of his fellow marines a "boy
from nowhere," is in the back row, second from left. Marine
Corps Research Center Archives, Quantico, Virginia.*

ginia, and later, Parris Island, South Carolina, for boot camp.[88] Most of them saw the South, for the first time, from the vantage point of military compounds and, perhaps, as they explored their surroundings during precious off-duty hours. None of them had escaped northern racism, though it may have escaped their conscious awareness, but seeing the racial codes of the South up close for the first time, they most likely thought about race in new ways.

Meanwhile, the evolving racial codes of various northern and midwestern settings, as well as national racial discourses, shaped the men who arrived at recruiting stations from Portsmouth, New Hampshire, to Des Moines, Iowa.[89] In Minnesota, for example, white racial constructs took shape in relation to conflict with Native Americans, notably the Great Sioux Uprising of 1862, at least as much as in relation to the conflict between North and South.[90] New York City, on the other hand, had a history of racial violence linked specifically to urban tensions arising out of class and ethnic conflict.[91] In the first decades of the twentieth century, race began to assume new meanings in places like Springfield, Illinois, where, in 1908, white rioters seemed to erase the legacy of Abraham Lincoln. The journalist William English Walling observed at the time, "a large part of the white population of Lincoln's home, supported largely by the farmers and miners of the neighboring towns, have initiated a permanent warfare with the negro race."[92] Rioters themselves pointed to African Americans' increasingly apparent self-assertion as a cause of the violence, as one white man reported to Walling, "Why, [they] come to think they were as good as we are."[93] As the northward migration of African Americans picked up speed and volume during the world war, racism flared and violence spread in other cities across the North.[94]

Indeed, as northern recruits were making their way south, the Ku Klux Klan was making its way north and becoming a national organization. By the 1920s the Klan's "100 percent Americanism" was equally at home in Pennsylvania and Indiana as in its birthplace, Tennessee. North and South, the Klan spread a vision of nationalism reserved for native-born Anglo-Saxons, a vision that scapegoated African Americans, Jews, Catholics, and immigrants. True, when the marines arrived in Haiti in 1915, the Klan was still a southern affair, but the social dislocations that would inflame racial hatreds were well under way in the North, and some of the racial and ethnic habits of mind that proved fertile ground for the Klan in the years to come were already well entrenched. The assumption, for example, that Americanness resided prototypically in the figure of the unmarked white, Anglo-Saxon Protestant male had deep roots on both sides of the Mason-Dixon Line.[95]

The recollections of a retired Marine Corps officer who had grown up in Minneapolis and had gone on to serve in the occupation as a young man provide a particularly striking example of the way in which any mark of difference could detract from the impression of a white man's American-ness. Looking back on his service under the command of Major Smedley D. Butler, Lieutenant General Merwin Hancock Silverthorn called the former head of the Haitian Gendarmerie "a great American." Yet, he qualified his statement of praise. For Butler had certain prominent "idiosyncrasies," among them, according to Silverthorn, his having been a Quaker. "I've never had the privilege of serving under a better leader than Smedley Butler," recalled the Minnesotan. "So I forgive him for [such] idiosyncrasies."[96] Smedley Darlington Butler, whose very name announced his roots in at least three long-established Pennsylvania families, could trace his "American origins" back to the year 1710, when Noble Butler arrived on this side of the Atlantic to join William Penn's great experiment.[97] If his Quaker heritage and beliefs could be viewed as a mark against his American-ness, a personal peculiarity that had to be forgiven, how, indeed, did other religious and ethnic differences square with American identity for men in the corps?

In addition to Quakers (Butler was surely not the only "fighting Quaker" in the Marine Corps), other men came to the corps with marked identities: German, Irish, Slav, Polish, Serbian, Jewish, and others.[98] Some immigrants themselves, some the children of immigrants, they represented the United States even as they were yet becoming part of it. For some, including former President Theodore Roosevelt, this combination seemed just right. With a war raging in Europe, and U.S. cities teeming with immigrants—between 1900 and 1915 alone, more than 14 million arrived in the United States—Roosevelt promoted a combined program of military preparedness and Americanization through universal male conscription. The bunk and mess would provide a shared space in which diverse Americans—old and new— would forge a common national identity and affiliation.[99]

Roosevelt's idea that immigrants should serve in the U.S. armed forces was not new, though his reasoning may have been. Indeed, despite nativist preferences, manpower shortages forced all branches of the service to enlist significant numbers of immigrants during the nineteenth century. With low pay and poor working conditions to offer its men, the Marine Corps, like the U.S. Army, faced high desertion rates.[100] As of 1895, the result was that in some parts of the country fully a quarter of the corps' enlistments were made up of immigrant aliens.[101]

The war with Spain turned things around to a significant extent but not entirely. A new image, born of glowing press reports on marines' participation in the war — from the bravery of an enlisted man on board the *Maine* in Havana Harbor to the martial successes of Huntington's Battalion at Guantanamo Bay — helped draw increasing numbers of men to Marine Corps recruiting stations.[102] Twenty percent pay raises for all enlisted men, and the creation of dozens of new petty officer billets, may also have added to the appeal of service with the corps and certainly boosted reenlistment rates.[103] As a result, recruiting became more selective and specifically sought out "Americans" over and above immigrants. As Marine Corps commandant George F. Elliot admonished one recruitment officer who continued to place advertisements in Polish-language newspapers in 1908, it was "not desired to enlist Poles in the Marine Corps as long as Americans are available."[104] Still, by 1915 increased staffing levels led to 25 percent shortages in enlisted personnel and 40 percent shortages among officers.[105]

Thus, despite the increased popularity and the increasingly selective approach to recruitment, Marine Corps rolls still carried surnames indicating diverse ethnic origins, and immigrants as well as the children of immigrants continued to sport the eagle, globe, and anchor.[106] To be sure, the process of Americanization began well before such young men arrived at recruit depots. Schooling in the United States had for some time been oriented toward that end: "health inspections, patriotic lessons, history classes, Protestant prayers, flag ceremonies, derogation of immigrant customs, and pageants were all put to the task."[107] One immigrant man recalled the role of history lessons in the process: "we learned about the Revolutionary War, the Civil War, and our founding fathers."[108] But individual marines carried with them to Haiti the local knowledge of their own ethnic communities, the memory of their actual fathers' lives and ways, and all the emotions attached to such knowledge and memory. Thus, Irish Americans no doubt considered their own participation in the occupation in the light of Ireland's relation to England.[109] And German Americans faced some challenging questions serving in Haiti while the United States debated whether to aid the British in their fight against "the Hun," and even more so once their fellow marines were themselves off for France. Lieutenant Adolph Miller, for one, thought carefully about the potential implications of his social contacts with German citizens in Port-au-Prince in 1915.[110]

While the Marine Corps continued to train more native-born than immigrant men, more Protestants than Catholics, to say nothing of Jews or Muslims, observers did not hesitate to highlight the presence of immigrants in the Marine Corps when they wanted to draw attention to military wrongdoing. This was, in part, a reflection of class tensions. The largest number of marines were young men who enlisted from the ranks of the civilian working poor and unemployed. In addition, certain prominent Marine Corps officers, including Major Smedley Butler, projected a roughneck image in contrast to the more refined and educated—indeed, the "effete"—figure of the naval officer. Thus, when news broke of the marines' misdeeds in Haiti, Christian moral crusaders expressed their outrage at the "so-called Americans," the "hyphenated low-brows" in the Marine Corps.[111] This sort of derogatory attitude toward the marines may have lent added weight to the American Red Cross's invitation to every marine in Haiti: "Everybody join, everybody become interested in your own Red Cross, be an American."[112]

If U.S. American identity was fragile, in different ways, for immigrants and native-born Americans, for northerners and southerners, and if it was vulnerable to challenge in the circumstances of the occupation, as I argue it was, this was perhaps especially so in the case of Pedro del Valle. Born in San Juan, Puerto Rico, in 1893, del Valle would have been about five when the United States claimed possession of his island country, taking it from Spain at the close of a war that began in Cuba.[113] Del Valle spent his childhood in Puerto Rico with the comforts of a middle-class home; his father was a doctor, his family had a cook, and perhaps other servants.[114] At seventeen, a year before the U.S. Congress extended limited citizenship rights to all Puerto Ricans, del Valle graduated from the U.S. Naval Academy and was commissioned as a second lieutenant in the Marine Corps.[115] Thus, in spite of the U.S. imperialist presence in his native land, del Valle embraced his connection to the United States.

Years after his participation in the occupation of Haiti, when Lieutenant General del Valle recorded an interview with Marine Corps historian Benis Frank, there seemed to be no hint of hesitation surrounding his U.S. American identity. Thus, del Valle responded to a question about the Marine Corps's participation in "civic action" around the world, with the statement that "we did it in Haiti and Santo Domingo and Nicaragua and to a certain extent in Cuba. It was part of the job . . . bringing order out of chaos."[116] And asked about the status of the Haitian infrastructure before the arrival of the marines in 1915, the lieutenant general replied, "You see, there was a French civilization there before ours."[117] "We" Americans brought order out of chaos in the Caribbean, he could easily claim; "our" civilization had been preceded only by that of the French.

Yet, evidence of a possible disjunction between his Puerto Rican experience and his newer national identity lightly punctuated his 1973 interview.

Consider this story, which presumably his parents told him: "I was a very young boy—I don't remember the incident—one of these crawling centipedes got up my leg here, and he chewed me up, and it hurt like hell. I screamed bloody murder. We had a black cook. She said, 'What's the matter?' Well, the old man had put all the gimmicks he had on there, and it still hurt to beat hell. 'Oh,' she said, 'just wait a minute.' She went out and took three kinds of herbs and mixed them together and mashed them up and put it on there—and whoosh, gone! They're close to these things, you see. It's so many thousands of years that we've been away from that sort of thing. But it survives even today."[118] Even as he asserted the fundamental distinction between "us" (Americans? whites? beneficiaries of Western education?) and "them" (Caribbean peasants in Haiti and Puerto Rico? people of African heritage? the uneducated?), he also marked his own distance from the "rational scientific temper" that Carl Van Doren had once attributed to white U.S. society. For this story related his belief in the healing practices of peasants, and thus the value of their knowledge, even as he distanced himself from them.[119]

Thus, from Smedley Butler, whose forbears could claim an American identity as far back as 1710, to Pedro del Valle, who could claim his U.S. American identity because the United States had claimed him, with his people, in an act of imperial possession, marines in Haiti negotiated their relationships to America across a wide variety of differences. Leaving home for the Caribbean—or traveling back to the Caribbean that was once one's home, in some few cases—marines traversed a world in which racial and national identities were yet fluid and, perhaps, becoming even more troubled.

BOYS AND MEN

The marines who went to Haiti between 1915 and 1934 were, then, all in their own ways American. At the same time, they were also, all in their own ways, men. Or, at least, they were becoming men. And if serving with the U.S. Marine Corps seemed likely to affirm a young man's racial and national identity, even more so did it hold out the promise of validating his dawning masculinity.[120] Indeed, in the martial ardor of the years following the U.S. war with Spain, young men increasingly looked to military service to develop and demonstrate physical prowess and to assert the kind of manly character that was held out to them as an essential element of citizenship.[121] If, however, race, ethnicity, and nation were shifting and troubled categories in the years leading up to and during the first U.S. occupation of Haiti, so too were the coordinates of gender, class, and sexuality shifting and troubled. Thus, American men staked their claims to manhood, in the United States and in Haiti, on uncertain ground.

Indeed, by 1915 some white men had been seeking terra firma for their manhood for several decades already and had done much to create the gender-charged atmosphere in which younger men would light out for the (now overseas) territories. During that time, a host of social, economic, and political changes were afoot, with implications for male status and identity on all levels. For white male political elites—wealthy and middle-class men with significant access to the power of the state—the resurgent woman's movement and the rise of male "others" in the political sphere posed special challenges. In the South, as noted above, the presence of African American men became increasingly difficult for the "New White Men" to ignore; in the North, working-class men and immigrants asserted themselves through labor unions and urban political machines.[122] At the same time, "organized womanhood" was on the move. Elite and middle-class women pressed for admission to full citizenship rights, including suffrage, and organized themselves as a significant political force—with the potential to influence legislation affecting men's lives—even without the vote. Working-class women raised their voices as well, in both suffrage campaigns and labor actions. Between 1895 and 1905, for example, women workers actively participated in 1,262 strikes, effecting 83 of those on their own.[123] Such challenges to the political and economic power of elite and middle-class men did much to create an atmosphere of anxiety and concern over the status of American manhood.

At the same time, the *social* relations of gender seemed to be askew. As wives, teachers, and moral reformers, elite and middle-class women seemed more than ever to determine the bounds of propriety for men as well as for other women. Elite and middle-class men thus began to fear becoming "overcivilized" and "sissified" at the hands of women.[124] Economic changes also fueled these fears, especially for middle-class men, reducing opportunities for individual initiative and entrepreneurship and increasing the ways in which they had to be subservient within larger bureaucratic structures.[125] Meanwhile, in a society organized in large part around an ideology of male breadwinning, economic change challenged working-class men in particular ways. Low wages, deskilling, unemployment, and a loss of control over the work process assaulted working-class men's sense of themselves as men.[126] Adding insult to injury, middle-class reformers, often women, blamed culturally "inferior" working-class men for the problems facing their families.[127] Thus, in different ways, men of various classes experienced challenges to their manhood in the decades surrounding the turn of the century.

In that context, both empire and military action emerged as favored paths for affirming the nation's virility. With them, too, came a panoply of cultural tools for protecting, bolstering, and celebrating both whiteness and manhood. Some of these had materialized in the last decades of the nineteenth century. Buffalo Bill's "Wild West," for example, dating back to 1882, presented a spectacle of military triumph over barbarian races on a vast untamed continent. The "White City" of Chicago's 1893 Columbia Exposition, on the other hand, served as a shrine to the technological genius and evolutionary superiority of the white man in America. Meanwhile, college football, which became a national craze in the 1890s, offered a ritual performance of virility in the making.[128] Other cultural supports for white manhood appeared in the wake of 1898, such as Theodore Roosevelt's narrative, *The Rough Riders*, recounting — and recasting — the battle of San Juan Hill as a monument to the robust integrity and leadership of white men in "the First United States Volunteer Cavalry."[129] The early twentieth century brought even more explicit images of powerful white physicality. Bernarr McFadden, for example, intended his body-building magazine, *Physical Culture*, to present a "wholesome and elevating" display of muscular male bodies.[130] And Edgar Rice Burroughs's 1912 novel *Tarzan of the Apes* effectively proclaimed, as Gail Bederman has shown, "that 'the white man's' potential for power and mastery was as limitless as the masculine perfection of Tarzan's body."[131] Whiteness had become an essential element of American manhood, and American men were poised to assert their mastery around the globe.

As white men thus recast their own virility in racial, martial, and imperial terms, some among them focused attention especially on the experience of boys — white boys, specifically — and on the nature of boyhood. Long enough had women placed undue constraints on boys' expression of primitive emotion and on their development of "the fighting instinct."[132] Whereas military action would serve the nation, such men believed, boyhood brawls, boxing, and discipline would serve young white men-in-the-making. "The nation that cannot fight is not worth its salts, no matter how cultivated and refined it might be," Theodore Roosevelt asserted, continuing, "it is just so with a boy."[133] And whereas empire, with its Darwinian encounter between civilized man and primitive savages, would strengthen the link between manliness and civilization, the primitive savagery of boyhood itself was encouraged and cultivated by such experts as the psychologist and educator G. Stanley Hall. Hall urged parents and teachers to allow boys to experience that youthful savagery: let them read "stories with bloodshed in them"; let them know "how it feels at the painful end of the rod"; and, above all, let them "double up their fists and fight back" when challenged.[134] Sharing with Roosevelt and Hall a belief in the value of primitive experience for cultivating masculinity, Daniel Carter Beard and William Thompson Seton founded the Boy Scouts of America in 1910 to provide boys with an opportunity to imbibe "the energy, frankness, and fellowship of the wilderness."[135] Thus, in the years leading up to and during the occupation of Haiti, white boys received boxing gloves as birthday gifts, mastered primitive survival skills as Scouts, and thrilled at adventure stories set in the wilds of Africa and on the distant shores of the Pacific.[136]

That a marine headed for Haiti should have fancied himself an Indian fighter or a latter-day colonial soldier-adventurer was, then, no mere coincidence. Indeed, young white men arrived at Marine Corps recruit depots and naval bases in the 1910s and 1920s with their heads full of images gathered from the culture of rough boyhood and imperial masculinity. Adventure stories, recruitment posters, press reports of American exploits overseas, and oral accounts of relatives and neighbors who had served in the military all contributed their part. Archer Vandegrift, for one, remembered the stories of his uncle returning home from war in 1898. He also recalled that before joining the Marine Corps he had read avidly about British military adventures around the world. "I was a keen G. A. Henty fan," he wrote years later in his memoir; "Henty wrote dozens of books about a young British sub-altern and I read them all. I fought with this fellow in India and in Canada and in the Boer War and on the Peninsula and in the Orange Wars—every place a British soldier ever fired a shot." "Sea stories," he recalled, "had fired my imagination. Now, suddenly, I was to become a Marine of those stories."[137] Other young men aspiring to manhood attempted to fill out the roles they imagined for themselves with the help of props and costumes, as one young lieutenant did, according to John Houston Craige: "With a boy's thirst for romantic trappings he bought himself elaborately ornamental boots of Spanish leather and carved holsters of the low-necked, Cheyenne type."[138] Though not all recruits could afford such props, even those motivated to enlist primarily by economic need could be spurred on by the popular image of the marine as an accomplished American jack-of-all-trades available to serve "from the Spanish Main to the Orient" or by the appeal of recruitment posters egging young men on: "If You Want to Fight!," they goaded, "Join the Marines."[139]

On the other hand, not every young man wanted to fight. Even if we grant that the relationship between maleness and violence was reinforced by diverse and overlapping discourses, so thoroughly as to appear natural—indeed, instinctive—we must not assume that men were equally and evenly conscripted by discourses of masculine bellicosity. Nor should we assume that all boys and men were successfully goaded to violence, either by neighborhood bullies or by military recruiters. For other imperatives—ideological, religious, and emotional—directed boys' and men's impulses, decisions, and actions.[140] Indeed, older discourses of manliness and alternative strains within dominant discourses of civilization inculcated more pacific codes of behavior. Moreover, having been goaded to violence and/or having been persuaded to adopt militarist values and a fighting spirit, men could rethink their relation to violence and reposition themselves in the world. Thus, even in the military (or perhaps especially there), we find critics of militarism.[141] And among the marines in Haiti were at least a few men reputed to be pacifists. One reportedly joined the corps during the world war, persuaded, at the time at least, that the cause was just and the war a necessary evil.[142] Thus, even with respect to aspects of gender identity that seemed to have been most successfully installed across the population, we must be attentive to the diverse social and cultural backgrounds, and to the diverse experiences, that shaped men's lives and their relationships to manhood and masculinity.

There was, of course, more to manhood than racial mastery, physical prowess, and a fighting spirit, even within the gender discourses articulated by militarist, empire-building men. For alongside the imperative to assert American manhood in the world at large was the equally essential call to be a man in the context of home and family. Indiana senator Albert J. Beveridge, a vocal proponent of U.S. military and economic expansion, made this point unequivocally in his 1908 book, *The Young Man and the World*. Beveridge dismissed out of hand the man whose "arm is not strong enough to protect a wife" and whose "shoulders are not broad enough to carry aloft [his] children." "The man who is not enough of a man to make a home, need not be counted," he declared flatly.[143] The idea articulated so pointedly by the senator, that a man was not a man until he took on paternal responsibilities, was not new.[144] The ideology of male breadwinning had been a distinguishing feature of the emerging middle class in the nineteenth century and was later embraced by workingmen in the call for a "family wage." It persisted as a defining feature of manhood, for men of both classes, into and beyond the Progressive Era.[145] Dominant discourses of fatherhood had, at the same time, always called for more than breadwinning. Then, in the early decades of the new century, middle-class men set about the business of overhauling the institution of fatherhood by expanding paternal responsibilities in the face of new challenges to male authority.[146] A new emphasis on "masculine domesticity" emerged, initially in suburban settings, but elsewhere as well. Fathers were to be "chums" with their children and were to play a special role in shaping their sons' masculinity.[147] In any case, even before fathers became "daddies," respectable men fathered families and supported them.[148]

The discourse of paternalism drew on this emerging constellation of cultural meanings surrounding fatherhood. It invited Americans, and particularly U.S. marines serving in Haiti, to stand in as father figures for a child nation. It offered such men the kind of status and prestige associated with fatherhood; to accept the offer, they had merely to see themselves in a paternal light. Thus, in order to understand how marines were likely to respond to the discourse of paternalism that dominated the occupation, it will be useful to ask who they were in relation to their own fathers, in relation to men who posed as paternal figures for them, and in relation to dominant ideologies of manhood and fatherhood. Who were they as sons, fathers, and potential fathers?

Among the men who went to Haiti, many undoubtedly remembered their fathers fondly. Some stayed in touch by letter while overseas. Some saw themselves as walking in their fathers' footsteps. Others saw themselves as seizing opportunities their fathers never had. Some, like Lieutenant Ivan Miller, whose father was postmaster of their small town of Versailles, Ohio, remembered the ways their fathers had helped them to become the men they were.[149] Southern fathers, in particular, had long sought to inculcate toughness and aggressiveness in their sons by encouraging them to ride, hunt, and fight.[150] Marines who joined the occupation in the late 1920s may even have been young enough to have benefited *as sons* from emerging norms of domestic masculinity, although for most marines who served in Haiti, this was probably not the case. Still, their fathers played key roles in their lives, providing moral leadership and material assistance as well as modeling authority, self-respect, and manly success on various levels.[151]

At the same time, as sons, boys and men of all classes almost certainly experienced the sting of subordination somewhere along the line. The insults of childhood may have been forgotten by the time a young man came to enlist, but patriarchal authority extended to fathers' control over their sons well into their twenties in some contexts.[152] Farmers' sons fled to the city, and in some cases to the military, to escape the work regime enforced by rural fathers. As one West Virginia teenager announced to a federal child

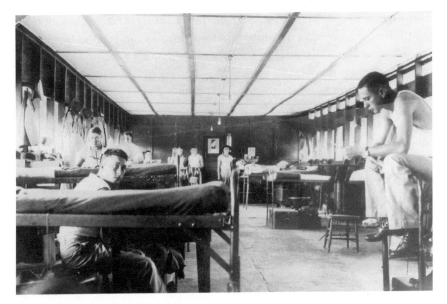

Figure 6. Marines in barracks, Port-au-Prince.
Marine Corps Research Center Archives, Quantico, Virginia.

labor investigator in the early 1920s, "I have to work myself to death and don't get nothing out of it; never get to go *nowhurs*. I don't like it and ain't goin' to stay."[153] Private John Wittek of Plainfield, New Jersey, wounded in action in Haiti in September 1915, may have felt the same way when he "ran away from home to join the marines."[154] Sociological studies conducted in the 1920s and 1930s confirmed that rural sons' resentment was directed specifically at paternal authority and discipline. For the urban sons of immigrant fathers, intergenerational conflict was exacerbated by the emphasis on Americanization within public schools. As one man commented, looking back on his schooling in New York City, "we were becoming Americans by learning how to be ashamed of our parents."[155] Sons born to New England wealth, too, chafed against the expectations of their fathers, expectations that could amount to requirements if a young man expected to come into his inheritance.

Men with experience as wage workers before joining the military also knew the subordination implicit in industrial paternalism. Increasingly routinized relations of production, combined with patronizing attempts to uplift workers, insulted workers' sense of manhood.[156] By the 1920s, industrial relations experts caught on and began advising employers that workingmen had rejected, in the words of one expert, "the so-called services so patronizingly rendered in the name of sweet charity."[157] As "self respecting, self-reliant men . . . they were right," wrote another; theirs was "a healthy, independent American attitude."[158] Thus, men who joined the marines had experienced the butt end of paternal authority, in various forms. As sons, both real and metaphorical, they knew its power dynamic all too well.

Some marines wielded paternal authority as fathers themselves. Some, like Smedley Butler, even brought their families to live with them in Haiti. Like the majority of U.S. men—wealthy, middle-class, and working-class alike—they most likely embraced the dominant ideology of manhood articulated by Senator Beveridge. Yet how widespread was this embrace within the Marine Corps? For if a majority of civilian men embraced the values associated with fatherhood, a smaller but significant segment of the male population specifically rejected breadwinning in favor of a culture of male camaraderie. In the late nineteenth and early twentieth centuries, approximately 40 percent of men sixteen years old and older were unmarried.[159] Most but not all of these men were in their teens, twenties, and early thirties, and many would eventually go on to marry despite their vigorous rejection of domesticity earlier on.[160] Whatever responsibilities they came to embrace later in life, however, many such men enlisted in the Marine Corps while still caught up in a spirited rejection of "respectable" norms of manhood. Thus, the call to shoulder the paternalist mantle in Haiti found some men eager, others willing, but many, no doubt, laughing at the very idea. Positioned differently as sons, fathers, and potential fathers, marines were not all equally disposed to appropriate or make use of the paternal vision of manhood embedded in their nation's dominant imperialist discourse.

As we have seen, the uncertain ground of male gender identity in the early twentieth century encompassed racial meanings, body images, capacities for violence, and dispositions toward fatherhood. In search of masculinity, men also had to contend with the shifting ground of class and sexuality. To explore this important context for the marines' experiences in Haiti, it will be useful to examine the world of young single men who rejected domesticity. For their elaboration of distinct norms for "rough," as opposed to "respectable," working-class manhood had, as it turns out, a significant impact on the development of masculinity and sexuality for all men.

The historian George Chauncey has provided a textured portrait of such rough, working-class, male communities as they appeared in urban settings in the decades surrounding the turn of the twentieth century.[161] Chauncey points out that they encompassed a variety of men untethered from their communities of origin: immigrant men intending to return home after a stint in America, or native-born migrant workers shuffling seasonally between countryside and city, many perhaps like F. W. Schmidt's "boy from nowhere." These dockworkers, construction workers, merchant marines, and sailors gathered in bars, poolrooms, and gambling dens. In such all-male social spaces, as well as in the homosocial contexts of their work lives, they developed codes of behavior and structures of identity foreign to respectable society. Such communities celebrated male solidarity, and, in Chauncey's words, "expressed mutual regard and reciprocity, perhaps most commonly through the custom of treating one's fellows to rounds of drinks."[162] Gambling table and poolroom rivalry as well as sexual braggadocio also afforded the men opportunities to perform their manhood for one another.

What was the relationship between this male subculture and the social world of the Marine Corps between 1915 and 1934? Several points of connection are relevant here. First, as I have suggested, rough, working-class male communities were part of the civilian world from which new recruits came to the corps. "Men on the move," in search of wages, adventures, and male solidarity, hoped to find all three in the military. The fact that enlistments rose with unemployment rates suggests that this connection grew stronger as alternative sources of livelihood dwindled. Second, while the rough male communities described by Chauncey had their locus in the civilian world, not infrequently they sprang up in the neighborhood of a navy yard and drew enlisted men into their midst. Indeed, the presence of sailors was particularly noted by other participants in these communities as well as by observers. Thus the boundaries between a rough civilian community and the social world of the military could be quite porous. Third, and most decisively, even if and when the social world of the Marine Corps was clearly separate and distinct from the civilian world described by Chauncey, it mirrored that world in significant ways.

The record of evidence left by marines substantiates this last point. Memoirs, for example, promise the revelation of gritty truths, possible only in a rough, male world. After twenty-seven years of service in the "old Marine Corps," Colonel Frederick May Wise wrote in 1929, "there are damned few of us left. We lived hard, drank hard, fought hard. . . . If I have learned anything in those years it was men."[163] Josephus Daniels, the prohibitionist secretary of the navy from 1913 to 1921, tried to curtail the hard drinking by decree but failed in his bid to reform that aspect of the service.[164] Still, like-minded officers noted what they regarded as a lack of morals among the men they commanded. Lieutenant Adolph Miller, for example, commented, in his diary, on men he considered a disgrace to the corps.[165] As an enlisted man, Faustin Wirkus had a different perspective. For the compul-

Figure 7. Marines at leisure in Haiti.
Marine Corps Research Center Archives, Quantico, Virginia.

sory religious services that were part of his training in 1914, "they always picked preachers who thought we were the lowest of the damned." And on the streets of Norfolk, "we were regarded as a godless crew and always would be."[166]

An ethos of male rivalry based on competitive claims to toughness and physical prowess—whether enacted on the battlefield or in a brothel—mirrored the rough civilian culture described by Chauncey. Marines' fast talk about women and yarns about brave deeds in battle echoed the barroom boasts of immigrants and migrant workers in Brooklyn, Philadelphia, and Norfolk.[167] Like Frederick Wise, Smedley Butler shared in and celebrated this ethos in his own memoir. He related, for example, a story about one of the very first encounters between marines and Haitian rebels in the north of Haiti. One evening, as the marines were eating supper—in their underwear, due to the heat—they received news that the Caco rebels were burning the railroad. As Butler told the tale, when he shouted "Who wants a fight?" the marines grabbed their guns and rushed to meet the rebels. According to Butler, the rebels fired first, but then the marines cut loose.

They were "baying like bloodhounds all through the bushes," the general recalled. "I kept blowing my whistle, and the bugler kept sounding 'To the rear,' and 'Cease firing,' but the men were in their element and nothing could stop them. Those undressed Marines went right on shooting at the Haitians." In this way, Butler represented the ethic of fearless, eager fighting, unchecked by the trappings or conventions of civilization, that gave shape to marines' tales up and down the rank and file.[168]

In the civilian world as well as in the military, the culture of rough working-class men attracted its share of middle- and upper-class hangers-on, men who found something there that was absent in the roles and conventions of their own class. Yet, cross-class relationships were complicated in different ways in the military. The Marine Corps, for example, was well aware of the "rituals of saloon conviviality" that celebrated and cemented horizontal ties among enlisted men. Commanding officers instructed new lieutenants to take care not to encroach on such rituals, and thus to avoid creating a false sense of equality across the strict hierarchical divide between an officer and his men.[169] At the same time, some officers, like Butler and Wise, styled themselves after the idea of "the soldier's general." Roughneck warrior leaders, willing to get their hands dirty in the field, appealed to enlisted men. Butler and Wise thus rejected the emerging naval standard of school-trained professional expertise, opting instead for gritty, charismatic leadership. As Hans Schmidt has argued, Butler "promoted a new Marine Corps mystique emphasizing physical stridency and egalitarian anti-intellectualism, at odds with the current trend to elitist bookish professionalism in the officer corps."[170] Butler judged his own deeds not by the praise he received from Washington but rather by the approbation of, as he wrote to his mother, "my men" for "that is the best criterion of a man's service."[171]

The divide between the soldier and the officer, which Butler and Wise sought to bridge, was illustrated in a 1931 novel about the marines, Irwin Franklyn's *Knights in the Cockpit: A Romantic Epic of the Flying Marines in Haiti.* At the outset, the hero, Rorrie O'Rourke, a sergeant and flying instructor at a Marine Corps training field in Pensacola, Florida, is offered a commission and refuses. Although O'Rourke "knew more about the tropics than any other Marine in the entire world," he was no officer "dandy." "He had nothing in common with those College men, born to the blood and shaped by a peculiar destiny to wear leather boots and silver spurs . . . 'give that commission to some dandy who needs a pair of spurs to keep his feet from slipping off a desk.' " Pressed by the knowledge that only he can overcome the Haitian rebels, however, O'Rourke agrees to lead an air offensive with his Tenth Squadron. Before they depart, the sergeant addresses his men, urging them to live up to the legacy of their predecessors. " 'We fought first and asked about it later—! That's the kind of timber I hope the new tenth squadron is made of—! Hard-fisted, hard-drinkin' sons of Satan —!' "[172]

If codes of masculinity seem to have been stable in all of this, on closer inspection we find that they were not in the least stable. Irwin Franklyn's use of the term "dandy" points to the fault line that was opening up into a chasm precisely during the decades of the Haitian occupation. For though it was a time-honored tradition among working-class men to insult middle-class men by calling them "dandy" and "pansy," working-class men's perception that they may need to defend themselves against such a charge was new.

Returning to Chauncey's portrait of the rough working-class male subculture, we learn more. For example, Chauncey tells us that the collective performance of manhood sometimes took the form of collective sexual violence. Such sexual conventions as the "lineup," in which a group of men would queue up, waiting their turn to penetrate a single woman in plain view of their fellows, enabled men to experience "manly solidarity" through the performance of sexual domination, according to Chauncey.[173] In some cases, however, a group of rough, manly men might queue up for sex, but not with a woman. At least one man known as a "fairy"—a feminine man who was willing to be sexually penetrated—reported having had sex with a group of men, one right after the other.[174] For the men in such a lineup, Chauncey has shown, there was no danger to their reputations as perfectly normal, masculine men. "Fairies," like women, could be the object of masculine dominance in such a sexual encounter because in these communities sexual identity had not settled into its modern pattern. Men were not "homosexual" or "heterosexual" or even "bisexual." As long as a man took the "active" role in the sexual encounter, he could be certain of his gender status—indeed, certain enough even to brag about his exploits, or perform them publicly, and thereby enhance his reputation as a man.[175] Moreover, as late as the 1930s, Alfred Kinsey's study of male sexuality showed that fully a quarter of the U.S. male population had had some significant homosexual experience, suggesting to Chauncey that the patterns he observes in New York City may have been common in other urban areas as well.[176] Even if Marine Corps training and discipline routed out such behavioral patterns, a highly questionable proposition, it seems likely that some significant number of men who enlisted were "normal" but not what we would now call "heterosexual."

Officers who styled themselves according to the rough culture of enlisted men most likely did not share this understanding of male sexuality with the men in their command. Indeed Chauncey points to a "growing antipathy of middle-class men toward both fairies and queers at the turn of the century," which was linked to the sense of gender crisis such men were experiencing at the time.[177] Chauncey explains that the fairy "provoked a high degree of anxiety and scorn among middle-class men because he embodied the very things middle-class men most feared about their gender status" and, further, that "the overtness of the fairy's sexual interest in men was even more unsettling, because it raised the possibility of a sexual component in . . . men's interactions." For men who had turned to the "celebration of male bodies and manly sociability" in response to a perceived crisis in masculinity, it would now be necessary to reject the possibility of homosexual desire actively and explicitly.[178] In short, what we now call homophobia emerged in a class-specific context, among middle-class men who fixed their gaze on working-class men's bodies and sought to keep that gaze free of any sexual taint. In that context, middle-class moral reformers characterized "open displays of homosexuality" as characteristic of "lowergrade" communities.[179] This was the sort of thing that went on, to use Faustin Wirkus's phrase, among "the lowest of the damned."

The process by which homophobia was articulated more clearly and spread more widely involved, among other things, a campaign in 1920 to rout out "fairies" from the Navy in Newport, Rhode Island.[180] A few years later, a newspaper reporting on Smedley Butler made a point of describing him as "strong-wristed," a clear reference to a physical gesture — the so-called limp wrist — that was becoming a sign of homosexuality.[181] The details of this process, which accompanied the emergence of gay male communities, are beyond the scope of this study. The point that is crucial for understanding the experience of marines in Haiti is that the field of meanings around which sexual identities were organized was changing. The days when men were men and fairies alone were queer were dwindling, giving way to the days when men would have to confine their sexual exploits to the "opposite" sex in order to guard their status as normal, newly defined in terms of heterosexuality. Here then was yet another way in which an American man's identity was up for grabs in the decades of the occupation.[182]

INDOCTRINATION

Arriving at recruit depots with this range of baggage and confusion, white U.S. boys and men soon found themselves caught up in the disciplinary regime of the U.S. Marine Corps. That regime had evolved significantly, with the corps itself, over the previous decades; it would be further refined and developed in the decades after the Haitian occupation began. Indeed, marines who landed in Haiti in July and August 1915 had been trained at several naval bases along the East Coast. Less than three months later, the Marine Corps established its own recruit training depot at Port Royal, South Carolina. A former naval station, the new training camp was renamed Parris Island in 1917.[183]

The traditional responsibilities of marines aboard Navy ships continued to dictate some elements of the training program, while others arose out of the corps's emerging function as an expeditionary force in support of colonial endeavors. Marines' original function, dating back to the corps's earliest years as a separate service, was to provide ships guards, or military police, to keep order among often unruly sailors. A second traditional function of the marines was to operate the secondary batteries of heavy artillery, the "five-inch guns" that marines talked about, on board naval vessels.[184] Marines were also intended to form the backbone of any landing party that might be necessary abroad. Thus they were valued both for maintaining shipboard order and for their skills as soldiers, and their training sought to prepare them for both roles. In keeping with the marines' role as military police, training had long emphasized discipline — unwavering obedience to orders, meticulous adherence to protocol, and spit-and-polish military presentation.[185] (This is not to say that such lessons took across the board; indeed in China in 1900, European observers of U.S. marines at work noted their "careless dress" and "casual discipline.")[186] To prepare them for soldiering, there was also a focus on equipment and drill. In the 1920s one USMC captain described old-timers, in particular, as men to whom "rifles were high and holy things."[187] With the advent of the .30 caliber Springfield rifle Model 1903, the corps stepped up its marksmanship program, offering badges and merit bonuses for the most skilled shooters.[188] The corps's new focus on expeditionary duty in the early twentieth century, moreover, led to an emphasis on the previously neglected areas of small-unit tactics and, later, battalion-sized maneuvers. Combat performance, for units as well as for individuals, would be projected as a key strength of the new Marine Corps cum "colonial infantry."[189]

Along with what they learned about uniforms and guns, salutes and maneuvers, protocol and survival, they learned, too, new ways of imagining themselves. They learned, to a greater or lesser extent, to relinquish their civilian identities and to assume with pride the mantle of the United States marine. A half-century later, a new generation of marines would articulate this aspect of training, which no doubt had been honed to a fine art in the years since Parris Island's founding. "They tore you down," one Marine veteran told the historian Christian Appy in the mid-1980s. "They tore every-thing civilian out of your entire existence—your speech, your thoughts, your sights, your memory—anything that was civilian they tore out and then they rebuilt you and made you over. . . . First they made you drop down to a piece of grit on the floor. Then they built you back up to being a marine."[190] Faustin Wirkus's lament at having been addressed as the "lowest of the damned" may well have reflected an early version of this process by which men were stripped of their civilian identities so that they could be remade as marines. Wirkus recalled his experience as a fresh recruit, soon to be a private in the Twenty-second Company; he had been told that he was "raw, very raw and unworthy material."[191]

Yet, it was from such "raw and unworthy material" that the corps built men who understood themselves as worthy of the name "marine." That sense of worth grew out of a training routine that sought, among other things, to inculcate a sense of belonging to the corps, to inspire that fidelity that has been the byword of the U.S. Marines: always faithful, "Semper Fi." Trained to present themselves in meticulous military formation for parades and reviews, marines came to know that their corps had always been a breed apart from the Navy, whose ranks they patrolled. Drilled on infantry tactics and marksmanship, they came to understand themselves as part of an elite fighting force. A relatively small, all-volunteer branch of the U.S. military, heralded in the press for heroic action and all-around ability, the Marine Corps was known for its selectivity.[192] It was the Marine Corps that "fur-nished guards of honor for the comings and goings of the Admiral and distinguished visitors" on any ship, Marine Corps captain John W. Thom-ason Jr. pointed out in 1926. Ask a marine to describe his corps, Thomason urged the reading public; "any private will assure you that the marines are a corps d'elite."[193]

While indoctrination into the Marine Corps was never as complete as Captain Thomason claimed, it was a many-pronged process that took place in informal as well as formal contexts.[194] Alongside drills and inspections, for example, fresh recruits were treated to stories passed down from more experienced marines, "traditions of things endured and things accom-plished, such as regiments hand down forever," Thomason called them.[195] Wirkus offered a sampling of the traditions handed down by his regiment: "yarns about starvation, jungle battles, Chinese knife men, back alley mur-der in foreign ports, women and rum."[196] Legends and lore, conveyed in the ritual spinning of yarns and telling of tales, helped bind individual marines, with affection and allegiance, to their regiments and to their corps. Other rituals operated by a different, more trying, logic. We know very little about the nature of hazing in the Navy and in the Marine Corps, but we know it took place. Asked whether he experienced hazing at the U.S. Naval Academy as an ordeal, Marine Corps brigadier general Ivan W. Miller responded only briefly. "Yes, there was a good bit of hazing," he confirmed, "but . . . it never bothered me much."[197] Yet hazing constituted a significant ritual in the informal processes of indoctrination by which marines were made. It was a ritual of subordination that presaged a marine's entrance into the ranks of those with a right to dominate; at times it may also have been a ritual of endurance involving the direct experience of violence. In keeping with G. Stanley Hall's theories on the cultivation of masculinity, the practical joke — that corollary and component of hazing — was viewed as "war, cruelty, and torture reduced to the level of play."[198]

How did military training, and the informal process of indoctrination that went along with it, prepare men for their roles as representatives of the United States in Haiti? How did they prepare marines to cross national boundaries and cultural divides? One striking feature of Marine Corps training, when considered in light of such questions, is the extent to which it cultivated a sense of separation from the civilian worlds from which the marines came. Marines, as we have seen, were taught to debase their former civilian selves and to vest their sense of worth in their status as marines. Yet, what did this imply about their fellow citizens who were not marines? Set apart from the civilian world — that is, from the nation they were to represent — marines could fall prey to a sense of disconnection from, and sometimes condescension toward, the nation. Marines' diaries, letters, memoirs, and oral histories express this sense of disconnection, which was often set in contrast to the sense of connection and belonging among marines.[199] American society might misunderstand them, muckraking journalists might distort their actions, even their government might forsake them, but common bonds held marines in a profound communion, always faithful.

To what extent did the discourse of paternalism shape the preparation of Marine Corps officers and enlisted men? Paternalism was built into Marine Corps relationships on several levels. It structured the relationship between officers and "men," between marines in their role as ships guards and the sailors whose behavior they monitored, and between marines and the people they would encounter overseas. As the historian Donald Mrozek has pointed out, "commitment to a moral code" and a "commitment to the intrinsic worth and practical benefits of hierarchy and authority" were fundamental to the perspectives of military officers during and after the Victorian era. These elements were, as we shall see in Chapter 3, important aspects of paternalism.[200] Moreover, during Josephus Daniels's term as secretary of the navy, paternalism was an especially important element of the expectations held out for officers. Middle-class values of manhood, including respectability, sobriety, moderation, and self-restraint were to be modeled by officers for the enlisted men under their tutelage.[201] The paternalist attitudes of marines toward sailors, on the other hand, were not always encouraged. Indeed, naval reformers had for some time been rankled by the forced infantilization of sailors effected by Marine Corps oversight on Navy vessels.[202] Finally, paternalism structured official attitudes and perspectives on the "natives" whom marines would be sent to discipline and assist. Thus, in a poem for the Marine Corps's *Recruiter's Bulletin* in April 1915, Private C. Hundertmark commented, with respect to "the people . . . of every country and clime":

> At times they raise trouble among themselves,
> And someone must intervene,
> Then the best man to send, so the President
>   says
> Is a United States Marine.[203]

By July 1915 U.S. presidents had found numerous occasions for calling out the marines in response to people around the world supposedly "raising trouble among themselves." Indeed, among the marines who went to Haiti were men with experience in China, the Philippines, Panama, Cuba, Nicaragua, and Mexico. For these men, Haiti would not present the first challenge to their sense of themselves as men and as Americans.[204] For others, like Private Faustin Wirkus, Haiti would be a first tour of duty, a first chance to learn about themselves in a foreign setting.

In his memoir, Wirkus described his first impressions on hearing that the Marines were headed southward. He got word that there was "something going on in Haiti — wherever that was — which required the 'Marines to land, and take the situation in hand.' " "There was," he continued, "a lot of backroom joking along that line. But none of us could seem to get any idea as to where this Haiti place was . . . somebody said Haiti was a land of black people — 'just like Africa.' " "The excited day dreams" of young recruits, Wirkus wrote, "were fed by the unending tales of those among us who had already seen sea duty and foreign duty."[205]

If marines boarded their ships, bound for Haiti, without much of a clue as to the whereabouts, no less, the cultural terrain, of that country, they did acquire some information on board. Marine officers searched the ships' libraries for books that might provide useful background on Haitian customs and traditions, and passed their new knowledge along to recruits en route to Haiti. They drilled their troops on practical matters such as the use of firearms, but also on the goals of the U.S. mission on Hispaniola and likely native responses.

On Friday, July 30, 1915, First Lieutenant Adolph Miller learned that he would sail for Port-au-Prince at 9:00 A.M. the next morning. From that day, Miller kept a "Personal Log," in which he recorded his thoughts, his reactions to events and to the people around him, and some of his daily activities.[206] Miller's log suggests something of the state of mind of a junior officer en route to Haiti. Called suddenly to leave his home, twenty-nine-year-old Adolph "Duff" Miller said good-bye to his wife, Holly, and noted that Mrs. Waller, the wife of a senior officer, had taken Holly under her wing.[207] Aboard the *Connecticut*, Miller instructed the troops by day, and by night, if it was too windy for movies on deck, he passed the time with his fellow officers. A few of them struck up a band with three mandolins, a banjo, and a piano, and others regaled one another with tales of their adventures.[208] A number of officers recounted old times together: there was a reunion of officers who served in China, Miller among them, and he remarked in his log, "It seems like a big family reunion."[209] Miller noted passing San Salvador, "the place where Columbus discovered America," and hearing news by radio of Pancho Villa's betrayal of the Americans: "Villa to U.S. to go to hell," he wrote on August 3.[210] Such comments framed the marines' passage to Haiti in the dual context of history and current hemispheric events — in particular, European discovery and conquest in the Americas, on the one hand, and "native" challenges to U.S. military and economic power, on the other.

Miller made a note of having instructed the company in the use of Colt automatics, but he did not remark on learning about Haitian customs.[211] His superior officer, Captain William P. (Deacon) Upshur, left a more detailed account of that activity: "En route to Haiti the officers of the Second Marines studied assiduously all that the ship's library contained about the Black Republic. Classes were held and the information obtained was passed on to the men by the company officers. Included in the information . . . were the statements that the Haitians were devotees of Voodooism and past masters in the art of poisoning their enemies."[212] For Upshur this was the lead-in to a comic tale about marine behavior in Port-au-Prince, illustrating, he thought, the "failure to verify information." Fearing the poison mastery of the natives, marines grabbed a Haitian man and "made him drink a pail of the water." Then, Upshur related, they stood watching for a long while to see if the Haitian would die, which he did not.[213]

One of the first things Miller notes in his log after arriving in Port-au-

Prince is precisely that the natives are masters at poisoning. Other comments Miller makes upon arrival in Haiti appear at first to be his own observations. Further consideration, in light of Deacon Upshur's discussion of shipboard learning, shows that Miller arrived with a host of ideas about the Haitians, which he then proceeded to "observe." Included among these were his observations with regard to Haitian women, about whom he wrote on his very first full day in Haiti: "All the native women are of easy virtue and all its accompanying evils."[214]

Looking back on his first trip to Haiti as a private on the USS *Tennessee*, Faustin Wirkus recalled his own indoctrination. The company officers described the events leading up to the American decision to intervene and warned the troops that they would be likely to encounter some resistance. Private Wirkus learned from them that Guillaume Sam was a "brute throwback to his jungle ancestry," who had ordered the butchering of political prisoners and was subsequently thrown to the mob by a "vigilance committee."[215] "We were told," Wirkus explained, that these events brought us to Haiti, and that the Monroe Doctrine justified it. "We were told that the mid-American and South American countries were not altogether willing for us to enforce this rule of ours and that probably the Haitian people would be inclined to resist its application. . . . But we were not told — because those in authority did not know themselves — how difficult was the problem of making the whole Haitian people friendly to our purposes."[216]

FIRST ENCOUNTERS

On July 28, 1915, the USS *Washington* steamed toward Port-au-Prince from the northern city of Cap Haïtien. After its brief foray in Mexico, the *Washington* had returned to Haitian waters to resume its watchful stance in relation to the developing unrest and potential disorder ashore. That afternoon, the admiral received word by radio that events were coming to a head. With two companies of marines and three companies of sailors on board, Caperton turned his ship to the south, under full steam, and headed for the capital.[217] The tragic events of July 26 and 27 had finally supplied the awaited pretext for an American landing. The *Washington*'s seasoned marines would soon come ashore at the capital.

Rosalvo Bobo, a medical doctor and statesman who was immensely popular among the Haitian poor, was leading his revolutionary forces toward the capital city, united on a platform of opposition to the threatened disgrace of an American receivership. As Bobo's forces gained momentum in the countryside, Port-au-Prince exploded with violence. The execution of 167 political prisoners effectively armed a crowd of city dwellers with the anguish, fury, and determination to bring down the president who was responsible for these political murders. The assassination of President Vilbrun Guillaume Sam left Haiti without a formally sanctioned, functioning government authority in the capital. With Port-au-Prince thus in turmoil, its population reeling from the events of the previous days, Admiral Caperton seized the opportunity to set in motion an invasion that had been planned months before.

Early in the evening of July 28, 330 marines and sailors disembarked at a beach just east of the Haitian Navy Yard, at Bizoton, immediately outside Port-au-Prince.[218] By 5:45 P.M., both battalions were ashore, and with covering fire ready from the USS *Washington* and several armed launches, they began their advance to the city. In double columns, flanking the streets through which they passed, the men held close to the sides of brick buildings for cover, evading guerrilla fire. As night began to fall, they approached the city, marines of the Second Battalion leading as advance guard, naval squads of the First Battalion following.[219] The officers who led each unit had rehearsed their routes in the previous months since the plans for the operation had been established.

Some years after his participation in the invasion, Marine Corps lieutenant colonel Harold Utley offered a detailed account of the landing operation and of the guerrilla response American forces encountered in their first few hours in Haiti. Haitians fired at marine squads from windows and rooftops along the route, according to Utley; marines were "compelled to open fire," in self-defense he implies, killing two Haitians and wounding ten. Utley described the Haitians' fire: "Many of the shots directed at the columns struck the walls of the buildings on one side of the street ahead of the column and ricocheted in such a manner as to strike the wall on the opposite side of the street in the rear of the tail of the column thus doing no harm. Had the columns been stronger, casualties might have occurred in the rear elements."[220] In Utley's view, the small size of the landing force, combined with the inaccuracy of Haitian fire, may have protected American lives. In fact, no marine or naval personnel were killed in this opening phase of the invasion.[221]

Utley's evaluation of the Marine Corps landing in Haiti was, on the whole, quite positive. It was "carefully planned and skillfully executed"; but most important, it was successful.[222] The landing force commander, Captain George Van Orden, faced some difficulties in getting Bobo's revolutionary committee to comply with his orders, but he handled with diplomacy what he did not yet have the armed strength to handle with force, settling for less desirable arrangements when necessary.[223] Reinforcements arrived within a week from Guantanamo Bay, Cuba, and from Philadelphia, increasing American forces to over 1,100 marines and sailors.[224] In the meanwhile, the men of the initial landing force faced significant physical and emotional challenges, according to Utley. "[T]he guard duty was exceedingly severe, some men having no opportunity to change their clothes for 72 hours at a stretch," he wrote later; "personnel, individually excellent, but untrained in special types of duty, are liable to 'crack' if put under a severe nervous strain for any considerable period" in such situations.[225]

As uniformed American men marched into Port-au-Prince on July 28, 1915, and in the days and weeks that followed, they seized the moment between two administrations by holding off the Bobo forces and claiming the necessity of filling this political vacuum. While top-ranking officers directed the overall movement of the troops to implement U.S. foreign policy objectives, individual marines confronted the cultural divide that separated them from Haitians and made palpable their identity as Americans.

Fresh recruits for the first time, and experienced marines once again, marked the differences between their nation and some other, their home and some foreign place. On arrival in Port-au-Prince, Adolph Miller noted the connection between this and previous military forays abroad with a simple reflection: "The island of Haiti is a beautiful spot," he wrote. "It reminds me somewhat of Hong Kong."[226] Some years later, another marine officer remarked on the connection between foreign service and American nationalism. "There is no patriot," wrote John Houston Craige, "like the confirmed globe-trotter."[227]

But nothing in Marine Corps training, nothing about the voyage to Haiti, nothing in the experience of landing on Haitian soil, prepared U.S. American men to make sense of the variety of Haitian responses to their arrival. Their first impressions and thoughts in Haiti reflected simply their training as an elite military force, their indoctrination into the purposes of U.S. foreign policy, and their beliefs about themselves and about people of African heritage at home and in this new setting. These impressions did not capture the Haitian frame of mind or attitude in the face of U.S. intervention.

Adolph Miller arrived on August 4 from Philadelphia with the rest of the Second Regiment. By the time he and the Fifteenth Company landed at the customshouse wharf, the Navy had taken control of the area. Miller took a detail of thirty men, loaded up four train cars with all the troops' gear, and rode through the city to the racetrack, where the men were to be quartered. In his diary, Miller recorded his impressions of the inhabitants' responses to him and his fellow marines: "The natives all cheered and seemed very glad to see us, although quite a number of brickbats were heaved at us from dark places along the line. . . . The native soldiers tried to put up some resistance but when they looked at us twice they changed their mind and departed."[228] Although Miller asserts that all the natives responded positively to the Marine presence, he immediately contradicts himself with references to "brickbats" and "native soldiers." Miller excluded acts of resistance and opposition to the American presence from his overall characterization of the Haitian reaction, despite the fact that he observed and even recorded those very acts of resistance. This was not a matter of reinterpreting history some years after the fact; Miller arrived in Haiti, observed these reactions, and made these notes on the very same day, August 4, 1915.

In the next few days, Miller took armed patrols around the city to enforce a Marine-imposed curfew, to confiscate arms from Haitians, and to collect intelligence as to where revolutionaries lived. He was surprised and humored by the reaction of two native soldiers whom he caught breaking the curfew: "When they saw us approaching . . . they started to yell, fell on their knees and begged us to let them go. They thought we were going to stand them up against a wall and shoot them."[229] Whether these Haitians were indeed afraid, or signaling the American presence to others nearby, we cannot know. Nor could Miller know what they thought, as he professed to, based simply on his observation of what they said and did.

Miller tells of frequent large demonstrations in the first few days after his arrival. On the morning of August 6, the Fifteenth Company rushed to the customshouse wharf to meet a Haitian gunboat and arrest the soldiers aboard. When the marines arrived on the scene, there was "an immense crowd at the Plaza." According to Miller, the marines cleared the crowd, took possession of the boat, and marched the soldiers off to the jail. But the crowd had not dispersed: "There were about 2000 people across the street. When the prisoners were marched off some of the crowd commenced shooting us up. When the shooting started the prisoners made a break for liberty. One was killed by a marine. We had great excitement for a few minutes but finally managed to quiet the crowd. The Haitians are a highly excitable people and fly off the handle at a moment's notice."[230] This passage illustrates the influence of racial assumptions regarding the emotionality of African peoples on one marine's direct observation and interpretation of Haitian responses.

A few hours after this incident, Dr. Rosalvo Bobo arrived in Port-au-Prince, and there was "another big demonstration by the crowd."[231] Miller's interpretation of the varied responses to Bobo and to the marines over the next few days reveals a great deal of confusion. Miller noted the enthusiasm of the "barefoot gang" or poorer Haitians for Dr. Bobo, who, he did not mention, was leading a revolution opposed to U.S. intervention. He also asserted, however, that "all the barefoot gang are glad to see us."[232]

Similar disjunctions mark the recollections of other marines. At times, they were exacerbated by the absence of any understanding of local cultural forms of expression. Without such local knowledge, marines and other U.S. Americans failed to draw any lines of connection between sniper bullets and brickbats, on the one hand, and other verbal and physical manifestations of popular dismay and disapproval, on the other. According to Fred McMillen, a naval officer who arrived on the *Tennessee*, the "bluejackets and marines" met with "little resistance from the population."[233] At the same time, he noted the difficulties he faced in trying to reorganize the port and customs activities at Petit Goave, a town of about 10,000; among the major obstacles he faced were "exasperating delays due to labor troubles" and "carnival days."[234]

McMillen reported that the customs officials and employees refused at first to work for the occupation forces. Although they eventually returned to work, McMillen continued to have difficulty finding tradespeople willing to contribute the necessary expertise to build a new customs office and to pave the streets around it. The actions (and inaction) of the workers described by McMillen thus conformed to the Haitian practice of "marronage," or protest through refusal to work.[235] McMillen gave no details relating to the "carnival days" that slowed down his work, yet this brief mention of carnival is suggestive of another Haitian custom, the peasant tradition of *rara*, a style of protest through song and theatrical public demonstration that continues to the present day.[236] Frederick Wise, posted to the smaller town of Jeremie, later wrote that he too "encountered passive resistance from the start." Wise noted that the Haitians of Jeremie were not in sympathy with the Bobo revolution, but, in his words, "they didn't particularly fancy our arrival either."[237]

Looking back on his own initial reaction to the Haitians, Faustin Wirkus provides some insight into the way in which expectation influenced American observation in Haiti. Wirkus remembered his first views of the city from the ship: "Before we were close enough to see that the seeming marble ramparts were sheds of corrugated iron and ramshackle whitewashed warehouses, the prospect was altogether romantic."[238] But once his company had landed and he had marched through the streets into the city, he had a very different impression: "It hurt. It stunk. Fairyland had turned into a pigsty. More than that. We were not welcome. We could feel it as distinctly as

OCCUPATION

we could smell the rot along the gutters. . . . Black faces lined the curbs across the street from the waterfront. They were blank of all emotion. White eyes gleamed. There was not a smile in sight. The opaque eyes in the black faces were not friendly. They seemed as indifferent as the lenses of cameras."[239] Wirkus later corrected himself: "They were not indifferent," he wrote. "They were merely on the alert to find out where they stood with us."[240] Wirkus acknowledged having viewed Haitians through the lens of his own disgust and discomfort with the situation: "My own distaste for the whole human picture was queerly influenced by the observation that the people were — as I had never seen people before — barefooted. . . . In my bewilderment I somehow blamed them for the horrid things on which they stood. . . . We were annoyed."[241] Wirkus saw blank stares and interpreted them as indifferent and alert, in turn. He acknowledged his own annoyance and the role it played in his understanding of the situation. Haitians who participated in this encounter had very different interpretations.

The reaction of many Haitians was captured by the title of Leon Laleau's literary protest against the occupation: *Le choc.*[242] The blank faces observed by Wirkus registered, too, in the memory of another Haitian writer, Roger Dorsinville, then a small boy at his mother's side. Looking back on his first view of the marines and their effect on the adults around him, he stated in his memoirs, "I remember my first 'marines' . . . it seems to me that it was the day they disembarked; I understood the newness of their presence by the stupefaction on the faces, and the silence suddenly all around me."[243] The child, Dorsinville went on, could register "nothing but the stupor, and then the resignation," evident on the faces of the adults around him. "The white soldiers," he later wrote, "had come to defile our independence: where were the ancestors? Finally, the ancestors were no more."[244]

In some respects, these were the first encounters between Haitians and U.S. Americans during the occupation. The marines and sailors who marched into Port-au-Prince on July 28, 1915, and those who arrived on the *Tennessee* and *Connecticut,* who confiscated Haitian arms and enforced the occupation curfew, who grabbed Haitians and made them drink pails of water, who patrolled the ports and seized the customs: these were the first U.S. Americans to represent the occupation to Haitian citizens and to collect impressions that they would pass on to others as they arrived. Haitians who fired at the invading marines, who demonstrated at the wharves, who stood silent in shock or cheered the U.S. troops, who participated in "labor troubles" and "carnival" protests: these were the first Haitians to have contact with U.S. Americans during the occupation, the first to react and to respond.

Yet these first encounters on Haitian soil were formed and weighed down with the baggage of history already at their moment of inception: the history of U.S. attitudes toward Haiti and of race relations at home; the history of the Haitians' attempts to maintain their independence against the odds; the young history of U.S. American forays on the world scene, in Cuba, in the Philippines, in China; the historical memory of each participant in the dialogue, struggle, cooperation, and conflict between the United States and Haiti during these years.

Moreover, these first encounters, heavy with the burden of so many pasts, would be repeated, with each new shipload of marines, with each arrival at a town or village, with each recruit into the Gendarmerie, with each insurgent captured, and so on. The U.S. occupation of Haiti from 1915 to 1934 was not a single conflict between two monolithic and singularly unified bodies; it was a struggle for identity and power waged in so many local instances, framed by a number of systemic factors, official acts, formal relationships, and informal structures. It was not only formed by policy, though policy framed it. It was not a series of isolated acts committed by individuals who had "cracked," though individual U.S. American men did break under the strain of it. It was not one singular act of resistance or welcome by the Haitian population, though many Haitians did fight it and some did support it, at least at first.

In the course of nineteen years, some marines formed significant relationships with the Haitians with whom they lived and worked. A few, perhaps more than we know, married Haitian women, raised Haitian families, and even became citizens of Haiti. Others, no doubt most, held themselves aloof from the nation they policed, seeking society only with their fellow U.S. Americans. Others still protested their assignment to this scorned nation — some peacefully, some with wrath and venom. One company of marines employed "a kind of a sit-down strike" to make their point; others resorted to the tools of their trade.[245]

Whether motivated by the desire to bridge the gap between two cultures or by the strategic need for information, some marines tried to learn what Haitians saw through eyes that seemed, in Wirkus's words, "indifferent as the lenses of cameras." Certainly, Marine Corps intelligence officers conducted extensive investigations to ascertain what Haitians thought. Yet, like Adolph Miller's "observations," the "intelligence" they gathered was always filtered through the lens of their own discursive frameworks. The official story was that the American occupiers had their finger on the pulse of Haitian society. Nervous white men, uncertain as to what awaited them should they fall into Haitian hands, belied that fiction.

Figure 8. Marine with Haitian woman, standing by a rural home.
Marine Corps Research Center Archives, Quantico, Virginia.

Even the final, formal encounter of the occupation, the ceremony of the marines' departure on August 15, 1934, was the scene of such uncertainty. As General Alfred H. Noble told the story some years later, "right toward the end, when we were about to get out of the country," rumors began to spread suggesting that the opposition was planning "to throw stones . . . and maybe shoot . . . and take credit for driving [us] out. . . . Well, it got some of our higher ups a little bit nervous. . . . They didn't know, nobody had any way of being sure just what the Haitians thought, you know. We thought we were on good terms with them, but now that we were going to leave they could see the old rattlesnake had had its fangs pulled." Noble, who had been chief of staff of the brigade, recalled that he alone among his peers held out for departing as scheduled "with the band playing and the flag flying." They did just that, in the end, and the whole thing came off surprisingly well, Noble thought, except that "the guns up in the fort didn't go off on time."[246]

As he reported this story to his interviewer in 1973, General Noble reflected on the impression he was making. "But that's just another tale," he commented. "You can cut that out later. Doesn't sound good anyway."[247] Indeed, it always sounded better to say that Americans knew the score. But facing the possibility of an embarrassment, or worse, on their final day, officers of the occupation paused, because, in truth, "nobody had any way of being sure just what the Haitians thought." Like Faustin Wirkus and Homer Overley, marines departing Haiti in the summer of 1934 still wondered.

PATERNALISM

METAPHORS OF FATHERHOOD

When Smedley Butler told a Senate investigating committee in October 1921 that he and his fellow marines had considered themselves the trustees "of a huge estate that belonged to minors," and that they had considered the Haitians their wards, he and his beloved Marine Corps were in the hot seat. The presidential election campaign of 1920 had provided an opening for critics of the occupation. Republican presidential candidate Warren G. Harding had made the most of a gaffe by Assistant Secretary of the Navy Franklin D. Roosevelt, who claimed to have personally authored the Haitian Constitution of 1918.[1] James Weldon Johnson, Herbert Seligmann, and Ernest Gruening had presented powerful indictments of the occupation in the pages of the *Nation*.[2] And worst of all — at least, from the marines' perspective — Marine Corps commandant George Barnett had, after being forced out of his position, wittingly or unwittingly disclosed to the public a series of documents suggesting that there had been "indiscriminate killing of natives" in Haiti.[3] As newspapers around the country picked up these stories and launched their own investigations, ordinary Americans penned indignant complaints for their leaders in Washington.[4] Concerned citizens asked congressmen and cabinet members to confirm or deny outrageous reports of marines governing Haiti by fear and intimidation and killing Haitians without the least provocation.[5] "Could this possibly be true," asked one writer, "at this stage of civilization?"[6] Another, who had participated in the world war, singled out Marine Corps officers and urged the administration to take disciplinary action against them. "When we have been willing to make such a sacrifice of life and to go to such a vast expense during the past six years for the sake of democratic institutions," he wrote, surely we must "guard against any danger of having these institutions overthrown by some of our own officers."[7]

In the face of such criticism, it is hardly surprising that Smedley Butler, now sporting the single star of a brigadier general, would present his corps and their actions in Haiti in the best possible light. Other officers, too, cast their previous actions as wholly consistent with the purportedly benign intentions of their government. Admiral Caperton, for example, reported an encouraging speech he had made to the Haitian president, Sudre Dartiguenave, on behalf of a treaty between the United States and Haiti in November 1915. According to the account he offered to the Senate six years after the fact, Caperton had laid before Dartiguenave a portrait of all that would be possible for Haiti with the friendship of the United States "if there is genuine cooperation on the part of Haitians." Haiti would be "a land of honor, peace, and contentment," the admiral had predicted, and Haitians would bring this about by their own efforts. The United States, he had assured the president, would merely "stand by as an elder brother to help and support."[8] Both Caperton and Butler wielded far more control than they implied in such speeches, but the ongoing work of the occupation, the future of naval appropriations, and the honor of the Marine Corps were hanging in the balance. In this context, paternalist rhetoric served crucial political ends.

When Smedley Butler wrote to his father in December 1915 he was also, in a sense, addressing Congress. He wrote from Port-au-Prince, using the plain Quaker "thee" and "thy" as was the custom in his family, "Thee is right, Father, it will be something in a man's life to have helped put a little nation on its feet."[9] Butler, then a major, had been in Haiti for four months and was embarking on one of the most significant institution-building projects of the occupation, the founding of the Gendarmerie d'Haïti. His father, Congressman Thomas S. Butler, sat on the House Naval Affairs Committee and was thus well positioned to foster his son's new project. In fact, congressional approval would be necessary for the young Butler's plans to go forward. On the other hand, in 1915 no immediate public controversy shaped Smedley Butler's accounts of the occupation. On all sides, at least in the U.S. context, the intervention in Haiti appeared to be a necessary and well-intentioned action. Smedley's 1915 statements to his father must be distinguished from his 1921 statements to the Senate in two other ways as well. First, he wrote to his father while he was in the midst of his work in Haiti. Second, congressman or not, it was his own father he was addressing. The correspondence between Smedley and Thomas Butler was thus at once political and deeply personal. Smedley's letters to his mother, Maud Darlington Butler, to his wife, Ethel C. P. Butler, and to family friends, in different ways, also resonated in more than one key.

For all these reasons, the letters of Major Smedley Darlington Butler from Haiti afford us an unusual glimpse of the discourse of paternalism at work. In letters to his father especially, we find Smedley Butler's articulation of paternalism as a moral and subjective framework for colonial administration side by side with the significance of fatherhood in his own personal relationships. If paternalism is an assertion of authority, superiority, and control expressed in the metaphor of a father's relationship with his children, then the confluence of policy issues, institution building, personal relationships, and discursive play in Butler's letters home may well illuminate some useful paths for our investigation. I use these letters, then, as a frame for my discussion of the ideology of paternalism as it took shape in Washington and in Haiti.

But let us begin by considering what led Butler and other Americans to Haiti in the first place. For Major Butler did not decide, of his own accord, to hop on a battleship and head for Cap Haïtien. Nor, for that matter, did Admiral Caperton author the decision to take control of Haiti, though he chose when and how to implement that decision and shaped U.S. policy toward Haiti in many important respects.[10] President Woodrow Wilson, in consultation with Secretary of State William Jennings Bryan and other advisers, made that crucial decision, if in a piecemeal way. Wilson approved the sending of warships and troops to Haiti on various occasions in 1914. He then resolved, bit by bit, between July 1914 and July 1915, to use those ships and troops decisively. He attempted to set in motion a U.S. occupation in October 1914, when Haitian president Oreste Zamor, his government faltering, had invited assistance on American terms, but Zamor's government fell before Wilson's decision could be carried out.[11] In early April 1915, more than three months before Admiral Caperton landed marines and sailors at Bizoton, President Wilson — still perplexed and hesitant, by his own account — nonetheless instructed Bryan directly that the United States must take control of Haiti and must move with dispatch to do so, declaring "the time to act is now."[12]

WOODROW WILSON AND THE BURDENS OF MORALISM

Two weeks later, Wilson set forth the logic — and the language — that Butler would embrace to explain the occupation to Congress. Speaking to the Associated Press at the Waldorf-Astoria Hotel in New York, Wilson's focus was the importance of American neutrality in relation to the European conflict and the unique role that the United States could play as a "mediating nation." America was "particularly free" to mediate because she had "no hampering ambitions as a world power," Wilson asserted. "We do not want a foot of anybody's territory." He went on to elaborate a fanciful revision of his country's history. "If we have been obliged by circumstances, or have considered ourselves to be obliged by circumstances, in the past, to take territory which we otherwise would not have thought of taking, I believe I am right in saying that we have considered it our duty to administer that territory, not for ourselves, but for the people living in it, and to put this burden upon our consciences — not to think that this thing is ours for our use, but to regard ourselves as trustees of the great business for those to whom it does really belong, trustees ready to hand it over to the *cestui que trust* at any time, when the business seems to make that possible and feasible."[13] Thus Wilson disclaimed all territorial ambition and cast the apparent territorial grabs of the past as selfless acts of paternalist obligation, evidence only of Americans' willingness to shoulder the white man's burden. As trustees of a "great business" really belonging to others, Americans, in Wilson's view, had been guided not by material interest but by obligation and the sound business principle of feasibility.

If U.S. citizens had been "obliged by circumstances" to shoulder the burden of trusteeship, according to Wilson, Latin Americans had been similarly obliged to hand over their "great business" to those "in the main field of modern enterprise and action," namely, Europeans and U.S. Americans. At the Southern Commercial Congress in Mobile, Alabama, a year and a half earlier, Wilson had addressed the more troubling implications of this side of the equation. "You do not hear of concessions to foreign capitalists in the United States," Wilson had told southern businessmen and politicians along with a handful of Latin American diplomats. "They are not granted concessions. They are invited to make investments. The work is ours, though they are welcome to invest in it." In contrast, "states that are obliged . . . to grant concessions" forfeit ownership and control over their own national development. The "always dangerous" and sometimes intolerable result, according to Wilson, was that the domestic affairs of these states inevitably came to be dominated by foreign interests.[14]

The happy news that Wilson brought to Mobile was that the recently opened Panama Canal promised to furnish the means by which Latin American states could, with the help of true friends, emancipate themselves from such subordination. The healthy trade that would result from the opening of the canal would foster "the dignity, the courage, the self-possession, the self-respect of the Latin American states." It would enable "an assertion of the splendid character which, in spite of [their] difficulties, they have again and again been able to demonstrate." In turn, this new circumstance, the opening up of this great trade route, would provide southern businessmen with a new field in which to display their manly character. "We must prove ourselves their friends and champions, upon terms of equality and honor," Wilson intoned, emphasizing that friendship must always be based "upon the terms of honor." Wilson appealed to his countrymen to claim for themselves the honor and righteousness that inheres in those who champion "the development of constitutional liberty in the world," assuring all present that nothing could be dearer "to the thoughtful men of America."[15]

Notwithstanding his attempt, at the Waldorf-Astoria Hotel, to bring the United States' past territorial acquisitions within the pretty logic of his own version of paternalism, Wilson in fact imagined that his foreign policy constituted a sharp departure from Theodore Roosevelt's big stick and William Howard Taft's dollar diplomacy. At Mobile, he marked that departure with a declaration renouncing military conquest and material interests as bases for U.S. policy toward Latin America and heralding the primacy of "human liberty and national opportunity" as guiding values. "I say this," he clarified, addressing his fellow Americans, "merely to fix in our consciousness what our real relationship with the rest of America is. It is the relationship of a family of mankind devoted to the development of true constitutional liberty."[16] Wilson underscored the moralism of his new approach with a millennial flourish at the end of his speech, making it seem rather a sermon than an address to diplomats and businessmen. The spiritual unity of the Americas was, Wilson believed, part of that slow but steady climb "that leads to the final uplands, [where] we shall get our ultimate view of the duties of mankind. We have breasted a considerable part of that climb and shall, presently — it may be in a generation or two — come out upon those great heights where there shines, unobstructed, the light of the justice of God."[17]

In his attempt to implant this moralism within existing foreign policy structures, Wilson felt that he faced significant obstacles. A month before his speech at Mobile, he wrote to Charles William Eliot, former president of Harvard University, of his difficulties with the diplomatic service. "We find that those who have been occupying delegations and embassies have been habituated to a point of view which is very different, indeed, from the point of view of the present administration. They have had the material interests of individuals and the United States very much more in mind than the moral and public considerations which it seems to us ought to control. They have been so bred in a different school that we have found, in several instances, that it was difficult for them to comprehend our point of view and purpose."[18] Diplomats in Haiti were no exception; December 1914 would find Wilson and Bryan chiding the U.S. minister to Haiti, Arthur Bailly-Blanchard, for failing to grasp the critical difference between U.S. control of Haitian customs, which Wilson and Bryan sought as a means to establish stable conditions for economic development and American investment generally, and the granting of particular concessions, in this case mining concessions to American prospectors. "Your proposition seems based upon a misunderstanding of this Government's position," Bryan wrote to Blanchard with Wilson's "entire approval." "While we desire to encourage in every proper way American investments in Haiti, we believe that this can be better done by contributing to stability and order than by favoring special concessions to Americans. American capital will gladly avail itself of business opportunities in Haiti when assured of the peace and quiet necessary for profitable production."[19] Thus, Wilson sought to promote American investment in Haiti and saw this as wholly consistent with "moral and public considerations." The burden of change rested in the difference between "special concessions" and healthy investment that could promote healthy economic development.

Yet, how big a change was this in fact? Looking back on Wilson's numerous military interventions in Latin America and the Caribbean from nearly a century later, his enforcement of the Monroe Doctrine seems not so very distinct from that of Roosevelt or Taft. Wilson himself remarked on the similarity between what he was overseeing in Haiti and Mexico in the summer of 1915 and what his bespectacled predecessor had done in Panama in 1903. He wrote to Colonel House on August 4, one week after marines and sailors disembarked in Haiti, "we are in danger of going a course not unlike that which Roosevelt followed on the isthmus."[20] If anything, Wilson's presidency stands out for its more extensive recourse to military intervention in Latin America.

INSTITUTIONAL CONTEXTS

To understand more fully the policy that brought U.S. forces ashore in Haiti in July 1915 and set them on the path toward a long occupation, we must look to the institutional traditions from which U.S. policy toward Haiti emerged and the institutional contexts in which it was implemented. As president, Wilson inherited a complex of state institutions whose very structure and history embodied particular discursive patterns and ideological perspectives. Assumptions about power and authority, about class and democracy, about race and gender, about private initiative and public goals, were embodied in the institutional forms of the federal government. The evolving liberal state — with its electoral system, its representative legislative structures, its Constitution and courts, its military and policing bodies, and its executive apparatus — established at once an institutional and a discursive framework within which Wilson's ideas and approaches to foreign policy took shape and were put into practice. Wilson butted up against some of the system's limitations and brought change to the federal government in crucial ways, but he was also shaped by the traditions he inherited. His paternalism was distinct from the paternalism of his predecessors, to be sure, but embedded within his — as within theirs — were the seeds of his repeated recourse to military force and private capital as fundamental foreign policy tools. A few examples from the military and economic spheres suffice to illustrate this point for now.

First, let us consider the structure of the military services and their relation to the policy-making apparatus in Washington. While the U.S. Army stood in readiness to defend the nation by engaging in warfare, both the Marine Corps and the U.S. Navy, with which the corps was institutionally linked, served peacetime functions.[21] The Navy served ongoing functions related to international commerce and the development of foreign policy. Even when no difficulty or potential conflict presented itself, the Navy had long supplied policy makers with essential information about ports of call visited by navy ships.[22] When conflicts did arise, a naval squadron or a gunboat could be dispatched "to protect American lives and property." In these different contexts, policy makers received information about local conditions filtered through the lens of naval perspectives, which were shaped, in part, as historian Richard Challener has noted, by naval officers' "general conservatism, dedication to discipline, and respect for hierarchical order in society." Consistent with these values, reports on Latin America and the Caribbean tended to embrace officers' scornful attitudes toward revolutionary disorder.[23] From the uss *Des Moines*, for example, came a 1908 report on civil disorder in Haiti, in which the author editorialized, "The one question is how long will the civilized nations permit such conditions to exist."[24]

Moreover, since 1900 the institution of the General Board had provided a means for the highest-ranking naval officers to weigh in on policy questions with the secretary of the navy. Naval perspectives were thus readily available as cabinet members conferred on policy options for which the Navy and/or the Marine Corps might be deployed. These included perspectives based on the professional and institutional objectives of the Navy, which were linked tightly to the Monroe Doctrine and to the newer policy of the Open Door. As the General Board stated in 1913, urging Secretary of the Navy Josephus Daniels to promote an expansive naval building program, the Monroe Doctrine is only as strong "as the armed and organized forces maintained to enforce it."[25] Leading naval doctrine, building on the ideas of naval officer and historian Alfred Thayer Mahan, linked the strength of the Navy with the U.S. potential for, and rise to, world power.[26] It was, in this sense, boldly imperialist. While the General Board failed to secure many of the institution-building measures it sought, it succeeded with others. The legacy of naval influence with previous administrations, as well as the impact of forceful personalities on the General Board in discussions with Secretary Daniels, continued to give the Navy a measure of influence, despite Wilson's commitment to civilian control over policy making.

Naval perspectives on the acquisition of Caribbean bases provide one example. For over a decade, naval planners emphasized the importance of keeping deepwater ports, such as Mole St. Nicholas in northwestern Haiti, out of European hands. As early as 1907 they elaborated a detailed plan for the seizure of that particular port to serve as an "advanced base" in the event of a military emergency.[27] The plan, developed in part in coordination with the Army, "provided that the Naval landing forces would be relieved by Army units 30 days after the initial seizure, and specific Army units were designated for permanent occupation duty."[28] Army planners apparently expressed some hesitation over the possibility of provoking war by so blatantly disregarding Haitian national integrity—that is, if the Haitians refused to accept American occupation. Yet, naval planners countered that, if it came to that, local guerrilla opposition could easily be overcome by the Army, if not initially by the Marines. After 1914, such "advanced base" schemes gave way to an emphasis within the General Board on acquiring Mole St. Nicholas on a permanent basis as a means to gaining "absolute American control of the Caribbean in the event of involvement in the European war."[29] Although Wilson, Bryan, and Daniels were, as Challener has pointed out, "motivated by a desire to prevent militarism and military values from infecting civilian policy," they accepted the strategic importance of Mole St. Nicholas to the United States and consistently demanded that successive Haitian governments—at the very least—refuse to cede or lease it to any European power.[30]

Another aspect of the U.S. military apparatus that was particularly significant for U.S. policy toward Haiti was the evolving nature, function, and importance of the Marine Corps. From its inception in 1798, the corps had a dual function: to serve as ships guards, keeping order among the naval ranks at sea, and to be available for shore duty as the president saw fit. Woodrow Wilson saw fit to use the Marines as no previous president had, and the corps was ready at hand as a versatile military tool available to enforce his policies.[31] The Marines were indeed, as they came to be called in the 1920s, "presidential troops."[32] The corps's tradition of serving as guards or policing troops dovetailed with Wilson's self-concept as an upholder of international law (even when Wilson himself was breaking international law).[33] Roosevelt had used the Army in Panama in 1903, with welcome implications for his reputation as an eager warrior. Prior to the occupation of Haiti, the Marine Corps had been used only once in a large-scale colonial effort—in Nicaragua in 1909. In Mexico, Haiti, and the Dominican Republic, Wilson turned repeatedly to the Marines to carry out the United States' self-appointed international police power, first asserted by Roosevelt in his 1904 corollary to the Monroe Doctrine. Wilson, no eager warrior, did not turn to the U.S. Army as had Roosevelt, but he did not shy away from the enforcement he felt was necessary to build his new world order based on political stability sufficient to support the expansion of capitalist trade networks. Its traditions made the Marines Corps the perfect tool.

More important than any of the various military factors, however, were the links between businessmen and bankers and the policy-making apparatus of the federal government. An absence of knowledge about Latin American affairs within the administration proper served to enhance those links. Neither Wilson nor Bryan had any significant knowledge of Haiti, nor was there much Latin American expertise in the Department of State.[34] Boaz W. Long, appointed chief of the Latin American Affairs Division by Bryan, was himself a businessman, who qualified as an expert on Latin America only because "his company had a branch office in Mexico City."[35] His assistant, Jordan H. Stabler, came from the diplomatic corps rather than the private sector, having served in Peru and Guatemala, but, most recently, in Sweden.[36] In lieu of a well-trained team in the Department of State, Wilson and Bryan came to rely upon bankers, railroad magnates, and other business leaders for guidance as they developed U.S. policy toward Haiti and other Latin American and Caribbean nations.

One striking example of this involved James P. McDonald, an American entrepreneur whose name, by 1912, had become "a household word" in the north of Haiti, according to Lemuel Livingston, the American consul at Cap Haïtien. Livingston reported to the Department of State that peasants there feared McDonald and "almost every unknown white man above the average in physical proportions" whom they supposed to be him.[37] In 1910 McDonald had taken over a railroad concession, which included the right to establish banana plantations on either side of the track, between Port-au-Prince and Cap Haïtien. Apart from the possibility that McDonald used bribery to obtain the concession in the first place, his engineers' manners offended the local elite and his plans threatened the local peasants who did not hold titles to the land they tilled.[38] Altogether, his presence inspired an impassioned nationalist response, and McDonald engaged in difficult struggles with Haitian peasants and with the Haitian government before the concession was taken over by a consortium headed by the W. R. Grace Company in 1911. Yet McDonald actively contributed to the Wilson administration's policy toward Haiti. Specifically, his formulation of the need for employment in Haiti became one of the central tenets of U.S. paternalism there.[39]

Thus, while Wilson insisted that he would brook no "special concessions" in his dealings with Latin American and Caribbean nations, his administration was keen to know what conditions would encourage U.S. investment in Haiti generally. In the spring of 1914 Jordan Stabler reported his findings on that question, gathered from representatives of the United Fruit Company. Their answer? A U.S. occupation, ensuring an end to the cycle of revolution.[40]

Bankers' connection to policy makers had been strengthened in the administration of Wilson's immediate predecessor, William Howard Taft. Concerned, as Wilson would be in time, with the economic influence of European powers in Latin America, Taft sought to reduce that influence by providing loans, through American banks, to financially troubled Latin American states. As Brenda Gayle Plummer has pointed out, this brought the banks into a more intimate relation with the policy-making structure of the federal government. Asked to extend loans to poor risks, bankers wanted "a stronger voice in policy formulation."[41] In 1909 the Department of State succeeded in persuading the National City Bank and Speyer and Company to throw their hats in the ring when there arose the possibility of a reorganization of the French-controlled Banque Nationale d'Haïti. Both financial institutions had extended loans to a German railroad concession in Haiti, and certainly Frank A. Vanderlip, president of the National City Bank, had great international ambitions, but neither institution initiated negotiations surrounding the Haitian National Bank.[42] By the time the deal was closed, American bankers held a 50 percent controlling interest.

Wilson balked at the actions of some banks, particularly in Mexico, and criticized them as he renounced material interest at Mobile in 1913, but he and Bryan came to rely on bankers and to accept their perspectives as legitimate bases for the development of U.S. policy toward Haiti.[43] The most significant figure to influence the Wilson administration in this connection was a personal friend of Boaz Long.[44] Roger L. Farnham was an officer of the National City Bank as well as vice president of the Haitian National Bank and president of an American-owned railroad company in Haiti. On January 22, 1914, Farnham gave Bryan the first of several crucial briefings on the Haitian situation, appealing to Bryan's sense of himself as a champion of commoners. Boaz Long underscored that appeal in a follow-up memorandum. "The political system which obtains throughout the country," he wrote, "constitutes a certain form of slavery for the masses, and no helping hand has been stretched out to the common people in an effort to improve their condition."[45] After another consultation with Farnham, in December of that year, Bryan arranged for a detachment of marines to escort $500,000 of Haitian government funds from the Haitian National Bank, via gunboat, to the National City Bank in New York. Shortly after receiving this assistance from the U.S. government, the Haitian Bank lowered its French flag and raised the Stars and Stripes, signaling that "it would henceforth be under the protection of the United States."[46] An even more crucial conference between Farnham and Bryan occurred in late March 1915. On that occasion, Farnham presented a highly dubious account of enemy cooperation between France and Germany whose object was to undermine the U.S. position in Haiti. He then added his own threat to remove American business interests from Haiti if there was to be no occupation.[47] It was this conference that precipitated an exchange between Bryan and Wilson, in which Wilson asserted that the United States must move quickly and efficiently to assume control of the Haitian government.[48]

In some ways, Wilson and his cabinet members seemed to deceive themselves about the intimate connections between private capital and public policy. In early January 1915 Bryan asked Wilson explicitly for guidance with regard to the bank. "There is probably sufficient ground for intervention, but I do not like the idea of forcibly interfering on purely business grounds," Bryan wrote. "I would like to know how far you think we ought to go in forcing the Bank's views and interests."[49] Wilson never responded directly, at least in writing, but implicitly affirmed the substantive agreement between his own conviction and the point pressed by the bank. We must tell the Haitians, Wilson responded, "as firmly and definitely as is consistent with courtesy and kindness that the United States cannot consent to stand by and permit revolutionary conditions constantly to exist there."[50] It is also striking that, at various points, American officials persisted in referring to the National Bank of Haiti as "the French bank."[51] It was, indeed, technically a French corporation; in that sense they were correct. Yet, as we have seen, after 1910, American banks and bankers held a controlling interest in the Haitian bank, and after 1914 the bank itself had hoisted an American flag to indicate its allegiance. It would have been equally correct to refer to the same institution as the "American bank" of Haiti. Referring to it as "the French bank" may well have helped to keep blinders on certain uncomfortable facts. Finally, Wilson knew well the sources of information and guidance on which his secretaries of state relied. Both Bryan and Lansing reported such information without hesitation. Yet Wilson wrote to his fiancée, Edith Bolling Galt, in early August 1915, just after the occupation began, "the small guiding threads of [the Haitian situation], the threads which really define the pattern of the whole transaction, I do not see clearly or at all, and I feel that I am rather blindly following the lead of the Secretary of State. I wonder what lead he is following?"[52] Whether sincere or disingenuous, Wilson's private remark to his fiancée resonates with an observation made of Wilson by a British diplomat in 1917, that "when any serious decision is taken, [he] always tries to unload the responsibility on to someone else."[53]

Fresh from his inauguration, President Wilson declared, on March 12, 1913, his commitment to international cooperation through "orderly processes of just government, based upon law, not upon arbitrary or irregular force."[54] Yet, for Wilson, "law" had two sides. On one hand, it underwrote the democratic egalitarianism at the heart of his rhetoric: the rule of law before which all are equal. On the other hand, it represented the authoritarian paternalism that ran like a central artery through the body of his discourse: the law of the father before whom one can only obey or be disciplined. Wilson confronted the contradiction between these two "laws" once the Marines had landed. "I fear we have not the legal authority to do what we apparently ought to do," he wrote to Robert Lansing, his new secretary of state, on August 4, 1915; "I suppose there is nothing for it but to take the bull by the horns and restore order."[55] At least one journalist called attention to Wilson's stern hand in Haiti; a *Literary Digest* editorial remarked, "small-boy Haiti is evidently going to receive, if not corporal punishment, at least the strictest sort of discipline."[56]

The job of meting out Wilson's discipline in Haiti would fall to a proud descendant of Virginia slaveholders, Colonel Littleton W. T. Waller. Smedley Butler's immediate commanding officer, as well as his friend and mentor, Waller was well known for his leadership in the ruthless campaign against Filipino insurgents, on the island of Samar in the fall of 1901.[57] In Haiti, he was committed to a policy of "positive firmness" with regard to the Cacos; "I know the nigger and how to handle him," he once wrote to John A. Lejeune, assistant commandant of the Marine Corps.[58] In April 1916 Waller, already brigade commander, would become the ranking officer resident in Haiti. As of December 1915, however, Admiral Caperton still held that position. Caperton, who originally hailed from Tennessee, was clearly no less interested in securing American control over Haiti, but he projected a more respectful and diplomatic attitude toward Haitian leaders and kept himself aloof from the daily business of "handling" the insurgency.[59] Therefore, when Smedley Butler wrote to his father that December, proud to be undertaking his new mission, he was operating under the leadership of two forceful and conflicting personalities, in an occupation taking shape under the direction of both diplomatic and military decision makers in Washington.

THY LOVING SON

Smedley Butler began his work with the Gendarmerie as a thirty-four-year-old man with a wife and three young children at home in Pennsylvania. He had been married for ten years and in that time he had lived with his family in the Philippines and in Panama as well as in his home state, though, of course, he had been absent for stretches of time, especially during the interventions in Nicaragua and Mexico.[60] While apart they carried on an affectionate and substantial correspondence; she was his "Bunny" and he was her "Daddie Piddie" (as in "Your loving, lonely, adoring, homesick, but slightly cheered up, Daddie Piddie").[61] Smedley had a daughter, named Ethel but known as Snooks, who was nine, and two sons, Smedley Jr., who was six, and Tom Dick, three (Figure 9).[62] The elder Smedley's reputation as a "bulldog marine" and a roughneck warrior hero was fairly well developed by this time, among his men and in the public eye, as well as — no doubt — in the eyes of his two young sons.[63] He had served in Cuba, the Philippines, China, Honduras, Panama, Nicaragua, and Mexico, and although he had been the butt of more than one joke about congressmen's sons and preferential treatment, he had made himself indispensable to the corps as a versatile colonial enforcer. He learned much as the young protégé of Colonel Waller, his mentor, friend, and, back in 1905, his best man.[64]

Writing to his father in December 1915, Smedley Butler evinced pride in his new project and embraced the paternal metaphor to express that pride. "For the past two weeks I have been working along hard with my little black Army and am beginning to like the little fellows," he wrote. He had "about 900" Haitians enlisted and was hopeful that they would do well, "in time, and as long as white men lead them."[65] If he still believed, as he had pro-

Figure 9. Smedley Butler with his family. Left to right: Smedley Sr., Smedley Jr., "Snooks," Ethel, and Tom Dick. Marine Corps Research Center Archives, Quantico, Virginia.

fessed to his father two months earlier, that Colonel Waller was his "ideal of a soldier" because he knew how "to end a row with a savage monkey," he did not employ that metaphor in this letter.[66] Instead, he acceded to his father's wisdom. Like helping his sons to walk for the first time and guiding them to adulthood, it would be a credit to his own manhood to raise up this "little nation."

In the coming months, Major Butler pressed forward with his work on an unofficial basis. At last, on May 3, 1916, the Haitian government took an important step toward legitimizing the Gendarmerie by ratifying the Haitian-American treaty, which the U.S. Senate had accepted in February.[67] Article X stated that "the Haitian government obligated itself . . . to create without delay an efficient constabulary, urban and rural, composed of native Haitians." "The constabulary shall be organized and officered by Americans," it continued, and "the Haitian government shall clothe *their officers* with the proper and necessary authority."[68] In plain English, "their officers" meant American marines. By treaty, then, Marine Corps officers and enlisted men serving in the Haitian Gendarmerie would be vested with the authority to act as an arm of the Haitian government, a representative, technically, of the Haitian president and, by extension, the Haitian people. They would be American men "clothed" as Haitian officers.

OCCUPATION

A few more steps were still necessary, however, for this diplomatic sleight of hand to be complete. For one thing, the U.S. Congress had to authorize officers and enlisted men of the U.S. military to serve, temporarily, under the authority of the president of Haiti. For another, there were details not covered in the treaty that were to be worked out in a separate Gendarmerie agreement. Neither of those steps had been completed when, on May 16, Smedley Butler reported to his father with bravado, "We had a cablegram last night announcing the Marine Corps Bill but whether it had passed the House or just been introduced we did not learn, however, we Gendarmes are all too busy to care much one way or another."[69] Here was the can-do, no-nonsense bulldog marine spirit that Smedley had exhibited so many times before. Whether or not the U.S. Congress had made it official, the marines themselves had "settled down to the hardest kind of work."[70] Never mind the bureaucratic detail that these were American marines and not, in fact, Haitian gendarmes. Smedley eagerly, and with humor, embraced his as-yet unofficial status as a Haitian officer.

When he wrote to Thomas Butler in May, Smedley had just returned from a trip to the States. While in Philadelphia he had taken the opportunity to lobby at least one of his father's colleagues in the House of Representatives for passage of the constabulary bill.[71] "Our Marines acting as Haitian officers are doing everything in their power to assist the native population," he wrote to Representative James R. Mann, a fellow Republican from Illinois. Reassuring Mann with regard to his constituency, Butler wrote, "all that is necessary is for our own people to realize what we're trying to do for this little republic."[72] By "our own people," of course, he meant the American public, but the younger Butler closed his letter on a different note. He offered to supply the congressman with "any further information which you desire" and to "come immediately to Washington at any time you say, for *we Haitians* want to get everybody we possibly can on our side of the fence."[73]

We Gendarmes. We Haitians. Smedley was indeed, on some level, embracing his new status. In the same vein, he opened his May 16 letter to his father, on the heels of his trip to Philadelphia, with a bit of wordplay: "Here I am," he wrote, "back in my native land." My native land? My home? My natives? Smedley Butler, the jokester, had found a pun he could not resist. If he had become Haitian as an officer of the Gendarmerie, then Haiti was surely his home, his "native land." He bounced his jest off the evocative nationalist phrase, invoking, at the same time, a whole train of connotations attaching to the word "native." The discourse of primitivism so natural to the schoolboys who would write Faustin Wirkus in 1929 gave life to Butler's witticism. But other meanings lurked there as well, not least, a sense of possession: *my* native land and even *my* natives, or, as he had called them a few months earlier in another letter home, "my little chocolate soldiers."[74]

When Smedley wrote to his father some months later, he was in a very different frame of mind. He was frustrated by a setback in his plans, occasioned by the Haitian government's refusal to sign on to the sweeping powers he had envisioned for himself and his Gendarmerie. He had wanted to have all public works and communications under his direction; it was now clear that this would not come through. "We lost our fight with the Haitians over the Gendarmerie agreement," he wrote.[75] His tone was now dead serious, as it has been back in January 1914, when he had experienced a similar kind of resentment at what he regarded as a significant diminution of his authority. At that time, when he had been ordered to leave Panama after four years of residence and prior to the opening of the canal, he communicated his "keen disappointment" to Secretary of the Navy Josephus Daniels. Butler had had his own "independent command" at Camp Elliott in Panama and was now being ordered to report as a shipboard officer with the Caribbean squadron for possible action in Mexico.[76] I have "spent the best years of my life here and the happiest and most successful," he wrote to Daniels, and now "have to go back to a subordinate position under some old fool."[77] Yet, if he had felt diminished by having to report to a naval officer in 1914, he regarded his new situation in Haiti as thoroughly degrading. "Instead of having practically the whole of Haiti to run," he wrote to his father on the first of October, "I am reduced to a very humiliating position, am simply the very subservient chief of a nigger police force."[78]

Here, in the distance traveled from "my little fellows" to "a nigger police force," the rhetoric of paternalism appears to break down.[79] Yet, the discourse of paternalism structured this epistolary outburst to the same degree that it structured Butler's expressions of fatherly pride in his gendarmes-in-the-making. For central to the logic of paternalism was the relation of power implicit in the father-child dyad. In the paternalist framework, the relation of father to child was not only marked by the care, guidance, protection, and affection of the father for the child, but also by the father's proprietary claims to, and mastery over, the child.

Haitian resistance to American mastery upset the would-be routine functioning of the discourse and forced open to view its uglier side. This process had begun to create cracks in the facade of paternalism months earlier, as may be seen in a letter Smedley Butler addressed to General John A. Lejeune in July. Haitian leaders continued to stall on the Gendarmerie agreement, which among other things specified the additional pay that would accrue to marines serving as Gendarmerie officers. American civilians work-

OCCUPATION

ing for the Haitian government had begun to draw their Haitian salaries. Butler, intent on pleading the case of his men (as well as his own), wrote "the rest of us, who have worked on an average of ten hours a day for seven or eight months for these negroes should be given the same privilege."[80] Butler's patience and good humor were wearing thin. "Non-commissioned officers performing duty in the bushes are certainly working like dogs for these wretched people," he wrote, "and I consider it an outrage that this government is not required to sign this agreement, and let them get their pay."[81] If Smedley's letters to his father were, to some extent, calculated in relation to political necessity, his letter to General Lejeune was strictly internal. One could argue, along these lines, that his letter to Lejeune was more honest. On the other hand, Major Butler wanted something from Lejeune, too. Claiming that it was an honor to work with gendarmes would have been rhetorically foolish in the context of this plea.

The Haitians' ultimate refusal to accede to Butler's demands for the Gendarmerie opened the cracks wider, and Smedley at last expressed his disgust to the congressman as well as the general. Marines serving as father figures to native gendarmes lived and worked in relatively close contact with their recruits. They were associated with Haitians more directly than marines garrisoned in Port-au-Prince or Cap Haïtien. Within the context of U.S. racism — and paternalism, it should be obvious, was always also racism — this relative intimacy between Americans and Haitians was palatable only because it took place within a rigid hierarchy. A sense of mastery enabled Butler and other marines to avoid the implication that they were themselves degraded by their association with a profoundly stigmatized racial other. Yet, when Butler felt that he faced a loss of mastery, he chafed at his intimacy with Haitians, now thrown into sharp relief. "My little black army" had become "these wretched people."

A further aspect of Smedley's October 1 letter to his father underscores the significance of domestic space in the discourse of paternalism. When his sense of degradation and anger came to the fore in that letter, he immediately turned his attention to the domestic and familial dimension of his life to explain why he would stay on to work with the Gendarmerie. He had been humiliated, he wrote, he would now be subservient to Haitians, and, he continued — in the very same run-on sentence — "were it not that I hope to save a little nest egg for the future, would leave the d——d job." "As it is," he went on, finally pausing to punctuate, "I have rented quite a nice house for Bunny and the Babies and have sent for them."[82] Turning quickly to his status as father and provider within his own "little family," Butler blunted the blow to his status as father and master over his "native land." We are reminded again of Smedley's January 1914 letter to his mother from Panama. For there, too, Butler drew a close connection between his domestic space and his military authority. Smarting at the loss of his command, he expressed his sense of injustice in terms of the loss of his "beautiful Camp and *home*," underlining *home* not once but twice. At the same time, removing him and his men was an injustice to the marines, "who took this place" and thereby had a right to it.[83]

Butler's frustration with the insufficiently pliant client government in Port-au-Prince continued into the next calendar year. "These wretched politicians," he wrote to his father on May 16, "do not intend to fall in with our American plans and ideas."[84] The previous month, the United States had entered the war against Germany, and Butler's desire to get to the front as quickly as possible undoubtedly accentuated his impatience with Haitian leaders. He expressed some regret at the prospect of leaving his work unfinished in Haiti: "I feel a little badly over leaving this poor wretched country in its present unsettled state," he wrote, "but it is the work of a lifetime."[85] Besides, the war beckoned him, promising a field for valor in action. If raising up a little nation was a credit to his manhood, all the more was this so of leaving to his sons a record of military honors, honestly won.

The prospect of fighting in France resonated with Smedley Butler's sense of his own manhood, and his manhood was, in his own mind, connected to the legacy he would leave to his sons. Back in August 1912, on the eve of what his biographer has called "his first dangerous assignment as a field-grade officer," he had written to his wife from Managua, "if anything should happen to me bring my Blessed Son [Smedley Jr.] up with the idea firmly planted in his head that his Dadda was not a coward."[86] After the action, he wrote again to his wife, this time somewhat embarrassed, "I am ashamed of my weakness in writing such rot to thee as I did before leaving Managua but everybody was sure . . . that we would have trouble."[87] For Butler, it was "rot" to express fear on the eve of battle, but he would return again to his concern for the legacy that he would leave to his son.

In the course of his first two years in Haiti, Butler tried to prevent that legacy from being diminished by what he regarded as a meaningless decoration. Some months before shipping off to Haiti, he had been informed that he would be receiving a Congressional Medal of Honor for his role in enemy action in Veracruz. What role that was, he could not imagine. The medal arrived for him in Port-au-Prince in February 1916, and he wrote to his mother that, even in his "most puffed up moments," he could "not remember a single action, or in fact any collection of actions, . . . that in the slightest degree warranted such a decoration. I did my duty as best I could in Vera

Cruz but there was absolutely nothing *heroic* in it."[88] Butler contrasted his record in Veracruz with his daring and leadership in a fight against Caco rebels at Fort Rivière, Haiti, in November 1915. For the latter action he would be happy to receive (and did in fact receive) the medal that he regarded as his "Country's greatest gift"; "should I get it I will accept with a feeling of satisfaction for my men think, so I understand, I deserve some such recognition and that is the best criterion of a man's service."[89] Butler tried, unsuccessfully, to refuse the medal awarded for Veracruz, and even asked his father to persuade Secretary Daniels to take it back. He explained his persistence in the letter to his mother: he did not want his sons (now two of them, Smedley Jr. and Tom Dick) to "proudly display this wretched medal, or rather wretchedly awarded, some time and have a bystander smile or wink — when they, my Boys, had always been under the impression that their father had honestly deserved all he left them."[90]

If his legacy to his sons, as well as his status as a father who could inspire pride in his sons, was on his mind as he wrote to his own father that day in May, his younger son was literally on his lap. Frightened of the family's butler, whom Smedley referred to as "Uncle Sam," Tom Dick was clamoring for some paternal care and attention. Yet, if his son was still young enough to show his fear, he was already playing the little warrior — that is, he was Butler's other sort of "little fellow." Thus Ethel despaired, Smedley reported to his father, about the possibility for world peace "when a precious little innocent thing like Tom Dick spends most of his time . . . aiming a make be-lieve cannon at birds and shouting 'boom.' "[91] Here was a moment freighted with the significance of fatherhood and masculinity in a colonial context. Here was Smedley Butler weighing his paternal obligations to Haiti and to his own sons, yearning to make his mark in war, getting a chuckle over the absurd inversion of power embodied in a black "Uncle Sam" frightening a small white boy, and waxing proud of his son, a little savage warrior claiming his dawning masculinity.[92] All this was in play as he addressed his own father, signing himself in the usual way, "Thy loving son," this time adding "and grandson," with the boy's mark following his own signature.[93]

Thus, as Smedley Butler embraced the paternal metaphor, he was en-sconced in the intertwined relations of power and affection surrounding fatherhood. When he wrote to his father, and for that matter to his mother, as a loving son, when he wrote to other congressmen as a loyal citizen, he could afford to play "Haiti" to their "America." "We Gendarmes" are all busy at work. "We Haitians" are eager for American support. Or, as he wrote on January 27, 1918, still heading up the Gendarmerie and now settled into the routine business of leading a nation in wartime, "we don't seem to be able to get rid of our coffee crop and are therefore very poor as a nation."[94] Shortly thereafter he received word that he would, finally, be on his way to France after a brief stopover in the States. "Thy little Family from Haiti," he wrote to his mother in March, should reach New York before the end of the month.[95] The occupation invited American men to adopt Haiti and to identify with Haitians as fathers identify with their sons. Butler accepted the invitation. In playful, calculated, and routine ways, he used that identification to perform his deference to his parents and to Congress. His performance, in turn, affirmed the power relations inherent in his own paternal role in Haiti. And, as we have seen, when his mastery was challenged in that context, all playfulness and deference disappeared, exposing the ugly underbelly of his paternalism.

THE LAW OF THE FATHER

Not all paternalists foregrounded the metaphors of fatherhood and childhood as explicitly as the American chief of the Haitian Gendarmerie. In contrast to Butler, Woodrow Wilson scrupulously avoided such blatant references to inequalities of power. His egalitarian rhetoric emphasized friendship rather than fatherhood. The United States and Latin America were neighbors, he said again and again, remarking, with regret, in 1915 "that it should have required a crisis of the world to show the Americas how truly they were neighbors to one another."[96] At Mobile, he said that the United States' real relationship with Latin America was "the relationship of a family of mankind," but he never mentioned fathers or children specifically — that is, he never specified who held authority within this "family." At the Waldorf-Astoria Hotel in New York, he used the term "trustees" to refer to U.S. Americans who had seized the land of others but, unlike Butler, he kept his metaphor in the realm of business relations among adults, never mentioning the supposed "wards" who would also, logically, have been affected by the transaction.

Indeed, when Wilson did make reference to "wards," it was to drive home the paternalist arrogance of one of his opponents in the presidential race of 1912 and thus to distance himself from such paternalism. Theodore Roosevelt's social welfare program — which included proposals for a federal workmen's compensation act, federal intervention in labor disputes, an expanded federal health program, and the use of tariffs "to insure fair wages to workers in industry" — would, Wilson charged, "make the people nothing more than mere wards and puppets of a National Board of Guardians, with such men as Frick and Gary as its supervising heads."[97] Speaking to an audience of workingmen in Buffalo, New York, two months before the election, he went on, "God forbid that in a democratic country we should resign the task of governing ourselves and hand the Government over to experts."[98] With this remarkable sleight of hand, Wilson aligned himself with the dignity and independence of white workingmen even as he refused to challenge the power of corporate owners' domination over labor. Moreover, Wilson's first administration would, in various ways, foster stronger ties between government and business. Yet, by denouncing Roosevelt's paternalism, Wilson could style himself a champion of "the liberties of the people."[99] "He urged every despondent workingman, who had no outlook but to sweat through his life to its very end," the *New York Times* reported the following day, "to take hope" in the Democratic platform, which would lead, he said, to a day "when every wage slave can look up and say to his fellow man: 'I, too, am of the free breed of American citizens.' "[100]

In other ways, too, Wilson's rhetoric sidestepped the more direct paternalist metaphors in favor of a democratic universalism that obscured inequalities and differences within the citizenry. The gender dimensions of Wilson's discourse, for example, can be glimpsed in his appeal to the honor of southern men at Mobile, but he made no direct reference to men as a group distinct from women. Only when pressed to address "the woman question" did Wilson explicitly acknowledge gender as a form of human difference in his public addresses.[101] Likewise, Wilson tried hard to erase racial matters from his explicit public speeches. His liberal rhetoric was nominally inclusive, insofar as it embraced "all" without naming any, a fact that helped him garner the support of a few key African American leaders in 1912.[102] Yet that same rhetoric worked a variety of exclusions by virtue of its silences and omissions as well as by the connotative weight of its metaphors. The term "wage slave," for example, bore a complex legacy of racial meaning, coming as it did out of the northern, white labor movement of the nineteenth century. My point is not simply that Wilson was racist and sexist. It is plain enough from his actions, as well as from his private correspondence, that he embraced racial and gender hierarchies; his approval of formal and systematic segregation in several branches of his administration is only one of the most obvious examples. My point, instead, is that such hierarchies were deeply embedded in the very rhetoric that seemed to reject them.

Paternalism — however obscured it may have been at times, either by the egalitarian aspects of his rhetoric or by his own explicit disavowal — was deeply embedded in Woodrow Wilson's liberal vision. In 1914 the obvious disjunction between his talk of equality and the newly institutionalized racism of his first administration led to a confrontation that would expose both his paternalism and the barely masked racial codes of his moralism. On two occasions, William Monroe Trotter, one of the African American leaders who had supported his election in 1912, led a delegation of African American Democrats to the White House to challenge segregation in the federal government. Trotter and his delegation first visited Wilson in November 1913 bearing a petition signed by 20,000 "Afro-Americans in thirty-eight states."[103] They returned a year later, on November 12, 1914, to press their case again, having witnessed no remedy to this institutionalized "public humiliation and degradation."[104] "Have you a 'new freedom' for white Americans," Trotter asked Wilson, "and a new slavery for your 'Afro-American *fellow citizens*'? God forbid."[105]

Wilson's reply betrayed the racial structure of his liberalism as it attempted to square institutionalized segregation with egalitarianism. Wilson began by speaking on behalf of "the American people, as a whole," by which, of course, he meant, white Americans. "I think that I am perfectly safe in stating," he ventured, "that the American people, as a whole, sincerely desire and wish to support, in every way they can, the advancement of the Negro race in America. They rejoice in the evidences of the really extraordinary advances that the race has made."[106] Thus, even as he attempted to counter Trotter's charge that he regarded African Americans as outside the circle of citizenship, he reinscribed the distinction between "the American people" and "the Negro race." "In my view," the president went on, still reaching for a complimentary tone, "the best way to help the Negro in America is to help him with his independence — to relieve him of his dependence upon the white element of our population, as he is relieving himself in splendid fashion."[107] The point of the segregation, Wilson insisted, was merely to remove the possibility of "any kind of friction" between the races within government offices, to prevent African American employees from being made "uncomfortable" by anything that a white employee might do, and vice versa.[108] Finally, Wilson addressed directly, and conceded, the implication that segregation implied some sort of inequality. "It is not a question of intrinsic equality," he explained, "because we all have human souls. We are absolutely equal in that respect. It is just at the present a question of economic equality — whether the Negro can do the same things with equal efficiency. Now, I think they are proving that they can. After they have proved it, a lot of things are going to solve themselves."[109]

Trotter's response pointed directly at the paternalism that Wilson refused to acknowledge. "We are not here as wards," he stated flatly. "We are not here as dependents. We are not here looking for charity or help. We are here as full-fledged American citizens, vouchsafed equality of citizenship by the federal Constitution."[110] Trotter recognized what was only implicit in Wilson's statement — that "economic equality" and "efficiency" functioned as codes for a kind of adult political status that Wilson attributed uniquely to whites. Equality was "intrinsic," but it was, for African Americans, a state to be realized at some future time when the race had sufficiently advanced, when they had proved themselves equal in ability to whites. For Wilson, the "advancement of the Negro race in America" was no basis at all for fostering the "fellowship" among equal citizens that Trotter called for. On the contrary, however "splendid" the progress of the race, the very need for "advancement" signified for Wilson that African Americans were still in the early stages of a process of political and economic development that Anglo-Saxons had mastered over generations and, indeed, centuries. This developmentalist racial framework enabled Wilson to embrace a notion of "equality" for all, while effectively reserving the full measure of citizenship to Americans of European — and not African — ancestry.

Wilson may have imagined that he was rigorous in his respectful attitude toward the African Americans who visited him that day, but he could not erase the racist and, for that matter, the gendered implications of his overarching political perspective. He may have used the word "man," as in "colored man," to describe an African American employee of the federal government, but Trotter heard "boy," with all the violence and condescension attached to that address.[111] No doubt feeling the temperature rise as he observed Trotter's as-yet nonverbal response, Wilson invoked yet another grid of racial and gender meanings — those associated with emotion and rationality — to temper Trotter's response: "we must not," he warned, "allow feelings to get the upper hands of our judgments."[112] Faced with such repeated, if indirect, assaults on his status as a rational, grown man, and thus a full and rightful citizen, Trotter finally brought gender to the surface, questioning Wilson's character as a man of faith. "We ought to to be truthful," he admonished the president. "I hope you want to be frank and true and not be false to your faith . . . you know it would be an unmanly thing to appear to be false."[113] Wilson endured Trotter's speech a bit longer, then showed him the door.[114]

Wilson's paternalism, which revealed itself with such clarity in this second meeting with Trotter, was not simply an isolated expression of racism, relevant only in interactions with African Americans. It was, instead, one of the organizing principles that lay at the heart of his political philosophy. It revealed itself, too, in his addresses to white Americans and in his elaboration of the meaning of leadership and democracy. In a talk at Swarthmore College, for example, Wilson praised William Penn, the "patron saint" of Swarthmore, "as a sort of spiritual knight, who went out upon his adventures to carry the torch that had been put in his hands so that other men might have the path illuminated for them which led to justice and to liberty. . . . This man Penn . . . crossed the ocean, not merely to establish estates in America, but to set up a free commonwealth in America and to show that he was of the lineage of those who had been bred in the best traditions of the human spirit . . . to see to it that every foot of this land should be the home of free, self-governed people, who should have no government whatever which did not rest upon the consent of the governed."[115] For Wilson, Penn embodied not only a political tradition but also a racial heritage. His conquest of America, in the name of freedom, showed that he was descended from "the lineage, the fine lineage, of those who have sought justice and right."[116] By virtue of that lineage, he could light the way for others less fortunate in their racial inheritance and, thus, in their ability to lead. Here, as elsewhere, Wilson identified justice, liberty, and democracy as markers of a unique Anglo-Saxon racial heritage.[117]

For Wilson, there was no irony in the proximity between conquest and self-government in this account of William Penn's great adventure. Wilson himself used the term "conquest" to describe Penn's accomplishment in bringing democracy to America. It was, of course, a righteous conquest, carried out in the name of justice, and it made way for others who shared Penn's fine lineage to take possession of the vast American continent, spreading liberty from coast to coast. Both the righteousness of the conquest and the vastness of the territory conquered testified, according to Wilson, to the greatness of the American people, for, as he said, "every race and every man is as big as the thing that he takes possession of."[118] Americans are right to boast, Wilson told Swarthmore students and faculty, about "the size of our own domain as a nation," for "the size of America is in some sense a standard of the size and capacity of the American people."[119] The historical fact of a vast and righteous conquest, then, verified the lineage that destined Americans for greatness.

If "the American people, as a whole" were especially fit to lead others down the path of justice and to support "the advancement" of those less fortunate, Latin Americans, as well as African Americans, were among those to be helped and supported. That is to say, Wilson regarded Latin Americans in the same racial light that he regarded African Americans. Thus, commiserating with his fiancée over a family disaster consisting of the fact that Edith's niece, Elizabeth, had announced her intention to marry a Panamanian man of apparently questionable family background, Wilson wrote, "it would be bad enough at best to have anyone we love marry into any Central American family, because there is the presumption that the blood is not unmixed." But, he cautioned, "we must not turn away from and abandon the girl, who is of *our* blood."[120] The racial issue was obvious to Wilson, and the fact that Latin Americans did not view themselves as racially inferior was apparently a source of some amusement to him. In August 1915, while pondering the impact of the United States' high-handed actions in Haiti, Wilson wrote privately, again to his fiancée, that "the effect on the rest of 'Latin America' of our course down there will not, we think, be serious, because, being negroes, they are not regarded as of the fraternity!"[121]

The developmentalist racial framework that constituted Wilson's paternalism was fundamental to his approach to Latin America. The United States had a special responsibility to its southern neighbors, Wilson felt. In the fall of 1913, revolutionary disturbances in Mexico drew Wilson's attention along these lines. Preparing an address to Congress in which he would argue the importance of U.S. intervention there, he wrote, "the paramount duty in the circumstances rests upon us, because of our long-established and universally recognized position with regard to the political development of the states of the Western Hemisphere."[122] Revolutionary disorder was, for Wilson, a sign that, in the words of the preeminent Wilson scholar, Arthur S. Link, "the peoples of northern Latin America" were not "much beyond the stage of political infancy."[123] Lacking "the fine lineage" of such as William Penn and his descendants, Mexico could seek "political development" only through tutelage, and the role of teacher fell to the United States by virtue of long-established tradition. Indeed, the very identity of the United States, Wilson asserted, depended on its willingness to shoulder such responsibilities. "We are bound," he wrote, "by every obligation of honour and by the compulsion of sacred interests *which go to the very foundations of our national life* to constitute ourselves the champions of constitutional government and of the integrity and independence of free states throughout America, North and South."[124]

Finally, Wilson's paternalism was, in important respects, consistent with his vision of a liberal international order based on capitalist economic development, free trade, and the rule of law. Sharing basic assumptions about white racial superiority with European imperialists, Wilson rejected the economic and political forms of traditional colonialism, but replaced them with a scheme equally founded upon racial hierarchy and political domination. As we have seen, Wilson's reverence for democratic forms was tied to a racial construct in which the genius for democracy signified a "fine lineage." Moreover, his commitment to liberty was tied to a framework of free-enterprise capitalism, in which the best men exercised initiative and efficiency without restraint, and in which others who had not yet proved themselves as men — those who had not yet proved their "economic equality" — developed under the leadership of enterprising white men.

Racial assumptions prevented Wilson, as well as other white capitalists, from seeing the value of economic models founded upon alternative notions of initiative and efficiency. To cite only the most pertinent example, the locally oriented subsistence agriculture cherished by Haitian peasants registered with American progressives as little more than a sign of backwardness. Its value as an optimal economic arrangement for a people at odds with international capitalism was inadmissible within a racial and class framework that denied black peasants the ability to determine their own interest.[125] The very notion of developmentalism — that the "less developed" countries should have the opportunity to develop along the lines of capitalism, supposedly following in the footsteps of the "more advanced" nations — presupposed that there was but one path toward progress and light. And this assumption — that the path followed by western European countries and by the United States was the proper path for all — was, among other things, a racial assumption. In this sense, racial hierarchy undergirded liberal developmentalism at every point.

The rule of law that Wilson championed as a path to world peace was, in turn, founded upon this racial framework. For this reason, it was no mere coincidence that nations finding themselves on the wrong side of the law came to be coded in racial terms. This was true, for example, for Germany during the First World War as well as for Latin American nations during this period. In this way, and perhaps in other ways as well, the legalist framework that Wilson intended to secure world peace and to guarantee the rights and self-determination of small nations carried within it the seeds and logic of domination. George Kennan made this observation — minus the racial aspect — in his critique of the idealist tradition of American foreign policy in 1951. "Whoever says there is a law," wrote Kennan, "must of course be indignant against the law-breaker and feel a moral superiority to him." Kennan continued, "And when such indignation spills over into military contest, it knows no bounds short of the reduction of the law-breaker to the point of complete submissiveness — namely, unconditional surrender. It is a curious thing, but it is true, that the legalistic approach to world affairs, rooted as it unquestionably is in a desire to do away with war and violence, makes violence more enduring, more terrible, and more destructive to political stability than did the older motives of national interest. A war fought in the name of high moral principle finds no early end short of some form of total domination."[126] Kennan's astute observation describes more or less accurately what happened in the United States occupation of Haiti. Kennan omitted the element of race, but he correctly identified as structural, rather than epiphenomenal, the sense of superiority and the right to control others held by those who defined and enforced international law and order.

The apparent contradiction between Wilson's authoritarian actions in Latin America and the Caribbean and the liberal political philosophy for which he is best known may be explained, in part, by these unstated, yet central, racialized structures of domination at the heart of liberalism. In this sense, Wilson's policy toward Haiti did not result from the failure of his liberal vision in this particular case but rather from the logical, if usually hidden, implications of that vision. Wilson may have been right to oppose "orderly processes of . . . government, based upon law" to the use of "arbitrary or irregular force." Indeed, he clung righteously to the idea of the law as the only proper basis for military action, even when the letter of the law provided insufficient grounds for the use of force, as in Haiti in 1914 and 1915. Nevertheless, his assumption that justice inhered in "orderly processes" of government, conceived within a framework of liberal developmentalism, ignored the systematic inscription of racial, class, and gender hierarchies within the law itself.

THE AMERICAN IDEA

The paternalist discourse of the occupation was sometimes blatant like Butler's, and sometimes coded like Wilson's, but throughout it had certain consistent features. Whether open to view or just below the surface, paternalism in Haiti always embodied the logic of domination that was revealed in Butler's angry outburst. It was based on the assumption that Haitians were, as yet, in the early stages of their evolutionary development as a people. It posited that Haiti would come into its own as a nation only after a period of tutelage under the guiding hand of that paternal figure known affectionately as Uncle Sam. These elements of paternalism revealed themselves in very different forms in occupied Haiti: in Captain Beach's characterization of the Haitian revolutionary leader, Dr. Rosalvo Bobo, as "a small schoolboy in the relentless grasp and power of a hard hearted master"; in State Department reports estimating "the mentality of the peasant" to be "that of a child between six and ten years of age"; in references to Haitian primitivism and savagery; but also in official plans for the efficient development of Haitian resources under American supervision.[127] For in its most pragmatic aspect, U.S. paternalism toward Haiti encompassed a program of economic as well as political development based on the assumptions and imperatives of international capitalism.

Occupation officials and policy makers in Washington tried hard to enlist Haitians into the logic of this paternalist-capitalist scheme, encountering more than a little resistance along the way. In a letter to his father, Smedley Butler railed against "these wretched politicians" who "do not intend to fall in with our American plans and ideas."[128] Farther removed from the daily power struggles between occupation officials and the U.S. client government, Woodrow Wilson was more sanguine about Haitian resistance, privately acknowledging his appreciation for the difficult position in which Haitian politicians found themselves. "Apparently the Haitian authorities are seeking to play fast and loose with us," he wrote to Edith Bolling Galt when Haitian cabinet members refused to sign onto the plan for a U.S. financial adviser; "I am wondering whether to blame them or not!" "The poor chaps," he had written to her a few days earlier, "are between the devil and the deep sea. They dare not offend us, and yet if they yielded to us their enemies would make a great case against them in any subsequent elections."[129] Meanwhile, Secretary of State Robert Lansing supplied the American chargé d'affaires with a series of carefully worded rationales for American control to be conveyed to Haitian leaders in government and civil society. The United States hoped, he wrote on August 18, 1915, "to aid in the establishment of peace . . . to give the people renewed trust and confidence and to inspire them into pursuits of industry and commerce."[130] Secretary of the Navy Josephus Daniels also repeatedly urged military representatives of the United States in Haiti to impress upon Haitians that Americans had come in the spirit of friendship to help their Haitian neighbors on the road to progress.[131] Caperton, as we have seen, hawked paternalism with Dartiguenave, and Beach led the effort, with more junior Marine Corps officers, to impress Haitians with the benevolent intentions of the American occupiers and the expansive possibilities that would come with their plans for Haiti.

Adolph Miller was one of the officers detailed to carry on this public relations campaign that was deemed so crucial to the occupation's success. In October, Miller and his company were transferred from Port-au-Prince to Fort Liberté, a small village east of Cap Haïtien, near the Santo Domingan border.[132] At Fort Liberté, Miller was responsible for getting public works projects under way as well as for convincing peasants to cooperate with the

Americans. He would travel through the countryside, gathering groups of peasants together to give them "encouraging talks." On December 11, he noted in his log, "arrived at Bédoux. . . . Sent for natives & held audience. Gave them a long talk on the 'American Idea in Haiti.' "[133]

Some sense of what Miller said, through his interpreter, to the peasants at Bédoux and other villages, may be gathered from an earlier log entry, written in Port-au-Prince, in which he explained: "The American Idea is this. As soon as the revenues commence to come into the Customs House we will employ several thousand natives to clean and pave the streets, put in sewers, a water supply system, and [an] electric light plant. We will pay the natives daily so that they can accumulate a little money and get the wrinkles out of their belleys [sic]. As soon as they find out that we will not stand for the [Haitian] Generals confiscating their farms, stealing their cattle, enforcing them into the army, they will be for us and will not revolt for a fortune."[134] While the public works projects undertaken at Bédoux would not be identical to those planned for the capital city, the underlying logic was the same. In Miller's formulation of the "American Idea," U.S. control of Haitian finances would benefit Haitians by allowing the creation of a public works program with Americans serving as the employer of Haitian wage laborers. These Haitian laborers would improve the material infrastructure of their country while putting food in their bellies and securing protection from elite Haitians who, he averred, had been the sole source of their problems to date. The "Generals," once vanquished by American military might, would no longer harass or coerce peasants, who, in turn, would no longer have reason to revolt.

The "American Idea" that Miller presented to his Haitian audiences was, in effect, a promise. At the center of this promise were two fundamental concepts: the state's guardianship of the peasant and the salutary nature of the wage relation. The Americans promised modernization achieved under U.S. management and direction by wage-earning Haitians. But beyond the infrastructural improvements that would be accomplished in this manner lay other supposed pots of gold. Occupation officials sought these improvements not as ends in themselves but as means to economic development. Electricity, plumbing, telephones, paved roads, and bridges would make two major changes possible. First, they would facilitate the establishment of stability because policing could be more effective with improvements in communication and transportation. Second, they would make possible increased American investment in the Haitian economy. This investment, in turn, would create more opportunities for wage labor.[135]

This was, of course, the local economic phase of Wilson's liberal internationalist vision. With technical assistance from the United States, the nations of the world could follow, in U.S. footsteps, a path that would lead away from isolation and toward modernization and integration into the international economy. The American idea entailed the establishment of a material infrastructure in Haiti to support such modernization as well as the creation of an efficient labor force to man the machinery of production. (Recall that the railroad entrepreneur James McDonald had helped to formulate this blueprint for Haiti's future.) Miller's version of Wilson's vision was also of a piece with Butler's plans for Haitian development under American paternal guidance and leadership. Inexperienced in matters of industrial and commercial business, Haiti would have to be carefully schooled. Never mind the fact that Haiti was the second independent nation of the Western Hemisphere, founded only twenty-nine years after the United States; within the paternalist framework, the United States was the adult nation nearest at hand to guide the "young" Haiti.

Haitians responded to this paternalist discourse in various ways. Some members of the elite embraced the language of paternalism, turning it to their own purposes. In August 1920, for example, G. F. Geffrard adopted it to frame an appeal to "the Government at Washington D.C." for more effective assistance to advance Haitian economic and political development. Geffrard began by affirming the Wilson administration's basic view of Haiti. "The experience of more than a century of civilization," he wrote, "has demonstrated that the Haitian, left to his own resources has not yet attained unto that degree of advancement where he would be capable of self government." He called, therefore, for "the definitive occupation of the country by the Americans . . . who can then apply their ideal program." Geffrard's letter acknowledged "the Haitian's animosity against the American" but attributed that animosity largely to the limitations Washington had placed on American action in Haiti. More effective assistance, he pleaded, would bring about the harmony "between occupier and occupied" that would be necessary "for the progressive evolution of our young nation." Haiti, he explained, must rely on "the philanthropy and generosity" of the United States, which has "given undeniable proofs of its ability [to bring stability] in Cuba, Puerto Rico, the Hawaiian islands and the Philippines." Describing Haitians as "a young and turbulent people who have been left to their devices," Geffrard echoed the paternalism of missionaries like W. F. Jordan who lamented Haiti's "road to ruin."[136]

Other Haitians adopted aspects of the paternalist framework but used them in a very different way to counter the abuses of the occupation. The *Courrier Haïtien* was described by one occupation official as "outspokenly

hostile both to the present Haitian government and to the American occupation"; its editors, Joseph Lanoue and Constant Vieux, were, according
to President Dartiguenave, essentially Cacos.[137] In the wake of what they
considered a cursory and wholly insufficient naval inquiry in 1920, Lanoue
and Vieux published a dispatch seeking a new convention between the two
countries, one that would give not more but less power to the occupation
and the Haitian government it supported. Yet, like Geffrard, Lanoue and
Vieux referred to Haiti as "our young country" when they were appealing to
U.S. officials for positive change. Like Geffrard, they too called on the discourse of civilization, but their formulation in no way implied that Haiti was
somehow outside its bounds. They expressed "the sincere desire of our
entire country to progress" and made their plea not only to Washington,
D.C., but also to be "placed before the Conscience of the civilized world."[138]

Other Haitian critics of the occupation rejected the language and logic
of paternalism altogether. The editor of *Les Annales Capoises*, for example,
printed an article with an altogether different tone. Published March 4,
1921, it included a wholesale condemnation of Woodrow Wilson, "a man of
baneful prejudices . . . may he be perpetually tormented by remorse[,] that
canker of a guilty conscience[,] have a sad and taciturn ending continually
gnashing his teeth, a prey to horrible hallucinations and believing himself to
be always pursued by the invisible specter of those of us who have died
martyrs to the cause of liberty." This author did not mince words and, in
fact, went further, according to Russell in a telegram to Marine Corps headquarters: "May he on his death bed eat 'les excréments de son vase.' "[139]
President Dartiguenave claimed, in response to such insults, that "liberty is
being smothered under licentiousness." Newspaper men were, he said, the
"agents of this anarchy." By allowing them to continue, the government and
the occupation were "demeaning themselves more and more each day."
Russell agreed, informing the Marine Corps commandant that the occupation was being "insulted in a most outrageous manner" and recommending
that the United States "act under martial law" to put a stop to the insults.[140]

Meanwhile, among the peasants, attitudes toward the occupation were
cautious at best, and there was, above all, the desire to avoid any form of
slavery. In the nineteenth century, Haitian peasants had struggled to establish a peasant economy and to resist forces urging them toward plantation
wage labor. Picking coffee and growing food for themselves and for the
market in their own garden plots afforded them greater levels of control
over their lives than plantation agriculture would allow. By 1915 peasants
were squeezed by exporters who kept the price of coffee depressed, but
peasant farming remained the occupation of choice. Peasants repeatedly

expressed their desire to farm and their rejection of the plantation model of agricultural work under the supervision of overseers. U.S. marines and other Americans living in or visiting the Haitian countryside failed to understand such preferences and expressed both amusement and consternation at the "primitive methods" employed by peasant farmers, who seemed wholly uninterested in more efficient technologies. Given the mounting economic difficulties facing Haitian peasants in the years leading up to and during the occupation (the same difficulties that fueled the Caco revolutions), it is not surprising that some peasants accepted plantation labor as one among several poor choices. Yet, the majority continued to vote with their feet, their backs, and their hands, for economic independence.[141]

If some level of Haitian cooperation was deemed important for the American idea to succeed, the involvement of American businessmen, experts in efficiency and economic development, was even more important — hence the publication, in 1918, of a pamphlet designed to present Haiti as an "island of opportunity" to potential U.S. investors. The author and photographer, Tamerlyn T. Chamberlain of the U.S. Navy, stated his intention to "give an idea of the many commercial and industrial possibilities in the Republic of Haiti . . . which await development in the near future." "Haiti offers a new field for commerce and industry," Chamberlain wrote in his introduction. "The industries of Haiti, at the present time, are chiefly . . . coffee, fruits, and some sugar cane. Dyewoods are exported in large quantities. There is now being erected . . . one of the largest and most modern sugar mills, by the Haitian-American Sugar Company, and in a comparatively short time, sugar will be the chief export. There are many undeveloped mineral resources throughout the island, and within easy access to the various seaports along the coast."[142] The advantages of investing in Haiti, argued Chamberlain, accrued from the commendable work of the U.S. occupation over the previous three years. He highlighted the formation of a police constabulary "unsurpassed in the Latin countries," as well as improvements in sanitary conditions and housing, and the protection afforded by the Haitian Coast Guard.[143]

A series of photographs presented as before-and-after shots illustrated the success of the occupation in creating an attractive area for investment. Chamberlain placed side by side one photograph of a rather impressive residential structure (home to an American) and another of a small Haitian shack, identifying them with the following captions: "One of the many Modern and Americanized Homes of Haiti . . . While this view shows the characteristic Haitian dwelling of previous years and customs."[144] While these two homes existed in the same temporal space of occupied Haiti, Chamberlain's

Figure 10. "A Civilian before Military training and after." From Port-au-Prince,
Haiti, *a pamphlet by Tamerlyn T. Chamberlain, U.S.N.*
Marine Corps Research Center Archives, Quantico, Virginia.

representation of them effectively marked one "future" and the other
"past." With another pair of photographs, Chamberlain sought to illustrate important changes in the population brought about by the American
presence. One shot presented a man dressed in rags, with his eyes cast
downward, standing on grass; the other showed a man, in a clean uniform,
standing at attention on what appears to be a paved street (Figure 10).
Chamberlain described them this way: "This reproduction shows the development accomplished by the American Marine Forces operating in Haiti. A
Civilian before Military training and after."[145] The new soldier promised
both effective police protection for American investments and a disciplined
population from which to draw a productive work force.

The occupation did have some success in inviting investors to participate
in the paternalist project in Haiti. In November 1920, Admiral H. S. Knapp
observed with pleasure a thriving cotton plantation near St. Michel, owned
and operated by the United West Indies Corporation. Admiral Knapp reported that the company was cultivating large tracts using modern methods
under the direction of "a resident engineer." "The spirit of the management," Knapp commented, "appears to be one of enlightened self interest,
with the desire to do something for the Haitians as well as to pay dividends.
The management does not pretend to be in Haiti for altruistic purposes, but

apparently has vision enough to realize that it is wiser to carry on in a way that will obtain the support of the people of Haiti themselves than to endeavor to wring the last dollar out of Haitian soil to go out of the country and into the pockets of foreign shareholders. I am told that the payment of wages by this company was the first payment of wages that has ever taken place in the valley on any but the very smallest scale."[146] The company, Knapp explained, "conducts a small school for about 70 children who are employed on the estate" and "is expecting within a few days to have a medical officer" for the plantation.[147] The best news of all was that, at least in this instance, "the American Idea" had come to pass. Knapp proudly reported that "many of the old Caco bands are now being employed on the plantation and have ceased entirely to be a source of trouble."[148]

The paternalism of the cotton plantation at St. Michel was wholly consistent with emerging progressive management practices, as well as with older racial political strategies, back in the States. During Reconstruction, white southerners of the patrician class had forged paternalist politics as a means to maintain their own political leadership in the face of African American enfranchisement and challenges to white rule.[149] More recently, northern corporate paternalism responded in part to an immigrant work force not yet socialized into a controlling "work ethic." It flourished, as David Montgomery has pointed out, especially during periods of prosperity when workers asserted their independence by taking time off and even quitting their jobs without regard for employers' production schedules.[150] The same logic informed American paternalism in Haiti; it was a strategy formed in response to the sort of "labor troubles" described by Fred McMillen and, more generally, in response to anticolonial resistance experienced by the United States in its recent colonial career.[151] Thus, if American corporate paternalism flourished especially in employers' attitudes toward immigrants in their adopted land, in Haiti paternalism found even more fertile ground in American attitudes toward black peasants in their homeland. Paternalism was, then, a language and an approach shared by progressive military figures in Haiti and potential investors in the United States.

Still, however sympathetic American industrial leaders were toward the paternalist outlook of the occupation, they did not flock to Haiti as occupation planners had hoped they would. The occupation never attracted U.S. investments on a large scale. Thus, while the occupation succeeded in transforming Haitian society and politics and to a great extent in bringing about the order that Wilson desired, it did not succeed in taking advantage of that order — that absence of revolutionary change — on behalf of U.S. investors, at least not in the short run.

Although U.S. paternalist discourses failed, on the whole, to persuade Haitians to sign on to American plans and ideas, and failed as well to attract large-scale U.S. investment to occupied Haiti, it succeeded, in crucial ways, in conscripting the marines assigned the task of carrying out the occupation.[152] Indeed, the aspect of paternalist discourse that chafed most for Haitians was precisely the element that appealed most to American military representatives in Haiti—that is, the occupied nation's supposed need for supervision by white men. Paternalist discourse appealed to marines as masters and managers; it addressed them in terms of their masculinity and manhood, their relation to fatherhood, their racial identity, their class aspirations, and their national pride. The success of this process of cultural conscription can be seen in the ways that marines observed Haitians and Haitian society within the framework of the dominant paternalist rhetoric. Paternalism was, then, an important part of the indoctrination of marines in Haiti. (The implications of this process are explored much more thoroughly in the next chapter.)

The American idea defined the role of Marine Corps officers and enlisted men in Haiti in terms of mastery and supervision. As such, its appeal may well have been reinforced by the fact that, both in the Marine Corps and in their lives back in the States, marines faced various forms of disempowerment. Within the military hierarchy, for example, enlisted men were confronted daily with the fact of their subordinate status, as Corporal Overley suggested in his reflections on his tour in Haiti. Officers, too, as we saw in the case of Major Butler's reaction to his transfer out of Panama, sometimes chafed at the command structure because it either limited their range of action or reminded them of their subordination. Evidence of this phenomenon lower down in the command structure may be found in Lieutenant Adolph Miller's diary, where he reveals the scarcity of information available to young officers regarding the progress of the occupation and the plans that higher officers had for them. On August 14, 1915, Miller noted, for example, "Capt. Van Orden dropped [in] around 11pm but would not give us a bit of dope."[153] One month later, he wrote, "there is a rumor floating around to the effect that the Army is coming down here to relieve us, and we will return home to our dear beloved U.S."[154] Yet, as we have seen, "home" could also harbor reminders either of subordination or of the precariousness of their status. Given the various challenges they had faced in the States—patriarchal fathers, oppressive employers, "feminist" women—young white men had many reasons to embrace a call to mastery, an invitation to serve as father figures to a people cast as children.[155]

Finally, policy makers used paternalist discourse to address the American public, especially once the occupation became a political fireball. Cabinet members responded to citizens' inquiries by assuring them, for example, that U.S. actions in Haiti were actuated only by "the American feeling of its trusteeship."[156] In one instance, faced with a radical critique of U.S. imperialism in Haiti and elsewhere in the Caribbean, the secretary of the navy echoed the structure of Wilson's paternalism as it was revealed in his conversation with William Monroe Trotter. Haiti must learn, Daniels told Walter Carrier of Lansing, Michigan, that "liberty must come by evolution and not revolution. Otherwise it is license and not the freedom of enlightenment."[157] Just as Wilson had effectively defined equality for African Americans as a state to be arrived at at some future time, Daniels defined liberty as a state to be claimed once a people had matured by a process of slow evolution. For a nation to claim liberty by revolution rather than by evolution was, for Daniels, oxymoronic. What they claimed would be not liberty but license and, indeed, even licentiousness (an ironic claim, of course, for an American). Daniels's articulation of paternalism in his response to Carrier illustrates the ways that evolutionary discourse, notions of primitivism and savagery, dovetailed with and contributed to other aspects of paternalist ideology.

THIS AMERICAN AFRICA

Paternalism enabled both Smedley Butler and Woodrow Wilson to blur the differences between America and Haiti, indeed between America and the Americas, at one moment, and then to reinforce those differences at another. For Butler, embracing his role as a Haitian officer and guiding his "little fellows" entailed a rhetorical suspension of the national differences that defined his American versus their Haitian identities. Referring to Haitians as "savage monkeys," on the other hand, posited a radical distance between civilized white Americans and savage black Haitians. Similarly for Wilson, hailing the unity of the Americas as part of "a family of mankind" temporarily erased national boundaries and racial differences, while pointing to "the fine lineage" of William Penn and the questionable family background of a young white woman's Panamanian suitor reinscribed them. These two sides of paternalism, separately and together, in different ways at different times, enabled the United States to claim power in Haiti.

The Reverend Wilhelm F. Jordan, a representative of the American Bible Society operating in Haiti in the early 1920s, brought together both sides of paternalism in one handy phrase. "This American Africa" he named Haiti, as he called on Christians to lend a hand to the occupation. "Politically, we are now acting the Good Samaritan to our badly wounded and exhausted neighbor," he declared.[158] Yet, much more needed to be done: "So few are those that are laboring in this American Africa, and so small are the bands of believers who are fighting the powers of darkness and evil that surround them."[159] Jordan's invitation highlighted, on one hand, the fact that Haiti was an *American* nation. In this sense, it emphasized a connection, a likeness, between Haiti and the United States. On the other hand, it likened Haiti to Africa and thus drew on the connotations of radical difference embedded in U.S. discourses of civilization and primitivism. We explore the implications of this apparent contradiction for marines serving in Haiti in Chapter 4. For now, let us consider some of the ways that each side of the contradiction facilitated U.S. goals in Haiti.

The U.S. occupation institutionalized paternalism's blurred boundaries most pointedly through the founding of the Haitian Gendarmerie, officered by Americans. The very existence of the Gendarmerie, with U.S. officers dressed in the authority of the Haitian state, entailed a kind of institutionalized confusion that was convenient indeed. Article X of the 1916 treaty laid out the lines of authority governing the actions of the new body: "The constabulary herein provided for, shall, under the direction of the Haitian government, have supervision and control of arms and ammunition, military supplies, and traffic therein, throughout the country."[160] But what part of the Haitian government would supervise this new body? Could Haitians decide for themselves which government officials would oversee the new Haitian military? Or could it only be the client president himself, who, with the approval of U.S. advisers, would authorize police and military action?

In fact, the Haitian government never exercised sovereign control over its nominal military force as long as the occupation persisted. During Smedley Butler's tenure as chief of the Gendarmerie, from December 1915 through April 1918, Butler himself served as the "adviser" most often at the president's side. Thus, the chief of the Gendarmerie effectively directed the president of the republic on key decisions, often by unorthodox means he called "undershirt diplomacy" in letters to his wife.[161] Butler's successor, U.S. Marine Corps colonel Alexander S. Williams, conducted himself with less bravado but no less authority. Williams commented, on his retirement from the post in July 1919, "that he had frequently an exceedingly difficult time deciding which of his two bosses he should obey," that is, the president of the republic or Marine Corps Headquarters in Washington.[162] Yet, it is abundantly clear that in practice he took his cues from Washington rather than Port-au-Prince.[163] As Williams retired, the Haitian government attempted to wrest proper control over the Gendarmerie; Dartiguenave created a new post within the Haitian government, that of prefect, vested with direct supervision of the Gendarmerie. His attempt was short-circuited at a meeting of the treaty officials, when the chief of the occupation, First Brigade Commander Louis McCarty Little, objected and successfully routed the Haitian effort.[164]

Smedley Butler stumbled over the institutionalized confusion that was the Gendarmerie in the course of his testimony before the Senate in 1921. He stated that, in January 1916, Colonel Waller notified him that "the Haitian Government had decided to give up trying to maintain law and order and had said, 'Now, you Americans do it with your Gendarmerie.' " Attorney Walter Bruce Howe asked Butler to clarify this: "What did the Haitians mean, then, by saying to the Americans to preserve order with *their* gendarmerie, when the gendarmerie was the Haitian gendarmerie?"[165] Butler may have misunderstood the question, but his next slip of the tongue was revealing: "It was the Haitian gendarmerie. We understood it to be an effort on their part to embarrass us, because they well knew that *our gendarmerie, or their gendarmerie that we were establishing for them* under the provisions of a treaty already confirmed, was not complete; but in two days we established 117 posts around the country."[166] Butler's slip highlights the useful and calculated blurring of identity that facilitated U.S. action in Haiti. Having styled himself as father figure to the new Haitian military and police force, Butler repeatedly took action, in the name of the Haitian government, well beyond anything reasonably comprehended within the language of the treaty. His mandate to form a constabulary, furthermore, came from a treaty adopted against the will of Haitian officials. Haitians and Americans both used the proper language to indicate whose Gendarmerie it was.

Making light of Butler's ambiguous position in Haiti, his superior officer, Colonel Littleton Waller, later related a story about a conversation with the "Haitian" military leader. According to Waller, Butler asked whether his new rank as major general in the Gendarmerie would favor him for a better seat at the officers' dining table. Waller said he replied that if Butler dined "as a Major of Marines, he would take his place according to rank," but if he dined as a Haitian general, then he could "feed" in the pantry with the servants.[167] Evident in Marine Corps humor such as this was the edge of disease caused by extensive cross-national playacting in the service of American military rule.

If metaphors of fatherhood, along with their institutional counterparts, blurred boundaries between Americans and Haitians, references to primitive savagery bolstered U.S. claims to power by inscribing profound dichotomies between the two nations and peoples. A very standard example of the exoticizing discourses that supported U.S. paternal claims to power in Haiti stands out as remarkable only because it was authored by a key player in the opening acts of the occupation and marketed as pulp fiction back in the States while the occupation was still under way. As secretary of the American legation in Port-au-Prince, Robert Beale Davis observed the revolutionary upheaval surrounding the overthrow of President Vilbrun Guillaume Sam in the days preceding the U.S. invasion. His telegraph reports of scenes of violence in the capital city brought Admiral Caperton and the uss *Washington* steaming toward Port-au-Prince.[168] Davis worked side by side with military representatives to establish U.S. control in the opening months of the intervention and in 1916, now as chargé d'affaires, signed the treaty that created a legal basis for the occupation.[169] Several years after his return from Haiti, Brentano's Publishing Company brought out [Robert] Beale Davis's sensational novel, *The Goat without Horns*.[170] A formulaic tale of romance amid tropical danger, Davis's novel replayed scenes he had recounted in formal memoranda, embellishing them amid purely fictional racial mysteries, Voodoo ceremonies, and tales of child sacrifice.

That a diplomatic representative of the United States would turn so readily to pulp fiction, as an outlet for the acts of imagination inspired by his tenure in "the Black Republic," highlights the cultural lens through which Americans came to "know" Haiti. Even more striking, perhaps, is the extent to which Americans' belief in Haitian primitivism and savagery shaped formal reports issued in the name of the occupation itself. One particularly striking example comes from the pen of John H. Russell, who in 1920, as chief of the occupation, relied on rumors of cannibalism and child sacrifice to serve as the linchpin in an argument for seizing control of the Haitian court system. Can "an American businessman . . . be assured of justice in the Haitian courts?" Russell asked at the start of his confidential memorandum to the secretary of the navy.[171]

Russell methodically elaborated twenty-four discrete points, designed to substantiate his not surprising conclusion. Point 12 cited the statement of a Haitian citizen that, with internal civil conflict still raging "in spite of the presence in their midst of a civilizing element," Haitians could hardly be expected to mete out justice, especially when their hearts are "full of bitterness against the Americans."[172] Point 14 cited statistics on literacy and related social indices, indicating that about 95 percent of the population "is bordering on a state of savagery, if not actually existing in such a state."[173] What constituted "a state of savagery" Russell did not specify. Not surprisingly, a good deal of his memorandum was devoted to an examination of Voodoo or "Vaudism," as he called it. Russell noted that the highly educated, as well as the less educated and the ignorant classes, participated in the religion, though secretly, and that "there appears to be among believers . . . a sort of Masonic feeling which naturally impels them to assist one another."[174] He cinched his case by indicating that there was, at that very moment, a Voodoo priest awaiting trial in Port-au-Prince who, "it is believed, sacrificed at least 12 or 15 children" for the purpose of eating their flesh and inviting others to do the same. "With such a condition," he concluded, "the probability of a white man obtaining justice in the courts is remote."[175] Effectively Russell argued that Haitians were cannibals and child killers who stuck up for one another, and for that reason American businessmen could not be assured justice. The larger implication of this argument, of course, was that the sort of legal system necessary to guarantee the property rights of American citizens, and thereby enable economic development, in Haiti would not be possible as long as Haitians remained in charge of the judicial system. The American idea, therefore, called for more thorough American control.

The discourse of civilization and savagery invoked by Robert Beale Davis and John Russell, and the metaphors of fatherhood invoked by Smedley Butler, represented two sides of the same paternalist coin. One posited a vast cultural distance between the United States and Haiti; the other emphasized the proximity and connection of the family relation that was supposed to have existed between them. Primitive Haitians, "bordering on a state of savagery," required the guidance and supervision of white men. Civilized Americans must shoulder the burden of this responsibility, bound as they were, according to Woodrow Wilson, "by every obligation of honour and by the compulsion of sacred interests . . . to constitute [themselves] the champions of . . . constitutional government." American businessmen stood ready to do their part for Haiti, Russell implied, but they required the protection of a proper legal system. Given the state of Haitian society, moreover, the "development of true constitutional liberty" could come about only under an American father figure.

In the context of the 1915–34 occupation of Haiti, metaphors of fatherhood were never simply figures of speech. Linked to a complex history of racial and gender connotation, such metaphors constituted a crucial part of the ideological machinery of the occupation. They functioned as mechanisms of power, enabling the construction of a temporary state apparatus sufficient to secure U.S. control over Haitian society and government. That apparatus — encompassing the First Brigade of the U.S. Marine Corps, the

U.S. legation in Port-au-Prince, the Gendarmerie d'Haïti, the new Haitian presidency, the provost courts, the official Haitian press, the Service d'Hygiène, and the Service Technique — owed its existence in part to the ideological work of paternalism. Crafted out of race, gender, and class relations in the United States, and fueled by deeply felt personal histories and local relations of power (which often had nothing to do with U.S. foreign policy), the language of paternalism underwrote the institutional machinery of the occupation.

Woodrow Wilson and Smedley Butler played key roles in the process by which that took place. For this reason, we have been interested in the language they used to represent their actions in public speeches and private musings. Butler did the hands-on work of building one of the most central institutions of the occupation, the Gendarmerie d'Haïti. His letters afford us an opportunity to see the operation of the discourse of paternalism in relation to his personal experience of fatherhood (as a father and as a son) and in relation to the crucial institution-building work he carried out. In his language, we see the blurring of identities that paternalism entailed, a blurring of identities that also enabled U.S. imperialism. We also see the tension between paternalism's outward face of benevolence and its central but concealed structure of power.

Having identified that tension so clearly in Butler's discourse, we can more readily recognize the same dynamic in Wilson's paternalism, despite his more carefully fashioned rhetoric. Although Wilson seldom used explicit metaphors of fatherhood, the paternalist trope was never far from the surface of his discourse. He rejected what he regarded as the obvious paternalism of government-sponsored social welfare legislation, but his vision of international cooperation and justice rested on metaphors of human development that infantilized some and accorded mastery to others.

In 1920 the contradiction between Butler's brand of free-wheeling "undershirt diplomacy" and Wilson's international vision, affirming the rights of small nations, threatened to rupture the whole operation. In the midst of the controversy, Navy Department advisers began to examine the legal basis for the U.S. military government in Haiti. Some among them attempted to square the occupation "as a matter of cold fact" with the tricky international legal questions posed by it.[176] At least one, however, a certain "Melling," confronted the obvious contradictions.[177] Melling voiced strong criticisms of the occupation as an inappropriate extension of military power. He criticized the continuance of martial law past the point where the United States had, by entering into a treaty with Haiti (and by other means), clearly acknowledged the existence of an independent Haitian state. To Melling it was patently clear that the citizens of Haiti did not approve of the U.S. military government there. In contrast to the stated goals of the occupation, he asserted, "the present military government does not preserve, but destroys any vestige of independence which the people of Haiti might claim."[178] Ultimately, Melling's analysis was rejected in favor of a more general justification for the continued use of provost courts and for the continuation of military government. Military rule was strengthened, moreover, by the appointment, in 1922, of Marine Corps colonel John H. Russell as high commissioner to Haiti, with the status of a direct diplomatic representative of the president of the United States.

Russell would rule Haiti with a firm grip for the next seven years. Protest would be forced largely below the surface, with public agitators jailed readily, local disturbances quashed, and U.S. Marine and Navy intelligence operations assessing the pulse of Haitian communities. Intelligence reports from the 1920s, as well as other evidence, continued to demonstrate — for those, like Mr. Melling, who cared to notice — that all was not well. As Gendarmerie first lieutenant Norman Poritz had reported from Le Trou in the wake of the Cacos' defeat, "the entire population it is thought does not like white people down in their heart [sic] and especially a white race maintaining a military rule over them."[179] And as J. L. Perkins reported from Aux Cayes, "the people in general respect the Gendarmerie and the Occupation because they know that there is force behind them."[180] Thus, as the occupation entered a new phase, paternalist rhetoric flourished untrammeled once again, secure in High Commissioner Russell's Pax Americana, until Haitian resistance burst open again in 1929.

MORAL BREAKDOWN

In his first sensational memoir of Haiti, *Black Bagdad*, John Houston Craige related the story of Marine Corps sergeant Ivan Virski. A respected guard at the U.S. legation in Port-au-Prince — according to Craige, "an efficient, sober and entirely reliable young man" — Virski turned up drunk at the waterfront one morning in the spring of 1927. He began shaking hands with the stevedores as they arrived for work; then, all at once, he pulled out an automatic pistol and shot the man whose hand he grasped. Having killed the Haitian "dead in his tracks," Virski turned and ran toward his post, shooting wildly and injuring two more people along the way. Arriving at the legation, he entered the building, climbed the stairs to the upper balcony, and from there "emptied a magazine of cartridges into the street." The Marine provost attributed Virski's spree to the unfortunate effects of alcohol, while opposition newspapers in Haiti decried yet another violent incident suffered at the hands of the American military. Tried by general court-martial for murder, Sergeant Virski was "pronounced insane" and sent back to the United States for hospitalization.[1]

Craige also told the story of Lieutenant South, the highest-ranking Gendarmerie officer, and the only marine, stationed at St. Michel. Lieutenant South "thought that he was king in the district," wrote Craige, "and of course, he was." Little by little, however, he began to show signs of wear, especially evident to the gendarmes with whom he interacted daily, though hidden well from his superior officer whom he saw less frequently. As the constant sound of drumming began to wear him down, South ordered his gendarmes to have it stopped. They did not succeed, and he began to imagine that he was under siege and in immediate danger. He sent a dispatch to his commanding officer requesting assistance, but before anyone arrived, he reached his limit. Advancing toward a Haitian gendarme, gun in hand, he was prepared to kill his subordinate, but something inside stopped him. South ran back to his room and barricaded his door.[2]

With the stories of Sergeant Virski and Lieutenant South, Captain Craige framed his discussion of American violence — or potential violence — against Haitians in terms of seemingly unique instances in which marines lost their emotional and mental balance. In this sense, he underscored the conclusions of formal investigations such as the Mayo Court and the Senate inquiry. In 1919 Admiral Mayo had found through his investigation only a "small number of isolated crimes or offenses" that had been committed by "a few individuals." "It was inevitable that some offenses would be committed," the admiral had reported, and "considering the conditions of service in Haiti, it is remarkable that the offenses were so few in number and that they all may be chargeable to the ordinary defects of human character."[3] In 1921 and 1922 the Senate inquiry had brought to light more extensive charges of violence than had the Mayo Court, but the Senate's conclusions similarly identified violence with particular individuals while exonerating the occupation as a whole.[4] In Craige's words, the Senate found that "there had been a few isolated instances of inhumanity by madmen and brutes, but these had been punished as soon as they had come to the attention of the authorities."[5] No marine in his right mind, Craige seemed to suggest, would do violence to decent Haitian citizens.

At the same time, Craige's account of what happened to Sergeant Virski and Lieutenant South suggested that their cases were not altogether isolated from one another. In Craige's view it was neither alcohol nor racist brutality that connected such incidents. Instead, Virski's spree and South's near miss were symptomatic of the mental and emotional degeneration that often afflicted or threatened to afflict white men on duty for any length of time near the equator. "To white men who stay south too long, something happens," wrote Craige: "the stolid slow up, the nervous blow up."[6] Craige described the symptoms of what he called "a mysterious, terrible psychological disorder": walking "queerly," mumbling, shaking one's head, waking terror-stricken, if one slept at all; these were the symptoms that caused one's messmates to say, "the tropics have got him."[7]

What about the tropics would "get" a man, according to Craige? The intense rays of the sun, the heat, and loneliness each played a part. Yet, as Craige went on to explain about Sergeant Virski's case, a woman might well be the source of the trouble. For Virski, the trouble was "Chiquita." According to Craige, Chiquita was a "Dominicaine," a prostitute from the Dominican Republic. With "eyes the brown of a butterfly's wing" and skin "the clear red-gold of the ripened orange," Chiquita was, Craige wrote, "a dream of loveliness." "Chiquita and her like seldom get into official reports," Craige noted, "but they have a way of influencing affairs for all of that."[8] He explained the effect she had on Ivan Virski: "Straying down into the byways of the native city, [the] young marine saw Chiquita one night as she danced. . . . The marine was lonely. The tropical sun had stimulated certain functions of his being and deadened others. In a temperate climate he would not have noticed such a woman. In Port-au-Prince he yearned for her with a desire that was an ache. His service pay, a pittance in the United States, made him a man of wealth in Haiti. The inevitable happened. Chiquita became his girl."[9] But when Chiquita "eloped" with a Haitian man, leaving the sergeant behind, "Virski had blown up."[10]

Lieutenant South's predicament differed from Virski's in some respects. Virski suffered in the city, for example, while South had to contend with life at an outpost of Haiti's interior. According to Craige, "he had been in the Gendarmerie for a couple of years, more than a year in the flea-bitten, sun-scorched village of St. Michel, where he was the sole representative of the white man's government.[11] He had no movies, no radio, none of the features of civilized life to which he was accustomed. He saw white faces rarely and white women hardly at all."[12] Thus, whereas the presence of a dark-skinned woman began Sergeant Virski's troubles, it was the absence of contact with white women, coupled with the constant sound of drumming, that drove Lieutenant South over the edge. But the disorder that afflicted both Sergeant Virski and Lieutenant South, in Craige's telling, was the same, for their violence resulted from the systematic biological realities of race, gender, and geography. These biological realities, for Craige, added up to a psychological disorder that afflicted white men too long in the tropics, particularly when isolated from white companionship, and especially when deprived of the civilizing influence of white women.

Whereas Craige emphasized the individual, psychological side of Marine Corps violence in occupied Haiti, Lieutenant Colonel Harold Utley pointed to the institutional and systemic side of military violence, or, as he preferred to call it, military force. Of course, these two former officers of the occupation ostensibly chose to write about U.S. American actions in Haiti for very different reasons. John Houston Craige, having served as the Marine Corps's director of public relations after his tour of duty in Haiti, hoped to create a sensation in 1933 with *Black Bagdad* and again in 1934 with *Cannibal Cousins*. Harold Utley's "Tactics and Techniques of Small Wars," on the other hand, was intended neither to titillate nor to play up the mystique of the Marine Corps, but to provide a systematic treatment of the Marines' experience with "small wars." He presented tactical wisdom accumulated through years of Marine Corps experience, in Haiti and elsewhere, for the guidance of future combatants in undeclared wars in former colonial settings. His narrative goals were to increase efficiency and to improve rates of success in reaching U.S. policy objectives.[13] Despite their differences in genre and intent, Craige and Utley, in distinct but complementary ways, commented on the nature of U.S. American violence in occupied Haiti.

Utley's discussion of military tactics and techniques acknowledged, of course, that undeclared wars in small tropical countries — or, as he sometimes called them, "wars that are not Wars" — nevertheless relied on the use of trained soldiers, guns, and gunboats. "In some instances," wrote Utley, "the mere occupation by an adequate force, sometimes as small as a section, of the affected area will suffice . . . to carry out our mission." "In other cases," he continued, "it will be necessary to overrun the entire country, as in HAITI in 1915."[14] Here, in the context of a frank discussion of military tactics, a former officer of the occupation forces stated plainly the character of the U.S. project in Haiti. Decision makers in the Marine Corps had no illusions about the necessity of force in accomplishing their mission. They did not expect Haitians to welcome them with open arms. They directed the movement of marine and naval personnel with a view to subduing local opposition and establishing American control with as much force as necessary. While journalists, politicians, radicals, and even disaffected brass may have described this force as "indiscriminate" and "excessive," in Utley's retrospective view the operation in Haiti simply required more force than many, perhaps most, other such operations.

Although Utley was primarily interested in conventions of military practice rather than in the actions of individual marines, his tactical manual also gestured toward the relationship between the institutional and the individual dimensions of violence. "The rules of Land Warfare for . . . Small Wars have not been, and probably never will be written," wrote Utley, because, in his view, judgment and experience rather than doctrine would always be the paramount guide. Yet, Utley's "Tactics and Techniques" was a step in the process by which small-wars doctrine was eventually codified — formalized — so that military action could rely less on the happenstance of individual experience. Moreover, as Hans Schmidt has argued, the occupation of Haiti was pivotal in the transition from the earlier roughneck conduct associated with the Indian wars and other unabashed colonial exploits to the more subtle imposition of U.S. control through client governments and counterinsurgency operations.[15] Thus, the mass of experience from which Utley drew encompassed a range of approaches to colonial warfare, carried on during a period of transformation in the United States' relationship to colonialism. In the roughneck spirit, marines prided themselves on getting the job done, by seat-of-the-pants methods where necessary; "undershirt diplomacy" was merely a newer — and only slightly more subtle — version of the informal means by which marines "took the situation in hand."

Utley's hesitation in the move toward doctrine suggests a framework for exploring the nature of violence in occupied Haiti. In what ways and to what extent did U.S. action in Haiti rely on formal military conventions and in what ways did it rely on the proclivities and personalities of individual officers and enlisted men? To understand the violence of U.S. imperialism in Haiti, we must ask how the formal and informal aspects of military practice interacted, how institutional and individual motivations challenged and/or reinforced one another. The move toward doctrine may have been especially complicated in the case of small wars, Utley seemed to suggest, for, as he cautioned his readers, in "wars that are not Wars, we are at peace no matter how thickly the bullets are flying."[16]

U.S. American paternalism flourished in Haiti in the space of this contradiction. Formally, the United States was at peace with Haiti. Consistent with this official state of affairs, paternalism conferred on the United States the status of an elder brother, in Haiti on a mission of paternal care and guidance. As Smedley Butler told the Senate in 1921, the idea was "to make out of Haiti a first-class black man's country." To clarify matters, attorney Walter Bruce Howe interrupted Butler, as the general held forth on this topic, and asked him to describe the enemy: "[With] whom did you have to contend . . . down there — [with] whom were you fighting?" Butler replied, "We were not really fighting anybody. We were endeavoring to overcome certain obstacles created by the political element, obstacles in the road of accomplishment of the object I have just pointed out."[17] "The political element" created "obstacles" for the occupation, but in the official story, there was no enemy, for there was no war.

Yet bullets flew. And the material realities of bullets and dead bodies took on specific meanings in the context of U.S. paternalism. First and foremost, official orders and reports surrounding military action were couched in terms of discipline and protection; "teaching the Cacos a lesson" was the oft-stated goal of military action in occupied Haiti. This was, of course, consistent with the punitive tradition of U.S. colonial wars in Central America and elsewhere; the Marine Corps did not invent the ugly side of paternalism especially for Haiti.[18] But training our lens on this particular occupation leads us to the connections between paternalism's affectionate and punitive iterations. Discipline was an especially key trope on both sides of the line between caring and violence. A wayward nation that had been left to its own devices for too long had to be brought into line. An affectionate paternal attitude was deemed appropriate in some instances. American Gendarmerie officers were encouraged, for example, to adopt such an attitude as they instructed their recruits in the use of the Springfield rifle. If they learn to shoot straight and do well in "the big inter-departmental shoot," urged an article in the *Gendarmerie News*, "tell them you will be proud of them."[19] Good advice for a father, no doubt, but affection could not do the whole job. There were good Haitians, and there were bad, and punitive discipline placed the latter at the wrong end of the Springfield rifle. No other approach, it was urged, could secure Haiti for its peaceful inhabitants.

In this way, the occupation hailed individual marines as would-be father figures, inviting them to adopt a stern paternal relation to bad Haitians and a protective relation to *bons habitants*. In the context of what Homer Overley called "a rotten undeclared war," such paternalist invocations could help marines make sense of their role and purpose. One lieutenant, who decided to join the Gendarmerie after hearing Butler talk about the humanitarian goals of the occupation — the need to "assist the Haitians in getting on their feet" — later commented, "we faced an obvious challenge, a country that needed our help."[20] Haiti needed discipline, protection, education, and economic support, according to the reigning discourse of the occupation. The war against the Cacos was a necessary step along the road to achieving "the American idea," and both phases of American assistance to Haiti embodied fatherly roles. Thus, by appealing to the marines' sense of manhood, the rhetoric of paternalism invited marines to make the imperialist project their own. By characterizing U.S. goals in terms of the subjective identity of the white male paterfamilias, paternalism encouraged marines to personalize the goals of the occupation.

Of course, the discourse of paternalism did not successfully hail all marines in Haiti. Nor could it successfully hail any of the marines all the time. Marines talked about killing, bagging, hunting, and bumping off Cacos.[21] Racial animosity and hatred fired marines' participation in the wars against the Cacos, and erupted as well outside the bounds of the war, as in the cases of Virski and South. Thus, bullets flew in Haiti not only because officers issued dispassionate tactical decisions about war maneuvers, and not only because marines wielded guns as tools of discipline and pedagogy, but also because a Sergeant Virski or a Lieutenant South or, for that matter, a Major Butler, could chafe against the limitations of his authority, the deprivations of his daily life, or his proximity to a racially stigmatized other. Indeed, paternalism called on marines—especially those serving as Gendarmerie officers—to integrate themselves into Haitian communities, to blur the lines between American self and Haitian other. The marines' authority over Haitians undoubtedly made more palatable the relative intimacy of paternalist relationships, but as we have seen, Haitians challenged that authority in various ways. While some marines may have arrived ready only to do battle with a racial enemy, others undoubtedly backed themselves into such corners as they faced daily assaults on the integrity of their whiteness.[22] In this sense, the paternalist framework of the occupation was implicated not only in paternalist violence, per se, but also in the "excesses" of violence that could not be contained within the language of discipline and protection.

The official occupation thus had a complicated relationship to the subjective experience of individual marines. In a sense, the occupation put marines in a position where they would erupt. The complexities of national, racial, and gender identity in the occupation—the marines' desire to affirm their whiteness, their masculinity, and their social distance from Haitians—created tensions that could not be fully managed by paternalist injunctions. What happened when the eruption occurred depended on its relation to the official military effort. If it fueled the marines' participation in field campaigns, if it "taught Cacos a lesson," and, above all, if it did not lead to bad publicity, then it could be harnessed for official uses and explained in terms of discipline and protection. If, on the other hand, it spilled over into the realm of civil society, or created a publicity mess for the occupation, then it was deemed "excessive" and chalked up to the vagaries of individual character. In this way, the relations of power that structured individual marines' subjective experience, what Foucault referred to as "the infinitesimal mechanisms of power," fueled the temporary machinery of the state that was the occupation. At the same time, such infinitesimal relations of power created potential obstacles in that the occupation had to rein in marines' power plays in order to uphold the paternalist fiction in interactions between marines and "peaceful natives."

The distinction between *bons habitants*, or peaceful inhabitants, and *mauvais habitants*, or Cacos, was especially crucial for managing these complex dynamics. Although Smedley Butler, who was so adept at rhetorical gymnastics, could elide the obvious fact of the war in Haiti in his Senate testimony, others could not erase it quite so handily. Frederick Spear of Fremont, Nebraska, who had served as a lieutenant in the Marine Corps in Haiti, thus answered Walter Bruce Howe's questions more straightforwardly. Were our forces "engaged in regular warfare"? Howe asked. "Yes," Spear told the Senate, we knew exactly who we were fighting and "what to expect from them." And did "the rules and customs of regular modern warfare" prevail? "Not entirely," Spear replied, because "those Cacos were very savage men, and if they had captured one of our marines they would probably have skinned him alive." When questioned as to the instructions he had received upon his arrival in Haiti, in the middle of the war against the Cacos, Spear told the Senate that he had received no formal instructions, but that he was shown "how to take charge" by other officers. "The attitude," as he understood it, "was that we were there to kill Cacos, and the quicker the better; but to be very careful about peaceful natives. When I went out to this town to take command, they instructed me, regardless of any belief that I held toward the black race, to be very careful . . . before taking command of the town, and work with [the magistrate], and not be antagonistic toward peaceful men. But all Cacos were to be killed. It was guerrilla warfare, as I understood it."[23] Thus, there was an enemy, and there was a savage war, but the paternalist fiction could be kept alive if a clear distinction was drawn between the peaceful inhabitants and the bad Cacos. That clear line required, in turn, that marines act on an official basis within the paternalist framework and put aside any personal animosity they may have had toward blacks. Thus, to vanquish Cacos, marines were enjoined to kill; but to govern, they were expected to set aside all motives that could be considered personal in nature.[24]

All this had implications both for the occupation and for the individual American men who carried it out. For individual marines, paternalism posed a choice. One could adopt Haiti and face the myriad questions and challenges of refiguring one's sense of oneself. John Balutansky of Pennsylvania chose this option in a rather permanent way. After completing his tour of duty in the early years of the occupation, he left his corps and his country to marry a Haitian woman and raise a Haitian family. His association with the occupation was a source of embarrassment and tension in his wife's family for some time to come, but, by marrying into that family, he himself became Haitian.[25] Other marines adopted Haiti in less permanent ways, but they too struggled with questions of identity and power. As we shall see, marines' fears of being skinned alive, or cannibalized, fed on these sorts of struggles. Violence offered an alternative for asserting one's sense of distance from the nation and the people one was sent to guide and care for. Whether experienced in terms of the paternalist injunctions to protect and discipline or as a rejection of paternalist rhetoric itself, such personal violence was an integral part of the occupation's overall structure of domination.

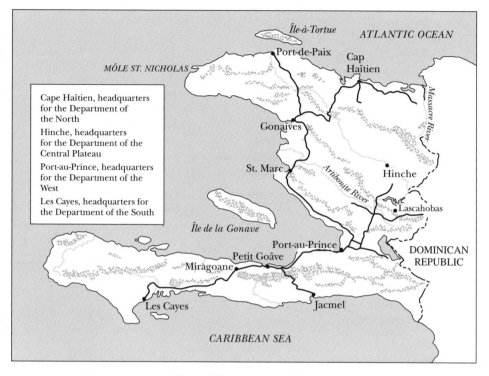

Map 3. The remapping of Haiti

For the occupation, the logic of paternalism shaped the conduct of this war with no name. First on paper, then on the ground, the occupation redrew the internal boundaries of Haiti in an attempt to realize the fiction of paternalism. Military cartographers literally remapped the country, dividing it into departments, districts, and subdistricts, which could be policed and managed more readily than the nation's traditional configuration.[26] Then, with Springfields and Browning automatics, the occupation attempted to mark out a clear line of distinction between the rebels and the population at large. In the early war against the Cacos, that is, in the first phase of U.S. military action in Haiti in 1915 and 1916, this strategy succeeded to a large extent. The war began to drive a wedge between the Cacos and their supporters. But the fiction of paternalism unraveled in the "excesses" of violence that attended the corvée. In response, a much larger part of the population turned toward the Cacos than ever had before, making the second phase of the Caco War, in fact if not in name, a war between nations. Thus, as Woodrow Wilson drew up the terms of peace in Europe, his "sea soldiers" waged war against Haiti.

The Cacos who fought to rid their country of U.S. marines carried with them a long tradition of rebellion and revolt. The taco, a small but fierce bird native to the island of Hispaniola, probably inspired the name of this tradition.[27] "God feeds the little birds" became the motto of some Cacos, including Charlemagne Péralte.[28] During the last campaigns of the Haitian Revolution, Cacos referred to former slaves who "harassed the French" as guerrilla irregulars in support of Christophe and Dessalines.[29] The phrase appeared again in the historical record in 1867, at which time it was the name given to small-holding peasants in the North around Cap Haïtien who took up arms under the leadership of "local chiefs" or "disaffected army officers" to challenge the government of President Sylvain Salnave. These Caco bands would remain in the vicinity of their homes, return to cultivation when government troops arrived in the area, and reassemble once the government forces had departed. Cacos would be paid for their service, with "opportunities for pillage" if not with cash. At the same time, according to David Nicholls, their activities were directed at "defending the interests of the masses."[30]

Between the Cacos' revolt of 1867 and the arrival of U.S. forces in Haiti in 1915, rural chiefs maintained reciprocity with Caco forces, calling on them in times of need. Peasants with small and medium-sized landholdings, in turn, viewed such revolutionary activity as an effective lever against the excesses of the national government, a kind of veto power against what they deemed unjust measures taken in Port-au-Prince.[31] In the years leading up to the occupation, as the government in Port-au-Prince bowed under increasing pressure from the great powers, especially the United States, peasant disaffection stepped up, and the revolutionary activity of the Cacos became much more frequent. Caco armies brought down one president after another, as each tried, unsuccessfully, to balance the requirements of foreign concessionnaires, the demands of the peasants, and their own political and economic aspirations.[32] In 1911, Caco bands opposed the granting of a concession for the McDonald railroad contract. With the advent of the occupation, the Cacos' revolt was now squarely aimed at the new central power in Haiti, the U.S. Marines and their client government.[33] Although the Cacos' activity was not originally nationalist in its orientation, as the occupation progressed the Cacos' activity took on an explicitly, and fervently, anti-American cast.

How did military representatives of the United States understand the Cacos and their activities? From the first days of the U.S. presence in Haiti, in reports telegrammed to Secretary of the Navy Josephus Daniels, Admiral Caperton set out his understanding of the Cacos, and his belief in the importance of subduing them in order to secure American control. "Large number Haitian revolutions due [to] existing professional soldiers called Cacos," reported Caperton on August 2; "Cacos are feared by all Haitians and practically control politics. About fifteen hundred Cacos now in Port-au-Prince. . . . Stable government not possible in Haiti until Cacos are disbanded and power broken. Such action now imperative [in] Port-au-Prince if United States desires to negotiate treaty for financial control [of] Haiti."[34] Caperton was correct, of course, about the Cacos' crucial role in the political process and about their objections to U.S. financial control of Haiti. Yet, on what basis did Caperton claim that the Cacos were "feared by all Haitians"? At that early stage of the occupation, the admiral's intelligence was largely limited to certain elite sources in Port-au-Prince. That some urban elites feared the Cacos was no doubt accurate, but Caperton's attribution of this fear to "all Haitians" was pure fiction.

Private Faustin Wirkus's understanding of the situation, based on his participation in curfew patrols in Port-au-Prince during the summer of 1915, provides another view. Wirkus later recalled how he and his fellow marines had understood their orders on these patrols. "Any Negro or any dark person out of doors after nine o'clock, whose behavior makes him seem like a sympathizer with Caco rebels, is to be shot on sight by the patrol, if he does not surrender."[35] How marines could shoot "on sight" and at the same time give someone an opportunity to surrender Wirkus did not make clear. Nor did he question the association between dark-skinned Haitians and supporters of the rebels. Yet, most interesting is Wirkus's challenge to Caperton's characterization of the Cacos as "professional soldiers" who stood apart from the rest of the population and were "feared by all Haitians." For Wirkus remembered that he had been on the lookout, not only for Cacos, but also for those who supported or sympathized with them.

In mid-August Caperton again emphasized the problem of the Cacos, claiming, it "will be the most difficult one for the United States to solve in Haiti." If so, was this because, as he wrote to Daniels, "these men have long been used to the wandering life of a bandit and to a life without work"?[36] Were the Cacos only or primarily "soldiers of fortune" or "bandits" with no interest in settling down to the farming life of a peasant and unwilling to do so without police supervision?[37]

From the relative distance of his ship, Caperton appears to have drawn a much more rigid distinction between Cacos and non-Caco inhabitants than might have been indicated by some of the reports he received from diplomatic personnel and subordinate officers operating on land. Presenting a contrast to Caperton's perspective, the U.S. consular agent at Port-de-Paix reported that the general population of that town "was entirely and openly hostile to the Government" and "ready to join the Cacos." The residents of Port-de-Paix, he warned, were about "to commence what they term 'guerre internationale' against [President] Dartiguenave and the American occupation." They were, he went on urgently, "very excited and inclined to excesses."[38] Marines arrived shortly thereafter to suppress the revolt. In Port-de-Paix, then, Cacos and non-Cacos joined forces, blurring the lines between inhabitant and insurgent, which Caperton sought to maintain. Here was, moreover, an early instance in which the United States faced serious opposition from residents who were not professional soldiers.

Glossing the complexities of popular resistance and cooperation in the face of U.S. military force, Caperton continued to report encouraging news as to the welcome marines received from inhabitants who were not Cacos. In late November, Caperton stated to Daniels that "Captain Campbell's company, which went to Hinche, found the population there and en route apparently delighted to see our troops."[39] Campbell's memoranda revealed, in contrast, a somewhat more complicated set of native reactions. At Hinche and Pignon, indeed, Campbell had some reason to believe the population welcomed them. At Pignon, he wrote, the chief of the arrondissement "stated that the people of Pignon looked upon us as liberators, as we were freeing the Haitians from slavery."[40] Shortly thereafter, Campbell submitted to his commanding officer his opinion that "the Chiefs at Pignon and Hinche appear to be good men and seem to be working in the interests of the government." These men did not approach the marines in a vacuum, however. Campbell's memo indicates what may have been at stake in making a good impression on the captain: "Am sending in a memoranda of what the Chief of the Arrondissement of Hinche says is due in salaries for his employees."[41] Given the level of control Caperton and his troops had succeeded in taking, militarily and financially, the allegiance of government employees may have been a poor indication of the sentiments of the population.[42] At Fort Liberté, Adolph Miller put a fine point on this dynamic when he noted in his personal log that his friend Bartlett had become the local "paymaster for the loyal Haitians."[43]

Captain Campbell's company diary also shows very clearly how systematic military violence shaped Haitian compliance with the occupation. On November 8, at Bertol, "the inhabitants all appeared friendly and displayed a white flag from their shacks." Campbell went on, "from questioning the women, it appears evident that the Cacos in the vicinity of Bertol are ready to quit. Through their women, I have tried to communicate to the Cacos the fact that, if in the future a single shot is fired by them, or if they . . . create any disturbance, we would return and burn all their houses and completely destroy their crops."[44] Earlier entries in the company diary confirm that these tactics had been used already. On November 3, Campbell wrote: "operated in eastward burning all shacks in that direction"; on November 4, he noted: "to Bahon, burned all shacks along route"; and on November 12, "burned many shacks . . . Lieutenant Clark burned district to River."[45] After the occupation, clergy at Dupity confirmed the destruction suffered by the town at the hands of the marines: "One detachment of the occupation ran into some rifle shots in the heights of Fond-Bleu. The Reprisals did not delay. The officer who commanded the detachment set fire to all the houses in the area. The chapel went up like the rest. Everything fell prey to the flames: chapel, presbytery, vestments, organ."[46] By early November, marine patrols had burned down villages throughout the areas in which the Cacos operated; marines had killed scores of Cacos and wounded many more. In this context, white flags and assurances that the Cacos were ready to quit conveyed defeat, but not delight.

These documents suggest that the marines' perceptions of inhabitants' attitudes toward the Cacos were inextricably bound up with the manner in which marine patrols operated to enforce acceptance of the occupation and rejection of the Cacos. Patrols operating in the North during the fall of 1915 followed orders to clear the country of "bandits." "Men with arms in hand, or gathered together in bands in the disaffected locations, are bandits and unless they surrender are liable to be shot," read one set of field orders. "All camps, forts, or strongholds occupied by Cacos are to be destroyed."[47] As a northern correspondent for a Port-au-Prince newspaper told the Senate committee in 1922, these tactics worked: "The Americans . . . burned all the houses having served as resting places for the Cacos, so that people drove them away themselves, knowing that they had everything to lose."[48] In this way, marine patrols drove a wedge between Caco forces and those who would support them.

Cacos employed similar tactics, perhaps on a more limited scale, pillaging and destroying the property of tradespeople who cooperated with the occupation government in an attempt to dissuade other potential collaborators.[49] Noting the parallel between Caco and Marine Corps operations, Wirkus asserted that peasants supported the Cacos simply to avoid reprisals: "they wanted safety. They sought it from the source that seemed most reliable at the time. Later they sought it from us all the time."[50] Yet, the sense of parity that Wirkus conveyed in this observation ignored significant differences in the relationships of the Cacos and the marines to the population at large. While Cacos used intimidating tactics to enforce solidarity, they could also rely on peasant opposition to onerous economic measures imposed by Port-au-Prince and, increasingly, on deeply held nationalist convictions. Support for the occupation government, on the other hand, may have been bolstered by the existence of families that had already crossed swords with the Cacos in previous campaigns, but it had little else to go on. Support for the occupation thus represented an accession to the superior military capabilities of the U.S. Marines. As Wirkus wrote regarding a later phase of the Caco War, acknowledging the economic dimensions of the peasants' revolutionary activity, "a lot of killing was necessary before one could start reasoning with the peasant whose hunger and general poverty had made him join the Cacos."[51] Official accounts offered a different view. The Cacos' violence was a sign of savagery, but the marines had come to Haïti to protect, not to bully.[52]

The categories Caperton employed to distinguish between hostile Cacos and friendly inhabitants imposed an artificial separation on the Haitian population. Caperton wrote to Daniels, "The Cacos against whom these operations have been undertaken, are bandits purely and simply, owing no allegiance to the Government or any political faction, but organized under petty chiefs for the sole purpose of stirring up strife against the Government and robbing, pillaging, and murdering innocent people."[53] Lieutenant General Merwin H. Silverthorn, looking back on the occupation from a distance of several decades, put this analysis in perspective. Asked about the Cacos, he responded, "They were called bandits. Now, during the so-called banana wars, any group of dissidents who weren't for the government were called bandits. They might be very honorable people with a different political feeling. Nevertheless they were bandits, and they were chased around the hills and shot at and killed whenever you could catch them."[54] Wirkus provided a more specific evaluation. He wrote, in stark contrast to Caperton's assessment: "The more I have learned about the Cacos, the less I have found that they deserved to be called bandits, or habitual criminals. They have always seemed to me to be foraging revolutionists rather than brigands; men who would rather steal than starve, but rather work honestly for wages than steal."[55] Referring to the red hatbands and pieces of cloth that Cacos proudly wore, Wirkus added his counterpoint to Caperton's view of the Cacos' politics: "The battle of the opposition against the established government is to them a battle of right against wrong. The red badge is in itself a declaration of a holy war against wrong and oppression."[56] Some inhabitants supported the Cacos' challenge to the occupation in the fall of 1915, and others did not. Yet as marine patrols succeeded, by violence and intimidation, in convincing people to reject the Cacos, Caperton's originally fictional separation between the Cacos and the population at large became increasingly material, at least for a time.

Alongside the campaign to drive a wedge between the Cacos and their supporters, marines also conducted offensive campaigns directly against the rebels. In raids on Caco camps, and in operations aimed at destroying centuries-old forts used by the Cacos, marines engaged in direct combat with the rebels. Caperton's reports to Daniels included tallies of Cacos killed, wounded, and captured in military campaigns throughout the North. Marines reported that the Cacos were not handy with rifles and often resorted to throwing rocks instead.[57] Trained marines had the better of them with wide disparities in numbers of campaign casualties. As the number of Haitian casualties mounted, Caperton tried to clarify the situation. On November 19, 1915, he issued the following statement: "the operations we have been conducting are purely of a defensive character for the preservation of law and order . . . and for the protection of life and property of the innocent farmers and tradesmen who form by far the majority of the population in the districts patrolled."[58] Yet Captain Campbell, who, as we have seen, had been out on patrols against the Cacos over the previous months, put a different spin on the Caco question in a letter to his mother, dated November 14: "We don't expect much fighting as we have taken most of it out of these people, but we will have to give them a few more lessons before they will know enough to quit."[59]

Secretary Daniels, whose understanding of the situation was more consistent with Campbell's, dispatched a telegram to Caperton immediately, ordering him to stop the killings: "Department strongly impressed with number Haitians killed. Department feels that a severe lesson has been taught Cacos and believes that a proper patrol can be maintained to preserve order and protect innocent persons without further offensive operations."[60] Despite Caperton's official reports, Secretary Daniels and the marines in the field knew well that they had been conducting an offensive campaign to enforce cooperation with the U.S. occupation. Consistent with the goals of a paternalist intervention, the language they used to describe that enforcement invoked the responsibilities of a father: in order to protect Haitians, marines had to teach them a lesson.

By early 1916 the success of months of marine patrols and counterinsurgency tactics led to a waning of Caco activity in the countryside. Marines had burned countless villages to the ground, destroyed most Haitian fortresses, and killed hundreds of Haitians. These were systematic acts of violence, directed against human beings and their property, but they caused no uproar in the United States. They fueled no political campaign, they caused no scandal in the press because these were deemed official and legitimate acts, carried out in the service of a righteous and benevolent intervention. An exposé focusing attention on the violence of these acts might have changed that perception, but none did. U.S. press coverage of the occupation focused instead on medals of honor won by Butler and others in campaigns against unruly Haitian insurgents. The political representation of the occupation as a protective, not destructive, intervention stood firm through this first phase of the war against the Cacos.

The paternalism of the occupation established its "moral" overtones: marines took on the unpleasant responsibility of killing Cacos in order to protect innocent Haitian farmers and tradespeople. The separation of the Cacos from the population at large was, then, essential to the ruling representation of the occupation as a paternalist undertaking. That separation occurred not only in Caperton's rhetoric but in local communities as well; by 1916 most Haitians knew what they had to lose if they closed ranks with the Cacos again. Whereas Caperton insisted on the defensive, protective nature of the killings, Secretary Daniels and Captain Campbell identified the offensive character of the operations by referring to them as teaching the Cacos a lesson. Here were two sides of the same paternalist coin.

A consciousness of the marines' official purpose in Haiti affected not only Caperton's rhetoric but also Daniel's orders and Campbell's actions in the field. Whatever strategic or economic goals paternalism may have served, it functioned on a day-to-day level to enable the violence necessary to secure U.S. control in Haiti and, at the same time, to uphold the marines' understanding of themselves as righteous Americans. Whether protecting innocent inhabitants or teaching Cacos a lesson, marines were carrying out the dictates of a paternalist undertaking. While their violent acts were deemed official — Campbell, for example, was following his field orders when he burned the shacks in his path — they were also, on another level, individual acts. U.S. Americans would carry this fact along with them into the next phase of the occupation, or over to Santo Domingo, or back to the States. As the contradictions of paternalist rule sharpened over the next few years, the dual nature of the marines' actions, both official and individual, would become increasingly apparent.

In this first phase of the Caco War, the Haitian Gendarmerie was on its way to becoming a major player in occupied Haiti. By the end of 1915 Butler had established more than 100 Gendarmerie posts around the country, and through 1918 he continued to build this hybrid Haitian-American military and police organization with Haitian men and American officers. Butler laid on a thick layer of paternalist rhetoric in the recruitment process; at the same time, a double paycheck provided the material incentive for marines to fold up their Marine Corps khakis and doff the uniform of the Gendarmerie, with nothing added to signify their double status.[61] "There will be some fat jobs for the bachelor officers," wrote Adolph Miller in his diary the day he learned about the arrangement.[62] Some enlisted men, too, could take advantage of the offer, because marines gained a rank or two over their status in the corps. Gunnery sergeants and first sergeants generally became first lieutenants in the Gendarmerie, while second lieutenants generally became captains.

Gendarmerie officers took on tremendous tasks and powerful roles. Posted to one or another district headquarters around the country, some marines-cum-gendarmes effectively served as military governors in their districts, enjoying little contact with, or assistance from, their fellow marines.[63] They oversaw public works projects, tax collection, police functions, judicial affairs, and military defense.[64] Merwin Silverthorn described his authority as a Gendarmerie captain and district commander for Aux Cayes: "A town was called a commune. I had 13 communes in this area, and I was the communal adviser to each of these communes. That meant that no ordinance passed by any of these communes . . . until I had approved it." He specified further, "I sat in on every meeting of the town council of Aux-Cayes, which is a city of 15,000 people" and approved every budget "for every commune in the whole district." In addition to his military and political responsibilities, he added, he had to oversee the justice system every time someone was arrested.[65] Other officers described their authority in even more stark terms.[66] By 1917, enough communes had complained to the government in Port-au-Prince about Gendarmerie officers' excessive control that the Haitian minister in Washington took it upon himself to convey these complaints to the State Department. "The American officers of the Haitian gendarmerie," he informed Jordan Stabler, "have extended their powers for the communal councils to such an extent that they wish to act as administrators of the commune and not rest within their powers . . . as intended by the president."[67]

Gendarmerie officers' status was double-edged as well as doubly paid. On one hand, their authority over Haitians bolstered crucial aspects of their identity as white men. The sense of mastery and superiority that was so essential to their understanding of themselves as set apart from the Haitian communities in which they lived was reinforced and maintained through their daily supervision of peasants and politicians alike. On the other hand, a tour in the Gendarmerie could be, as Silverthorn described it, "man-killing work." "You were isolated; you were out in the hills; you had no social contacts. All of your work was done in Creole or in French."[68] Perhaps this is why Adolph Miller opted to turn down such a "fat job"; "I wouldn't have one for $1000 a month extra," he wrote.[69] In this connection, in his interview for the Marine Corps oral history project, Lieutenant General Silverthorn told a story very much like the one that Captain Craige told about Lieutenant South. When he took over at Aux Cayes, said Silverthorn, "the former commander had lost his mind, had killed a native, and had been relieved under guard" only to commit suicide by jumping out "the porthole of the ship that was taking him to the States."[70] Silverthorn took over, he said, with only a handful of white people in the vicinity and only one American woman — his wife.[71]

These marines lived and worked with Haitians on a day-to-day basis, and when occupation officials instituted the corvée, these marines carried it out. Beginning in August 1916, they took on the responsibility for enforcing corvée labor for the purpose of constructing roads to facilitate military control in the countryside.[72] Orders to the Gendarmerie officers specified that inhabitants were to be paid wages, fed, and not taken out of the vicinity of their homes.[73] While occupation officials professed that wages and meals would be welcomed by the peasants, for many Haitians forced labor simply resembled too closely the slavery they abhorred. On top of this, the prom-ised wages and meals were not always forthcoming. In St. Marc, in 1918, it was reported that corvée laborers received "1 gourde or, in American money, about 20 cents a week; without any food."[74]

The methods employed by Gendarmerie officers to enforce the corvée were fueled by racism and the rank desire for mastery and no doubt were inflamed by Haitian resistance. The process itself reinforced Haitians' belief that this was indeed a new form of slavery. Gendarmes took peasants forcibly from their homes, roped them together, and used brutal discipline with the corvée gangs. Capsine Altidor, from the town of Maïssade, in the North, testified before the Senate committee while it was in Haiti that a group of gendarmes, including "one white man," came to his house on June 8, 1917, and took his son "for the corvée." "They struck him on the head and made him lose a quantity of blood," Altidor explained, before taking him to the Gendarmerie office. He never saw his son again.[75]

European American Baptist missionary L. Ton Evans testified that on a Sunday morning in June 1918, on his way to church, he had witnessed inhabitants, including "native preachers" and members of his own congregation "roped tightly and cruelly together, and driven like slaves" toward the Gendarmerie headquarters. As a rule, Evans explained to the committee, gendarmes, acting "under official orders of the marines, would catch, arrest, and rope the natives and drive them to prison, and from prison to work on the roads, and under such conditions often cruelly deal with them."[76] Evans testified that he had witnessed these practices, or evidence of them, in several different regions of the country. In Jacmel, in the South, he visited the prison and the hospital, where, as he told the senators, "I was startled to see two or more prisoners with their arms like jelly or raw beef and being treated by our American doctor." When Evans asked the marine captain what had been the cause of their condition, the captain explained that it was "the roping business connected with the corvée." According to the doctor, Evans added, such cases occurred constantly and were "a disgrace to the United States."[77] The reverend testified further as to the brutal use of corvée workers: "I have seen in the gangs at work men, for merely turning their head and without the slightest provocation as far as I could see struck until actually stunned." Evans told of dead bodies "exposed and naked for days," that he had seen "lying around."[78] He could not say for sure that they had been the bodies of corvée workers who had been killed by gendarmes, but he believed this to be the case.

Senator Atlee Pomerene, anxious to establish the extent of marines' involvement with the violent practices associated with the corvée, asked Evans directly: "You do not mean that our Marines used violence?" Evans responded affirmatively, but explained that he had never seen a marine strike a peasant. He attributed this to the likelihood that marines would want to avoid behaving that way in front of a Christian missionary. He added, however, that the marines "give the orders and see that they are carried out." Evans further asserted to the committee: "I verily believe that more [Haitians] have met their deaths through the corvée thus illegally practiced, willfully or ignorantly, by marines and gendarmes and acquiesced in by those in supreme command and at Washington than were killed in open conflict with the Cacos, if it was not indeed the chief cause and mainstay of Cacoism."[79]

In response to reports of abuses, Colonel Russell, who had recently become commander of the Marine brigade in Haiti, ordered the corvée ended in October 1918. It continued, however, in the North. When investigations revealed this fact, occupation officials insisted that it had been carried out illegally by one particular Gendarmerie officer, Colonel Clark H. Wells, a Marine Corps major and district commander for the North.[80] The Senate inquiry later established that Wells had known about, and allowed, the brutal treatment and killing of corvée laborers. Clark Wells was never tried by court-martial.[81]

Even after the end of the corvée in the North, other forms of coerced labor persisted. Gendarmerie officers routinely employed prisoners as laborers on public works projects, and even sometimes made arrests in order to have sufficient labor. There was no shortage of possible charges to levy against less-than-fully compliant peasants; cursing Americans, for example, could bring nine months' jail time in occupied Haiti.[82] In at least one instance, Selden Kennedy, the district commander at Hinche, talked openly about this practice; years later, Major General Bennett Puryear, who had served as a colonel in the Gendarmerie d'Haïti between 1925 and 1928, recalled his explanation. If a Gendarmerie captain had building projects that needed completion and an insufficient number of prisoners to do the job, he would go to the local judge and "tell him he needs so many prisoners" and "tell him to go out and get them." Then men without machetes — that is, those that appeared not to be working actively — would be picked up and put to work.[83] Another district commander, Louis B. "Chesty" Puller, who went on to make a name for himself in the Pacific War and again at Inchon, told his biographer about the severe conditions under which prisoners labored to build a new barracks for the gendarmes at St. Marc. "For months the men quarried stone, cut it into rough blocks, and bore it under Puller's watchful eye. Dozens of them broke down under the burdens, and were useless for the work. A few of them died." "I may go to hell for this," Puller is reported to have said to a visiting officer.[84]

ROUTINES OF VIOLENCE, 1918–1921

By 1918, the Cacos' war against the occupation had resumed with renewed dedication and force in response to the escalation of abuses associated with the corvée. As the Union Patriotique explained a few years later, "internal peace could not be preserved because the permanent and brutal violation of individual rights of Haitian citizens was a perpetual provocation to revolt."[85] Simply put, the corvée drove Haitians to the Cacos. In turn, the fiction that Cacos were shiftless peasants stirred up by elite agitators became more difficult to uphold. As one marine officer explained in an oral history interview, it was obvious that the insurgents "were natives who had lived in these areas; and, because of the corvée, a lot of them had taken to the mountains and joined the bandits."[86] At the same time, Haitians who did not fight with the Cacos offered more consistent support for the rebels than they had before.[87] The lines between the Cacos and their supporters, and between their supporters and the general population, thus became harder to clarify by rhetorical or military means, although the attempt was made.

The Marine Corps, with the help of its offspring, the Gendarmerie d'Haïti, prosecuted the war with determination, while offering money, food, and "bon habitant passes" to those rebels who would agree to lay down their arms. But this time, success would be hard won. The Cacos, organized under the leadership of Charlemagne Péralte, "the Commander in Chief of the Forces Operating Against the Americans," Benoit Batraville, and other key leaders, fought with spirit and tenacity to reclaim "Haiti for the Haitians."[88] Some wore "holy virgin scapulars and medals blessed in Saut D'Eau" to sustain them in the liberation of their country.[89] More solidly than before, they were, as Péralte called them, a "patriot army."

In response to the renewed vigor of the Cacos, marines themselves fought more viciously, taking them farther and farther away from any semblance of paternalist affection. "Chesty" Puller later recalled that when he first arrived in Haiti, in June 1919, "the orders down there were: the prisons are filled; we don't want any more prisoners." The implications of such orders were clear enough, and Puller's memories are corroborated by documents from the files of the secretary of the navy.[90] Historian Arthur S. Link described the escalation of the war against the Cacos this way: "The process of pacification, which had begun so easily soon became almost a war of extermination, as the Haitians fought back fanatically, and the job was not completed until some two thousand of them had been shot."[91] In fact, more than 3,000 Haitians, and possibly thousands more, were killed in military campaigns against the Cacos, with even higher numbers wounded. In addition, Link failed to understand what was at stake for Haitians in the conflict; he could see only excessive and unreasonable zeal. Yet Link's summary account of the second phase of the Caco War is instructive, for it echoes a long imperialist tradition of projecting violence onto savage natives.[92] It was the Haitians' fanaticism, this implied, not the Americans' brutality, that upped the ante of violence in the conflict. Link thus shifted the onus for creating what was "almost a war of extermination" from the marines who did the killing to the Haitians who were killed.

In keeping with this imperialist tradition, marines themselves attributed

Figure 11. Caco leader: Valerius Pierre.
Marine Corps Research Center Archives, Quantico, Virginia.

Figure 12. Unidentified Caco leader.
Marine Corps Research Center Archives, Quantico, Virginia.

the escalation of violence to the savage nature of a primitive people. As former lieutenant Spear told the Senate, "we knew what to expect" from the rebels so that "the rules and customs of regular modern warfare" could not prevail. The comments of two officers who served in the latter years of the occupation highlight this same dynamic. Asked whether he ever saw any indication of American brutality in occupied Haiti, Brigadier General Ivan W. Miller, who was in Haiti for the final year of the occupation, was quick to clarify the situation. He explained that "there was some talk about some brutality, but then you have to remember that what we consider brutality among people in the United States is different from what they considered brutality. Those people, particularly at that time there, their idea of brutality was entirely different from ours. They had no conception of kindness or helping people."[93] And "helping people" was, of course, exactly what the marines were there to do, as General Lemuel C. Shepherd, who served in the Gendarmerie from 1929 to 1934, stated. "We wanted to establish law and order" and to "clean up" a backward country. "I have a soft spot in my heart for my four years in Haiti," said Shepherd, recalling his relationships with the gendarmes who served under his command. Yet Shepherd likened the war against "Charlemagne and his Cacos" to the "Frontier fighting" or "Indian fighting" of the nineteenth century and to the war in Vietnam, which was under way at the time of his interview. "[Y]ou've got to fight that kind of war in the way that they're waging it on you," he said, calling for the development and training of client armies for counterinsurgency purposes; "a white man can't do it."[94]

Yet white men did do it, or at least they fought with the brutality they attributed to those they sought to vanquish.[95] Indeed, none of the wars mentioned by Shepherd, not the so-called Indian wars, the war in Haiti, or the war in Vietnam, could have taken place without white men, that is, without the discourses of whiteness and manhood or, later, masculinity, that made white men who they were.[96] Moreover, in conjunction with discourses of sexuality, civilization, and national identity, discourses of race and gender shaped and directed U.S. marines' experience of and conduct in the most violent phases of the occupation. By examining the meanings associated with violence in the second stage of the Caco War, we may begin to glimpse the relationships among broad cultural patterns, individual experience, and the hard material realities of bullets and bodies. The words marines used to describe their actions in battle, and their feelings and thoughts about what they were doing, may shed light on the processes by which identity and consciousness took shape in that context. As this stage of the Caco War intensified, individual marines reflected upon matters of race, morality, identity, and motivation. In the face of official paternalism, native hostility, and bad press for their corps, they struggled to maintain their sense of themselves. Their reflections from the field may help us understand the meanings surrounding violence, and the manner in which subjective individual and group identities were challenged in the context of this violent international conflict.

Faustin Wirkus left behind a particularly rich and reflective record of his consciousness in battle. Wirkus left Haiti a private in the Marine Corps in 1916, to return two years later as a sergeant. In April 1919 Wirkus was commissioned as a second lieutenant in the Gendarmerie. Facing battle for the first time (he had served in Port-au-Prince for his first stint in the country), Wirkus considered his actions, as he trained his sights on a Caco leader leaving his camp: "something in this man's coolness in facing fire . . . made me lower my gun. I had never killed a man before, I grew a little sick at the thought of taking a life like this — this, I thought, would be murder."[97] Wirkus later explained that his qualms had been misplaced. "Olivier," the Caco leader he let slip away, continued his hostile acts and brought many Haitians along with him, only to die in battle at a later date. If he had been able to shoot when he first had seen the man, he thought, he would have saved those lives.[98] Nonetheless, Wirkus raised the issue of interpretation. Did killing an enemy leader constitute murder? Not necessarily, Wirkus seemed to suggest, if it saved the lives of his peasant followers. Wirkus's reflections suggested the way in which context seemed to shift the moral weight and meaning of a violent act in battle.

In other passages of his memoir, Wirkus made explicit some of the thought processes that contributed to the marines' dehumanization of Cacos in battle. Whereas other marines spoke of "hunting" Cacos, Wirkus articulated the intellectual process involved in that attitude.[99] On one occasion, he noted that seeing Cacos raiding a village, they "seemed more like frightened animals than armed enemies."[100] And coming on a few Haitians in a thicket, he wrote, "often I have come on wild animals in a wilderness which has not been troubled by hunters, where the four-footed creatures acted exactly the same way — standing still instinctively to avoid attention."[101]

Wirkus also articulated the connection between racial attitudes at home and the experience of killing Cacos in battle. He described a battle in which the Cacos hid behind a line of boulders located in front of a tall "chalk-like cliff." "Every time a black head appeared over the top or around the side of a boulder," he wrote, "it was as clearly outlined as a bull's eye on a painted target." Wirkus related his thoughts as he proceeded to aim and shoot: "I steadied down to my job of popping at black heads, which appeared very much as those behind the 'hit the nigger and get a cigar' games at American amusement parks."[102] Here, despite his earlier reasoning, the Haitian rebels became simply targets, utterly dehumanized. Killing came to seem like an amusement. The racism that placed white men back home in front of a beebee gun and an image of a black man resounded in this foreign context, challenging the logic of paternalism that earlier helped him pull the trigger. And the resonance of racist sport, of killing as amusement, can be observed in the discourse of other marines who, as we have seen, referred to their military activity in Haiti as "hunting Cacos."

Wirkus thus demonstrated the connection between racial attitudes at home and the experience of killing Cacos in battle. Marines who shot at Cacos while under fire, as Wirkus describes here, did not, in so doing, carry on "indiscriminate killing." They were, presumably, waging a most traditional form of warfare. Yet the likeness between this activity and the sport of shooting images of blacks at home did not escape them, whether or not it was present to them on a conscious level, as in Wirkus's case. Thus, racism both contributed to and undermined the paternalist tone of the occupation. Seeing people of African heritage as children enabled marines to imagine themselves acting on protective and disciplinary motivations. Seeing them as targets, however, did not.

Wirkus's dissection of his own engagement with paternalism and violence lends insight to the processes by which marines negotiated these complexities, but his account, written some years after the fact, and written for publication, tells too neat and tidy a story. In the face of paternalism's contradictions, in the face of a foreign and seemingly threatening culture, in the face of one's own doubt, marines confronted the war's escalation — and their own violence — with much less certainty. Homer Overley's lingering sense of doubt seems more telling, in this respect, than Wirkus's careful explanations. Letters home, written at the time, also reveal the sense of confusion marines must have felt. In a letter to his mother, for example, "Chesty" Puller admitted his surprise at receiving a medal from the Haitian government for killing Cacos. Puller wrote, "You may rest assured I was relieved when I found out that I had been ordered to Port-au-Prince to be decorated for killing Cacos and not to be court-martialled for the same."[103]

Such confusion contributed to the sense of separation marines felt from their home country as they faced the difficulties of field campaigns and battles. Marine patrols took to the mountains for a week or two at a time, with little sleep and sometimes little food. They "hid out in the daytime and traveled at night," ever watchful. One marine described it as "sweaty, backbreaking work." At the same time, the sounds of conches and drums, associ-

Figure 13. Marines with prisoner.
Marine Corps Research Center Archives, Quantico, Virginia.

ated with Vodou ceremonies poorly understood by the marines, were unsettling and demoralizing. Stories of cannibalism added a gruesome twist that gave marines the "jitters."[104]

In this context, marines could find U.S. press coverage of marine atrocities jarring. "Chesty" Puller, in a letter to a friend back in the States, expressed his frustration over Americans who misunderstood the occupation and made a fuss over something that seemed to him inconsequential: "every once in a while some misguided fool up in the States, who knows nothing of the trouble here, sets up a howl over a few black bandits being knocked off."[105] Homer Overley recalled how painful it was to hear about such reports, knowing (he thought) that the papers never told the stories of cannibalism that plagued marines daily. And Faustin Wirkus claimed that he burned all his unofficial field notes for fear that they would fall into the hands of someone who might not understand the situation.[106]

In light of the moral confusion, normative dissonance, and emotional difficulty expressed by these men, it is especially notable that marines seem to have had a good deal of autonomy in the field, particularly when operating as officers in the Gendarmerie. Upon joining three other Gendarmerie officers in Perodin, Sergeant Wirkus recalled being told, "It's everybody for himself up here. . . . Each man takes his orders in his own way." Wirkus told of one Gendarmerie officer, named Williston, who devised his own methods. Williston had made it his trademark to collect the hats of all those he killed. He stacked them on a pole as a visible body count and as a weapon of intimidation. Another officer explained to Wirkus: "Williston believes that orders to 'get' a Caco (or a bandit) mean literally . . . 'You had best get him before he first gets you.' So Williston 'gets' every Caco he sees with a touch of red about his clothing. . . . It's going to get him into trouble, sometime, because he's apt to 'get' somebody he shouldn't."[107] Here, Wirkus suggested, was a story of "indiscriminate killing." What distinguished Williston from other marines in the field, according to Wirkus, was that Williston failed to draw proper distinctions between appropriate and inappropriate victims in battle.

This failure to maintain the proper distinctions between one category of Haitians and another was precisely the issue at stake in the scandal over "indiscriminate killing." To conduct successfully a counterinsurgency campaign in the context of a paternalist foreign intervention necessitated the maintenance of several crucial analytic distinctions, between, for example, acceptable and unacceptable forms of violence, honorable and dishonorable motivations and purposes, and appropriate and inappropriate victims. Yet these distinctions, if they had ever been clear, were certainly breaking down, in the face of Haitian resistance, in the second phase of the war against the Cacos.

On October 15, 1919, Colonel Russell issued confidential orders to stop such activities if they in fact were going on. The "alleged charge" was that "troops in the field have declared and carried on what is commonly known as an 'open season' where care is not taken to determine whether or not the natives encountered are bandits or 'good citizens' and where houses have been ruthlessly burned merely because they were unoccupied and native property otherwise destroyed."[108] Russell's confidential orders identified a process long in the making; however, his concurrent address to the population attempted to deal with the problems that resulted simply by declaring them nonexistent. "The occupation is determined to enforce only the laws of Haiti and have them respected, and it will assure its entire protection to all the good and peaceable citizens while it will drive out the bandits."[109] His statement reaffirmed the distinctions that were crucial to the paternalist ideal: good citizens and bandits were mutually exclusive categories; Americans were present in Haiti in order to protect good citizens; the occupation was in no way an outside imposition; it was a benevolent presence.

This declaration would not be sufficient to erase Haitian indignation over the usurpations and abuses they experienced. Nor would it change the nature of violence in occupied Haiti. A year later, Russell issued yet another in his series of confidential memoranda. It instructed "officers attached to this Brigade" that when and where their responsibilities should bring them "in contact with the Haitian people such duty will be performed with the minimum of harshness compatible with the situation."[110] Clarifying the logic of this order, for those who would not be apt to understand it, he continued, "There are two good reasons for this: personal self respect and a regard for decency and human kindness on the part of the Officer, in the first place, and public expediency in the interest of his own government, in the second place." "No people with any spirit can view the occupation of their territory by the troops of another nation in any light other than as a heavy blow to their pride; considerate treatment may soften the blow, but harshness is bound to harden it into resentment that goes to defeat the larger interests of the occupying nation. . . . It is plain that American officers should exert every effort to gain the confidence and goodwill of the Haitian people, without in any way relaxing firmness where firmness is required."[111] In this way, the brigade commander attempted to shore up the distinctions that alone could maintain the benevolent face of paternalism. But the Caco War had come to defy the justifications of protection and discipline. Violence that had rested on the ability to discriminate among — that is, to discern — appropriate forms, victims, purposes, had become indiscriminate. Nothing short of conquest would restore the fiction of paternal care.

In the meanwhile, neither the violence, nor talk about it, could be contained. The event that led to the most damaging disclosures, that led, indeed, to public charges of "indiscriminate killing," did not take place on the field of battle, but rather in the woods behind a prison in the vicinity of Hinche. On May 22, 1919, a Marine Corps noncommissioned officer (NCO) and Gendarmerie lieutenant named Louis A. Brokaw led two marine privates, three gendarmes, and two prisoners out back of the prison into those woods. Brokaw is said to have ordered the prisoners to dig graves, one each, and then to stand in front of those graves. He then ordered Private Walter E. Johnson and Private John J. McQuilkin, along with the gendarmes, to shoot the two prisoners. Subsequent court-martial trials for Johnson and McQuilkin established that the two enlisted men shot at but did not kill the prisoners. "[D]oubting his authority to order such an execution, but fearing to disobey orders, [they] shot 'wide' so as not to kill," read one statement of the case. Then Brokaw, "seeing the prisoners were still alive," shot and killed them "with his own pistol." The privates on trial were convicted of striking the prisoners. Lieutenant Brokaw was never tried by court-martial because "he was adjudged insane."[112]

This killing was, by all accounts, a startling atrocity. Critics of the occupation, who learned of it, saw it as emblematic of a corrupt intervention; Colonel Russell also viewed it as a horrible event, from a public relations standpoint, as well as in other ways. As far as we know, he did not see the court-martial records before they were passed along to General Barnett. Buried in those records, General Barnett found something more startling than the event itself. Marine Corps Lieutenant Spear, whom we have met, serving as defense counsel for Private Johnson, had argued that neither his client, nor Private McQuilkin, should be judged too harshly for their actions, for they were merely following a general custom. "He had himself seen many similar cases."[113]

Responding to the revelations contained in the court-martial record, Barnett sent a stern "personal and confidential" letter to Colonel Russell ordering an end to the corvée and an investigation with all "guilty parties brought to justice." "The court-martial of one private for the killing of a native prisoner brought out a statement by his counsel that showed me that practically indiscriminate killing of the natives has gone on for some time," wrote Barnett. "Judging by the knowledge gained only from the cases that have been brought before me, . . . the Marine Corps has been sadly lacking in right and justice, and I look to you to see that this is corrected and corrected at once."[114] This was the letter that made its way to the American press, just five months before a presidential election, when George Barnett stepped down as commandant of the corps. Frederick Wise, then commandant of the Gendarmerie, later wrote that these events led to the idea that "the shooting of natives in Haiti was comparatively ordinary routine."[115] Was it?

We have seen how "the shooting of natives" in the war against the Cacos led to a blurring of distinctions separating righteous warfare from indiscriminate killing. Shooting natives also accompanied the practice of burning inhabitants' homes in campaigns against the Cacos, although the shooting was often invisible in official descriptions of that activity. Heraux Belloni of Maïssade testified before the Senate committee that he had seen a group of gendarmes, led by a white man, shoot his mother and burn down their house. Belloni escaped from the house without being hit; from the nearby ravine where he hid, he saw his dead father slumped against the tree to which he was tied.[116]

There were other instances, besides the notorious case of Johnson and

McQuilkin, in which gendarmes or marines shot prisoners. Some documents and testimony that emerged at the Senate hearings pointed to the widespread practice of shooting prisoners. Marine Corps major Thomas C. Turner conducted an investigation at Maïssade after the Johnson and McQuilkin case came to light. Upon concluding his investigation, he reported that he questioned many gendarmes and marines; "while they all admitted of hearing many rumors of murdering Caco prisoners none of them were able to testify under oath that such was so. . . . Almost everyone stationed in Haiti during the early part of this year seemed to have some knowledge of the fact that both marines and gendarmes were killing prisoners. It was very difficult to get any witnesses to testify directly as, in the opinion of the undersigned, they were all equally culpable."[117] "That there were killings and many of them is undoubtedly true," wrote Turner. His report concluded, however, that all of these many killings could be "directly traced to Major Clark H. Wells," the same man who continued to enforce the corvée after receiving orders to stop it. Turner believed that because the Gendarmerie officers were noncommissioned officers in the Marine Corps, they had a deeply ingrained sense of obedience to senior officers. Wells instructed them, wrote Turner, "to bump off Caco prisoners, and they carried their orders out to the best of their ability."[118]

Wells was not alone in his culpability. Beside the cases discussed by Turner, there are several other instances of marines or gendarmes shooting prisoners that have made it into the historical record. One Haitian gendarme was court-martialed for shooting three prisoners "in cold blood" after two others escaped from him. It was determined that the murders were committed in an attempt to silence the victims. The gendarme in question was sentenced to death, and the execution was carried out swiftly in order to send a message to other gendarmes, or so it was claimed.[119]

Cases involving Americans did not come to justice in the same way — swiftly or at all. Louis Cukela, a Marine Corps lieutenant who had won a Medal of Honor as a sergeant in France, executed a group of prisoners "in the middle of a Marine camp," according to one superior officer. Cukela was "transferred but not court-martialed."[120] "Chesty" Puller's biographer asserts that Puller was proud of having shot the "minor Caco chief" who told him about Sergeant Lawrence Muth's death; at the time, Puller claimed that he shot the Caco chief because he tried to escape.[121]

In addition, marines serving under Major Wells, like those serving under Sergeant Brokaw, made their own decisions about "bumping off" prisoners. Herman Hanneken, who would soon gain considerable renown and respect for capturing and killing Charlemagne Péralte, clearly made his own decision when he killed a Caco leader whom he had taken prisoner while on patrol in the vicinity of Hinche. Hanneken reported this with arresting frankness to Major Wells on February 15, 1919. "[A]fter a running fight up a mountain five Cacos were killed and *as Marius was proving a hindrance I killed him,*" he wrote in a field operations report. Wells subsequently squirreled the report away in his personal files.[122]

The Reverend L. Ton Evans testified to other incidents of violence. He had, he asserted, heard marines "boastfully speak of their killing, or, as they termed it, bagging Cacos on shooting expeditions."[123] He described a dead body being carried openly through the streets of St. Marc for the purpose of terrorizing the inhabitants. As a man of the cloth, Evans learned about some abuses from remorseful marines. A lieutenant from Petite Rivière had told him about killings there, and others had told him of lesser acts of violence. "Many of our American marine officers have confessed to me that when they came first to Haiti, inexperienced, somewhat prejudiced, ignorant of their language . . . they often misunderstood them, [and] wrongly abused these men."[124] According to Evans's testimony, Captain Kenny, who "had a reputation for brutality" at St. Marc, had "admitted his error" to the reverend. Another marine who had bragged about killing Haitians told Evans "that he was sick and disgusted with the way things were in Haiti," and was looking forward to going back to the States, where he "would be done forever with this kind of life."[125]

Evans spent the last days of 1918, and the opening days of 1919, in a prison cell at St. Marc having been arrested by order of Kenny's successor, Captain Fitzgerald Brown, and subsequently charged with rebellion against the U.S. occupation. Evans had been raising questions about the violence of the marines and gendarmes in the district, and was firmly of the belief that drink was behind it. Captain Brown was one of the prime targets of his criticisms. In prison, Evans claimed, he observed evidence of abuse and torture. One man "had his back beaten into a kind of jelly," according to Evans. When Evans asked another prisoner how it had happened, he was told "that this American Captain Brown, in another of his drunken rages had pounded this man." Evans reported seeing female prisoners with "their heads held under spigots by gendarmes and otherwise tortured."[126] In addition to what he saw, Evans claimed that he heard even more: "I could hear the yelling and groaning of native prisoners, as well as their being cruelly beaten and pounded. . . . Many a time these yells and groans would cease, and then a scuffle, whispering, and the sound like if they were carrying out a dead body."[127] Evans attributed these beatings to gendarmes, but held Brown responsible for them.

Sexual violence also came to light during this second phase of the war against the Cacos, though it was not confined to that period. Marines "prowling for liquor and women" during off-duty hours resulted in repeated conflicts with Haitian citizens from the outset, suggesting to U.S. officials that the misbehavior of enlisted men was the primary source of friction between the occupation and the population.[128] "Marines often immoral," Secretary of the Navy Josephus Daniels noted in his diary in August 1920; Daniels looked into the possibility of bringing the Young Men's Christian Association (YMCA) to Haiti to address the problem.[129] His relatively mild response was consistent with the occupation as a whole, despite the fact that U.S. officials touted American standards of decency in contrast to Haitian immorality.[130] In fact, Americans' repeated deprecation of Haitian women did much to create and maintain an atmosphere in which rape would go unrecognized, unnamed, and, of course, unpunished. Consistent with racialized definitions of rape prevailing in the United States, Captain Craige commented, "rape, I believe, implies a lack of consent. I never heard of a case where consent was lacking in Haiti's black belt."[131] In this context, it would fall to African Americans to insist on the severity and the extent of sexual violence by marines against Haitian women and young girls. Indeed, it was the Reverend S. E. Churchstone-Lord, American pastor of the African Methodist Episcopal Church in Port-au-Prince, who charged marines, in May 1920, with systematic rape in Haiti. "In one night alone in the 'Bisquet' section of Port-au-Prince nine little girls from 8 to 12 years old died from the raping of American soldiers," Churchstone-Lord stated and the *Chicago Defender* reported. Nor was it only enlisted men who were involved, Churchstone-Lord made clear, for white officers of the Gendarmerie, he also charged, compelled native gendarmes "to procure native women for use of the whites as concubines."[132]

In all these ways, violence was, in fact, a "comparatively ordinary routine" in occupied Haiti. The routine of violence began in 1915, in field campaigns against the Cacos; it took on new forms as peasants resisted the corvée; and with the resurgence of the Cacos it exploded beyond the boundaries of corvée enforcement and military campaign. Rape and sexual harassment, though they went on without comment by Americans for the most part, characterized the occupation from the beginning, but came to light following the use of the corvée and the resurgence of the Caco rebellion. The routine of violence affected all marines, though not all in the same way. Not all marines committed atrocities; it is possible that a relatively small number participated in the most extreme forms of violence outside the conduct of military campaigns.

What roles did alcohol and insanity play in the atrocities that did occur? While these were undoubtedly very real factors in some cases, they do not explain why violence took place, or what subjective and cultural processes led individual U.S. American men to participate actively in and to perpetuate the routine of violence. The question is why, when American men in Haiti became drunk or mentally unbalanced, did their behavior take the particular form it did? Other American men in Haiti struggled with the challenges of the occupation, including the routine of violence, to very different ends. Their experiences, and the ways in which their stories became woven into Marine Corps legends, may shed light on the cultural dimensions of violence in occupied Haiti.

THAT NAMELESS DREAD

Marines, like Louis Brokaw, who committed atrocities and were found innocent by reason of insanity were judged, in effect, to have lost their normal subjective state. This loss, it was reasoned, caused them to commit actions for which they could not be held responsible. Leaving aside, for the moment, the question as to whether this "insanity" was a politically expedient fabrication, the claim raised the issue of identity and its fragility in various occupation contexts. However expedient a fabrication it may have been in some instances, it reflected the experience of marines facing a very real subjective challenge: how to maintain one's sense of oneself amid the collapse of meanings and distinctions essential to one's identity; how to maintain one's sense of oneself as a white man, and as an American, in occupied Haiti.

We have seen how this challenge affected some marines in Haiti, causing them to remark on the separation they felt from their home country as they faced the difficulties of battle: Overley, who resented criticism of the marines, attempted to maintain a sense of humanity in the field and feared losing his head; Wirkus burned his notes for fear of being misunderstood and later articulated many of the challenges facing marines in Haiti; Puller lost hold of the importance of distinguishing one act of violence from another, one "type" of Haitian from another, and ultimately committed violent acts in a variety of contexts; Louis Cukela, an immigrant to the United States, felt betrayed by having to be in Haiti and took it out on a group of Haitian prisoners. These marines grappled with the subjective and cultural dilemmas presented by the occupation. Some lost their heads, so to speak. So far, we have focused most directly on marines as they committed acts of violence, and as they considered what was at stake in committing these acts. Yet some marines (and sometimes these same marines) resolved the tension between recognizing and denying the humanity of the Haitian people by taking seriously the paternalist promises of the occupation. In doing so, however, these marines were not clear of the subjective difficulties facing their fellow soldiers, for there was more than one way to lose one's head in occupied Haiti.

Stories about men who allowed themselves, in various ways, to come close to Haiti and Haitians reveal something of the texture of the marines' subjective and emotional investments in whiteness, masculinity, and Americanness, that is, in their own identities. Marines who were captured by the Cacos, marines who joined the Gendarmerie and perhaps embraced too thoroughly their status as Haitian officers, marines who took up with Haitian women, and those who learned Creole and mixed easily with Haitians in conversation were apt to become the subjects of Marine Corps lore. Vehicles for the expression of marines' fears and preoccupations, such stories connected the threads of racial, gender, and nationalist discourses that framed the experience of marines in occupied Haiti. Perhaps this is why they became the stuff of Marine Corps legend, and, in turn, lent themselves to popular consumption back in the States as pulp horror fiction.

By addressing the fears and uncertainties raised by the myriad boundary crossings required of white men occupying a black nation, marines' horror stories served to shore up their racial, gender, and national identity. Returning home after a brief tour in Haiti in 1924, Lieutenant Arthur J. Burks parlayed these stories into lurid tales, laying the groundwork for his career as a popular and prolific pulp fiction writer.[133] In several stories, Burks's heroes were marines who, "following the lure which calls always to the adventurous," found themselves shuddering with terror in their "innermost being."[134] "As one with many another normal American," Burks wrote of his fictional Lloyd Chandler, "just to think of Haiti's short and bloody past was to be filled with horror and a nameless dread."[135] Burks's stories, and the lore from which he drew his material, enabled marines to mark the distance between themselves and Haitians when the logic of paternalism and the material fact of their presence in Haiti threatened to collapse that distance. Such stories were cautionary tales that affirmed whiteness and manhood as well as a sense of belonging to America. Ironically but predictably, similar stories, when told by Haitians, became yet another occasion for Americans to replay the paternalist narrative. Thus, upon hearing that Haitian peasants feared that Americans had come to cannibalize them, Colonel Russell reported to General Barnett, "The Haitians, as you no doubt know, are a very hysterical people. Hundreds of rumors are circulated among them daily that are simply ridiculous, but, like children, they believe them and," the colonel added, echoing the language of his own troops, "completely lose their heads."[136]

The most literal way for an American to lose his head in Haiti, according to Marine Corps lore, was to be captured by Haitians. An experienced Gendarmerie officer warned "Chesty" Puller, when he received his commission as a lieutenant in the Haitian constabulary, that the Cacos would bloody their wounded enemies: "They slash the face to ribbons, and tear the body apart. You will see."[137] Marines warned one another that they could lose their skin in Haiti, too, as we know, for example, from Frederick Spear's Senate testimony and from Lester Dessez's oral history interview. "It was a grim affair for those caught by the revolutionaries," recalled Brigadier General Dessez some years later, "for they were usually skinned alive."[138] Yet, tales of cannibalism were perhaps most frequent and certainly most detailed in blood and gore.

"Chesty" Puller was only one of many who recounted the story of Sergeant Lawrence Muth. Benoit Batraville was said to have eaten a piece of Muth's heart to obtain his courage and strength. In a letter to a friend back in the States, Puller wrote of Muth's death: "In the fight with the Cacos a few weeks back Muth got his. The Marines and Gendarmes left him when they retreated (damn them). I surely hope he was dead when the black men got to him. . . . The next day, a large force hiked over to the scene. There wasn't a piece of flesh or bone as large as my hand. His head is stuck up on the end of a pole somewhere now, out in the hills."[139] In his memoir, Puller told of his search for the truth of what happened to Muth. After "talking with literally hundreds of the bandits, hearing their versions of combats in which he had fought," Puller claimed to have learned about Muth from a "minor Caco chief" named Charlieuse. Puller attributes to Charlieuse these words: "We were four chiefs to make the sacrifice. As always we took off the head from the Leftenant, and cut up his body. . . . Then we opened the chest . . . and took out the heart. It was very large. And we ate of it, each of the four chiefs, to partake of the courage of your Leftenant Muth. It was a glorious day."[140] The considerable lore surrounding Sergeant Muth's death encompassed many versions of his story. The official history of Muth's regiment described the search for Muth's body as revealing "a gruesome discovery — the mutilated remains of Sergeant Lawrence Muth, minus the head and heart, the latter purportedly eaten by the Cacos."[141]

Yet, marines could lose themselves without even being captured. When Faustin Wirkus arrived in Perodin, for example, he was struck by the physical appearance of the Americans he met there. There were three marines serving as Gendarmerie officers at that location, Philip Neuhaus, Samuel Williston, and a man named Kelly; it was Williston who proudly stacked native hats on a pole to count the number of Haitians he had killed.[142] Wirkus later wrote: "They were unlike any marines, officers or men, I had ever seen. Their eyes were sunken in their heads. They had bedraggled, untrimmed whiskers; their uniforms hung about them, slack and creaseless. They wore native hats of plaited straw. (Their campaign hats had been lost in the jungles.)"[143] These marines, according to Wirkus, were transformed by their experience in the jungle with the Gendarmerie. They had lost their resemblance to other marines. With eyes "sunken in their heads," they, like Sergeant Virski and Lieutenant South, showed physical signs of wear. Like Virski and South, too, they had experienced a sort of moral breakdown; they committed, or ran the risk of committing, indiscriminate acts of violence.

Losing his likeness to other Americans, facing moral breakdown, a marine in the Gendarmerie risked losing his sense of himself. Wirkus tells us too that Neuhaus, Kelly, and Williston had changed hats. Having lost their "campaign hats" in the jungle, they had replaced these with the native equivalent. Wirkus's description makes literal one of the changes these men had undergone. By joining the Gendarmerie, they had changed hats; while they continued technically to serve in the Marines, they had become "Haitian" officers. They commanded Haitians; they lived and fought every day with, and against, Haitians. Their world had become Haitian.

John Houston Craige, who told the stories of Virski and South, at times feared that he was himself on the path to "nervous degeneration and collapse." He wrote, "all was going well with me, officially, but personally, I was beginning to be conscious of a change." Daily contact with Haitians, and participation in the affairs of their daily lives, Craige explained, had brought him too close to Haiti. "I worked and sweated and suffered with them, country-folks and townspeople, through rains and heat for more than three years. I ruled them and tried to civilize them. I saw them born, saw them die and went to their funerals."[144] Craige had accepted the paternalist mantle, but eventually it took its toll.

While Craige did not seem to fear becoming uncontrollably violent, he did notice he was beginning to believe some of the things he had previously considered "Voodoo" superstition. He felt that he "had got to know the Haitians too well" and it was beginning to affect his fundamental belief system. "The drums were always throbbing. . . . It wore on my nerves. Savage customs seldom fail to affect the nerves of a white man who stays long enough in a primitive country to begin to know too much about his savages."[145]

Figure 14. Faustin Wirkus with a Haitian man.
Marine Corps Research Center Archives, Quantico, Virginia.

Perhaps this is why, when asserting his sympathy for Haitians and his long-standing sympathy toward blacks in general, Craige managed to affirm his own identity in the same breath: "My family has lived in Pennsylvania for more than two hundred years and my father and his brothers fought in the Union Army."[146] Jack Craige felt he had to leave Haiti in order to remember who he was: a United States Marine Corps captain, but also an Episcopal minister, a journalist, a Philadelphian, and, through it all, a white man and an American.

Faustin Wirkus experienced some of the same tensions. Wirkus took over as the sole white Gendarmerie officer at Perodin after Neuhaus, Kelly, and Williston were called to other posts. Wirkus had been in this position at Perodin for five months, patrolling the area with gendarmes, then settling down "to routine duty," when he began to feel uneasy. "I was not right with myself," he wrote later. "I was worn down and bothered by months of hunting Cacos . . . [and by] the constant worry of breaking them up, driving [them] back, and killing them."[147] The tensions surrounding his own violence had worn him down, but there was more. He had been living and

Figure 15. Faustin Wirkus with a Haitian woman.
Marine Corps Research Center Archives, Quantico, Virginia.

fighting with Haitian gendarmes, and he characterized his role in paternal-ist terms that sounded much like Craige's: "Under the strain of acting as go-between for birth and death and after being father and big brother . . . to our Haitian friends, my weight alone had dropped from 160 to 135 pounds."[148] Like Craige, Wirkus recognized the tension between having sympathy for the Haitians and losing one's sense of oneself. Wirkus articu-lated that tension more pointedly than Craige. "I felt that I was, as we had a way of saying in the Marines, on the way to 'go native.' Now it is a good thing, as an administrator and a governor and as a policeman, to 'go native' so far as an understanding of the persons over whom one has jurisdiction is con-cerned. But it is a very bad thing to let that sympathy and understanding take the place of one's own natural common sense and training and educa-tion."[149] An American man serving at an isolated post in the Gendarmerie had to resist, in Wirkus's words, "becoming in his own consciousness an albino Haitian."[150]

Salty tales that passed around among marines and sailors featured men who had indeed given up their "own common sense and training and education" — generally to live with native women. "Marines who have seen Asiatic and South American or other far-flung service call those who fall victim to such influence 'beach combers,' " wrote Wirkus. "I had read a lot of such moral breakdowns."[151] Among the beachcombers who had "gone native" in Haiti, according to one leatherneck yarn, was a sailor who ended up at a Voodoo ceremony, drunk on rum and "spread out on some planks," with drums pounding and lighted candles all around. " 'Had a little money then,' " said the sailor to a young Marine Corps lieutenant, " 'and took up with a . . . gal living in a damn little mud and straw shack. Liquor was cheap, anyhow, and I sure swallowed plenty.' He scratched his head and spat reflectively to leeward. 'Might have been there yet if I'd kept my snoot out of that voodoo business. . . . Mind your step,' " the sailor warned, " 'even marines don't go fooling around with them . . . when they get on this voodoo stuff.' "[152]

Among the tales John Houston Craige related was a very different story about a beachcomber who thought of himself as a sort of racial missionary. The man claimed to have fathered 246 children in two years in an attempt to whiten the black race. "The negroes in the United States are nearly half white already," Craige quoted the man as saying, "in another 200 years there will be hardly any negroes, recognizable as such. The race problem will have disappeared. Meantime, it is the duty of every patriotic American and every white man who loves his race to speed the process." For Craige, this beachcomber was a man who had held on to his identity even as he was perceived by his countrymen as having disappeared into the native population. Telling his story, Craige seemed to be literalizing the relationship between paternalism and "going native." Yet, "white men," said Craige, "called him a 'white negro,' and considered him a disgrace."[153] "Taking up with" Haitian women, it seemed, would lead a man to disgrace or insanity if not to a more horrible end. No wonder Wirkus felt that he confronted an especially dangerous situation when he felt himself drawn to "Marie of Carzal." "I felt myself slipping," he wrote. "If there was one thing fixed in my mind, it was to stay away from Carzal — and Marie."[154]

The term "moral breakdown," as it was used by Faustin Wirkus, seems to have encompassed many possible meanings; it was a term with a great deal of slippage. Did it refer to the sorts of moral breakdown Josephus Daniels had in mind when he commented, "marines often immoral"? Did it refer to the kind of moral breakdowns that Sergeant Virski suffered, the breakdown of all distinctions between when and when not to shoot and kill natives, or between which natives to kill and which to protect? Did it refer to the kind of breakdown that led some American men to forget themselves and "go native"? Or were all these forms of moral breakdown somehow related? Did one imply the other? Wirkus's use of the term suggests that there were indeed connections, at least within the cultural framework available to marines in Haiti, between "going native" the way Williston did when he shot Haitians indiscriminately and "going native" the way Balutansky did when he took a Haitian wife.

Women may have seemed an important link in the process of going native because they often served as a key to intercultural contact. Women sometimes served as guides through areas of Haiti unknown to the marines.[155] Prostitutes, familiar with both the marines and the Cacos, sometimes helped the marines to identify insurgents. Haitian and other Caribbean women who lived with marines, moreover, helped them master the native tongue, a crucial step in the process of getting to know the people. L. Ton Evans told the Senate that he did not know "of a single case of an American living with a Haitian or colored woman, with the exception of some of the captains and lieutenants of American marines in the gendarmerie, and most of who in these cases were English-speaking Negro women from surrounding islands living in Haiti and able to assist white Americans with the native through the French patois."[156] Marines, furthermore, would sometimes refer to a woman who slept with a marine as a "sleeping dictionary."[157]

Learning Creole could transform a marine's relationship with gendarmes, prisoners, and local inhabitants. Overley's attempts at humanity in the field were made possible by his ability to speak directly to the Haitians he encountered. Marines who learned to converse in Creole improved their chances of reducing friction on a local, day-to-day level and enabled themselves to learn more about Haitians and Haitian culture. Breaking down some of the boundaries between marines and "natives," in turn, enabled marines to play paternalist roles in their adopted communities in Haiti. Considering marines' fears of losing hold of their own identity, this may not always have seemed like a positive thing.

While learning Creole could assist marines in improving relations with Haitians, it could also give them tools necessary for some military operations. The most extraordinary example of this was the capture and killing of Charlemagne Péralte.[158] According to official accounts, as well as Marine Corps lore, William R. Button and Herman H. Hanneken, commissioned respectively as a first lieutenant and a captain in the Gendarmerie, were sufficiently versed in Creole and knowledgeable about Haitian customs to pass as Haitians in order to penetrate a Caco camp and kill Péralte.[159] According to Craige, "Button was one of the most remarkable men we have ever had in the Gendarmerie. He could speak all varieties of Creole. He loved to wander in native disguises and could pass as a Haitian of any class.

Figure 16. Herman Hanneken and William R. Button of the Gendarmerie. Lieutenant Hanneken and Sergeant Button received medals from President Dartiguenave for capturing and killing Charlemagne Péralte. Marine Corps Research Center Archives, Quantico, Virginia.

One of his favorite disguises was that of a market-woman."[160] The evening of October 31, 1919, Hanneken and Button were said to have "stripped and blackened themselves all over with burnt cork."[161] Then they led a party of seventeen gendarmes, all disguised as Cacos, to raid the Caco leader's camp. The party carried Péralte's body out of the bush, and marines later circulated a photograph of the slain leader in "an attempt to demoralize the guerrillas." As historian Hans Schmidt has pointed out, however, the image became a symbol of Péralte's martyrdom and a "continuing source of inspiration to nationalists" (Figure 17).[162]

Herman Hanneken and William Button walked a fine line (as Burks would suggest). They learned enough about Haitians and their language to use it successfully against Haitians, without letting their (spatial or cultural) proximity to the "natives" get them first. Those who learned about the Haitians and used that knowledge not to defeat but to join Haitians in a paternalist project ran an even greater risk of losing their balance. In either case, marines perceived excessive contact with Haitians as a dangerous proposition. A closer look at stories about marines who were supposedly eaten by cannibals serves to demonstrate this point. For Lawrence Muth and Mike Morris, the two marines featured as victims in these stories, both made a point of learning Creole and familiarizing themselves with Haitian culture. Both marines also, as the stories go, expressed a good deal of sympathy for Haitians in general and Cacos in particular.

Muth learned Creole in order to gather intelligence useful for the campaigns against the Cacos in 1919 and 1920. Craige explained, "Muth threw himself heart and soul into the business of gaining information. He rapidly mastered the art of Creole conversation. He loved to gossip with country people and women of the market places. . . . Muth's sallies brought gales of laughter [from the market women]."[163] In some versions of the story of Sergeant Muth, he has a conversation with the Caco chief, Benoit Batraville, before he dies. Batraville speaks for Haitians when he says, "Mon general, you are a blanc and we are negres. We do not understand your ways and you do not understand ours. You came from over the water to fight us in our country. . . . We think you have come to take our country and make us slaves. We want to keep our country and our freedom. We intend to drive the blancs to the sea." Muth is said to have replied, "it is true that I am a blanc and you are negres, but I can see a little with Haitian eyes. . . . You are soldiers and it is right that you should fight for your country. . . . Only remember that if you kill me, other blancs will come."[164] Was learning to "see a little with Haitian eyes" Muth's fatal mistake?

In *Black Bagdad*, Craige tells Mike Morris's story as told to him by Ser-

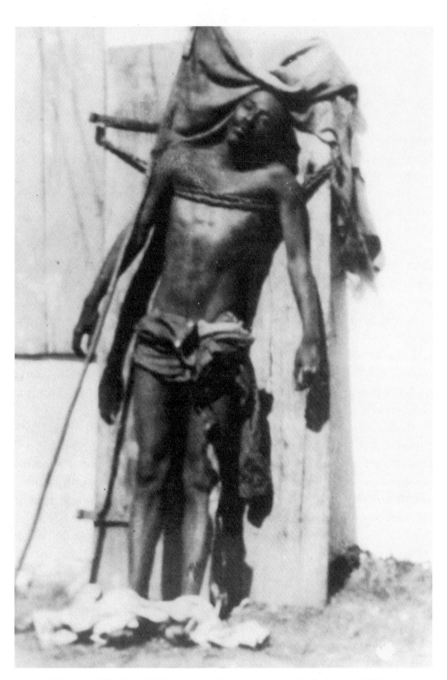

Figure 17. The body of Charlemagne Péralte, as it was displayed to the Haitian people. Marine Corps Research Center Archives, Quantico, Virginia.

geant Francis Patrick (Pat) Kelly, a captain in the Gendarmerie. "Mike tried to fraternize with the natives around Hinche and the prisoners. He told them he was their brother and he wanted to be kind to them. . . . He spoke a little French and soon picked up enough Creole to get along. . . . He loved to play the harmonica . . . [and] soon picked up a lot of the native meringues and learned a lot about their meaning." Mike's parents and teachers, Kelly explained, began "preparing him for the cannibal's pot" from an early age, by raising him to believe in nonresistance. Yet, when the United States entered the world war, he became a marine, because he felt the cause was just, and "in spite of his teachings, he had a good bit of manhood." When the war ended, Mike Morris landed in Haiti, despite his beliefs. He believed, according to Kelly, that "we had no business in Haiti; that the occupation was imperialism and tyranny." According to Pat Kelly, Mike Morris "was a consistent idealist, and they ate him for it."[165]

According to these stories, Morris and Muth, for different reasons, learned about the Haitians and developed sympathetic perspectives with which to view the conflict with the Cacos. Perhaps these stories of cannibalism were cautionary tales for marines who risked being consumed by another culture. Cannibalism reminded marines, with the force of deeply felt emotion, to be vigilant about maintaining boundaries, even, or especially, when they themselves were breaching those boundaries. The stories of Muth and Morris suggest that the salience of cannibalism for marines had something to do with the fragility of national and racial identity in a paternalist occupation.

Arthur J. Burks wove several lurid tales from the various threads of Marine Corps legend and lore associated with Haiti. Populated with unlucky marines captured and skinned alive, brave white men who black their skin to penetrate the Haitian "jungle" and avenge the deaths of their murdered and mutilated buddies, lustful and dangerous ebony women, and Haitian politicians who turn out to be Voodoo-worshiping cannibals, these stories rejected out of hand the logic of paternalism.[166] There was nothing in these stories of that condescending affection some marines expressed toward Haitian peasants. Burks had one protagonist use the phrase "the poor fellow" to refer to a Haitian man, the villain of the piece, but the reference comes only after "the poor fellow" is found dead at the bottom of a cliff, "mashed beyond all human resemblance."[167] The terms with which Burks and his American heroes described live Haitians uniformly conveyed the most pointed hatred and derision, straight from the lexicon of homegrown racism; they were "dull and stupid" beings, "beasts of prey," vengeful "master-rogues," great black brutes, aged idiots, and loathsome women.[168]

The white men in Burks's stories were marines who came dangerously close to Haiti — too close, in some cases. They were brave and curious young men, beckoned by distant fires and drums, who ventured forth in search of "answers to strange questions which no white man had ever asked."[169] "One of them lies at this moment in a distant cemetery," wrote Burks in a story called "Black Medicine"; "his nude body was found on the hillside which supports Petionville, mutilated as though it had been torn by the remorseless fangs of wild beasts."[170] In "Voodoo," Burks described more precisely the brutal murder of a young bugler, Charlie "Music" Hepner. His "clothing had been stripped from his body and the little Music had literally been skinned alive! From just above his ankles the flesh had been cut to the bone and stripped off over his feet, apparently, as the hunter skins the hide from a rabbit's leg!"[171] Here, then, was the fear expressed by Frederick Spear and Lester Dessez, rendered in rather gory detail.

It was, perhaps, redundant for Burks to specify, in "Black Medicine," that the soldier's body was "nude" while also telling his readers that the body was torn to shreds. His attention to detail in "Voodoo" was perhaps more logical, yet still notable. For the image of American men stripped bare in the wilds of Haiti resonates with marines' repeated references to the uniforms that clothed them as marines and as gendarmes. It was, after all, in part the state of Williston's uniform — "hung about [him], slack and creaseless" — that alarmed Wirkus when he first arrived at Perodin. And the legendary William Button, who with Herman Hanneken succeeded in infiltrating a Caco camp to capture Charlemagne Péralte, prepared himself in part by learning Creole and donning Haitian garb. Button even, in some cases, engaged in a kind of double cross-dressing, when he passed, or so said some, as a Haitian market woman. In another of Burks's stories, moreover, he refers to beachcombers as men "outside the uniform and without visible means of support" who have become "pariahs" in the eyes of other white men.[172] The marine's uniform, a sign of status, identity, and American authority, marked white men's bodies in crucial ways. It was, in a sense, another layer of whiteness, saturated also with military masculinity and emblems of national identity. When marines gave it up — by allowing themselves to be "clothed" instead with "the authority of the Haitian state," by losing their sense of discipline in the field, or by searching for answers to questions white men should not ask — they risked being stripped of the signs it carried. Thus the stripping and subsequent skinning of Charlie Hepner were two steps in the same process. Together, they vividly illustrated the danger of losing one's white skin, and all the gendered and national meanings associated with it, in the so-called jungles of Haiti.[173]

The white men who sought to avenge these deaths, these challenges to American men's authority and status in Haiti, also had to venture into dangerous territory. They, too, ran risks as they crossed boundaries. In "Voodoo," Rodney Davis sets out to find the monster responsible for the death and mutilation of his "young friend and protege," Charlie Hepner.[174] To do so, he must first go to Port-au-Prince "to study the patois" and, with no uniform to distinguish him from a self-exiled beachcomber, he must mix with the population and learn enough to identify and locate Hepner's killer.[175] Burks describes Davis's fear as distinct from any possibility of hesitation on the field of battle. "Death in itself is not so horrible to a soldier. In the field he walks always by the monster's side, growing callous to the thought of dying, even with his boots on, unshriven. But when death is attended with such gory details as those which attended little Hepner, it is something else again."[176] In "Black Medicine," Burks explains his protagonist's fearlessness when faced with the facts of the Petionville murder. "Chandler, a true American, had a duty to perform, perhaps some lives to save; and the knowledge that this was so drove all lesser thoughts from his mind."[177] Moreover, "he did not wish to be known, even to himself, as a chap who feared the shadows."[178] Yet, in both stories, the heroes, too, begin to face the dissolution of boundaries. As Chandler "visualized back country jungles which had never known the touch of a white man's boot," it was as if "something of the awesome and menacing spirit of the Black Republic seemed to enter into him."[179] And in "Voodoo," by the time Davis arrives at the site of a Voodoo ceremony, now accompanied by his fellow marines, he has begun to take on the lust for violence and revenge that characterized more naturally the monster he sought. "Even before they had reached the scene, each man knew that he was soon to look upon some unspeakable horror. And not the least of the horrors was the appearance of Davis himself. He had become in a few moments a graven marble image, cold as starshine, with eyes that saw but one thing, that recognized neither superior nor bunkie. A creature with but one aim in life and no hope beyond that aim. An automaton. A mechanical creature made to rend and destroy."[180] Finally, when Davis sets out on the trail to find and kill Cerimarie Sam, "the greatest monster in all of Haiti," he does so, in a riff on the story of Hanneken and Button, with "every inch of his skin dyed ebony, lips thickened with injections of parafin."[181]

Burks paints Cerimarie Sam's monstrosity in vivid colors. Who is this black man who deprives the American of his white skin? Davis finds his answer, predictably, in a Voodoo temple. A Voodoo priestess (or, Maman Loi) sets the scene in which the full extent of Sam's monstrosity will be revealed. Burks describes the dance of the priestess in lurid prose, then asserts: "The lust of the beast is clean because it is natural. The natural emotion of man is clean because it is sacred. But the lust expressed in the dance of the Maman Loi was the lust of a man or woman for a beast— horrible, revolting, inexpressible in words."[182] For Burks, such a horror, "inexpressible in words," could be expressed only through the figure of a black woman of unrestrained sexuality.

In another story, Burks explains the usefulness of the evil priestess as a device for evoking what he calls "that nameless dread" that filled white men's hearts when they thought of Haiti: "An evil man is a common thing, for there are many such, and of various degrees of evil. Yet it seems that there are no depths too deep for a woman who has penetrated the veil of evil. For that reason an evil woman seems to typify unmentionable horror— especially if she be a voodoo priestess."[183] This is precisely the function of the priestess in the story called "Voodoo": to express the "inexpressible," to mention the "unmentionable." What follows is the usual absurd and quasi-pornographic account of a Voodoo ceremony: the priest (Cerimarie Sam) brings in the "goat without horns" for sacrifice (in this case, a "nude girl of sixteen or so"), opens a vein in her neck, inciting blood frenzy in the gathered crowd, and the ceremony proceeds, "to its inevitable conclusion. . . . Men and women, one with the other, forced themselves far, far down below the level of beasts — in the name of the most terrible religion."[184] For Burks, Voodoo is without question or hesitation "the most terrible religion"; it signifies the absence of that ordered sexuality on which civilization ultimately rests.

When Cerimarie Sam approaches Rodney Davis, the American marine reacts instantly, leaping "atop the monster, this beast in human guise that murdered children; who had children by whatsoever woman he desired and attended none of them; who had even offered some of these children, on occasion, as sacrifices to the serpent."[185] With Rodney Davis's righteous attack, then, Burks puts a fine point on the evil of Cerimarie Sam and the horror of Voodoo. It is child-murder, it is the violent rejection and destruction of the family by the Haitian man, it is the destructive lust expressed in the figure of a black woman who represents both blackness and female sexuality unleashed.

Burks's Haiti was a site of sexual excess, gender disorder, and primitive savagery; it was a land characterized by the effective absence of the family as a basis for social order. In Burks's telling, the grotesque horror of Haiti showed the obvious and urgent need for American rule there. At the same time, Burks's story foregrounded the danger inherent in such a place as he

OCCUPATION

described: the consequence of failing to reign in black and female excesses was evident in the death of Charlie Hepner, whose white identity was violently ripped from him.

VIOLENCE AND PATERNALISM

Paternalism called on marines to take up a variety of roles in Haiti as if they were an integral part of a Haitian family. When they first arrived, marines participated in military campaigns against insurgents, officially understood as wayward children who required discipline. Teaching the Cacos a lesson also enabled the Marine Corps to represent its actions as protective of most Haitians, viewed as *bons habitants,* or good citizens. The rhetoric of paternalism rested on the separation of insurgents from the majority of the population. Although this condition, according to American rhetoric, had existed all along, it was, in fact, produced by the violent but sanctioned actions of the marines.

After defeating the Cacos in 1916, marines turned to the project of building a viable infrastructure and creating the social and political stability necessary to support economic investment in Haiti. U.S. officials saw two innovations as crucial to this project: a native constabulary, officered and trained by Americans, and a corvée to make possible the construction of a network of passable roads. As occupation officials pursued these two measures, however, U.S. marines confronted head on the difficulties of their new roles. Taking up posts around the country, American Gendarmerie officers moved into Haitian communities, enforced the occupation's vision of an improved Haitian society, and confronted growing resistance on the part of the inhabitants. They grappled with the implications of living in Haiti for an extended period of time, knowing little, but perhaps learning, about Haitian culture, getting to know individual gendarmes and other residents, fearing the Cacos, sometimes wanting to be elsewhere, and acting on, or confronting, one way or another, their own beliefs about race and national identity. At the same time, they followed orders predicated on a set of analytical distinctions that were in the process of breaking down. The incidence of physical violence in Haiti was a logical consequence of these tensions.

These events did not occur in the same ways all over Haiti. Local conditions and individual personalities led some aspects of the process to be emphasized in one district or town, others elsewhere. Yet the paternalist project of the occupation laid the groundwork for these tensions everywhere in Haiti, and the creation of an American-officered Gendarmerie heightened the tensions that some marines would face. As the Mayo Court suggested in its 1920 report, marines who served in the Gendarmerie faced particularly difficult challenges. Lieutenant Adolph Miller's reaction on hearing that there would soon be positions available in the constabulary was telling: no amount of money would persuade him to take on such an ambiguous role.

Having examined U.S. American violence in Haiti — in its various forms — in light of the subjective experiences, fears, and concerns of individual marines, let us consider the interpretations of violence offered by contemporary commentators on, and participants in, the occupation. Was the marines' violence evidence of a bald attempt by the United States to subdue a foreign nation for the purposes of economic exploitation and strategic advantage, as Walter Carrier and other radicals believed? Was some amount of individual violence the inevitable result of human nature even in a regulated situation, as the Mayo Court reported? Or, as James Weldon Johnson suggested, was American violence in Haiti the expression abroad of racism learned at home? Did the absence of white women and the presence of women of color have anything at all to do with the violence? Was there, as Craige suggested, something in the circumstances of the occupation that led men, systematically, to crack?

The violent acts of U.S. marines in Haiti were not simply the isolated acts of individuals, nor were they simply the direct expression of an official and systematic imperialism. The first explanation ignores the context of sanctioned violence and the breakdown of meaning separating the sanctioned and the unsanctioned. The second tells us nothing about how individual men or groups of men were conscripted into an official process that masked, but rested upon, violence. Explaining these acts as the obvious consequence of sending racist marines to Haiti is also insufficient. Marines were shaped by the racism of their particular regional, class, and cultural contexts as well as by the racism of the Marine Corps itself. They necessarily brought racist constructs and dispositions with them to Haiti, but American men did not simply export domestic racism. The experience of going to Haiti, living and fighting in the occupation, and grappling with the conflicting dictates of paternalism and violent repression had profound effects on the marines' racism: bringing it to consciousness for some, reinforcing it for others, challenging some aspects of it for many. American racial constructs were transformed and reinforced in specific and significant ways in Haiti.

Perhaps John Houston Craige's understanding of the place of violence in the occupation is most illuminating. For while his analysis rested on a Darwinian concept of race, he acknowledged and explored the subjective processes that attended an individual American man's participation in the larger project of the occupation. He saw violence, not as an isolated, individual phenomenon, but as part of a broader systematic process. Craige presented that process in biological terms; his stories nonetheless bring to light important links between individual subjective processes and broader cultural dynamics. Those links remind us, in turn, that imperialism can never be an unmediated expression of armed might. Culture, consciousness, and identity both direct and are affected by, among other things, the taking up of arms and the harming of human bodies.

Physical violence in occupied Haiti was part of a cultural process brought on by the unequal meeting of these two "nations," the United States and Haiti. "Going native," to various degrees in various contexts, was part of that same process. The official dictates of a paternalist occupation sent marines off on paths that would lead at one bend toward violence, at another toward a loss of self, and in some places toward both. Individual men found their way through the maze that process created, sometimes doing untold damage along the way. By the time they left Haiti, they were transformed in significant ways, and so too were the two nations transformed.

AFTERMATH

HAITI'S APPEAL

HAITI GETS AN AUDIENCE

If marines in Haiti, through daily contact with a people they considered primitive, confronted the fragility of their own "civilized" selves, they also provided avenues for other U.S. Americans to have a version of that experience without leaving the country. For their presence in Haiti, and the resistance it engendered, called attention to the "black republic" in the United States. And as U.S. citizens (and consumers) took an interest in Haitian affairs, Haiti became not only a point of protest, but also, with new vigor, an object of cultural fascination — indeed, an object of desire, a valuable commodity. Haiti's cachet derived in part from the ways in which it came to serve as a means for negotiating the politics of race, gender, sexuality, and national identity. Its career in U.S. American culture illustrates the process by which a foreign intervention could itself intervene in domestic cultural politics.

This chapter examines the particular historical moment in which Haiti came to the attention of the American public and begins to chart the subsequent path of Haiti's career in the United States. We begin with James Weldon Johnson and Eugene O'Neill, the two writers whose work shaped that initial moment, in different but overlapping ways. The complex cultural politics embedded in Johnson's journalism and O'Neill's hit play, *The Emperor Jones*, helps us understand the appeal of Haiti as it took shape in 1920 and developed over the course of the next two decades. Relations of power at work in the occupation facilitated U.S. Americans' appropriation of Haitian themes, and such cultural appropriations in turn effaced those very relations of power. The chapter closes with a consideration of two popular cultural texts, a novel and a film, that illustrate how Haiti continued to serve as a means to negotiate domestic cultural politics in the United

States. Throughout this chapter, we will be concerned with the tensions between political protest and cultural fascination, between critique and commodification.

In 1920 Haitian nationalists and their U.S. allies finally got a hearing in the United States. Haitian leaders had attempted to get Washington's attention earlier, most notably at Versailles, where Wilson claimed to stand for the rights of small nations everywhere, but to no avail. Journalists posted to Haiti were also hobbled in their attempts to get word out about what was going on in that particular small nation, as one Associated Press correspondent told Herbert Seligmann of the *Nation* in April 1920. "Owing to military censorship," he "had found it impossible in the preceding three years . . . to send a single cable dispatch concerning military operations in Haiti to the United States."[1] As one frustrated civil rights activist asserted, "Who knows what we're doing [in Haiti]? No newspaper tells us, and of our self-appointed trusteeship no account is rendered to us or by us."[2]

A few newspapers and magazines did express disapproval of U.S. intervention in Haiti right from the start.[3] By 1917 a few more Americans had become disenchanted with the occupation; in February of that year, the *Nation* initiated its editorial protests, which would henceforth be consistent.[4] "This is imperialism of the rankest kind," wrote Oswald Garrison Villard, the magazine's editor. In the next couple of years, word of the marines' irregularities filtered back to the States, and by 1920 most journalists caught on that something was seriously amiss with Washington's plan for benevolent assistance to the black republic.[5] Missionaries were key players in this process. AME Minister S. E. Churchstone-Lord made a plea for change to Secretary of State Lansing as early as October 1915 and subsequently reported on the occupation in the Chicago *Defender*.[6] By 1918 the white evangelist L. Ton Evans of the Lott Carey Mission Society was also an outspoken critic of the occupation.[7]

But if evidence against the occupation was mounting, other changes were at least equally significant in turning the tide of public opinion. As Brenda Plummer has argued, "the timing of the occupation was especially significant." By 1918 and 1919 a rising militancy growing out of African Americans' experience with the war in Europe, and sparked by the violence that met black soldiers upon their return to the States, occasioned a shift in African Americans' perspective on Haiti. "The spirit of the times made Haiti an important issue," according to Plummer; "the Bloody Summers of 1918 and 1919, the agitation for a federal anti-lynching bill, and the rise of militant nationalism put racial matters at the forefront."[8] And as African Americans' perspectives shifted, their protests played an increasing role in making Haiti a matter of public controversy.

At last, with the heat of a presidential election campaign as a catalyst, marines' casual comments about their own actions in Haiti began to reverberate in churches and meeting halls, in press rooms and legislative offices, back in the States. Journalists and concerned citizens alike took up the pen to express their dismay over what Seligmann called a "militarist and imperialist burlesque" on the ideals for which the United States fought in the Great War.[9] In 1918 James Weldon Johnson had managed to interest Theodore Roosevelt in this Democratic foreign policy debacle. Now, with elections coming, the Republican Party supported Johnson's fact-finding mission to Haiti, and Candidate Harding took up the cudgel in his campaign for the presidency.[10]

As Johnson's activism picked up steam, Eugene O'Neill turned his attention to Haiti as well. He got hold of several histories of Haiti and became fascinated by stories of black kings and emperors. Then, drawing on the history and mythology associated with Haiti's King Henri Christophe, as well as on his own experiences abroad, O'Neill crafted a dramatic representation of the consequences of one man's imperial grab for power in the Caribbean. His fate, like the fate that some white men in Haiti just then feared, was the dissolution of his civilized self in the face of "formless fears." *The Emperor Jones* centered not on white marines, however, but on a black man, an escaped convict turned emperor of a West Indian island, thanks to his boast that he could be killed only by a silver bullet. The action takes place on the day of his fall from power, and the play chronicles his flight through the forest and his simultaneous psychological degeneration.[11] A complex and contradictory text, *The Emperor Jones* conveyed a radical critique of imperialism as economic exploitation even as it participated in the discourses of civilization and exotic primitivism that sustained the occupation in Haiti. Yet, despite its critical elements, the play ultimately served to erase the relations of power that enabled imperialist theft and helped to turn Haiti into a salable commodity in the United States.

O'Neill's play provides a window onto U.S. America's renewed fascination with Haiti in the 1920s. Haiti would become salable especially because of its uses for white Americans, the ways it seemed to facilitate white struggles with modern selfhood. But the complex racial implications of the play, as well as its gender politics, illustrate the appeal of Haiti for African Americans, too. Viewed side by side with Johnson's important articles and with a series of subsequent popularizations of the story of Haiti's King Henri

Christophe, O'Neill's play begins to show us how the gender and race constructs of paternalism would be both reinforced and deconstructed, variously, in an unpredictable chain of cultural events precipitated by the imperialist moment, that is, both by its acts of domination and by their critique. But before we turn to the dramatic and cultural dynamics of *The Emperor Jones*, let us first consider James Weldon Johnson's road to Haiti, his discussion of the occupation, and his representation of the Haitian people in his series for the *Nation*, "Self-Determining Haiti."

JAMES WELDON JOHNSON'S HAITI

James Weldon Johnson was not the first African American to speak out for Haiti, but once he set his mind to the task, he was a most determined ally. By July 1915, when the marines landed, Johnson had made a name for himself as a poet, a songwriter, a novelist, and a journalist. He was a member of the NAACP and, as writer of the *New York Age* editorial page, he was, to use his own term, a key "propagandist" for the race.[12] Yet Haiti passed many months under U.S. rule before Johnson was moved to protest. That Johnson was not only a writer and a race leader but also a former diplomat no doubt influenced his thinking. Having served as U.S. consul in Puerto Cabello, Venezuela, and Corinto, Nicaragua, he was used to thinking in terms of the United States' strategic interests.[13] During his time in Nicaragua, moreover, he had himself been "part of the military and diplomatic machinations" of U.S. policy, for he played a key role during the Marines' 1912 landing at Corinto and subsequent action to maintain a pro–United States government in Managua.[14] In 1915, Johnson urged black Americans not to jump to the conclusion that U.S. intervention in Haiti represented merely another instance of white racism, pointing instead to the clear problem of Haitian political instability.[15] In the immediate aftermath of the marines' arrival in the black republic he wrote in the *Age*, "each time [Haiti] suffers from revolution and lawlessness we experience a feeling of almost personal disappointment."[16] Thus, Johnson, like most Americans, was slow to criticize U.S. policy in Haiti.

In December 1916, however, Johnson became the new field secretary of the NAACP, which brought him into close association with both blacks and whites who took a different view of the occupation. W. E. B. Du Bois, editor of the *Crisis*, the NAACP organ, had been quick to respond to the new occupation.[17] Du Bois wrote to Wilson, within days of the invasion, urging him to do nothing without "the cordial support of the Haytian people" nor without assuring "ten million American citizens of Negro descent . . . that we have no designs on the political independence of the island and no desire to exploit it ruthlessly for the sake of selfish business interests here."[18] Moorfield Storey, a longtime anti-imperialist activist and the (white) president of the NAACP, was also outraged by the Marines' invasion of Haiti and hoped to whip up popular protest. But, as he lamented to a friend in September 1915, "it is very hard to get people to consider anything except the war" in Europe.[19] In contrast, Booker T. Washington — patron of the *New York Age* — offered only muted criticism of the occupation.[20] He expressed concern over the marines' racism and the danger of their "shooting civilization" into Haitians, but he saw the occupation as a necessary evil, a result of Haitians' own failures.[21] Du Bois later commented on this approach, which Johnson had also taken at the *Age*: African Americans "must cease to think of Liberia and Haiti as failures in government," he wrote. "These are [among] the pictures of each other which white people have painted for us and which with engaging naiveté we accept, and then proceed to laugh at each other and criticize each other before we make any attempt to learn the truth."[22]

In the next couple of years, as Johnson was settling into his new post as NAACP field secretary, the political atmosphere of New York's African American communities shifted in crucial ways. On a world scale, the U.S. entry into World War I in April 1917 and the Russian Revolution in November of that same year both played a role in transforming racial politics. Marcus Garvey's Universal Negro Improvement Association (UNIA), founded in Jamaica a few years earlier, established a base in Harlem in 1917. More locally, but with profound implications, the same year also saw the founding of another new institution in Harlem: A. Philip Randolph and Chandler Owen's socialist publication, the *Messenger*. Randolph and Owen, who had made names for themselves as soapbox orators, put forth a bold challenge to established African American leadership. "Patriotism has no appeal to us," they wrote in their inaugural issue, "justice has. Party has no weight with us; principle has. Loyalty is meaningless; it depends on what one is loyal to."[23] The inaugural issue also carried a short story by Lovett Fort-Whiteman about a Haitian woman who avenges her lover's death at the hands of an American marine.[24] Fort-Whiteman's tale pointedly conveyed the radical paper's opposition to the occupation, in keeping with the editors' critique of capitalist and imperialist wars.[25] Garvey's UNIA, and its newspaper, the *Negro World*, called for black initiative and racial unity and tapped the history of Haiti as a means to convey their message. "[W]e have achieved nothing by way of our own initiative," Garvey told an audience in 1919, "we have achieved nothing, except in the Republic of Haiti, where one Negro repelled [the white man] and established an independent republic." Garvey thanked God for Toussaint L'Ouverture, and drew a parallel between the work of that singularly great black leader and the work now facing the UNIA. Whereas he "was able to inspire the other men of his country to carry on the work until Haiti was made a free country, so today we have inspired not one, not two, but hundreds of thousands to carry out the work even if they imprison one or kill one."[26]

In this changing political context, Johnson began to reevaluate his position on Haiti. News of American "undershirt diplomacy" in the matter of Haiti's constitution now seemed to wake him to the travesty that was being played out in the name of strategic necessity and benevolent guidance. Indeed, he began to see the occupation, just as he had warned others not to see it, as whole-cloth white racism, linked intimately with the domestic racism he was determined to outflank. Thus, by 1918 — still well before most others — Johnson took up the cause of Haitian self-determination.[27] As his organization sought the means to press for change in U.S. policy, Johnson approached Theodore Roosevelt, and later Hamilton Fish Jr., of the Republican Party, to seek support for an investigative trip to occupied Haiti.[28] The venture failed to materialize in 1918, but two years later Johnson was on his way to Haiti for a two-month investigation.

In Haiti, Johnson met with Haitian leaders in Port-au-Prince, from President Dartiguenave and lesser officials of the occupation government to disaffected politicians and dissident nationalist leaders. He also traveled to the interior and talked with peasants in the countryside. Both the urban elite and the rural peasantry made a positive impression on him. He talked, too, with U.S. marines, who spoke casually of rape, killing, and torture.[29] "Many of the things which the Haitians rightfully consider cruel and brutal," Johnson wrote in his report to the NAACP Board of Directors, "American marines consider, I might say funny."[30] Of the marines serving in the Gendarmerie he wrote, "Many of these men are rough, uncouth, and uneducated, and a great number from the South, are violently steeped in color prejudice."[31] But Johnson did not lay blame solely with racist marines; indeed, his analysis of the occupation featured prominently the "most sinister" role of the National City Bank in making U.S. Haitian policy.[32] "To know the reasons for the present political situation in Haiti," he began his exposé, "it is necessary, among other things, to know that the National City Bank of New York is very much interested in Haiti."[33] To counter such sinister forces, Johnson urged Haitian nationalist leaders to organize "without distinction as to party" and to come together "for the defense of their interests."[34] Johnson's visit to Haiti inaugurated a crucial alliance between the Patriotic Union, which had been founded by Georges Sylvain in the immediate wake of the invasion, and the NAACP.[35]

Back in the States, Johnson became an indefatigable champion of Haitian independence. In addition to writing his series for the *Nation*, Johnson pressed the issue with Republicans in Congress, including Henry Cabot Lodge and Medill McCormick; reached out across the political divide by contacting Marcus Garvey; worked in coalition with anti-imperialist whites in the Popular Government League and the Foreign Policy Association; founded, with Moorfield Storey, the Haiti–Santo Domingo Independence Society; and spoke to numerous African American clubs and organizations to foster protest against the occupation.[36] Johnson's work for Haiti inspired and encouraged protest from an impressive array of prominent activists, reformers, and public figures, including Mary Church Terrell, Nannie Helen Burroughs, Mary McLeod Bethune, Addie Hunton, Helena Hill Weed, Felix Adler, Henry Sloan Coffin, Ernest Gruening, Felix Frankfurter, Emily Greene Balch, Paul H. Douglas, and Lewis S. Gannett, among others.[37]

Most crucially, in the summer and fall of 1920 Johnson cultivated Warren G. Harding's interest in Haiti, particularly once it became clear that this was the single issue, among all those put forth by the NAACP for the Republican platform, in which the candidate showed any interest.[38] Harding saw the Haitian question, Johnson later wrote, as a "gift right off the Christmas tree."[39] With Johnson's help, he made political capital of Wilson's most glaring foreign policy contradiction, opening it up to public view on a broader scale than ever before. Harding's harassment of the Democrats also helped to force Secretary of the Navy Josephus Daniels, at long last, to institute the naval inquiry headed by Admiral Mayo.[40] A more thorough airing of American wrongs came with the full-scale Senate inquiry of late 1921 and early 1922, headed by Medill McCormick. Neither one resulted in the changes that Johnson and others at the NAACP hoped to bring about, but both helped to bring Haiti more fully into the public eye.

While Johnson's party politicking and coalition building challenged the occupation politically, his series for the *Nation* sought to undermine its ideological framework. "Self-Determining Haiti" challenged paternalism not simply by emphasizing the marines' brutality, or by pointing to a bank's self-interest, but more generally by seeking to shift readers' point of view on U.S. policy. Johnson invited his readers to understand Haitian perspectives on the occupation in ways that were unimaginable within the paternalist frame. He showed Haitians not as grateful (or, for that matter, ungrateful) wards, but as fully competent political subjects who had explicitly and repeatedly refused to grant control of Haitian affairs to the United States. Haitians saw, according to Johnson, that what Americans wanted they would take by brute force, and that, in keeping with that observation, the U.S.-imposed convention of 1916 "demands everything of Haiti and gives nothing."[41] They saw, too, that their long-standing constitutional provision barring alien land ownership was rooted soundly in the very principle of self-determination that the United States invoked as it went about forcibly overturning that provision. (Johnson also implicitly contrasted the logic of Haiti's now defeated laws against alien land ownership with their more nefarious counterparts in California.)[42]

Haitian perspectives on progress, as it was embodied in assistance offered by the occupation, structured Johnson's exposé. Thus while "the building of the road from Port-au-Prince to Cape Haitian" figured as "the most important achievement" of the occupation in the second of four articles, Johnson offered his readers a view of the road, not from the seat of an automobile, but rather from the perspective of the pedestrian whose primary assets, a donkey and two pigs, had just been run down.[43] He also asked his readers to see the implications of the road for Haitians "of education and culture," like "Charlemagne Péralte [who] was forced to work in convict garb on the streets of Cape Haitian."[44] "From the point of view of the National City Bank," Johnson wrote in his third article, "the institution has not only done nothing which is not wholly legitimate, proper, and according to the canons of big business throughout the world, but has actually performed constructive and generous service to a backward and uncivilized people in attempting to promote their railways, to develop their country, and to shape soundly their finance. That Mr. Farnham and those associated with him hold these views sincerely, there is no doubt. But that the Haitians, after over 100 years of self-government and liberty, contemplating the slaughter of 3,000 of their sons, the loss of their political and economic freedom, without compensating advantages which they can appreciate, feel very differently, is equally true."[45]

Johnson challenged paternalism most pointedly by calling attention to the implications of the occupation for Haitian families. Whereas Wilhelm F. Jordan and other supporters of the occupation suggested that Haiti's problems stemmed, at least in part, from a lax sexual order in which marriage meant little, Johnson emphasized, throughout his analysis, the destruction of the Haitian family by U.S. policies and actions. Discussing the central issue of Haitian finances, for example, Johnson asserted that, "for over a hundred years [Haiti] scrupulously paid its external and internal debt . . . until five years ago when under the financial guardianship of the United States interest on both the internal and, with one exception, external debt was defaulted."[46] France held most of the external debt and, being under obligation to the United States itself, could not protest. The internal debt, however, was held by Haitian citizens, Johnson explained, Haitian government bonds being more or less equivalent to "United States, state, and municipal bonds." "Non-payment of these securities," Johnson asserted, "has placed many families in absolute want."[47]

If U.S. financial policy in Haiti, dictated by the National City Bank, thus dealt damaging blows to middle-class and upper-class Haitian families, peasant families in the countryside were even more vulnerable to the ravages of the occupation. Discussing the corvée, Johnson likened American action to "the African slave raids of past centuries." "And slavery it was," he wrote, "though temporary. By day or by night, from the bosom of their families, from their little farms . . . Haitians were seized and forcibly taken to toil for months in far sections of the country. Their terror-stricken families meanwhile were often in total ignorance of the fate of their husbands, fathers, brothers."[48] Likening the occupation to slavery specifically in its destruction of the black family, Johnson undermined U.S. claims to paternalism. Whereas pro-occupation writers figured Haiti as an orphan in need of a foster father, Johnson wrote, in contrast, "if the United States should leave Haiti today, it would leave more than a thousand widows and orphans of its own making."[49]

In an article in the *Crisis*, Johnson took another swing at the conceit of paternalism. If contemporary Haitian fathers were killed and kidnapped by U.S. Marines, the occupation could not so readily deprive Haitians of their historical fathers. Answering the question of Haiti's paternity that was implied by the discourse of paternalism, Johnson said, in effect, Haiti has concrete evidence of a most impressive father, one of the founding fathers of the Haitian revolution: King Henri Christophe. That evidence could be seen in Christophe's Citadel, built "in the first decade of the nineteenth-century . . . to quarter 30,000 soldiers" and "to serve as a stronghold against the French," should they return "to retake Haiti."[50] Johnson recalled his visit to the Citadel: "As I stood on the highest point, where the sheer drop from the walls was more than two thousand feet, and looked out over the rich plains of Northern Haiti, I was impressed with the thought that, if ever a man had the right to feel himself a king, that man was Christophe when he walked around the parapets of his citadel."[51] Haiti, Johnson made quite clear, was not lacking founding fathers; Christophe's Citadel, which he urged Americans to visit, stood as a monument to a proud Haitian paternity. Johnson's critique of the occupation, then, rested on the damage done to Haitian fathers and their families by the U.S. military presence; his defense of Haiti likewise stood firm on the proud patriarchal heritage of the Haitian past.

The ideology of black masculinity expressed in Johnson's portrait of Christophe employed class and gender codes to further racial goals. In 1906, as an African American man representing the U.S. consulate in Puerto Cabello, Venezuela, Johnson had been frustrated by his observation that Venezuelan men of obvious African ancestry achieved significant accomplishments in education and statesmanship without identifying themselves in terms of race.[52] In Henri Christophe, by contrast, Johnson found a "race man" to top all others.[53] A proud black man committed to defending the black nation he had fathered, Christophe was, for Johnson, the truest kind of man, a man who "had the right to feel himself a king." Like Christophe himself, Johnson linked his claims to black manhood with claims to European-style civilization.

Johnson's critique of exoticism, like his critique of paternalism, also relied on this link between manliness and civilization. In response to those who would denigrate Haitian men on the basis of their nation's supposed primitivism, Johnson emphasized Haiti's likeness to Europe. In contrast to the Spanish influence one finds in Latin America, he remarked, "Port-au-Prince is rather a city of the French or Italian Riviera. . . . Cosmopolitan yet quaint, with an old-world atmosphere yet a charm of its own, one gets throughout the feeling of continental European life."[54] And for those who considered Haitian men ill-equipped to govern, Johnson drew out points of likeness between Haiti's shortcomings and those of the United States. "Haitian history has been all too bloody," Johnson conceded, but a "writer might visit our own country and clip from our daily press accounts of murders, robberies on the principal streets of our larger cities, strike violence, race riots, lynching, and burnings at the stake of human beings, and write a book to prove that life is absolutely unsafe in the United States."[55] And " 'graft' has been plentiful [in Haiti], shocking at times," he admitted, "but who in America, where the Tammany machines and the municipal rings are notorious, will dare to point the finger of scorn at Haiti in this connection."[56]

Johnson's ideology of black masculinity was more explicit in his account of elite society in Port-au-Prince. "Haitian intellectuals — poets, essayists, novelists, historians, critics," Johnson informed his readers, gathered at the Cercle Bellevue, which was characterized by "the courteous, friendly atmosphere of a men's club."[57] There one might encounter "a dozen or more contemporary Haitian men of letters whose work may be measured by world standards."[58] And as a guest at any one of "hundreds of beautiful villas," wrote Johnson, the visitor finds that among "the well-to-do . . . the majority have been educated in France; they are cultured, brilliant conversationally, and thoroughly enjoy their social life. The women dress well. Many are beautiful and all vivacious and chic."[59] Thus Haitian society was distinguished, according to Johnson, by worldly men and ornamental women. Measured in class terms, "the best Haitian society" had nothing at all in common with the primitive land of white racist fantasies.

If, as I have argued, exoticism relied on a reductive and stereotypical opposition between a civilized self and a primitive other, Johnson's reply decisively rejected race and nation as bases for such an opposition. "[E]ducated, cultured, and intellectual [Haitians] are not accidental and sporadic offshoots of the Haitian people," Johnson insisted; "they *are* the Haitian people."[60] Judge Haiti by their accomplishments. Yet, his approach left room for a certain brand of primitivism in his account of the Haitian poor. Johnson acknowledged an opposition between the civilized and the primitive in occupied Haiti, but located it along the axis of class rather than race or nation. "The masses of the Haitian people are . . . industrious and thrifty," wrote Johnson, answering charges that rural peasants sought to avoid labor. "For a woman to walk five to ten miles with a great load of produce on her head which may barely realize her a dollar is doubtless primitive, and a wasteful expenditure of energy, but it is not a sign of laziness."[61] Similarly, Johnson described the "long rows of wooden shanties, the curious little booths around the market" in the capital city as "no less picturesque and no more primitive . . . than similar quarters in Naples, in Lisbon, in Marseilles."[62] To Johnson the Haitian poor were primitive, to be sure, but no more so than the southern European poor.

In their own way, moreover, the Haitian poor added something by way of "local color" to their nation's cultural wealth. "[N]o less picturesque" as well as "no more primitive" than their southern European counterparts, Haiti's poor urban neighborhoods were, Johnson said, "more justifiable than the great slums of civilization's centers — London and New York, which are totally without aesthetic redemption." Thus "scantily clad children, magnificent in body" ran in and out of the market at the waterfront in Port-au-Prince.[63] And among the peasants in the countryside — people "with a profound sense of beauty and harmony" — "an aesthetic touch is never lacking."[64] Those "primitive" and inefficient market women, moreover, made "perhaps the deepest impression" on Johnson. "Magnificent as they file along the country roads by scores and by hundreds on their way to the town markets," he wrote, "with white or colored turbaned heads, gold-loop-ringed ears, they stride along straight and lithe, almost haughtily, carrying themselves like so many Queens of Sheba."[65] Johnson's notion of "aesthetic redemption" suggested that "quaint" Haitian peasants justified themselves by their value as objects to be admired, if not by their economic efficiency. Their worth resided, in part, in the visual pleasure they offered to the visitor.

This aspect of Johnson's discourse on Haiti is especially interesting in light of the authors whom Johnson proudly claimed to have influenced. Looking back on his visit to Haiti and his promotion of the island nation back in the States, Johnson proudly assessed his influence on the growth of American attention to Haiti. "I think I may claim that I rediscovered it for the United States," he wrote in his autobiography in 1933. "What I said and wrote was in some degree responsible for a new literary interest in Haiti. John W. Vandercook talked with me about Christophe and his citadel before he went down and wrote his book, *Black Majesty*; and William B. Seabrook talked with me about Haiti before he went down and wrote *The Magic Island*. Among my friends and acquaintances my trip started a sort of pilgrimage to the Black Republic."[66] Yet Vandercook and especially Seabrook would promote exoticized portraits that would attract widespread attention to Haiti as a primitive preserve within a modern empire. There is some irony in the fact that while Johnson sought to dispel negative attitudes toward the black nation, in drawing American attention to the "picturesque" he too contributed to the creation of an exotic object called Haiti.

EUGENE O'NEILL'S PATH TO *THE EMPEROR JONES*

Like Johnson, Eugene O'Neill came to write about Haiti having accumulated his own experiences of American empire.[67] In October 1909, in San Francisco Harbor, Eugene O'Neill had boarded a fruit company vessel, bound for Central America to collect a shipment of bananas for American consumption.[68] O'Neill himself was headed for Honduras, where he would make his way through the jungle laden down with "a cartridge belt around [his] waist and a Colt revolver at one hip . . . a bandolier over one shoulder . . . a carbine slung over the other and . . . a machete dangling from the other side of [his] belt."[69] O'Neill and his companion were in search of gold, which they never found. He returned to the States with malaria — and with a classic set of stereotypes to describe Central American peasants: "The natives are the lowest ignorant bunch of brainless bipeds that ever polluted a land or retarded its future," he wrote to his parents from Guajiniquil, Honduras.[70] He left again the following year: "Sixty five days on a Norwegian barque, Boston to Buenos Aires," he later wrote. "In Argentine I worked at various occupations — in the draughting department of the Westinghouse Electrical Company, in the wool house of a [Swift Company] packing plant at La Plata, in the office of the Singer Sewing Machine Company in Buenos Aires."[71]

O'Neill had seen the burgeoning U.S. economic empire as a worker, not as a gentleman of leisure. After returning to the States in 1911, he cultivated a critical perspective on American politics and, according to cultural historian Joel Pfister, "savored imagining himself as radical." He signed his letters, "Yours for the Revolution," wrote "radical poems," and voted for Socialist Eugene Debs in 1912.[72] O'Neill wrote for the New London *Telegraph* during this time, and according to another of his biographers, "covered socialist events with partisan feeling."[73] This radicalism gave him a rather different context in which to develop his perspectives on U.S. imperialism.

O'Neill stumbled on Haitian history as he sat drinking at a hotel barroom, at least as he told the story.[74] It was the late teens, and the occupation was under way. By then, O'Neill had studied drama at Harvard in 1914 and 1915. He was spending time largely in New York City and Provincetown, writing, observing, and drinking. His interest in the left persisted, and his circle in Greenwich Village included white labor radicals and anarchists, as well as African Americans and Italians, whom he dubbed "true native Villagers."[75] At the barroom of the Garden Hotel across from Madison Square Garden, he was a regular among "fight promoters, circus people, . . . gamblers and racketeers."[76] In the *Bartender's Guide* distributed to regulars such as himself, O'Neill made notes of his conversations and observations.[77]

Sometime in the winter of 1919, O'Neill made note of a story he heard from "an old circus man," named Jack Croak, who had been "traveling with a tent show through the West Indies." "He told me a story current in Haiti concerning the late President Sam," O'Neill wrote. "This was to the effect that Sam had said they'd never get him with a lead bullet; that he would get himself first with a silver one." Croak gave O'Neill "a coin with Sam's features on it," which the playwright kept "as a pocket piece."[78]

In the course of the following year and a half, building on this story — ostensibly about President Sam, but actually long associated with Henri Christophe — O'Neill got the idea for what was to become *The Emperor Jones*.[79] He prepared to write the play by reading about Toussaint L'Ouverture, Henri Christophe, and the Haitian Revolution. O'Neill claimed that when he came upon the uses of the drum while reading about religious feasts in the Congo, the heart of the play took shape, but his use of the drum also resonated with the histories of Haiti he had read. As another American noted a decade later, "Eugene O'Neill arranged that the distant drum should beat continuously all through the play. That made the drama Haitian more than all the scenery and the lines."[80] And the play came together sub-stantially during the summer months of 1920, precisely when news of the marines' misdeeds in Haiti was making election season headlines. In September, O'Neill composed it in only two weeks, dating it October 2, 1920.[81]

Finally, O'Neill drew directly from the title of James Weldon Johnson's *Nation* exposé for his prefatory note for the play. "Self-Determining Haiti," Johnson called his series, pointing to the obvious contradiction between Wilson's high-flown claims to protect the rights of small nations and the bare facts of what his administration was overseeing in one particular small nation. O'Neill used the phrase to set the stage for his drama: "The action of the play takes place on an island in the West Indies as yet not self-determined by White Marines. The form of native government is, for the time being, an Empire."[82]

DRAMATIC AMBIGUITIES

On the eve of election day 1920, at the Playwright's Theater in Greenwich Village, Charles S. Gilpin commanded an "avalanche of applause" for his opening-night performance as the emperor (Figure 18).[83] For those eager to see progress for African American actors, there seemed to be much to cheer, for Gilpin took a leading part that, in the past, would almost certainly have gone to a white actor in blackface.[84] He also made the most of the role; reviewers said that his was a "performance of heroic stature" and that he should be "ranked with the greatest artists of the American stage."[85] On the other hand, he played a scoundrel and a cheat, and the narrative followed his demise. As we shall see, the play's ambiguities did not end there. Indeed, with its contradictory implications for the politics of race, gender, and empire, it is perhaps especially fitting that *The Emperor Jones* was the first major artistic translation of the U.S. occupation of Haiti in the United States.

The emperor's identity is constructed out of a grid of references to Haitian, African American, and U.S. American culture, the last of these in its dominant, racially unmarked iteration. His character also highlights connections between race and masculinity in important ways. In order to appreciate more fully O'Neill's use of the black male figure, and his use of Haiti, we must consider the complexity of racial, national, and gender references in the play. For O'Neill conceived of Brutus Jones not as an "African American" character, but as a "full-blooded negro," and that marker was as wholly ambiguous with respect to national identity as it was absolute with respect to race. Out of this ambiguity, I argue, came the richness of *The Emperor Jones* as

Figure 18. Charles Gilpin as the Emperor Jones. © *Jessie Tarbox Beals. Courtesy
Howard Greenberg Gallery, New York City; photograph, Yale Collection of
American Literature, Beinecke Rare Book and Manuscript Library.*

a modernist text that helped to launch Haiti on a new phase of its career in U.S. American culture — for better and for worse.

When the play opens, Brutus Jones is "a tall, powerfully-built" black man, resplendent in his emperor's uniform, "sprayed with brass buttons, heavy gold chevrons on the shoulders, gold braid on the collar," and more. If his sartorial excess is intended in part to be comic, O'Neill qualifies this by indicating that "there is something not altogether ridiculous about his grandeur. He has a way of carrying it off."[86] Indeed, he shows contempt easily, and his powerful gaze is sufficient to cow a white man. If Jones is a "full-blooded negro," he is also, at the same time, the very embodiment of powerful manhood, holding wealth, title, and the reins of state power.[87] Jones displays the confidence of a man who has picked himself up by his own bootstraps, embraced his new status, and defined himself in terms of his newfound power. When reminded of his former troubles, he shoots back, "What I was den is one thing. What I is now's another."[88] Yet, the emperor, as Aaron Douglas depicted him in one of his 1926 illustrations for *Theatre Arts Monthly*, is about to slip off his throne (Figure 19).[89]

If the Emperor Jones is, for the time being at least, a figure for powerful manhood, the island nation that is destined to be "self-determined by White Marines" is, in contrast, represented initially by a fearful, bare-footed, old "native negro woman."[90] Yet, it is this cowering, supplicating embodiment of abject weakness who announces the imminent demise of the emperor. She does so, moreover, in O'Neill's version of "native" speech, a dialect that evokes the speech patterns of Native American Indians, as imagined within classic racist stereotypes. "Him Emperor — Great Father . . . Him sleep after eat."[91] And while the "Great Father" sleeps, she tells her white interrogator, and the audience, the natives have taken to the hills to beat the drum and prepare for revolution. This linguistic invocation of U.S. paternalism toward native peoples, suggestive of the relationship between Native Americans and the "Great Father at Washington," is one of several textual details that serve to associate Brutus Jones's imperial power with the United States and with his U.S. American identity.[92] Thus, this opening encounter between an old native woman and a white man, "the Cockney trader," who evinces contempt for the emperor behind his back, but tries to be prudent in his presence, foregrounds not only matters of race and gender, but also questions of national identity.

The Emperor Jones unfolds in eight scenes. The first and longest consists primarily of a conversation between the emperor, Brutus Jones, and the crooked Cockney trader, Smithers. In it we learn something of Jones's history in the States. He had been a Baptist and a Pullman porter, but having

Figure 19. Aaron Douglas, Untitled. Illustration of The Emperor Jones *for* Theatre Arts Monthly, *1926. Private collection.*

Figure 20. Aaron Douglas, Forest Fear. *Illustration of* The Emperor Jones *for* Theatre Arts Monthly, *1926. Private collection.*

killed another black man in a craps game, Jones landed in a chain gang; having then killed the prison guard and filed the chain from his ankle, he escaped, stowed away, and landed on the island.[93] After hooking up with Smithers and participating in his dishonest racket, Jones survives a gunshot fired by a native. The shot misses him, but Brutus Jones convinces the native that he can only be killed by a silver bullet. Through this legend, the American ex-convict ascends to the throne, becoming the Emperor Jones. From that advantageous position, his theft takes the form of exorbitant taxes, as Smithers reminds him, exclaiming, "You've squeezed 'em dry!"[94]

The remaining seven scenes, which form the heart of the play, are devoted to the Emperor Jones's undoing. To the steady and ever-so-slightly accelerating sound of the native drumbeat, Jones sets out for the coast, attempting to follow a path through the forest that he has laid in preparation for this moment. His pistol chamber is full, with five lead bullets and the last one made of silver, for himself, if it should come to that. But as he proceeds, he encounters, one by one, a series of haunts at which he fires all six shots. In turn he comes upon "the little formless fears"; Jeff, the man he killed over a craps game; the prison guard on the chain gang; an auctioneer and planters at a slave auction, in which he is on the block; slaves in the hold of a ship; and, finally, a witch doctor and crocodile monster back in Africa. By dawn, Brutus Jones has gone and come full circle, back to the edge of the forest where he started, and there the native soldiers kill him with the silver bullets they have fashioned in secret from coins of the empire.

While Brutus Jones's African American identity is most explicit, his association with Haiti is unmistakable insofar as his character is pieced together from various fragments of Haitian history and lore. We have seen how O'Neill came by this store of material. His readings on Haitian history would have very likely included books like Hesketh Prichard's *Where Black Rules White* and Lothrop Stoddard's history of the Haitian Revolution. From such books he would have learned that Haiti's first head of state, Jean Jacques Dessalines, called himself "Emperor"; he may or may not have known that a second nineteenth-century Haitian leader, Faustin Soulouque, did likewise. He would have read about color divisions in Haiti and known that Dessalines was a black man, not a mulatto, and thus a "full-blooded negro" like Brutus Jones. O'Neill learned, too, the startling history that caught Johnson's attention, that Henri Christophe established himself as king, ruled Haiti surrounded by a court of nobles, and built an astonishing fortress high on a mountain. Of course, Prichard and his like saw in the Citadel evidence of monstrosity rather than masculine accomplishment.[95] Jones's silver bullet ruse also came from Christophe's legend, although, as O'Neill learned it from Sam Croak, the circus man, it was a story about a more recent Haitian leader, President Sam.

Brutus Jones's association with a racially unmarked version of American culture is more subtly implied. O'Neill's initial description of Jones, for example, identifies him with American frontier masculinity, even as it reproduces a racist opposition between blackness and American identity. "His features are typically negroid," reads the playscript, "yet there is something decidedly distinctive about his face — an underlying strength of will, a hardy, self-reliant confidence in himself that inspires respect."[96] Similarly, the emperor's costume, while ostentatiously European for the most part, sports a "pearl-handled revolver" and "boots with brass spurs."[97]

Moreover, despite the Haitian origins of the silver bullet story, in Smithers's view it is simply "Yankee bluff." Jones responds, as if to confirm this identification of American bravado, "Ain't a man talkin' big what makes him big — long as he makes folks believe it?"[98] Eugene O'Neill drew this image of masculine bravado from his own vast experience in the rough male world described by historian George Chauncey, for O'Neill had been a denizen of that world in his teens and twenties.[99] Another version of this bravado appeared a year later in his play, *The Hairy Ape*, which O'Neill called "a direct descendant of *Jones*."[100] The lead character of that primitivist piece is another "big talker." A white man whose face is often blackened with coal dust, he resembles a "Neanderthal," with his "natural stooping posture," overdeveloped back and shoulder muscles, long powerful arms, and "low, receding brow."[101] O'Neill named him, pointedly, Yank.

If O'Neill cast Brutus Jones as an "American" figure through his frontier spirit and paraphernalia, his masculine braggadocio, and his success as a self-made man, he was American too in his thieving. In this sense, references to Jones's American identity are central to O'Neill's criticism of U.S. imperialism in the Caribbean. The dialogue between Smithers and Jones in scene 1, in particular, reveals the extent to which Brutus Jones has learned the crooked ways of white folks back in the States. As they review the history of their swindling on the island, Jones reminds Smithers that he has used his government power to protect the Cockney trader, "Ain't I . . . winked at all de crooked tradin' you been doin' right out in de broad day. Sho' I has — and me makin' laws to stop it at de same time!"[102] Smithers reminds Jones in turn that the emperor himself broke the laws just as fast as he made them.[103]

Jones's next response echoed an analysis set forth several decades earlier by African American author Anna Julia Cooper. In *A Voice from the South*, Cooper had written, "If your own father was a pirate, a robber, a murderer, his hands are dyed in red blood, and you don't say very much about it. But if your great great great grandfather's grandfather stole and pillaged and slew, and you can prove it, your blood has become blue and you are at great pains to establish the relationship."[104] The words O'Neill put in Brutus Jones's mouth pointed to a similar irony: "Ain't I de Emperor? De laws don't go for him. . . . You heah what I tells you, Smithers. Dere's little stealin' like you does, and dere's big stealin' like I does. For de little stealin' dey gits you in jail soon or late. For de big stealin' dey makes you Emperor and puts you in de Hall o' Fame when you croaks. . . . If dey's one thing I learns in ten years on de Pullman ca's listenin' to de white quality talk, it's dat same fact."[105] This indictment of capitalism both at home, and as carried abroad by the self-proclaimed emperor, was reinforced by O'Neill's reference to Johnson's *Nation* series in his prefatory note to the play, presumably included on the program that was handed out to theatergoers.

If Jones's American side provided O'Neill with opportunities to criticize capitalism and imperialism, his Haitian side did likewise. Thus, when a white man (Smithers) tries to take credit for getting Jones on his feet and setting him on the path to success, Jones responds with a pointed rejection of such paternalist claims. "You didn't let me in on yo' crooked work out a' no kind feelin's dat time. . . . I was wu'th money to you, dat's de reason."[106]

Yet, while O'Neill made a point of articulating these critiques of capitalism, imperialism, and paternalism, in line with his long-standing interest in socialist and anarchist ideas, his play was not simply or even primarily written in a critical, political mode. Indeed, far from taking the side of the island's natives, the play manifested the same contempt for them that O'Neill had exhibited toward Honduran peasants in 1909. His belief, cultivated in that context, that "native" revolutions were "comic opera" affairs ultimately overshadowed the critical, political moments I have so far highlighted.[107]

Still, the significance of *The Emperor Jones* in relation to the U.S. occupation of Haiti does not lie only in its stance for or against capitalism, imperialism, or paternalism. It is significant for the ways it mobilized images of Haiti in the United States. The play's ambiguities and its reception illustrate white Americans' investment in Haiti, and in black bodies, as objects of fascination, sources of liberation, means for negotiating the demands of their own social and political context. At the same time, they also show the strategies whites employed in an attempt to keep these ever more fascinating objects—Haitians and African Americans—from seeing themselves as subjects, and thus forcing a redefinition of the national self. As we shall see, the attempt was abortive.

O'Neill's play served several apparently contradictory ends for its white audiences. First, it represented the troubling ambiguities raised by empire building and colonial adventuring. The prefatory notes presented these ambiguities, which men who had been abroad had encountered in diverse ways. For if "the form of native government" could be an empire headed by a nonnative, indeed by an American, then where did the "native" end and the "nation" begin? If a West Indian island could be "self-determined by White Marines," then what did that say about the relationship between "White Marines" and the "self" of the island? Smedley Butler had played with these very terms and confusions as chief of the Gendarmerie d'Haïti. Now *The Emperor Jones* seemed to equate "White Marines" with native West Indians and African Americans with self-reliant frontiersmen. In this sense, it opened up the troubling question, Who and what is an American?

O'Neill's comments on his own tropical adventures, as well as those of other white men, suggest the possibility that he employed a black character to say something about white men and the challenge to selfhood they sometimes experienced in the tropics. Regarding *The Emperor Jones*, O'Neill later recalled, "the effect of the tropical forest on the human imagination was honestly come by. It was the result of my own experience while prospecting for gold in Spanish Honduras."[108] In 1909, foreshadowing the kinds of racial playacting in which marines in Haiti later engaged, O'Neill had written to his parents from Honduras, "I am as brown as a native and am growing a mustache in order to look absolutely as shiftless and dirty as the best of them."[109] A few years later, he described Theodore Roosevelt, perhaps the most prominent white colonialist figure of the time, using similarly boundary-blurring language. In the New London *Telegraph*, Roosevelt became "the hero of the jungle." "Colonel Theodore Roosevelt, who is jocosely described by various names ranging from Bwana Tumbo to Chief Running Bull, passed through here on the eastbound limited at 3:38 yesterday afternoon."[110]

At the same time, representations of Haiti did not appeal only to white men who had been abroad in the tropics. Indeed, some white men went to the tropics to resolve struggles born on home ground. As economic change challenged long-held conceptions of manliness and individuality by subordinating men to machines, and as world war challenged national pieties about civilization and progress, whites looked to racial others in new ways — as sources of liberation. As James Clifford has argued, modernist primitivism took hold in the 1920s, as "a series of stereotypes long associated with backwardness and inferiority acquired positive connotations and came to stand for liberation and spontaneity, for a simultaneous recovery of ancient sources and an access to true modernity."[111] The importance of liberation suggests a contrast between two of O'Neill's primitivist plays, *The Hairy Ape* and *The Emperor Jones*. For if, in the former, the white "Yank" and his fellow workers are caged in a prison of steel (trusts) from beginning to end, in the latter the black "Brutus" has broken his chains, fled for his life, and landed on his feet—at least for a time. The ambiguity of Jones's national identity allowed whites to access this element of the play, while providing them, too, with an escape—from the potential implications of their investment in a black character. Within such a frame, whites could be encouraged to identify with black characters as a means to plumb the depths of their own souls, as O'Neill explicitly hoped his audiences would do.[112]

The fantasy of liberated masculinity, vested in black bodies like those of Charles Gilpin and Paul Robeson, had, nevertheless, to be contained.[113] And all the more was this so because representations of Haiti served a third and perhaps most crucial end, namely, to triangulate domestic racial and gender struggles.[114] In Johnson's use of Christophe, as in O'Neill's insistence on Jones's demise, Haiti served as a foil for contests over black men's political fitness in the United States. Projecting this question onto Haiti, Jones's fate dramatized the argument that had been made by Hesketh Prichard, calling for an intervention in Haiti some years before. "Can the negro rule himself?" Prichard had asked, concluding, "he has shown no signs whatever which can fairly entitle him to the benefit of the doubt that has for so long hung about the question."[115] Thus, just as Smedley Butler's paternalism had its ugly side, so O'Neill's ambiguities ultimately had to be resolved. As Hazel Carby has argued, O'Neill displaced the threat of black masculinity and African American political leadership onto the realm of the psychological.[116]

Finally, O'Neill's staging of Brutus Jones's demise bears scrutiny. For as he makes his way through the forest, Jones strips down, by stages, losing first his Panama hat, then his coat, shoes, and pants, leaving him finally "naked except for the fur of some small animal tied about his waist."[117] Joel Pfister says of this "strip-tease that actors Charles Gilpin and Paul Robeson performed when playing Jones" that it "identified them with a sexuality that white audiences could both fascinate themselves with as an embodiment of their own psychological primitivism, yet at the same time spurn as 'nothing more than a prancing darky onstage.'"[118] Yet it also represented the stripping away of those markers of civilization, manhood, and national identity—no more brass spurs, no more honorific regalia, in which category the marines included pants. Thus, the emperor's "strip-tease" resonated with the discourses and experiences of the marines in Haiti. For uniforms and insignia vested men with authority, and as marines divested themselves of these habiliments—in various ways—they confronted the subjective chal-

Figure 21. Puppet production of The Emperor Jones. *Photograph by Helen Liebman. Yale Collection of American Literature, Beinecke Rare Book and Manuscript Library.*

lenges that sometimes led to "indiscriminate" violence. In Smedley Butler's telling, their own stripping down could represent a return to elemental masculinity: marines in their underwear were ripe for a fight. Yet, if Brutus Jones exhibited his bare chest and legs in order to allow white audiences a fantasy of black masculinity, a "dark lyric of the flesh," in the words of one reviewer, his stripping down also disarmed him, so that, in the end, he was reduced to a mass of quivering, unmanly emotionality.[119]

O'Neill's *The Emperor Jones* illustrates a fundamental contrast between the discourses of paternalism and exoticism, despite their usual alliance in support of U.S. imperialism. To be sure, paternalism fired an American fascination with the exotic by creating a context in which U.S. citizens could appropriate and commodify Haitian culture, the process to which this chapter turns next. Exoticism, in turn, reinforced paternalism by focusing American attention on the differences between the two cultures, often expressed as primitive shortcomings in Haitian life, which justified a paternal American presence in Haiti. Yet the differences are crucial. For whereas paternalism inscribed U.S. Americans into Haiti's domestic landscape as needed and

AFTERMATH

welcome family members, exoticism inscribed Haiti into U.S. American culture as an explicitly foreign and unfamiliar entity. As O'Neill's play suggests, Americans created a cultural space for Haiti in the United States premised on Haiti's very foreignness. And while some Americans challenged the discourse of exoticism, the prevailing terms of Haiti's incorporation into American culture emphasized the cultural dissonance between the two nations in a manner that served to justify U.S. political and economic control in Haiti. Thus, paternalism and exoticism, the two reigning tropes of U.S. contact with Haiti, mirrored and reproduced the political asymmetries of the occupation itself.

The enormous appeal of *The Emperor Jones* with black and white audiences alike signaled both the allure of primitivism among some sectors of the white population and the hunger for serious and meaningful cultural representation among African Americans. These contrasting desires contributed to the growth of white attention to black subjects during the 1920s, evidenced in the appearance of publishers like Boni and Liveright, who sought out "black" material by white and black writers. The presence of U.S. marines in Haiti and in other tropical settings provided grist for such a mill.

The "avalanche of applause" that met *The Emperor Jones* on opening night at the Playwright's Theatre spilled over into the days, months, and years to come. The day following the opening, the Provincetown Players were met with 1,500 new subscription requests. After its highly acclaimed first run in Greenwich Village, the play opened again at the Selwyn Theatre on Broadway on December 27, and later at the Princess Theatre, and ran for over 200 shows on Broadway.[120] *The Emperor Jones* found its way to print as soon as January 1921, when *Theatre Arts Magazine* published the full text along with an extended review, and later that year, Boni and Liveright brought out two editions of the play, one illustrated by Alexander King.[121] A two-year road tour followed the play's extensive Broadway run, and in 1925 New York was treated to a revival, with Paul Robeson leading the cast. The play was also staged over and over again by smaller companies, uptown and outside New York, especially those hungry for African American themes.[122] In time, *The Emperor Jones* would make its way to radio, opera, film, and even puppetry (Figure 21).[123]

White and black audiences both had reasons to stand and cheer for the Emperor Jones, at least for a time. Indeed, some African Americans welcomed O'Neill's serious treatment of African American themes at first; *The Emperor Jones* represented a marked improvement over earlier dramatic fare. It presented a strong black lead character who, for one thing, could put whites in their place. In the first scene, for example, on detecting a note of disrespect in Smithers's voice, Brutus Jones, reaching for his revolver, remonstrates, "Talk polite, white man!"[124] If the play seemed to accommodate certain stereotypes, moreover, it also dramatized the oppression of slavery through scenes of the Middle Passage and the auction block. Perhaps most important, as we have seen, the Provincetown Players abandoned customary racial practice by employing an African American actor for an important lead role. "Progress in the building of a black theatre," Jervis Anderson has noted, "had been made through the efforts of a white playwright."[125]

There was, however, some very pointed criticism in the African American press. One review asserted unequivocally, " 'The Emperor Jones' is the kind of play that should never be staged under any circumstances, regardless of theories, because it portrays the worst traits of the bad element of both races."[126] W. E. B. Du Bois, writing in the *Crisis,* disagreed. Calling *The Emperor Jones* "a splendid tragedy," Du Bois countered: "No more complete misunderstanding of this play or of the aim of Art could well be written." "The white artist looking in on the colored world, if he be wise and discerning, may often see the beauty, tragedy and comedy more truly than we dare."[127] But, as historian David Levering Lewis has pointed out, African Americans admitted to themselves more often than to their white friends and patrons their dislike of the exotic primitivism evident in white writing on "the Negro." George Schuyler, an editor of the *Messenger,* said publicly what others would not; he criticized whites for writing about the African American as if, "even when he appears to be civilized, it is only necessary to beat a tom-tom or wave a rabbit's foot and he is ready to strip off his Hart Schaffner & Marx suit, grab a spear and ride off wild-eyed on the back of a crocodile."[128] In time, too, Charles Gilpin would begin to take liberties with his lines, refusing to use the word "nigger" as called for in the script.

The success of the play with white U.S. audiences, moreover, hinged on the racist perceptions and longings that fueled modernist primitivism.[129] White reviewers, including Alexander Woollcott of the *New York Times* and Kenneth McGowan of the *Globe,* made this clear. To Woollcott, the play was "an extraordinarily striking and dramatic study of panic fear."[130] McGowan called it "a study of personal and racial psychology of real imaginative truth." Specifically, he noted, "The moment when he [Jones] raises his naked body against the moonlit sky and prays is such a dark lyric of the flesh, such a cry of the primitive being, as I have never seen in the theatre."[131] A year and a half later, reviewing *The Hairy Ape,* another O'Neill play dealing with a similar theme, but centering on a white character, Lawrence Remner of the *New York Herald Tribune* compared the new play with *The Emperor Jones* unfavorably. "[I]t was much more exciting game to see the negro usurper beaten by fate," wrote Remner. "He was such a clever rascal."[132]

The appropriation of Haitian images and themes by white writers and artists began in the twenties, burgeoned in the thirties, and continued into the following decades. O'Neill's use of the Sam/Christophe legend about the silver bullet was an early version of this appropriation, one that shared some characteristics with the later trend, but which also shows important contrasts. While O'Neill, on the face of it, portrayed the atavistic demise of a black man, at the same time, his lead character was really a fusion of Haitian and American, black and white. *The Emperor Jones* blurred the lines between black Haitian and white American, and this blurring of identities would not come to characterize the most sensational representations of the twenties and thirties. Those representations would instead emphasize exotic otherness; they would, in fact, come to emphasize those very elements of O'Neill's play that made it so popular with white audiences, despite the playwright's textual nuances. "It was," as theater critic Lawrence Remner had written, "much more exciting game to see the negro usurper beaten by fate."

European Americans' attraction to primitive themes therefore fashioned a new chapter in the history of American racism. Attending to Afro-American and Afro-Caribbean themes, U.S. whites could depart from a tradition of racist hostility while maintaining a fundamental commitment to racial hierarchies and essential racial identities. They could criticize their own culture or explore previously unexplored aspects of their own personalities through their fascination with primitive others. But in doing so, they would further reinforce some of the very tenets of the racist traditions they appeared to reject.

It is important to note that while white audiences continued to respond favorably to *The Emperor Jones* through the 1920s and into the 1930s, African American audiences, to the extent that they had not immediately rejected the play, more generally soured to its racism over the years. In 1940 Langston Hughes recalled a Harlem audience heckling actor Jules Bledsoe so thoroughly that he resorted to lecturing them — in the middle of his performance — on "manners in the theater." To his dismay, the audience continued to "howl with laughter."[133]

Given the politics of the gaze at work in the play's performance for white audiences, we can imagine a set of meanings quite distinct from those O'Neill must have intended as we listen to the words he wrote for Brutus Jones, standing atop the auctioneer's block, in scene 5. Listen to Brutus Jones, as a figure for Haiti, addressing his white American audiences: "What

you all doin', white folks? What's all dis? What you lookin' at me fo'? . . . Is dis
a auction? Is you sellin' me like dey uster before de war?"

THE COMMODIFICATION OF HAITI

If protests against the occupation brought Haiti to the attention of the
American public, and if O'Neill's primitivist rendering of Haiti made visible,
and cultivated, white investments in Haiti as an object of fascination and
desire, the occupation itself created myriad opportunities for marines to
indulge this fascination. Indeed, relations of power at work in the occupation gave marines access to Haitians—their bodies and their services—as
well as to Haitian cultural objects and lore. Ironically, this turned out to be
more profitable, at least in the short run, than the development of Haitian
agricultural or manufacturing pursuits.

As the Provincetown Players took their highly successful show on the road,
and as *The Emperor Jones* proceeded to sell theater tickets, magazines, books,
and more, plans for economic prosperity in Haiti did not proceed apace. By
1922, the Haitian American Sugar Company (HASCO) was in receivership,
and investment in cotton by the United West Indies Corporation had failed
completely.[134] While HASCO revived over the next seven years, attempts to
attract diverse American interests to Haiti, and speculation as to the extraordinary natural wealth of the island, led to only a limited number of investments.[135] Through the Service Technique de l'Agriculture, established by
the occupation in 1923, U.S. officials "encouraged the diversification of
crops" and successfully promoted the cultivation of sisal.[136] Pineapple investments, promising at first, came to naught after a struggle for solvency.[137]
"The American Idea" had failed, but the Marine Corps stayed on.

The U.S. Marine Corps enjoyed a period of ease and autonomy in Haiti
for seven years following the reorganization of the occupation in 1922.
Officers' memoirs and diaries reveal mornings of military exercises, local
administration, and public works supervision, and afternoons of reading,
sports, and leisure. Polo, boxing, golf, basketball, and baseball maintained
the competitive and physically active spirit of the marines. The leisurely
pace of the occupation in this new phase also left marines and other American officials with time to pursue their interest in learning about "Voodoo"
and other aspects of Haitian culture.

The relations of power at work in occupied Haiti also gave marines access
to Haitian cultural artifacts. In an attempt to modernize and rationalize Haitian society as preparation for its integration into international economic

networks, occupation officials banned Vodou ceremonies in Haiti. Marines would raid places of worship, called hounforts, and confiscate drums and other ritual objects ostensibly to interrupt this now illegal practice. Katherine Dunham recalled that when she arrived in Haiti in 1936, "not long after the exodus of the Marines, there were still baptized drums hidden in hollow tree trunks and behind waterfalls."[138] Although some ritual objects were then burned, many were sent back to the States, or kept, as souvenirs. Captain John Houston Craige, for example, had collected four drums, "a mass of beads," and what he called "ghost-rattles" by the time he left Haiti.[139] Making Vodou illegal also gave American authorities a good deal of leverage on the local level, because they could make "exceptions" and allow ceremonies to take place in exchange for needed cooperation on development projects. This was a widespread practice; in fact, French anthropologist Alfred Métraux suggested that the ban on Vodou was largely observed in the breach, and that the main enforcement activity was, indeed, the confiscation of drums.[140] In this way, military power facilitated the production of Haitian cultural objects as exotic commodities for circulation and exchange in the United States. Thus, while disciplining Haitians for their supposed backwardness, marines could indulge their own desire for the exotic.

The occupation brought American civilians, as well as marines and naval personnel, to Haiti, and they too could enjoy a taste of the exotic while working there. In 1926, for example, Frank Resler Crumbie, formerly president of the Rockland County Trust Company back in Nyack, New York, took up a post as customs inspector at Cap Haïtien.[141] Formally appointed by Haitian president Louis Borno, upon the recommendation of U.S. president Calvin Coolidge, Crumbie worked with other U.S. nationals to rationalize Haitian finances in order to pay Haiti's debts and create viable links to international commerce. Whereas by day, he thereby participated in his government's modernization efforts, by night, and on his own time, he avidly pursued his interest in Voodoo, collecting books and artifacts and interviewing Haitians on the subject when he could find those who would speak of it.[142]

When President Hoover sent a commission to Haiti to investigate the occupation and recommend a course of action regarding its possible discontinuation, La Presse, a Haitian newspaper, accused Crumbie and other "employees of the tax office" of "malicious manoeuvering in order to dazzle and impress members of the commission. . . . Mr. Crumbie is buying drums with drumheads on which the fur is preserved. They will be given as gifts to members of the commission and will be illustrations of the mentality of a people who they say are profoundly attached to voodoo."[143] For members of

Figure 22. Captain John Houston Craige, author of Black Bagdad *and* Cannibal Cousins, *posing with drums. Marine Corps Research Center Archives, Quantico, Virginia.*

the Haitian elite, the American fascination with Voodoo often connoted a lack of respect for the accomplishments of cultured Haitians and an insistence on defining Haitian culture in terms of primitivism.

In another sense, Haitians themselves became commodities for U.S. Americans in occupied Haiti. Captain Craige, for example, spoke of his servant, Destiné, as his "first venture in black ivory."[144] Marines need not have attained a captain's rank, furthermore, in order to invest in servants. As Craige said of Sergeant Virski, "his service pay, a pittance in the United States, made him a man of wealth in Haiti."[145]

Haitians who took advantage of the economic opportunities represented by Americans' desire for various kinds of services were not literally rendered objects or commodities. They chose to work with Americans, whether out of necessity or for some other reason. They also set the terms of their own employment in various ways. As workers they resisted their employers' control with myriad strategies that would be interpreted, in some cases, simply as laziness or as part of a primitive way of life. Thus, to suggest that Haitians themselves became commodities for Americans is to address the significance of the transaction for white Americans rather than for Haitians. Americans viewed Haitian servants and prostitutes as commodities insofar as the latter could be bought and sold and insofar as they could confer upon the "buyer" a sense of status and identity linked to class, race, gender, and sexuality.

Prostitutes, like household servants, enabled U.S. Marines and other American men in Haiti to shore up their own sense of masculinity and class status. Although it is unlikely that prostitution was unknown to Port-au-Prince before the U.S. occupation, as one Haitian critic claimed, still the sex industry grew with the extraordinary infusion of American money and men into the capital city. The occupation's attempts to create order, furthermore, did not extend to this aspect of public life. In September 1915 Lieutenant Adolph Miller, guarding the American Legation, refused a request for assistance from a local policeman "to help raid a red-light house." On the advice of the Marine provost martial, Miller informed the local lawman that this was an internal matter, and of no concern to the Marine Corps.[146] Within the month, marines were making rounds in these districts but, whether they were searching for rebels or for fun, they were not out to close down the illicit operations. "Turnage made a reconnaissance of the red-light district with mounted patrols," Miller noted in his personal log, "nothing exciting."[147]

By 1918 U.S. naval doctors were busy investigating and treating the spread of syphilis and other venereal diseases in Haiti.[148] In the mid-twenties, U.S. observers noted the "obvious" presence of the "illegitimate children of soldiers and native women."[149] "A man may drink and carouse with black or white," said one member of the Women's International League for Peace and Freedom (WILPF) delegation to Haiti in 1926; "let him, however, offer honorable marriage to a Haitian girl, and he has performed an act 'unbecoming to a soldier and a gentleman.' "[150] By the time of the WILPF investigation into the effects of the occupation on Haiti in 1926, Port-au-Prince could boast "147 registered saloons and drinking places," all of them "places of open prostitution." "Girls invade Port-au-Prince and Cap Haïtien," asserted one Haitian critic, "lured by the dollars of the marines."[151]

Finally, in addition to the material objects funneled back to the States from Haiti, and the servants and prostitutes who came to be seen as objects of exchange within Haitian borders, Americans transformed the very idea of Haiti into an object of value in capitalist exchange. A number of marines and other U.S. officials wrote memoirs or fiction based on their experiences, observations, and fantasies in and of Haiti. In doing so, they cashed in on, and contributed to, Americans' fascination with the exotic. Marines also sometimes served as tour guides to visitors, who would then return to the States to tell of Haiti's lure. Thus, where U.S. fruit, cotton, oil, and rubber producers failed to find profitable commodities in occupied Haiti, U.S. publishers succeeded, and a host of other cultural enterprises would follow their lead.[152] Moreover, the marketing of Haiti and Haitian culture in the United States would obscure the very relations of power that put Haitian stories, images, and objects in circulation in U.S. cultural markets.[153]

Former lieutenant A. J. Burks, whose stories expressed so vividly the fears of his fellow leathernecks in Haiti, provides a pointed example. Burks turned his experiences as a marine into a lucrative business. He served only a short time in Haiti, but upon returning to the States, he immediately began to churn out short stories based on Marine Corps lore about the black republic. He went on to write thirty-five books and over 1,200 stories. Earning from his writing close to $40,000 during each year of the Great Depression, A. J. Burks came to be known as the "speed merchant of the pulps."[154]

As if responding directly to James Weldon Johnson and Marcus Garvey, who looked to Haitian leaders as part of a proud black heritage, Burks turned to those very Haitian figures to fashion his horrific villains. For Burks, Christophe was "the greatest monster in all history" and "the tale of Toussaint" was "a tale of beastly lust, brute aggrandizement, freedom from restraint for men with the passions of wild animals, the strength of the savage, and the bloodlust of followers of the green serpent."[155] In *Weird Tales* and other pulp horror magazines, Haiti would become a familiar setting for ghastly murders and gruesome goings-on. In time, the same motif would appear on radio in Orson Welles's popular show, *The Shadow*, and on screen in films such as *White Zombie*.[156]

Reaching for a more respectful tone than *Weird Tales*, John Vandercook's lively biography of Henri Christophe, *Black Majesty*, celebrated the Haitian

king as a proud and dignified figure. Vandercook pointedly recognized Christophe's manhood, even as he participated in primitivist discourses to some extent. The final passage emphasized that he was known to those he left behind not as "King," or "Majesty, or Henry, or Christophe," but simply as " 'L'Homme.' The Man."[157] Mahlon Blaine's illustration for the book's cover, on the other hand, seems more appropriate to Burks's stories than to Vandercook's biography (Figure 23). A popular Literary Guild selection and a "blue ribbon book" for 1928, *Black Majesty* introduced Christophe to thousands of American readers, building on and popularizing another version of the Emperor Jones.[158]

In books and magazines, on stage and on screen, in radio drama and in song, in advertising and in the fine arts, countless images of black kings and emperors populated U.S. American culture in the 1920s and 1930s. A giant and fierce Christophe, arms akimbo, phallic sword prominently displayed, legs astride a steamship, helped to sell Colombian Line cruises for $944 a day (and up). "Colombian Line alone presents Sans Souci and The Citadel . . . palace and fortress of Haiti's King Henri Christophe . . . Two added attractions at no added cruise cost" (Figure 24).[159] Those who were not inclined to travel, on the other hand, could transform the interior of their own homes with images of Christophe's court on "scenic wallpaper" (Figure 25). Katzenbach and Warren, Inc., of New York City advertised "A Visit to King Christophe," designed by Nicholas de Molas, for $600 per set of nine strips, in a limited edition of 100 sets.[160] Where Eugene O'Neill had blended the splendor of his emperor in full regalia with the spectacle of his naked body by staging a striptease, Katzenbach and Warren evoked both images in their description of one of the wallpaper panels. "A detachment of Christophe's fabulous regiment of six-foot 'Les Dahomeys,' resplendent in their opera-bouffe uniforms, point their bare black toes toward the sea, into which, legend has it, they would march to a salty death at their King's command" (Figure 26).[161]

The Marine Corps itself effected a most remarkable act of cultural appropriation in 1929. Building on Vandercook's work, the corps published a pamphlet entitled *Citadel of Christophe: Famous Ruler of Haiti* (Figure 27).[162] The pamphlet's cover informed potential readers that it was part of the "Marine Corps Travel Series." "Romance wraps its mantle around Haiti's greatest monument," the text began, and it went on to describe "this impressive structure" and its "picturesque ruler."[163] A final page focused not on Christophe but on "The Globe Trotting Marines." "Marines are world travelers," it proudly announced. "They have virtually followed the trail of Columbus through the Caribbean."[164]

Figure 23. Mahlon Blaine, cover of John Vandercook's popular book,
Black Majesty. *Courtesy of Harper Collins Publishers.*

*Figure 24. Colombian Line, "Cruise the West Indies." Haitiana Collection,
University of Florida Library, Gainesville, Florida.*

Shrouding the Marine Corps in all the romance of Christophe and all the
glory of Columbus, the pamphlet served as a tool for recruiting and public
relations. Haiti, it claimed, "offers a never-ending source of information" to
"the wideawake Marine" who is "keen to learn the customs and some of the
history of the countries he visits." "No country in the Western Hemisphere
has had a more vivid or picturesque history. Small wonder that the Marines
are attracted to the Citadel of Christophe. It stands as a monument to an
interesting personality, who by sheer force of character won a place for
himself among the outstanding figures of American history."[165] In this way,
the U.S. Marines Corps appropriated the "Citadel of Christophe" as a
means to establish the romance and glory of their presence in Haiti — and to
market itself at a time when military appropriations were not perceived as a
priority. Moreover, the Marine Corps chose to blur the distinction between

A VISIT TO KING CHRISTOPHE

A Scenic Wallpaper

designed by

Nicholas de Molas

Katzenbach and Warren, Inc.

49 East 53rd Street   *New York City*

Chicago   *Boston*   *Los Angeles*

Figure 25. Scenic wallpaper, "A Visit to King Christophe." Haitiana Collection, University of Florida Library, Gainesville, Florida.

Figure 26. Scenic wallpaper, panels 5–8. Haitiana Collection,
University of Florida Library, Gainesville, Florida.

Haitian and "American," in the best Wilsonian tradition, even as it persisted in an unjust occupation. The pamphlet is remarkable for the boldness with which it effaced the relations of power that constituted the occupation, but it was typical of U.S. appropriations of Haiti precisely for that erasure.

This use of Christophe reached vast numbers of Americans, moreover, as Marine Corps public relations materials were used to shape the image of the corps in popular culture and news reporting.[166] In 1929 a general strike against the occupation and the killing of Haitian protesters at a rally in Aux Cayes raised troubles once more for the Marine Corps's image. Hearst Metrotone newsreels proudly presented the "first sound films from the Black Republic, where a recent clash between the U.S. Marines and natives led President Hoover" to call for an inquiry.[167] Yet, if there was potentially trouble for the marines, there was no trouble for America, as Metrotone assured its viewers. As the camera pans over the city of Port-au-Prince from an airplane, the voice-over announces, "President Louis Borno welcomes the Metrotone aerial expedition, showing no hostility towards America."[168]

Four years later, Metrotone was back in Haiti, this time with good news for the marines as well as for America. "Metrotone takes you on a . . . flight with the Leathernecks. You are now flying over Port-au-Prince, . . . but we are bound for the mountains . . . toward the interior, where our goal awaits us. Here is a wonder of the world, the Citadel of Christophe, begun in 1801 and completed after the King's death. And it's Uncle Sam's Marine aces that give

Figure 27. U.S. Marine Corps Travel Series, Citadel of Christophe. *Schomburg Center for Research on Black Culture, New York.*

us this tour."[169] Later that year, Metrotone invoked the Citadel again, this time to mark the accomplishment of the Marine brigade as it "bid farewell to Haiti" on August 15, 1934. The Citadel of "the Emperor Crystal [*sic*] . . . now stands in a land of peace, thanks to a job done well. . . . No hard feelings, just a hearty goodbye to Uncle Sam's boys who brought order out of chaos."[170]

MURDEROUS WOMEN AND SOULLESS MEN

In Johnson's articles, O'Neill's play, and Burks's stories, Haiti functioned as a proving ground for men, a site for struggles over racialized versions of masculinity. Those struggles continued to be worked out through Haitian characters and in narratives set in Haiti, but cultural texts taking off from Haitian themes also addressed themselves to women's proper place. In the 1925 novel, *The Goat without Horns*, and the 1932 film, *White Zombie*, the politics of race and gender would revolve around the fate of a woman under a monstrous spell. At stake, in both cases, was the proper domestic affection of a wife for her husband and a mother for her child. In the novel, in particular, the very integrity of Western civilization hung in the balance. And if Johnson's essays and O'Neill's play embodied tensions between political critique and visions of an exotic Haiti, these cultural texts showed more pointedly how exoticism itself could be the very vehicle of critique.

Authored by the former U.S. chargé d'affaires in Haiti, Robert Beale Davis, *The Goat without Horns* presented racist sensationalism as a vehicle for a broad critique of American society and the failure of Western values, evident in the carnage of world war. When, by the end of the novel, the Haitians' "primitive brutality" has come to the surface, Davis has one character suggest that they were, at least, "no worse than their civilized brothers who were, right now, making a shambles of Europe." At the same time, the narrative reveals a crucial difference between a brutal primitive society and a civilized nation that has fallen into warfare. That difference turns on the organization of gender and sexuality in Western civilization.

For Davis, romance, marriage, and family relations constituted the foundation of all that was right with Euro-American society. What threatened well-ordered sexuality therefore threatened the West. Davis took aim at feminists, whom he associated singularly with that grave danger, a liberated sexuality. Failing to mind their place in the world, modern women played with fire. Davis excoriated women whom he saw as constantly "meddling with something [they] only halfway know about" and "emancipated women" whose "sex psychology goes no deeper than the blatantly physical."[171] Such women had "done their best to kill [romance]," his protagonist laments, and apparently the killing would not stop there.[172] But if this sort of running commentary pinned the blame on feminists, the narrative presented yet another collective villain.

Davis's protagonist is Felix Blaine, a Wall Street financier, attempting to take a rest from business matters with a visit to Port-au-Prince. In Haiti, he falls in love with the beautiful and charming Thérèse Simone and plans to take her away from the island and marry her. Yet, if Blaine assumes that his fiancée is a white woman, his assumption is soon thrown into doubt. Spying on a Voodoo ceremony from the bush, Felix Blaine sees his own Thérèse at the center of the (lurid) action. The mystery of Thérèse Simone's racial and national identity adds a note of racial suspense to the plot. With Felix Blaine, however, readers learn that Thérèse is white, and that her presence in the midst of the Voodoo ceremony may be explained by the fact that she is under the power of a native spell. Knowing this, Haitian "society" shuns her, but the peasants will not allow her to leave the island — not until she performs the final ceremonial act for which she is needed.

Davis's Haitian natives recall with pride the bloodshed of their long ago revolution and now intend to effect another, this time on a world scale.[173] Black magic is their chosen weapon, and a white woman must be the pawn of their power play. For the natives believe that "when a white child, a baby boy, is brought to the altar and a knife [is] plunged into his heart by a white woman," then and only then, white power will come to an end, and "the blacks will reign supreme."[174] Thérèse, of course, has been chosen to serve as the agent of this world transformation.

Felix and Thérèse try to get away from the island, but they are thwarted at one turn and another by zealous natives, chief among them Thérèse's lifelong and trusted servant, Ida. As they contrive new plans for their escape, Port-au-Prince breaks out in revolution (and Davis provides graphic descriptions of the violence involved). Against this backdrop, the lovers' efforts are finally redeemed by none other than the USS *Washington* and the United States Marines.

What the marines prevented, in this telling, was nothing less than the demise of white power and what was left of Western civilization. By landing to quell the violence of the Haitian mob and by allowing the white couple to escape, the U.S. military is shown to have prevented the ultimate violence, the violation of the sacred racial-maternal bond between white woman and white (male) baby. In this way, Davis's narrative emphasized the centrality of that bond as a fundamental underpinning of white racial integrity. Feminist assertions of sexual and economic independence, on the other hand, were cast as threats to that racial integrity. Despite the madness of the war in Europe, the righteousness of the U.S. military is established as the marines restore to safety the integrity of the white family.[175]

The Goat without Horns did not reap the profits Burks saw from his sustained literary enterprise. Nor did it establish its author as a significant literary figure, as *The Emperor Jones* had done for O'Neill. But like those earlier examples of exoticizing Haitiana, Davis's novel enabled his readers to indulge in primitive fantasies even as they reviled the primitive. At the same time, it went beyond those texts by articulating more precisely the link between racial and gender ideologies that seemed to be threatened, at home and abroad, in an all-too-modern world.

The onset of the Great Depression compounded postwar dissatisfaction with Western civilization, and cast the politics of race and gender in a new light. In that context, white sensationalism focused more consistently on a new figure taken from Haitian culture — and promptly made over to serve white American uses — the zombie. In the 1930s, myriad cultural forms (e.g., novels, short stories, memoirs, travel narratives, plays, and films) made use of the belief that, in Haiti, the dead could be made to rise in their soulless bodies and would then be subordinated to the will of a master. These images could be threatening: monstrous, once-dead black men rising up, embodying white fears of black revolt at home as well as abroad.

But the zombie could also serve as a sign for the powerlessness that white men and women felt in the face of economic struggle. In the early 1930s, William Seabrook likened the zombie image to the modern man who is little more than "a cog in a wheel."[176] And one 1930s New York City newspaper columnist defended his fellow New Yorkers by insisting that they were not simply "a species of zombie."[177] The figure of the zombie generally became less threatening and more amusing over the course of the decade. Moreover, as white discourses began to merge diverse racial "others" into a single, fluid and generic, exotic object, they tended to emphasize less the specific horrors that had been attributed to Haiti since the early years of the occupation.[178] Hence the opening, at the 1940 World's Fair, of the Zombie Restaurant, decorated in "a South Sea motif."[179] The zombie theme, whether in a mood of horror or humor, could give muted expression to a growing dissatisfaction with American society.

In the 1930s this highly salable image, based originally on Haitian material, found a place in the burgeoning film industry, giving rise eventually to a distinct subgenre of horror film — the zombie flick. Like the Zombie Restaurant with its South Sea motif, later zombie flicks dropped direct references to Haiti, but Edward and Victor Halperin set their 1932 screen hit, *White Zombie*, in a dark and mysterious Haiti. Starring Bela Lugosi as the zombie master, the film drew directly on William Seabrook's account of Haitian "magic."[180] No doubt, it was a long way from Eugene O'Neill to the Halperin brothers, and from Charles Gilpin to the cast of *White Zombie* (about which *Time* wrote, "the acting . . . suggests that there may be some grounds for believing in zombies"). Yet, in this popular "jitter and gooseflesh" film of 1932, as in the popular primitivist play of 1920, the uses of Haiti turned, significantly, on racial and gender politics.[181]

Like *The Goat without Horns*, *White Zombie* told the story a white man and his betrothed, whose nuptial bliss is delayed by Haitian evil. In this case, the wedding is on schedule, but a white rival seeks the new wife's affections. He turns for assistance to "Murder Legendre," a dark, widow-peaked Bela Lugosi, who lives — reminiscent of Henri Christophe — in a castle atop a mountain. Legendre turns Madeline (the new wife) into a zombie, promising Charles Beaumont (the rival) that this alone will secure her for him.[182] But Legendre turns next to Beaumont himself, who begins to realize that he is the object of the evil man's attentions. Legendre then reveals his intention to turn Beaumont into his own zombie. "I have taken a fancy to you," is Legendre's come-on line, followed by a toast, "To the future, Monsieur."[183]

Madeline and Charles are not the only white zombies in *White Zombie*. Those who have been previously zombified and enslaved are, significantly, white men. Their bulging eyes could perhaps suggest stereotypical images of African Americans, but their darkened skins are more reminiscent of O'Neill's "hairy ape," Yank, and his fellow workers, than of Brutus Jones. Legendre's zombie-workers were once powerful men: a minister of the interior, a captain of the Gendarmerie, a brigand chief, a witch doctor, and an executioner. Now, he says of them, "they work faithfully; they're not afraid of long hours."[184] Indeed, the mighty have fallen; Legendre's zombies now labor in his sugar mill. As *Time* noted, "Bela's zombie factory is going full blast. Corpses carry baskets, grind the mill, do the upstairs work."[185] One film critic judged the scenes in the sugar mill as the most successful aspect of the film. The "native zombies" he saw as especially effective: "Around the primitive mills they turn like so many black, white-eyed, emasculated Samsons. They walk around in death-like groups, emotionless, lethargic and quite frightening."[186] Haiti is the locus and source of evil, but also provides, in the figure of the zombie, a vehicle for commenting on an industrial civilization that threatens to turn men into "a species of zombie."

We see, in the bedraggled figures of these once powerful men, hauling baskets and working the mill machinery, what may be in store for the wealthy and refined Charles Beaumont. Even the imposing masculine figure of the very tall actor Frederick Peters, weighing in at 250 pounds, is cowed by Legendre, and is reduced, like the others, to his enslavement at the mill.[187] But Charles's fate is made even more palpable by the film's suggestion of his forthcoming sexual powerlessness, as a man to whom Legendre has "taken a fancy." Legendre's domination over other "emasculated" men, exhibited most graphically in slave labor at the mill, takes on, in this toast to Charles, an aura of sexual domination. *Time* overlooked this detail, as it commented in a tone of ridicule, "Bela Lugosi, who looks like a comic imbecile, can make his jawbones rigid and show the whites of his eyes. These abilities qualify him to make strong men cower and women swoon."[188]

White Zombie made use of Haiti as a racialized backdrop for a drama that involved nominally white characters, or at least characters played by white actors. The Halperin brothers employed African Americans as extras on the film, but Haitian as well as American characters were played by white actors. Whether we can consider them to have performed in blackface is another question, but if so, this was not blackface of a traditional sort. In this sense, the film erased Haiti's blackness, just as it erased the fact of the occupation, still ongoing in 1932 when the film was made.[189] Still, in the racial context of the early 1930s, there may have been some ambiguity about the now swarthy zombies and the dark-haired zombie master.[190] *Time* noted that Lugosi was a Hungarian immigrant who had played, as his first American role, a "Spanish Apache" in *The Red Poppy*.[191] But whatever racial ambiguity may have attended the Halperins' Haitian monsters, there is no question that the "evil that lurks" there is the evil of Voodoo black magic, the evil that was associated particularly with Haiti.

The central drama that is played out against this background surrounds the apparent sundering of the heterosexual union between the new husband and wife, Neil and Madeline. Without her, Neil loses himself, wandering the roads in a drunken stupor, feverish, calling her name. With the help of a trusted doctor, Neil makes his way through the jungle and up to the castle, only to be confronted by his own wife. For here again, as in Davis's pulp novel, is a white woman with a knife in her hand. Murder Legendre has ordered Madeline to kill her husband, and powerless as the zombie she is, she seeks out her husband to do her (new) master's bidding. Someone, perhaps the good doctor, grasps her arm just in time.[192] Madeline wakes from her zombie state, as if from a dream, once Charles Beaumont and Legendre have fallen to their common death from a portico. White man and wife are reunited at last.

If controversy over the occupation, inflamed by the 1920 election season, opened a space for protest against the occupation, it also launched Haiti on a new career in U.S. American culture. And if for Johnson the fathers of Haitian independence offered a proud heritage, for white playwrights, novelists, short-story writers, radio programmers, and film makers, as well as for their audiences, Haiti offered racial material of an altogether different nature. Haiti's appeal, for those who would applaud its revolutionary history, as for those who would render revolutionary heroes as monsters and zombie masters, rested, at least in part, on the resources it made available for negotiating the politics of race, gender, sexuality, and national identity. Contests for meaning waged in Haiti's name, moreover, would continue beyond the final withdrawal of the Marines in August 1934. Since the long occupation, Haiti has continued to serve, in more and less veiled ways, as a reflection of U.S. American fears and desires, and thus as a salable commodity.[193]

6

MAPPING MEMORY AND DESIRE

HAITI IN THE LAND OF THE PURITANS

Like the protagonist of Agnes Tait's 1934 short story, Edna Taft "had to go to Haiti."[1] She had been wanting to go to Haiti, she said, practically her whole life; in 1937 she made it happen. A single white woman from an old New England family, Taft met with resistance from family members when she proposed the idea. But she was not of a mind to be stopped by convention or appearances. Indeed, as she told the story, in an account of her trip published later that year, she set out for her adventure in the black nation unchaperoned. This was to be a very personal adventure, something akin to a rendezvous.[2]

Edna Taft located her desire for Haiti in the folds of her childhood memory and in the dark past of her family's history in America. She recalled — and recounted in a preface to her narrative — leafing through the family Bible as a child and stumbling upon the yellowed pages of a diary that had been stashed there years before. The young Edna was not the first to come upon these pages, for they were "dog-eared by much handling." They had been torn from the diary of Zacharias Raymond, a slave trader, and one of Taft's early American ancestors. The entries told how Raymond's travels had taken him "from the steamy, torrid swamps of the African Slave Coast to an enchanting island named Saint-Domingue."[3] "When I was a child," wrote Taft, "I used to pore over these entries, dreaming childish dreams and strange fancies."[4]

Taft's "childish dreams and strange fancies" took her to the cities and towns where her great-great-great-grandfather had sold his human cargo. He had been to Cap-François, first port of call for slave traders, but also "Saint Marks, Port-au-Prince, Jeremie, L'Anse d'Enhault, Donna Maria, Aux Cayes and Jacquemel [sic]" — for he was "a shrewd Yankee" and knew he would get a better price further south. "The names of these places were magic words to my young, unformed mind," Taft mused.[5] The landscape, as it appeared in Zacharias Raymond's handwriting, held its own allure for her. "The few torn pages," she wrote, "told of a lovely land of lofty, 'folded' green mountains, emerald verdure, brilliant sapphire skies and stately palms swaying at the water's edge." But the "magic" of the towns was more explicitly racialized and gendered, for there one found "beautiful women of mixed blood."[6] Cap-François, she learned from her ancestor's private writing, was "an exceedingly wicked tropical city where adventurous men of many nations succumbed to the lure of gambling, rum and beautiful quadroon and octoroon girls whose seductive charms were famed throughout the Caribbean."[7]

Edna Taft's description of Zacharias Raymond's diary is striking in part because of the way it framed her narrative of Haiti. She accounted for her own desire for Haiti as having been kindled by reading those "few torn pages." "I spent hours searching enchanting atlases and gazing intensely at the globe of the world, seeking a tiny country named Haiti . . . and exulting jubilantly when I had found it," she wrote. "I offer this book as the result of impressions gained in the fulfillment of those early desires."[8]

Taft employed Zacharias Raymond's diary as a literary device that promised the revelation of some deeply personal truth. Consistent with modern psychological discourse, Taft's narrative figured that truth as a defining core of selfhood and identity organized in terms of sexuality. The diary promised to illuminate a sexualized space of interiority that could reveal something essential about who Zacharias Raymond had been and, perhaps, about who Edna Taft was. Yet that interior realm that existed in Taft's memories, and in Raymond's diary entries, was not only sexual; it was also fundamentally structured by racial and national differences. For what Taft found in her family Bible revealed, in faded ink, a sexualized reality called Saint Domingue, peopled by racialized women famed for their "seductive charms" and white men who "succumbed" to their lure.

That reality, moreover, stood at the very foundation of Taft's American family history. The slave-trading ancestor tucked away in the family Bible in a prominent New England home hinted at something less than pure in the land of the Puritans. Taft made that analysis explicit in her preface. "Zacharias had prospered in his pernicious trade: he had acquired many rich acres; he owned the first brick house erected in town; he was respected by his fellow citizens; he was a pillar of the church; and his frugality enabled Zacharias's descendants to live in ease and social prominence for many generations."[9] Here then, at the heart of that New England heritage that defined America for so many whites in the United States, was Haiti.[10]

Finally, Taft's marker for that heritage, the family Bible, was nothing less than an icon of Protestant domesticity. As such, it signified not only a racial, national, and class lineage, but also the very "Christian home life" that paternalist narratives claimed was lacking in Haiti. If the family Bible was a defining presence in "American homes," that presence was, in Taft's telling, a site of struggle, a representation of domesticity haunted by sexuality and race, haunted, indeed, by Haiti.

Taft's book, *A Puritan in Voodoo-Land*, was one of dozens of accounts of white Americans' travels and experiences in Haiti, written during or shortly after the long U.S. occupation there.[11] Many of these accounts — indeed, the majority — responded affirmatively to the paternalist invitation to cultivate an imperial consciousness. Yet, as Taft's refiguring of American "puritanism" suggests, the discourses that emerged from this process did not simply reproduce the paternalism that launched it. As white Americans grappled with the cultural and material implications of the occupation, they reformulated their relationship to U.S. imperialism, just as the political forms of that imperialism were themselves being reformulated in Haiti and elsewhere in the 1920s and 1930s.[12]

The cultural contexts in which U.S. Americans grappled with their relation to Haiti also shifted over the course of these decades, in part through the successive layering of discourses on Haiti. Travel writers like Edna Taft framed Haiti in new ways in relation, for example, to the intertwined development of the fields of psychology and anthropology and in relation to popular versions of those developments.[13] In the modern age of sexual liberalism, American interpreters and popularizers of psychoanalysis in the 1920s and early 1930s addressed the tensions surrounding flapper sexuality and family life.[14] Meanwhile, at Columbia University, Franz Boas placed the concept of cultural relativism at the center of his anthropological investigations and teaching, cultivating a dynamic group of students and colleagues.[15] And anthropologists and sociologists in the 1930s melded psychological questions with sociohistorical investigations in ways that gave rise to the study of "culture and personality."[16] Elsie Clews Parsons, George Eaton Simpson, Melville Herskovits, and Zora Neale Hurston participated in these academic discourses in part through their studies of Haiti. Popular travel writers, like academic anthropologists, would articulate the U.S. American desire for Haiti in new ways in relation to these emerging contexts.[17]

The four accounts of Haiti examined in this chapter all laid claim to an exotic Haiti figured largely in terms of race and sexuality. Their authors were all white Americans, and none of them was part of the formal state apparatus of the occupation.[18] They visited Haiti between 1918 and 1938 — three of them while the occupation was under way, one within a few years after the marines' withdrawal. All four, in their own ways, imagined Haiti as an integral part of an American empire, notwithstanding the fact that one of them was a self-proclaimed "anti-imperialist," who explicitly opposed the use of military force to establish or maintain U.S. influence. Two women and two men, one Texan and one Virginian, one from Massachusetts and one from Maryland, their accounts of race and sexuality in Haiti took divergent paths. Nonetheless, the travel writings of Samuel Guy Inman, Blair Niles, William Seabrook, and Edna Taft serve to illustrate some of the ways Americans used Haiti to claim, at once, their empire and their modern selves.

ON TOUR WITH THE MARINES

Samuel Guy Inman did not intend to write merely a popular and entertaining account of his travels in Haiti and the Dominican Republic. A lay minister and teacher with the progressive Christian fellowship known as the "Disciples of Christ," and a leader in the North American Protestant missionary movement, Inman had loftier goals and a more urgent sense of what was needed.[19] Like the evangelist Wilhelm Jordan, who would shortly make his call for missionary work in the "American Africa," Inman sought to mobilize the forces of civilization to assist Haiti. Indeed, the Texas-born, forty-three-year-old, white father of five saw Haiti as a "very dark spot on the horizon of the United States."[20] Thus locating Haiti on America's "horizon," he insisted that it was within the purview of caring "Christian" citizens of the United States to do something about that darkness. Although he would come, in time, to revise and complicate his understanding of Haiti, *Through Santo Domingo and Haiti: A Cruise with the Marines*, published in 1920, figured the black nation as an uncivilized backwater very much in need of American attention.[21]

This is not to say that Inman supported the occupation he saw at such close range as he traveled through the Haitian countryside in 1918, at the very height of the United States' undeclared Caribbean war. Having spent the better part of ten years as a missionary in Mexico, in part during that country's revolution, he rejected U.S. military intervention in Latin America as a solution to the region's problems.[22] Inman's 1920 account of his travels in Haiti and the Dominican Republic conveyed his opposition to the military occupations then under way in both countries. Missionaries rather than marines were the proper agents of civilization, according to Inman. He intended his travelogue to serve as a practical handbook for men of the cloth and other dedicated church members who would turn their attention to these Caribbean nations in need.[23]

In Inman's view, Haiti's darkness was nowhere more evident than in the absence of sexual morality to be found in that island nation. Haiti's need for missionary attention could be seen most readily, in particular, in the near absence, among the country people in Haiti, of any regard for marriage "in our sense of the word." "Here is one country," he wrote, striking a main chord of paternalist discourse, "where statistics on legitimacy are not kept."[24] For Inman, female "purity" and "modesty" were at the heart of civilization, and in this respect Haitians in the remote country districts were desperately in need of education. That women slept by the side of the road was just one sign of that lack of modesty. Dances marked by "the abandonment characteristic of animals," in which "body and song alike exhibit brazen proposals" provided an even more upsetting spectacle for Inman.[25] Haitians "are unmoral rather than immoral," he declared, "as they seem to have no conception of any high standards of life."[26]

If Inman knew just what to think about Haitian "darkness," if he arrived in Haiti ready to witness sexual immorality, all that he saw with the marines, and heard from them, seemed to confirm his perspective. Inman's "cruise with the marines" took him first to the port of Cap Haïtien, where he reported, as he advised other visitors to do, "to the local American officer in command."[27] Inman's discussion of the overland tour that followed gave prominence to the perspectives and concerns of the young marines who escorted him through Haiti, and of those he met along the way. "It is not hard," he wrote, "to believe anything that one is told about the degradation of the country people."[28] Traveling with marines through war-torn areas of Haiti, Inman seemed to share his companions' disgust with the local population. He quoted "one American boy stationed at Plaisance," who urged him to " 'Look at these people, just look at these people we have to live with.' "[29]

When marines looked at Haitians through the cultural lens of paternalism, what they saw was, by turns, disturbing and thrilling. Their critiques of Haitian home life featured references to the unnaturally hard toil expected of Haitian women by lazy, unmanly Haitian men.[30] Samuel Guy Inman may or may not have heard them sing their traditional leatherneck lament, revised for the Haitian setting:

> In the land of sloth and vice
> Where they never heard of ice
> Where the donkeys and the women work all day
> Where the land is full of ants

And the men don't wear their pants
It is here the soldier sings his evening lay.[31]

In song they damned the unmasculine Cacos they had to fight and pined for home in their chorus:

Underneath the boiling sun
Let them have their Benet gun
And return us to our beloved homes.[32]

As each verse enumerated the villainy and unworthiness of the Haitian Cacos, the marines' chorus brought them back to the contrast of their own cultural values, embodied in properly gendered settings, namely, "our beloved homes."

At the same time, marines' "perceptions" of Haitian gender disorder were convenient indeed for men who wanted to prove their masculinity by dominating women. As we have seen, U.S. marines raped and sexually harassed Haitian women during their tenure in the Caribbean. Other marines deplored such behavior, holding their uniform (and their humanity) above it. Together, however, those who sexually violated Haitian women and those who did not colluded in a collective project: the discursive construction of the Haitian woman as exotic and promiscuous.

Inman's assessment of "moral life" in Haiti shaped his analysis of what was wrong with the occupation and, at the same time, formed the basis of his defense of the marines. Thus, while he criticized the "military standpoint" from which "it is natural to regard all life as cheap," he emphasized the specific moral conditions that led "American boys" to commit "repulsive acts" in Haiti.[33] "Who will throw the first stone at a man who is compelled to live away from all that is pure and noble, without religious or moral influence of any kind, without books or recreation often, without even a baseball or a victrola, in the midst of the vilest native life, where men have little virtue and the women small sense of shame?"[34] As John Houston Craige would later suggest, so Inman insisted that the company of Haitian women and the absence of white American women was a crucial problem for U.S. marines in Haiti. "If necessary for a few months under extraordinary conditions, it should certainly not be permitted through the years that men cannot get into a pure atmosphere or see good women of their own race or hear a moral exhortation for two or three years, as happens with some of our men here."[35] If "a baseball or a victrola" might have helped a bit in their absence, Christianity and white women Inman ranked as fundamental moral requirements for American men.

AFTERMATH

These women do nearly all the manual labor that is done in the island —

A typical country woman riding her burro —

Figure 28. Lieutenant Arthur B. Jacques's portrait of "a typical country woman riding her burro." Marine Corps Research Center Archives, Quantico, Virginia.

Inman's critique of the occupation, based in part on his concern for the young white men stranded in Haiti without white women, in no way precluded his adoption of their perspective regarding the rebels they sought to vanquish. Inman reported, for example, a story he learned from an officer, "of a prisoner that had just been brought in from the hills, who acted just like an animal, eating the mud on his arms and trying to chew the rope with which he was bound."[36] Prefiguring pulp fiction writers who would turn Haitians into inhuman beings and outright monsters, Inman later told of a rebel who was brought into camp after being shot. "A gendarme was probing for the bullet," he wrote, "with what looked to me like a needle used to sew up potato sacks. The blood was flowing profusely as the probe went here and there, but the man lay as still as though absolutely nothing was going on." "After seeing that," he continued, "I was more ready to believe the stories of how they kept on coming after they had been shot in a way that would be fatal to an ordinary man."[37]

In light of marines' confusion regarding the distinction between groups of people whom Corporal Homer Overley lumped together as "Cacos and Voodoes [sic]," and in light of the difficulty marines faced in distinguishing between dangerous Cacos and peaceful inhabitants, Inman's understanding of Voodoo is especially revealing. "It is said," he reported without noting who said it, "that the result of Voodoo worship is plainly registered on the faces of those who participate in it, making them look like devils."[38]

The similarities between Inman's practical "handbook" and the sensationalist work of later travel and fiction writers extended also to his description of the Voodoo ceremony itself. Inman reported on this matter-of-factly, as though he had seen it, which he admitted he had not. "A ceremony very much like the Mass is used at the beginning," he wrote. "Afterward the child which is to be sacrificed is brought in and at a certain stage it is killed, its heart being taken out and the participants drinking of its blood." "The more recent form of the ceremony," Inman added casually, "substitutes a goat for a child."[39]

Inman also seemed to share with the marines the "thrill" of "getting into bandit country."[40] Missionary and marines alike imagined themselves in the image of the white man exploring Africa, Inman suggested. Speaking for the whole party, he wrote, "all the time we were in the country districts, and a good deal of the time we were in the cities, we felt that we were in the heart of Africa." Yet, even that "dark continent," where other American missionaries labored, could not suggest the level of "vice and disease," or the challenge to "rule and discipline" that Americans faced in Haiti, according to Inman.[41]

Inman argued, in effect, that paternalism should be left to ministers and missionaries, particularly in Haiti, where the population was "less amenable to rule and discipline than their African progenitors," and where the men sent to fill out the paternal role lacked the moral context (or training) necessary to do it properly. Inman's opposition to the occupation rested on the supposed degradation of the Haitian people, the same idea that, for others, made the occupation necessary in the first place. In this way, Inman's protest played into the very same cultural patterns that resulted in the popular vilification of Haiti and Haitians in the United States. Moreover, Inman's use of notions of sexual order to critique U.S. policy fell in line with statements made in support of the occupation that also rested on a view of Haiti as a land of sexual excess and gender disorder. Finally, despite the differences between missionary tracts and popular exotic fiction, Inman's texts exhibited Haitian "exotica" in forms remarkably similar to those later found in pulp fiction and Hollywood film.

In the course of the 1920s, Samuel Guy Inman would pursue his interest and concern for Haiti through reading, discussion, and, in 1929, another trip to the still occupied nation. By 1930, when he published another book on the questions of conquest and missionary assistance in the Caribbean, he had come to a rather more complex view of the problems facing Haiti and avenues for their solution, as we will see in the final chapter.

While Inman was moving away from the exoticism that marked his early writing on Haiti, the rest of his nation was moving rapidly toward it. By the mid-twenties, tourism in Haiti was beginning to be advertised. At the same time, U.S. travel writing was ready to explore further — and to play out — the links between paternalism and exoticism in U.S. approaches to Haiti.

By 1926 the *Herald Tribune* could describe Haiti as a picturesque place of leisure, and indeed, other newspapers and magazines joined in praising Haiti's virtues as a vacation spot for Americans. Characterizing the Caribbean island nation as a haven for the weary, adventurous, or simply curious traveler, American newspapers and magazines in the 1920s featured Haiti as a tranquil, safe, and rewarding destination, while holding out its mysterious and exotic allure. Not until the thirties would steamship companies really focus on promoting vacations in Haiti, but by 1929 would-be travelers felt the pull of the island nation, having been exposed to the possibilities: an exhilarating hike up to the Citadel of King Henri Christophe; a picturesque stroll through the market; a venturesome evening of Haitian rum, dance, and song in a Port-au-Prince nightclub.

"Housekeeping in Haiti," announced a back-page headline in the *New York Herald Tribune* in October 1926, "Is both Picturesque and Leisurely;

Markets Offer Colorful Wares at Penny Prices."[42] The article that followed addressed itself to middle-class American women who might consider a family sojourn in the black republic, enticing them with the promise of ease, lovely scenery, and inexpensive souvenirs. Indeed, a dollar went farther in Port-au-Prince than in Philadelphia, afforded more in Cap Haïtien than in Chicago. New Yorkers and others returned home loaded with sisal baskets, mahogany trinkets, and colorful cottons, all purchased with little more than spare change.

Between 1918 and 1926 Americans began to tame the Haiti they had created; they reined in its wild side, as they understood it. As marine "pacification" made Haiti safe for American travel, early concerns over, and fascination with, what was perceived as Haitian sexual excess and gender disorder turned into a highly marketable brand of excitement. By the 1930s the narratives of returning marines and travelers presented Haiti's sights and wonders, in turns, as picturesque, comic, horrific, and even disgusting, yet always somehow strangely alluring.

BLAIR NILES AND "AFRICA'S ELDEST DAUGHTER"

Blair Niles's *Black Haiti: A Biography of Africa's Eldest Daughter*, one of the most revealing travel narratives of the 1920s, made explicit many of the tensions that characterized U.S. discourses on Haiti. Published the year of WILPF's investigation, and considered by Emily Balch to be a "charming book," Niles's account of her travels offered a mix of cultural relativism and racial essentialism that praised "Black Haiti" precisely for its very blackness.[43] While maintaining a fairly tempered attitude toward the "advisory Nordic occupation," as she called it, Niles criticized the assumption of cultural superiority that underlay American paternalism in Haiti. Like others, Niles presented the Caribbean nation in terms of gendered social relations and exotic sexuality. Unlike others, she explored in detail the specular aspects of U.S. exoticism, illuminating the ways in which increasing numbers of Americans found "aesthetic redemption" in Haiti. For these reasons and others, Niles's account lends further insight into the cultural dynamics of U.S. travel in occupied Haiti.

Born fifteen years after the close of the Civil War, Blair Rice Crenshaw was raised on a Virginia plantation, owned by her father, and worked by a large number of tenant sharecroppers. Niles, then, like many other white Americans who would come to write on Haiti during the occupation, developed an acquaintance with cultural variation before ever leaving the States.[44] Married first to William Beebe, a naturalist, then to Robert Niles, an architect and photographer, Blair Niles traveled extensively in the South Pacific and South America with Beebe before making a trip to Haiti with her second husband in 1925.[45]

In preparation for her trip, Niles read whatever she could find on Haitian politics, history, and culture.[46] In addition, besides newspapers, magazines, and books, Niles, like Eugene O'Neill, had verbal sources to augment her understanding of Haiti. By this time Niles lived in New York City, where, she later wrote, she had made the acquaintance of "a sea-captain, temporarily out of command, and filling in the interval by running the lift in a New York apartment house."[47] Having been to Haiti recently, the captain warned her against the trip.

Niles began *Black Haiti* with a brief account of the captain's repeated warnings. After several such conversations, he finally explained that when he had last been in Haiti, a native man had approached and threatened him. According to the captain, the Haitian's words had been, " 'If I could get you alone, . . . I'd cut out your heart and eat it.' " Having done more research while in Haiti, and having read quite a number of Haitian authors, Niles cited the poet, Hannibal Price, regarding "the incurable levity of his countrymen," who would play jokes on foreigners by leveling such threats.[48] She commented further, "now that I know Haiti I can see how irresistible a target for Haitian raillery the big blond captain had been as in his white uniform he walked the sun-flooded streets of Port-au-Prince." Opening her travel narrative thus, Niles set her own book apart from much popular writing on Haiti to date.[49] This, she effectively declared, will not be a lurid tale of cannibalism. On the contrary, Niles's discussion of cannibalism was more an attempt to understand the cultural dynamics that produced such tales. Racial antagonism, according to Niles, played a crucial role in this process; she wrote, "I could hear the laughter" of the Haitian who had played this joke, "And there was bitterness as well as mockery" in it.[50]

Shortly after arriving in Cap Haïtien, Blair Niles had an encounter that seemed to her to illuminate further the process that resulted in such bitter mockery. Niles saw, "perched on the edge of a sidewalk," a small boy carefully enunciating the words, "Ca-lam-i-té, Mo-ral-i-té, Ti-mid-i-té, Se-gur-i-té." "Enchanted by this little person who . . . oblivious of passers-by, read to himself such serious words, I cried out to the photographer that I must have him."[51] As Robert Niles focused the shot, however, "an elderly mulatto man" interjected, proclaiming, "I oppose myself. . . . I will not have the child put on a post card and labelled a 'monkey'! . . . I will not have it!" Niles mused over the effect of the incident on the little boy and concluded that "the idea of race animosity had been planted."[52]

Yet, where Niles drew from this incident a lesson about race animosity, her account of it illuminates another dimension of intercultural contact in occupied Haiti. The elderly man was apparently conscious of the practices by which Americans were turning his country and his people into exotic commodities and, particularly, into spectacles designed to produce visual pleasure by reproducing and reinforcing quaint and racist images of Haiti. Niles's own travel narrative, furthermore, illustrates and documents the very process highlighted by the elderly man's protests.

Distancing herself from the other American travelers with whom she arrived in Haiti, Niles contrasted their respective itineraries. She sought not "sights" but instead "the living echo of the streets," not the daytime Haiti, but "the dream Haiti," "the Haiti of drum and dance."[53] She sought always to go "into the interior," geographically and psychologically.[54] Refusing to settle for "histories composed at long range, by authors far removed in color, in environment and inheritance," Niles visited Madame Viard's book-shop in Port-au-Prince and sought out books on Haiti wherever possible. She wrote, "All this seeking of mine is for the things that Haitians have written. I want to know what they have thought and felt in the years of their dramatic existence as Haitians."[55] Niles imagined her book as an extended inquiry into Haitian subjectivity, an attempt to ascertain the truth of Haitian racial consciousness.

As Niles's own literary and travel itinerary brought her a deeper under-standing of Haiti, along the way she caricatured the surface view available to the less inquisitive traveler. The singers she saw and heard at night would be "by day but men and women; cast in the familiar Ethiopian mold; teakwood people with ivory for teeth and for the whites of their eyes."[56] By day, Niles seemed to imply, one could see but statues in Haiti, if not postcards, still little more than teakwood tokens such as tourists might buy as souvenirs at the "Haitian Curio Shop" in Port-au-Prince.[57]

In contrast to the depth of understanding she sought in her travels, Niles emphasized the quality of appearances on first arriving in one port or an-other. Landing at Cap Haïtien, for example, the scenes she noticed seemed to her to partake "of the quality of Art."[58] In Petit Goave, Niles wrote, the market people "appear in the white light merely as brightly colored pup-pets; part of some sun-flooded spectacle, staged about the bluest of all the blue bays of all pageant worlds."[59] "You remember only the light," she said of the coastal town, "light of so intense a clarity that you see the surging life as purely objective." "One is conscious of no subjective profundities. Reality has slipped from life. Surely the oranges piled in golden heaps on the ground are but baubles, intended only to be looked at."[60] On first arriving, Niles suggested, a visitor could be so taken with the sense of visual pleasure that human beings and objects alike would appear merely as part of a vast spectacle. "So does the gay sun blind one to realities," she wrote, "burlesquing even the surfaces, and obliterating the depths; denying that there are profundities where still lives the song of Africa."[61]

If, in the bright light of a coastal town, one gained no sense of Haitian "subjective profundities," then travels "into the interior" would shift the visitor's focus, allowing one to plumb the depths of Haitian culture. Niles explored Haitian subjectivities by observing and engaging cultural expression in a variety of forms, including poetry, history, religion, dance, and song. If poetry and history could be obtained at Madame Viard's in Port-au-Prince, one had to travel inland, Niles implied, in order to experience Haitian religion, song, and dance. Accordingly, one night Niles and her husband ventured into the hills, where, not far from the capital, they joined a gathering of dancing peasants.[62]

The dance they observed this night she called the "love dance," and, according to Niles, it transformed reality and time, highlighting the essential identities of the sexes.[63] Niles described the bodily movements of the dancers and the instruments used including "the long Voodoo drum, the voice of which so profoundly stirs them that its use has been made illegal." All of a sudden, "it is no longer the year 1925. It is the sixth day of creation; the day when 'male and female created He them.'"[64] Here then was "the Haiti of drum and dance," the "true" Haiti in which elemental gender differences were stark and unmistakable, in which sexuality was central to cultural expression. For Niles, sexuality as a kind of ultimate subjective truth here belied the initial impression of Haiti as mere spectacle.

This reading of the "truth" of Haiti, furthermore, marked a shift away from the interpretations of missionaries and marines earlier in the decade. These observers had perceived a kind of gender abnormality in Haitian social patterns surrounding work and sexuality. Critics like James Weldon Johnson had portrayed any irregularities in Haitian family life as the result of American imperialism. Unlike either, Niles instead focused on Haitian sexuality as revealing the most natural, unadorned truth of male and female identities. For Niles, this was a welcome contrast to American civilization.

Joining the dancing peasants, then, Niles asserted, "We became absorbed by the crowd, assimilated, blotted out." For travelers, then, as well as for marines with a different understanding of Haiti, probing the depths of Haitian culture could entail, at least temporarily, an erasure of selfhood. For Niles, however, this self-abnegation was a welcome change, enabling her to receive the gifts of Haitian song and dance: "great gifts," she called them, "which their race might make to a drab and waiting world."[65]

If dance and music seemed to reveal to Niles some of the essential truth of race and sex, her exploration of Haitian patriotism emphasized the importance of these truths for understanding national identity. For Niles, this exploration, like her ventures into the Haitian hills, proceeded in spatial terms, as she guided her reader through the landscape. "You wander through the familiar fields of patriotism," she wrote, "where Anglo-Saxon and Africo-French can meet understandingly." "You wander into areas of domestic affection where the landscape is placidly familiar." Yet, she noted, there were marked differences, for whereas American patriotism was "semi-religious," Haitian national sentiment was "a personal passion, like love."[66]

Drawing on the history books she had gathered, Niles presented this passion as fed by the spirit of the Haitian revolutionary leader Dessalines. The pride and defiance that, as a slave, brought the violence of slavery fully to bear on his body, Niles explained, resulted in "fustigations" or wounds that would always serve to rekindle his rage and resentment.[67] The rage of Dessalines and his people supplied a fundamental contrast to the patriotism familiar to Americans, according to Niles. Coming upon it, she wrote, "you enter a dark and bitter land, a devastated region, such as your race, if you are of Nordic origin, has never known." "You begin then to know that you have come upon a journey; that you are in an exotic land" characterized by "a vibrant patriotism and fierce defiant pride of race."[68]

Continuing her guided tour of Haitian patriotic passion, Niles warned her readers that their ultimate destination would be the most shocking. "If you are a typical Anglo-Saxon, accepting without question your inheritance, it is in the final region of sexual morality, into which inevitably your explorations lead, that you find yourself most alien." Niles's explanation for this, ultimately, is the dual inheritance of France and Africa, and "the actual blood of France" that courses through the veins of Haiti.[69]

Here, of course, is that familiar trope of American writing on Haiti: blood, the signifier at once of race, inheritance, identity, and family. If Haiti was the child of France and Africa, suggested Niles, this was so by virtue of the "actual blood" coursing through her veins. One must understand this in order to understand the "landscape" of "domestic affection" that is Haitian patriotism. The terms "blood" and "domestic affection," furthermore, indicated the centrality for Niles, as for other American writers, of the family as a fundamental construct informing the discourse of national identity.

Of course, U.S. Americans were not alone in using the idea of the human family to represent Haitian identity. In fact, Niles relied on Haitian writers for some of her most pointed metaphors. Beauvais Lespinasse supplied the phrase "fille ainée de l'Afrique," and Niles borrowed the characterization for both her subtitle and her epigraph. He wrote, "Haiti, eldest daughter of Africa, views her history and her civilization as the first page in the rehabilitation of her race."[70] Lespinasse's words served to establish right from the outset Niles's intention to praise Haiti. Niles also quoted the poet Devieux to qualify the relation between parent (Africa) and child (Haiti); Devieux described Haitians as "an orphan people, brutally torn from the cradle of their race."[71] Here, as in James Weldon Johnson's account, Haiti is orphaned as a result of the brutalities of Western imperialism.

Yet, here we are not simply reading Lespinasse and Devieux. We must consider not only the content of the quotes, but their selection by Niles and their incorporation into her text. What was the effect of her appropriation of their words for this travel narrative? By characterizing her text as "a biography of Africa's eldest daughter," she thus personified Haiti and defined "her" primarily in terms of gender and parentage. Haiti's direct lineal connection to Africa, accented by the "blood" of France, and her essentially gendered female identity, served to highlight the appeal of the black nation as an object of desire. Niles used Haitian writers to establish the appeal of Haiti in contrast to the industrialized civilization of the United States. After discussing Devieux and other Haitian poets, she concluded that "in Haiti the mingling of France with Africa was like giving to Africa a drink of Champagne: with the result that the personality of Haiti is singularly vital."[72] "Gifts of rhythm and of imagery and of joy," wrote Niles, in what by now is a tired trio of stereotypes, were the "race inheritance" of Haiti.[73]

If Niles appeared to discover racial truths that separated Haiti and the United States, evidenced in the elemental passion of Haitian patriotism, in her sense of herself as alien amid the sexual morality of Haiti, in the "exotic" nature of Haitian race pride, still the racial and cultural chasms between Haiti and the United States need not, to her mind, remain unbridged. She may not have had her postcard-like image of the serious little boy from Cap Haïtien, but she left the interior with its contours and landmarks "mapped in [her] memory." Reemerging from the interior, arriving for a second time at Cap Haïtien, she wrote, "this time, I was arriving in the mood of memory." "Haiti had become," she wrote, "an intimate experience, an integral part of personal living, taking its place among remembered things." "Only in travel," furthermore, could history "come thus sensuously alive, that it appears with the reality of personal memory."[74] Niles appropriated Haiti to the point of internalizing it, claiming its subjectivity as her own.

Niles's appropriation of Haitian culture, her acceptance of its "gifts," led her to object to certain aspects of the occupation and to its rhetorical justification on the grounds that Haiti was a backward and degraded land. "Americanization should stop with order and science," she wrote; "it must not stifle the song in hearts that yet remember how to set life to music."[75] Yet, if Americans had much to learn from Haiti, as Niles repeatedly suggested, the daytime Haiti also had to learn from the occupation. For all its implicit criticism of American civilization, *Black Haiti* portrayed the paternalist American presence as useful in creating enough calm and clarity in which the value of Haiti's African culture could be appreciated by Americans. Niles herself, after all, had access to Haiti and to Madame Viard's bookshop in part because of the presence of an "advisory Nordic occupation." She concluded that it was, finally, in the "transient tranquillity of paternalism" that one could fully discern the relative merits of Haitian culture, and in turn the limits that had to be placed on U.S. modernization efforts in Haiti.[76]

Niles's qualified approval of the American military presence developed as she began to sympathize and identify with a U.S. Marine Corps lieutenant serving as a Gendarmerie captain in the Haitian interior. Niles introduced the "tall lean man" in khaki as he stood on a hilltop, among Haitian ruins, overlooking the district he commanded. With "loving pride," according to Niles, the marine began to speak: " 'All this,' he was saying, 'is my district . . . as far as you can see.' " Niles was immediately struck by two characteristics of the marine who thus boasted of "his land," namely, his integrity and his whiteness. She conceded the existence of widespread Haitian resistance to white proprietorship in Haiti, but contrasted the Haitians' image of the white man "as the symbol of a dealer in human flesh," the personification of "the wheel and the whip," with her own image of this trustworthy and responsible custodian of Haitian society.[77]

Like Niles, the marine lieutenant had gone into interiors and, in so doing, had shed his mask of marine bravado. "It is only a lonely Marine that will drop the mask, and to find him you have to go into interiors. In the midst of his fellows he is ever the rollicking, swashbuckling, 'goddam'; enthusiastic only about a drink or a woman; vastly superior to all dark races; and even contemptuous of any whites not hailing from the land sanctified by his own nativity."[78] In contrast, this man was thoughtful and temperate. Yet it turned out that this man "was one of those who had been charged with atrocities." He "had won my trust," wrote Niles; "I who generally speaking disbelieve in Marines, I who am unalterably opposed to capital punishment" had come to trust a man who had ordered the execution of a Haitian rebel.[79] Niles's trust in the lieutenant, moreover, survived this revelation. He was, she concluded, "the sort of man who was merry with dogs, a man who won the confidence of his negro orderly, a man who loved the power of his job, but who was skeptical about omniscience in the matter of civilizations."[80] He was, in short, a man who seemed to share Niles's sense of the appeal of Haitian culture and who, like Niles, had Haiti "mapped in [his] memory." These similarities suggest the possibility of another: did Niles also share the marine's proprietary feeling for Haiti?

In contrast to the lieutenant, Niles discusses an American woman in Haiti, "a pale little wife" she met at another "Gendarmerie Captain's bungalow." "Like many exiles, especially exiled women, this girl had an infinitely detached way of talking about her environment. You felt that it seemed unreal to her and that she spoke of it much as she might have alluded to the vague details of a dream. I am sure that in her mind, etched in exact detail were the streets and shops and moving picture houses of some little town in the States, a town inhabited by the only real people there were in the world."[81] Like the tourists who saw only "teakwood people," the "pale little wife" never gained the ability to see past surface appearances. In the midst of Haiti's bountiful cultural gifts, she insisted on clinging to the details of her hometown and allowing her exotic surroundings to pass her by with an air of unreality.

Niles's attention to surface appearances in Haiti seems to have been part of a rhetorical strategy designed to underline her own more probing look at Haiti. Yet, although she may have insisted that she succeeded in plumbing the nation's depths, Niles presented a view of Haiti that still conformed to the character of a staged spectacle. Relating the story of Dessalines's assassination, for example, Niles explained that the emperor had arranged to be met at the bridge called Pont-Rouge by a loyal officer named Gedeon. How would the assassins overcome this obstacle? Could they find a convincing impostor? Niles concluded, "As in a melodrama there would have been an adjutant-major strongly resembling Gedeon, so there was his counterpart at Pont-Rouge." It was, she wrote, "as though in the very facts of their history the blacks could never escape drama; as though they were pawns in the hands of an omnipotent playwright."[82] If all of her seeking led her to "interiors" that belied Haiti's surface "burlesque," at the same time Niles's travels seemed to confirm that one authentic race truth evident in Haiti was indeed the dramatic burlesque inherent in Haitian history and culture.

Niles pointed to several different modes of interacting with Haiti as an

American. One was illustrated by the "pale little wife" of a Gendarmerie captain, who maintained "an infinitely detached way of talking" about Haiti. Colorless as she was, she failed to internalize any of what she saw around her. Like other exiled women, the land of her exile was not "mapped in [her] memory," as it was mapped in Niles's. The Gendarmerie captain, on the other hand, had himself gone into interiors. Shedding the "mask" worn by marines in the capital city, his humanity shone through as he stood atop a hill looking out at the surrounding countryside and proclaiming, "this is all my district." Finally, Niles described herself, atop the Citadel and looking down after her own exploration and internalization of Haitian interiors. She compared herself to a hawk hovering above the land. Then she invoked the memory of other appropriations: that of Columbus, of the buccaneers, of Napoleon. Mackandal and Toussaint had fought for independence on the grounds she viewed from the Citadel, but now goods were exported under American supervision out of the port towns in her hawk's-eye view. Her language, whether or not by conscious decision, likened her own appropriation with the others. Niles concluded with the "world-question" of whether European American civilization had much to offer or could even justify itself. It was clear to her, however, that Haiti had a great deal to offer, and she urged other U.S. Americans to get it, if they could.

WILLIAM SEABROOK'S "MAGIC ISLAND"

By the late twenties, a handful of travel writers were getting what they thought Haiti had to offer, and passing it along to other Americans on a larger and larger scale with the help of newspapers, magazines, and book clubs.[83] The Literary Guild, as we have seen, featured two books dealing with Haiti among its "main selections": John Vandercook's *Black Majesty*, in 1928, and William Seabrook's *The Magic Island*, in 1929. Both books developed an extensive popular audience in the months and years following their publication and selection by the guild, and the latter achieved best-seller status, introducing a relatively broad U.S. readership to Haiti and Voodoo as exotic cultural commodities.[84] The *New York Herald Tribune* said of *The Magic Island*: "Here in its own field is the book of the year."[85]

In 1927, at the age of forty-one, William Buehler Seabrook was a journalist turned world traveler and writer, with some experience in advertising. Having just published his first book, *Adventures in Arabia*, Seabrook now expressed his desire to travel to Haiti and to get at the truth of Voodoo. He had "turned Arab" to write about Arabia, he announced to his publisher, and now he would "turn Negro" to write about Haiti.[86] Like Blair Niles, Seabrook set out to write a sympathetic book about the Caribbean nation, one that would emphasize the appeal of a primitive culture for Americans who were in danger of becoming "mechanical, soulless robots."[87]

The original object of the former journalist's investigation, then, was not the success or failure of the military intervention. At the same time, traveling through Haiti during the occupation would necessarily lead William Seabrook, as it had led James Weldon Johnson, Samuel Guy Inman, and Blair Niles, to the marines. Seabrook's evaluation of the occupation, to the extent that he treated it directly in his final account, was mixed. He praised its accomplishments with "roads, sewers, hospitals, sanitation, stabilized currency, economic prosperity, and political peace," but criticized the American attempt to inculcate "race-consciousness" in the Haitian upper classes by teaching them "their proper place." Seabrook focused on the racist attitudes and behaviors of U.S. Marine Corps officers in Haiti, particularly those who, from the capital city, supervised what he termed, sometimes ironically, "our own benevolent American protectorate."[88]

Ultimately, however, Seabrook's narrative reflected a belief in the value of U.S. military paternalism in Haiti. His Haiti was an orphaned island ready to welcome a benevolent American "Papa Blanc" or white father. Unlike some apologists for the occupation, Seabrook refused to defend U.S. intervention by denying the validity or integrity of Haitian culture. Setting himself apart from such writers, he professed his desire to defend Haiti and its customs, and repeatedly proclaimed their value, particularly in contrast to the empty routine of modern American civilization. At the same time, with a journalist's desire to bring out "the story" in what he wrote, and with an advertiser's eye for "the hook," Seabrook consistently emphasized what, for American readers, would be the new, the different, and, especially, the shocking in Haitian life as he perceived it. Partly by virtue of this sensational approach, *The Magic Island* ultimately buttressed the claims of U.S. paternalism with graphic illustrations (in words and pictures) of Haiti's disturbing otherness.

The core of Seabrook's exposé on Haiti concerned the intimate relationship between sexuality and racial identity, evidenced in the primitive beliefs and practices of the Haitian peasant folk. Eight years earlier, Samuel Guy Inman had attended to matters of gender and sexuality as crucial for understanding the Haitian people out of a desire to change them. In contrast, Seabrook, like Niles, shifted the discourse toward the celebration of an essential African racial identity fully revealed in an exotic sexuality. Seabrook, to a much greater extent than Niles, presented an unflinching examination of the sexual content attributed to "blackness." His quest for the secrets of Voodoo would provide the vehicle for this presentation.

Like Samuel Guy Inman, then, Seabrook was particularly interested in the religious question in Haiti. Unlike him, of course, Seabrook sought not to Christianize Haiti but to learn from Voodoo, to get at some truth about himself by escaping the strictures of civilization as he knew it. Whereas for Inman superstition could be overcome by Christianity, for Seabrook civilization could be overcome by exposure to the authentic belief of a primitive people. He wrote: "Better a papaloi [Vodou priest] in Haiti with blood-stained hands who believes in his living gods than a frock-coated minister on Fifth Avenue reducing Christ to a solar myth and rationalizing the immaculate conception." Seabrook sought not "rational ethics and human brotherly love," however useful they might be, but rather a kind of primal religious experience. "Let religion have its bloody sacrifices," he wrote, "yes, even human sacrifices, if thus our souls may be kept alive."[89]

By returning to the primitive roots of civilization and learning what truth lay there, Seabrook suggested, Western man could free himself. It was therefore essential that *The Magic Island* establish the connection between Haiti in 1928 and the origins of Western civilization. To this end, Seabrook pointed out the likeness of particular aspects of Haitian culture with scenes and figures drawn from Judaic, Christian, and Greek texts. Those aspects of Haitian Voodoo that seemed most foreign to white Americans were most likely to come in for this treatment in his book. Thus, the sacrifice of a large bird he described in a manner suggestive of Zeus visiting Leda in the form of a swan and impregnating her. Likewise a girl whom, it appeared, was about to be sacrificed, was, for Seabrook, like "Jephtha's daughter doomed to die by her own father" or, more accurately, like "Isaac bound by Abraham on Mount Moriah."[90] Haiti was "a world of marvels, miracles, and wonders," he wrote, "in which gods spoke from burning bushes, as on Sinai." Seabrook explained Voodoo as a syncretic religion, a melding of different traditions and symbols to create a new religious form, just as, he pointed out, indeed, even Christianity had been at one time, drawing as it had on pagan rituals.[91]

By establishing such similarities, Seabrook also reinforced the image of Haiti as a preserve of human primitivism, a land where adventurous white men could revisit the savage childhood of their own race. Like big game hunting in Africa, exploring the mysteries of Voodoo in Haiti could serve to affirm racial and gender identity for white American males.[92] It was in this role that Haiti presented one of its most alluring aspects. In turn, the affirmation of a primitive cross-racial connection served, for Seabrook, to justify the cultural appropriation of Haiti. Seabrook thus explained his connection to "the Voodoo holy of holies," the priestess who would show him the mysteries of Voodoo, this way: "Between Maman Celie and me there was a bond which I cannot analyze or hope to make others understand. . . . We had both felt it almost from our first contact. It was as if we had known each other always, had at some past time been united by the mystical equivalent of an umbilical cord; as if I had suckled in infancy at her dark breasts, had wandered far, and was now returning home."[93] In Seabrook's telling, the exotic priestess evoked in him a return to the primitive infancy of man, and she too felt the power of that connection. As a result, he confidently asserted, she would not worry about what he might write, for "whatever might grow treelike from my interest," she would know, "its roots were buried in soil common to us both."[94]

Despite this confident assertion, however, the published text belied Seabrook's simply stated intentions. Indeed, his Haiti was by turns, "sweet . . . impenetrable . . . monstrous . . . obscene . . . hairy . . . black . . . forbidding." Seabrook professed his desire to exonerate Voodoo from the unfairness with which it had been discussed in the past. Yet he praised it, in his words, "despite up-cropping naivetes, savageries, grotesqueries, superstitious mumbo-jumbo, and at times deliberate witch-doctor charlatan trickiness that must be included too if I am to keep this record honest."[95] Seabrook compared his own reactions to a Voodoo ceremony with those of the "literary traditional white stranger" looking on with revulsion; he saw the beauty in it, he said, even though it was savage.[96]

In Seabrook's text, then, Haiti served as a literalized spatial representation of the Freudian unconscious, a place where the family romance and the earlier experience of polymorphous sexuality could be revisited and unshackled. Yet, this literalization also fixed Haiti's discursive association with the developmental stage of childhood. If Haiti could serve as the realm of childhood in relation to an American adulthood, furthermore, it would become clear, in turn, that the United States could provide a useful adult presence in that realm. Here, then, was the logic of paternalism, an integral part of a text claiming to exonerate and value Haiti's black culture.

That logic emerged in a variety of contexts within Seabrook's narrative. His very first lines of text, for example, raised the question of Haiti's paternity and suggested the mystery of its racial identity. Seabrook opened *The Magic Island* by introducing the reader to Louis, his "devoted yard boy," the book's first figure for Haiti. It is clear from the outset that Louis is a troubling and almost schizophrenic character, for though he is humble and devoted, there is also something distinctly evil about him. After an extensive discussion of Louis and his oddities, Seabrook indicated how important this character had been for his own understanding of Haiti. He wrote: "And what has all this to do with the dark mysteries of Voodoo? you may ask, but I suspect that you already know. It was humble Louis and none other who set my feet in the path which led finally through river, desert, and jungle, across hideous ravines and gorges, over the mountains and beyond the clouds, and at last to the Voodoo Holy of Holies. These are not metaphors," Seabrook pointedly asserted. "The topography of Haiti is a tropical-upheaved, tumbled-towering madland of paradises and infernos."[97] The schizophrenic Louis, then, was a key figure in Seabrook's understanding of the literal "madland," which he called "the Magic Island." By introducing the author to the *mamaloi* (priestess) whose rites and magic practices he would describe, Louis would be the first to unlock the secrets of Voodoo for traveler and reader alike.

Bearing all this in mind, let us now turn to the first words Seabrook used to introduce the reader to Louis and to Haiti: "Louis, son of Catharine Ozias of Orblanche, paternity unknown — and thus without a surname was he inscribed in the Haitian civil register."[98] The first trouble with Louis, then, was that he had no father. Like Haiti, Seabrook seemed to imply, he was a fatherless child, whose very identity was itself a mystery. Did "the actual blood of France" course through Haiti's veins, as Blair Niles had recently asserted? Seabrook preferred to leave the question open, at least, so far as the backcountry peasants were concerned. Upon arriving in the remote mountain village that was Louis's home, however, Seabrook declared, "It might have been in the friendly heart of Africa."[99]

In an impassioned response to *The Magic Island*, Jean Price-Mars, now Haiti's foremost ethnologist, assailed the credibility of Seabrook's account of this village. "That Mr. Seabrook may have succeeded in winning the confidence of a Maman Celie, I am willing to concede to him, on the condition, however, that he does not dramatize the situation by depicting to us the peasant community whose guest he has been as a nook lost in the highest and most inaccessible mountains, isolated from all communication with urban centers."[100] Price-Mars explained, "These conditions render his account absolutely improbable," for "there is not a single peasant in a true rural centre who would consent to organize real Voodoo ceremonies for the sole pleasure of a stranger." Calling Seabrook's account of the rites he claims to have observed in this village "only half true," Price-Mars detailed some of the gross discrepancies between the ceremonies depicted in *The Magic Island* and those that actually took place in rural Haiti.[101]

Jean Price-Mars's objections to Seabrook's sensationalism rested in part on the presence of such half truths. "I am forced to remark that this book is throughout very amusing and very cruel — amusing, on account of the material replete with savage humor, and abominable, because the American reader, and even the Haitian reader who is not in a position to check up on the facts advanced, is drawn to ask himself: 'Is what he relates true? In any case, these grewsome facts, such as are recorded, seem likely if they are not true.' "[102] Indeed, U.S. reviewers of Seabrook's book accepted much of its tone as accurate, even when they questioned some of the facts. The sociologist Robert Redfield, for example, suggested, "Admit the probability that some of the blood and blackness and much of the persistent rhythm of the tomtoms is merely good stage direction. It is, in the vernacular, just hooey. . . . It is, nevertheless, a safe guess that the book more vividly conveys to the reader the character of Haiti" than would a "painstaking" academic account.[103]

Price-Mars's objections notwithstanding, it was in this mountain village, according to Seabrook, that he first learned the secrets of Voodoo under the guidance of Maman Celie, who appeared to be the most powerful presence in the area. Although he described the village as "primitive and patriarchal," Seabrook emphasized the role of the mamaloi in local governance. "The little community," he wrote, "was ruled by Maman Celie and Papa Theodore, her venerable, less active husband."[104] In contrast to earlier characterizations of Haitian men as dominating their wives, Papa Theodore, it appeared, in no way impinged on Maman Celie's reign. Seabrook's narrative thus cleared the way for a lurid tale of female power and primitive sexuality, couched, of course, in terms of a defense of Haitian culture.

William Seabrook effectively narrated parts of *The Magic Island* through two voices: one he attributed to himself, the "I" of the narrative; the other spoke through Seabrook, but only appeared in the third person, a kind of ever present absence in the text. The second voice that effectively narrated Seabrook's account was the voice of "the literary-traditional white stranger." Thus, describing a Voodoo ceremony, Seabrook could assert: "And now the literary-traditional white stranger who spied from hiding in the forest, had such a one lurked near by, would have seen all the wildest tales of Voodoo fiction justified."[105] The description that followed conformed precisely to the formula of "literary-traditional" accounts of Voodoo, complete with "writhing black bodies," "white teeth and eyeballs gleaming," and couples fleeing the circle "to share and slake their ecstasy." Accompanying a grotesque drawing on the opposite page, moreover, was an excerpted phrase from this description: "blood-maddened, sex-maddened, god-maddened . . . [they] danced their dark saturnalia." "Seabrook" returns as narrator moments later, reminding the reader that the tone of this description was not intended to reflect the author's perspective: "Thus also my unspying eyes beheld this scene in actuality," he wrote, "but I did not experience the revulsion which literary tradition prescribes."[106]

Here and elsewhere, Seabrook's descriptions of Haiti, Haitian customs, and "the Haitian people" turn out to be discourses on the relationship between observer and observed, American visitor and Haitian host. A recurrent theme in these discourses is the terror of the white male observer in a savage and sexual land. Seabrook's discussions of animal sacrifice, high on Price-Mars's list of sensationalist inaccuracies in *The Magic Island*, illustrate this dynamic.

For Seabrook, the act of sacrifice was always a sexual act and the sacrificial animal was always male. Thus, his description of a ceremony in which Maman Celie sacrifices a bird with "great white wings," a bird that "seemed larger and more powerful than she." Seabrook wrote: "bird and woman seemed to mingle struggling in a monstrous, mythical embrace. But her fatal hands were still upon its throat, and in that swan-like simulacre of the deed which for the male is always like a little death, it died."[107] Here, Seabrook seemed to identify with the "little death" of the sacrificial white bird.

Elsewhere, he described the preparations for a ceremony in which a small white he-goat was to be sacrificed, after which he turned to the memory of his own reaction to the ceremony. "There is," he wrote, "one small thing . . . acid-etched so deeply that it will leave some lines, I think, when my brain lies rotting. . . . It was the sound of the terrorized shrill bleating of the white he-goat, tethered out there in the shadows, as it pierced through yet was always dominated, sometimes drowned by the female howling choral of the women. It caused something that was elemental male in me, something deeper than anything the word sex usually defines, to shiver in the grip of an icy terror."[108] Seabrook's identification with white bird and white he-goat suggests something of the racial dimensions of the terror he professed. His next lines confirmed this suggestion, by denying it: "Nor had this any connection with the fact that I, a white man, knelt there among these swaying blacks who would presently become blood-frenzied. They were my friends. It was a terror of something blacker and more implacable than they — a terror of the dark, all-engulfing womb."[109] While denying that his terror derived from any fear of the individual "blacks" who surrounded him, Seabrook reinforced the interconnectedness of racial and sexual connotations in his portrait of Haiti. Even blacker than the blacks themselves, he asserted, was the terrifying female presence, represented by the "howling female choral of the women." Likewise, as slayer of the white bird, Maman Celie, with whom Seabrook earlier expressed a deep "umbilical" connection, now represented the terror of the womb. Later on in the text, he would describe a Haitian song about the curse of a woman, emphasizing that it did not refer to the work of a sorceress; "it meant simply the fatal lure of the female."[110]

Following his confession of fear at the sacrifice of the white he-goat, Seabrook apologized to the reader for inserting himself into the narrative this way. "But I forget that I am writing the description of a Voodoo ceremonial in the Haitian mountains, and that excursions among the terrors aroused by elemental nightmares in my own soul are an unwarranted interruption."[111] Far from constituting unwarranted interruptions, in fact, Seabrook's "excursions" into his "own soul" were necessary threads in the fabric of *The Magic Island*. These threads of text were essential, moreover, to the author's construction of an object called "Haiti." *The Magic Island* stands as a crucial piece of evidence attesting to the historical creation of that object through white American observation and discourse during and after the U.S. occupation.

One of Seabrook's summary characterizations of "the Haitian people" toward the end of his narrative underscores this point. He began by explaining: "they are a little comic, a little ludicrous, they are easily vulnerable to a certain sort of caricature." With these phrases, Seabrook himself seemed cognizant of the presence of the white observer, who would, presumably, be the one to draw the caricature. He went on, however, to describe his perception of the true, if sometimes buried, nature of the Haitian people: "then suddenly from time to time something that is essential in the color and texture of their souls—essential perhaps too in the color and texture of their skins—something more than atavistic savagery, but which may trace none the less to their ancestral Africa, dark mother of mysteries—some quality surges to the surface of group or individual."[112] Erasing the distinction between these two aspects of the Haitian people, the illustrator Alexander King provided a visual caricature of the "dark mother of mysteries" to which Seabrook referred. King's "Africa" was a grotesque, horned, black female figure suckling two black human figures, one each at her oversized breasts. King's illustration, while not strictly representative of the line of Seabrook's text, which it supposedly "illustrated," does reflect aspects of the overall narrative, which characterized Haiti as an overwhelming, terrifying, and sometimes grotesque female presence.

Seabrook contrasted the Haiti that could be caricatured as comic or ludicrous with the true Haiti "that suddenly from time to time . . . surges to the surface. . . . When this happens," he went on to explain, "we others are in the presence of a thing . . . which strikes terror and sometimes awe."[113]

What is especially notable here, and what is striking throughout *The Magic Island*, is that "we others" are present in the first place. Thus, Seabrook's travel narrative transported the U.S. American reader to Haiti in 1929 to observe the "bloody rites"; to see a human girl placed on, and then removed from, the altar of sacrifice; to watch as "the zombies shuffled through the marketplace, recognizing neither father nor wife nor mother."[114]

Like former chargé Robert Beale Davis in his novel, *The Goat without Horns*, Seabrook's lurid and titillating tale of a land where soulless beings recognized "neither father nor wife nor mother" promoted the belief in a benevolent U.S. military paternalism in Haiti. In other ways as well, *The Magic Island* suggested the logic of paternalism. Seabrook portrayed Haiti as an orphaned nation whose French origins were hazy and mysterious at best, but whose maternal connection to Africa remained strong. The influence of mother Africa was everywhere in sight in Seabrook's Haiti, personified in Maman Celie and other dangerous females. That Seabrook professed his respect and admiration for Haitian culture did not detract from this simultaneous characterization of Haiti as grotesquely feminine. In these ways and others, Seabrook's Haiti called out for a fatherly male presence, and suggested that U.S. marines, when they were not too caught up in their own blatant racism, could fill that urgent need.

Into this paternal vacuum walked Faustin Wirkus, in Seabrook's telling. The marine sergeant, who as a lieutenant in the Gendarmerie serving on Île de la Gonave, was to receive dozens of letters from American schoolboys, had been "crowned Wirkus king of La Gonave," according to Seabrook.[115] *The Magic Island* described a ceremony in which the natives greeted Wirkus as "Le Roi" with great pomp and circumstance. He described Queen Ti Meminne, who had ruled La Gonave alone prior to Wirkus's arrival, and who welcomed the new king along with everyone else.[116]

Seabrook's chapters on Wirkus rounded out the fantasy he was providing especially for his white male readers. "To hold undisputed sway on some remote tropical island set like a green jewel amid the coral reefs of summer seas — how many boys have dreamed of it, and how many grown men, civilization tired."[117] He elaborated on this point two years later, in the introduction to Wirkus's book, "Every boy ever born, if he is any good, wants, among other things, to be king of a tropical island. . . . Every man, also, sometimes, whether millionaire or day laborer, wants to be king, that is, a supreme ego . . . instead of being a highly polished or dirty cog in a wheel. Every man (who isn't dead on his feet like a zombie) perhaps wants to be God. Most of us are continually caught in wheels, and are never the mainspring. Wirkus, for a while, was the mainspring. Wirkus for a while — for ten thousand people — was God."[118] The story of "The White King of La Gonave," according to Seabrook, fulfilled the fantasy of the supreme ego. As an "antidote to civilization," Seabrook's Haiti, and particularly Wirkus's La Gonave, offered a welcome escape. By inviting readers to identify with Wirkus, a farmer boy turned tropical king, Seabrook personalized and promoted the ideology of imperialist paternalism and the lure of an exoticized, feminine Haiti.

SEXUALITY AND RACE IN EDNA TAFT'S "VOODOO-LAND"

Like Samuel Guy Inman, Blair Niles, and William Seabrook, Edna Taft projected onto Haiti an empire of the imagination, in which modern Americans could confront the tensions between race and sexuality. Inman had advised his readers to make their way to Haiti in order to counter the primitive sexual expression they would find there. Niles and Seabrook had, in different ways, urged their readers to take that reality in and remake themselves through it. Edna Taft, in common with Seabrook, transported her readers to an exotic Haiti that was both an object of desire and a source of fear, "repellant yet alluring . . . fascinating, yet frightening."[119]

Yet, if Taft's "Voodoo-land" resembled Seabrook's "magic island" in the boldness of its sensationalism, it departed from that model in one crucial way. For whereas Seabrook's salacious narrative appealed particularly to modern white men, Taft's sought to represent the desires and fantasies of modern white women. Haiti's racial landscape would be crucial to that project. Indeed, a white woman's narrative of lost innocence occasioned by contact with the empire, *A Puritan in Voodoo-Land* linked sexual awakening with racial mingling and with the violence of Haitian history.[120] Taft eroticized race, recast gender and sexuality, and used her narrative of Haiti's supposed racial and sexual landscape to assert herself as a modern female sexual subject. In effect, she appropriated the discourse of exotic primitivism to assert female desire. The consequences and implications of this response to paternalism were several. Before we turn to these, however, let us take a closer look at Taft's account of her awakening in Haiti.

Setting out for her promiscuous adventure, Taft marked her own innocence both by her lack of familiarity with people of African heritage and by references to girlhood. "I would meet and associate with colored people," she wrote, "something I had never done before in my life. I guessed that I was going to feel very much like Alice in Wonderland."[121] Taft narrated the process by which she tested her own boundaries, marking her emotional reactions to various sorts of intermingling. Anticipating the "intimacy" that would necessarily be involved in dancing with a Haitian man, she claimed to have "dreaded the ordeal."[122] She thought of her uncle's warning against just this sort of event, and of her father who "would turn over in his grave." Yet, her first dance partner in Haiti, she recalled, "was like a tall, broadshouldered bronze statue. Phidias or Praxiteles would have gloried in such a model," she mused, for this man "had a splendid athlete's body."[123] She danced with a half dozen or a dozen men that same evening, and professed herself "more confused than ever" as to her prejudices and opinions by the end of the night.[124]

Confused she may have been, but it is clear enough that her racism outlived the anticipated "ordeal." Further on in her narrative, she described her anticipation of another "new experience." She wrote, "I had danced with colored people; I had eaten with colored people. And now I was to sleep barely twenty feet away from a colored girl. A lovely girl, to be sure. But colored, none the less."[125] Thus Taft's loss of innocence entailed racial mingling with women as well as with men. And just as dancing with Haitian men had allowed her to see the fine, broad shoulders of Haitian masculinity, so sleeping in close proximity to a Haitian girl introduced her to a long line of proud Haitian heroines, for her roommate that night was, she said, "a true feminist." Upon hearing the story of Marie Jeanne, who "bayonet in hand, at the head of seven hundred Haitians, carved her way through nearly eighteen thousand French soldiers" at Crête-à-Pierrot, Taft "jumped out of bed and lighted her candle to examine the picture of this indomitable woman."[126]

Thus, Taft found in Haiti strong women and statuesque men, but it was the landscape itself that lured her into a tryst. Indeed, upon her arrival at her first Port-au-Prince hotel, she found herself drawn to an "enchanted grove" with an open-air *bassin*. "I could not resist its alluring invitation," she wrote, "I tossed on a negligé and caught up a towel. I hastened back to the beckoning *bassin*, entered the enclosure, and slid the cumbersome iron bolt on the gate. As I leaned back against the wall, out of breath and panting, the scene before me smote my senses vividly. . . . Here and there a bit of bright blue sky peeked though the tracery of feathery palm fronds and boughs clad with large, leathery, dark green leaves. . . . I threw off my negligé and stepped over to the beryl green water, in answer to the beckoning fingers of light."[127]

And if Taft found pleasure in the "magic pool," if she cast her encounter with "feathery" fronds and dark "leathery" leaves as an erotic interlude, the sexualized Haiti that she discovered through her travels was also a realm of danger. Yet, it was into this realm of danger that she sought to venture, for her "greatest desire of all," she said, was to be led "before the altar, to the wild throbbing" of the Voodoo drums.[128] In this great desire, she admitted, she was disappointed. "Such mysteries were not for foreigners, least of all for women," she wrote. "And foreign females who did not mind their own business were apt to be sorry."[129]

This was no idle threat, Taft assured her reader, with reference to white women in Haiti's past, who had indeed found themselves in a position to "be sorry." Drawing on a narrative of the Haitian Revolution written by a white Frenchman, and published in Philadelphia in 1927, Taft provided a portrait of "bestial black soldiery" unleashed on white women in the wake of the former slaves' victory. "The wealthy women," wrote Taft, "those delicately nurtured and of noble lineage, were taken by the officers, who, after they had sated their criminal lust, murdered these unhappy females with indescribable tortures. The women of the lower classes were abandoned to the fury and passions of the black rabble."[130] Taft almost acknowledged the rape of slave women by masters, in that she used the word "violence" to describe what these white men had done, but her description hedged on that point while emphasizing, again, black rapists. "The mulatto aristocracy owed its origins to violence," she wrote, specifying "lustful relations between white masters and black slavewomen; and the infinitely more outrageous, shameful, but secret, subjection of white girls — hardly more than children — to concupiscent young negro slaves." Echoing (and reinscribing) paternalist discourses, Taft called this a "double heritage of illegitimacy."[131] With these passages, Taft emphasized the connection between sexuality and violence.

Taft's inability to acknowledge the rape of black women was wholly consistent with the dominant construction of rape as a racial crime in the United States. Within the dominant cultural framework that defined rape, only white women could be the target and victim of that crime, while the African American man was the archetypal figure for the rapist.[132] African American women had for many decades protested that cultural framework, and the violence that it generated and justified, including both the rape of African American women and the lynching of African American men.[133]

Taft's inability to acknowledge the rape of black women seems to have had a more specific anchor in that it flowed from the logic of her investment in Haiti as a sexualized realm and, especially, in black women as vessels of sexuality. For Taft waged her battle for white female sexual self-assertion by mobilizing stereotypes about black women. Writing about Haitian prostitutes, for example, Taft asserted that their "dark" bodies "held the secret of all the unquenchable passions of torrid lands."[134] Taft sought to claim those "unquenchable passions" as a means to assert her modern sexual self in contrast to the puritanism of a bygone Victorian era. In this respect, Taft's narrative may shed light on other white women's refusal to acknowledge the rape of black women.

Taft's comments on lynching are also significant. In the years and months leading up to Taft's trip, racial violence was in the news. A new wave of lynchings had taken hold earlier in the decade. The 1934 lynching of Claude Neal in Marianna, Florida, in particular, had received nationwide press coverage. The NAACP had launched its campaign for federal antilynching legislation. Indeed, a new bill had been introduced in Congress, to that end, in 1937, the very year that Taft left for Haiti.[135] That year, too, a Gallup poll revealed widespread support for such legislation around the country.[136]

Although clear majorities of Americans declared their opposition to the vicious racism embodied in lynching, Taft took occasion, in her narrative on Haiti, to hedge on that question, just as she had hedged on the rape of black women. What she learned about the history of conflict between black and mulatto Haitians, she turned to this end: "Racial prejudice and intolerance, I found out, were nothing in the United States compared to the violent, undying hatred the negroes and mulattoes of Haiti bore each other." Taft dismissed U.S. American racial violence, claiming that in terms of "savage ferocity," "lynchings and race riots at home . . . could not hold a candle" to the violence Haitians directed against one another.[137]

Given Taft's preoccupation with racial crossings as titillating fare, her refusal to declare her opposition to lynching seems also to be linked to her use of Haiti, and of race, to assert her sexuality. Her reflections on interracial marriage in Haiti also seem striking in relation to the racial-sexual nexus of lynching debates in the United States. "If through his virility, charm, and cleverness, a Haitian man succeeded in acquiring such a rare prize as a white American wife, immediately after marriage, the prize lost its value, while the colored husband retained all the glory and honor of the capture."[138] Here, she thought, was surely "the strangest twist in this interracial marriage tangle. . . . Queer, is it not?"[139] Here and elsewhere, Taft's fascination with Haiti seemed to arise in part out of her attempt to reckon with the implications of U.S. discourses on rape and lynching for white women's sexual selfhood.

Finally, in and through the process of projecting race and sexuality onto Haiti, Taft produced a discourse of selfhood that linked her own interiority to the foreign context of empire. Like Niles, who had Haiti "mapped" in her memory, and like Seabrook, with terrifying images of Voodoo "acid-etched" in his brain, Taft had the sounds of a market woman's strident call echoing in her "subconsciousness." "Years later," she warned her reader, and "two thousand miles away, you will hear her cry, lifelike and clear, within your subconsciousness."[140]

Taft's account of her decision to leave Haiti is significant in this respect. "My nerves were jangled," she wrote. "Maybe it was the relentless rhythm of the nightly drumming in the hills that had beaten its way into my subconsciousness."[141] But her final decision to leave she attributed to a powerful dream, in which she found herself "before a pair of colossal gates." She explained, "just before I reached them, they invariably slammed shut in my face. And a deep voice chanted, 'Too late! Too late!' A chorus of voices behind the barred gates chanted, 'Keep her out, Papa Legba!' . . . Then, 'Accursed blanche!' But I persisted, and pounded on the gates with my bare fists. . . . When I continued beating upon the closed portals, Papa Legba, the Opener of the Gates, yelled at me, in a furious voice, 'Go away, accursed white woman! Or I shall send Papa Damballa's snakes after you!' And, all of a sudden, slimy green serpents were weaving in and out between my bare legs. Papa Legba started to shout again, but his voice, as I gradually struggled to consciousness, assumed the shrill, rasping tones of the market women calling their wares, as they strode to the markets in the hour that just precedes day break."[142]

Here again, Taft drew the parallel between her own experience and that of Zacharias Raymond, who left Cap-François, that "vile sink of iniquity," with the "shrill voice" of a worn-out prostitute ringing in his ears, "You will never forget Saint-Domingue!"[143]

Responding thus to paternalism and related discourses, Taft's narrative performed cultural work with potential implications for personal, national, and international politics. Like the other narratives examined in this chapter, it shaped personal politics insofar as it helped to elaborate a racialized psychological discourse of sexuality and selfhood. Taft's use of her ancestor's alleged diary framed her book in these terms. Taft's sexual self-assertion also engaged national politics in that it took up, directly and indirectly, the debate over federal antilynching legislation. Taft's trip to Haiti provided her with a context in which to explore both racial violence and interracial sexuality.

Finally, Taft's narrative implicated her in the culture of U.S. imperialism. That culture was based on the imperialist relationship between Haiti and the United States, and it perpetuated the cultural framework of hierarchy and disrespect that underpinned the relationship, now embodied in U.S. control of Haitian finances. Inman, Niles, and Seabrook, as we have seen, reinscribed the logic of imperialist paternalism even as they declared their "disbelief in marines." Writing four years after the marines' withdrawal, but while the United States still exercised financial supervision of Haitian affairs, Taft implicitly affirmed Haiti's need for guidance.

Taft's narrative had implications for international politics insofar as it participated in the culture of U.S. imperialism in relation to Haiti. It helped to shape the cultural framework that continued to underwrite U.S. economic control of Haiti and possibly other imperialist ventures as well. While *A Puritan in Voodoo-Land* most likely did not reach a very wide audience (certainly it did not get the attention that Seabrook's narrative received), it illustrates, nonetheless, the ends to which the occupation's rhetoric would be taken, in the hands of an elite white woman.[144]

Many of the stories U.S. Americans told upon their return from Haiti between 1918 and 1938 resembled the stories told by Sir Spencer St. John in the previous century and by Hesketh Prichard at the turn of the twentieth. But in the 1920s and 1930s U.S. American travelers told these stories in new ways and to new ends. In 1938, as in 1918 and earlier, U.S. Americans experienced and described Haiti in terms of race, gender, and sexuality. The tone of their discourses, however, had shifted. By celebrating the primitive sexual expression of a specifically racialized object called "the Haitian people," Blair Niles, William Seabrook, Edna Taft, and others articulated some of the links between the "discovery" of the unconscious and the claiming of an empire. "[T]he people of the United States," said Carl Van Doren, "should be reminded that they are . . . citizens of an empire."[145] Exotic discourses on "the black nation" accomplished this end by mapping the repressed truth of sexuality onto the geographical space called "Haiti."

RACE, REVOLUTION, AND NATIONAL IDENTITY

LANGSTON HUGHES IN HAITI

Langston Hughes arrived in Haiti in the spring of 1931 on a boat filled with Haitian sugarcane workers returning home from Cuba.[1] Twenty-nine years old, with a first novel published and a few hundred dollars from a Harmon Foundation grant in his pocket, Hughes had what he needed, but it was a lump sum, not a steady income. Besides, the Depression was on, and Hughes had recently lost the support of his wealthy white New York patron, Charlotte Osgood Mason. "She wanted me to be more African than Harlem — primitive in the simple, intuitive and noble sense of the word," he wrote later. "I couldn't be, having grown up in Kansas City, Chicago and Cleveland. So that winter had left me ill in my soul." He went to Haiti, he said, to gather his wits.[2] "[I]n Haiti I began to puzzle out how I, a Negro, could make a living in America from writing."[3]

In addition to his Harmon Award, Hughes arrived in Port-au-Prince with several letters of introduction "to the cultural and political elite." He had letters from James Weldon Johnson, Walter White, and Arthur Spingarn, all associated with the NAACP. He had a letter, too, from William Seabrook.[4] Perhaps there is some irony in the fact that Langston Hughes traveled to Haiti, in part, to sort out his relationship to the primitivism demanded by white audiences, and did so carrying a letter of introduction from William Seabrook.[5] Yet, Hughes noted none. That this should go unremarked, in turn, suggests the extent to which U.S. Americans — "white" and "black" —

functioned at that moment in a cultural milieu drenched with primitive exoticism. In any case, Hughes never used the letter.[6]

Like other U.S. American visitors to Haiti, Hughes sought out "voodoo dances," though he found only one, for "real voodoo dances are not easy for tourists to see." His description of the dance as "serious in mood" and "too self-centered to be vulgar" provided a contrast to the usual sensationalist fare. He emphasized the solitary and ritualistic nature of the movement "even when they dance in couples."[7] But Hughes accepted the richness and profundity that Blair Niles had attributed to Haitian peasants, writing, for example, "the black Haitians of the soil seem to remember Africa in their souls and far-off ancestral tribes where each man and each woman danced alone."[8] Hughes preferred wakes to dances, for there "the companions of the deceased gathered to play the games and sing the songs the dead person liked, and to eat the food and drink the drinks he would have drunk in life."[9] Hughes was after the ways of the Haitian folk, and he found them well represented at such events.

Langston Hughes's account of the Haitian people responded to the prevailing racism of U.S. discourses by placing the Haitian situation in its international contexts. Thus, he wrote that in the nineteenth century, the "upper classes developed a political caste that ruled badly—yet no worse than many another ruling class in other lands."[10] In 1915, he went on, "the American Marines came to Haiti to collect American loans, and were there when I came."[11] Indeed, Hughes had been rankled by the white marines who had checked his passport and permitted him to disembark in Port-au-Prince.[12] Haiti, he wrote in an article for the *Crisis* upon his return to the States, "has its hair caught in the white fingers of unsympathetic foreigners, and the Haitian people live today under a sort of military dictatorship backed by American guns. They are not free."[13]

In this light, Hughes recast the marines' characterization of the Haitian peasants as "people without shoes." "Haiti was a land full of people without shoes," he wrote, "black people, whose feet walked the dusty roads to market in the early morning, or trod softly on the bare floors of hotels, serving foreign guests. Barefooted ones tending the rice and cane fields under the hot sun, climbing mountains slopes, baking coffee beans, wading through surf to fishing boats on the blue sea. All of the work that kept Haiti alive, paid the interest on American loans, and enriched foreign traders, was done by people without shoes."[14] He sent a sharp critique from Haiti to the *New Masses*, a radical political, art, and literary magazine back in the States: "Hayti today: a fruit tree for Wall Street, a mango for the occupation, coffee for foreign cups, and poverty for its own black workers and peasants."[15]

For Langston Hughes, the "people without shoes" were, above all, proud and independent, and he saw that spirit embodied in the Citadel, which he visited three times in one trip to Haiti. Like James Weldon Johnson, Hughes was taken with the sheer masculinity expressed by the massive fortress. "The Citadel is in ruins," he wrote. "But it is one of the lustiest ruins in the world, rearing its husky shoulders out of a mountain with all the strength of the dreams that went into its making more than a century ago."[16] "The fact that beauty as well as strength went into its making is cause for further wonderment, for the Citadel is majestic, graceful in every proportion, with wide inner staircases and noble doorways of stone, curving battlements, spacious chambers and a maze of intricate cellars, dungeons, terraces and parade grounds."[17] Hughes would return to this theme in his creative work over the next decade and beyond.[18]

Langston Hughes found — in the Citadel — the answer to the questions that had plagued him in the winter of 1930–31, when he had lost his patron. "I did not want to write for the pulps, or turn out fake 'true' stories to tell under anonymous names. . . . I did not want to bat out slick non-Negro short stories in competition with a thousand other commercial writers. . . . I wanted to write seriously and as well as I knew how about the Negro people, and make that kind of writing earn for me a living."[19] Hughes puzzled out something significant about his relation to the United States, and about the relation of his own writing to his Americanness, as he ascended "wide inner staircases" and passed through "noble doorways of stone." For Hughes, and for many other African Americans, the legacy of the Haitian Revolution would help to remake race in America.

To understand the context and impact of that remaking of race, this chapter examines anti-imperialism, critiques of exoticism, and African American responses to the discourse of paternalism in the 1920s and 1930s. We begin with some of the social, political, and institutional contexts of interracial anti-imperialist collaboration and antiracist activism. We have seen the importance of the NAACP and of the liberal press on both counts, and of the UNIA for antiracism, though not for interracial efforts. Other important — and overlapping — contexts included the postmigration urban North, the nascent Haitian immigrant community in the United States, the international women's movement, and the radical left.[20] These were among the varied sources of protest against the occupation. Critiques of exotic primitivism emerged in those contexts, too, though not consistently. Such critiques — again partial and problematic though they were — were also grounded in the academic discipline of anthropology and in the popular turn to folklore and folkways in the 1930s.

The social and political reconfigurations of the Depression decade provide one more set of keys to understanding the emergence of a new emphasis on the Haitian Revolution of 1791–1804. Langston Hughes wandered up to the Citadel in 1931 and brought his images of proud black masculinity home to a very different cultural landscape than had James Weldon Johnson in 1920. Hughes and others could now build on Johnson's work in new ways, unsettling, through discussions of Haitian history and culture, hegemonic interpretations of American identity.

Through such discussions, African Americans challenged prevailing conceptions of race and national identity in the United States. Moreover, in confronting racist cultural constructs, African American writers and artists explicitly and implicitly addressed themselves to the uses of gender and sexuality in hegemonic discourses of domination. In doing so, they sometimes reinscribed — and occasionally challenged — gender inequalities, while laying the groundwork for the transformation of race relations in the decades to come. The chapter closes with an extended consideration of one such challenge: Zora Neale Hurston's *Tell My Horse*.

THE CONTEXTS OF ANTI-IMPERIALISM IN THE 1920S

During the U.S. occupation of Haiti, the NAACP and the UNIA functioned in a broad context that encompassed the significance of the Great Migration and the growth of national African American organizations. The first fifteen years of this long occupation coincided with tremendous social and cultural change for African Americans. In 1915, the year of the Marines' invasion of Haiti, the Great Migration was beginning. Over the next five years, thousands of southern African Americans would follow family members who had migrated, or would themselves lead the way to northern cities to escape the increasing difficulties of their southern lives. According to one historian, African Americans who left the South in the late teens saw migration as an opportunity to claim the rights and privileges of American citizenship — specifically, as black Americans.[21] The "Promised Land" fell short of their expectations, bringing low wages, unhealthy industrial working conditions, exclusion from skilled trades, high rents, residential segregation and overcrowding, race riots, and a host of other problems to replace the boll weevil, disfranchisement, lynching, sexual harassment, rape, and other sometimes deadly trials of the South.[22]

The concentration of African Americans in urban centers and the strengthening of black organizations, however, created new possibilities for political and cultural assertion. The civil rights orientation of the NAACP and the black nationalism of Marcus Garvey's UNIA would both contribute to the articulation of African Americans' desires for themselves and for Haiti in the 1920s.[23] Garvey's working-class constituency would be drawn especially from the urban North. In addition, the creation of an economic base within black communities combined with white patronage to make possible the flourishing of African American cultural expression in some urban settings, notably Harlem and Chicago. In these contexts, African Americans could come together to protest U.S. actions in Haiti and to reflect on the significance of the Haitian situation.

Within this urban context, particularly in New York, a Haitian immigrant community also began to take root as educated Haitians fled the repressive conditions of the occupation.[24] From the States they could mount a campaign of protest against the occupation in alliance with African American and progressive white organizations. During the 1920s, the Patriotic Union thus established its presence in the United States.[25] The transnational Haitian community headquartered in New York also drew on links established through the emigration of African Americans to Haiti in the previous century. The American-Haitian Benevolent Club, representing the Haitian descendants of those emigrants, protested not the occupation as a whole but the deployment of racist white marines to conduct the occupation. They called for the exclusive use of African American troops to carry out U.S. policy in Haiti.[26]

At the same time, the base of strength in the North also strengthened national African American organizations. In addition to the NAACP, the National Negro Press Association and the National Association of Colored Women (NACW) also weighed in on the Haitian question.[27] The Harding administration responded to such protests by appointing a black man, Napoleon Marshall, as a clerk for the U.S. Legation in Port-au-Prince. As Brenda Plummer has pointed out, Harding's action backfired when Marshall, isolated from his white superiors, "became a vocal opponent of the occupation."[28] He and his wife, Harriet Gibbs Marshall, worked to help Haitians organize effective opposition to the occupation.[29]

The international women's movement also provided a crucial context for protest against the occupation, particularly through its intersection with the national activism of African American women. The International Council of Women (ICW) had been founded in 1888 in order to unite women from around the world in a common effort on behalf of human welfare, with special attention to issues affecting women.[30] Frances Willard, charismatic leader of the white "woman movement," leading but inconstant white ally to

African American women, had served as the international organization's first chairperson.[31] The NACW, founded in 1896, was probably first represented at an international congress of the ICW in 1904, when Mary Church Terrell attended the Berlin congress.[32] In 1920 members of the NACW seeking to take a more active role in international affairs and to influence U.S. policy in Africa and the Caribbean joined the International Council of Women.[33] Racism within the ICW and its affiliated white women's organizations, and specifically the racist treatment of NACW representatives, Mary Talbert and Dr. Mary F. Waring, at the 1920 congress in Paris, led the NACW to found the International Council of Women of the Darker Races.[34]

In 1922 the International Council of Women of the Darker Races met in Washington, D.C., with representatives from North America, Africa, Asia, and the Caribbean, including Haiti.[35] The convention set forth the organization's statement of purpose, having "as its object the economic, social, and political welfare of the women of all the darker races."[36] The council elected officers, including Margaret M. Washington (widow of Booker T. Washington) as president and Addie W. Hunton as first vice president. As Cynthia Neverdon-Morton has noted, "the principal activity for the remainder of 1922 was to be an investigation of the status of women and children in Haiti. Emily Williams was sent to Haiti to study women there; her trip was partially financed by the Council, and her report was submitted to the general body at the 1923 convention," which met again in Washington, D.C., in August of that year.[37]

Another branch of the international women's movement, the Women's International League for Peace and Freedom (WILPF), founded in 1915, would both foster significant interracial work against the occupation and find a larger and more influential audience for its views. In 1925 Haitian members of that organization requested that WILPF undertake an investigation of the occupation.[38] WILPF put together an interracial delegation with representatives from its own U.S. section as well as from the International Council of Women of the Darker Races, and several other organizations. Emily Greene Balch of WILPF's U.S. section led the delegation. It also included Addie Hunton, now president of the International Council of Women of the Darker Races and vice president of the NACW, and Charlotte Atwood, a prominent African American clubwoman and high school teacher from Washington, D.C. Two University of Chicago professors were included: Zonia Baber, a white woman who taught geography at the School of Education, who was also a WILPF member, and Paul H. Douglas, who was an economist in the field of industrial relations. Douglas, a white man, was a member of the Foreign Service Committee of the Society of Friends, and a socialist—though not advertised as such—and would later become a U.S. senator. Finally, Grace (Mrs. J. Harold) Watson of Pennsylvania represented the Fellowship of Reconciliation, a Christian peace organization.[39] In February 1926 this delegation traveled to Haiti to observe and evaluate U.S. rule there.

Occupied Haiti, the report of the group's findings and recommendations, edited by Emily Greene Balch, covered a wide array of issues, including finances, land tenure, racial relations, public order, civil liberty, education, public health, and freedom of the press.[40] Specific problems existed in all these areas, yet "even more than they anticipated," Balch declared on behalf of the whole delegation, "they found the problem in Haiti to consist not in individual instances of misused power, but in the fundamental fact of the armed occupation of the country."[41] "There has been for some time a drift towards imperialism," Balch concluded, and in this regard, she asserted, "our actions in Haiti are perhaps most flagrant." U.S. officials, Balch charged, were training Haitians "to subordinate themselves" and "to accept military control as the supreme law."[42] "The determining element in the situation," wrote Balch, "is that it rests on force, . . . [which] makes American rule deeply repugnant to all Haitians that still prize the independence that they have suffered so much to win and maintain."[43]

Like James Weldon Johnson, Balch drew on the discursive framework of paternalism to present WILPF's case against the occupation. As the editor of *Occupied Haiti*, she chose, as an epigraph for the volume, a quote from Sidney George Fisher's *True History of the American Revolution*. "No community of people, naturally separated from others . . . by any strong circumstances," Fisher had asserted, "ever willingly remains a colony." He had gone on to specify that some members of every community that seeks independence will, however, fail to participate in the dominant trend. Quoting Fisher, Balch drew an implicit parallel to the pro-American faction in Haiti. "There will always be a loyalist party," she quoted him as saying, "just as there will always be a certain number of individuals who prefer to live in lodgings, or in other people's houses, and do not want a family."[44] The metaphor of the family, as well as the memory of the American Revolution, served to call to the reader's mind dearly held values. The majority of Haitians—those who still prized their independence—would never prefer to live in other people's houses, as Fisher had put it; they do want a family, Balch seemed to be insisting, and not a family headed by Uncle Sam.[45]

If the (interracial) international women's movement provided one internationalist alternative to paternalism, the radical left provided another. This has often been overlooked because, in the relatively conservative political atmosphere of the 1920s, radicals did not always advertise themselves as such, nor did liberals who participated in radical organizations.[46] Emily Greene Balch, for example, very carefully subtitled WILPF's important volume, *Occupied Haiti*, "Being the report of the Committee of Six disinterested Americans representing organizations exclusively American, who, having personally studied conditions in Haiti in 1926, favor the restoration of the Independence of the Negro Republic."[47] The political expediency of this characterization of the delegation is clear enough, particularly in the jingoistic context of the 1920s. Balch opted not to mention the fact that the liberal Paul H. Douglas was, for example, associated with the Socialist Party's Intercollegiate Socialist Society (ISS), which had chapters on sixty college and university campuses by 1923. Pointing this out would hardly have helped to secure for Balch the personal meeting she desired, and did in fact have, with President Calvin Coolidge.[48] Yet, the ISS may well have provided a significant vehicle for cultivating oppositional perspectives on U.S. foreign policy. In addition to Douglas, ISS members included others who were outspoken in opposition to the occupation of Haiti, such as Roger Baldwin of the American Civil Liberties Union, Freda Kirchwey, then editor of the *Nation*, Lewis Gannett, and Paxton Hibben.[49]

The American Communist Party (CP-USA), then known as the Workers (Communist) Party, was famously systematic in covering its tracks in order to promote critical perspectives on capitalism and imperialism. For this reason, and perhaps for other reasons, too, historians continue to minimize or ignore altogether its role in domestic opposition to the occupation. Yet the Communist Party played a significant role in antioccupation protests in the 1920s.

The party called for a "program of uniting all revolutionary working-class movements in the home countries of imperialism with the National Liberation struggles in the oppressed colonial and semi-colonial countries."[50] "In our case," recalled a leader in the party's "Anti-Imperialist Department" from the 1920s, that meant "independence for Puerto Rico, liquidation of the Guantanamo Naval base in Cuba, withdrawal of U.S. forces from Haiti and the Dominican Republic and an end to all U.S. exploitation in Latin America and the Philippine islands. We also called for a free China."[51]

In keeping with regular party practices, the Anti-Imperialist Department functioned largely through a "front organization," which was not nominally associated with the Communists. Charles Phillips, who was known as Manuel Gomez in the 1920s, first established a section of the Communist front organization, known as the All-America Anti-Imperialist League (Liga Antiimperialista de las Americas) in Mexico in 1925.[52] Later that year he established the U.S. section in Chicago. He found a handful of radicals at the Chicago Bureau of the Federated Press news service, who gave the league publicity.[53] He found a "wealthy Chicago liberal" to fund the league's activities, which consisted primarily of putting out "propaganda" against U.S. imperialism in the Caribbean and elsewhere.[54] The league also secured the support of William Pickens of the NAACP, Robert Morss Lovett of the University of Chicago, Roger Baldwin, Freda Kirchwey, and other liberals and radicals.[55] The Haitian Patriotic Union organized a banquet to honor Phillips, alias Gomez, as secretary of the All-America Anti-Imperialist League in September 1928.[56]

Besides the activities of the Anti-Imperialist Department and its better known "pro-communist" partner, the Anti-Imperialist League, the Communist Party sponsored conferences and generated literature to promote critical discussion of imperialism in Haiti and elsewhere. Party member Joseph Freeman and party sympathizer Scott Nearing, for example, coauthored the important 1927 volume, *Dollar Diplomacy: A Study of American Imperialism*, with a substantial focus on Haiti.[57] Nearing, together with Philips and several other members and sympathizers, also attended the 1927 Conference against Colonial Oppression and Imperialism in Brussels, organized by the party.[58]

Other radical organizations also spoke out against the occupation, some founded as pro-Communist "front" organizations, such as the American Negro Labor Congress (later called the League of Struggle for Negro Rights), headed by former *Messenger* writer, Lovett Fort-Whiteman.[59] The *New Masses*, the magazine where Langston Hughes published his comments on the occupation, was also a Communist organization, which shared quarters with the Anti-Imperialist League, after it moved to New York in 1927.[60] The Vanguard Press would publish, in 1934, an important antiracist account of the Haitian Revolution. Given the centrality of the Communist critique of U.S. imperialism in the work of the party, it is not surprising that African American newspapers across the country learned about the 1929 Aux Cayes massacre from a press release sent out immediately by the CP-USA.[61]

To be sure, there were other contexts shaping anti-imperialist protest in the 1920s. The African American press played a crucial role throughout the decade. The Pan-African movement drew attention to the connections between European colonialism in Africa and U.S. actions in Haiti. Protestant missionaries continued to provide critical commentary on the occupation.[62] The Catholic Welfare Association of the United States spoke out against the U.S. attempt to establish "a network of American-owned plantations through which Haitian small farm owners will be turned into peons and day laborers."[63] Two dozen prominent lawyers reviewed the record of the Senate inquiry and declared in one voice that the occupation violated "traditional American principles . . . international law . . . every tenet of fair and equal dealing between independent sovereign nations, and . . . American professions of international good faith."[64]

WHITE U.S. AMERICANS AND THE STRUGGLE AGAINST RACISM IN THE 1930S

If in 1920 Samuel Guy Inman had known just what to think about the relationship between black Haiti and white America, by 1930 the issues had become more complicated. In that ten-year period, Inman had earned two graduate degrees, one from Columbia and the other from Texas Christian University, and had read widely about U.S. imperialism in the Caribbean and in Latin America. He had read not only WILPF's account of Haiti but also William Seabrook's. Blair Niles's *Black Haiti* had made quite an impression on him, as had John Vandercook's *Black Majesty*.[65] He had observed the Harlem Renaissance with great interest and had followed the progress of Pan-African Congresses from Europe to West Africa to South Africa.[66] He had both organized and participated himself in several inter-American conferences and had gained a new measure of respect for Latin American and Caribbean peoples.

By 1930 Inman opposed not only military domination but also the assumption of white superiority, in which he had himself participated so thoroughly ten years earlier. By that time, in his mind, the biggest question relevant to U.S. relations with Haiti was neither what path that nation should follow, nor how to prevent Haiti from dragging white men down, but "whether the white man can eliminate some of his racial superiority complex."[67]

Retelling the story of his 1918 trip to Haiti in a new book, *Trailing the Conquistadores*, Inman's emphasis had clearly shifted. He still recalled having been disturbed by the sight of Haitian men and women dancing, but now he explained that the "nude" dance performance, which he had found most disturbing, had been "staged by one of our fellow-countrymen."[68] He still saw the peasants as primitive, but now he marveled at the contrast between primitive and modern with a distinct note of modernist appreciation. When he and his companion had needed to cross the Massacre River, he now recalled, "ten husky Haitians, stripped of the bothersome trappings of civilization, hoisted the car on their shoulders and slipping and sliding, yelling, cursing and laughing, finally made the opposite shore. Such a mixture of modern and of 'darkest Africa' one could not have imagined."[69] "Darkest Africa" had come into qualifying quotation marks, while the "high standards of life" Inman had held so dear ten years before had now become "bothersome trappings."[70]

As this retelling suggests, Inman's newfound appreciation for the primitive enabled him to reevaluate his racial perspective and assumptions. Yet, it left him still moving within the grooves of exoticizing discourses. Indeed, Inman seemed to become invested in those discourses in new ways, even as he tried to develop a critical perspective on them. Thus, knowing the formulaic patterns of U.S. narratives, he began his chapter on Haiti with an incantation, "Drums, shadows, forests, mystery—Haiti!," followed by a scene of drumming and dancing. The scene served as a lead-in to a series of questions framed by cultural relativism. "Superstition? Ignorance? Inferiority? Challenge to superior whites to drive out, with swift hard blows, such indecent sorcery?" And his answer marked the distance he had traveled, and his hopes for effective cross-cultural communication. "As long as the white man, who has his own superstition and revelries, his prejudice against other races, goes to Haiti to destroy Voodoo by force and teach the Negro his inferior place, so long the white man will fail with the Negro."[71]

In contrast to the racist superstition he attributed to other white men, Inman found himself identifying with the drummer in this primitive scene, and the gendered terms on which he did so illuminate his new investment in primitivism. What is striking about Inman's description of this supposed Voodoo ceremony in the forest is that the actors are male. Rather than emphasizing the relations between men and women, Inman now told a story about a drummer and "his companions." In the course of their revelries, these men get to "see" a "long line of African girls who respond to every emotion invoked by the drummer with movements of their arms, their feet, their hips."[72] Through this process, Inman told readers of his new volume, the drummer and his companions "received into themselves the wisdom of the serpents" and "the strength of the bull."[73] Here, then, was a newly configured story about gender in a primitive land. Here was a drumbeat to which Inman felt he could respond. Indeed, he wrote, "heart and body begin answering to the rhythm," not specifying whose heart and whose body responded so readily.[74] Vesting primitive Haitian men with virility and masculine dignity, Inman was now eager to distance himself from what Blair Niles had called "omniscience in the matter of civilization."

Inman attributed masculinity to the drummer in other ways as well. He associated the drum with the history of the Haitian struggle for liberty, which came alive for him when he read *Black Majesty*. And if the drum was a figure for primitive masculinity in one scene, it was nothing less than a brilliant technology in another. One of many slaves who "came from noble families, accustomed in Africa to rule," Inman told his readers, was Mackendal (*sic*). "One day he disappeared into the forest, and the drums began to wireless mysterious messages to the slaves. To the planters the drums only announced a dance; the Africans must be allowed to satisfy their craving for rhythm. To the slaves, however, the drums meant another meeting . . . and renewed dreams of freedom."[75] "Toussaint, Dessalines, Christophe," moreover, all "listened to the drums," and all were "strong native leaders."[76]

Samuel Guy Inman hoped to underline the positive message he saw in Vandercook's biography of Christophe, but he also sought to shift his readers' attitudes toward contemporary Haitian leaders. He drew attention to Haiti's "distinguished literary men, international lawyers, and devoted leaders. This small cultured class," he wrote, "has much real talent and character." As if to comment on his own earlier work, he noted, "Their morals and culture, being Latin rather than Anglo-Saxon, are easily underestimated by a provincial Nordic." But, he assured his reader, "Family life among them is often most beautiful." Inman rejected commonplace American judgments of the Haitian elite in terms of their treatment of the peasants. "Relations between the rich land owner and the peasants are often found to contain praiseworthy conditions not found on the surface."[77]

While Inman still saw in Haiti a need for Christianity and Christian uplift, he now believed that Haiti would find what it needed through its association with other people of African heritage rather than from white missionaries. "The problem of Haiti cannot be considered apart from the world problem of the Negro," he insisted. People of African heritage were, he saw, "developing a world consciousness. The Pan African movement, the West African and South African conferences, the National Association for the Advancement of Colored People in America, the Union Patriotique d'Haïti, the Garvey movement in Jamaica, and the movement for Federation of British West Indies Negroes, are among the most important signs."[78] Inman hailed the NAACP's "aggressive program of protest against racial abuses" as well as its assistance to the people of Haiti. He also linked this growing "political self consciousness" with the artistic achievements of the Harlem Renaissance. "The Negro," he declared, "has found himself and his people in possession of the power to create."[79]

Moreover, while this "awakening of the Negro" had been "particularly noticeable since the World War," that same period found white Americans in a state of affliction. Thus, Inman rounded out his new chapter on Haiti with a diagnosis. "Dr. Haven Emerson warns us," he wrote, that "we are creating . . . conditions as unbearable for human beings in peace as the conditions which existed in front-line trenches during the World War. Much of the wreckage of mind and nerve today is due to fear, which is induced in no small degree by unemployment, by depression, by the sudden realization of people capable of working for their living that there is no place for them in this vaunted modern civilization."[80] In contrast, as Inman now saw, Haiti was full of "spaces where God lurks, hidden from eyes too blind to see that which does not move."[81]

It is possible that Guy Endore knew Samuel Guy Inman when they were both at Columbia in the early 1920s, Endore as an eager undergraduate with radical views, Inman as an older graduate student, a lecturer, and an outspoken peace activist. Inman would soon publish "Imperialistic America," an important critique of U.S. policy in Haiti and elsewhere, in the *Atlantic Monthly*.[82] Endore would graduate and make his living as a translator, biographer, and novelist in New York. Sometime after the stock market crash, Endore landed in Hollywood as a screenwriter working for several major studios. (He would later be blacklisted for his connection to the Communist Party.)[83] It was in this context that he wrote *Babouk*.

In 1934, the Vanguard Press brought out Guy Endore's historical novel about Boukman, the early revolutionary leader of Saint Domingue (called by the fictional name "Babouk," which also provides the book's title). Like Inman, Endore called attention to the prevailing images of Africa and Haiti against which he wrote: "Who has not read a hundred stories, seen a dozen plays, of the dreadful tomtom of the savages[?] A thousand authors have blathered of the dreadful tomtom of the blacks, the terror of the jungle. How one's spine shivers in a cozy room to read of dark jungle sorcery, of the black man's cruel witchcraft. . . . But it is the white man's drum, backed by lash and chain, by gun and cannon, that has girdled the globe."[84] By calling attention to the fictional vilification of blacks in exotic discourses, and by contrasting that fiction with the violent reality of imperialism, Endore leveled harsh criticism at the United States for its actions in Haiti. At the same time, his narrative call for revolution replicated the sexual emphasis of earlier exotic discourses.

More subtly critical of U.S. actions in Haiti, the anthropologist Melville Herskovits offered a direct critique of the exoticism that so pervaded white discussions of Haiti. Having traveled to Haiti in 1934 with a scholarly expedition from Columbia and Northwestern Universities, Herskovits was in a good position to challenge the tradition of exoticism when, in 1935, yet another travel narrative appeared, this one entitled *Voodoo Fire in Haiti*.[85]

Seeing Herskovits's review of the travelogue, Alfred A. Knopf solicited from the anthropologist a book-length treatment of the Haitian theme, and the 1937 volume, *Life in a Haitian Valley*, resulted.[86]

Herskovits's ethnology directly challenged much of the sensational literature on Haiti to date. The "picture of the Haitian" that he attempted to draw for his readers was, at least in part, that "of a man going about his affairs in a matter-of-fact fashion."[87] Herskovits also sought to provide careful elaboration of African and European influences in Haitian culture. In response to those who associated Haiti with sexual immorality, he pointed to the influence of "the sex customs of the Créoles and other Europeans" as crucial sources.[88] Similarly, he traced Haitian magic practices equally to European as to African roots.[89] Thus, Herskovits found in Haiti evidence of cultural retentions from both Europe and Africa. He suggested, moreover, that this was in all likelihood true of African Americans as well as of Haitians.

On the other hand, despite his impassioned critique, Herskovits reinscribed the idea of an inherent instability in Haitian culture. His analysis not only emphasized Haiti's dual cultural inheritance from Europe and Africa but also posited an inherent ambivalence between the two, which supposedly structured the Haitian "personality." Where Langston Hughes identified imperialism and class conflict as the heart of Haiti's problem, Herskovits found a "psychological conflict" that was "being waged within the frame of Haitian society." He identified, for example, an "absence of graphic and plastic arts" in Haiti, which revealed "the anatomy of this inner conflict of traditions, since it is important to recognize that the suppression of these forms of the prevalent African tradition would seem to have lost to the Haitian an important outlet for the resolution of inner tensions caused by pent-up drives."[90]

Herskovits concluded that, "[a]s regards the Haitian, it must be recognized that the two ancestral elements in his civilization have never been completely merged. As a result, his outwardly smoothly functioning life is full of inner conflict, so that he has to raise his defenses in order to make his adjustment within the historical and cultural combination of differing modes of life that constitute his civilization."[91] Ironically, this attribution of psychological conflict, an ingrained "socialized ambivalence," mirrored the discourses of William Seabrook and Frederick Wise, who called into question Haiti's paternity and, in that connection, insisted on the instability of Haitian identity.[92] Like the discourses of exoticism that Herskovits rejected, his own analysis displaced relations of power — social and economic conflict — onto a recently discovered psychological realm.[93]

AFTERMATH

Another challenge to the discourse of exoticism came from the folklorist Harold Courlander, who published his first book on Haiti in 1939, at the end of the period I am examining here. In *Haiti Singing*, Courlander tried to "understand the subtleties and tangent ways of Haitian thinking" with assistance from a host of Haitian friends.[94] He presented Vodou not as a primitive and violent set of rites, but as "a highly formalized and sophisticated attitude toward life," which he considered to be at once both less and more than a religion.[95] Far from reducing Haiti to "Voodoo," Courlander sought an understanding of the ways in which Vodou related to diverse aspects of Haitian experience: "This is not all that goes on in Haiti, but this is the reason for everything else," he wrote. "It is for this . . . that men slave all day in dusty lime pits, or perhaps in the cane fields of a rich foreigner, for twenty cents a day."[96] Finally, challenging the discourse of Robert Beale Davis, A. J. Burks, and others, Courlander insisted that Vodou is a thing of the family.

Yet, how did *Haiti Singing* resonate in 1939? Despite the differences that set it apart from exoticizing texts, at the same time it underscored stereotypic notions of blacks as closer to nature, and naturally happy, having special access to joy as whites could not. Like Blair Niles's *Black Haiti*, Courlander's sometimes sensitive work was caught within prevailing cultural definitions of race, even as it tried to shift those definitions.

His next book on Haiti, a children's book entitled *Uncle Bouqui of Haiti*, demonstrated the crucial matter of context in starker terms.[97] Based on the Haitian folk tales about Bouki and Malice, the sharp trickster, in some respects, Courlander's *Uncle Bouqui* resembled parts of Jean Price-Mars's *Ainsi parla l'oncle*.[98] Yet, in the U.S. American context, *Uncle Bouqui* presented a familiar stereotype of a big stupid black man as the central comic figure in the stories. The contrast between *Haiti Singing* and *Uncle Bouqui*, then, is startling, insofar as one works hard trying to avoid falling into received stereotypes, while the other tumbles headlong into them.

The complexities attending any evaluation of the work of Inman, Endore, Herskovits, and Courlander on Haitian themes suggests the importance of context for understanding racial ideology. These white authors grappled with race in ways that challenged and, to some extent, shifted the status quo. At the same time, they were produced by the cultural context that bolstered the status quo. So too, though in different ways, were the African American writers to whom we turn next.

Although I have been discussing "white writers" and will now go on to discuss "black writers," it would be misleading to suggest that instances of U.S. attention to Haiti could be neatly categorized according to the racial identity of each writer or artist who contributed to the playing out of this cultural fascination. On the contrary, white and black authors, artists, publishers, actors, and audiences participated in complex ways in negotiations over racial identity as they participated in diverse but related discourses on Haiti. James Weldon Johnson was proud to have influenced William Seabrook. Black actors presented a dramatic version of *Babouk*. Orson Welles directed a "black" version of Macbeth, set in Haiti.[99] White publishers brought out the work of Langston Hughes, Zora Neale Hurston, and Rayford Logan. And, as we shall see, a white college dean asked the African American author Arna Bontemps to renounce racial politics by burning a book written by a white man, John Vandercook's best-selling *Black Majesty*.[100] Bearing in mind this complexity, let us turn now to the national and international contexts in which African American writers turned to the Haitian Revolution and its leaders in the 1930s.

HAITIAN HISTORY AND A WORLD IN CRISIS

Between 1920 and 1940, the legacy of the Haitian Revolution was transformed. It shifted, first, as a result of African Americans' increased contact with Haiti during the occupation and, second, as a result of the social changes of the Depression years. But to understand how African Americans' relationship to Haiti changed, we must look not only to the national context of the Depression, or to the bilateral relationship between Haitians and U.S. Americans, but also to the international contexts of the radical left and the Pan-African movement. For what Johnson, Du Bois, and other African Americans began in the teens and twenties, a pair of Trinidadians, George Padmore and C. L. R. James, carried forward, along with dozens of other men and women of African heritage in the United States, in the Caribbean, and elsewhere.

Addressing the NAACP after his return from Haiti, James Weldon Johnson brought Henri Christophe to the attention of African Americans in 1920. He also noted the disparaging view of Christophe that many African Americans had held up to that time: "We, too, have been snobs — laughing at Haiti because we knew no better — simply taking as true the lies that have been told about her. . . . How many of us have not laughed at Christophe's court?"[101] Johnson now countered such ridicule with a respectful and heroic portrait of the black king. No longer laughing at Christophe's court, Johnson lauded Christophe's leadership in the struggle to establish a black nation, and in the attainment of prosperity for that nation. He appealed to African Americans to revise their view of Christophe; the new portrait he suggested was that of a strong black man. In the context of American racism, and particularly in light of the racist attacks against black manhood embodied in lynching, this was a significant assertion of race pride. But, for all the literary and cultural ferment of the African American Renaissance, the 1920s saw relatively little attention to Haitian history by black writers. Where it existed, it usually focused, like Johnson's discussions of Christophe, on the stature of an individual leader.[102] This emphasis would shift dramatically in the 1930s. It would remain for that decade to link this black hero with the revolution he led.

To understand this shift, let us consider, first, the social context in which African Americans reflected on Haitian history, and how that context changed with the onset of the Depression. The majority of African Americans in the 1920s already suffered from severe economic hardship, and indeed a significant part of the U.S. population survived on annual income levels below the official poverty line of $2,000. At the same time, the considerable wealth of those in the upper echelons of the economy created the impression of nationwide prosperity and kept attention focused away from social problems. This bifurcation in the social structure affected black as well as white communities, particularly in cities where African American artists benefited from the interest of wealthy patrons, both African American and white. In those same cities, working-class and poor African Americans were more likely to participate in Garvey's back-to-Africa movement than to put their faith in an interracial civil rights organization like the NAACP.

The onset of the Depression shifted the context for African American cultural expression and political participation in the United States. While reducing the financial means available to support many African American writers and artists, the social changes following the Great Crash of 1929 opened up new possibilities for social criticism and for the articulation of race and class consciousness by black writers.

As the Great Depression caused so many more U.S. Americans to join the ranks of the struggling and disaffected, new possibilities opened up also for interracial alliances on local and national levels. Ultimately, the work of white Communists in alliance with African Americans and the economic opportunities opened up by the New Deal, however limited they were, both contributed to rising expectations on the part of African Americans with respect to the benefits of political association with whites.[103] According to historian Nancy J. Weiss, the contributions of the New Deal to such rising expectations led to substantial increases in African American voter participation and to the founding of black civic and political leagues where none existed before.[104]

In this context, African American attention to Haitian history expanded to reflect not only the assertion of race pride but also, simultaneously, the possibility of revolutionary change. In 1930, for example, Harriet Gibbs Marshall, the wife of Napoleon Marshall, would write a history of Haiti for young people, focusing on the Revolution, "[so] that they may know the inspiring details and thrilling victories that enabled the unlettered masses . . . to drive the foreigners from their shores, to proclaim their independence and establish a Republic."[105] Thus, in Depression America, Haiti spoke to black citizens in ways that were newly compelling.

Not surprisingly, other African American writers and artists of the 1930s joined Marshall in passing on the proud heritage of the Haitian Revolution and the rich treasure of Haitian history and culture. Langston Hughes and his friend and fellow Harlem Renaissance author, Arna Bontemps, focused on Haiti together, in a children's book called *Popo and Fifina*, and separately in poems, plays, and novels.[106] Rayford Logan began to focus his scholarly attention on Haiti and Haitian history.[107] Jacob Lawrence used images of the Haitian Revolution and of the Citadel in murals and paintings (Figure 29).[108] Katherine Dunham and Lavinia Williams studied Haitian dance, and Zora Neale Hurston, Haitian folklore.[109] Sculptor Augusta Savage responded to African American men's fascination with the masculinity of the Citadel with a feminine image of freedom, which she called *La Citadelle* (Figure 30).[110] Others took advantage of New Deal arts projects either to study Haiti or to present Haitian themes to African American audiences.

At the same time, George Padmore and C. L. R. James turned their attention to Haiti. Padmore, an active member of the Communist Party, did so mostly from the Soviet Union until 1935, when he left there disenchanted because the Communists, interested in aligning themselves with England and France in opposition to fascism, now seemed to be watering down their critiques of Western imperialism and racism.[111] Padmore went to London, where he worked with James organizing support for Ethiopia, in the wake of the Italian invasion of that nation.[112] By this time, James had done some research on the history of the Haitian Revolution and had written a play based on the story of Toussaint L'Ouverture.[113] By 1938 he would complete his "grand narrative" of the Revolution, *The Black Jacobins*.[114] In Haitian history, as Grant Farred has pointed out, James found a model for popular revolution in which white and black, metropolis and periphery, could come together to put right a world in crisis.[115]

The early 1930s found another key international figure in London, Paul Robeson. Robeson had met with considerable fame in connection with his stage performances of *The Emperor Jones*.[116] In 1933 he would return to the

Figure 29. Jacob Lawrence, "The General," from the Toussaint L'Ouverture series. Courtesy of the estate of Jacob Lawrence and the Francine Seders Gallery; print, Spradling Ames.

Figure 30. Augusta Savage, La Citadelle — Freedom, *bronze sculpture,
14 ½ in. (h). Howard University Gallery of Art, Washington, D.C.*

States for the film version, with Jones Beach, Long Island, standing in for the
Caribbean coast. By that time he and James were acquainted, and soon
Robeson would come to know Padmore, who would do a stint as an amateur
performer, alongside Robeson, in a play called *Stevedore*.[117] By the early
1930s Robeson was moving toward a more radical stance, although publicly
he defended his artistic decision to make the film version of O'Neill's
play.[118]

With Paul Robeson in London, C. L. R. James pursued his research on

AFTERMATH

Toussaint L'Ouverture and the Haitian Revolution against a background formed in part by O'Neill's representation of Haitian history. James would come to the United States in 1938, and his work on the Haitian Revolution would be greeted with excitement by African Americans. But the connection between James's radicalism and U.S. American discourses on Haiti had been established already — overseas.

RACE AND REVOLUTION

Meanwhile, African Americans were themselves engaged in the project of rehabilitating Haiti's history and reputation. In books for young readers, Harriet Gibbs Marshall, Langston Hughes, and Arna Bontemps responded to the exoticism of prevailing U.S. discourses on Haiti by providing an alternative. Introducing *The Story of Haiti*, Harriet Gibbs Marshall wrote: "the writer, with a real sense of duty after the privilege of a lengthy sojourn in the little Republic of Haiti, presents this story to give the young people of all lands and especially English-speaking nations, a concise and correct history of the struggles and laudable achievements of the Haitian people."[119] Foremost among those achievements was the successful attainment of freedom from slavery through revolutionary struggle. A large portion of the book focused on the Revolution, and within that focus, Marshall emphasized the leadership of Toussaint L'Ouverture.

Without explicitly addressing the discourse of exoticism, Marshall challenged it through her portrait of Toussaint. His success lay not only in having led a revolution, she wrote: "Though vanquished in war by superior power, his life was a success in that he demonstrated for all time what a slave and black man could accomplish, and left to the coming generation a heritage sublime."[120] For Marshall, the success of Toussaint's life was also evident in his domestic life: "He married Suzanne Simon and adopted her son, Placide. His [Toussaint's] home life, directed by a devoted husband and affectionate father, seemed to be nearly ideal."[121]

This attempt to reverse the effects of sensational discourses on Haiti was evident too in *Popo and Fifina*, the children's book coauthored by Langston Hughes and Arna Bontemps. Challenging the discourse of paternalism as laid out by a host of white writers, Hughes and Bontemps's story emphasized strong paternal figures in the Haitian family and in Haitian history. Challenging the notion that Haiti embodied a threatening, untamed sexuality, the story was set in a solid nuclear-family context.

Popo and Fifina (ostensibly about a Haitian boy and his sister) follows the adventures of Popo as he learns the ways of his culture and the history of his people. Popo moves with his family to Cape Haiti (Cap Haïtien) because his parents, who had been peasant farmers, "had grown tired of the life of their lonely hillside."[122] In town, Popo's father could become a fisherman, while his mother could tend the home and visit the market. Popo notes the presence of U.S. marines in the town, and comments on the American factory, at which, he is sure, he would not like to work.[123] In time, Popo begins to learn a trade, and it is during his apprenticeship to his uncle (a carpenter) that Popo and the reader learn the central lesson of Haitian history: the proud heritage of Henri Christophe and the great Citadel, which protected the hard-won freedom of the Haitian people.[124]

The themes of black manhood, racial pride, and revolutionary possibility evident in these works for young readers also pervaded African American cultural expression directed to adults in the Depression decade. In addition, two other closely linked though apparently contradictory themes appeared in many of the novels, plays, and histories intended for adult audiences. One was the unprecedented expression of violence toward whites; the other, the expectation of interracial respect and alliance. Taken together, these themes marked the arrival of a new stage in the history of contestations over U.S. American national identity.

The historical novels of Arna Bontemps, one based on an American slave revolt inspired by the Haitian Revolution and one about the Haitian Revolution itself, brought together the themes of violence and interracial alliance, as well as the emphasis on black manhood, racial pride, and revolutionary possibility. In Bontemps's accounts, white allies play crucial roles as the central black figures in each novel assert themselves and claim their freedom (or attempt to do so) through violent revolution. Bontemps's novels reconstructed a nonracial Enlightenment vision of the nation, while presenting Gabriel Prosser and Toussaint L'Ouverture as powerful and imposing black leaders.

The path by which Arna Bontemps came to write about the Haitian Revolution illustrates the way in which exposure to Haitian history and culture contributed to the matrix of African American radicalism in the 1930s. A central figure in the Harlem Renaissance, Bontemps began to learn about Haitian history in that context. When he lost his teaching position after the Crash, he packed up his family and moved to Alabama, where he managed to secure a teaching position at a small Adventist college.[125] Bontemps kept up his friendship with fellow Harlem writer Langston Hughes. When Hughes returned from Haiti in 1931 with the idea for *Popo and Fifina*, the two set out to coauthor the little book, Bontemps learning about Haiti from Hughes and doing much of the writing himself.[126]

That same year, in the town of Scottsboro, Alabama, nine young black men were unjustly accused of raping two white women. The Scottsboro trial, which was held in nearby Decatur, brought "Communists and agitators," including Bontemps's vocal friend, Langston Hughes, to the area; it was in this context that the college dean suggested that Bontemps demonstrate "a clean break with unrest in the world" by burning his "race-conscious and provocative" books, including Vandercook's *Black Majesty*.[127] Bontemps not only refused to burn any books but also decided it was best to leave the college as quickly as possible.[128]

Meanwhile, Bontemps had begun to think about writing a novel based on the slave revolts that had been attempted in the United States. He had been inspired by reading slave narratives at Fisk University, where he had had the opportunity to visit three other friends from his Harlem years: Charles S. Johnson, James Weldon Johnson, and Arthur Schomburg.[129] After the book-burning request, Bontemps and his family headed to Watts, California, where, in cramped quarters, he began to compose *Black Thunder*.

A fictionalized account of the Gabriel Prosser revolt in Virginia in 1800, *Black Thunder* presented the Haitian Revolution as the model and inspiration for revolt in this country. Bontemps looked to the Enlightenment ideals of the French Revolution, as carried forth by Toussaint L'Ouverture in Haiti, for a new basis on which to establish race relations in the American context. While the novel focused on several black figures who led or participated in the revolt, it also treated with importance several white Jacobin characters who expressed sympathy for the slaves.

As literary critic Arnold Rampersad has pointed out, Bontemps linked the radical Jacobin tradition with the struggles of the slaves by highlighting the importance of the Haitian Revolution. In this way, he expressed "his deepening respect for radicalism, and his growing outrage at how blacks were treated and had been treated from time immemorial in the United States."[130] *Black Thunder* met with enormous success among African American readers and reviewers, including Richard Wright, who hailed the novel for its presentation of a black revolutionary tradition.[131]

Several years later, Bontemps published another historical novel, this one dealing directly with the Haitian Revolution. While *Black Thunder* had suggested the importance of white allies and Western intellectual traditions in slave revolts, *Drums at Dusk* placed these at center stage. This novel presented Toussaint, the leader of the blacks, as an important but secondary character; the central figure in *Drums* was the fictional Diron Desautels, a white man and a member of the Amis des Noirs, who actively assisted the slave revolution.[132] At one point, the novel finds Diron in the midst of a crowd of whites attempting to escape from the blacks just after the uprising begins. Diron breaks away from the crowd in order to "meet the slaves alone" and "take his chances as an individual."[133] In many respects, *Drums* seems to be an extended discourse on the possibilities for interracial alliances in the midst of revolutionary struggle.

If Bontemps suggested the possibility of productive and liberating alliances with whites, he also emphasized some of the most brutal aspects of white oppression. In particular, Bontemps drew attention to the extent to which white power was expressed through sexuality and sexual violence. In *Drums at Dusk*, immediately after the uprising begins, one young female slave encounters her master's cousin and representative, the Count de Sacy, in a hallway as she is abandoning her household duties. They begin to brawl and she is relentless in her attacks, biting and scratching with all her might. He eventually leaves, beaten, exhausted, and she rests on the floor a moment. Toussaint arrives at the scene and, seeing her, is alarmed. "She had the look of one who had been ravished; but when Toussaint squinted questioningly, she quickly corrected him. It wasn't what he thought."[134]

Later on, de Sacy, having been run off his cousin's plantation, having escaped only by disguising himself as a black man, rapes a mulatto woman in an attempt to maintain a sense of his disintegrating power.[135] Shortly after the rape, de Sacy is caught, and his captors, in a sense, rape him too. " 'What are you doing?' the count cried, feeling the clothes torn from his waist downward. 'Just inserting a little gun powder,' a slave replied. . . . The count felt himself torn apart by crude implements devised to help accommodate the charge. A moment later, fainting away, he ceased to struggle or to protest."[136]

In Bontemps's telling, the struggle for power between the revolting slaves and the white slave owners was waged, at least in part, in terms of gender and sexuality. In response to the depredations of slavery, the slaves not only killed de Sacy but deprived him of his manhood precisely as they did so. Bontemps's description of this violent action, along with similarly violent scenes in *Black Thunder*, indicated the arrival of a new phase in African American cultural expression, a phase in which the Haitian Revolution would facilitate the representation of black violence against whites to an unprecedented extent.

As in Bontemps's novels, other 1930s African American discourses on the Haitian Revolution juxtaposed fierce, sometimes violent, expressions of race pride with stories about white allies who served the cause of black freedom. This juxtaposition was indicative of the process by which African American writers began to imagine the possibility of a new national political community in the United States. As white Communists reached out to blacks with a vision of interracial class solidarity, and as white Democrats appeared to champion the cause of racial justice through economic opportunity, black artists fashioned a new vision of African American life. No longer a separatist Garveyite vision, this new vision projected life in an America characterized by interracial cooperation and, at the same time, the uncompromising assertion of African American race pride. The Haitian Revolution offered a useful point of departure for elaborating this vision.

FEDERAL THEATRE

If the New Deal contributed to a politics of rising expectations with respect to life in the United States, it also provided material support for African American writers and artists who would articulate new ways of imagining and creating the national community. Through its several branches, the Works Progress Administration funded black writers, painters, actors, dancers, and other artists, many of whom would focus attention on Haiti. One undertaking of the Federal Writers Project, for example, was a history of the influence of the Haitian Revolution on New York. Employees of the project researched a variety of historical materials in order to show the myriad forms of that influence.[137]

The Federal Theatre Project, founded in 1935, with several "Negro" units, including one in Harlem and one in Los Angeles, provided numerous opportunities for African American artists to consider the relevance of Haitian themes for their own lives. One of the most successful of all Federal Theatre productions was undoubtedly the Harlem unit's *Macbeth*. Directed by Orson Welles and informally dubbed "Voodoo Macbeth," the play was set in nineteenth-century Haiti.[138]

One of the Los Angeles productions was a play called *Black Empire*, which focused on the final days of Henri Christophe's reign as king of Haiti. *Black Empire* was an unabashed polemic on race pride in which a French spy would eventually abandon his mission and confess to a dying Christophe: "I came to rob and ridicule a negro, my brave Henri! I leave your unhappy empire paying tribute to a great man."[139] Other dramatic fare on the Haitian Revolution and its leaders, from the Federal Theatre and from smaller, local theaters, included *Babouk* (based on the novel by Guy Endore), *Opener of*

Doors, Toussaint L'Ouverture, Dessalines, Christophe, Christophe's Daughter, King Henry, and *Genifrede,* as well as Langston Hughes's *Drums of Haiti* and *Troubled Island* and C. L. R. James's *Black Majesty*.[140]

Another play, called simply *Haiti*, illustrates further the ways in which representations of the Haitian Revolution reflected changing struggles over U.S. American national identity between 1915 and 1940. The play, whose long and unexpected career spanned almost this entire period, was written in 1917 by a white southern newspaper reporter named William Dubois. Set in the final years of the Revolution, Dubois's drama was a morality play about the grave dangers of miscegenation. By creating a class of mulatto freedmen, Dubois believed, the French in colonial Saint Domingue had brought on their own tragic and bloody downfall.[141]

The story revolved around a romance between one French officer and the wife of another. This wife and lover is Odette, and as the play unfolds it becomes clear that Odette is not as she appears; she is not white. What is worse — for the French, and for the intended audience — her father is a spy for Christophe and Toussaint. When Odette realizes her true identity, in Dubois's original version, she follows her atavistic impulses and betrays both husband and lover, leading to the utter defeat of the French army.[142]

It was not until 1937 that anyone seems to have read Dubois's script with an eye to staging it. The man who did was Maurice Clark, the African American director of the Federal Theatre Project's Harlem unit. Needless to say, Clark's audience would contrast sharply with the audience for which the play had been intended. Clark sat down with Dubois (who was now a reporter for the *New York Times*) and described how he wanted to revise the play for production. Dubois, though he was considerably disturbed by the proposed revisions, agreed to them all, insisting only — in deference to his original theme — that no black and white hands could touch on stage. Clark agreed to that condition.[143]

By the time *Haiti* hit the stage of the Lafayette Theatre in Harlem on March 2, 1938, it had been utterly transformed. No longer a play about the tragic demise of the French, it was now a dramatization of the black struggle for freedom. True to her newly discovered racial identity, the revised Odette proudly assists Christophe and his black troops. By the end of the evening, most of the cast crowded onto the stage for the final scene of revolutionary triumph, much to the delight of the audience. That night, *Haiti* could boast eight curtain calls.[144]

Neither did the audience wait for the curtain to register its approval of the action on stage. On that opening night, and for more than 100 nights to follow, Harlem theatergoers saw blacks beating up whites on stage. And as the actors—the strapping Rex Ingram and Canada Lee—brought their fists down on the whites, voices from the audience could be heard encouraging the action: "Give him a lick for me!" "Hit him again!" "Man, that's it, that's it!"[145] On opening night, one reviewer noted that, when the Revolution triumphs, the audience burst into "deep-throated applause."[146] That same night, however, when the curtain rose, black and white actors, to the dismay of the original playwright, took their bows, eight times over, side by side, and hand in hand.[147]

Over 72,000 people came to see these scenes reenacted over the next four months—in New York alone.[148] The play then went on to Chicago, Cleveland, and Hartford. In keeping with the Federal Theatre Project's tradition of using the stage as a "living newspaper," this play's headlines announced, in different ways, both the possibility for interracial collaboration and the frustration, anger, and growing race consciousness of African Americans in the 1930s.

Such headlines, funded by federal tax money, were sure to draw fire, and draw fire they did. Congressman J. Parnell Thomas, a member of the House Un-American Activities Committee (then called the Dies Committee for its first chair, Texas Democrat Martin Dies), picked out *Haiti* and two other Federal Theatre plays as evidence of the "un-American activity" of the New Deal arts project. *Haiti*, according to J. Parnell Thomas, had "communistic leanings" and showed that the Federal Theatre Project was "one more link in the vast unparalleled New Deal propaganda machine."[149] Not more than a few months after the play closed, the Federal Theatre Project was brought before the Dies Committee for a series of hearings that led, ultimately, to the closing down of the entire project, coast to coast.[150]

So, what was "un-American" about the play called *Haiti*? How might we make sense of this conflict over competing conceptions of American national identity, expressed in relation to a drama of revolutionary Haiti? Hadn't the Haitian Revolution, like the American Revolution, been an anticolonial struggle for national independence? And hadn't the Haitians fought to end slavery, just as Americans had fought to do so, even at the cost of splitting their Union asunder? It was the bold representation of antiwhite violence that marked the play as a target for those appointed to ferret out the "un-American" in American cultural expression. Here was a challenge to the association between whiteness and American identity, a challenge couched in terms of Haitian history, and articulated by African Americans with financial assistance from the government itself.

The production and reception of *Haiti* in 1938 was indicative of important changes in the uses of Haitian history and culture for African Americans in the 1930s. While, in the 1920s, African Americans could express race pride through portraits of powerful individual figures like Christophe, during the Depression decade, the Haitian Revolution would facilitate the articulation of black demands for rights and for respect from whites. In that sense, 1930s African American discourses on Haiti did indeed challenge hegemonic conceptions of "America," for they were discourses on American national identity that sought to undermine the racial status quo. As we have seen, African American writers often contended with questions of gender and sexuality—with varying results—as they articulated this challenge.

ZORA NEALE HURSTON'S GODS AND HORSES

Zora Neale Hurston's challenge to prevailing U.S. discourses on Haiti and "America" stood apart. Notably, Hurston refused to criticize directly the racism and exploitation involved in the U.S. occupation of Haiti. Hurston's anthropological study of Haiti and Jamaica, *Tell My Horse*, also played right into the prevailing themes of exotic primitivism evident in popular white discourses on Haiti over the previous decade. On the other hand, Hurston presented a subtle critique of the gendered ideology that underlay American action in, and white writing about, Haiti. Through a variety of literary turns, Hurston challenged the very meanings she appeared to reinscribe. In the process, she laid bare a number of the assumptions underlying white and black discussions of race and U.S. national identity.[151]

This subtlety was undoubtedly lost on many readers, as it was lost on the sensational author, William Seabrook, who sought vindication for his own exotic discourses in *Tell My Horse*. Writing his autobiography in the early 1940s, Seabrook recalled the doubt that Melville Herskovits had cast on the veracity of *The Magic Island*. "I hope," Seabrook wrote, "that in the interval he [Herskovits] has chanced to read a book, published a little while after his, entitled *Tell My Horse*, by Zora Hurston."[152] "It was a lucky break for me that her book, which no sea-level ethnologist has presumed to doubt, contained page after page, the complete circumstantial verification of the scenes and ceremonies I'd described in mine."[153] "Circumstantial" was indeed the key word in Seabrook's evaluation of Hurston's work.

Hurston's study of "Voodoo and Life in Haiti" presented stories about zombies and Voodoo ceremonies shrouded in language that made it hard to know whether she was reporting "fact" or lore. It was as if she had said to the reader, "You want something exotic? I'll give you something exotic!"[154]

While Seabrook regretted Herskovits's critique and gloried in what he took to be Hurston's vindication of his own work, neither *Life in a Haitian Valley* (as we have seen) nor *Tell My Horse* could ultimately be characterized simply by its apparent rejection or confirmation of Seabrook's sensational claims. Both works offered complex meditations on the prevailing themes in American discussions of Haiti; both also commented on the relevance and implications of those themes for Americans and American culture.

Two points concerning the framework within which Hurston presented her study will be especially important for understanding the complexity of her text and its relationship to the historical and cultural moment in which she wrote. Both suggest that Hurston was conscious of the white audience that would receive her work. First, Hurston dedicated the book to Carl Van Vechten, whom she called "God's image of a friend." The fascination that Van Vechten, a leading white patron and promoter of Harlem Renaissance writers, felt for African Americans grew from his perception of the primitive nature of the black race. This became clear in his controversial 1926 novel *Nigger Heaven*.[155] While many Harlemites rejected Van Vechten after the novel's publication and kept him out of some of the clubs he had frequented for several years, he finally gained readmittance to his favorite night spot — on Zora Hurston's arm.[156] By dedicating her study of Jamaica and Haiti to Van Vechten, Hurston implicitly announced her awareness of the white audience that would, in part, structure her text.

Second, an examination of that aspect of Vodou from which Hurston drew her title suggests that on one level Hurston may have directed the book to an audience that she perceived (or that, she believed, perceived itself) as more powerful than Hurston. Moreover, it appears that the book may have constituted for Hurston a kind of back talk against the authority of that audience. Hurston took her title from the formulaic utterance of a Haitian god, or *loa*, Papa Guedé, whose primary characteristic is the audacity of his back talk. Through his "mounts" or "horses" — that is, those he possesses — Guedé talks back brazenly to the powerful, beginning always with the words, "Tell my horse . . ."[157]

When not deriving from the authentic voice of Guedé, this phrase serves as a mask enabling self-expression, a voice one may take on in order to speak one's mind under the guise of possession.[158] Hurston explained, "You can see him in the market-women, in the domestic servant who now and then appears before her employer 'mounted' by this god who takes occasion to say many stinging things to the boss." Guedé is "the deification of the common people," Hurston told her readers.[159] The elites don't worship Guedé, though they fear him, because they are among the most likely of his targets. When a "horse" possessed by Guedé makes "devastating revelations," Hurston explains, "the common comment is 'Guedé pas dras' (Guedé is not a sheet), that is, Guedé covers up nothing. It seems to be his mission to expose and reveal."[160] Guedé speaks with a sharp tongue, then, ready to loose damaging gossip, about a boss or a government official, as the occasion demands.

Whereas Guedé speaks through and for the common people of Haiti, so that they may express themselves on the unfairness and inequalities with which they contend, the common people of Haiti seem to speak through Hurston's ethnology, beginning with the words of Guedé, in the title, *Tell My Horse*. Moreover, whereas, according to Hurston, Guedé "covers up nothing," Guedé's words in Hurston's title may cover up quite a lot, even as they reveal a critical, subversive voice in her text. At the very least, Hurston's title suggests the complexity of her own utterance, for it raises the question: whose voice is it that follows the words "Tell my horse"?

In connection with the issues raised by Hurston's title, it is especially interesting to consider the one and only instance in which a human being is possessed by Guedé in Hurston's study. "A tragic case of a Guedé mount happened near Pont Beudet," wrote Hurston. "A woman known to be a Lesbian was 'mounted' one afternoon. The spirit announced through her mouth, 'Tell my horse I have told this woman repeatedly to stop making love to women. It is a vile thing and I object to it. Tell my horse that this woman promised me twice that she would never do such a thing again, but each time she has broken her word to me as soon as she could find a woman suitable for her purpose. But she has made love to women for the last time. She has lied to Guedé for the last time. Tell my horse to tell that woman I am going to kill her today. She will not lie again.' The woman pranced and galloped like a horse to a great mango tree, climbed it far up among the top limbs and dived off and broke her neck."[161] Hurston's account bears a striking resemblance to another story involving a Haitian woman who was living in the Dominican Republic in the 1920s. The woman, a *manbo* (priestess) who was a lesbian, angered another male *loa*—Ogou, the warrior—by neglecting him and giving gifts to women instead.[162] (Anthropologist Karen McCarthy Brown explains that Ogou is associated with military power in Haitian history. The U.S. occupation of 1915–34, she points out, provided additional material for stories of "promise and betrayal" by the handsome soldier who could also be "untrustworthy" and "wantonly violent.") In this *manbo*'s story, as in the story told by Hurston, the struggle between a male *loa* and his unresponsive horse ended in the woman's death.[163]

Reading Hurston's title and story together, it is as if, through her voice, Guedé is saying: "Tell my horse it is futile to defy openly a male god who requires allegiance and obedience." Or, like the market women who feign possession, is it Hurston herself suggesting that futility? In any case, *Tell My Horse* openly conforms to the dictates of exoticism and paternalism; only subtly and under cover, only through multiple voices, storytelling, and trickster strategies, does it challenge the dominant tropes or themes of white discourses on Haiti.

In light of the textual framework I have suggested, let us consider Hurston's stance with respect to the righteousness of the U.S. military occupation, ended three years before Hurston's trip to Haiti. On the most obvious level, *Tell My Horse* is striking for its enthusiastic and emphatic defense of the occupation. Consider, for example, the following: "For four hundred years the blacks of Haiti had yearned for peace . . . but it eluded them and it vanished from their hands. A prophet could have foretold it was to come to them from another land and another people utterly unlike the Haitian people in any respect." Or consider this fictional rendering of a peasant response to the coming American invasion: "One black peasant woman fell upon her knees with her arms outstretched like a crucifix and cried, 'They say that the white man is coming to rule Haiti again. The black man is so cruel to his own, let the white man come!' " Or: "The smoke from the funnels of the U.S.S. *Washington* [one of the U.S. naval vessels that carried the marines to Haiti] was a black plume with a white hope."[164] Contrast these with Langston Hughes's description of Haiti under the U.S. occupation. Hurston's characterizations of the occupation bore a greater resemblance to the descriptions written by marines themselves, in contrast to those of Hughes or James Weldon Johnson.

Hurston was certainly aware of African American efforts on behalf of Haiti, as she indicates in a passage condemning Haitian president Stenio Vincent. Vincent lies outright, she writes, when he "announces himself as the Second Deliverer of Haiti. . . . He knows that the N.A.A.C.P., *The Nation* and certain other organizations had a great deal more to do with the withdrawal of the Marines than Vincent did and much more than they are given credit for." While this passage suggests that Hurston thought credit was in fact due to these groups for bringing an end to the occupation, in the next breath, she asserts that "nobody wanted the Marines to go."[165]

How are we to understand these passages? To dismiss such bold statements in retrospective support of the occupation would be absurd. Yet some contradictions within the text are worth noting. On one hand, Hurston asserts that Haiti would be saved from itself by a people, namely Americans, with whom they had nothing in common. On the other, she repeatedly mentions similarities between the two countries: both have populations of black folk who want food, shelter, and clothing; both have had, as she put it, "empty wind bags" for race leaders; both experience bloodshed at the hands of some form of organized crime, which cannot be, or has not been, stopped by agents of the law; both harbor hypocrites who publicly condemn something (whiskey in one case, Voodoo in the other) but privately support it; and so on.[166] Thus in small ways, throughout the text, national differences are diminished.

Another similarity emerges if we consider statements made by Hurston in *Mules and Men*, her collection of the folklore of African Americans, in which she discusses the role of the trickster in interactions with whites.[167] Literary critic Barbara Johnson draws our attention to Hurston's explanation of this practice.[168] Hurston writes, "The theory behind our tactics: 'The white man is always trying to know into someone else's business. All right, I'll set something outside the door of my mind for him to play with and handle.' "[169] In *Tell My Horse* Hurston discusses "the habit of lying," which she calls "the most striking phenomenon in Haiti to a visiting American." She shows that it takes many forms and distinguishes between the lies of the rich and the lies of the peasants. The lies of the rich are transparent, as when, "under the very sound of the Voodoo drums, the upper class Haitian will tell you that there is no such thing as Voodoo in Haiti, and that all that has been written about it is nothing but the malicious lies of foreigners."[170] The Haitian peasant, on the other hand, "often fancies himself to be Ti Malice, the sharp trickster of Haitian folklore."[171] In Haiti, then, as in the United States, African Americans, according to Hurston, play the trickster and tell tales — to white audiences, that is.

The similarities between Haiti and the United States return again and again, like subversive eruptions, defying Hurston's characterization of the American people as "utterly unlike the Haitian people in any respect."[172] At other points in the text, minor anecdotes appear to undermine Hurston's stated position on the occupation. Bearing in mind the figure of the trickster, consider the following tidbits, taken from a chapter devoted to Île de la Gonave. Hurston introduces these by describing her desire "to see the Kingdom of Faustin Wirkus," because "William Seabrook in his *Magic Island* had fired my imagination with his account of the White King."[173] It's hard to believe this is not tongue-in-cheek.

First, Hurston related the story of a stone that was possessed by Papa Guedé. (She explains that *loa* do not only possess human beings.) As we know, Papa Guedé is a special god, one who, through his mounts, talks back audaciously to the powerful. This famous stone "had so much power," Hurston explained, "that it urinated." Papa Guedé insisted that it be clothed and so his devotees put a little dress on the stone. Hurston goes on: "One of the American officers of the Occupation named Whitney saw it. . . . It was a curious idol and he wanted it for himself. The Haitian guard attached to Whitney's station told him that it would urinate and not to put it on his desk but he did so in spite of warning and on several occasions he found his desk wet."[174] The second incident took place at Anse-à-Galets, the port of La Gonave, where a sergeant of the Garde d'Haïti was stationed. Hurston hears him swearing in English and remarks that he must be "a black Marine." He responds by announcing, "I am a black Marine. I speak like one always. Perhaps you would like me to kill something for you."[175]

The tricksterlike play of voices in these anecdotes suggests the possibility that Hurston's apparent support for paternalist justifications of the occupation masked a deeper critique. This textual evidence should not be taken to mean that Hurston was "really" some sort of radical in reactionary garb. Hurston's conservatism was evidenced in many other contexts, and her surface collusion with exotic and paternalist discourses had an effect on the cultural construction of race in the 1930s, whatever subtlety historians and literary critics now find in her work.

At the same time, recognizing the complexity of Hurston's textual ruminations on Haiti, and on the U.S. role there, provides insight into the complicated ways in which the occupation and its cultural aftermath affected racial politics in the United States. One New York newspaper, for example, reported on Hurston's return from Haiti: "After eleven months in the dark jungles back of Port-au-Prince, chanting voodoo chants, drinking the blood of the sacrificial goat and worshipping with descendants of the African slaves whose people were bred in the Congo, Miss Hurston returns a believer in voodooism."[176] If the idea of an accomplished black female intellectual might have seemed threatening to some white readers, the reporter allayed any such fears, by noting that, "Despite her degree from Barnard, the books she has written, the Columbia and Guggenheim Fellowships which she has won, Miss Hurston is a happy-go-lucky pagan."[177] By helping to generate increased interest in "the exotic," American activity in Haiti led to increased white interest in African Americans who, like Zora Neale Hurston, could also be seen as exotic. If that interest created opportunities for Hurston or for others, those opportunities were limited severely and were, at the same time, damaging, as they revised and perpetuated new forms of U.S. American racism.

Seizing such opportunities, Hurston could articulate, in however muted a form, a challenge to hegemonic discourses that no one else put forth. The limits of that challenge, even in its muted form, become evident as we further examine Hurston's reflections on gender and national identity, as manifested in her between-the-lines critique of the discourse of paternity and paternalism.

Tell My Horse opens with a consideration of paternity and illegitimacy in another Afro-Caribbean context. Her first chapter finds Hurston in Jamaica, about which she comments, with characteristic Hurston flair, "Jamaica is the land where a rooster lays an egg."[178] Hurston is struck by what she perceives as the desire of so many Jamaicans to be white and to "look English." "Sometimes it is so far-fetched," she writes, "that one is reminded of that line from 'Of Thee I Sing,' where the French Ambassador boasts, 'She is the illegitimate daughter of the illegitimate son of the illegitimate nephew of the great Napoleon.' " "In Jamaica," she continues, "just substitute the word Englishman for Napoleon and you have the situation."[179] In this context, Hurston suggests that the glorification of white paternal ancestry effaces the very existence of black mothers; she writes, "When a Jamaican is born of a black woman and some English or Scotsman, the black mother is literally and figuratively kept out of sight as far as possible, but no one is allowed to forget that white father, however questionable the circumstances of birth. You hear about 'My father this and my father that, and my father who was English you know,' until you get the impression that he or she had no mother. . . . You get the impression that these virile Englishmen do not require women to reproduce."[180] One aspect of Hurston's challenge to the discourse of paternalism, and its more specific variation, the discourse of paternity, this passage suggests, is the explicit reintroduction of the black mother, and of the "maternal" heritage of Africa, into discourses about Caribbean identities. Although writing at this point about a different Caribbean island, Hurston thus opens the book with a hint at her oppositional stance with respect to the question of cultural paternity; she closes with a much more extended consideration of the issue.

Toward the end of *Tell My Horse*, Hurston devotes a chapter to Dr. Reser, an American living in the town of Pont Beudet, not far from Port-au-Prince. Reser, who had been a pharmacist's mate in the U.S. Navy, but never actually a doctor, was now an officer of the state insane asylum there. Why, we readers wonder, in a book about Jamaica and Haiti, do we come across an entire chapter devoted to an American ex-military man? Could it be, as Hurston suggests, that "A piece about Haiti without Doctor Reser would be lacking in flavor?"[181] I doubt anyone getting to this point in *Tell My Horse* would miss the "flavor." There is more to it.

Dr. Reser, I argue, provided Hurston with a device with which to articulate her challenge to the discourse of paternity and paternalism. Through her extended discussion of Reser, Hurston refused the logic that saw Haiti as a nation without a stable identity, one that required a paternal American presence. At the same time, Hurston lay bare the gender dimensions of that logic.

Dr. Reser, it turns out, is a *houngan*, a Vodou priest.[182] According to Hurston, most Americans who want to write a book about Haiti, upon arriving in the country, simply pay a visit to Dr. Reser, get a few stories, and return home to write their books. Hurston assures her readers that she does not visit Reser for this purpose, because she is perfectly capable of collecting folklore on her own, directly from Haitians.

Instead of using Reser to get information about others in Haiti, she wrote about Reser himself, and by making a white American ex-military man the object of her analysis, Hurston also turned the tables on the discourse of the exotic. "I am breaking a promise by writing this," Hurston informed her readers, "and the cocks may be crowing because of it, but all the cocks in creation can crow three times if they must. I am going to say something about Dr. Reser."[183]

Leaving aside for the moment the potentially gendered meanings of cocks crowing on account of her broken promise, I should mention here that Hurston's readers don't ever learn what promise she has, ostensibly, broken. The answer lies in some edited scraps of text from which I learned that Reser had an American family, a wife and daughter back in the States. They are nowhere mentioned in the version of *Tell My Horse* published by J. B. Lippincott. Reser asked Hurston not to talk about him for fear that his reputation would ruin his daughter's future. But Hurston assures her would-be readers, still in the unpublished text, "I have no fear whatever for little Miss Reser's future. The public does not go around being nasty to pretty, spunky and talented young girls because their fathers go native in a way."[184] Thus, in her original text, one of the first things Hurston tells about Reser is that he is a father, and a father who has gone native "in a way."

Following immediately on the heels of this revelation, Hurston raises the subject of the white father figure (Papa Blanc), using the story of Faustin Wirkus, whom William Seabrook had dubbed "The White King of La Gonave." As she put it, "I tackled him [Reser] one day on the business of being a white king of Haiti."

> "Now in all the adventure tales I have ever read, the natives, finding a white man among them, always assume that he is a god, and at *least* make him a king. Here you have been in Haiti for eleven years . . . and still no kingly crown. How is that?"

"Well, I tell you Zora, if you show yourself sincere, the Haitians will make a good friend of a white man, but hardly a king. They just don't run to royalty."

"Not even a *white* man?"

"Not even a white man . . ."

I sat bolt upright at that. He had his mouth open and he was making broad statements.[185]

Reser articulates something that we readers sense throughout much of *Tell My Horse*, that there seems to be some question as to Zora Hurston's sincerity. What we suspected when we first came across her reference to Wirkus, that she didn't buy the story for a moment, is here seconded by Reser's aside, "Zora, if you show yourself sincere . . ."

Hurston used storytelling in her chapter on Reser to further elaborate this subtle suggestion of a critique, but, as we have already seen, not all the stories made it into the published version of the text. One story that was edited out prior to publication centers on Reser's domestic life in Pont Beudet. We know from the published text that Reser lives on the premises of the insane asylum. The edited text informs us that Dr. Reser's mistress, Cecile, lives nearby with her adopted daughter, Rose. Rose's birth mother, we learn by and by, is an inmate at the asylum.[186]

One day Rose, Cecile, Reser, and Zora Hurston are together on Reser's porch, and, Hurston tells us, "Little Rose had learned new dance steps which she would presently show her 'daddy.' "[187] In Hurston's telling, Cecile teases Rose about insisting that Reser is her father. Here is the conversation between mother and adopted daughter:

> "How can you think Dr. Reser is your papa, Rose? Look at him and look at yourself. See, he is very white with blue eyes while you are very black with black eyes. He cannot be your father."
>
> "Oh yes he is my papa, too."
>
> "But look at the difference in your color, Rose, you have nothing like Dr. Reser. That white man cannot be the father to a black little girl like you."[188]

A Haitian woman, mistress to a white American man, tells her adopted daughter that no, the white man is not, and could never be, her father.

Here is the question of Haitian paternity literalized. Reser's fatherhood and his paternal roles, which figure centrally in these edited scraps of text, take their place in Hurston's challenge to the white U.S. American discourse of paternity. Whereas Seabrook and company focus their analytic attention on the orphan or illegitimate child, deprived of a coherent identity due to the ambiguity of paternity, Hurston sets the analytical eye on an American (formerly of the U.S. military) whose role as a father is at issue. Hurston's stories about Reser's two "daughter figures" effectively pose the question: Whose father is he? Hurston thus reverses the picture offered by Seabrook and the marines.

Not only is Reser's paternal role questioned, so is his nationality, and the ambiguity over his national identity structures the entire chapter. Hurston informs her readers at the outset that although, "by the calendar," Reser came to Haiti eleven years earlier, from the United States, with the Marine Corps, "in soul he came from Africa with the rest of the people."[189] But then, she continues, "in spite of his having become more haitian than american, having let his American wife and children return to the United States and leave him with his peace in Haiti, his American feelings come down on him now and then."[190] Reser's identity is anything but stable — he is an American, but really more Haitian than American because he has gone native in a way. In addition, whereas for Seabrook, the family members' identities are defined by the father, for Hurston, the father is defined by the family; thus, by letting his American wife and family return to the United States, Reser became "more Haitian than American."

Hurston's discussion of Reser is interrupted periodically by the inmates "who wandered about the grounds [of the asylum]," says Hurston, "and occasionally came up to the screened porch to beg a cigarette or say something that seemed important to their crippled minds."[191] The chatter of the inmates provides the material for another story with which Hurston then elaborates her discourse on national identity.

Hurston informs her readers that "The insane patients would be depended upon to yell something startling every so often." She mentions "One tall lanky patient [who] . . . hung around the porch and kept reciting the tales of Fontaine." And "One Syrian, formerly a merchant in Port-au-Prince, kept standing with his face against the porch wishing Dr. Reser well. . . . 'Doctor Reser! Doctor Reser! I like for you to have a very good eating . . .'" and the Syrian went on, "'I tell the man, "You pay five dollars duty to the American government every time you leave pork [i.e., a pig] in the street."'"[192]

Back on the porch, Hurston "fell to wondering what part of the United States Dr. Reser came from." He tells her that he is from "Lapland," to which she responds, "I thought you said you were an American." He assures her that he is — he is from the land where Missouri laps over Arkansas. And with that, Dr. Reser breaks into "the brogue of the hill-billy" and begins to recite "about folk heroes."[193] Here is Hurston's account of what ensues, starting with Reser's tale:

> "Yes, I'm the guy that chewed the wad the goat eat that butted the bull off the bridge!"
>
> Just then the Syrian hurried up to the porch and called: "Dr. Reser! Dr. Reser! The soldiers of Monte Carlo killed the Dead Sea, then they built the Casino!"
>
> "Thanks for the information," Dr. Reser replied.
>
> The patient who spent all of his waking hours quoting Fontaine's fables came to the porch too. I had laughed heartily at Dr. Reser's quotations from the folk lore of the Ozarks, and perhaps our merriment attracted them. Another patient came up and began to babble the Haitian folk tales about Brother Bouki and Ti Malice.
>
> Dr. Reser went on: "Raised on six shooters till I got big enough to eat growed shotguns. I warmed up the gulf of Mexico and bathe therein. I mount the wild ass and hop from crag to crag. I swim the Mississippi River from end to end with five hundred pound shot in my teeth! Airy dad gummed man that don't believe it, I'll hold him by the neck and leave him wiggle his fool self to death."
>
> "Dr. Reser! Dr. Reser!" The Syrian attracts attention to himself. "They have horse racing in Palestine. The horses have contracts in Jewish and Arabic and English and the Jewish horse must be second. It's political."
>
> The man who recited Fontaine pointed his stagnant eyes on the porch and babbled on as if he raced with the man who was talking about Ti Malice and Bouki, but he had a weaker voice. So we heard very distinctly:
>
> "Of course, Bouki was very angry with Ti Malice for what he had done and Ti Malice was afraid, so he ran away very fast until he came to a fence. The fence had a hole in it, but the hole was not very big, but Malice tried to get through — "
>
> "Dr. Reser! Dr. *Reser*! Never speak to a person with tired physinomic! I drive car for five years without license and the United States Government was very content."
>
> "Are they annoying you?" Dr. Reser asked me. "They never worry *me* at all."
>
> "Oh no," I answered. "It is very interesting. Let them go on."[194]

On one level, "the folk-heroes of the Ozarks" may serve to illustrate for Hurston Reser's American identity, but at the same time this folklore marks a regional identity more than a national identity — it shows him coming from a particular part of the country, not as identifying with the nation as a cohesive unit.

Furthermore, the apparently marginal chatter and hollering of these inmates are central to Hurston's elaboration of the instability of national identity. It is impossible for Reser to recite the folklore that defines him, without calling into play the tales and fables and ruminations of three inmates in particular: one, representing French Enlightenment culture, reciting the fables of Fontaine; one, representing Haiti's African roots, reciting the tales of Bouki and Malice; and one, representing Haiti's most recently acquired blood heritage, the Syrian immigrant merchant who carries on about two colonial-imperial references — the American government and the mandate of Palestine. In 1936 and 1937, Palestine was a British mandate embroiled in riots and civil strife. The Syrian's juxtaposition of statements about the U.S. government in Haiti and politics in Palestine serves as a reminder of the international relations of power at work defining the very possibilities of nationhood and national identity for colonial and neo-colonial subjects. Syrians in Haiti, moreover, had a complicated relationship to national identity in that many had claimed U.S. citizenship and looked to the United States for diplomatic protection when anti-Syrian sentiment surged, especially during times of economic constriction.[195] The insane asylum provided the perfect backdrop, then, for Hurston's extended textual rumination on shifts, transformations, and instabilities in subjective national identity.

By the end of the chapter, it is Reser's Haitian identity that is affirmed as he discusses the experience of possession. Hurston explains: "A new personality burned up the one that had eaten supper with us. . . . Before our very eyes, he walked out of his Nordic body and changed. Whatever the stuff of which the soul of Haiti is made; he was that. You could see the snake god of Dahomey hovering about him. Africa was in his tones. He throbbed and glowed. He used English words but he talked to me from another continent. He was dancing before his gods and the fire of Shango played about him."[196] Reser (or Hurston) has effected a complete transformation. No longer American at all, Reser is made of the stuff of the soul of Haiti. The father's identity is not stable.

Dr. Reser, I suggest, served as a vehicle for Hurston's critique of the gendered discourse of paternity, which posed Papa Blanc as the savior of an illegitimate child/nation in need of a father. If, in marines' accounts, white father figures with stable identities are welcomed by a childlike country suffering from an identity complex ever since its French white fathers left its black and mulatto mothers to raise the new nation alone, then in Hurston's refiguring of the story the child's identity is not problematic; it is the supposed father who suffers from a confused national identity.

Throughout *Tell My Horse*, storytelling, or telling tales in the style of Ti Malice, serves as a means of expressing a subtle critique of hegemonic U.S. discourses that Hurston refused to challenge in a straightforward "scholarly" manner. Replete with contradictions, Hurston's study of Haiti and Jamaica reinforced exotic discourses, while critiquing them in the same breath. Attributing her own words to a powerful Haitian god named Papa Guedé, Hurston put forth a critique of paternalism that, however subtle it was, focused on gender dimensions in ways no other writer did.

Why did the themes of Haitian culture and history resonate so much in the experience of U.S. Americans, and how did these themes resonate differently for different groups (and individuals) at different times? How did the legacy of the occupation help Americans to make sense of, and to reshape, their own nation? What, in short, were the consequences of U.S. foreign policy in Haiti for the construction of class, race, gender, and sexual categories at home?

The occupation of Haiti did not, in and of itself, bring about paternalism, racism, race pride, exoticism, gender inequalities, modern sexualities, psychological discourses, or U.S. nationalism, but it provided a host of cultural vehicles with which U.S. Americans would come to express, bolster, or challenge each of these. In turn, these diverse articulations led to the destabilizing of American national identity as it had been known, and to the consolidation of new visions of "America," laying the groundwork for future political struggles. Finally, in the shifting salience of Haiti for Americans between 1915 and 1940, in conflicts over the meaning and substance of U.S. American identity, in the reimagining of a national political community, we can begin to trace the impact of foreign policy on the experience of Americans who may never leave the United States.

CONCLUSION

The first U.S. military occupation of Haiti grew out of a culture of imperialism whose genesis and history were never separate and distinct from the nation itself. That culture had taken root in the very idea of an "America" settled and ruled by people of European heritage. Over the course of several centuries it had shifted, but persisted, producing a changing collection of overlapping imperial and anti-imperial discourses. By 1915, it had given rise to a familiar yet specific cultural framework, a twentieth-century discourse of interventionist paternalism. That discourse constituted a significant part of the cultural armament of the nineteen-year-long occupation of Haiti. The extended U.S. military presence in Haiti, in turn, did much to transform the culture from which it arose.

The occupation attempted to conscript U.S. marines and other Americans into the racialized and gendered narrative of paternalism. This cultural history of the occupation has tried to show the partial success of that process and the unintended consequences of that success, including forms of violence that exceeded the bounds of military propriety, such as they were, but that flowed logically from the terms and structures of paternalism. I have been interested in showing how the military and economic project of the occupation itself relied on this cultural process, especially as it affected marines, enlisting them in the business of carrying out U.S. imperial aims.

At the same time, this book has also been about the failure of cultural conscription. The occupation, that is, the state apparatus established to control Haiti, could never control the entire discursive terrain in relation to which it had to function. Other discourses crowded the field, and marines and other U.S. Americans as well as Haitians could draw on the variety of available discourses to resist cultural conscription within the imperial project of the United States. In fact, the encounter with Haiti and Haitians occasioned by the occupation itself reminded U.S. Americans of new and forgotten cultural resources — narratives and images associated with Haiti and with the Haitian past. These, in turn, became the basis for articulating new ways of understanding race, gender, sexuality, and Americanness. The creative processes of conscription and resistance that emerged in and through the occupation gave rise to new subjective formations and, as such, enabled both the extension of U.S. imperialism and challenges to domestic relations of power.

Thus, in both its successes and its failures, interventionist paternalism left a profound stamp on the United States as well as on Haiti. Indeed, it was an integral part of Woodrow Wilson's wholly racialized vision of liberal internationalism, and as fully as the rest of that vision, it laid the groundwork for one of the dominant foreign policy traditions of the United States in the twentieth century. Interventionist paternalism in its Haitian iteration revealed, to be sure, the ugly underbelly of that tradition, which has led others to dismiss its importance for understanding the central lines of Wilson's foreign policy. But as we saw in the letters of Major Smedley Butler, there was a fine line between seeing Haiti as "a little nation" one could be proud to raise up and as a land of wretched people one had violently to control. Preparing nations for participation in an international legal order was a tricky business. Wilson's legalism, as George Kennan pointed out, carried the seeds of extreme violence.

Paternalism's imprint on the United States has been visible, moreover, not only in foreign-policy-making tradition, but also in the cultural politics of race and gender at home — in both senses of the word "home." Indeed, the rhetoric of paternalism had its roots in the changing social organization of gender and race in the United States. It appealed to deeply ingrained sets of beliefs about righteous masculinity, feminine domesticity, and white race privilege precisely at a time when the racial dimension of U.S. American gender ideologies was coming to the surface and when racial and gender hierarchies were being challenged in multiple ways.

For twenty-five years prior to the U.S. invasion of Haiti, African American women had been actively organizing and articulating challenges to a social order structured by racial and gender inequalities. After the turn of the century, organized political activity on the part of African American men and white women was also on the rise. In the context of increasingly visible African American and feminist challenges to the social, economic, political, and cultural predominance of white men in the teens and twenties, the call to take up the paternalist mantle in Haiti seems to have had a particularly compelling resonance for some white U.S. men. In this context, policy makers could call on heavily gendered and racialized ideological constructions to enable imperialist (economic and military) projects like the occupation of Haiti.

By characterizing U.S. goals in Haiti in terms of the subjective identity of white men under attack, paternalism became an effective tool for enlisting those men in the project of imposing U.S. rule. Policy makers called on marines to serve as benevolent but stern father figures in Haiti. They appealed to the racial consciousness of whites who might feel proud to lend a helping hand to a supposedly less capable, backward people, or who might appreciate the need to discipline a childlike people whose revolutionary misbehavior had gotten well out of hand. By evoking the paternal image, policy makers also appealed to the marines' sense of manhood, to their understanding of a man's responsibility to his family. In these senses, the rhetoric and ideology of paternalism called into play a cultural disposition made up of racial and gender consciousness.

That disposition was reinforced by the systematic indoctrination of marines with respect to the fatherly intentions of U.S. policy. In training, marines learned that Haitian peasants participated in political revolts solely out of compulsion, due either to elite intimidation or financial need. "The American Idea," as Lieutenant Adolph Miller called it in his personal log, was to protect the poor black peasants from the mulatto elite and to provide the blacks with wage work under American supervision. Protection, education, and discipline were among the dominant themes employed in both unofficial and official Marine Corps discourses: in personal letters, journals, memoirs, songs, and cartoon drawings, as well as in field orders, reports of military campaigns, administrative memoranda, and testimony before the Senate. Marines who left a record of their time in Haiti often described their work, to themselves, to each other, and to their nation, in terms of these themes.

Thus, the ideology of paternalism was the central discursive construction that supported the U.S. presence in Haiti. Paternalism was the rhetoric used to justify the intervention, but I have argued that it was more than "mere rhetoric." It was the cultural and ideological framework within which U.S. imperialism in Haiti would be conceived and carried out. It was the cultural fabric of the occupation, a fabric that helped to determine the material practices of the thousands of marines and the scores of sailors and nonmilitary personnel who ruled Haiti for nineteen years.

As we have seen, in the hands of white U.S. American men dislocated to Haiti between 1915 and 1934, that cultural and ideological framework would prove deadly. In so many ways, when marines shipped off for Haiti, the ground was already shifting underneath their feet. The subjective challenges they faced once they were in Haiti would compound the problem. In some ways, these challenges mirrored the struggles with which other U.S. Americans would contend in the wake of the occupation. In other ways, the challenges marines faced were brutally distinct.

Wilhelm Jordan's characterization of Haiti as "this American Africa" suggested some of the questions that would be raised by U.S. contact with Haiti, for marines and others: questions of national and cultural definition. Jordan's choice of words pointed to a likeness that would haunt some white Americans as they compared and contrasted the mainland nation and its island neighbor. Neither was simply "white" or "black"; both, particularly by virtue of being located in the Americas, were creole nations, composed of a mix of racial and cultural elements. This fact was useful for policy makers and politicians, but it was troubling indeed for men in the field.

The white U.S. marines who arrived in Haiti in and after 1915 were armed — if inadequately — with a nationalism that posited the inherent stability and racial basis of U.S. American identity. Yet, these marines were probably the first to experience the challenge to American identity that the occupation, and its paternalist rhetoric, would pose. Thrust into a foreign context to carry out an intervention justified by, and organized according to, a notion of benevolent paternalism, marines — particularly those stationed in the Haitian countryside — were encouraged to take up the role of father to what was considered a child nation. We have seen that this paternalist injunction had contradictory implications. On the one hand, it degraded Haitians and justified violence committed under the guise of necessary discipline; on the other hand, it suggested the efficacy of learning Creole and inserting oneself into "native" society. It also encouraged some marines to develop a high degree of sympathy toward the Haitians with whom they lived.

This aspect of service in Haiti could be frightening. Marines spoke of the dangers inherent in developing too much sympathy for the Haitians. We may recall Sergeant Faustin Wirkus's assertion that an American man serving in the occupation had to resist "becoming in his own consciousness an albino Haitian." Marines' fears of being consumed by another culture came out in stories of cannibalism, in which the victim was always a marine who had crossed over the cultural line separating "Americans" from "Haitians." Stories of cannibalism reminded marines of the need for vigilance in maintaining cultural boundaries, particularly when they themselves were breaching political boundaries.

If marines (and their naval cohorts) were the first Americans to confront the challenges Haiti would pose, they were certainly not the last. During and after the occupation of Haiti, U.S. travel writers, journalists, novelists, playwrights, anthropologists, and others contributed to the ongoing negotiation of American identity through their reflections on the United States' relationship to Haiti. Exotic renderings of the Caribbean nation effectively defined Haiti as outside the bounds of the American nation, even as Haiti came to have a more and more substantial place in white cultural expression in the United States. Indeed, by the late 1920s Haiti had become a hot commodity in American popular culture.

Popular U.S. discourses on Haiti established the ambiguous place of the so-called black nation both inside and outside "America": inside the American empire, yet outside the American nation; outside the nation, yet increasingly central to national self-definition. This ambiguity sustained the hegemonic version of U.S. national identity as fundamentally white, fundamentally European American, even as the political reach of the U.S. government extended, in Carl Van Doren's words, to "isthmuses and islands far away from New York . . . or Oregon."

To the extent that the literature on Haiti helped to redefine America as an empire and no longer "merely" a republic, this subjective perception of national greatness and international power affected African Americans as well as whites. At the same time, U.S. attention to Haiti provided cultural resources to African Americans for their challenge to the dominant association between whiteness and American identity. In the essays of Langston Hughes, in the novels of Arna Bontemps, in the plays of the Federal Theatre Project, and elsewhere, African American readers and audiences could find increasingly pointed expressions of anger over racist oppression and expectation with respect to meaningful participation in American society. Through representations of the Haitian Revolution, African American writers and artists challenged the ideology of white domination in the 1930s, setting the stage for a more thorough reshaping of racial politics in the decades to come.

Yet, if, as I have argued here, racial and gender hierarchies enabled U.S. actions in Haiti, the occupation, in turn, enabled the deployment of a cultural line of defense against domestic black and feminist challenges to the status quo. By explicitly linking race and gender hierarchies in fiction, film, travel narratives, and the like, imperialist discourses surrounding the occupation intervened in domestic cultural and political struggles. Specifically, discussions of Haiti contributed to a defense of white supremacy conceived in terms of gender and sexuality. As white American men in Haiti confronted a social order structured in unfamiliar ways (unfamiliar particularly in terms of gender norms), they produced racist and exoticized representations of Haitian men and women. These representations, in turn, fueled reactionary discourses in the United States during the 1920s and 1930s. The sexual and gender disorder attributed to "the black republic" by writers like Beale Davis and William Seabrook provided striking contrasts to the normative image of the white American male-headed household. By establishing a dichotomy between gender disorder in Haiti and gender order in the United States, paternalist and exoticizing discourses on Haiti posited the male-headed nuclear-family household as the gendered basis of U.S. power in the world.

The ironies of this discursive sleight of hand stand out if we consider that, during the first half of the twentieth century, colonial (or neocolonial) relationships increasingly made possible the image of the prosperous nuclear family that came to signify "the American way of life." They did so by providing raw materials, consumer goods, and wealth to the United States, all necessary ingredients for a high standard of living. Through the discourse of paternalism, however, that way of life, with the nuclear family as its centerpiece, came to be seen, not as the result, but as the basis of U.S. American power in the world. In the decades following the end of the occupation, this ideological reversal would have profound effects on race and gender politics in the United States.

At the same time, the racialized politics of gender and sexuality had contradictory implications. From Eugene O'Neill's *The Emperor Jones* to Zora Neale Hurston's *Tell My Horse*, Haiti served as a locus of struggle over the politics of masculinity and other implications of interventionist paternalism's gender politics. White men and women also used Haiti as the means to claim modern sexualities and to articulate racialized psychological discourses of selfhood. Thus the occupation contributed to the reshaping of gender and sexuality in the United States. In fundamental ways, this reshaping was inextricably linked to racial and national questions. Examining the cultural dimensions of an imperialist venture has enabled us to see some of the complexity of this intertwining.

The U.S. occupation of Haiti contributed to both the bolstering and the reshaping of prevailing conceptions of national identity for individual marines and other U.S. Americans between 1915 and 1940. On the one hand, the first military occupation of Haiti was not just an instance of U.S. imperialism but also a motor for it. It propelled the cultural logic of "American greatness" in a variety of ways. On the other hand, the cultural implications of the occupation in the United States provided the means for U.S. Americans in and out of the military to shake the structure of gendered, racial, and sexual meanings on which a hegemonic conception of U.S. national identity had rested. The consequences of this process were at once far-reaching and diffuse.

If in some respects the occupation helped the United States to remake imperialism, to make it more resilient and versatile, it also led to the destabilizing of U.S. American cultural forms. (The idea of America as a white nation provides only one example.) This destabilizing took place, not all at once, as though a monolithic structure had been unsteadied by an earthquake, but repeatedly and in varied ways. It took place in so many local encounters and personal conflicts, in the daily relations of power that gave form and substance to military endeavors, in the myriad doubts, questions, and possibilities raised by contact with another culture and another nation. And though the effects were not felt in one fell swoop, they did, nonetheless, help to shape the course of domestic cultural and political expression in profound ways. Between 1915 and 1940, Americans began to redefine the boundaries of their own national community, in part, through their discussions of Haiti.

Eugene O'Neill and Zora Neale Hurston, *The Emperor Jones* and *Tell My Horse*, suggest some of the ways that individual subjectivities and imperialist discourses criss-crossed one another in the context of the occupation and its aftermath in the United States. And if O'Neill and Hurston provide us with particularly complex examples, others, too, were bound up with the cultural fabric of paternalism and exoticism, whether they thought they were shredding that fabric or donning it with pride. Try as we may, we will not find a single historical actor untainted by the dominant discourses that shaped this history. Butler, Wilson, Overley, Wirkus, Inman, Seabrook, Niles, and Craige were implicated, of course — but so, too, were Johnson, Balch, Hughes, Bontemps, Robeson, Herskovits, and James. Nonetheless, in the web of discourses they engaged, produced, and were produced by, we will find the seeds of future troubles for "America."

NOTES

ABBREVIATIONS

AMPAS
  Academy of Motion Picture Arts and Sciences, Margaret Herrick Library, Beverly
  Hills, Calif.
Crumbie Papers
  Frank Crumbie Papers, Caribbean Collection, University of Florida Library,
  Gainesville, Fla.
FRUS
  United States Department of State, *Foreign Relations of the United States.* Washington,
  D.C.: Government Printing Office, 1913–34.
HMD
  United States Marine Corps, History and Museums Division, Washington, D.C.
Miller Log
  Adolph B. Miller, Personal Log, Haiti, Adolph B. Miller Papers, PC 196, Personal
  Papers Collection, United States Marine Corps, History and Museums Division,
  Washington, D.C.
NA
  National Archives, Washington, D.C.
Overley Papers
  Homer L. Overley Papers, PC 1099, Personal Papers Collection, United States Marine
  Corps, History and Museums Division, Washington, D.C.
PPC
  Personal Papers Collection, United States Marine Corps, History and Museums
  Division, Washington, D.C. (*Note*: After I did the research for this book, the Personal
  Papers Collection was moved from Washington, D.C., to the Marine Corps Research
  Center Archives, Quantico, Va.)
RG 45
  Record Group 45, Naval Records Collection, National Archives, Washington, D.C.
RG 80
  Record Group 80, General Correspondence, National Archives, Washington, D.C.
RG 127
  Record Group 127, Records of the United States Marines Corps, National Archives,
  Washington, D.C.
Senate Hearings
  United States Senate, Inquiry into Occupation and Administration of Haiti and
  Santo Domingo, *Hearings before a Select Committee on Haiti and Santo Domingo.* 67th
  Cong., 1st and 2nd sess., 1922. 2 vols. Washington, D.C.: Government Printing
  Office, 1922.

UCLA

   The UCLA Film and Television Archive, Los Angeles, Calif.

Venzon MS

   Anne Cipriano Venzon, "The Letters of Smedley D. Butler," Ph.D. diss., Princeton
   University, 1982, copy in Anne C. Venzon Papers, PC 2364, Personal Papers
   Collection, United States Marine Corps, History and Museums Division,
   Washington, D.C.

Wilson Papers

   Arthur S. Link, ed. *The Papers of Woodrow Wilson*. 69 vols. Princeton, N.J.: Princeton
   University Press, 1978.

Wirkus Papers

   Faustin E. Wirkus Papers, PC 1518, folder 1: "Haiti Letters," Personal Papers
   Collection, United States Marine Corps, History and Museums Division,
   Washington, D.C.

PROLOGUE

1. Seabrook, *The Magic Island*.
2. Wirkus and Dudley, *The White King of La Gonave*.
3. Craige, *Black Bagdad*, and *Cannibal Cousins*.
4. Butler, *Old Gimlet Eye*, and Burke Davis, *Marine!*
5. Overley, "A Marine Patrol," folder 8: "Manuscript," Overley Papers, and Miller Log,
   May 14, 1916.
6. See, for example, Chandler Campbell, "Diary 13th Company," folder 1: "Diary of
   Activities, Haiti, 1915," Alex O. Campbell Papers, PC 55, PPC.
7. Seabrook, *The Magic Island*, 173.
8. C. William Dize to Faustin Wirkus, October 3, 1929, Wirkus Papers.
9. Gordon Haverstock to Faustin Wirkus, October [1929], Wirkus Papers.
10. Donald Pifer to Faustin Wirkus, October 3, 1929, Wirkus Papers.
11. Paul Redman to Faustin Wirkus, October 8, 1929, Wirkus Papers.
12. See, for example, Robert McKnight to Faustin Wirkus, October 3, 1929, Wirkus
    Papers.
13. C. William Dize to Faustin Wirkus, October 3, 1929, Wirkus Papers.
14. Dwight Fonny to Faustin Wirkus, October 3, 1929, Wirkus Papers.
15. Redfield, review of *The Magic Island*, 315–17.
16. Van Doren, "Why the Editorial Board Selected *The Magic Island*," 3.
17. Benedict Anderson, *Imagined Communities*.
18. For others, it was indeed a matter of debate. See, for example, Freeman and Nearing,
    Dollar Diplomacy.
19. Sacco explores this connection in "Winner Takes All: The Contexts of Conquest and
    Collecting in the Museums of Pierre Eugene Du Simitiere and Charles Willson Peale,
    1779–1796." See also Kaplan and Pease, *Cultures of United States Imperialism*.
20. This is not to suggest that it was inconceivable for all. Indeed, Puerto Rican statehood
    was a matter of active debate.
21. Van Doren, "Why the Editorial Board Selected *The Magic Island*," 3.
22. Adam Wertz to Faustin Wirkus, October 4, 1929, Wirkus Papers.
23. Said, *Culture and Imperialism*.

1. Schmidt, *The United States Occupation of Haiti*, 64–81. On the debt question, see Lundahl, *Peasants and Poverty*, 371–72. For contrasting contemporary accounts, see James Weldon Johnson, "Government of, by, and for the National City Bank," 295, and Harold Davis, *Black Democracy*, 198–200.

2. Marine Corps commandant George Barnett initially reported 3,250 Haitian deaths to Secretary of the Navy Josephus Daniels, only to claim later that the figure resulted from a math error, and that he should have said 2,250. Hans Schmidt's accounting of casualty reports in the war against the Cacos totals 3,071. Schmidt, *The United States Occupation of Haiti*, 103. Trouillot states that at least 6,000 peasants were killed by the USMC and the Gendarmerie during the war, and that another 5,500 died in "forced labor camps." Trouillot, *Haiti, State against Nation*, 106. See also Kethly Millet, "Okipasyon Ameriken ak Abitan Ayisyen," 18, and *Les paysans haïtiens et l'occupation américaine, 1915–1930*; Bellegarde, *Pour une Haïti heureuse*, 25; Moral, *Le paysan haïtien*.

3. See McCrocklin, *Garde d'Haïti: Twenty Years of Organization and Training by the United States Marine Corps, 1915–1934*.

4. Statement of Admiral William B. Caperton, 1921, Senate Hearings, 1:392; "Wards of the United States," 143–77; Coffey, "A Brief History of the Intervention in Haiti"; Dunlap, "Carrying the Gospel of Health to Haiti."

5. Schmidt, *The United States Occupation of Haiti*, 135–53; Gaillard, *Hinche mise en croix*.

6. Laguerre, *The Military and Society in Haiti*, 71; Weatherly, "Haiti: An Experiment in Pragmatism," 359.

7. Painter, *Standing at Armageddon*; Montgomery, *The Fall of the House of Labor*; Steinson, *American Women's Activism in World War I*; Tuttle, *Race Riot: Chicago in the Red Summer of 1919*; Shapiro, *White Violence and Black Response*.

8. See, for example, Rafael, "White Love," 185–218; Kaplan, "Black and Blue on San Juan Hill," 219–36.

9. Magdaline Shannon, *Jean Price-Mars, the Haitian Elite and the American Occupation*.

10. Paul Woyshner, "The Missionary," *Marines Magazine* (April 1917), HMD; reproduced in Schmidt, *The United States Occupation of Haiti*, illustrations found between 134 and 135.

11. Wirkus and Dudley, *The White King of La Gonave*, 108–9.

12. Senate Hearings, 1:516.

13. My analysis of marines' "experience" in Haiti owes much to the work of Joan W. Scott. See especially Scott, " 'Experience,' " 26–28, 33.

14. Langley, *The Banana Wars*, 223; see also Heinl and Heinl, *Written in Blood*. Harold Palmer Davis, evaluating the financial policies of the occupation from the perspective of 1936, commented, "it is absolutely inexcusable that Americans who have had every opportunity to learn the truth of the situation should have either openly or by innuendo suggested that the American policy in Haiti, or the conduct of any one of the responsible American officials, was in any manner influenced by any other than a sincere, if perhaps sometimes misguided, effort to carry out the expressed objects of the Haitian-American treaty for the benefit of the Haitian people as a whole." Harold Davis, *Black Democracy*, 200.

15. Schmidt, *The United States Occupation of Haiti*, 42–63; Perkins, *Constraint of Empire*, 122–23; Fernandez, *Cruising the Caribbean*, 92–105. Healy, *Gunboat Diplomacy in the Wilson Era*, pays scant attention to paternalism. Like Schmidt in *The United States*

Occupation of Haiti and Perkins, Healy emphasizes the strategic goals of the occupation, but points out that Admiral Caperton succeeded in keeping casualty levels remarkably low in the first year of the occupation.

16. Schmidt, *Maverick Marine*, 84.

17. In *Roll, Jordan, Roll*, Eugene Genovese linked paternalism to discipline as well as to the moral justification of a system of exploitation. While Genovese figured paternalism as the "reigning ideal" of an entire "social system," and thus as a relation *between* masters and slaves, which shaped both parties fundamentally, my analysis interrogates paternalism as a discourse of domination that shaped those assigned to carry it out. The extent and the ways in which Haitians made use of this discourse remains to be examined, although some limited and tentative speculations will be offered here. Genovese, *Roll, Jordan, Roll*, 3–25, 70–86, 482–94, 658–60, 661–65. Cf. Morgan, *Slave Counterpoint*, 257–96. Morgan distinguishes between "patriarchalism," the "dominant social ethos and cultural metaphor of seventeenth- and early-eighteenth-century Anglo-America," and paternalism, which emerged later in that context. Patriarchalism emphasized "control, obedience, discipline, and severity" in the master's relationship with his slaves, though it "also involved protection, guardianship, and reciprocal obligations." The gentler ethos and metaphor of paternalism, according to Morgan, rested on the emergence of sentimentalism, evangelicalism, and humanitarianism, but also, ironically, on the exclusion of slaves from the rights-bearing community. Thus, for Morgan "[a]ustere patriarchalism slowly gave way to mellow paternalism." My own discussion of U.S. interventionist paternalism sees the austere and the mellow as two sides of the same twentieth-century coin. Other discussions of paternalism that I found helpful include Tone, *The Business of Benevolence*; Hetherington, *British Paternalism and Africa, 1920–1940*, especially chap. 3, "The Meaning of Colonial Trusteeship"; McLaurin, *Paternalism and Protest*; and Roberts, *Paternalism in Early Victorian England*. See also Jackman, *The Velvet Glove*.

18. Brenda Gayle Plummer acknowledges the significance of culture in international politics and diplomacy with a similar metaphor. She refers to U.S. historical literature about Haiti in the first decades of the twentieth century as an "instrument of power" that worked in tandem with commerce to shape linkages between the United States and Haiti. See Plummer, *Haiti and the Great Powers*, 67. Indeed, culture is integral to Plummer's analyses of U.S. relations with Haiti before, during, and after the occupation. See Plummer, *Haiti and the United States*. In *The United States Occupation of Haiti*, Hans Schmidt also addresses culture as a significant element in the history of the occupation. But Schmidt casts culture primarily as an undermining factor, a force that not only detracted from, but unraveled the intended materialist and progressive character of the U.S. mission in Haiti, rather than as a shaping force. Schmidt's biography of Smedley Butler makes culture more central to his analysis of the transformation of military practice. See *Maverick Marine*. My own work builds on the insights of both Schmidt and Plummer and indeed is possible because of their pioneering studies.

19. Wilentz, *Chants Democratic*, 4–5.

20. Genovese, *Roll, Jordan, Roll*; Morgan, *Slave Counterpoint*; Cheyfitz, "Savage Law," 109–28, and *The Poetics of Imperialism*; Rogin, *Fathers and Children*; and Pike, *The United States and Latin America*, 168–71.

21. Montgomery, *The Fall of the House of Labor*, 309.

22. Tone, *The Business of Benevolence*, 237–38.

23. The language of wards and trusteeship dates back to the 1890s. See Kidd, *Control of the*

Tropics, 51–60; Hetherington, *British Paternalism and Africa*, 45–57. A prior example from U.S. discourse on Haiti was "Wards of the United States." A later example was Blair Niles, *Black Haiti*.

24. Jordon, *Crusading in the West Indies*, 79.

25. See, for example, Osterhout, "A Little-Known Marvel."

26. Burks, *Black Medicine*. See also Robert Jones, *The Shudder Pulps: A History of the Weird Menace Magazines of the 1930s*, and Weinberg, *The Weird Tales Story*.

27. Blassingame, "The Press and American Intervention in Haiti and the Dominican Republic, 1904–1920," 36–37.

28. Addams, *Peace and Bread in Time of War*, 54–55; Du Bois, "Hayti," 291, in Aptheker, *Selections from the Crisis*, 1:106; Fort-Whiteman, "Nemesis," 23–25.

29. James Weldon Johnson, "Self-Determining Haiti."

30. James Weldon Johnson, *Along This Way*, 352.

31. O'Neill, *The Emperor Jones*; Vandercook, *Black Majesty*; Seabrook, *The Magic Island*; Hughes, *I Wonder as I Wander*. In the 1940s Mercer Cook wrote on Haitian literature and on education in Haiti and collaborated with various Haitian authors. See, for example, Cook and Bellegarde, *The Haitian-American Anthology*, and Roumain, *Masters of the Dew*.

32. "A Visit to King Christophe: A Scenic Wallpaper Designed by Nicholas de Molas," Katzenbach and Warren, Inc., New York City, n.d., advertising leaflet, 3 pp., Scrapbook 3, Crumbie Papers; Helen Damrosch Tee-Van, F. Edwin Church, and Vladimir Perfielieff, *Haiti: Portraits, Landscapes, Submarines*, gallery announcement for a show by three painters who accompanied the naturalist William Beebe on his expedition to Haiti in 1927, Scrapbook 2, Crumbie Papers; Theatre Program for Kenneth Webb's *Zombie*, performed in 1932 at the Biltmore Theatre in New York City, Scrapbook 4, Crumbie Papers; Lu Duble, *The Haitian Negro: Sculpture*, gallery announcement for a show by a white, female, U.S. American sculptor, at the Marie Sterner Galleries in New York City, and unidentified newspaper clippings reviewing Duble's work, all in Scrapbook 5, Crumbie Papers; Lucius Beebe, "Invoking Aid of Voodoo Gods, Schwab Offers a New Thriller," *New York Herald Tribune*, September 10, 1934, clipping, Blue Scrapbook, Crumbie Papers.

33. See, for example, Augur, "Drums at Night"; Cranston, "Wings"; Harold Davis, "Sunlight on Voodoo Mysteries"; Foster, "Drums of Black Haiti"; Frankfurter, "Haiti and Intervention"; Gayer, "Hispaniola Rediscovered"; Knox, "Homemaking around the Globe"; Nock, "The Bright Isle"; Osterhout, "A Little-Known Marvel"; Tait, "The Petals Fall Slowly"; Taylor, "The Last Sacrifice"; Wirkus and Lanier, "The Black Pope of Voodoo."

34. Taft, *A Puritan in Voodoo Land*; Orson Welles's *The Shadow*, Street and Smith Editorial Records Collection, Syracuse, N.Y.; Fossett, "Listening to Empire: Lamont Cranston and 'The Shadow' Go Abroad"; *White Zombie* (1932); *I Walked with a Zombie* (1943).

35. Tait, "The Petals Fall Slowly."

36. George Stocking, "Matthew Arnold, E. B. Tylor, and the Uses of Invention," quoted in Young, *Colonial Desire*, 45 (see also 29–54); Raymond Williams, *Keywords*, 87–93.

37. See, for example, Ferguson et al., *Out There*.

38. Rosaldo, *Culture and Truth*, 207–8. See also Anzaldúa, *Borderlands*.

39. Ibid., 217.

40. Scott, "Deconstructing Equality-versus-Difference," 135. See also Scott, "Gender: A Useful Category for Historical Analysis."

41. Poovey, *Uneven Developments*, 3–4.

42. On missionary paternalism in diverse institutional contexts, see Clymer, *Protestant Missionaries in the Philippines*; Hunter, *The Gospel of Gentility*; Patricia Hill, *The World Their Household*; Higginbotham, *Righteous Discontent*, 92–94; Gilmore, *Gender and Jim Crow*, 150–57. On U.S. Navy perspectives, see Challener, *Admirals, Generals, and American Foreign Policy*, 12–45. See also Scranton, "Varieties of Paternalism," 235–57.

43. The career of paternalism was in this sense fractured. As we shall see, it was also marked by ambivalence, for what I have called "aspirations" may also be described in terms of "anxieties." See Young, *White Mythologies*, 142–43; Bhabha, "Of Mimicry and Man," 19.

44. Foucault, "Two Lectures," in *Power/Knowledge*, 99. "[T]he important thing is not to attempt some kind of deduction of power starting from its centre and aimed at the discovery of the extent to which it permeates into the base, of the degree to which it reproduces itself down to and including the most molecular elements of society. One must rather conduct an ascending analysis of power, starting, that is, from its infinitesimal mechanisms, which each have their own history, their own trajectory, their own techniques and tactics, and then see how these mechanisms of power have been — and continue to be — invested, colonized, utilized, involuted, transformed, displaced, extended etc., by ever more general mechanisms and by forms of global domination."

45. Poovey, *Uneven Developments*, 3.

46. Karen Barad's theorization of materiality offers an important corrective to much "discourse analysis" and provides a helpful framework for exploring the relationship between the "cultural" and the "material," between human and machine, and, in this case, between a man and his gun. See Barad, "Getting Real," 87–128.

47. Indeed, the tenacity of dominant cultural values and meanings, for good and ill, is a crucial area for historical investigation.

48. On the spaces between and beyond, see, for example, Chauncey, *Gay New York*, 47–63.

49. Joan Scott calls attention to "the complex and changing discursive processes by which identities are ascribed, resisted, or embraced and which processes themselves are unremarked, indeed achieve their effect because they aren't noticed." Scott, " 'Experience,' " 33. See also Spivak, *In Other Worlds*, 142.

50. Raymond Williams called attention to "residual and emergent cultures." He wrote, "By 'residual,' I mean that some experiences, meanings and values, which cannot be verified or cannot be expressed in terms of the dominant culture, are nevertheless lived and practised on the basis of the residue — cultural as well as social — of some previous social formation. . . . By 'emergent,' I mean . . . that new meanings and values, new practices, new significances and experiences, are continually being created." Raymond Williams, "Base and Superstructure," 415–16.

51. Ginzburg, *The Cheese and the Worms*, xx–xxi.

52. This relationship is explored in Richard Johnson, "What Is Cultural Studies Anyway?," 38–80. See also Frow and Morris, "Australian Cultural Studies," 344–67.

53. To say that such discourses are overdetermined in this sense is not, however, to say that they are fundamentally stable. Building on the work of Homi Bhabha, Robert Young discusses the process by which apparently hegemonic representations reveal their instabilities in colonial contexts. The "mastery" of colonial discourse, he concludes, "is always asserted, but is also always slipping, ceaselessly displaced, never complete." Young, *White Mythologies*, 145.

54. Williams also used the phrase "structures of feeling" to indicate something that is "at the very edge of semantic availability." Raymond Williams, *Marxism and Literature*,

132–33; Rosaldo, *Culture and Truth*, 106. See also Raymond Williams, *What I Came to Say*, 195–225.

55. Rosaldo, *Culture and Truth*, 106–7.

56. Comaroff and Comaroff, *Of Revelation and Revolution*, 1:29.

57. Or what Scott calls "reading for the 'literary.' " See " 'Experience,' " 36.

58. They also help us step out of tidy oppositions between imperialist oppressors and anti-imperialist champions of the oppressed. Close readings belie easy distinctions between those who wielded and those who resisted paternalist logics. See Bhabha, "Difference, Discrimination, and the Discourse of Colonialism," 198.

59. Plummer, *Haiti and the United States*, 19. See Logan, *Diplomatic Relations of the United States with Haiti*.

60. Logan, *Diplomatic Relations of the United States with Haiti*, 176–79; Elkins and McKitrick, *The Age of Federalism*, 662.

61. Hunt, *Haiti's Influence on Antebellum America*.

62. It should be noted, however, that African Americans had an ambivalent relationship to Haiti, a point to which we will return.

63. Plummer, *Haiti and the United States*, 26–31.

64. Ibid., 46–48. See also Staudenraus, *The African Colonization Movement, 1816–1865*, 247; Floyd Miller, *The Search for a Black Nationality*, 108–9, 232–49.

65. Plummer, *Haiti and the United States*, 50–52.

66. Logan, *Diplomatic Relations of the United States with Haiti*, 322–32. Logan points out that Seward articulated an early version of the Roosevelt Corollary (328) and contemplated annexation of Hispaniola in 1868 (329).

67. Ibid., 341, 426.

68. Langley, *The United States and the Caribbean in the Twentieth Century*, 69.

69. Plummer, *Haiti and the Great Powers*, 87.

70. Ibid., 98, 166, 198. In 1904 U.S. military intelligence operations in Haiti were also stepped up with the assignment of an African American army officer, Captain Charles Young, as military attaché for the American legation. See ibid., 81.

71. Manigat, "La substitution de la prépondérance américaine à la prépondérance français en Haïti au debut de XXe siècle," 321–55; Plummer, *Haiti and the Great Powers*.

72. Link, *Wilson: The Struggle for Neutrality*, 524; see also *Wilson Papers*.

73. Captain Edward Beach manuscript, RG 45, Subject Files 1911–27, box 1000, pp. 140–43, NA, cited by Fernandez, *Cruising the Caribbean*, 103.

74. Millspaugh, *Haiti under American Control, 1915–1930*, 38.

75. Cited in Daniels to Wilson, August 3, 1915, *Wilson Papers*, 34:70.

76. Caperton to Wilson, August 11, 1915, *Wilson Papers*, 34:165.

77. Millspaugh, *Haiti under American Control*, 41–42.

78. Lansing to Wilson, August 13, 1915, *Wilson Papers*, 34:183.

79. Schmidt, *The United States Occupation of Haiti*, 100.

80. Ibid., 192.

81. Ibid., 195n.

82. Ibid., 196.

83. Victor G. Hoiser, quoted in the Journals of W. Cameron Forbes, typescript, vol. 3, 39, Library of Congress, Washington, D.C.

84. Ibid.

85. Schmidt, *The United States Occupation of Haiti*, 219.

86. Laguerre, *The Military and Society in Haiti*, 72; Trouillot, *Haiti, State against Nation*, 102, 152.

CHAPTER 2

1. Homer L. Overley, "Where Are They Now?," folder 3: "Poetry, Death of Sergeant Muth," Overley Papers.

2. Ibid., and "Death of Sergeant Muth," 2, folder 3: "Poetry, Death of Sergeant Muth," Overley Papers.

3. Overley, "A Marine Patrol," 10, folder 8: "Manuscript," Overley Papers.

4. Ibid., 24–25, and "Where Are They Now?"

5. Overley, "Death of Sergeant Muth," 1–2.

6. Ibid., 1, and "Where Are They Now?"

7. Overley, "Death of Sergeant Muth," 1, and "Where Are They Now?"

8. Overley, "Death of Sergeant Muth," 1–2.

9. Overley, "A Marine Patrol," 24–25.

10. Ibid., 2, 4.

11. Ibid., 3, 10–11.

12. Ibid., 11.

13. [No author], "An Enlisted Man's Account," 1, folder (unnumbered): "Papers, 1915–1919," Vincent E. Stack Papers, PC 104, PPC.

14. Chandler Campbell, "Diary 13th Company," November 8, 1915, folder 1: "Diary of Activities, Haiti, 1915," Alex O. Campbell Papers, PC 55, PPC.

15. Overley, "Death of Sergeant Muth," 1–2.

16. Fouchard, *The Haitian Maroons*; Mintz, *Caribbean Transformations*, 152–54.

17. The story of Bois Caiman has been an important element in Haitian history, both as lived and written in Haiti, and as it has been constructed by outsiders who have sought to deride Haiti. The origins and significance of the story are much debated. See Dayan, *Haiti, History, and the Gods*, 29–30; Geggus, *Slavery, War, and Revolution*, 40, and "La cérémonie du Bois-Caïman," 59–78; Hoffmann, "Histoire, mythe et idéologie," 9–34. See also Bellegarde-Smith, *Haiti: The Breached Citadel*, 26, 40; Métraux, *Voodoo in Haiti*, 42.

18. The sound of the *lanbi* (conch) is recorded on the first track of *Rhythms of Rapture* (compact disc, 1995).

19. Smith, "Traditional Peasant Groups."

20. Conches used in battle would have been hidden from view, but conches were also used decoratively.

21. W. E. Eaton, "The Service d'Hygiène," *Gendarmerie News* 1, no. 3 (November 1, 1921): 5–6, copy in RG 80, box 240, location 5526, NA.

22. Stoddard, *The French Revolution in San Domingo*; Prichard, *Where Black Rules White*; St. John, *Hayti, or the Black Republic*. Marines and sailors received shipboard indoctrination as to prevailing European and European American interpretations of Haitian history. In contrast, Haitian interpretations emphasized the brutality of French slavery, the heroism of Haitian revolutionary leaders, and the agency and determination of the slaves.

23. Smith, "Traditional Peasant Groups."

24. Ibid.

25. Thanks to Liza McAlister for bringing this to my attention.

26. This Haitian Creole phrase was discussed by the audience at the Haitian Studies Association annual conference, Tufts University, Medford, Mass., October 1991. It translates as "Dessalines is riding me," which refers to Dessalines as a *lwa* (*loa*, god, spirit) who is taking over the body of the speaker, as in possession. Another Creole

phrase that corresponds to this, and resonates as well with the same history, is "koupe tèt, boule kay" (cut off the heads and burn the houses). On Dessalines as a *lwa kreyòl* or Creole god, see Dayan, *Haiti, History, and the Gods*, 30–31, 39.

27. Brown, *Mama Lola*, 273n.

28. Desmangles, *Faces of the Gods*, xi; McAlister, *Angels in the Mirror*, 6. Brown, *Mama Lola*, 273n, notes that in Haiti, "the term Vodou more commonly refers to a particular drum rhythm." Several alternative spellings of Vodou (e.g., Vodoun, Vodun) have been used in the past. I have chosen to follow the official orthography for Haitian Creole, developed by Yves Dejean and adopted in 1986, which uses the phonetically correct "Vodou." See Desmangles, *Faces of the Gods*, xi–xii. Elsewhere, I use the word "Voodoo" to refer to the exotic phantasm that sensational writers constructed through their discourses on Haiti. The relationship between what is experienced and understood by those who serve the spirits and what is observed and imagined by those who do not is much more complex than is suggested by this distinction between Vodou and Voodoo. The importance of that complexity notwithstanding, I use this terminology to emphasize the specificity of Voodoo as imagined and observed by U.S. Americans in contrast to the sacred forms and practices of Haitians.

29. See Desmangles, *Faces of the Gods*, for an analysis of the relationship between Vodou and Roman Catholicism in Haiti. Desmangles calls Vodou "the folk religion of Haiti," which "pervades the framework of Haitian culture," even as Haitians embrace Catholicism as their own (1). Alfred Métraux refers to Vodou as "a conglomeration of beliefs and rites of African origin, which, having been closely mixed with Catholic practice, has come to be the religion of the greater part of the peasants and the urban proletariat of the black republic of Haiti." *Voodoo in Haiti*, 15. Sidney Mintz, in his introduction to Métraux's classic study, states "that *vaudou*, like any other complex of beliefs and practices, is a vital, living body of ideas and behaviors, carried in time by its practitioners, and responsive to the changing character of social life" (13). Building on Mintz, Joan Dayan emphasizes the "intensely intellectual" and creative nature of Vodou, arguing, in *Haiti, History, and the Gods*, "that vodou practices must be viewed as ritual reenactments of Haiti's colonial past, even more than as retentions from Africa" (xvii).

30. Brown, *Mama Lola*, 36.

31. See, for example, Julian C. Smith, Oral History Transcript, 45, HMD.

32. Miller Log, October 16 and 17, 1915; Merwin H. Silverthorn, Oral History Transcript, 161–62, HMD; Pedro del Valle, Oral History Transcript, 60, HMD.

33. Del Valle, Oral History Transcript, 56; Silverthorn, Oral History Transcript, 165.

34. Gordon Lewis, *Main Currents in Caribbean Thought*, 252.

35. Nicholls, *Dessalines to Duvalier*, 87–102; Gordon Lewis, *Main Currents in Caribbean Thought*.

36. James, *The Black Jacobins*, 86–89.

37. On women who served as soldiers in the Revolution, see Bellegarde-Smith, *Haiti: The Breached Citadel*, 26; Nicholls, "Holding the Purse-Strings," in *Haiti in Caribbean Context*, 122.

38. Geggus, *Slavery, War, and Revolution*, 23; James, *The Black Jacobins*, 241–42, asserts that one-third of the black population of Saint Domingue died during the Revolution.

39. Logan, *Diplomatic Relations of the United States with Haiti*, 111; Geggus, "The Haitian Revolution," 41; Bellegarde-Smith, *Haiti: The Breached Citadel*, 42–43.

40. The phrase is from James, *The Black Jacobins*, 241. Note that Napoleon recognized Toussaint as the governor of Saint Domingue.

41. Dupuy, *Haiti in the World Economy*, 54–57.

42. James, *The Black Jacobins*, 242.

43. Note that plantation agriculture had been devastated by the war.

44. James, *The Black Jacobins*, 240.

45. Dupuy, *Haiti in the World Economy*, 75–76. Those who were considered *blan* (*blancs*, white) included French people of all classes, but did not include a Polish regiment that had defected from Napoleon's army to fight for the Revolution. The Polish soldiers became integrated into the Haitian population and, skin color notwithstanding, were not considered *blan*. Nicholls, *Dessalines to Duvalier*, 35–36.

46. Mintz, "Slavery and the Rise of Peasantries," 226–28, and *Caribbean Transformations*, 40–41, 147–54; Dupuy, *Haiti in the World Economy*, 62–63.

47. Dessalines concentrated between three-quarters and nine-tenths of Haitian land in government hands. Moya Pons, "The Land Question." See also Dupuy, *Haiti in the World Economy*, 76–77. Dupuy points out that slaves "fled to the mountains" to find unclaimed land, particularly after Dessalines's fall (96).

48. That is, local needs for subsistence but also for cash. Mintz, *Caribbean Transformations*, 274: "Peasants cultivate with three goals in mind: cash income from world market commodities . . . ; cash income from items produced for local sale and consumption; and subsistence. While they are heavily involved in production for sale, their crop choices and land-use patterns rest fundamentally on a subsistence orientation. All grow a substantial part of their own food." Mintz also states: "Haiti's history of slavery, and the acquisition of access to land through revolution, has perhaps given a special symbolic significance to landowning." Finally: "In the course of the century [following the Revolution], the Haitian people laid claim to their own soil, while population growth and the adoption of the French tradition of equal inheritance progressively reduced the average size of holdings."

49. Sidney Mintz has described this process as the creation of a "reconstituted peasantry." That is, African-born former slaves, together with the descendants of Africans, having survived slavery, were able to reconstitute themselves as a "peasantry whose ways of life combined elements of the African and American Indian past, as well as considerable European . . . influence, in new cultural constellations." Mintz, *Caribbean Transformations*, 268.

50. For various explanations of the assassination of Dessalines, see Dayan, *Haiti, History, and the Gods*, 26–27; Dupuy, *Haiti in the World Economy*, 81; Nicholls, *Dessalines to Duvalier*, 38. Following the assassination, Henri Christophe was elected to a four-year term as president, but the Constituent Assembly that elected him attempted to restrain his control over government functions. After failing in his attempt to take more complete control of the government by force, Christophe headed for the North, and there established a separate constitutional state. Pétion, who had overseen the creation of the new constitution in Port-au-Prince, was subsequently elected president of the republic in 1807. Dupuy, *Haiti in the World Economy*, 86; Trouillot, *Haiti, State against Nation*, 47; Nicholls, *Dessalines to Duvalier*, 40. *Ancien libres* refers to those who had been *affranchis*, or free people of color, prior to the Revolution. *Nouveau libres* refers to those freed by the Revolution.

51. Pétion instituted various land distribution schemes beginning in 1809. Mintz, "Slavery and the Rise of Peasantries," 227. Murray, "The Evolution of Haitian Peasant Land Tenure: Agrarian Adaptation to Population Growth," 1:79. Murray sees Pétion's policies as the recognition of a fait accompli on the part of the peasants. Moya Pons, "The Land Question." Moya Pons argues that Pétion effectively returned the

land that had been confiscated by Dessalines to the mulatto class from whom it had been taken.

52. Historians disagree as to exactly how divergent were the intentions of Pétion and Christophe with regard to economic development. Dupuy, *Haiti in the World Economy*, 88, emphasizes the contrast between "the militarization of . . . labor relations" that led to a significantly stronger economy under Christophe and the more liberal labor policies of Pétion. Nicholls cautions that the propaganda put out by each state, drawing the other in starkly oppositional terms, exaggerated the differences between North and South. *Dessalines to Duvalier*, 40–60. Christophe signed into law an act to break up the estates in 1807, Nicholls also points out, though he did not put it into effect for another ten years. Nicholls, "Economic Dependence and Political Autonomy, 1804–1915," in *Haiti in Caribbean Context*, 83–120.

53. Boyer had become president in the South upon Pétion's death in 1818. Christophe committed suicide in the wake of escalating protests against his iron rule. Dupuy, *Haiti in the World Economy*, 98. On elite attempts to reestablish control over the peasantry, see ibid., 85–113.

54. Dupuy argues that this was a Pyrrhic victory, in that the new (or "reconstituted," in Mintz's view) peasantry was integrated into, and always subordinate to, a larger, exploitative economy. Dupuy, *Haiti in the World Economy*, 62, 96, 103. See also Mintz, *Caribbean Transformations*, 132; Moya Pons, "The Land Question."

55. Mintz, *Caribbean Transformations*, 275; Nicholls, "Holding the Purse-Strings," in *Haiti in Caribbean Context*, 122–23, 125–26.

56. See Nicholls, "The Wisdom of Salomon," in *Haiti in Caribbean Context*, 36–47.

57. Nicholls, "Rural Protest and Peasant Revolt," in *Haiti in Caribbean Context*, 167–85.

58. Joseph Lanoue and Constant Vieux, "The Real Desiderata of the Haitian People," translation of article from *Le Courrier Haïtien*, November 30, 1920, RG 80, box 240, location 5526-321:24, NA.

59. They did seek to extract profit, and some did evince disdain for their countrymen, yet these points must be seen in their larger context.

60. Trouillot, *Haiti, State against Nation*, 50.

61. Ibid., 50–51.

62. And despite a pointed plea from Massachusetts senator Timothy Pickering on behalf of the new nation. Pickering wrote Jefferson on February 24, 1806, "If Frenchmen . . . could find an apologist in you for cruel excesses of which the world had furnished no example, — are the hapless, the wretched Haytians ('guilty,' indeed, 'of a skin not coloured like our own' but) *emancipated*, and by a great National Act declared Free . . . are these men, not merely to be abandoned to their own efforts, but to be deprived of those necessary supplies which . . . they have been accustomed to receive from the UStates, and without which they cannot subsist? . . . And what will be their *rights* under the law of nations? Seeing [that] we, by an act of Government, take part with their enemies, to reduce them to submission by *starving them!* . . . Save then your country, Sir, while you may, from such ignominy and thraldom." Quoted in Elkins and McKitrick, *The Age of Federalism*, 662. Formal relations between the United States and Haiti would not be reestablished until 1861.

63. Kemedjio, "Entre le Larousse et le dollar: De l'occupation américaine de 1915 à l'Afrique post-totalitaire."

64. Dupuy, *Haiti in the World Economy*, 94.

65. Moya Pons, "The Land Question."

66. Trouillot, *Haiti, State against Nation*; Nicholls, *Dessalines to Duvalier*. Political struggles

were couched in terms of color divisions, though such divisions overlaid class in complex ways.

67. Manigat, "La substitution," 321–55.

68. Magdaline Shannon, *Jean Price-Mars, the Haitian Elite and the American Occupation*, 42.

69. Ibid.

70. Some commentators have claimed that the U.S. Navy sent disproportionate numbers of southern men to Haiti based on the belief that southerners would know how to "handle" Haitians. The claim was put forth in print by Leyburn, *The Haitian People*, 103n. Leyburn did not document his assertion. This historical controversy is ably addressed by Schmidt, *The United States Occupation of Haiti*, 143–45. See also M. Dean Havron et al., "Constabulary Capabilities for Low-Level Conflict," 44 (Report prepared for the Office of Naval Research, April 1969, Archives of the United States Naval War College, Newport, R.I.), quoted in Huggins, *Political Policing*, 26–28. Schmidt concludes that no one has yet made a compelling argument to substantiate the claim based on the available evidence. But he states that, "whether or not there was a disproportionately large number of Southern marines in Haiti, the fact that many observers felt that this was the case indicates that Southerners and Southern racial codes were conspicuous."

71. See Nelson, *National Manhood*, on the significance of identification with the president. Wilson was born December 28, 1856, in Staunton, Virginia; his family moved to Augusta, Georgia, before he was one year old, and from Augusta to Columbia, South Carolina, when he was fourteen. His father, the Reverend Joseph Ruggles Wilson, supported the Confederacy. Freud and Bullitt, *Thomas Woodrow Wilson*, 5.

72. Gilmore, *Gender and Jim Crow*, 63; Silber, *The Romance of Reunion*.

73. Rutherford, *Wrongs of History Righted*, 361.

74. Vandegrift, *Once a Marine*, 21, 23.

75. Gilmore, *Gender and Jim Crow*, 3.

76. Rutherford, *Wrongs of History Righted*, 362.

77. Lester A. Dessez, Oral History Transcript, 1b-2, HMD.

78. For this reason, it is quite likely that the interracial proximity of the occupation would sit differently with them than with northerners.

79. See Williamson, *A Rage for Order*.

80. Gilmore, *Gender and Jim Crow*. This mythology shaped relations between U.S. marines and Haitians especially after the arrival of U.S. wives. See Schmidt, *The United States Occupation of Haiti*, 136–39.

81. Lionel Hogu commented on this in conversation with the author, Boston, July 11, 1996.

82. Testimony of Smedley D. Butler, Senate Hearings, 1:517.

83. Barker was secretary of the Tennessee Society of Washington at the time. Chaffin was an Army officer. A. D. Chaffin to Robert Barker, October 28, 1929, Robert Barker Papers, PC 42, PPC.

84. As of 1910, the Marine Corps's "Advanced Base Forces" had two centers of operation, one on the East Coast of the United States, the other in the Philippines at Olongapo. By 1911, the East Coast operation was concentrated in Philadelphia, where equipment and supplies were stored and officers were trained. Fleming, Austin, and Braley, *Quantico: Crossroads of the Marine Corps*, 21. The marines who served in Haiti were part of this East Coast operation. They came from the South, the North, and the Midwest. My research did not turn up any evidence that marines from west of the Mississippi became part of the East Coast operation and landed in Haiti, although it is possible

that some did. According to Allan Millett, prior to the war of 1898, "marines were still recruited along the eastern seaboard, as they had been since the 1790s." After 1898, the Marine Corps expanded "its system of recruiting stations inland from both coasts and [turned] itself into a truly national institution." Allan Millett, *Semper Fidelis*, 118n, 136.

85. See Chapter 4.

86. F. W. Schmidt to Mrs. F. W. Schmidt, Postcard, undated, folder: "Horse Marines Envelope," F. W. Schmidt Papers, PC 1433, PPC.

87. Chauncey, *Gay New York*, 77; Nels Anderson, *Men on the Move.*

88. Before October 1915, recruits from east of the Mississippi landed at the East Coast training compound in Norfolk, Virginia. In 1915, a new Marine Corps Recruit Depot at Parris Island, South Carolina, took over the training of new recruits. Marines shipped off for Haiti from Norfolk and from Philadelphia. Fleming, Austin, and Braley, *Quantico: Crossroads of the Marine Corps*, 21.

89. It is important to emphasize the extent to which racial codes were indeed evolving. Racism consolidated northern white identities and stigmatized African Americans in singular ways prior to, as well as after, the 1890s, but the word "race" was still a relatively fluid term in the years surrounding the turn of the century. Racial discourse had not yet settled exclusively onto the black-white axis, the singular "color line," that W. E. B. Du Bois identified as the problem of America in the twentieth century. See Du Bois, *The Souls of Black Folk*. Thus, Jacob Riis, in his 1902 portrait of New York City, could speak of the Irish race, the Italian race, and the German race, as well as the "black" and "yellow" races. See Riis, *How the Other Half Lives*. And the noted psychologist and expert on adolescence, G. Stanley Hall, could envision a future American race of supermen, which would in time evolve from the current "mongrel" whites he saw around him in the mid-1890s. White Americans constituted a mongrel people, for Hall, because their bloodlines contained a diverse racial inheritance. One young man, for example, might carry German, Scottish, English, and Scandinavian blood. Thus, even as Hall participated in establishing an absolute opposition between black and white, his racial theory exposed a "seething" disunity within the evolving category of whiteness. See Bederman, *Manliness and Civilization*, 105–6. See also Jacobson, *Whiteness of a Different Color.*

90. Calloway, *Our Hearts Fell to the Ground*, 89–96; Gary Anderson and Woolworth, *Through Dakota Eyes*, 23–27, 55–56, 237; Utley, *The Indian Frontier of the American West, 1846–1890.*

91. Bernstein, *The New York Draft Riots*; Shapiro, *White Violence and Black Response*, 93–96, on the race riot of 1900. New York was also one of the few places in the East where the racial mix included a significant minority enclave of Chinese Americans.

92. William English Walling, "The Race War in the North," *Independent*, September 3, 1908, 529, quoted in Shapiro, *White Violence and Black Response*, 103.

93. Walling, "The Race War in the North," *Independent*, September 3, 1908, 530, quoted in Shapiro, *White Violence and Black Response*, 103.

94. Tuttle, *Race Riot: Chicago in the Red Summer of 1919.*

95. See Nelson, *National Manhood.*

96. Silverthorn, Oral History Transcript, 184–85. Silverthorn's impression of Smedley Butler as idiosyncratic was no doubt exacerbated by Butler's singular position as a distinguished Marine Corps general who became, in the 1930s, an outspoken anti-imperialist and isolationist. Nonetheless, Silverthorn's use of the term "idiosyncrasy" specifically to describe Butler's Quaker identity calls for comment.

97. Schmidt, *Maverick Marine*, 6.

98. Overley, "Where Are They Now?," makes reference to a Jewish marine. I found no references to or evidence of Italians in the First Brigade. Folder 8: "Manuscript," Overley Papers.

99. Painter, *Standing at Armageddon*, 298; Kennedy, *Over Here*, 17–18; Mooney and Lyman, "Some Phases of the Compulsory Military Training Movement, 1914–1920," 41. Henry L. Stimson and Leonard Wood, among others, shared Roosevelt's view.

100. Allan Millett, *Semper Fidelis*, 103. Millett puts nineteenth-century desertion rates for the Marine Corps at 25–33 percent, annually.

101. Ibid., 118. See *Manchester Union*, March 18, 1895, cited by Allan Millett, *Semper Fidelis*, 682 n. 8.

102. Allan Millett, *Semper Fidelis*, 129, 134, 136, 175. The Marine Corps benefited, to be sure, from the new martial spirit that grew out of the U.S. experience of the war. See Hoganson, *Fighting for American Manhood*, 17–32. Yet, as Millett points out, Marine Corps enlistment rates outstripped those of the army and navy.

103. Allan Millett, *Semper Fidelis*, 136, 175. Millett states that in 1899, "Congress approved the new enlisted rank of 'gunnery sergeant,' thus creating 72 billets for specialists in handling naval ordnance; at the time gunnery sergeants were the highest paid ($35 monthly) noncommissioned officers in the Corps. Additional sergeants-major and quartermaster sergeants were [also] authorized."

104. Major General Commandant George F. Elliot, quoted in Allan Millett, *Semper Fidelis*, 175.

105. Coletta, *A Survey of U.S. Naval Affairs, 1865–1917*, 185.

106. The "eagle, globe, and anchor" refers to the insignia of the Marine Corps. Immigrants may have been disproportionately reenlistees, given the increasing selectivity of the corps in the years leading up to the occupation.

107. Griswold, *Fatherhood in America*, 82; Tyack, *The One Best System*, 230.

108. Stephan Brumberg, *Going to America, Going to School*, 75–78, as quoted in Griswold, *Fatherhood in America*, 83.

109. For Irish American perspectives on earlier phases of U.S. imperialism, see Jacobson, *Special Sorrows*, 177–216, and Doyle, *Irish Americans, Native Rights and National Empires*.

110. Miller Log, August 13, 1915; September 10, 18, 1915.

111. Charles S. Simmington to the Secretary of the Navy, with enclosure, February 26, 1921, RG 80, box 240, location 5526-321:27, NA. Clipping enclosed: "The Haiti Scandal," *Record of Christian Work*, March 1921.

112. "The American Red Cross," *Gendarmerie News* (Port-au-Prince, Haiti) 1, no. 3 (November 1, 1921): 9. Copy in RG 80, box 240, location 5526-327:18, NA.

113. Del Valle, Oral History Transcript, prefatory comments, page unnumbered. Del Valle was born August 28, 1893. The United States acquired Puerto Rico after the war with Spain. The war ended in August 1898; the treaty declaring the transfer of Puerto Rico from Spain to the United States was ratified by the U.S. Senate in January 1899. On Puerto Ricans' embrace of U.S. rule, see Findlay, *Imposing Decency*, especially 112–15, 116–17.

114. Del Valle, Oral History Transcript, 62.

115. Ibid., prefatory comments, page unnumbered.

116. Ibid., 54.

117. Ibid., 55.

118. Ibid., 62.

119. Van Doren, "Why the Editorial Board Selected *The Magic Island*," 3. This story could perhaps find parallels in the accounts of white southerners reflecting on their own childhood proximity to African American folk culture.

120. Bederman addresses the specific significance of the terms "masculinity" and "manliness"; see *Manliness and Civilization*, 17–19.

121. Hoganson writes, about the years following the war with Spain, "The postwar eagerness to link martial capacity to political authority . . . suggested that self government was not an inherent right, but rather, one that rested on a specific kind of manly character." She suggests further that "the fourteen-year gap between 1896 and 1910 in which no states granted women full suffrage . . . can be explained in part by the strengthened conviction that full citizenship belongs only to those who could fight for their country." *Fighting for American Manhood*, 125, 130.

122. On "New White Men" and their response to African American men in southern politics, see Gilmore, *Gender and Jim Crow*, 64–73. On unions and masculinity, see Baron, "Questions of Gender." See also Higham, "The Reorientation of American Culture"; Filene, *Him/Her/Self*; Griffen, "Reconstructing Masculinity from the Evangelical Revivals to the Waning of Progressivism"; Bederman, *Manliness and Civilization*; Hoganson, *Fighting for American Manhood*; Griswold, *Fatherhood in America*; Marsh, "Suburban Men and Masculine Domesticity"; Cott, "On Men's History and Women's History."

123. James Green, *The World of the Worker*, 44. On working-class women in suffrage campaigns, see DuBois, "Working Women, Class Relations, and Suffrage Militance"; Orleck, *Common Sense and a Little Fire*, 87–120.

124. Chauncey, *Gay New York*, 112; Lears, *No Place of Grace*, 4.

125. Chauncey, *Gay New York*, 111; Bederman, *Manliness and Civilization*, 12–13.

126. See Griswold, *Fatherhood in America*, 35–85; Baron, "Questions of Gender"; and Montgomery, *The Fall of the House of Labor*.

127. Of course, such men did cause problems for their families when they drank excessively and became violent with their wives and children, just as elite and middle-class men who became violent caused problems for their families. The point here is that reformers targeted poor, working-class, and immigrant men, labeling them as "inferior" and failing to address the class dynamics surrounding their overbearing patriarchal power. See Griswold, *Fatherhood in America*, 60–62. See also Elizabeth Pleck, *Domestic Tyranny*.

128. On the "Wild West," see Slotkin, "Buffalo Bill's 'Wild West' "; on the White City, see Bederman, *Manliness and Civilization*, 31–35, 36–40; on football, see Bederman, *Manliness and Civilization*, 15, Harvey Green, *Fit for America*, and Mrozek, *Sport and American Mentality*.

129. On *The Rough Riders*, see Kaplan, "Black and Blue on San Juan Hill." Cf. Hoganson, who emphasizes the unifying, fraternal legacy of the Rough Riders, in *Fighting for American Manhood*, 142.

130. On McFadden, see Chauncey, *Gay New York*, 116.

131. Bederman, *Manliness and Civilization*, 221.

132. Rotundo, *American Manhood*, 252; G. Stanley Hall, "Feminization in Schools and Home: The Undue Influence of Women Teachers — The Need of Different Training for the Sexes," *World's Work* 16 (1908): 10–38, quoted in Rotundo, *American Manhood*, 354 n. 14; Stearns, "Men, Boys, and Anger," 83, 84; Bederman, *Manliness and Civilization*, 16. On other boy-focused groups, see Chauncey, *Gay New York*, 116.

133. Kimmel, *Manhood in America*, 166.

134. Bederman, *Manliness and Civilization*, 98–99; G. Stanley Hall, "The Education of the Heart (Abstract)," *Kindergarten Magazine* 2 (May 1899): 593, quoted in Bederman, *Manliness and Civilization*, 264 n. 74.

135. On the Boy Scouts, see Rotundo, *American Manhood*, 228; Beard, *Hardly a Man Is Now Alive*, 351–61; Kimmel, *Manhood in America*; Mcleod, *Building Character in the American Boy*.

136. On boxing gloves as gifts, see Stearns, "Men, Boys, and Anger," 84. On adventure stories, see Martin Green, *The Adventurous Male*; Ely, *The Road to Armageddon*; Richards, *Imperialism and Juvenile Literature*. On Tarzan, first published in 1914, see Bederman, *Manliness and Civilization*, 219–32; Torgovnick, *Gone Primitive*, 42–72.

137. Vandegrift, *Once a Marine*, 24–25.

138. Craige, *Black Bagdad*, 88.

139. Allan Millett, *Semper Fidelis*, 175, 177. See also Lindsay, *This High Name*.

140. See Lynd, *Nonviolence in America*; Bederman, *Manliness and Civilization*; Mrozek, "The Habit of Victory."

141. Homer Overley, Smedley Butler, and William Baheri are a few of the marines who served in Haiti who left some record of their opposition to militarism. Baheri, a former enlisted man who went to Haiti as a teenager, was deeply affected by the sight of a Haitian woman and her children crying as they watched their husband and father be caught and shot. Leo Dougherty has interviewed William Baheri, and I thank him for sharing this information with me. In his biography of Butler, Hans Schmidt concludes that the famous marine's "1930s recantation is best understood as evolving from experiences within the military and in civilian police work, rather than from outside ideological influences." Schmidt, *Maverick Marine*, 249. More recently, we may think of such organizations as Vietnam Veterans for Peace.

142. Craige, *Black Bagdad*, 98–102. For other marines' attitudes toward such men, see Chapter 4.

143. Beveridge, *The Young Man and the World*, 156, quoted in Hoganson, *Fighting for American Manhood*, 155.

144. Conversely, in the mid-1890s, G. Stanley Hall saw adolescence as the onset of manhood because it introduced the possibility of paternity, and thus linked a young man to the future of the race. See Bederman, *Manliness and Civilization*, 103–4.

145. On breadwinning and fatherhood, see Griswold, *Fatherhood in America*; Filene, *Him/Her/Self*; Rotundo, *American Manhood*.

146. The coterie of responsibilities assigned to fathers in the nineteenth century varied by region. On fatherhood in the nineteenth-century North, see Frank, *Life with Father*. On fatherhood in the nineteenth-century South, see Wyatt-Brown, *Southern Honor*; Stowe, *Intimacy and Power in the Old South*; Burton, *In My Father's House Are Many Mansions*; Censer, *North Carolina Planters and Their Children*; Cashin, *A Family Venture*. On the transformation of fatherhood in the first half of the twentieth century, see Griswold, *Fatherhood in America*; LaRossa, *The Modernization of Fatherhood*. Robert Griswold suggests that among those challenges was the challenge posed by the state, which increasingly intervened in family matters, reducing paternal authority and rendering "paternal autonomy . . . illusory." See Griswold, *Fatherhood in America*, 7.

147. See Marsh, "Suburban Men and Masculine Domesticity," especially 122, 126.

148. Indeed, the state enforced such respectability. During the years immediately preceding the U.S. occupation of Haiti, progressive reformers focused public attention on the importance of paternal responsibility and the necessity of disciplinary coercion to bring wayward fathers into line. Robert Griswold points out that "in the first

decade of the new century, eleven states made desertion or non-support of destitute families a felony; eighteen increased the fine and/or the length of imprisonment for these crimes; others allowed third parties to bring suits, permitted wives to testify against husbands, and granted probation agents the power to apprehend the deserter and oversee his conduct. By 1920 a third of the nation's states and territories had taken steps to ensure that men fulfilled their half of the family bargain." This suggests that the dominant discursive framework for the United States' approach to Haiti was worked out earlier in the context of domestic paternalism. See Griswold, *Fatherhood in America*, 63–64.

149. Ivan Miller remembered that his father's friendship with one of Ohio's congressmen led to his admission to the U.S. Naval Academy. Ivan W. Miller, Oral History Transcript, 2–3, HMD.

150. Griswold, *Fatherhood in America*, 19.

151. Ibid., 26, 38.

152. On the insults of childhood, see, for example, Stoler, *Race and the Education of Desire*, 151–52. See also Kett, *Rites of Passage*. On early-twentieth-century U.S. American fathers expanding their authority over their children into their twenties, see Griswold, *Fatherhood in America*, 38.

153. Clopper, *Rural Child Welfare: An Inquiry by the National Child Labor Committee*, 85, quoted in Griswold, *Fatherhood in America*, 28.

154. "Old Jersey Marine Guard Gains Purple Heart," unidentified newspaper clipping, folder 1: "1982 Dissertation for Princeton History Department by Anne Cipriano Venzon," Anne C. Venzon Papers, PC 2364, PPC.

155. Covello, *The Teacher in the Urban Community*, 41, 43, quoted in Griswold, *Fatherhood in America*, 84. See also Bernard Weiss, *American Education and European Immigrants: 1840–1940*, 61–77.

156. Montgomery, *The Fall of the House of Labor*, on Taylorism; Tone, *The Business of Benevolence*, on industrial paternalism.

157. Maxwell Droke, "Shall We Say Farewell to 'Welfare?,' " *Industrial Management* 66 (October 1923): 206, quoted in Tone, *The Business of Benevolence*, 237–38.

158. Charles A. Lippincott, "Promoting Employee Team Work and Welfare without Paternalism," *Industrial Management* 71 (March 1926): 147, quoted in Tone, *The Business of Benevolence*, 239.

159. Chauncey, *Gay New York*, 76.

160. Ibid., 76–80, especially 79.

161. Chauncey focuses on New York City but offers important clues for our understanding of the rough culture of single men in other urban areas. He points out, for example, that working-class male communities "began to disappear in the 1920s, when the sex ratios of immigrant communities started to stabilize." Immigration legislation "made it difficult for immigrant workers to enter the United States for brief periods of work." At the same time, "the number of seamen in the city began to decline as New York's port declined, and the number of transient workers (or hoboes) dropped throughout the country in the 1920s, as economic and technological production, and the expansion of auto transport, reduced the need for them." See Chauncey, *Gay New York*, 78. See also Nels Anderson, *Men on the Move*, 2–5, 12.

162. Chauncey, *Gay New York*, 79–80.

163. Wise, *A Marine Tells It to You*, frontispiece.

164. Coletta, "Josephus Daniels," in *American Secretaries of the Navy*, 2:527–28.

165. Miller Log, May 3, 1916.

166. Wirkus and Dudley, *The White King of La Gonave*, 9–10.

167. Scottman, "A Marine Remembers Haiti," 22–23.

168. Butler, *Old Gimlet Eye*, 184. This is not to suggest that enlisted men's boasts would have taken the same form.

169. "Thou Shalt Not: Hints to Newly Commissioned Officers," pamphlet, folder 2: Untitled, William Rossiter Papers, PC 113, PPC.

170. Schmidt, *Maverick Marine*, 1.

171. Smedley D. Butler to Maud Darlington Butler, February 21, 1916, Venzon MS, 203. Also see Chapter 3.

172. Franklyn, *Knights in the Cockpit*, 6.

173. Chauncey, *Gay New York*, 84–85.

174. Ibid. While, on rare occasions, a lineup may have been a financially profitable scheme orchestrated by a prostitute, most often the event was nothing short of out-and-out gang rape.

175. Ibid., 81.

176. Ibid., 118–19. Further support for this argument may be found in Linn's discussion of homosexuality in the U.S. Army in the early-twentieth-century Pacific. Linn's evidence is from the records of General Courts-Martial. *Guardians of Empire*, 130–33.

177. Chauncey, *Gay New York*, 115–18.

178. Ibid., 115–16.

179. Ibid., 79.

180. See Chauncey, "Christian Brotherhood or Sexual Perversion?," and Murphy, *Perverts by Official Order*.

181. Schmidt, *Maverick Marine*, 174. The article on Butler was from 1927.

182. Together, the work of George Chauncey and Donald Mrozek may illuminate the breakdown of values among marines in Haiti, which constitutes the focus of Chapter 4. Mrozek claims that "[t]he hardihood of military life . . . protected male friendship from insinuations of homosexuality" ("The Habit of Victory," 222). He claims, further, that the military provided an institutional context in which the display and even the flamboyant spectacle of the manly body could be indulged in without the anxieties that attended civilian middle-class men's pleasure in looking at manly bodies. As Mrozek points out, "military display had its own history and justification" (222). Yet military display — the proper display of the uniform, for example — was precisely what fell apart in the field in Haiti. As the usual structures of proper military form fell away, could it be that anxieties held at bay by such forms could emerge and trouble the marines' sense of self?

183. Fleming, Austin, and Braley, *Quantico: Crossroads of the Marine Corps*, 20–21; Sweetman, *American Naval History*, 132. See also Champie, *A Brief History of the Marine Corps Recruit Depot, Parris Island, S.C.*

184. Thomason, *Fix Bayonets!*, xix.

185. Allan Millett, *Semper Fidelis*, xvii.

186. Ibid., 162.

187. Thomason, *Fix Bayonets!*, x.

188. Allan Millett, *Semper Fidelis*, 176.

189. Ibid., xvii, 145–50.

190. Gene Holiday, quoted in Appy, *Working-Class War*, 86. See also Butler, *War Is a Racket*, 28.

191. Wirkus and Dudley, *The White King of La Gonave*, 9–10.

192. Showalter, "Evolution of the U.S. Marine Corps as a Military Elite," 44–58.

193. Thomason, *Fix Bayonets!*, xix.

194. Homer Overley's use of the word "gyrene," a derogatory term used to describe marines, at least raises the question of the extent to which marines maintained their sense of worth. We shall return to this idea in Chapter 4.

195. Thomason, *Fix Bayonets!*, xiv.

196. Wirkus and Dudley, *The White King of La Gonave*, 9–10.

197. Miller, Oral History Transcript, 4.

198. Hall, quoted by Kimmel, *Manhood in America*, 163–64. Hazing was one particular "tradition of things endured," in Thomason's phrase.

199. See Chapter 4.

200. Mrozek, "The Habit of Victory," 222. Mrozek comments on the process of "softening" that was part of military indoctrination: "It is crucial to note that U.S. military officers were at least as likely to need cultivation of the gentler skills than of aggressive attitudes and physical prowess and they were similarly diligent to see that their men followed the same pattern. Since Victorian manliness was not mere brute strength and unrestricted will, it was equally important to develop the sense of restraint to instill an instinct for balance and to cultivate the habit of grace under pressure. Military courage and manliness thus inspired a rhetoric of 'softening' as much as 'toughening,' especially since the armed forces tended to draw so much of their manpower from outside the middle and upper classes" (224).

201. Cronon, *The Cabinet Diaries of Josephus Daniels*, 331, 553. A representative of the YMCA did visit Haiti to assess morale and help plan an appropriate training program. See Inman, *Trailing the Conquistadores*, 117–18.

202. Allan Millett, *Semper Fidelis*, 142.

203. Private C. Hundertmark, "The United States Marine," *Recruiter's Bulletin* (April 1915), cited in Allan Millett, *Semper Fidelis*, 145.

204. Regimental histories provide important information about the background (and lore) that some experienced marines brought with them to Haiti. The First Regiment, for example, was initially composed of several battalions that had been in the Philippines prior to 1900, when it was first organized. The First Marines also served in China, Panama, Cuba, Mexico, Puerto Rico, and the Dominican Republic as well as in Haiti. Littleton W. T. Waller, Eli K. Cole, Smedley D. Butler, Deacon Upshur, Frederick Wise, Adolph Miller, George Osterhout, and Merwin Silverthorn all served with the First Regiment in Haiti. Johnstone, *A Brief History of the 1st Marines*. See also Kane, *A Brief History of the 2d Marines*; Santelli, *A Brief History of the 8th Marines*; Buckner, *A Brief History of the 10th Marines*.

205. Wirkus and Dudley, *The White King of La Gonave*, 12–13.

206. Miller Log, July 30, 1915–June 24, 1916.

207. Ibid., July 31, 1915. For nickname, see Postcard, box 13, folder: "Naval Academy, 1905–1909," Adolph B. Miller Papers, PC 196, PPC. Cynthia Enloe has commented on the important but largely unacknowledged labor performed for the military by officers' wives acting in this manner. See Enloe, *Bananas, Beaches, and Bases*, and *Maneuvers*. On military wives in occupied Haiti, see Schmidt, *The United States Occupation of Haiti*, 136–39; Dessez, Oral History Transcript; Silverthorn, Oral History Transcript; Miller Log, June 3 and 8, November 26, December 2, 1916.

208. Miller Log, August 1, 1915–June 24, 1916.

209. Ibid.

210. Ibid., August 3, 1915.

211. Ibid., August 1, 1915.
212. Deacon P. Upshur, quoted in Harold H. Utley, "The Tactics and Techniques of Small Wars," 14, unpublished typescript, Harold H. Utley Papers, PPC. Books dealing with Haiti and Haitian history available at the time included St. John, *Hayti, or the Black Republic*; Prichard, *Where Black Rules White*; Johnston, *The Negro in the New World*; Bonsal, *The American Mediterranean*; and Stoddard, *The French Revolution in Santo Domingo*. Prichard's volume was among those read by Adolph Miller while he was in Haiti. See Miller Log, January 9, 1916.
213. Deacon P. Upshur, quoted in Utley, "The Tactics and Techniques of Small Wars," 14.
214. Miller Log, August 5, 1915.
215. Wirkus and Dudley, *The White King of La Gonave*, 19.
216. Ibid.
217. Healy, *Gunboat Diplomacy in the Wilson Era*, 53.
218. Utley, "The Tactics and Techniques of Small Wars."
219. Ibid., 94, 95, 97.
220. Ibid., 95, 98.
221. Ibid., 95.
222. Ibid., 100.
223. Utley describes Van Orden's handling of the refusal by the revolutionary committee to allow U.S. forces to use the Caserne barracks. Ibid., 99.
224. Healy, *Gunboat Diplomacy in the Wilson Era*, 66–67, 77, 88–89.
225. Utley, "The Tactics and Techniques of Small Wars," 100.
226. Miller Log, August 5, 1915.
227. Craige, *Black Bagdad*, 176.
228. Miller Log, August 4, 1915.
229. Miller Log, August 5 and 8, 1915.
230. Miller Log, August 6, 1915.
231. Ibid.
232. Miller Log, August 10 and 9, 1915, respectively.
233. McMillen, "Some Haitian Recollections," 522.
234. Ibid., 522–23.
235. This use of "marronage" derives from the same word that refers to the maroon tradition discussed earlier. See Fouchard, *The Haitian Maroons*.
236. On rara, see McAlister, " 'Men Moun Yo: Here Are the People,' " and "New York Lavalas and the Emergence of Rara."
237. Wise, *A Marine Tells It to You*, 132–33.
238. Wirkus and Dudley, *The White King of La Gonave*, 15.
239. Ibid., 17.
240. Ibid., 20.
241. Ibid., 17.
242. Laleau, *Le choc*. Laleau's title translates as *The Shock*.
243. Dorsinville, *Marche arrière*, 16. "[J]e me souviens clairment de mes premiers 'marines' par un matin de soleil, et il me semble que c'était le jour de leur débarquement; je percevais leur nouveauté à la stupéfaction des visages, au silence soudain autour de moi." Translation by the author.
244. Ibid., 27. "[L]'enfant n'a enregistré que la stupeur des visages, puis la résignation évidemment. . . . Des soldats blancs étaient venus salir l'indépendance: où étaient les aïeux? Finalement les aïeux n'étaient plus."
245. On the sit-down strike, see Julian C. Smith, Oral History Transcript, 52, HMD.

246. Alfred H. Noble, Oral History Transcript, 56–57, HMD.

247. Ibid., 57.

CHAPTER 3

1. Schmidt, *Maverick Marine*, 91.

2. Seligmann, "The Conquest of Haiti"; James Weldon Johnson, "Self-Determining Haiti."

3. Schmidt, *Maverick Marine*, 110–28, especially 117. Brig. General George Barnett, "Report of Affairs in Haiti, June 1915–June 1920," RG 45, ZWA-7, box 1000, folder 4, NA. See also various documents in the George Barnett Papers, PPC.

4. "The Real Desiderata of the Haitian People," translation of article from *Le Courrier Haïtien*, RG 80, box 240, location 5526-321:24, NA. See also Blassingame, "The Press and the American Intervention"; Plummer, "The Afro-American Response"; and the correspondence files of the Secretary of the Navy in RG 80, NA.

5. "U.S. Rules Haiti by Fear, Says Brooklyn Attorney," *New York Globe*, July 15, 1920. Copy located in RG 80, location 5526-279, NA.

6. J. Deerlson (illeg.) to Secretary of the Navy, August 2, 1920, RG 80, location 5526-282: 6, NA.

7. Waldo A. Amos to Newton D. Baker, Secretary of War, RG 80, location 5526-279, NA.

8. Testimony of Admiral William B. Caperton, 1921, Senate Hearings, 1:392. See also Perkins, *Constraint of Empire*, 122.

9. Smedley D. Butler to Thomas S. Butler, December 23, 1915, Venzon MS, 198.

10. Healy, *Gunboat Diplomacy in the Wilson Era*.

11. Link, *Wilson: The Struggle for Neutrality*, 524.

12. Wilson to Bryan, April 5, 1915, *Wilson Papers*, 32:479.

13. Wilson, "Remarks to the Associated Press in New York," April 20, 1915, in *Wilson Papers*, 33:39. The metaphor of trusteeship dated back, at least, to Benjamin Kidd's 1898 work *Control of the Tropics*. See also Porter, *Critics of Empire*, and Hetherington, *British Paternalism and Africa*.

14. Wilson, "An Address on Latin American Policy in Mobile, Alabama" [October 27, 1913], *Wilson Papers*, 28:448–53.

15. Ibid., 448–53.

16. Ibid., 451.

17. Ibid., 452.

18. Wilson to Eliot, September 17, 1913, *Wilson Papers*, 28:280.

19. Bryan to Blanchard, December 18, 1914, *Wilson Papers*, 31:486–87. Note that Wilson qualified Bryan's original draft by adding the word "special."

20. Wilson to Edward Mandel House, August 4, 1915, *Wilson Papers*, 34:80.

21. A separate Corps of Marines was established in 1798, initially drawn from the ranks of the Army. A more central institutional ambiguity arose from the fact that marines were intended as ships guards for the Navy, but also put at the president's disposal. In the nineteenth century marines were used as police forces in Washington, D.C., and in certain other domestic contexts, notably in Brooklyn's "Irishtown" between 1867 and 1871 and during labor uprisings, most conspicuously in the Great Uprising of 1877. Meanwhile the corps had its own separate commandant, but that commandant reported to the secretary of the navy. Around the turn of the century, naval reformers sought to remove ships guards from navy vessels and various plans were

floated for reorganizing the Marine Corps; some called for integrating it into the Regular Army. The corps emerged from those institutional battles with all its functions intact, only to be redefined — and indeed strengthened — in the context of U.S. colonial wars in the Pacific and the Caribbean. Allan Millett, *Semper Fidelis*.

22. Challener, *Admirals, Generals and American Foreign Policy*, 65.

23. Ibid., 20.

24. Commander John Shipley, USS *Des Moines*, to Sec. Navy, December 19, 1908, RG 45, Navy Area Files, 1900–1911, NA, quoted in Langley, *The Banana Wars*, 124.

25. Challener, *Admirals, Generals and American Foreign Policy*, 18.

26. Mahan, *The Influence of Sea Power upon World History*.

27. Challener, *Admirals, Generals and American Foreign Policy*, 42–44.

28. Ibid., 44.

29. Ibid., 45, 399.

30. Ibid., 365.

31. Allan Millett, *Semper Fidelis*, 29–30.

32. Schmidt, *Maverick Marine*, 126.

33. This tradition included the use of the Marine Corps troops in the domestic arena, especially in Washington, D.C. High, "The Marine Corps and Crowd Control," 113–35. Note that in the decades leading up to this time, the National Guard had largely taken over that function in the domestic context.

34. Link, *Wilson: The Struggle for Neutrality*, 497.

35. Ibid., 499.

36. Ibid., 499 n. 5.

37. Livingston to Assistant Secretary of State, May 15, 1912, DF 711.38/14, cited in Plummer, *Haiti and the Great Powers, 1902–1915*, 159.

38. Schmidt, *The United States Occupation of Haiti*, 37; Plummer, *Haiti and the Great Powers*, 159.

39. McDonald to Lansing, August 2, 1915, *Wilson Papers*, 34:68.

40. Stabler to Bryan, May 13, 1914, SD 838.00/1667, cited in Schmidt, *The United States Occupation of Haiti*, 53.

41. Plummer, *Haiti and the Great Powers*, 146.

42. Ibid., 148; cf. Schmidt, *The United States Occupation of Haiti*, 39. Schmidt argues that the initiative was concurrently taken by the State Department, the bankers, and Germans.

43. It is possible that Wilson's legislative baby, the Federal Reserve Act of 1913, though intended to provide the federal government with a measure of control over the banks, also contributed to the close connection between banking leaders and Washington policy makers and to the influence of the bankers. See Dawley, *Struggles for Justice*, 147. On Wilson's attitudes toward large corporations, see Weinstein, *The Corporate Ideal in the Liberal State*, 162–65.

44. Link, *Wilson: The Struggle for Neutrality*, 518.

45. Long to Bryan, January 23, 1914, cited in Link, *Wilson: The Struggle for Neutrality*, 519.

46. Schmidt, *The United States Occupation of Haiti*, 60–61.

47. Link, *Wilson: The Struggle for Neutrality*, 530; Schmidt, *The United States Occupation of Haiti*, 53.

48. Wilson to Bryan, April 5, 1915, *Wilson Papers*, 32:479.

49. Bryan to Wilson, January 7, 1915, *Wilson Papers*, 32:27–28.

50. Wilson to Bryan, January 13, 1915, *Wilson Papers*, 32:62.

51. See, for example, Lansing to Wilson, August 13, 1915, *Wilson Papers*, 34:184.

52. Wilson to Edith Bolling Galt, August 8, 1915, *Wilson Papers*, 34:139. Or soon-to-be fiancée — they were secretly engaged in the late summer but did not announce the engagement until October. Heckscher, *Woodrow Wilson*, 347–57.

53. Thomas B. Hohler, quoted in Wells, "New Perspectives on Wilsonian Diplomacy," 396.

54. Quoted in Millspaugh, *Haiti under American Control*, 26.

55. Wilson to Lansing, August 4, 1915, *Wilson Papers*, 34:78.

56. *Literary Digest* 51 (August 14, 1915): 456, as cited by Healy, *Gunboat Diplomacy*, 155.

57. Allan Millett, *Semper Fidelis*, 153–54. Waller's commanding officer, Brigadier General Jacob H. Smith, had ordered a battalion of Marines, led by Waller, to "turn Samar into a 'howling wilderness.'" Waller led a vigorous and exhausting campaign, at the end of which he ordered the summary execution of eleven Filipinos. Waller was court-martialed for murder, but not convicted, despite "persuasive" evidence.

58. Schmidt, *Maverick Marine*, 84.

59. Healy, *Gunboat Diplomacy*, 6, 15, 62–81.

60. Smedley and Ethel were married in June 1905. Schmidt, *Maverick Marine*, 32.

61. Smedley D. Butler to Ethel C. P. Butler, March 2, 1916, Venzon MS, 205.

62. Schmidt, *Maverick Marine*, 33, 39, 59.

63. For example, ibid., 71, 74.

64. Ibid., 32.

65. Smedley D. Butler to Thomas S. Butler, December 23, 1915, Venzon MS, 198.

66. Schmidt, *Maverick Marine*, 84.

67. Schmidt, *The United States Occupation of Haiti*, 77. A separate agreement regarding the administration of the Gendarmerie was yet to come. See Evans, *Treaties and Other International Agreements of the United States*, 663, 671–72.

68. Ibid., 663 (emphasis added).

69. Smedley D. Butler to Thomas S. Butler, May 16, 1916, Venzon MS, 211. The law passed Congress on June 12. Millspaugh, *Haiti under American Control*, 64.

70. Smedley D. Butler to Thomas S. Butler, May 16, 1916, Venzon MS, 211. This was not the first time the younger Butler had commanded the military force of another country. He had written his wife from Nicaragua, for example, "this morning I practically took command of the Government Army of about 4,000 men and have been issuing instructions . . . all day — this move of mine must not become public for I really have no authority for such a course but it is the only way for this Government to win." Schmidt, *Maverick Marine*, 45.

71. H.R. 12835, "A bill to allow officers and enlisted men of the Navy and Marine Corps to serve under the government of the Republic of Haiti." Venzon MS, 209–10.

72. Smedley D. Butler to James R. Mann, April 4, 1916, Venzon MS, 207, 209.

73. Ibid. (emphasis added).

74. Schmidt, *Maverick Marine*, 84.

75. Smedley D. Butler to Thomas S. Butler, October 1, 1916, Venzon MS, 226.

76. Schmidt, *Maverick Marine*, 60.

77. Ibid., 39, 60.

78. Smedley D. Butler to Thomas S. Butler, October 1, 1916, Venzon MS, 226–27.

79. In his biography of Smedley Butler, Hans Schmidt handles this disjunction by characterizing the outright racial slur as an exception. For Schmidt, it was an aberration from the overall pattern of paternalism in Butler's letters, an expression of temporary despair resulting from the loss of a particular "political skirmish"; Butler's pride in his achievements with the Gendarmerie was paramount. Schmidt, *Maverick Marine*, 92.

80. Smedley D. Butler to John A. Lejeune, July 13, 1916, Venzon MS, 218.
81. Ibid.
82. Smedley D. Butler to Thomas S. Butler, October 1, 1916, Venzon MS, 226–27.
83. Schmidt, *Maverick Marine*, 60.
84. Smedley D. Butler to Thomas S. Butler, May 16, 1917, Venzon MS, 230.
85. Ibid.
86. Schmidt, *Maverick Marine*, 45–46. Schmidt calls this "a rare and vaguely hysterical streak of bombast."
87. Ibid., 47.
88. Smedley D. Butler to Maud Darlington Butler, February 21, 1916, Venzon MS, 203 (emphasis in original).
89. Ibid.
90. Ibid.
91. Smedley D. Butler to Thomas S. Butler, May 16, 1917, Venzon MS, 231.
92. See Bederman, *Manliness and Civilization*, 97–98, on G. Stanley Hall's prescription that boys should play at war and savagery as a way to ensure their civilized manliness.
93. Smedley D. Butler to Thomas S. Butler, May 16, 1917, Venzon MS, 231.
94. Smedley D. Butler to Thomas S. Butler and Maud Darlington Butler, January 27, 1918, Venzon MS, 239.
95. Smedley D. Butler to Maud Darlington Butler, March 2, 1918, Venzon MS, 240.
96. Wilson, "A Welcome to the Pan-American Financial Conference," *Wilson Papers*, 33:245–46.
97. "Insure fair wages" is from Link, *Woodrow Wilson and the Progressive Era*, 20; "make the people nothing more" is from *New York Times*, September 3, 1912, 3, cols. 2–3.
98. *New York Times*, September 3, 1912, 3, cols. 2–3.
99. Ibid.
100. Ibid.
101. Steinson, *American Women's Activism in World War I*.
102. According to Oswald Garrison Villard, candidate Wilson pledged in 1912 to be "President of all the people." But when he was invited by Villard and W. E. B. Du Bois to clarify the implications of this statement with respect to African American voters, he demurred. Lewis, *W. E. B. Du Bois: Biography of a Race*, 423. African Americans who supported Wilson in 1912 included Du Bois, William Monroe Trotter, Bishop Walters, Max Barber, Byron Gunner, and Milton Waldron.
103. "An Address to the President by William Monroe Trotter," November 12, 1914, *Wilson Papers*, 31:298; for a record of the November 1913 meeting, see William Monroe Trotter's Address to the President and Wilson's Reply and a Dialogue, November 6, 1913, *Wilson Papers*, 28:491–500, especially 498, re: number of signatures on the petition.
104. "An Address to the President by William Monroe Trotter," November 12, 1914, *Wilson Papers*, 31:299.
105. Ibid., 300 (emphasis added).
106. Ibid., 301.
107. Ibid.
108. Ibid., 302.
109. Ibid., 303.
110. Ibid.
111. Ibid., 302.

112. Ibid., 303.

113. Ibid.

114. Ibid., 306. For public reaction to Wilson's meeting with Trotter, see Lewis, *W. E. B. Du Bois: Biography of a Race*, 511–12.

115. Wilson, "A Talk at Swarthmore College," October 25, 1913, *Wilson Papers*, 28:440–41.

116. Ibid., 441.

117. See also Horsman, *Race and Manifest Destiny*.

118. Wilson, "A Talk at Swarthmore College," October 25, 1913, *Wilson Papers*, 28:441.

119. Ibid.

120. Wilson to Edith Bolling Galt, August 19, 1915, *Wilson Papers*, 34:254 (emphasis in the original).

121. Wilson to Edith Bolling Galt, August 15, 1915, *Wilson Papers*, 34:209.

122. Wilson, "A Draft of an Address to Congress," [ca. October 31, 1913], *Wilson Papers*, 28:480.

123. Link, *Wilson: The Struggle for Neutrality*, 479. Link seems to have shared Wilson's paternalist perspective on Latin America, or at least he manifested little critical distance on it. Yet, he summed it up very well, directly employing the metaphors of childhood and maturity that Wilson carefully avoided. Wilson, he wrote, had "certain strong convictions about the general political development of mankind and the responsibilities that great powers had for less advanced neighbors. . . . He believed that democracy was the highest form of political life and that peoples could rise to its mature level only through generations of experience or tutelage. He did not believe that peoples of northern Latin America were much beyond the stage of political infancy; and he assumed that it was his responsibility as well as his privilege to teach his unenlightened neighbors how to write good constitutions and elect wise leaders." Link, *Wilson: The Struggle for Neutrality*, 479. Other historians join Link in uncritically replaying the paternalism of the United States toward Latin America and, in particular, toward Haiti.

124. Wilson, "A Draft of an Address to Congress," [ca. October 31, 1913], *Wilson Papers*, 28:480 (emphasis added).

125. Mintz, "Slavery and the Rise of Peasantries."

126. Kennan, *American Diplomacy, 1900–1950*, 98–99.

127. Captain Edward Beach manuscript, RG 45, Subject Files 1911–27, box 1,000, 140–43, NA, cited by Fernandez, *Cruising the Caribbean*, 103; Department of State, Report Covering Haiti, 41–42, Hoover Library, cited by Fernandez, *Cruising the Caribbean*, 116–17; Schmidt, *United States Occupation of Haiti*, 174–88.

128. Smedley D. Butler to Thomas S. Butler, May 16, 1917, Venzon MS, 230.

129. Wilson to Edith Bolling Galt, August 30, 1915, *Wilson Papers*, 34:367; Wilson to Edith Bolling Galt, [ca. August 24, 1915], *Wilson Papers*, 34:311.

130. Telegram, Secretary of State to Chargé Davis, August 18, 1915, *FRUS*, 1915, 434. "You may use the following as your views of the motives and purposes of the Government of the United States," he wrote on August 22, 1915, "to establish a stable government and lasting domestic peace . . . so that the Haitian people may safely enjoy their full rights of life, liberty and property and all patriotic citizens may be encouraged to participate in the development of their country." Telegram, Secretary of State to Chargé Davis, August 22, 1915, *FRUS*, 1915, 435–36.

131. Secretary of the Navy Josephus Daniels urged Navy and Marine Corps officers "to

regard themselves as friendly brothers of Haitians sent there to help these neighbor people." *New York Times*, October 6, 1920, 2, cited in Schmidt, *The United States Occupation of Haiti*, 78.

132. Miller Log, October 10, 1915.

133. Miller Log, December 11, 1915.

134. Miller Log, September 5, 1915.

135. Note that, as secretary of state, William Jennings Bryan's orientation toward a kind of "public dollar diplomacy" would have emphasized primarily the use of U.S. government funding for Haitian development projects, so as to protect against the abuse of policy. Langley, *The Banana Wars*, 122; also see Rosenberg on "chosen instruments," *Spreading the American Dream*, 59–62, 72–73. Lansing and Wilson agreed that private investment must also be part of the plan, although, as we have seen, Wilson tried to be careful not to seem partial to U.S. investors.

136. G. F. Geffrard to "the Government at Washington D.C." via John H. Russell, [ca. August 15, 1920], RG 80, box 239, location 5526-298, NA. Russell forwarded this letter to Daniels with his endorsement. No wonder, given that Geffrard argued forcefully for empowering the occupation, and in particular recommended that Washington "proclaim the Chief of the American Occupation Military Governor of the Republic with the rank of President of the Cabinet."

137. Telegram, USS *New Hampshire* (Knapp) to Secretary of the Navy, December 4, 1920, RG 80, box 240, location 5526-321:16, NA.

138. Telegram, Senior U.S. Naval Representative in Haiti (Knapp) to Secretary of the Navy, December 4, 1920, RG 80, box 240, location 5526-321:24, NA. The *Courrier Haïtien*'s dispatch prompted another round of exchanges over whether and how the occupation should suppress such oppositional speech. Gail Bederman examines Ida B. Wells's similar use of the discourse of "civilization" in "'Civilization,' the Decline of Middle-Class Manliness, and Ida B. Wells's Anti-Lynching Campaign."

139. Telegram, Brigade Port-au-Prince to Marcorps, March 14, 1921, RG 80, box 240, location 5526-321:28, NA. The French phrase translates approximately to "the scum of his own chamber pot." When occupation officials failed, so obviously, to conscript Haitians into the paternalist framework, they resorted straightaway to censorship.

140. Ibid.

141. Harold Palmer Davis, "A Brief Analysis of the Haitian People in Connection with Plans for Educational Development," Port-au-Prince, January 21, 1921, unpublished typescript essay, 10 pp., RG 80, box 241, location 5526-363 1/2, NA.

142. Tamerlyn T. Chamberlain, U.S.N., *Port-au-Prince, Haiti* (n.p., [1918]), 1, folder: "Unidentified Papers," Fred S. Robillard Papers, PPC.

143. Ibid.

144. Ibid., 18–19.

145. Ibid., 32.

146. H. S. Knapp to Secretary of the Navy, November 8, 1920, RG 80, box 240, location 5526-331, NA.

147. Ibid.

148. Ibid.

149. Gilmore, *Gender and Jim Crow*, 62.

150. David Montgomery highlights 1909 and 1912–13 as periods of prosperity with high rates of turnover and absenteeism. Montgomery, *The Fall of the House of Labor*, 239. See also Tone, *The Business of Benevolence*.

151. McMillen, "Some Haitian Recollections"; on anticolonial troubles, see, for example, Rafael, "White Love."

152. Archer A. Vandegrift, for example, later described his work in the Gendarmerie as "a civil counterpart to the work of Christian missionaries who were devoting their lives to these people." Vandegrift, *Once a Marine*, 58. Arthur B. Jacques also referred to "the marines as missionaries." A. B. Jacques, untitled manuscript, box 2, folder 10, Arthur B. Jacques Papers, PC 873, PPC.

153. Miller Log, August 14, 1915.

154. Miller Log, August 14 and September 10, 1915.

155. Only two years before the occupation began, the word "feminism" emerged, for the first time, to name the growing challenge to masculine power. See Cott, *The Grounding of Modern Feminism*, 13.

156. Josephus Daniels to Mr. [*sic*] M. J. Exner, August 26, 1920, RG 80, box 240, location 5526-282:7, NA. Note that M. J. Exner did not identify herself or himself by gender.

157. Draft of letter to Walter Carrier, n.d., RG 80, box 240, location 5526-325:16, NA.

158. Jordan, *Crusading in the West Indies*, 79.

159. Ibid., 98.

160. Evans, *Treaties and Other International Agreements of the United States of America*, 663.

161. Smedley D. Butler to Ethel C. P. Butler, July 16, 1916, Venzon MS, 221. See also Renda, "This American Africa," 82–83.

162. Louis McCarty Little to Edwin Denby, April 8, 1921, RG 80, box 241, location 5526-363 1/2, NA.

163. Although it may also be argued that he made up his own rules.

164. Louis McCarty Little, Daily Diary Report, July 28, 1919, RG 45, entry WA-7, box 742, folder 8, NA.

165. Senate Hearings, 1:514.

166. Ibid. (emphasis added).

167. Schmidt, *Maverick Marine*, 84.

168. Telegram, Chargé Davis to the Secretary of State, July 27, 1915, *FRUS*, 1915, 474–75; Plummer, *Haiti and the Great Powers*, 220.

169. Evans, *Treaties and Other International Agreements of the United States of America*, 663.

170. Beale Davis, *The Goat without Horns*. We will return to Davis's novel in a later chapter in order to address more closely the racial and gender dynamics of his text and its relation to race and gender politics in the United States.

171. John H. Russell, Memorandum on the Judicial System of Haiti, March 16, 1920, RG 80, Secretary of the Navy, General Correspondence, 1916–26, box 239, location 5526-254:1, NA. Note that Russell was brigade commander at the time, not yet high commissioner; Daniels was secretary of the navy.

172. Ibid., 4.

173. Ibid., 5.

174. Ibid., 6.

175. Ibid.

176. Memorandum for the Judge Advocate General, June 30, 1920, initialed "E," RG 80, box 240, location 5526-280, NA.

177. Memorandum Re: Military Commissions in Haiti, July 3, 1920, signed "Melling," RG 80, box 240, location 5526-280, NA.

178. Ibid., 4. Melling's memo is especially interesting because it focused so much detailed attention on the act of Congress by which officers and enlisted men of the Navy and Marine Corps were authorized to serve as officers in the Haitian military. The very

fact that the Congress of the United States had had to authorize these men to serve under another government proved, for Melling, that another government not only existed but was acknowledged and recognized by the government of the United States. If these officers and enlisted men were simply to govern Haiti under the authority of the U.S. military government in Haiti, then no special authorization would have been needed. Thus, for Melling, the American-officered Gendarmerie confirmed the illegality of maintaining martial law in Haiti.

179. Norman Poritz, First Lieutenant, Gendarmerie d'Haïti, Intelligence Report for Le Trou, October 31, 1921, RG 127, entry 165, box 1, folder 10-3: "Summary of Gendarmerie — 1921," NA.

180. District Commander, Aux Cayes, to Department Commander, Department of the South, December 22, 1921, RG 127, entry 165, box 1, folder 10-3: "Summary of Gendarmerie — 1921," NA.

CHAPTER 4

1. Craige, *Black Bagdad*, 195–96. For another account of a marine out of control with a gun at the waterfront, see Miller Log, September 7, 1915.

2. Craige, *Black Bagdad*, 90.

3. Admiral Henry T. Mayo, "Conclusions," reprinted in Senate Hearings, 1:435. The Mayo Court's conclusions cited only "two unjustifiable homicides" and "16 other serious acts of violence," all of which had been properly prosecuted prior to the naval inquiry.

4. Schmidt, *The United States Occupation of Haiti*, 122.

5. Craige, *Cannibal Cousins*, 87.

6. Craige, *Black Bagdad*, 193.

7. Ibid., 82–83.

8. Ibid., 193–94.

9. Ibid., 194.

10. Ibid., 197.

11. Commanding officers expressed concern about marines who spent long periods of time isolated from other Americans. Brigade Commander John Russell noted, for example, that "too long a period in Haiti, especially at isolated posts is apt to cause one to loose ones [*sic*] perspective." Brigade Commander to Major General Commandant, Memorandum re: "Length of tour of duty of officers and enlisted men attached to the Gendarmerie d'Haïti," December 13, 1920, RG 127, box 1, location 1375, NA.

12. Craige, *Black Bagdad*, 88.

13. Harold H. Utley, "The Tactics and Techniques of Small Wars," unpublished typescript, Harold H. Utley Papers, PPC.

14. Ibid., 5 (capitalization as in the original).

15. Schmidt, *Maverick Marine*, 74–95.

16. Utley, "The Tactics and Techniques of Small Wars," 8.

17. Testimony of General Smedley D. Butler, Senate Hearings, 1:518.

18. The punitive approach to military action in Central America was especially urged by Assistant Secretary of State F. M. Huntington Wilson. In 1912, for example, Wilson urged that swift and decisive military action should be brought to bear on Nicaraguan rebels so that "the moral effect upon the whole revolution-ridden region of Central America and the Caribbean should be greatest." Quoted in Challener, *Admi-*

rals, Generals and American Foreign Policy, 306. Hans Schmidt refers to "Huntington Wilson's moral purgation of Nicaragua." See Schmidt, *Maverick Marine*, 51–52, 62.

19. *Gendarmerie News* (Port-au-Prince) 1, no. 3 (November 1, 1921): 7, copy in Secretary of the Navy, General Correspondence, RG 80, box 240, location 5526-327:18, NA.

20. Vandegrift, *Once a Marine*, 49; Schmidt, *Maverick Marine*, 84–85.

21. Maj. Gen. Commandant to the Secretary of the Navy, November 2, 1920, typescript memorandum, RG 80, box 240, location 5526-321, NA. This memo states: "There is evidence that Maj. Clark H. Wells . . . on or about November 2, 1918, . . . gave orders over the telephone from Cape Haitian to Frederick C. Baker, at that time a private in the Marine Corps and a captain in the Gendarmerie d'Haïti, to 'bump off,' meaning to kill, prisoners; that on or about March 19, 1919, he gave Capt. George D. Hamilton orders to kill any man Capt. Hamilton thought to be a Caco and not to bring him to prison; that, at diverse times, during the period November 1, 1918, to March 31, 1919, he gave orders to his juniors to suppress reports of any unfavorable conditions in regards to the state of peace in the department of the North."

22. Simple cross-cultural misunderstanding also contributed to this dynamic. For example, see Chapter 2 re: *neg*, the Creole word for "guy."

23. Testimony of Frederick Spear, Senate Hearings, 1:589.

24. Some Haitians identified marines' racism in just these terms, as actuated by "motives of a personal nature." See RG 80, various documents, location 5526, NA.

25. Conversation with Edwidge Balutansky and Kathleen Balutansky, Port-au-Prince, Haiti, October 31, 1998. Note that according to Haitian law, by marrying into a Haitian family, one acquires Haitian citizenship. Adolph Miller noted the marriage of "Ex-Pvt. King" to a "very wealthy Haitian girl." See Miller Log, November 29, 1916.

26. Laguerre, *Military and Society*, 71–72.

27. Nicholls, "Rural Protest and Peasant Revolt," 180, 261n; Nicholls, *Dessalines to Duvalier*, 284n; Gaillard, *Les cents jours*, 58n.

28. Charlemagne Péralte to British Consul, copy included in Albertus W. Catlin, Daily Diary Reports, July 5, 1919, RG 45, entry WA-7, box 742, NA.

29. Nicholls, "Rural Protest and Peasant Revolt," 180.

30. Ibid., 185. By "the masses," Nicholls means "the middle class of peasants rather than the very poor" (180). The *rural* base of the Cacos must also be emphasized for, as Nicholls tells us, in 1867 Salnave counted among his supporters "the urban proletariat and sub-proletariat, particularly . . . women" (179).

31. On the significance of regionalism prior to the U.S. occupation of 1915–34, see Trouillot, *Haiti, State against Nation*, 96–97. See also Laguerre, *Military and Society*, 70, and Nicholls, "Rural Protest and Peasant Revolt," 183–84.

32. Plummer, *Haiti and the Great Powers*, 163–64; Nicholls, *Dessalines to Duvalier*, 142.

33. Laguerre, *Military and Society*, 70.

34. To this end, Caperton urgently requested that another regiment of marines be sent to Haiti in addition to the regiment that was already en route on board the USS *Connecticut*. Admiral Caperton to Secretary of the Navy, August 2, 1915, *FRUS*, 1915, 477.

35. Wirkus and Dudley, *The White King of La Gonave*, 28.

36. Admiral Caperton to the Secretary of the Navy, August 16, 1915, *FRUS*, 1915, 489.

37. Regimental histories described the Cacos as "soldiers of fortune." See, for example, Kane, *A Brief History of the 2d Marines*, 7.

38. Admiral Caperton to the Secretary of the Navy, August 16, 1915, *FRUS*, 1915, 489. Caperton included this in a report, which was then forwarded by the acting secretary of the navy, W. S. Benson, to the secretary of state, September 11, 1915.

39. Admiral Caperton to the Secretary of the Navy, November 29, 1915, *FRUS*, 1915, 496.

40. Chandler Campbell, Memorandum to Commanding Officer (Colonel Cole), November 28, 1915, folder 2: "Operations of 13th Co., Artillery BN, Haiti, S-N15," Alex O. Campbell Papers, PC 55, PPC.

41. Ibid.

42. Indeed, Hinche was a center of Caco activity in the later stages of the war. Gaillard, *Hinche mise en croix*. In 1996, several residents and former residents of Hinche stated that either they or their parents had been adamantly opposed to the presence of U.S. marines when they first arrived, though relations improved in the years following the end of the war against the Cacos. One woman described a fistfight between her father and a marine who threatened the household. Hector LaPaix, interview by the author, tape recording, Hinche, August 20, 1996; Escan Jean-Marie and Hector LaPaix, interview by the author, tape recording, Hinche, August 21, 1996; Remy Garcia, interview by the author, tape recording, Hinche, August 21, 1996; Anonymous (female), interview by the author, Hinche, August 22, 1996.

43. Miller Log, October 11, 1915.

44. Chandler Campbell, "Diary 13th Company," folder 1: "Diary of Activities, Haiti, 1915," Alex O. Campbell Papers, PC 55, PPC.

45. Ibid., November 3, 4, 12, 1915.

46. Monseigneur Jan, *Monographie des paroisses du Cap-Haïtien* (n.d.), quoted in Gaillard, *Premier écrasement du cacoïsme*, 162.

47. Eli K. Cole, Field Order, No. 9, October 29, 1915, folder 1: "Diary of Activities in Haiti, 1915 [with enclosures]," Alex O. Campbell Papers, PC 55, PPC.

48. Senate Hearings, 2:1685–86. The correspondent worked for *Le Matin*.

49. Gaillard, *Premier écrasement du cacoïsme*, 167.

50. Wirkus and Dudley, *The White King of La Gonave*, 91. The legacy of bitter conflict continues between families that supported the revolutionary activity of the Cacos and those that experienced their wrath after collaborating with the marines. This was addressed by the audience following the panel on Reconstructing Histories at the Haitian Studies Association third annual conference, Tufts University, October 18, 1991.

51. Wirkus and Dudley, *The White King of La Gonave*, 87–88.

52. In contrast, in his small-wars manual, Harold Utley included such coercive measures in his list of methods "used in the past by civilized nations in like situations," which could reasonably serve as a guide for U.S. action. His list included, for example, "the killing or wounding or capture of those opposed to us and the destruction of their property; the destruction of the property of those who aid or abet those hostile to us; the laying waste of entire sections inhabited by people generally supporting those hostile to us." Utley, "The Tactics and Techniques of Small Wars," 5.

53. Caperton to Daniels, November 19, 1915, *FRUS*, 1915, 495.

54. Merwin H. Silverthorn, Oral History Transcript, 170, HMD. At the same time, Silverthorn asserted that the Cacos were "out-and-out outlaws." He stated that he based this opinion on his "contact with many marines who served and chased them." Silverthorn arrived in Haiti in 1923, well after the Cacos were vanquished.

55. Wirkus and Dudley, *The White King of La Gonave*, 21.

56. Ibid., 22.

57. Testimony of Major General George Barnett, Senate Hearings, 1:423.

58. Caperton to Daniels, November 19, 1915, *FRUS*, 1915, 495.

59. Chandler Campbell to his mother, November 14, 1915, folder 1: "Diary of Activities, Haiti, 1915," Alex O. Campbell Papers, PC 55, PPC.

60. Daniels to Caperton, November 20, 1915, *FRUS, 1915*, 493.

61. Silverthorn, Oral History Transcript, 142.

62. Miller Log, October 3, 1915. Married marines also took advantage of the arrangement.

63. Laguerre, *Military and Society*, 71. "Gendarmerie captains normally commanded districts, Gendarmerie lieutenants normally commanded sub-districts, and noncommissioned officers were placed at outposts 'at strategic points.'" See also McCrocklin, *Garde d'Haïti*, 82.

64. Other marines in the Gendarmerie continued to serve primarily military roles with their units.

65. Silverthorn, Oral History Transcript, 147.

66. John Houston Craige and Faustin Wirkus, to name only two examples.

67. Memorandum by Jordan H. Stabler, October 26, 1917, RG 80, box 233, location 5526-33:2, NA. The brigade commander asked Dartiguenave whether he had approved this communication, and the president stated "that the minister had no authority whatsoever to make any such complaint." Brigade Commander to the Bureau of Operations, Navy Department, November 3, 1917, RG 80, box 233, location 5526-33:2, NA.

68. Silverthorn, Oral History Transcript, 142.

69. Miller Log, October 3, 1915.

70. Silverthorn, Oral History Transcript, 145.

71. Ibid., 152.

72. Gaillard, *La république autoritaire*, 274.

73. Schmidt, *The United States Occupation of Haiti*, 100–101.

74. Testimony of L. Ton Evans, Senate Hearings, 1:164.

75. Testimony of Capsine Altidor, Senate Hearings, 2:911.

76. Testimony of L. Ton Evans, Senate Hearings, 1:166, 164, respectively.

77. Ibid., 166.

78. Ibid., 164–65.

79. Ibid., 163–64. Roger Gaillard corroborates Evans's observation in his multivolume history of the occupation, *Les blancs débarquent*.

80. Testimony of Brigadier General Albertus W. Catlin, Senate Hearings, 1:651. Hans Schmidt has pointed out that this was precisely the area in which the occupation required roads most urgently, because this was the area of greatest Caco activity. See Schmidt, *The United States Occupation of Haiti*, 101.

81. Testimony of Major General George Barnett, Senate Hearings, 1:431; see also testimony of Brigadier General Albertus W. Catlin, Senate Hearings, 1:667–69.

82. "Tabulation Statement of All Convictions in the Provost Court, Port de Paix, Haiti, from September 1915 [to March 14, 1916]," RG 80, box 233, location 5526-39, NA. This is one of several documents with the same location number.

83. Bennett Puryear Jr., Oral History Transcript, 73, HMD.

84. Burke Davis, *Marine!*, 45. Labor violence was not limited to work settings under the administration of marines. L. Ton Evans testified that an American contractor with the Haitian American Sugar Company boasted to him about his own "brutality toward those who worked under him, and killed one or two." Testimony of L. Ton Evans, Senate Hearings, 1:241.

85. "Memoir on the Political, Economic, and Financial Conditions Existing in the Re-

public of Haiti under the American Occupation, by the Delegates to the United States of the Union Patriotique d'Haïti," Senate Hearings, 1:14. The delegates presented this memoir to the State Department and to the Senate Foreign Relations Committee.

86. Gerald C. Thomas, Oral History Transcript, 376–77, cited in Santelli, *A Brief History of the 8th Marines*, 9.

87. Santelli, *A Brief History of the 8th Marines*, 9. In March 1920, L. Ton Evans informed Secretary of the Navy Daniels, "conditions have been allowed to grow rapidly worse . . . [so that the Caco forces are] having the sympathy more and more of the moderate, intelligent, and educated and better class of Haitians, who have lost respect for and confidence in our American occupation." See L. Ton Evans to Josephus Daniels, reprinted in Senate Hearings, 1:137.

88. Testimony of Brigadier General Albertus Catlin, Senate Hearings, 1:666; Wise, *A Marine Tells It to You*, 305. Péralte claimed to have 30,000 followers; Catlin estimated that he had closer to 5,000, not all armed. See Senate Hearings, 1:428, 652.

89. Laguerre, *Voodoo and Politics in Haiti*, 97–98.

90. Lewis B. Puller, Oral History Transcript, 44, HMD. Internal naval investigations uncovered evidence that Lieutenant Colonel Alexander S. Williams, Gendarmerie commandant from May 2, 1918, through July 18, 1919, was said to have instructed at least one Gendarmerie officer "that no Provost prisoners were wanted" and that if he "found that any of the prisoners were 'Cacos' and actually had arms in their possession to do away with them." Major General Commandant (John A. Lejeune) to the Secretary of the Navy (Josephus Daniels), November 2, 1920, RG 80, box 240, location 5526-321, NA. This memorandum stated that there was "insufficient evidence for bringing Lieutenant Colonel Williams to trial." It also named other Marine Corps–Gendarmerie officers implicated in passing on orders to "bump off" Cacos, including, notably, Clark Wells.

91. Link, *Woodrow Wilson and the Progressive Era*, 102.

92. See, for example, Hoganson, *Fighting for American Manhood*, 134. Sources for figures on the number of Haitians killed are given in Chapter 1, n. 2.

93. Ivan W. Miller, Oral History Transcript, 31, HMD.

94. Lemuel C. Shepherd, Oral History Transcript, 197–201, 366, HMD.

95. For an excellent account of this process in another context, see Lepore, *The Name of War: King Phillip's War and the Origins of American Identity*.

96. Bederman, *Manliness and Civilization*; Kaplan, "Black and Blue on San Juan Hill"; Hoganson, *Fighting for American Manhood*; Jeffords, *The Remasculinization of America*.

97. Wirkus and Dudley, *The White King of La Gonave*, 64.

98. Ibid., 102.

99. James Weldon Johnson, *Along This Way*, 349.

100. Wirkus and Dudley, *The White King of La Gonave*, 64.

101. Ibid., 40.

102. Ibid., 66–67, 68.

103. Burke Davis, *Marine!*, 43.

104. "Sweaty, backbreaking work" is from Gerald C. Thomas, "Memoir, 1919–41," 5, Gerald C. Thomas Papers, PC 1447, PPC; "jitters" is from Craige, *Black Bagdad*, 229.

105. Burke Davis, *Marine!*, 43.

106. Wirkus and Dudley, *The White King of La Gonave*, 20.

107. Ibid., 50.

108. John H. Russell, Confidential Order, October 15, 1919, reprinted in Senate Hearings, 1:429.

109. John H. Russell, "New Address to the Population," Senate Hearings, 1:429.

110. John H. Russell, Brigade Commander, to the Commanding Officers of the 2nd Regiment and the 8th Regiment, September 15, 1920, RG 80, box 237, location 5526-39:338, NA. Even these orders placed the marines' activities in a relatively benign light by mentioning the burning of unoccupied houses and the destruction of property without mentioning the killings that sometimes went along with these activities. In contrast, Haitians testified before the Senate Committee that family members had been shot and left to die inside the houses as they burned. See, for example, Testimony of Mme. Celicourt Rosier, Senate Hearings, 2:909–11.

111. John H. Russell, Brigade Commander, to the Commanding Officers of the 2nd Regiment and the 8th Regiment, September 15, 1920, RG 80, box 237, location 5526-39:338, NA.

112. Major Edwin N. McClellan, Senate Hearings, 1:433. USMC major McClellan participated in the hearings "as custodian of certain reports and correspondence taken from Navy and Marine Corps files." Senate Hearings, 1:3.

113. Testimony of Major General George Barnett, Senate Hearings, 1:425.

114. Major General Commandant (Barnett) to Colonel John H. Russell, October 2, 1919, George Barnett Papers, PPC.

115. See also Testimony of Frederick Wise, Senate Hearings, 1:304; Wise, A Marine Tells It to You, 304.

116. Testimony of Heraux Belloni, Senate Hearings, 2:916–20.

117. "Confidential Memorandum, Major Thomas C. Turner to Brigade Commander (Russell), Re: Report of Investigation of certain irregularities alleged to have been committed by officers and enlisted men in the Republic of Haiti," reprinted in Senate Hearings, 1:472.

118. Ibid.

119. McCrocklin, Garde d'Haïti, 100–101.

120. Allan Millett, Semper Fidelis, 199; Gerald C. Thomas, Oral History Transcript, 68–79; Wise, A Marine Tells It to You, 301–35.

121. Burke Davis, Marine!, 44–45.

122. Emphasis added. The paragraph from which this comes reads as follows: "At 5 a.m. the morning of the 15th captured Marius a chief and delegate of Charlemagne, with a Gras rifle 5 r of ammunition and a letter from Charlemagne and also a letter written to General Adema. I judged that there was a band close by and reconnoitered and ran upon 25–30 Cacos under General Adema and after a running fight up a mountain five Cacos were killed and as Marius was proving a hindrance I killed him. There were also several wounded as noted by the blood that was seen on the stones on the mountainsides." Capt. H. Hanneken G. d'H. to Department Commander, Dept. of the Cape, February 15, 1919, ms. memorandum, RG 127, box 1, folder: "Papers taken from locked drawer . . . ," location 173, NA. A note in the file explains: "Papers taken from locked drawer in the Dept. Commander's desk at Cape Haitian and a report from Capt. Hanneken taken from Personal files, Wells, at Cape."

123. Testimony of L. Ton Evans, Senate Hearings, 1:181.

124. Ibid., 245, 247.

125. Ibid., 248–49, 247, respectively. USMC sergeant Charles E. Kenny was commissioned as a captain in the Gendarmerie. "Enlisted Men on Duty as Officers of the Haitien Gendarmerie," December 2, 1918, RG 127, box 81, location 53094, NA.

126. Testimony of L. Ton Evans, Senate Hearings, 1:247.

127. Ibid., 246.

128. Allan Millett, *Semper Fidelis*, 199; Millett notes: "The basic source on the atrocity question is the collection of documents and testimony of investigating officer Major T. C. Turner and Colonel A. S. Williams," Senate Hearings, 1:457–509, 595–606.

129. Josephus Daniels, Diary, August 28, 1920, in Cronon, *The Cabinet Diaries of Josephus Daniels*, 553. See also Inman, *Trailing the Conquistadores*, 117–18.

130. Individual officers also prided themselves on their own standards of decency, and deplored the misbehavior of enlisted men as so many blemishes on the fine reputation of their corps. See, for example, Miller Log, May 3, 1916.

131. Craige, *Cannibal Cousins*, 124.

132. "U.S. Troops Attack Haitian Girls," *Chicago Defender*, May 15, 1920. The Records of the U.S. Marine Corps contain complaints of Haitian citizens against the occupation and some material regarding investigations of these complaints. One such case involved two young girls, Rose and Nanine Guadagnoli, who complained of being harassed at gunpoint by several marines. See Brigade Intelligence Officer to Brigade Commander, August 19, 1919, "Investigation of the Guadagnoli Case," RG 127, box 3, folder 60-0: "Investigations 1915–1922," NA.

133. Burks went on to write thirty-five books and over 1,200 stories. As we shall see, he earned an impressive income from his writing during each year of the Great Depression. See Chapter 5.

134. Burks, "Black Medicine," 152–53, 146.

135. Ibid., 146.

136. John H. Russell to Maj. General George Barnett, October 17, 1919, reprinted in Senate Hearings, 1:428.

137. Burke Davis, *Marine!*, 44.

138. Lester A. Dessez, Oral History Transcript, 25, HMD.

139. Burke Davis, *Marine!*, 44.

140. Ibid.

141. Santelli, *A Brief History of the 8th Marines*, 7. Julian C. Smith recalled that an interpreter in Miragoane told him, in 1915–16, "that when Christmas time came he could take me out and get me a nice meal of human flesh if I wanted it for Christmas. He said, 'There'll be plenty of them cooked out in the hills.' I said, 'How do you tell?' He said, 'You can tell human flesh. It bubbles all over when you boil it.'" Julian C. Smith, Oral History Transcript, 35, HMD.

142. USMC private Samuel I. Williston was commissioned as a second lieutenant in the Gendarmerie. USMC private Philip Neuhaus was commissioned as a first lieutenant in the Gendarmerie. It is not clear which Kelly Wirkus was referring to. First Sergeant Patrick F. Kelly was commissioned as a Gendarmerie captain; Private Julian A. Kelly was commissioned as a second lieutenant. "Enlisted Men on Duty as Officers of the Haitien Gendarmerie," December 2, 1918, RG 127, box 81, location 53094, NA.

143. Wirkus and Dudley, *The White King of La Gonave*, 48.

144. Craige, *Black Bagdad*, 231.

145. Ibid.

146. Ibid., 230.

147. Wirkus and Dudley, *The White King of La Gonave*, 108, 111.

148. Ibid., 108–9.

149. Ibid., 108.

150. Ibid., 109.

151. Ibid., 108.

152. Scottman, "A Marine Remembers Haiti," 22–23.

153. Craige, *Black Bagdad*, 201–3.

154. Wirkus and Dudley, *The White King of La Gonave*, 116, 123–24. Carzal is a town in Central Haiti near Arcahie.

155. Campbell, "Diary 13th Company," November 8, 1915, Campbell Papers, PPC.

156. Testimony of L. Ton Evans, Senate Hearings, 1:197.

157. Wirkus and Dudley, *The White King of La Gonave*, 74.

158. For another example, see Santelli, *A Brief History of the 8th Marines*, 9–10.

159. McCrocklin, *Garde d'Haïti*, 117. Although this lore has passed into official histories of the occupation, the effectiveness of Hanneken's and Button's disguises may have had a great deal more to do with the cover of night and the seventeen Haitians who surrounded them on this expedition than is generally acknowledged.

160. Craige, *Cannibal Cousins*, 67.

161. Wise, *A Marine Tells It to You*, 321.

162. Schmidt, *The United States Occupation of Haiti*, 102.

163. Craige, *Cannibal Cousins*, 67.

164. Ibid., 72–73.

165. Craige, *Black Bagdad*, 99–102.

166. Arthur J. Burks's "Voodoo" and "Black Medicine" originally appeared in *Weird Tales* magazine, December 1924 and August 1925, respectively; both are reprinted in Burks, *Black Medicine*, 120–25 and 144–84.

167. Burks, "Voodoo," 125.

168. Burks, *Black Medicine*, 122, 135, 137, 166, 170. These references are from Burks's stories entitled "Black Medicine," "Voodoo," "Thus Spake the Prophetess," and "Luisma's Return."

169. Burks, "Black Medicine," 152–53, 145.

170. Ibid., 153.

171. Burks, "Voodoo," 121.

172. Ibid.

173. In light of the significance of clothing and the troubling implications of cross-national and cross-racial playacting that I have described, it is especially interesting that marines staged blackface minstrel shows in Haiti. Marines of the Second Regiment, present in Haiti from 1915 to 1934, left a record of such entertainment in the form of a program announcing "The Marine Masqueraders present Coontown Nights" by the "Burnt Cork Company." Folder 2, William Rossiter Papers, PC 113, PPC. On blackface minstrelsy as a manifestation of fascination with blacks and black culture and as a means to produce whiteness, in different U.S. contexts, see Roediger, *The Wages of Whiteness*, 115–27; Lott, *Love and Theft*, especially 97; Erenberg, *Steppin' Out*, 73; Lipsitz, *Time Passages*, 64.

174. Burks, "Voodoo," 120.

175. Ibid., 121.

176. Ibid.

177. Burks, "Black Medicine," 179.

178. Ibid., 151.

179. Ibid., 145.

180. Burks, "Voodoo," 121. Burks's language resonates, in different ways, with that of Stephen Alexis and Smedley Butler. Alexis, in his novel of protest against the occupation, *Le nègre masqué*, wrote, "One morning, mechanical man, you're going to wake up," quoted in Dash, *Haiti and the United States*, 39. In *War Is a Racket*, Butler wrote,

"Boys with a normal viewpoint were taken out of the fields and offices and factories and classrooms and put into the ranks. . . . We used them for a couple of years and trained them to think nothing at all of killing or of being killed" (28).

181. Burks, "Voodoo," 121–22.

182. Ibid., 123.

183. Burks, "Black Medicine," 170.

184. Burks, "Voodoo," 124.

185. Ibid., 125.

CHAPTER 5

1. Seligmann, "The Conquest of Haiti," 35.

2. Hixson, *Moorfield Storey and the Abolitionist Tradition*, 72.

3. *Crisis* 10 (September 1915): 232; 11 (November 1915): 30–32. Newspapers included the New York *Evening Post* and the Springfield *Republican*. Blassingame, "The Press and American Intervention," 39. See also *Literary Digest* 51 (September 4, 1915): 456–57, and *Current Opinion* 59 (October 1915): 223–25.

4. *Nation* 104 (February 8, 1917): 152–53; cf. *Nation* 101 (September 13, 1915): 371, and (September 30, 1915): 397.

5. Blassingame, "The Press and American Intervention," 27–43.

6. Plummer, "The Afro-American Response," 130–31; "U.S. Troops Attack Haitian Girls," *Chicago Defender*, May 15, 1920.

7. Plummer, "The Afro-American Response," 131.

8. Ibid.

9. Seligmann, "The Conquest of Haiti," 35. For citizens' responses, see, for example, the correspondence files of the secretary of the navy, RG 80, NA.

10. Levy, *James Weldon Johnson*, 203, 205; Plummer, "The Afro-American Response," 132.

11. O'Neill, *The Emperor Jones*, 1030–61.

12. Levy, *James Weldon Johnson*, 71, 152, 154, 179. Johnson was also a former school principal and a lawyer.

13. Ibid., 109, 113.

14. Ibid., 117–18, 155; James Weldon Johnson, *Along This Way*, 276–89. The Navy also participated in the Nicaragua intervention, which took place from August to October 1912; see Allan Millett, *Semper Fidelis*, 170.

15. Levy, *James Weldon Johnson*, 202.

16. *New York Age*, August 5, 1915; Plummer, "The Afro-American Response," 127.

17. W. E. B. Du Bois, *Crisis* 10 (September 1915): 232; 11 (November 1915): 30–32; Plummer, "The Afro-American Response," 131.

18. W. E. B. Du Bois to Woodrow Wilson, August 3, 1915, reprinted in *The Correspondence of W. E. B. Du Bois*, 1:212. On NAACP efforts to persuade the Wilson administration to change its course in Haiti immediately after the occupation, see also Kellogg, *NAACP*, 1:284–88.

19. Hixson, *Moorfield Storey and the Abolitionist Tradition*, 72.

20. Levy, *James Weldon Johnson*, 103. Washington subsidized the paper but did not publicize that fact.

21. Washington, "Haiti and the United States," 681; Blassingame, "The Press and American Intervention," 36; Washington, "Speech to the National Negro Business League," August 18, 1915, reprinted in Wintz, *African American Political Thought*, 77.

22. W. E. B. Du Bois, "Pan-Africa and New Racial Philosophy," 247, 262.

23. Jervis Anderson, *A. Philip Randolph*, 77, 83.

24. Fort-Whiteman, "Nemesis," 23–25. This was the first issue with this title; Randolph and Owen took over the *Hotel Messenger* from its previous publisher.

25. Jervis Anderson, *This Was Harlem*, 106, and *A. Philip Randolph*, 101.

26. Marcus Garvey, "Address to UNIA Supporters in Philadelphia," October 21, 1919, reprinted in Wintz, *African American Political Thought*, 200.

27. Levy, *James Weldon Johnson*, 202–4.

28. Ibid.

29. Johnson, "What the United States Has Accomplished," 266.

30. Quoted in Plummer, "The Afro-American Response," 132.

31. James Weldon Johnson, "What the United States Has Accomplished," 266.

32. James Weldon Johnson, "The American Occupation," 237.

33. Ibid., 236.

34. Dantes Bellegarde, quoted in Logan, "James Weldon Johnson and Haiti," 396.

35. James Weldon Johnson, *Along This Way*, 348. Johnson says he urged Sylvain to form an organization along the lines of the NAACP.

36. Plummer, "The Afro-American Response," 133; Hixson, *Moorfield Storey and the Abolitionist Tradition*, 273, 272.

37. Neverdon-Morton, *Afro-American Women of the South*, 200; Plummer, "The Afro-American Response," 133n.

38. Levy, *James Weldon Johnson*, 208–9.

39. Ibid., 209; James Weldon Johnson, *Along This Way*, 359.

40. Levy, *James Weldon Johnson*, 210.

41. James Weldon Johnson, "The American Occupation," 236–37.

42. Ibid., 237.

43. James Weldon Johnson, "What the United States Has Accomplished," 265, 266.

44. Ibid., 265.

45. James Weldon Johnson, "Government of, by, and for the National City Bank," 297.

46. Inman, *Through Santo Domingo and Haiti*, 59; James Weldon Johnson, "Government of, by, and for the National City Bank," 295.

47. Ibid.

48. James Weldon Johnson, "What the United States Has Accomplished," 265.

49. Ibid., 267.

50. James Weldon Johnson, *Along This Way*, 351.

51. James Weldon Johnson, "The Truth about Haiti," 218, and *Along This Way*, 352.

52. Levy, *James Weldon Johnson*, 111.

53. Carby, *Race Men*, 9–41. Hazel Carby examines the articulation of black masculinity and leadership qualities, embodied in that term, in the work of W. E. B. Du Bois and Cornel West.

54. James Weldon Johnson, "The Haitian People," 345.

55. Ibid., 347.

56. Ibid.

57. Ibid., 346.

58. Ibid.

59. Ibid., 345–46.

60. Ibid., 346 (emphasis in the original).

61. Ibid.

62. Ibid., 345.

63. Ibid.

64. Ibid.

65. Ibid., 346.

66. James Weldon Johnson, *Along This Way*, 352.

67. O'Neill saw his experience as an important resource for his drama. In 1914 he wrote to a professor of drama with whom he hoped to work, "if varied experience be a help to a prospective dramatist I may justly claim that asset for I have worked my way around the world as a seaman on merchant vessels and held various positions in different foreign countries." Eugene G. O'Neill to George Pierce Baker, July 16, 1914, in Cargill, Fagin, and Fisher, *O'Neill and His Plays*, 19–20.

68. Frenz, *Eugene O'Neill*, 10.

69. Gelb and Gelb, *O'Neill*, 134.

70. O'Neill to James and Ella O'Neill, December 25, 1909, in O'Neill, *Selected Letters*, 19–20.

71. O'Neill to Barrett H. Clark, 1919, in Clark, *Eugene O'Neill*, 10. See also O'Neill to Waldo Frank, April 1917, in O'Neill, *Selected Letters*, 78–79.

72. Pfister, *Staging Depth*, 106.

73. Ibid.; Sheaffer, *O'Neill*, 239.

74. A play about Christophe by William Edgar Easton, *Christophe: A Tragedy in Prose of Imperial Haiti*, had been staged in Harlem in 1912, but it is not clear whether O'Neill knew about that performance. Easton had also written a play about Dessalines. Errol Hill, *Black Heroes*, 4.

75. Barrett Clark, *Eugene O'Neill*, 29.

76. Gelb and Gelb, *O'Neill*, 294.

77. Ibid., 439.

78. Ibid., 438–39.

79. It is not clear whether Croak was speaking of Simon Sam, president of Haiti from 1896 to 1902, or about Vilbrun Guillaume Sam, whose assassination in July 1915 precipitated the U.S. invasion.

80. Inman, *Trailing the Conquistadores*, 103.

81. Sheaffer, *O'Neill*, 29.

82. O'Neill, *The Emperor Jones*, 1030.

83. Gelb and Gelb, *O'Neill*, 446; Sheaffer, *O'Neill*, 33. Charles Gilpin was awarded a William E. Harmon Award "for Distinguished Achievement among Negroes" for his performance in the play. Reynolds and Wright, *Against the Odds*, 13.

84. Pfister, *Staging Depth*, 121–37; Jervis Anderson, *This Was Harlem*, 114.

85. Heywood Broun of the *Tribune*, quoted in Sheaffer, *O'Neill*, 33; *New Republic*, quoted in Jervis Anderson, *This Was Harlem*, 114.

86. O'Neill, *The Emperor Jones*, 1033.

87. Ibid., 1033, 1034.

88. Ibid., 1034.

89. On Douglas's illustrations of *The Emperor Jones* for *Theatre Arts Monthly*, see Kirschke, *Aaron Douglas*, 84–85.

90. O'Neill, *The Emperor Jones*, 1031.

91. Ibid., 1032.

92. The phrase is from James Weldon Johnson, commenting on another play in *Black Manhattan*, 183. See also Pfister, *Staging Depth*, 132.

93. Pullman porters enjoyed a good deal of status as "folk heroes" and "pillars of society" in African American communities. See Harris, *Keeping the Faith*, 15.

94. O'Neill, *The Emperor Jones*, 1035.

95. Prichard, *Where Black Rules White*, 248, 263.

96. O'Neill, *The Emperor Jones*, 1033.

97. Ibid.

98. Ibid., 1036.

99. See Chapter 2.

100. Quoted in Barrett Clark, *Eugene O'Neill*, 83.

101. O'Neill, *The Hairy Ape*, 121.

102. O'Neill, *The Emperor Jones*, 1035.

103. Ibid.

104. Cooper, *A Voice from the South*, 103–4. For a discussion of Cooper's analysis of internal and external colonization, as reflected in this quote, see Carby, *Reconstructing Womanhood*, 105.

105. O'Neill, *The Emperor Jones*, 1035. DuBose Heyward, who wrote the scenario for the film based on O'Neill's play, attempted to make this association more explicit in the screen version, which was produced in 1933. He explained, "I added the character of the earlier Jones, as I had imagined it, and by throwing his character into contact with the disintegrating power of our white civilization, broke Jones down from the rather simple Southern Negro to the shrewd, grafting Negro of the play. I rather enjoyed making him a black counterpart of our own big business pirate." In the context of the early 1930s, this critique of U.S. American civilization was more commonplace, but Heyward developed it by drawing on elements of the story that were fully present in O'Neill's playscript. DuBose Heyward, quoted in William Lewis and Max J. Herzberg, "Study Guide for the Screen Production of the Emperor Jones," Production File: *The Emperor Jones*, AMPAS.

106. O'Neill, *The Emperor Jones*, 1034.

107. O'Neill to James and Ella O'Neill, December 25, 1909, in O'Neill, *Selected Letters*, 20.

108. Gelb and Gelb, *O'Neill*, 135.

109. O'Neill to James and Ella O'Neill, November 9, 1909, in O'Neill, *Selected Letters*, 19.

110. Quoted in Gelb and Gelb, *O'Neill*, 198.

111. Clifford, "Negrophilia," 901.

112. Eugene O'Neill to Arthur Hobson Quinn, April 3, 1925, in O'Neill, *Selected Letters*, 195.

113. Carby, *Race Men*, 45–83.

114. On the "triangulation" of domestic racial struggles in an imperial context, see Kaplan, "Imperial Triangles."

115. Prichard, *Where Black Rules White*, 357, 368.

116. Carby, *Race Men*, 77–79. VèVè Clark has also argued that *The Emperor Jones* "reframed the action [of the Haitian Revolution] in psychological rather than political terms." "Haiti's Tragic Overture," 8.

117. O'Neill, *The Emperor Jones*, 1047 (hat), 1049 (coat), 1052 (shoes), 1055 (pants).

118. Pfister, *Staging Depth*, 130.

119. Thanks to Gail Bederman for suggesting this phrase.

120. Gelb and Gelb, *O'Neill*, 448.

121. Ibid., 652.

122. See, for example, Rampersad, *The Life of Langston Hughes*, 186.

123. For radio, see Gelb and Gelb, *O'Neill*, 720; for film (United Artists 1933), see Orlandello, *O'Neill on Film*, 51–65; for opera, see Lawrence Gilman, "The Emperor Jones as Opera," *New York Herald Tribune*, January 8, 1933; for puppetry, see Helen Lieb-

man, photographs, box 145, folder 2581, Eugene O'Neill Papers, Yale Collection of American Literature, Beinecke Rare Book and Manuscript Library, Yale University, New Haven, Conn.

124. O'Neill, *Emperor Jones*, 1034. In the film version, the production code barred a certain scene, depicting activity only alluded to in the play, from being shown on screen because it depicted a black man (Jones) killing a white man (the prison guard).

125. Jervis Anderson, *This Was Harlem*, 114.

126. Quoted in W. E. B. Du Bois, "Criteria of Negro Art," 290.

127. Ibid.

128. George Schuyler, quoted in Lewis, *When Harlem Was in Vogue*, 92.

129. Carby, *Race Men*, 48; Clifford, "Negrophilia," 901–2.

130. Alexander Woollcott, review of *The Emperor Jones*, *New York Times*, November 7, 1920.

131. Kenneth McGowan, review of *The Emperor Jones*, *Globe*, November 4, 1920. McGowan had been a founder of the Provincetown Playhouse; see Lewis, *When Harlem Was in Vogue*, 104.

132. Lawrence Remner, review of *The Hairy Ape*, *New York Herald Tribune*, March 10, 1922. After decades of criticism emphasizing the brilliance and innovation of *The Emperor Jones* for its treatment of "racial psychology," or as O'Neill biographer Barrett Clark put it, for its "magnificent presentment of fear in the breast of a half-civilized Negro," the early 1970s saw a decided turn in critical judgment. Barrett Clark, *Eugene O'Neill*, 72. In 1971 Nathan Huggins, writing about the play in connection with the Harlem Renaissance, argued that "O'Neill used Negro characters in *The Emperor Jones* . . . to make general statements about humanity." Nathan Huggins, *Harlem Renaissance*, 297–98. In 1973 O'Neill biographer Louis Sheaffer echoed Huggins's assessment: "O'Neill was not trying to demonstrate that the American black is only a short step from his African ancestors; he was suggesting something more universal — that an apprehensive primitive being lurks just below the surface of us all." Sheaffer, *O'Neill*, 30. Perhaps, this new interpretation seemed to suggest, when Kenneth McGowan praised Brutus Jones's prayer as "such a dark lyric of the flesh, such a cry of the primitive being," what touched him was the likeness he recognized, intuitively, with his own "primitive being." Yet, McGowan aptly called it "a dark lyric of the flesh," and the proximity of darkness and flesh in the reviewer's language was quite pointed, conscious or not. If "the primitive being" was meant to be universal, he still had to be represented in the figure of a black man in order to evoke the desired response from a white audience in New York in 1920.

133. Hughes, *The Big Sea*, 258–59.

134. Schmidt, *The United States Occupation of Haiti*, 171; Kuser, *Haiti: Its Dawn of Progress after Years in a Night of Revolution*, 93; Harold Davis, *Black Democracy*, 283.

135. As Brenda Plummer puts it, "corporate interest in the black republic flickered." Plummer, *Haiti and the United States*, 110; see also 109–17. On the fortunes and failures of U.S. economic enterprises in occupied Haiti, see also Munro, *The United States and the Caribbean Republics*, 98–107.

136. Plummer, *Haiti and the United States*, 110.

137. Ibid., 282.

138. Dunham, *Island Possessed*, 3.

139. Craige, *Black Bagdad*, 275. See also Miller Log, October 16 and 17, 1915; Merwin H. Silverthorn, Oral History Transcript, 161–62, HMD.

140. Métraux, *Voodoo in Haiti*, 59; Mervin, "A Voodoo Drum from Haiti," 123–25.

141. Frank Resler Crumbie, business cards, box C-1, folder 5, Crumbie Papers.

142. See Frank Crumbie's extensive collection, Crumbie Papers.

143. *La Presse*, March 8, 1930, Scrapbook 6, Crumbie Papers.

144. Craige, *Black Bagdad*, 4.

145. Ibid., 194.

146. Miller Log, September 14, 1915.

147. Miller Log, September 29, 1915.

148. Koltes and Albrecht, "Prevalence of Syphilis in Haiti"; see also the comments of Perceval Thoby, quoted in Balch, *Occupied Haiti*, 119.

149. Balch, *Occupied Haiti*, 135.

150. Quoted in ibid., 116.

151. Ibid., 19. Some marines appear to have used their dollars to pay women to drop their dresses. See, for example, Arthur B. Jacques's collection of photographs, including many shots of women and girls, some with their dresses literally dropped to the ground around their feet. Folder 15: "Photographs," Arthur B. Jacques Papers, PC 873, PPC.

152. Helen Delpar's account of the "enormous vogue of things Mexican," especially between 1927 and 1935, provides an important counterpoint to this story. Delpar argues that while the Mexican vogue "was rooted in cultural issues, . . . it would not have flowered without the marked improvement in diplomatic relations between the two countries that occurred in the late 1920s." Delpar, *The Enormous Vogue of Things Mexican*, 55. In the late 1920s, U.S. "diplomatic relations" with Haiti engaged not an independent government but a client state operating under a U.S. high commissioner. In this context, the "enormous vogue of things Haitian" was fueled by opposition to U.S. rule by Haitians and their U.S. American allies as well as by close and cordial diplomatic relations.

153. For a detailed analysis of the ways in which *National Geographic* magazine effected this erasure of power relations, see Lutz and Collins, *Reading National Geographic*. For the contributions of *National Geographic* to discourses on Haiti and the U.S. occupation there, see "Wards of the United States" (1916); Osterhout, "A Little-Known Marvel" (1920); Gayer, "Hispaniola Rediscovered" (1931); Craige, "Haitian Vignettes" (1934).

154. Robert Jones, *The Shudder Pulps*, 83–84; *The National Cyclopedia of American Biography*, 58:590.

155. Burks, "Luisma's Return," 126; "Thus Spake the Prophetess," 136. In "Voodoo," the story discussed in Chapter 3, Burks seems to have named the evil papaloi, Cerimarie Sam, after Haiti's last president, Vilbrun Guillaume Sam (125). All stories appear in *Black Medicine*.

156. Fossett, "Listening to Empire: Lamont Cranston and 'The Shadow' Go Abroad." See also "Isle of Fear," Radioscript, October 30, 1938, *The Shadow* Radio Series, Street and Smith Editorial Records Collection, Street and Smith Archives, Syracuse University, Syracuse, N.Y.

157. Vandercook, *Black Majesty*, 203. Christophe's manhood resided, in part, in his willingness and ability to do manual labor. In this sense, Vandercook addressed one of the main points of contention between Haitian elites and the U.S. occupation. See, for example, p. 10 and the illustration facing p. 172.

158. Although Vandercook's emphasis on Christophe's manhood in *Black Majesty* contradicted the emphasis of Blaine's cover illustration, Vandercook's later writing did not. His 1938 travel guide, *Caribbee Cruise*, explained the demise of Saint Domingue this

way: "The French planters wanted only healthy blacks and men of good physique, for the work of the cane fields was hard and they were willing to pay accordingly. So they got the pick of Africa. . . . It was the labor of Frankenstein. Heedlessly, incalculably, they built their ruin. The high-priced breed they bought had strength in it and seeds of greatness" (88).

159. Colombian Line advertisement, unidentified newspaper clipping, Scrapbook 3, Crumbie Papers.

160. "A Visit to King Christophe: A Scenic Wallpaper designed by Nicholas de Molas," Katzenbach and Warren, Inc., New York City, n.d., advertising leaflet, 3 pages, Scrapbook 3, Crumbie Papers.

161. Ibid., 2.

162. U.S. Marine Corps, *Citadel of Christophe: Famous Ruler of Haiti*, Schomburg Clipping File: "Haiti—Travel and Description," Schomburg Center for Research on Black Culture, New York.

163. Ibid., 1.

164. Ibid., final page, unnumbered.

165. Ibid.

166. See Lindsay, *This High Name*.

167. Hoover appointed a commission headed by Cameron W. Forbes to look into the status of the occupation. He did not, as Metrotone reported, call for a congressional inquiry. Spector, *W. Cameron Forbes and the Hoover Commission to Haiti*. "Metrotone at the Front in Haiti," Newsreels, vol. 1, no. 222, December 14, 1929, Hearst Metrotone News Collection, UCLA. See also "New Revolt in Haiti," vol. 3, issue 35 (excerpt), December 10, 1929, MGM International Newsreel, UCLA.

168. "Metrotone at the Front in Haiti," Newsreels, vol. 1, no. 222, December 14, 1929, Hearst Metrotone News Collection, UCLA.

169. "U.S. Marines Test Wings over Haiti," Newsreels, vol. 5, no. 248, March 3, 1934, Hearst Metrotone News Collection, UCLA.

170. "Haiti, Coolidge, Batista, Trujillo," Newsreels, CS 205, December 1929 to December 1942, Hearst Metrotone News Collection, UCLA.

171. Beale Davis, *The Goat without Horns*, 123, 176–77.

172. Ibid., 176–77.

173. Davis was right to link Haitian self-assertion in the face of white power with a world-scale effort to overturn white supremacy. The Pan-African Congress that met in Europe in the aftermath of World War I attempted to organize people of African heritage precisely to that end. As a U.S. diplomat and a white Virginian, Davis was probably aware of these developments and their potential consequences for his own racial privilege.

174. Beale Davis, *The Goat without Horns*, 230.

175. Davis was not the first to link the power of Voodoo with the politics of women's maternal role. In the 1917 Lasky-Paramount film *Unconquered*, with Fannie Ward, Voodoo prompts the near murder of a small boy, providing his mother, from whom he has been taken by a court order, with the opportunity to prove her willingness to sacrifice herself (literally). She is saved, and the boy is restored to her. Edward Weitzel, "Lasky-Paramount Releases," *Moving Picture World*, June 2, 1917, clipping, Production File: *Unconquered*, AMPAS.

176. William Seabrook, preface to *The White King of La Gonave*, by Wirkus and Dudley, xii.

177. Scrapbook 4, item 5, unidentified newspaper clipping, Crumbie Papers.

178. Torgovnick has emphasized the versatility of "the primitive" as a signifier in Euro-

American discourses. See *Gone Primitive*, 9–10. With respect to American discourses on Haiti, Plummer reaches similar conclusions in *Haiti and the United States*.

179. Scrapbook 6, p. 4, unidentified newspaper clipping, May 1940, Crumbie Papers. Hollywood's use of the zombie similarly merged diverse "primitive" locales and signifiers. Islands filled with "lost souls" could evoke Haiti and the South Pacific all at once. And while some screenwriters were "plunged into research on Haitian voodoo," as Ardel Wray recalled in relation to the 1943 RKO Picture *I Walked with a Zombie*, other writers mixed stereotypes and stock images with abandon. Commenting on Paramount's 1940 comedy *The Ghost Breakers*, with Bob Hope and Paulette Goddard, Idwel Jones commented, "Casting about for a new source of shudders, the dramatists found it in this zombie business we have been hearing about in Cuba." The setting for this comic take on zombies was "an island off the coast of Cuba," known as "Black Island." Ardel Wray, quoted in Los Angeles County Museum of Art, "The RKO Years," n.d., Production File: *I Walked with a Zombie*, AMPAS. Idwel Jones, "Production Information," August 1, 1940, Production File: *The Ghost Breakers*, AMPAS. See also "The Ghost Breakers," *Movie Story*, ca. 1940, clipping, Production File: *The Ghost Breakers*, AMPAS.

180. Review of *White Zombie*, *Time*, August 8, 1932.

181. Ibid. Note that the term "jitter" has its origins in a Mandingo word related to dance. The term seems to have been fairly new to common American English in the 1920s. Stuart Berg Flexner dates it to 1925. Clarence Major dates it to the seventeenth century in African American usage. See Flexner, *Listening to America*, 91; Major, *Juba to Jive*, 259.

182. Price and Turner, "White Zombie," 35; Frank, *Horror Movies*, 88. Madge Bellamy played Madeline Short; Robert Frazer played Charles Beaumont.

183. Price and Turner, "White Zombie," 38.

184. Ibid., 39.

185. Review of *White Zombie*, *Time*, August 8, 1932.

186. John S. Cohen, "The New Talkie," unidentified clipping, July 29, 1932, Scrapbook 2, Crumbie Papers.

187. Price and Turner, "White Zombie," 39.

188. Review of *White Zombie*, *Time*, August 8, 1932.

189. For another interpretation, see Tony Williams, "White Zombie, Haitian Horror," 20.

190. See Jacobson, *Whiteness of a Different Color*, 91–125.

191. Review of *White Zombie*, *Time*, August 8, 1932.

192. See Price and Turner, "White Zombie," 36.

193. While I was writing this book, I met a literary agent at a party. When she learned that I was writing about Haiti, her eyes lit up, and she handed me her card. "Haiti!," she said with great excitement, "Haiti sells! Romania? You can't give it away. But Haiti sells!"

CHAPTER 6

1. Tait, "The Petals Fall Slowly"; see Chapter 1.

2. Taft spent about six months in Haiti, beginning in December 1937. Taft, *A Puritan in Voodoo-Land*, 29.

3. Ibid., 11–12.

4. Ibid., 11.

5. Ibid., 12.

6. Ibid.

7. Ibid. Taft did not state directly that her own ancestor had "succumbed" as had other men, but she at least left her readers wondering. For Zacharias Raymond had taken a hand in freeing "an unbelievably beautiful young octoroon girl named Adoree Chery" who had escaped from a brutal French master. Raymond "had secreted her in the hold" of his ship and taken her to "Santiago de Cuba," where, Taft added, "her descendants doubtless live to this very day" (ibid., 13).

8. Ibid., 12–13.

9. Ibid., 11.

10. Amy Kaplan has shown that Perry Miller used Africa to frame his discourse on the Puritans in *Errand into the Wilderness*; see Kaplan, "Left Alone with America," 3–11.

11. Another book-length travel account is Loederer, *Voodoo Fire in Haiti*. For a sampling of travel journalism, see Arthur Ruhl, "Haytian Odds and Ends," *New York Herald Tribune*, May 8, 1932, and Harold Denny, "Proud Haiti Demands Her Old Freedom," *New York Times Magazine*, October 9, 1932, both in Scrapbook 2, Crumbie Papers, and Nock, "The Bright Isle," 552–59. See also Laguerre, *The Complete Haitiana*.

12. See Schmidt, *Maverick Marine*, 2–4, and Chapters 2–4 above.

13. Buhle emphasizes the cross-fertilization between these two fields in *Feminism and Its Discontents*, 100–101.

14. Ibid., 90–95. See, for example, Tridon, *Psychoanalysis and Love*; Dell, *Love in the Machine Age*; and the essays collected by Calverton and Schmalhausen in *Sex in Civilization, The New Generation*, and *Women's Coming of Age*.

15. This group included Elsie Clews Parsons, George Eaton Simpson, Melville Herskovits, and Zora Neale Hurston. On Boas and his students, see Barkan, *The Retreat of Scientific Racism*, 76–95, and Herskovits, *Franz Boas*.

16. Buhle, *Feminism and Its Discontents*, 98.

17. I am particularly interested in the ways that U.S. American writing on Haiti "manufactured desire" in terms of race and sexuality. See Stoler, *Race and the Education of Desire*, 167–77.

18. Samuel Guy Inman was perhaps most closely related to that apparatus in that he traveled to Haiti with a representative of the YMCA's Committee on Training Camps, whose goal was to advise the Marine Corps on matters related to morale and training. Inman, *Trailing the Conquistadores*, 117–18.

19. Inman dissented from dominant North American Protestant missionary views and practices by championing mission work in Latin America. With others, he founded the Committee on Cooperation with Latin America in 1910; he also served as its secretary for many years. See Koll, "Samuel Guy Inman: Venturer in Inter-American Friendship," 45–66. The Disciples of Christ was a nondenominational Christian fellowship, founded in the context of U.S. westward "expansion." In the 1920s, its members tended toward populist and progressive perspectives, emphasizing education and lay ministry. It was constituted as a denomination in the late 1950s and is now known as "The Christian Church (Disciples of Christ)." See Colby Hall, *Texas Disciples*.

20. Inman, *Through Santo Domingo and Haiti*, 85. For miscellaneous biographical information on Inman, see *Who Was Who in America*, vol. 4, *1961–1968* (Chicago: Marquis-Who's Who, 1968), 482.

21. For Inman's revised perspective, see his *Trailing the Conquistadores*. See also Chapter 7 below.

22. Gerald Anderson, *Biographical Dictionary of Christian Missions*, 319.

23. Inman, *Through Santo Domingo and Haiti*, 58; see also his "The Present Situation in the Caribbean," 289–317.

24. Inman, *Through Santo Domingo and Haiti*, 59.

25. Inman, *Trailing the Conquistadores*, 122.

26. Inman, *Through Santo Domingo and Haiti*, 79.

27. Inman, "The Present Situation in the Caribbean," 294.

28. Inman, *Through Santo Domingo and Haiti*, 79.

29. Ibid., 64.

30. Like the American evangelical women about whom historian Joan Jacobs Brumberg has written, American men in Haiti contrasted the "domestic oppression" of women in this foreign setting with what they believed to be the relatively emancipated lives and domestic happiness of women in the United States. See Brumberg, "Zenanas and Girlless Villages," 347–71.

31. Miller Log, Song on first page (unnumbered).

32. Ibid.

33. Inman, *Through Santo Domingo and Haiti*, 70, and *Trailing the Conquistadores*, 122.

34. Inman, *Through Santo Domingo and Haiti*, 71.

35. Ibid.

36. Ibid., 59–60.

37. Ibid., 69.

38. Ibid., 79.

39. Ibid.

40. Ibid., 64 and 63, respectively.

41. Ibid., 58, 85.

42. "Housekeeping in Haiti," *New York Herald Tribune*, October 24, 1926.

43. Balch, *Occupied Haiti*, 114.

44. One biographical sketch suggests that "exposure to the black tenants on her father's plantation" gave her "sensitivity to alien cultures." Buchanan, "Blair Rice Niles," 267.

45. Ibid. William Beebe led a scientific expedition to Haiti in 1927. Beebe, *Beneath Tropic Seas*, 199. Robert Niles also wrote about Haiti after the 1925 trip with Blair Niles. See Robert Niles, "An Architect's View of the Fortress of the Black King Christophe."

46. Buchanan, "Blair Rice Niles," 267. See also the list of "Authorities Consulted," included in Blair Niles, *Black Haiti*, 319–25.

47. Blair Niles, *Black Haiti*, 3.

48. Ibid., 4.

49. See, for example, Prichard, *Where Black Rules White* (1900); Ober, *A Guide to the West Indies and Bermuda* (1908); Fisk, *The West Indies* (1911); Bonsal, *The American Mediterranean* (1912); Franck, *Roaming through the West Indies* (1920); and the book that influenced all of them, St. John, *Hayti, or the Black Republic* (1884). Brenda Plummer identifies these, along with Seabrook's book, Taft's, and others, as "a literature of condemnation," which constituted one of the "instruments of power" deployed in U.S. relations with Haiti.

50. Blair Niles, *Black Haiti*, 5.

51. Ibid., 9.

52. Ibid., 10, 11.

53. Ibid., 14, 21.

54. Ibid., 136.

55. Ibid., 64 and 62, respectively. Niles's characterization of Haitians' "dramatic existence" resonates with the broad impact of Eugene O'Neill's *Emperor Jones*.

56. Blair Niles, *Black Haiti*, 155.

57. See the photograph by Phillip Hiss, Photographs File, Crumbie Papers.

58. Blair Niles, *Black Haiti*, 13.

59. Ibid., 126.

60. Ibid., 126–27.

61. Ibid., 135.

62. Ibid., 24.

63. Ibid., 25.

64. Ibid., 22.

65. Ibid., 24 and 23, respectively.

66. Ibid., 100.

67. Ibid., 64–65.

68. Ibid., 100–101.

69. Ibid., 102.

70. Ibid., title page.

71. Ibid., 133–34.

72. Ibid., 102.

73. Ibid., 23.

74. Ibid., 190, 191, 199.

75. Ibid., 154.

76. Ibid., 21, 309.

77. Ibid., 159, 160.

78. Ibid., 161.

79. Ibid., 167, 168.

80. Ibid., 169.

81. Ibid., 139–40.

82. Ibid., 71.

83. On the early history of the Book-of-the-Month Club, with references to the Literary Guild, see Rubin, *The Making of Middlebrow Culture*, 93–147.

84. Selection by one of the two popular book clubs, Literary Guild and Book-of-the-Month Club, boosted sales in bookstores as well as ensuring distribution to guild or club members. See ibid., 96–97.

85. Review of *The Magic Island*, *New York Herald Tribune*, January 8, 1929.

86. Seabrook, *No Hiding Place*, 273.

87. Seabrook, *The Magic Island*, 42.

88. Ibid., 127.

89. Ibid., 62.

90. Ibid., 60, 63.

91. Ibid., 12, 34.

92. See Haraway, "Teddy Bear Patriarchy," in *Primate Visions*, 26–58.

93. Seabrook, *The Magic Island*, 28, and *No Hiding Place*, 280.

94. Seabrook, *The Magic Island*, 31.

95. Ibid., 11–12, 13.

96. Ibid., 42.

97. Ibid., 11.

98. Ibid., 7.

99. Ibid., 17.

100. Jean Price-Mars, *Une tape de l'évolution Haïtienne*, excerpted in Joseph Williams, *Voodoos and Obeahs*, xv.

101. Ibid., xvi.

102. Ibid., xiv.

103. Redfield, review of *The Magic Island*, 317.

104. Seabrook, *The Magic Island*, 28.

105. Ibid., 42.

106. Ibid., 43 and 42, respectively.

107. Ibid., 60.

108. Ibid., 37.

109. Ibid.

110. Ibid., 223.

111. Ibid., 37.

112. Ibid., 277.

113. Ibid.

114. Ibid., 99.

115. Ibid., 172.

116. Seabrook made it clear to the reader that king and queen did not have to be married in Haiti, and indeed that this royal pair was not so joined. Ibid., 193.

117. Ibid., 171.

118. Wirkus and Dudley, *The White King of La Gonave*, xii–xiii.

119. Taft, *A Puritan in Voodoo-Land*, 16.

120. Other women writers, notably fiction writers, also used Haiti to claim or to project modern sexuality. See Adelaide Wilson, *First Woman*, and Forbes, *Women Called Wild*. For another account of the mutually constitutive links between race and sexuality, see Somerville, *Queering the Color Line*.

121. Taft, *A Puritan in Voodoo-Land*, 29.

122. Ibid., 42.

123. Ibid., 42–43.

124. Ibid., 44–45.

125. Ibid., 108.

126. Ibid., 110–11.

127. Ibid., 22–23.

128. Ibid., 374.

129. Ibid., 375.

130. Ibid., 362. See Chazotte, *The Black Rebellion in Haiti*. C. L. R. James acknowledged the rape of white women by black soldiers after the defeat of the French. His account linked such violence to a sense of revenge wrought by years of rape and violence by white masters against slave women and men. " 'Vengeance!' was their war-cry. . . . Yet, in all the records of that time, there is no single instance of such fiendish tortures as . . . blowing [white men] up with gunpowder" (*The Black Jacobins*, 89). Arna Bontemps would pick up on this image; see Chapter 7 for more on images of rape and revolution.

131. Taft, *A Puritan in Voodoo-Land*, 370.

132. Haag, *Consent*, 143, 160; Freedman, "The Response to the Sexual Psychopath," 83–106.

133. See Bederman, " 'Civilization,' the Decline of Middle-Class Manliness, and Ida B. Wells's Anti-Lynching Campaign."

134. Taft, *A Puritan in Voodoo-Land*, 83.

135. Shapiro, *White Violence and Black Response*, 282–83.

136. Ibid., 283. According to Shapiro, support for the legislation extended to the South.

The Costigan-Wagner bill was introduced in 1934, the Wagner-Van Nuys-Gavagan bill in 1937.

137. Taft, *A Puritan in Voodoo-Land*, 372.
138. Ibid., 105.
139. Ibid.
140. Ibid., 68.
141. Ibid., 368.
142. Ibid., 368–69.
143. Ibid., 397–98.
144. Tebbel, *The Golden Age*, 430. Tebbel estimates that successful travel books in the 1930s sold between 3,000 and 5,000 copies (in the first printing), and *A Puritan in Voodoo-Land* received mixed reviews. The *Springfield Republican*, December 20, 1938, 8, called it "agreeably readable," but the *New York Times Book Review*, January 15, 1939, 3, judged it "naïve," and the *Boston Transcript*, December 17, 1938, 2, held its nose, finding it "sickening," "rank and uncultivated," and "shockingly superficial."
145. Van Doren, "Why the Editorial Board Selected *The Magic Island*," 3.

CHAPTER 7

1. Rampersad, *The Life of Langston Hughes*, 204.
2. Hughes, *I Wonder as I Wander*, 5. The novel was *Not Without Laughter*. On the Harmon Foundation's support for African American achievement, especially in the field of visual arts, see Reynolds and Wright, *Against the Odds*. Charlotte Osgood Mason, who preferred to be called "Godmother," also patronized Zora Neale Hurston.
3. Hughes, *I Wonder as I Wander*, 4.
4. Ibid., 15.
5. See Chapter 6.
6. Hughes, *I Wonder as I Wander*, 15. He did use a letter from Walter White introducing him to the Haitian novelist Jacques Roumain, whose novel, *Gouverneurs de la rosée*, he later translated. See Roumain, *Masters of the Dew*.
7. Hughes, *I Wonder as I Wander*, 22.
8. Ibid. Hughes explicitly praised Blair Niles's *Black Haiti* as well as Vandercook's *Black Majesty*. See *I Wonder as I Wander*, 16.
9. Hughes, *I Wonder as I Wander*, 23.
10. Ibid., 27.
11. Ibid.
12. Rampersad, *The Life of Langston Hughes*, 204.
13. Hughes, "White Shadows in a Black Land," 157.
14. Hughes, *I Wonder as I Wander*, 27. Hughes acknowledged the significance, for people of any means at all, not only of shoes, but also of coats, in light of Haitian history. "Strange, bourgeois and a little pathetic, I found this accent on clothes and shoes in an undeveloped land, where the average wage was then thirty cents a day, and where the sun blazed like fury. Articles of clothing in Haiti were not cheap. Taxes were high, jobs scarce, wages low, so the doubtful step upward to the dignity of leather between one's feet and the earth, or a coat between one's body and the sun, was a step not easily to be achieved. But perhaps a coat and a pair of shoes had more meaning than that inherent in their mere possession. And perhaps that meaning was

something carried over from the long-ago days of the white masters, who wore coats and shoes — and had force and power. Perhaps they were symbols" (28).

15. Hughes, "A People without Shoes," 469; Rampersad, introduction to *I Wonder as I Wander*, by Hughes, xviii.
16. Hughes, *I Wonder as I Wander*, 26–27.
17. Ibid., 27.
18. Errol Hill writes that Hughes "first produced *Drums of Haiti* in 1935, revised it in 1936 as *Troubled Island*, turned this version into an opera with music by William Grant Still in 1949, and his final revision . . . was completed in 1963." Hill, *Black Heroes*, 4.
19. Hughes, *I Wonder as I Wander*, 5.
20. Protest also emerged out of the Pan-African movement, the peace movement, the African American press, white liberal organizations like the Popular Government League, the Foreign Policy Association, religious communities, and, as we saw in Chapter 3, the institutions of the state itself. This list is not intended to be exhaustive, nor will the present work attempt a thorough investigation of all of these contexts. More work remains to be done to fill out our understanding of each one and of the relations among these, along with others not mentioned here.
21. Grossman, *Land of Hope*, 8.
22. Marks, *Farewell — We're Good and Gone*, 146; Hine, "Rape and the Inner Lives of Black Women," 343.
23. Haiti provided one of the only issues around which these two organizations would join forces. Plummer, "Afro-American Response," 133.
24. Ibid., 138–39.
25. Shipman, *It Had to Be Revolution*, 168.
26. Plummer, "Afro-American Response," 135. The American-Haitian Benevolent Club "represented the descendants of Americans who had emigrated to Haiti in the 1850s and 1860s."
27. Ibid., 135; Neverdon-Morton, *Afro-American Women of the South*, 198.
28. Plummer, "Afro-American Response," 135.
29. Ibid., 135, 138.
30. See Rupp, *Worlds of Women*, 13–50.
31. On Willard's work with southern African American women and on her conflict with Ida B. Wells, see Gilmore, *Gender and Jim Crow*, 46, 49–50, 56–57, and Ware, *Beyond the Pale*, 198–215.
32. Neverdon-Morton, *Afro-American Women of the South*, 198.
33. Ibid.
34. Ibid.
35. The one representative from Asia was from Ceylon, now Sri Lanka. Ibid., 200.
36. Ibid. See also "Booker T.'s Wife Heads World Order," *Chicago Defender*, August 26, 1922.
37. Neverdon-Morton, *Afro-American Women of the South*, 200.
38. Balch, *Occupied Haiti*, v.
39. Ibid., viii.
40. Two of the fifteen chapters were coauthored by Balch and Hunton.
41. Balch, *Occupied Haiti*, vii.
42. Ibid., 149, 153.
43. Ibid., 152.
44. Ibid., iii.

45. *Occupied Haiti* refused all exoticism, though Balch considered Niles's book "charming."

46. On conservatism in the 1920s, see Higham, *Strangers in the Land*; Blee, *Women of the Klan*; Marsden, *Fundamentalism and American Culture.*

47. Balch, *Occupied Haiti,* 11.

48. On the ISS, see David Shannon, *The Socialist Party of America,* 54–56.

49. Ibid., 56.

50. Shipman, *It Had to Be Revolution,* 153–54.

51. Ibid., 154.

52. Phillips was also later known as Charles Shipman. Ibid., 155.

53. Carl Haessler, Leland Olds, and Art Shields. Ibid., 157.

54. Ibid. The patron was William H. Holly.

55. The Anti-Imperialist League letterhead included the names William Pickens, Roger Baldwin, Robert Morss Lovett, Paxton Hibben, Lewis Gannett, Freda Kirchwey, Arthur Garfield Hays, Scott Nearing, William C. Foster, William F. Dunne, and Manuel Gomez. Ibid.

56. Ibid., 168.

57. Nearing and Freeman, *Dollar Diplomacy*. Philips described Freeman as "an old reliable of the party's agitprop establishment." See Shipman, *It Had to Be Revolution,* 151, 181.

58. Shipman, *It Had to Be Revolution,* 162. Others who attended were Roger Baldwin, Richard B. Moore, and Chi Ch'ao-ting. Moore and Chi were party members.

59. Plummer, "The Afro-American Response," 137; Shipman, *It Had to Be Revolution,* 165. Fort-Whiteman was active in the Communist Party in New York through the 1920s. He then moved to the Soviet Union, married there, and nine years later died in one of Stalin's prisons, having been convicted of "Anti-Soviet agitation." Klehr, Haynes, and Anderson, *The Soviet World of American Communism,* 218–27.

60. Shipman, *It Had to Be Revolution,* 166.

61. Plummer, "Afro-American Response," 140.

62. Samuel Guy Inman, to whom we shall now turn, is a key example. See Inman, "Imperialistic America," and *Trailing the Conquistadores.* In conjunction with the latter, the Disciples of Christ also created a study guide to facilitate education on questions of racism and imperialism raised by Inman's book. See Hinman, *Our Caribbean Neighbors.* See also Stowell, *Between the Americas,* and Rycroft, *On This Foundation.*

63. Inman, *Trailing the Conquistadores,* 216. See also Montavon, *Haiti, Past and Present,* published by the Catholic Association for International Peace.

64. Inman, *Trailing the Conquistadores,* 44–45. The lawyers, members of the Foreign Policy Association, included Raymond B. Fosdick, Lewis Marshall, Charles B. Howland, Judge Frederick A. Henry, and Moorfield Storey. Charles B. Howland was the author of *Survey of American Foreign Relations.* See also Hixson, *Moorfield Storey and the Abolitionist Tradition,* 73; Bausman and Bettman, *The Seizure of Haiti by the United States*; and Buell, *The American Occupation of Haiti.*

65. Inman, *Trailing the Conquistadores,* 107–8, 122.

66. Ibid., 131, 132.

67. Ibid., 133.

68. Ibid., 122.

69. Ibid., 118.

70. Cf. Inman, *Through Santo Domingo and Haiti,* 58, 79.

71. Inman, *Trailing the Conquistadores,* 104.

72. Ibid., 103–4.
73. Ibid., 104.
74. Ibid., 103.
75. Ibid., 106.
76. Ibid., 114, 115.
77. All quotations in this paragraph are from ibid., 130.
78. Ibid., 131–32.
79. Ibid., 132.
80. Ibid., 133–34.
81. Inman, *Trailing the Conquistadores*, 131, quoting Señor de Madariaga.
82. Inman, "Imperialistic America." The essay was also excerpted in a collection of anti-imperialist writings published in 1928; see Hopkins and Alexander, *Machine Gun Diplomacy*, 143–50.
83. Gaspar and Trouillot, "History, Fiction, and the Slave Experience," 184.
84. Endore, *Babouk*, 295–96.
85. Herskovits, "Voodoo Nonsense," 308; Loederer, *Voodoo Fire in Haiti*.
86. Herskovits, *Life in a Haitian Valley*. Herskovits was neither first nor last among anthropologists who sought to defend Haiti by debunking racist views. Elsie Clews Parsons weighed in against the occupation in the relatively early days of 1917, conducted fieldwork there in 1926, and provided financial support to others interested in the folklore of Haiti, including Harold Courlander. Zumwalt, *Wealth and Rebellion*, 191, 204–5. For Parsons's Haitian folklore, and for her criticisms of the occupation, see Parsons, "Injustice to Haitians," *New York Times*, January 7, 1917; "Spirituals from the 'American' Colony of Samana Bay, Santo Domingo"; and "The People in Hayti," *New York Herald Tribune*, December 15, 1929, Scrapbook 1, Crumbie Papers. George Eaton Simpson was another anthropologist who actively sought to debunk racist views of Haiti. See Simpson, "The Vodoun Service in Northern Haiti," and "Haitian Peasant Economy." See also "Scientist Defends Haiti's Voodoo; Holds 'Magic' Benefits the Natives," *New York Times*, December 29, 1938, Scrapbook 5, Crumbie Papers.
87. Herskovits, *Life in a Haitian Valley*, xviii–xix.
88. Ibid., 46.
89. Ibid., 266.
90. Ibid., 293.
91. Ibid., 295.
92. Ibid.
93. Further complexities of Herskovits's ethnographic relationship to Haiti are revealed in Kate Ramsey's astute reading of the extensive correspondence between Herskovits and Katherine Dunham, while she was in Haiti in 1936 doing fieldwork as a graduate student. Ramsey, "Melville J. Herskovits, Katherine Dunham, and the Politics of African Diasporic Dance Anthropology." See also Dunham, *Island Possessed*.
94. Courlander, *Haiti Singing*, vii. See also Courlander, "Haiti's Political Folksongs," and *The Drum and the Hoe*. Laura Bowman and Antoine Leroy also collected Haitian music and folklore in the late 1930s. See Bowman and Leroy, *The Voice of Haiti*.
95. Courlander, *Haiti Singing*, 6.
96. Ibid., 1–2.
97. Courlander, *Uncle Bouqui of Haiti*.
98. Price-Mars, *Ainsi parla l'oncle*.
99. Welles, *Orson Welles on Shakespeare*.

100. Bontemps, "Introduction to the 1968 Edition," in Bontemps, *Black Thunder*, xxviii. Bontemps was asked to burn most of the books in his small library, but a few were indicated by name, including Vandercook's *Black Majesty*.

101. James Weldon Johnson, "Haitian Notes," 163, James Weldon Johnson Papers, Yale Collection of American Literature, Beinecke Rare Book and Manuscript Library, Yale University, New Haven, Conn.

102. See, for example, Leslie Pickney Hill's 1928 play, *Toussaint L'Ouverture*. One notable exception was Arthur Alfonso Schomburg. See Schomburg, *Military Services Rendered by the Haitians in the North and South American Wars for Independence*.

103. In 1937, for example, Reverend Adam Clayton Powell remarked that the Communist National Negro Congress was the "only mass organization dedicated to our problem here in America." Quoted in Naison, *Communists in Harlem*, 199.

104. Weiss, *Farewell to the Party of Lincoln*; see, for example, 206, 228–29, 268, 293.

105. Marshall, *The Story of Haiti*, 7.

106. Bontemps and Hughes, *Popo and Fifina*; Bontemps, *Black Thunder*, and *Drums at Dusk*; Hughes, "Troubled Island," and "Emperor of Haiti"; see playscripts in the Billy Rose Theatre Collection, New York Public Library for the Performing Arts, New York, N.Y.

107. Logan, "Education in Haiti," and *Diplomatic Relations of the United States with Haiti*.

108. Wheat, *Jacob Lawrence*, 39–41, 52–53; Driskell, *Two Centuries of Black American Art*, 184–85.

109. Dunham, *Island Possessed*; Yarborough, *Haiti-Dance*.

110. The full title of the piece is "La Citadelle — Freedom." Reynolds and Wright, *Against the Odds*, 251–52.

111. Padmore, "The Revolt in Haiti," and *Haiti, an American Slave Colony*; Farred, "First Stop, Port-au-Prince," 229.

112. The organization that James founded Padmore later led, and, in that context, both men developed important relationships with African leaders, including Kwame Nkrumah of Ghana. Boggs, *Living for Change*, 46; Farred, "First Stop, Port-au-Prince," 238.

113. James, *Black Majesty*; Duberman, *Paul Robeson*, 194; Boggs, *Living for Change*, 46. The play is variously referred to by the titles "Toussaint L'Ouverture," "Black Majesty," and, in its revised and published version, "The Black Jacobins." See Grimshaw, *The C. L. R. James Reader*.

114. Said, *Culture and Imperialism*, 251.

115. Farred, "First Stop, Port-au-Prince," 236–37. See also Kelley, introduction to *A History of Negro Revolt*, by C. L. R. James; Farred, *Rethinking C. L. R. James*; Robinson, *Black Marxism*; Said, *Culture and Imperialism*, 245–61.

116. Duberman, *Paul Robeson*, 74.

117. Amy Ashwood Garvey, Marcus Garvey's ex-wife, was another of the amateur actors in that production, and Amy Garvey was also active with James and Padmore in their work for Ethiopia.

118. Thomas Cripps sees the film as having been successful at conveying the tragedy of racism. "Robeson's Jones overawes the picture and gives it heroic dimensions," he claims. "When Jones dies in a revolt, he is not a Pullman toady or a high-roller under the stairwell; he is a black king dying in pain and rage at his demeaning fall." Cripps, *Slow Fade to Black*, 216–17. Some contemporary viewers would have agreed. In their study guide on the film, for example, William Lewis and Max J. Herzberg highlighted the ways in which the film established the integrity of Brutus Jones through

an early scene in a church and the use of spirituals in the score (by J. Rosamond Johnson). They pointed also to the contrast between that integrity and the character of the three white men in the film, "Harrington, a corrupt financier; Smithers, a corrupt trader; and the brutal prison guard. . . . Compared to them," they noted, Brutus Jones "compels sympathy." Lewis and Herzberg, "Study Guide for the Screen Production of the Emperor Jones," Production File: *The Emperor Jones*, AMPAS.

119. Marshall, *The Story of Haiti*, 7.

120. Ibid., 62.

121. Ibid., 46.

122. Bontemps and Hughes, *Popo and Fifina*, 1.

123. Ibid., 35.

124. Ibid., 78.

125. Rampersad, "Introduction to the 1992 Edition," in Bontemps, *Black Thunder*, x.

126. Bontemps and Hughes, *The Letters of Langston Hughes and Arna Bontemps*.

127. Bontemps, "Introduction to the 1968 Edition," in Bontemps, *Black Thunder*, xxviii.

128. Jones, *Renaissance Man*.

129. Bontemps, "Introduction to the 1968 Edition," in Bontemps, *Black Thunder*, xxv. Both James Weldon Johnson and Arthur Schomburg had written about Haiti and the Haitian Revolution.

130. Rampersad, "Introduction to the 1992 Edition," in Bontemps, *Black Thunder*, xiii.

131. Jones, *Renaissance Man*, 81.

132. On the Amis des Noirs, see David Brion Davis, *The Problem of Slavery in the Age of Revolution*, 96–100.

133. Bontemps, *Drums at Dusk*, 158.

134. Ibid., 142.

135. Ibid., 200–201.

136. Ibid., 205.

137. See, for example, Oakley Johnson, "Influence of Haitian Revolution on New York," Research for "Negroes of New York," WPA Writers' Project, Schomburg Center for Research on Black Culture, New York.

138. The large crowd outside the theater on opening night attracted the attention of the police. Gill, *White Grease Paint on Black Performers*, 26.

139. Christine Ames, *Black Empire*, act 3, p. 14. Unpublished playscript in Billy Rose Theatre Collection, New York Public Library for the Performing Arts, New York, N.Y.

140. William Edgar Easton, *Dessalines* (1893) and *Christophe* (1911); Leslie Hill, *Toussaint L'Ouverture* (1918); May Miller, *Christophe's Daughter* (n.d.); Allen C. Miller, *Opener of Doors* (1923); Helen Webb Harris, *Genifrede, the Daughter of L'Ouverture* (1935). See Belcher, "The Place of the Negro in the Evolution of the American Theatre," xv, xvi. John Mathews and Clarence White also wrote an opera, *Ouanga* (1920). See VèVè Clark, "Haiti's Tragic Overture," 36. Other 1930s plays focusing on Haitian themes provided minor "opportunities" for African American actors, including two plays called *Zombie*, one (1929) by Natalie Scott, another (1932) by Kenneth Webb, which was performed at the Biltmore Theatre in New York, as well as *Dance with Your Gods* (1934), by Laurence Schwab. See "Biltmore Theatre: Zombie," Program, New York: New York Theatre Program Corporation, 1932, Scrapbook 4, Crumbie Papers; Lucius Beebe, "Invoking Aid of Voodoo Gods, Schwab Offers a New Thriller," *New York Herald Tribune*, September 30, 1934, Blue Scrapbook, Crumbie Papers; Scott, *Zombie*, in Isaacs, *Plays of American Life and Fantasy*. African American film makers also took up Haitian themes in *Black Majesty* (1932, Southland Pictures, copy available at the

Southwest Film/Video Archives, Southern Methodist University, Dallas, Tex.) and *Drums O' Voodoo* (1933, International Stage Play Pictures). See Jones, *Black Cinema Treasures*, 191–232; Cripps, *Slow Fade to Black*, 325–26.

141. O'Connor and Brown, *Free, Adult, and Uncensored*, 119.

142. William Dubois, "Complete Working Script of 'Haiti' by William Du Bois [*sic*]," Billy Rose Theatre Collection, New York Public Library for the Performing Arts, New York, N.Y.

143. Maurice Clark, quoted in O'Connor and Brown, *Free, Adult, and Uncensored*, 119.

144. Dubois, *Haiti*; and "Production Notes" for *Haiti*, Billy Rose Theatre Collection, New York Public Library for the Performing Arts, New York, N.Y. Dubois's script also dispensed with the battle scene, in which the ex-slaves are victorious, in two minutes of dialogue. Maurice Clark rewrote the scene to put the emphasis on the victory Dubois had lamented. "Climactic Scene of a Big Battle Gave Him a Fight," unidentified newspaper clipping, March 27, 1938, Scrapbook 4, Crumbie Papers.

145. Mitchell, *Black Drama*, 103.

146. Review of *Haiti*, *Time*, March 14, 1938.

147. Maurice Clark, quoted in O'Connor and Brown, *Free, Adult, and Uncensored*, 119.

148. Gill, *White Grease Paint on Black Performers*, 99.

149. Fenwick Library, *The Federal Theatre Project*, 31.

150. Gill, *White Grease Paint on Black Performers*, 31.

151. For other readings of Hurston's Haitian anthropology, see Mikell, "When Horses Talk," and Hernandez, "Multiple Subjectivities and Strategies of Positionality." A radically different account of Hurston's politics may be found in Delbanco, "The Political Incorrectness of Zora Neale Hurston."

152. Seabrook, *No Hiding Place*, 282.

153. Ibid., 283.

154. See, for example, Hurston's discussion of zombies, *Tell My Horse*, 179–98. All quotes from Hurston's manuscript are used with permission of the Estate of Zora Neale Hurston.

155. Van Vechten, *Nigger Heaven*. See also Lewis, *When Harlem Was in Vogue*, 184–89.

156. Rampersad, *Life of Langston Hughes*, 135.

157. Hurston, *Tell My Horse*, 64.

158. Ibid., 221.

159. Ibid., 219.

160. Ibid., 223.

161. Ibid., 222.

162. Brown, *Mama Lola*, 206–7.

163. Ibid., 94–95, 235, 207, respectively.

164. Hurston, *Tell My Horse*, 65, 71, 72.

165. Ibid., 86, 87.

166. Ibid., 77, 75, 204, and 91, respectively.

167. Hurston, *Mules and Men*.

168. Barbara Johnson, "Thresholds of Difference," 317–28.

169. Hurston, *Mules and Men*, 4–5, quoted in Barbara Johnson, "Thresholds of Difference," 325.

170. Hurston, *Tell My Horse*, 81, 83.

171. Ibid., 82.

172. Ibid., 65.

173. Ibid., 134.

174. Ibid., 136.

175. Ibid., 137.

176. Helen Worden, "Voodoo Lore Is Brought Here from Haiti by Woman Who Was Converted after Worshipping with Natives," *New York World-Telegram*, October 1938.

177. Ibid.

178. Hurston, *Tell My Horse*, 6.

179. Ibid., 6–7.

180. Ibid., 8.

181. Ibid., 245.

182. Ibid., 246.

183. Ibid., 245.

184. Zora Neale Hurston, "Tell My Horse," unpublished manuscript, folder 27, Zora Neale Hurston Papers, Yale Collection of American Literature, Beinecke Rare Book and Manuscript Library, Yale University, New Haven, Conn. Used with permission of the estate of Zora Neale Hurston.

185. Hurston, *Tell My Horse*, 246, 247.

186. Hurston, "Tell My Horse."

187. Ibid.

188. Ibid.

189. Hurston, *Tell My Horse*, 246.

190. Hurston, "Tell My Horse" (capitalization as in original).

191. Hurston, *Tell My Horse*, 246.

192. Ibid., 246, 248.

193. Ibid., 253.

194. Ibid., 253–54.

195. Syrians in Haiti faced resentment from native Haitians, especially during times of economic constriction. Plummer cites a Haitian exporter, Camille Devereux, who happened to be in New York when the *Times* was reporting on anti-Syrian agitation in Haiti. Devereux "claimed the situation in Haiti was analogous to the anti-Chinese feeling in the United States." Plummer, "Black and White in the Caribbean," 1:176, and 155–89. The reference to Syrians is also interesting in light of the role Syrian merchants played, prior to the occupation, as sometimes "the sole representatives of American commerce" in Haiti. Plummer, *Haiti and the Great Powers*, 173. Plummer concludes that the "Syrians' activities in Haiti . . . cannot be understood apart from the ambitions and interests of the diverse powers which supported and opposed them. The United States' decision to represent even those Syrians who were still Ottoman subjects and others of dubious nationality indicated a growing commitment to this group as an important link to American penetration of the country." Plummer, "Black and White in the Caribbean," 1:177. See also Plummer, "Race, Nationality, and Trade."

196. Hurston, *Tell My Horse*, 257.

BIBLIOGRAPHY

PRIMARY SOURCES

Manuscript Collections
Beverly Hills, California
    Margaret Herrick Library, Academy of Motion Picture Arts and Sciences
        Production Files
        The Emperor Jones
        Ghost Breakers
        Island of Lost Souls
        I Walked with a Zombie
        Revolt of the Zombies
        Unconquered
        White Zombie
Gainesville, Florida
    Caribbean Collection, University of Florida Library
        Frank Crumbie Papers
        Haitiana Collection
Los Angeles, California
    Hearst Metrotone News Collection, UCLA Film and Television Archive
        Newsreels
New Haven, Connecticut
    Yale Collection of American Literature, Beinecke Rare Book and Manuscript Library,
        Yale University
        Zora Neale Hurston Papers
        James Weldon Johnson Papers
        Eugene O'Neill Papers
        Walter White Papers
Newport, Rhode Island
    Archives of the United States Naval War College
        Report prepared for the Office of Naval Research, April 1969
New York, New York
    Billy Rose Theatre Collection, New York Public Library for the Performing Arts
        "Black Empire" playscript (Christine Ames)
        "Emperor of Haiti" playscript (Langston Hughes)
        "Haiti" playscript (William DuBois [*sic*])
        "Troubled Island" playscript (Langston Hughes)
    Schomburg Center for Research on Black Culture
        Clipping Files, Haiti
        WPA Writers' Project

Syracuse, New York
  Street and Smith Editorial Records Collection, Street and Smith Archives, Syracuse
    University
  The Shadow Radio Series
Washington, D.C.
  Library of Congress
    Journals of W. Cameron Forbes
  National Archives
    Record Group 45, Naval Records Collection of the Office of Naval Records and
      Library
    Record Group 80, Secretary of the Navy
      General Correspondence, 1916–26
    Record Group 127, Records of the United States Marine Corps
  United States Marine Corps, History and Museums Division
    Oral History Collection
      Lieutenant General Pedro A. del Valle
      Brigadier General Lester A. Dessez
      Brigadier General Ivan W. Miller
      General Alfred H. Noble
      Lieutenant General Lewis B. Puller and Colonel William A. Lee
      Major General Bennett Puryear Jr.
      General Lemuel C. Shepherd
      Lieutenant General Merwin H. Silverthorn
      Lieutenant General Julian C. Smith
    Personal Papers Collection
      Robert B. Barker Papers
      George Barnett Papers
      Alex O. Campbell Papers
      Arthur B. Jacques Papers
      Adolph B. Miller Papers
      Homer L. Overley Papers
      Fred S. Robillard Papers
      William Rossiter Papers
      F. W. Schmidt Papers
      Vincent E. Stack Papers
      Gerald C. Thomas Papers
      Harold H. Utley Papers
      Anne C. Venzon Papers
      Faustin E. Wirkus Papers

Interviews and Personal Communications

Anonymous (female). Interview by the author. Hinche, August 22, 1996.

Asad, Marcel. Interview by the author, tape recording. Port-au-Prince, August 14, 1996.

Balutansky, Edwidge, and Kathleen Balutansky. Conversation with the author. Port-au-
    Prince, October 31, 1998.

Dougherty, Leo J., III. Telephone conversation with the author. November 4, 1998.

Gaillard, Roger. Conversation with the author. Port-au-Prince, August 15, 1996.

Garcia, Remy. Interview by the author, tape recording. Hinche, August 21, 1996.

Hogu, Lionel. Conversation with the author. Boston, Mass., July 11, 1996.

Jean-Marie, Escan, and Hector LaPaix. Interview by the author, tape recording. Hinche, August 21, 1996.

LaPaix, Hector. Interview by the author, tape recording. Hinche, August 20, 1996.

Sam, Max. Interview by the author, tape recording. Port-au-Prince, August 12, 1996.

Journals, Newspapers, and Periodicals

American Architect	Negro World
Amsterdam News	New York Age
Chicago Defender	New York Globe
Le Courrier Haïtien	New York Herald Tribune
Crisis	New York Times
Gendarmerie News	New York World-Telegram
Herald Tribune Independent	Record of Christian Work
Leatherneck	Recruiter's Bulletin
Literary Digest	Theatre Arts Monthly
Marines Magazine	Time Magazine
Messenger	Variety
Nation	Wings, The Magazine of the Literary Guild
National Geographic	World's Work
Navy Medical Bulletin	

Published Works

Addams, Jane. *Peace and Bread in Time of War*. New York: King's Crown Press, 1945.

Alexis, Stephen. *Le nègre masqué*. Port-au-Prince: Imprimerie de l'État, 1933.

Anderson, Gary Clayton, and Alan L. Woolworth, eds. *Through Dakota Eyes: Narrative Accounts of the Minnesota Indian War of 1862*. St. Paul: Minnesota Historical Society Press, 1988.

Anderson, Nels. *Men on the Move*. Chicago: University of Chicago Press, 1940.

Aptheker, Herbert, ed. *The Correspondence of W. E. B. Du Bois*. Vol. 1, *Selections, 1877–1934*. Amherst: University of Massachusetts Press, 1973.

——. *Selections from the Crisis*. Vol. 1. Millwood, N.Y.: Kraus-Thomson, 1983.

Augur, Helen. "Drums at Night." *American Magazine* (November 1940).

Balch, Emily Greene. "Social Values in Haiti." In *Beyond Nationalism: The Social Thought of Emily Greene Balch*, edited by Mercedes M. Randall. New York: Twayne, 1972.

——, ed. *Occupied Haiti*. 1927. Reprint, New York: Garland, 1972.

Bausman, Frederic, and Alfred Bettman. *The Seizure of Haiti by the United States*. New York: Foreign Policy Association, 1922.

Beard, Daniel Carter. *Hardly a Man Is Now Alive: The Autobiography of Dan Beard*. New York: Doubleday, Doran, 1939.

Beebe, Charles William. *Beneath Tropic Seas: A Record of Diving among the Coral Reefs of Haiti*. New York: G. P. Putman's Sons, 1928.

Bedford-Jones, H. *Drums of Dumbala*. New York: Covic-Friede, 1932.

Bellegarde, Dantès. *L'occupation américaine d'Haïti: Ses conséquences morales et économiques*. 1929. Reprint, Pétion-Ville, Haïti: Editions Lumière, 1996.

——. *Pour une Haïti heureuse*. Port-au-Prince: Imprimerie Chéraquit, 1927.

Beveridge, Albert J. *The Young Man and the World*. New York: D. Appleton, 1905.

Bingham, Hiram. "The Future of the Monroe Doctrine." *Journal of International Relations* 10 (April 1920): 392–403.

Boggs, Grace Lee. *Living for Change: An Autobiography*. Minneapolis: University of Minnesota Press, 1998.

Bonsal, Stephen. *The American Mediterranean*. New York: Moffat, Yard, 1912.

Bontemps, Arna Wendell. *Black Thunder*. 1936. Reprint, Boston: Beacon Press, 1992.

——. *Drums at Dusk*. New York: Macmillan, 1939.

Bontemps, Arna, and Langston Hughes. *The Letters of Langston Hughes and Arna Bontemps*. Edited by Charles H. Nichols. New York: Dodd and Mead, 1980.

——. *Popo and Fifina: Children of Haiti*. New York: Macmillan, 1932.

Bowman, Laura, and Antoine Leroy. *The Voice of Haiti: Original Native Ceremonial Songs, Voodoo Chants, Drumbeats, Stories and Traditions of the Haitian People*. New York: Clarence Williams Music Publishing, 1938.

Brierre, Jean F. *Le petit soldat*. Port-au-Prince: Imprimerie Haïtienne, 1934.

Buell, Raymond Leslie. *The American Occupation of Haiti*. New York: Foreign Policy Association, 1929.

Burks, Arthur J. "Voodoo," "Luisma's Return," "Thus Spake the Prophetess," and "Black Medicine." In *Black Medicine*, 120–84. Sauk City, Wisc.: Arkham House, 1966.

Butler, Smedley D. "General Butler Tells the World." *Christian Century* 47 (January 1, 1930): 5–6.

——. *Old Gimlet Eye, As Told to Lowell Thomas*. New York: Farrar and Rinehart, 1933.

——. *War Is a Racket*. New York: Roundtable Press, 1935.

Calixte, Demosthene P. *Haiti: The Cavalry of a Soldier*. New York: Wendell Malliet, 1939.

Calloway, Colin G., ed. *Our Hearts Fell to the Ground: Plains Indian Views of How the West Was Lost*. Boston: Bedford Books, 1996.

Calverton, V. F., and Samuel Schmalhausen, eds. *The New Generation: The Intimate Problems of Modern Parents and Children*. New York: Macaulay, 1931.

——. *Sex in Civilization*. New York: Macaulay, 1929.

——. *Women's Coming of Age: A Symposium*. New York: H. Liveright, 1931.

Chamberlain, George Agnew. *The Silver Cord*. New York: G. P. Putnam's Sons, 1927.

Chazotte, Peter Stephen. *The Black Rebellion in Haiti*. Philadelphia: Privately published, 1927.

Clark, Barrett. *Eugene O'Neill: The Man and His Plays*. 1926. Reprint, New York: Dover, 1967.

Clopper, Edward N. *Rural Child Welfare: An Inquiry by the National Child Labor Committee*. New York: Macmillan, 1922.

Coffey, Robert B. "A Brief History of the Intervention in Haiti." *U.S. Naval Institute Proceedings* 48 (August 1922): 1325–44.

Cook, Mercer. *Education in Haiti*. Washington, D.C.: Federal Security Agency, Office of Education, 1948.

——. "Trends in Recent Haitian Literature." *Journal of Negro History* 32 (April 1947): 220–31.

Cook, Mercer, and Dantès Bellegarde. *The Haitian-American Anthology: Haitian Readings from American Authors*. Port-au-Prince: Imprimerie de l'État, 1944.

Cooper, Anna Julia. *A Voice from the South*. 1892. Reprint, New York: Oxford University Press, 1988.

Courlander, Harold. *The Drum and the Hoe: Life and Lore of the Haitian People*. Berkeley: University of California Press, 1960.

——. *Haiti Singing*. Chapel Hill: University of North Carolina Press, 1939.

——. "Haiti's Political Folksongs." *Opportunity* 19, no. 4 (April 1941): 114–18.

——. *Uncle Bouqui of Haiti*. New York: William Morrow, 1942.

Craige, John Houston. *Black Bagdad: The Arabian Nights Adventures of a Marine Captain in Haiti*. New York: Minton, Balch, 1933.

———. *Cannibal Cousins*. New York: Minton, Balch, 1934.

———. "Haitian Vignettes." *National Geographic* 66 (October 1934): 435–85.

———. *What Every Citizen Should Know about the Marines*. New York: W. W. Norton, 1941.

Cranston, Claudia. "Wings." *Good Housekeeping* 101 (July 1935): 26–27; (August 1935): 38–39.

Cronon, E. David. *The Cabinet Diaries of Josephus Daniels, 1913–1921*. Lincoln: University of Nebraska Press, 1963.

Davis, Beale. *The Goat without Horns*. New York: Brentano's, 1925.

Davis, Burke. *Marine! The Life of Lieutenant General Lewis B. (Chesty) Puller, U.S.M.C. (Ret.)*. Boston: Little, Brown, 1962.

Davis, Harold P. *Black Democracy: The Story of Haiti*. 1928. Rev. ed., New York: Dodge, 1936.

———. "Facts about Haiti." *World's Markets* (February 1924).

———. "Sunlight on Voodoo Mysteries." *Travel* 73 (May 1939): 34–37.

Dell, Floyd. *Love in the Machine Age: A Psychological Study of the Transition from Patriarchal Society*. New York: Farrar and Rinehart, 1930.

Detweiler, Charles. *The Waiting Isles: Baptist Missions in the Caribbean*. Philadelphia: Judson Press, 1930.

Dorsinville, Roger. *Marche arrière*. Outremont, Quebec: Collectif Paroles, 1986.

Douglas, Paul H. "The American Occupation of Haiti, I." *Political Science Quarterly* 42 (1927): 255–56.

———. *In the Fullness of Time: The Memoirs of Paul H. Douglas*. New York: Harcourt, 1971.

Du Bois, W. E. B. *Against Racism: Unpublished Essays, Papers, and Addresses, 1887–1961*. Edited by Herbert Aptheker. Amherst: University of Massachusetts Press, 1985.

———. *The Correspondence of W. E. B. Du Bois*. Edited by Herbert Aptheker. Vol. 1, *Selections, 1877–1934*. Amherst: University of Massachusetts Press, 1973.

———. "Criteria of Negro Art." *Crisis* 32 (October 1926): 290–97.

———. "Hayti." *Crisis* 10 (October 1915): 291.

———. "Pan-Africa and New Racial Philosophy." *Crisis* 40 (November 1933): 247, 262.

———. *The Souls of Black Folk*. 1903. Reprint, New York: Vintage Books, 1990.

———. *W. E. B. Du Bois: A Reader*. Edited by David Levering Lewis. New York: Henry Holt, 1995.

Dubois, William. *Haiti*. In *Federal Theatre Project Plays*. Vol. 1. New York: Random House, 1938.

Dunham, Katherine. *Island Possessed*. Garden City, N.Y.: Doubleday, 1969.

Dunlap, Maurice. "Carrying the Gospel of Health to Haiti." *American Review of Reviews* 78 (September 1928): 296–301.

Endore, Guy. *Babouk*. New York: Vanguard Press, 1934.

———. *King of Paris*. New York: Simon and Schuster, 1956.

Evans, C. I. *Treaties and Other International Agreements of the United States of America, 1776–1949*. Vol. 8. Washington, D.C.: Department of State, 1971.

Fisk, Amos Kidder. *The West Indies*. New York: Putnam's Sons, 1902.

Forbes, Rosita. *Women Called Wild*. New York: E. P. Dutton, 1937.

Fort-Whiteman, Lovett. "Nemesis." *Messenger* 1, no. 11 (November 1917): 23–25.

Foster, Harry L. "Drums of Black Haiti." *Travel* 52 (November 1928): 37–39.

Franck, Harry. *Roaming through the West Indies*. New York: Century, 1920.

Frankfurter, Felix. "Haiti and Intervention." *New Republic* 25 (December 15, 1920): 71–72.

Franklyn, Irwin R. *Knights in the Cockpit: A Romantic Epic of the Flying Marines in Haiti*. New York: Dial Press, 1931.

Gayer, Jacob. "Hispaniola Rediscovered." *National Geographic Magazine* 59 (January 1931): 80–112.

Gray, William S., and Ruth Monroe. *The Reading Interests and Habits of Adults: A Preliminary Report*. New York: Macmillan, 1929.

Grimshaw, Anna, ed. *The C. L. R. James Reader*. London: Blackwell, 1992.

Gruening, Ernest. "At Last We're Getting Out of Haiti." *Nation* 138 (June 20, 1934): 700–701.

———. "The Conquest of Haiti and Santo Domingo." *Current History* 15 (March 1922): 885–96.

———. Editorials. *Nation* 111 (July 1–December 31, 1920): 231, 337, 436, 493, 517, 678, 720, 765.

———. *Many Battles: The Autobiography of Ernest Gruening*. New York: Liveright, 1973.

Hale, William Harlan. *Hannibal Hooker: His Death and Adventures*. New York: Random House, 1939.

Hall, Robert Burnett. "The Société Congo of the Ile à Gonave." *American Anthropologist* 31 (1929): 685–700.

Herskovits, Melville. *Life in a Haitian Valley*. New York: Alfred A. Knopf, 1937.

———. "Voodoo Nonsense." Review of *Voodoo Fire in Haiti*, by Richard Loederer. *Nation* 141 (September 11, 1935): 308.

Hill, Errol. *Black Heroes: Seven Plays*. New York: Applause Theatre Book Publishers, 1989.

Hill, Leslie Pickney. *Toussaint L'Ouverture*. 1918. Reprint, Boston: Christopher Publishing House, 1928.

Hilton, John. "Tramp in Haiti." *Spicy Adventure Stories* 12 (September 1940): 19–29, 107–8.

Hinman, George Warren. *Our Caribbean Neighbors: A Course for Adult Study Groups, based primarily on "Trailing the Conquistadors," by Samuel Guy Inman*. New York: Council for Home Missions and Missionary Education Movement, 1930.

Holly, Theodora. "Rich Haiti Awaits Wise Development." *Negro World* (March 14, 1925): 4.

Holt, Gavin. *Drums Beat at Night*. New York: Hodder and Stoughton, 1932.

Hopkins, J. A. H., and Melinda Alexander. *Machine Gun Diplomacy*. New York: Lewis Copeland, 1928.

Howland, Charles B. *Survey of American Foreign Relations*. New Haven: Yale University Press, 1929.

Hughes, Langston. *The Big Sea*. New York: Knopf, 1940.

———. *I Wonder as I Wander*. 1956. Reprint, New York: Hill and Wang, 1984.

———. "A Letter from Haiti." *New Masses* 7 (July 1931): 9.

———. *Not Without Laughter*. 1930. Reprint, New York: Collier Books, 1985.

———. "A People without Shoes: The Haitian Masses." In *Negro Anthology*, edited by Nancy Cunard, 468–70. 1934. Reprint, New York: Negro Universities Press, 1969.

———. *Troubled Island*. An opera in three acts by William Grant Still. Libretto by Langston Hughes. New York: Leeds Music Corporation, 1949.

———. "White Shadows in a Black Land." *Crisis* 39 (May 1932): 157.

Hurston, Zora Neale. *Mules and Men*. Bloomington: Indiana University Press, 1978.

———. *Tell My Horse: Voodoo and Life in Haiti and Jamaica*. 1938. Reprint, New York: Harper and Row, 1990.

Inman, Samuel Guy. "Imperialistic America." *Atlantic Monthly* 134 (July–December 1925): 107.

———. "The Present Situation in the Caribbean." *Journal of International Relations* 11 (October 1920): 289–317.

———. *Through Santo Domingo and Haiti: A Cruise with the Marines.* New York: Committee on Cooperation with Latin America, 1920.

———. *Trailing the Conquistadores.* New York: Friendship Press, 1930.

Isaacs, J. R., ed. *Plays of American Life and Fantasy.* New York: Coward, McCann, 1929.

James, C. L. R. *The Black Jacobins: Toussaint L'Ouverture and the San Domingo Revolution.* 1938. Reprint, New York: Random House, 1963.

———. *Black Majesty.* In *The C. L. R. James Reader,* edited by Anna Grimshaw, 67–111. London: Blackwell, 1992.

Jesse, F. Tennyson. *Moonraker; or, The Female Pirate and Her Friends.* New York: Alfred A. Knopf, 1927.

Johnson, James Weldon. *Along This Way: The Autobiography of James Weldon Johnson.* 1933. Reprint, New York: Penguin, 1990.

———. "The American Occupation." Part 1 of "Self-Determining Haiti." *Nation* 111 (August 28, 1920): 236–38.

———. *Black Manhattan.* New York: Alfred A. Knopf, 1930.

———. "Government of, by, and for the National City Bank." Part 3 of "Self-Determining Haiti." *Nation* 111 (September 11, 1920): 295–97.

———. "The Haitian People." Part 4 of "Self-Determining Haiti." *Nation* 111 (September 25, 1920): 345–47.

———. "Self-Determining Haiti." 4 parts. *Nation* 111 (August 28–September 25, 1920): 236–38, 265–67, 295–97, 345–47.

———. "The Truth about Haiti." *Crisis* 20 (September 1920): 217–24.

———. "What the United States Has Accomplished." Part 2 of "Self-Determining Haiti." *Nation* 111 (September 4, 1920): 265–67.

Johnston, Harry. *The Negro in the New World.* New York, 1910.

Jordon, W. F. *Crusading in the West Indies.* New York: Fleming H. Revell, 1922.

Kelsey, Carl. *The American Intervention in Haiti and the Dominican Republic.* Philadelphia: Annals of the American Academy of Political and Social Science, 1921.

Kidd, Benjamin. *Control of the Tropics.* London: Macmillan, 1898.

Knox, Katherine Jenckes. "Homemaking around the Globe." *American Home* 11 (January 1934): 78–79.

Koltes, F. X., and A. Albrecht. "Prevalence of Syphilis in Haiti." *Naval Medical Bulletin* 12 (July 1918).

Kuser, J. Dryden. *Haiti: Its Dawn of Progress after Years in a Night of Revolution.* Boston: Richard G. Badger, 1921.

Laleau, Leon. *Le choc: Chronique haïtienne des années 1915–1918.* 1932. Reprint, Port-au-Prince: Imprimerie Centrale, 1975.

Lewis, David Levering. *W. E. B. Du Bois: A Reader.* New York: Henry Holt, 1995.

Leyburn, James G. *The Haitian People.* New Haven: Yale University Press, 1941.

———. "The Making of a Black Nation." In *Studies in the Science of Society,* edited by George P. Murdoch, 377–94. New Haven: Yale University Press, 1937.

Link, Arthur S., ed. *The Papers of Woodrow Wilson.* 69 vols. Princeton, N.J.: Princeton University Press, 1978.

Loederer, Richard. *Voodoo Fire in Haiti.* New York: Literary Guild, 1935.

Logan, Rayford M. *The Diplomatic Relations of the United States with Haiti, 1776–1891.* Chapel Hill: University of North Carolina Press, 1941. Reprint, New York: Kraus Reprint, 1969.

———. "Education in Haiti." *Journal of Negro History* 15 (October 1930): 401–60.

———. "Haiti: The Native Point of View." *Southern Workman* 58, no. 1 (January 1929): 36–40.

———. "The Haze in Haiti." *Nation* 124 (March 16, 1927): 281–83.

MacCorkle, William A. *The Monroe Doctrine in Its Relation to Haiti.* New York: Neale Publishing, 1915.

Mahan, Alfred Thayer. *The Influence of Sea Power upon World History, 1660–1783.* Boston: Little, Brown, 1890.

Marshall, Harriet Gibbs. *The Story of Haiti.* Boston: Christopher Publishing House, 1930.

McCormick, Medill. "Our Failure in Haiti." *Nation* 111 (December 1, 1920): 615–16.

McMillen, Fred E. "Some Haitian Recollections." *United States Naval Institute Proceedings* 62 (April 1936): 522–36.

"Memoir of the Political, Economic, and Financial Conditions Existing in the Republic of Haiti under the American Occupation by the Delegates to the U.S. of the Union Patriotique d'Haïti." *Nation* 112 (May 25, 1921).

Mervin, Bruce W. "A Voodoo Drum from Haiti." *University of Pennsylvania Museum Journal* 8 (1917): 123–25.

Millspaugh, Arthur C. *Haiti under American Control, 1915–1930.* Boston: World Peace Foundation, 1931.

Montague, Ludwell Lee. *Haiti and the United States, 1714–1938.* Durham, N.C.: Duke University Press, 1940.

Montavon, William Frederick. *Haiti, Past and Present.* Washington, D.C.: Catholic Association for International Peace, 1930.

Munro, Dana Gardner. *Intervention and Dollar Diplomacy in the Caribbean, 1900–1921.* Princeton, N.J.: Princeton University Press, 1964.

———. *The United States and the Caribbean Republics, 1921–1933.* Princeton, N.J.: Princeton University Press, 1974.

Nearing, Scott, and J. Freeman. *Dollar Diplomacy: A Study in American Imperialism.* New York: B. W. Huebsch and the Viking Press, 1925.

Newcombe, Covelle. *Black Fire: The Story of Henri-Christophe.* New York: Longmans, Green, 1940.

Niles, Blair Rice. *Black Haiti: A Biography of Africa's Eldest Daughter.* New York: G. P. Putnam's Sons, 1926.

Niles, Robert. "An Architect's View of the Fortress of the Black King Christophe." *Journal of American Institute of Architects* 164 (April 1928): 147.

Nock, Albert J. "The Bright Isle." *Atlantic Monthly* 159 (1937): 552–59.

Ober, F. A. *A Guide to the West Indies and Bermuda.* New York, 1908.

O'Neill, Eugene. *The Emperor Jones.* In *Eugene O'Neill: Complete Plays, 1913–1920,* with notes by Travis Bogard. New York: Library of America, 1988.

———. *The Hairy Ape.* In *Eugene O'Neill: Complete Plays, 1920–1931,* with notes by Travis Bogard. New York: Library of America, 1988.

———. *Selected Letters of Eugene O'Neill.* Edited by Travis Bogard and Jackson R. Bryer. New Haven: Yale University Press, 1988.

Osterhout, George H., Jr. "A Little-Known Marvel of the Western Hemisphere: Christophe's Citadel." *National Geographic Magazine* (December 1920).

Padmore, George. *Folklore of the Antilles, French and English*. 2 vols. American Folk-Lore Society, Memoir 26. New York: American Folk-Lore Society, 1933.

———. *Haiti, an American Slave Colony*. Moscow: Centrizdat, 1931.

———. "The Revolt in Haiti." *Labour Monthly* (London) 12 (June 1930): 356–66.

Parsons, Elsie Clews. *Spirit Cult in Haiti*. Paris, 1928.

———. "Spirituals from the 'American' Colony of Samana Bay, Santo Domingo." *Journal of American Folklore* 41 (1928): 525–28.

Price-Mars, Jean. *Ainsi parla l'oncle*. 1928. Translated as *So Spoke the Uncle*, by Magdaline W. Shannon. Washington, D.C.: Three Continents Press, 1983.

———. *La vocation de l'élite*. Port-au-Prince: Edmond Chenet, 1919. Reprint, Port-au-Prince: Ateliers Fardin, [c. 1977].

Prichard, Hesketh. *Where Black Rules White: A Journey across and about Hayti*. New York: Westminster, 1900.

Redfield, Robert. Review of *The Magic Island* and *An Account of the "Witch" Murder Trial, York, Pennsylvania, January 7–9, 1929*. *American Journal of Sociology* 35, no. 2 (September 1929): 315–17.

Riis, Jacob. *How the Other Half Lives*. Edited by David Leviatin. New York: Bedford Books, 1996.

Riley, Woodbridge. Review of *The Magic Island*. *Yale Review* 19 (September 1929): 185–87.

Robillard, Fred S. *As Robie Remembers*. Bridgeport, Conn.: Wright's Investors' Service, 1969.

Rodman, Selden. *The Revolutionists: A Tragedy in Three Acts*. New York: Duell, Sloan and Pearce, 1942.

Roumain, Jacques. *Masters of the Dew*. Translated by Langston Hughes and Mercer Cook. 1941. Reprint, New York: Collier Books, 1971.

Ruhl, Arthur. "What America Is Doing for Haiti." *Current History* (August 1925).

Rutherford, Mildred Lewis. *Wrongs of History Righted*. Atlanta, Ga.: United Daughters of the Confederacy, 1914.

Rycroft, W. Stanley. *On This Foundation: The Evangelical Witness in Latin America*. New York: Friendship Press, [1942].

St. John, Sir Spenser. *Hayti, or the Black Republic*. 1884. Reprint, London: Frank Cass, 1971.

Schoenrich, Otto. *Santo Domingo: A Country with a Future*. New York, 1918.

Schomburg, Arthur Alfonso. *Military Services Rendered by the Haitians in the North and South American Wars for Independence*. Nashville: AME Sunday School Union, 1921.

Scottman, Drake. "A Marine Remembers Haiti." *Leatherneck* 26 (February 1943): 22–23.

Seabrook, William B. *The Magic Island*. New York: Harcourt, Brace, 1929.

———. *No Hiding Place: An Autobiography*. New York: J. B. Lippincott, 1942.

Seaman, Augusta H. *The Charlemonte Crest: A Mystery of Modern Haiti*. Garden City, N.Y.: Doubleday, Doran, 1930.

Seligmann, Herbert. "The Conquest of Haiti." *Nation* 111 (July 10, 1920): 35.

Shipman, Charles. *It Had to Be Revolution: Memoirs of an American Radical*. Ithaca, N.Y.: Cornell University Press, 1993.

Simpson, George Eaton. "Haitian Peasant Economy." *Journal of Negro History* 25 (1940): 498–519.

———. "The Vodoun Service in Northern Haiti." *American Anthropologist* 42 (1940): 236–54.

Stoddard, T. Lothrop. *The French Revolution in San Domingo*. Boston: Houghton Mifflin, 1914.

Stowell, Jay S. *Between the Americas*. New York: Council for Home Missions and Missionary Education Movement, 1930.

Sylvain, Georges. *Dix années de lutte pour la liberté, 1915–1925*. Port-au-Prince: Henri Deschamps, 1950.

Taft, Edna. *A Puritan in Voodoo Land*. Philadelphia: Penn Publishing, 1938.

Tait, Agnes. "The Petals Fall Slowly." *New Yorker* (October 6, 1934).

Taylor, J. G. "The Last Sacrifice." *Astounding Stories*, December 1933.

Thomason, John W., Jr. *Fix Bayonets!* New York: Charles Scribner's Sons, 1926.

Thorpe, George C. "American Achievements in Santo Domingo, Haiti, and the Virgin Islands." *Journal of International Relations* 11 (October 1920): 63–86.

Tridon, André. *Psychoanalysis and Love*. New York: Brentano's, 1922.

United States Department of Commerce. *Haiti: An Economic Survey*. Trade Information Bulletin no. 264, Supplement to Commerce Reports, Published by the Bureau of Foreign and Domestic Commerce, August 25, 1924. Washington, D.C.: Government Printing Office, 1924.

United States Department of State. *Papers Relating to the Foreign Relations of the United States*. Washington, D.C.: Government Printing Office, 1913–34.

United States Senate. Inquiry into Occupation and Administration of Haiti and Santo Domingo. *Hearings before a Select Committee on Haiti and Santo Domingo*. 67th Cong., 1st and 2nd sess., 1922. 2 vols. Washington, D.C.: Government Printing Office, 1922.

Valcin, Virgile. *La blanche négresse*. Port-au-Prince: V. Valcin, [c. 1934].

Vandegrift, Alexander Archer. *Once a Marine: The Memoirs of General A. A. Vandegrift, United States Marine Corps*. As told to Robert B. Asprey. New York: Norton, 1964.

Vandercook, John. *Black Majesty*. New York: Literary Guild of America, 1928.

——. *Caribbee Cruise: A Guide to the West Indies*. New York: Reynal and Hitchcock, 1938.

Van Doren, Carl. "Why the Editorial Board Selected *The Magic Island*." *Wings* 3, no. 1 (January 1929): 2–7.

Van Vechten, Carl. *Nigger Heaven*. 1926. Reprint, New York: Harper and Row, 1971.

"Wards of the United States." *National Geographic Magazine* 30 (August 1916): 143–77.

Washington, Booker T. "Haiti and the United States." *Outlook* 111 (November 17, 1915): 681.

Waxman, Percy. *The Black Napoleon*. New York: Harcourt and Brace, 1931.

Weatherly, Ulysses G. "Haiti: An Experiment in Pragmatism." *American Journal of Sociology* 32, no. 3 (1926): 353–66.

Welles, Orson. *Orson Welles on Shakespeare: The WPA and the Mercury Theatre Playscripts*. Edited by Richard France. New York: Greenwood Press, 1990.

Williams, Joseph J. *Voodoos and Obeahs: Phases of West Indian Witchcraft*. New York: Dial Press, 1932.

Williams, Paul W. *The American Policy of Intervention and the Monroe Doctrine with Special Reference to the Military Occupation of Haiti and the Dominican Republic*. Cambridge, Mass.: Harvard University Press, 1925.

Wilson, Adelaide. *First Woman*. New York: McCauley, 1933.

Wilson, Woodrow. *The Papers of Woodrow Wilson*. Edited by Arthur S. Link. 69 vols. Princeton, N.J.: Princeton University Press, 1966–94.

Wintz, Cary D., ed. *African American Political Thought, 1890–1930: Washington, Du Bois, Garvey, and Randolph*. Armonk, N.Y.: M. E. Sharpe, 1996.

Wirkus, Faustin, and Taney Dudley. *The White King of La Gonave*. Garden City, N.Y.: Garden City Publishing, 1931.

Wirkus, Faustin, and H. W. Lanier. "The Black Pope of Voodoo." *Harper's Magazine* 168
(December 1933): 38–49; (January 1934): 189–98.
Wise, Frederick M. *A Marine Tells It to You.* New York: J. H. Sears, 1929.
Yarborough, Lavinia Williams. *Haiti-Dance.* Frankfurt am Main: Bronners Druckerai,
1959.

Other Media
Angels in the Mirror. Compact disc and book. Roslyn, N.Y.: Ellipsis Arts, 1997.
The Emperor Jones. Film. United Artists, 1933.
I Walked with a Zombie. Film. RKO Radio Pictures, 1943.
Revolt of the Zombies. Film. United Artists, 1936.
Rhythms of Rapture: Sacred Music of Haitian Vodou. Compact disc. Smithsonian/Folkways,
1995.
White Zombie. Film. United Artists, 1932.

SECONDARY SOURCES

Anderson, Benedict. *Imagined Communities: Reflections on the Origin and Spread of
Nationalism.* London: Verso, 1986.
Anderson, Gerald H., ed. *Biographical Dictionary of Christian Missions.* New York:
Macmillan Reference USA, 1998.
Anderson, Jervis. *A. Philip Randolph: A Biographical Portrait.* New York: Harcourt Brace
Jovanovich, 1972.
———. *This Was Harlem, 1900–1950.* New York: Farrar Straus Giroux, Noonday Press,
1981.
Anderson, Warwick. "The Trespass Speaks: White Masculinity and Colonial
Breakdown." *American Historical Review* 102 (December 1997): 1343–70.
Antoine, Jacques C. *Jean Price-Mars and Haiti.* Washington, D.C.: Three Continents Press,
1981.
Anzaldúa, Gloria. *Borderlands: The New Mestiza.* San Francisco: Aunt Lutte Books,
1987.
Appy, Christian G. *Working-Class War: American Combat Soldiers and Vietnam.* Chapel Hill:
University of North Carolina Press, 1993.
Arciniegas, German. *El continente de siete colores: Historia de la cultura en America Latina.*
Buenos Aires: Editorial Sudamericana, 1965.
Barad, Karen. "Getting Real: Techno-Scientific Practices and the Materialization of
Reality." *Differences: A Journal of Feminist Cultural Studies* 10, no. 2 (1998): 87–128.
Barkan, Elazar. *The Retreat of Scientific Racism: Changing Concepts of Race in Britain and the
U.S. between the World Wars.* New York: Cambridge University Press, 1992.
Baron, Ava. "Questions of Gender: Deskilling and Demasculinization in the U.S.
Printing Industry, 1830–1915." *Gender and History* 1 (Summer 1989): 178–99.
Bederman, Gail. "'Civilization,' the Decline of Middle-Class Manliness, and Ida B.
Wells's Anti-Lynching Campaign." In *Gender and American History*, edited by Barbara
Melosh, 207–39. New York: Routledge, 1993.
———. *Manliness and Civilization: A Cultural History of Gender and Race in the United States,
1880–1917.* Chicago: University of Chicago Press, 1995.
Behar, Ruth, and Deborah A. Gordon, eds. *Women Writing Culture.* Berkeley: University of
California Press, 1995.

Beisner, Robert L. "AHR Forum: American Imperialism: The Worst Chapter in Almost Any Book: Comments." *American Historical Review* 83 (June 1978): 672–78.

Belcher, Fannin Saffore, Jr. "The Place of the Negro in the Evolution of the American Theatre." Ph.D. dissertation, Yale University, 1945.

Bellegarde-Smith, Patrick. *Haiti: The Breached Citadel.* Boulder, Colo.: Westview Press, 1990.

Bemis, Samuel Flagg. " 'America' and 'Americans.' " *Yale Review* 57 (1968): 321–36.

Bernstein, Iver. *The New York Draft Riots: Their Significance for American Society and Politics in the Age of the Civil War.* New York: Oxford University Press, 1990.

Bhabha, Homi K. "Difference, Discrimination, and the Discourse of Colonialism." In *The Politics of Theory*, edited by Francis Barker et al. Colchester: University of Essex, 1983.

———. "Of Mimicry and Man: The Ambivalence of Colonial Discourse." *October* 28 (1984): 125–33.

Blassingame, John. "The Press and American Intervention in Haiti and the Dominican Republic, 1904–1920." *Caribbean Studies* 9, no. 2 (July 1969): 27–43.

Blee, Kathleen M. *Women of the Klan: Racism and Gender in the 1920s.* Berkeley: University of California Press, 1991.

Brands, H. W. *Bound to Empire: The United States and the Philippines.* New York: Oxford University Press, 1992.

Brown, Karen McCarthy. *Mama Lola: A Vodou Priestess in Brooklyn.* Berkeley: University of California Press, 1991.

Brumberg, Joan Jacobs. "Zenanas and Girlless Villages: The Ethnology of American Evangelical Women, 1870–1910." *Journal of American History* 69 (September 1982): 347–71.

Brumberg, Stephan F. *Going to America, Going to School: The Jewish Immigrant Public School Encounter in Turn-of-the-Century New York City.* New York: Praeger, 1986.

Buchanan, Harriette Cuttino. "Blair Rice Niles." In *American Women Writers*, edited by Lina Mainiero, 3:267. New York: Frederick Ungar, 1981.

Buckner, David N. *A Brief History of the 10th Marines.* Washington, D.C.: History and Museums Division, Headquarters, USMC, 1981.

Buhle, Mari Jo. *Feminism and Its Discontents: A Century of Struggle with Psychoanalysis.* Cambridge, Mass.: Harvard University Press, 1998.

Burton, Orville Vernon. *In My Father's House Are Many Mansions: Family and Community in Edgefield, South Carolina.* Chapel Hill: University of North Carolina Press, 1985.

Calloway, Helen. *Gender, Culture, and Empire: European Women in Colonial Nigeria.* London: Macmillan, 1987.

Carby, Hazel. *Race Men.* Cambridge, Mass.: Harvard University Press, 1998.

———. *Reconstructing Womanhood: The Emergence of the Afro-American Woman Novelist.* New York: Oxford University Press, 1987.

Cargill, Oscar, N. Bryllion Fagin, and William J. Fisher, eds. *O'Neill and His Plays: Four Decades of Criticism.* New York: New York University Press, 1961.

Cashin, Joan E. *A Family Venture: Men and Women of the Southern Frontier.* New York: Oxford University Press, 1991.

Censer, Jane Turner. *North Carolina Planters and Their Children, 1800–1860.* Baton Rouge: Louisiana State University Press, 1984.

Challener, Richard D. *Admirals, Generals, and American Foreign Policy, 1898–1914.* Princeton, N.J.: Princeton University Press, 1973.

Champie, Elmore A. *A Brief History of the Marine Corps Recruit Depot, Parris Island, S.C., 1891–1962.* Washington, D.C.: Historical Division, Headquarters, USMC, 1962.

Chancy, Myriam J. A. *Framing Silence: Revolutionary Novels by Haitian Women.* New Brunswick, N.J.: Rutgers University Press, 1997.

Chauncey, George. "Christian Brotherhood or Sexual Perversion? Homosexual Identities and the Construction of Sexual Boundaries in the World War I Era." In *Gender and American History,* edited by Barbara Melosh, 72–105. New York: Routledge, 1993.

———. *Gay New York: Gender, Urban Culture, and the Making of the Gay Male World, 1890–1940.* New York: Basic Books, 1994.

Cheyfitz, Eric. *The Poetics of Imperialism: Translation and Colonization from "The Tempest" to "Tarzan."* New York: Oxford University Press, 1991.

———. "Savage Law: The Plot against American Indians in *Johnson and Graham's Lessee v. M'Intosh* and *The Pioneers.*" In *Cultures of United States Imperialism,* edited by Amy Kaplan and Donald E. Pease, 109–28. Durham, N.C.: Duke University Press, 1993.

Chrisman, Laura. "The Imperial Unconscious? Representations of Imperial Discourse." In *Colonial Discourse and Post-Colonial Theory,* edited by Patrick Williams and Laura Chrisman, 498–516. New York: Columbia University Press, 1994.

Clark, VèVè. "Haiti's Tragic Overture: (Mis)Representations of the Haitian Revolution in World Drama (1796–1975)." In *Representing Revolution: Essays on Reflections of the French Revolution in Literature, Historiography, and Art,* edited by James Heffernan. Hanover, N.H.: University Press of New England, 1991.

———. "When Womb Waters Break: The Emergence of Haitian New Theatre (1953–1987)." *Callaloo* 15, no. 3 (Summer 1992): 778–86.

Clifford, James. "Negrophilia." In *A New History of French Literature,* edited by Denis Hollier, 901–8. Cambridge, Mass.: Harvard University Press, 1989.

———. *The Predicament of Culture: Twentieth-Century Ethnography, Literature, and Art.* Cambridge, Mass.: Harvard University Press, 1988.

Clymer, Kenton J. *Protestant Missionaries in the Philippines, 1898–1916: An Inquiry into the American Colonial Mentality.* Urbana: University of Illinois Press, 1986.

Coletta, Paolo E. *American Secretaries of the Navy.* Vol. 2, *1913–1972.* Annapolis, Md.: Naval Institute Press, 1980.

———. *A Survey of U.S. Naval Affairs, 1865–1917.* Lanham, Md.: University Press of America, 1987.

Comaroff, Jean, and John Comaroff. *Of Revelation and Revolution: Christianity, Colonialism, and Consciousness in South Africa.* 2 vols. Chicago: University of Chicago Press, 1991.

Corvington, Georges. *Port-au-Prince au cours des ans. La capitale d'Haïti sous l'occupation: 1915–1922.* Port-au-Prince: Imprimerie Henri Deschamps, 1984.

Costigliola, Frank. " 'Unceasing Pressure for Penetration': Gender, Pathology, and Emotion in George Kennan's Formation of the Cold War." *Journal of American History* 83 (March 1997): 1309–39.

Cott, Nancy F. *The Grounding of Modern Feminism.* New Haven: Yale University Press, 1987.

———. "On Men's History and Women's History." In *Meanings for Manhood: Constructions of Masculinity in Victorian America,* edited by Mark C. Carnes and Clyde Griffen, 204–19. Chicago: University of Chicago Press, 1990.

Covello, Leonard. *The Teacher in the Urban Community.* Totowa, N.J.: Littlefield, Adams, 1970.

Cripps, Thomas. *Slow Fade to Black: The Negro in American Film, 1900–1942.* New York: Oxford University Press, 1993.

Dash, J. Michael. *Haiti and the United States: National Stereotypes and the Literary Imagination.* London: Macmillan, 1988.

Davis, David Brion. *The Problem of Slavery in the Age of Revolution*. Ithaca, N.Y.: Cornell University Press, 1975.

Dawley, Alan. *Struggles for Justice: Social Responsibility and the Liberal State*. Cambridge, Mass.: Belknap Press of Harvard University Press, 1991.

Dayan, Joan. "Erzulie: A Women's History of Haiti?" In *Postcolonial Subjects: Francophone Women Writers*, edited by Mary Jean Green et al., 42–60. Minneapolis: University of Minnesota Press, 1996.

———. *Haiti, History, and the Gods*. Berkeley: University of California Press, 1995.

de Lauretis, Teresa. *Technologies of Gender: Essays on Theory, Film, and Fiction*. Bloomington: Indiana University Press, 1987.

Delbanco, Andrew. "The Political Incorrectness of Zora Neale Hurston." In *Required Reading: Why Our American Classics Matter Now*, 189–206. New York: Farrar, Straus and Giroux, 1997.

Delpar, Helen. *The Enormous Vogue of Things Mexican: Cultural Relations between the United States and Mexico, 1920–1935*. Tuscaloosa: University of Alabama Press, 1992.

Desmangles, Leslie. *Faces of the Gods: Vodou and Roman Catholicism in Haiti*. Chapel Hill: University of North Carolina Press, 1992.

Doyle, David Noel. *Irish Americans, Native Rights and National Empires: The Structure, Divisions and Attitudes of the Catholic Minority in the Decade of Expansion, 1890–1901*. New York: Arno Press, 1976.

Drinnon, Richard. *Facing West: Indian Hating and Empire Building*. New York: Schocken Books, 1980.

Driskell, David C. *Two Centuries of Black American Art*. New York: Alfred A. Knopf, 1976.

Duberman, Martin Bauml. *Paul Robeson: A Biography*. New York: Ballantine, 1989.

DuBois, Ellen Carol. "Working Women, Class Relations, and Suffrage Militance: Harriot Stanton Blatch and the New York Woman Suffrage Movement, 1894–1909." In *Unequal Sisters: A Multicultural Reader in U.S. Women's History*, edited by Ellen Carol DuBois and Vicki L. Ruiz, 176–94. New York: Routledge, 1990.

Dupuy, Alex. *Haiti in the World Economy: Class, Race, and Underdevelopment since 1700*. Boulder, Colo.: Westview Press, 1989.

Elkins, Stanley, and Eric McKitrick. *The Age of Federalism: The Early American Republic, 1788–1800*. New York: Oxford University Press, 1993.

Ellsworth, Harry Allanson. *One Hundred Eighty Landings of United States Marines, 1800–1934*. Washington, D.C.: History and Museums Division, Headquarters, USMC, 1974.

Ely, Cecil Degrotte. *The Road to Armageddon: The Martial Spirit in English Popular Literature, 1870–1914*. Durham, N.C.: Duke University Press, 1987.

Enloe, Cynthia. *Bananas, Beaches, Bases*. Berkeley: University of California Press, 1989.

———. *Maneuvers*. Berkeley: University of California Press, 2000.

Erenberg, Lewis A. *Steppin' Out: New York Nightlife and the Transformation of American Culture, 1890–1930*. Chicago: University of Chicago Press, 1981.

Farred, Grant. "First Stop, Port-au-Prince: Mapping Postcolonial Africa through Toussaint L'Ouverture and His Black Jacobins." In *The Politics of Culture in the Shadow of Capital*, edited by Lisa Lowe and David Lloyd, 227–47. Durham, N.C.: Duke University Press, 1997.

———, ed. *Rethinking C. L. R. James*. Cambridge, Mass.: Basil Blackwell Publishers, 1996.

Fenwick Library, George Mason University. *The Federal Theatre Project: A Catalog-Calendar of Productions*. New York: Greenwood Press, 1986.

Ferguson, Russell, et al., eds. *Out There: Marginalization and Contemporary Cultures*. New York: New Museum of Contemporary Art and MIT Press, 1990.

Fernandez, Ronald. *Cruising the Caribbean: U.S. Influence and Intervention in the Twentieth Century*. Monroe, Maine: Common Courage Press, 1994.

Field, James A., Jr. "AHR Forum: American Imperialism: The Worst Chapter in Almost Any Book: Comments." *American Historical Review* 83 (June 1978): 644–68.

Filene, Peter. *Him/Her/Self: Gender in Modern America*. 3rd ed. Baltimore: Johns Hopkins University Press, 1986.

Findlay, Eileen J. Suárez. *Imposing Decency: The Politics of Sexuality and Race in Puerto Rico, 1870–1920*. Durham, N.C.: Duke University Press, 1999.

Fleming, Charles A., Robin L. Austin, and Charles A. Braley III. *Quantico: Crossroads of the Marine Corps*. Washington, D.C.: History and Museums Division, Headquarters, USMC, 1979.

Flexner, Stuart Berg. *Listening to America: An Illustrated History of Words and Phrases from Our Lively and Splendid Past*. New York: Simon and Schuster, 1982.

Fossett, Judith Jackson. "Listening to Empire: Lamont Cranston and 'The Shadow' Go Abroad." Paper presented at the panel on Writing Empire: A Roundtable of Critical Historiographies. American Studies Association annual meeting, Seattle, November 1998.

Foster, Catherine. *Women for All Seasons: The Story of the Women's International League for Peace and Freedom*. Athens: University of Georgia Press, 1989.

Foucault, Michel. *Power/Knowledge: Selected Interviews and Other Writings, 1972–1977*. Edited by Colin Gordon. New York: Pantheon Books, 1980.

Fouchard, Jean. *The Haitian Maroons: Liberty or Death*. Translated by A. Faulkner Watts. New York: E. W. Blyden Press, [c. 1981].

Frank, Alan G. *Horror Movies: Tales of Terror in the Cinema*. N.p.: Cathay Books, 1974.

Frank, Stephen. *Life with Father: Parenthood and Masculinity in the Nineteenth-Century American North*. Baltimore: Johns Hopkins University Press, 1998.

Freedman, Estelle. "The Response to the Sexual Psychopath, 1920–1960." *Journal of American History* 74 (June 1987): 83–106.

Frenz, Horst. *Eugene O'Neill*. New York: Frederick Ungar, 1971.

Freud, Sigmund, and William C. Bullitt. *Thomas Woodrow Wilson, Twenty-Eighth President of the United States: A Psychological Study*. Boston: Houghton, Mifflin, 1967.

Frow, John, and Meaghan Morris. "Australian Cultural Studies." In *What Is Cultural Studies? A Reader*, edited by John Storey, 344–67. London: Arnold, 1996.

Gaillard, Roger. *Les blancs débarquent*. 7 vols. Port-au-Prince: Various publishers, 1973–85.

———. *Les cents jours de Rosalvo Bobo*. Vol. 2 of *Les blancs débarquent*. Port-au-Prince: Presse Nacionales, 1973.

———. *Hinche mise en croix*. Vol. 5 of *Les blancs débarquent*. Port-au-Prince: Roger Gaillard, 1984.

———. *Premier écrasement du cacoïsme*. Vol. 3 of *Les blancs débarquent*. N.p.: Imprimerie Natal, 1981.

———. *La république autoritaire*. Vol. 4 of *Les blancs débarquent*. Port-au-Prince: R. Gaillard, 1982.

Gaspar, David Barry, and Michel-Rolph Trouillot. "History, Fiction, and the Slave Experience." Afterword to *Babouk*, by Guy Endore. New York: Monthly Review Press, 1991.

Gearheart, Suzanne. "Colonialism, Psychoanalysis, and Cultural Criticism: The Problem of Interiorization in the Work of Albert Memmi." In *"Culture" and the Problem of the Disciplines*, edited by John Carlos Rowe, 171–97. New York: Columbia University Press, 1998.

Geggus, David Patrick. "La cérémonie du Bois-Caïman." *Chemins Critiques* 2, no. 3 (May 1992): 59–78.

———. "The Haitian Revolution." In *The Modern Caribbean*, edited by Franklin W. Knight and Colin A. Palmer, 21–50. Chapel Hill: University of North Carolina Press, 1989.

———. *Slavery, War, and Revolution: The British Occupation of Saint Domingue, 1793–1798*. Oxford: Clarendon Press, 1982.

Gelb, Arthur, and Barbara Gelb. *O'Neill*. New York: Harper and Brothers, 1960.

Genovese, Eugene. *Roll, Jordan, Roll: The World the Slaves Made*. New York: Vintage Books, 1976.

Gill, Glenda. *White Grease Paint on Black Performers: A Study of the Federal Theatre, 1935–1939*. New York: Peter Lang, 1988.

Gilmore, Glenda Elizabeth. *Gender and Jim Crow: Women and the Politics of White Supremacy in North Carolina, 1896–1920*. Chapel Hill: University of North Carolina Press, 1996.

Gindine, Yvette. "Images of the American in Haitian Literature during the Occupation, 1915–1934." *Caribbean Studies* 14 (1974): 37–52.

Ginzburg, Carlo. *The Cheese and the Worms: The Cosmos of a Sixteenth-Century Miller*. Translated by John Tedeschi and Anne Tedeschi. New York: Penguin Books, 1983.

Green, Harvey. *Fit for America: Health, Fitness, Sport, and American Society*. New York: Pantheon Books, 1986.

Green, James R. *The World of the Worker: Labor in Twentieth-Century America*. New York: Hill and Wang, 1980.

Green, Martin. *The Adventurous Male: Chapters in the History of the White Male Mind*. University Park: Pennsylvania State University Press, 1993.

———. *Dreams of Adventure, Deeds of Empire*. New York: Basic Books, 1979.

Griffen, Clyde. "Reconstructing Masculinity from the Evangelical Revivals to the Waning of Progressivism: A Speculative Synthesis." In *Meanings for Manhood: Constructions of Masculinity in Victorian America*, edited by Mark C. Carnes and Clyde Griffen, 183–203. Chicago: University of Chicago Press, 1990.

Griswold, Robert L. *Fatherhood in America: A History*. New York: Basic Books, 1993.

Grossman, James R. *Land of Hope: Chicago, Black Southerners, and the Great Migration*. Chicago: University of Chicago Press, 1989.

Haag, Pamela. *Consent: Sexual Rights and the Transformation of American Liberalism*. Ithaca, N.Y.: Cornell University Press, 1999.

Hall, Colby D. *Texas Disciples*. Fort Worth: Texas Christian University Press, 1953.

Hall, Stuart. "C. L. R. James: A Portrait." In *C. L. R. James's Caribbean*, edited by Paget Henry and Paul Buhle, 3–16. Durham, N.C.: Duke University Press, 1992.

———. "The Rediscovery of 'Ideology.' " In *Culture, Society and the Media*, edited by Michael Gurevitch et al., 56–90. London: Methuen, 1982.

Haraway, Donna. *Primate Visions: Gender, Race, and Nature in the World of Modern Science*. New York: Routledge, 1989.

Harris, William H. *Keeping the Faith: A. Philip Randolph, Milton P. Webster, and the Brotherhood of Sleeping Car Porters, 1925–37*. Urbana: University of Illinois Press, 1977.

Healy, David. *Drive to Hegemony: The United States in the Caribbean, 1898–1917*. Madison: University of Wisconsin Press, 1988.

———. *Gunboat Diplomacy in the Wilson Era: The U.S. Navy in Haiti, 1915–1916*. Madison: University of Wisconsin Press, 1976.

Heckscher, August. *Woodrow Wilson*. New York: Charles Scribner's Sons, Macmillan, 1991.

Heinl, Robert Debs, and Nancy Gordon Heinl. *Written in Blood: The Story of the Haitian People, 1492–1971*. Boston: Houghton Mifflin, 1978.

Hemenway, Robert E. *Zora Neale Hurston: A Literary Biography*. Urbana: University of Illinois Press, 1977.

Hernandez, Graciela. "Multiple Subjectivities and Strategies of Positionality: Zora Neale Hurston's Experimental Ethnographies." In *Women Writing Culture*, edited by Ruth Behar and Deborah A. Gordon. Berkeley: University of California Press, 1995.

Herskovits, Melville J. *Franz Boas: The Science of Man in the Making*. New York: Scribner, 1953.

Hetherington, Penelope. *British Paternalism and Africa, 1920–1940*. London: Frank Cass, 1978.

Higginbotham, Evelyn Brooks. *Righteous Discontent: The Women's Movement in the Black Baptist Church, 1880–1920*. Cambridge, Mass.: Harvard University Press, 1993.

High, James. "The Marine Corps and Crowd Control: Training and Experience." In *Bayonets in the Streets*, edited by Robin D. S. Higham, 113–35. Lawrence: University Press of Kansas, 1969.

Higham, John. "The Reorientation of American Culture in the 1890s." In *Writing American History*, 73–102. Bloomington: Indiana University Press, 1970.

———. *Strangers in the Land: Patterns of American Nativism, 1860–1925*. New Brunswick, N.J.: Rutgers University Press, 1955.

Hill, Patricia. *The World Their Household: The American Woman's Foreign Mission Movement and Cultural Transformation, 1870–1920*. Ann Arbor: University of Michigan Press, 1985.

Hine, Darlene Clark. "Rape and the Inner Lives of Black Women in the Middle West: Preliminary Thoughts on the Culture of Dissemblance." In *Unequal Sisters: A Multicultural Reader in U.S. Women's History*, 2nd ed., edited by Vicki Ruiz and Ellen Carol DuBois, 342–47. New York: Routledge, 1994.

Hixson, William B., Jr. *Moorfield Storey and the Abolitionist Tradition*. New York: Oxford University Press, 1972.

Hoffmann, François. "Histoire, mythe et idéologie: La cérémonie du Bois-Caïman." *Études créoles: Culture, langue, société* 13, no. 1 (1990): 9–34.

Hogan, Michael J. *America in the World: The Historiography of American Foreign Relations since 1941*. New York: Cambridge University Press, 1996.

Hoganson, Kristin L. *Fighting for American Manhood: How Gender Politics Provoked the Spanish-American and Philippine-American Wars*. New Haven: Yale University Press, 1988.

Horsman, Reginald. *Race and Manifest Destiny: The Origins of American Radical Anglo-Saxonism*. Cambridge, Mass.: Harvard University Press, 1981.

Huggins, Martha K. *Political Policing: The United States and Latin America*. Durham, N.C.: Duke University Press, 1998.

Huggins, Nathan Irvin. *Harlem Renaissance*. New York: Oxford University Press, 1971.

Hunt, Alfred N. *Haiti's Influence on Antebellum America: Slumbering Volcano in the Caribbean*. Baton Rouge: Louisiana State University Press, 1988.

Hunter, Jane. *The Gospel of Gentility: American Women Missionaries in Turn-of-the-Century China*. New Haven: Yale University Press, 1984.

Iriye, Akira. "Culture and Power: International Relations as Intercultural Relations." *Diplomatic History* 3 (1979): 115–28.

———. "A Round Table: Explaining the History of American Foreign Relations — Culture." *Journal of American History* 77 (June 1990): 99–107.

Jackman, Mary R. *The Velvet Glove: Paternalism and Conflict in Gender, Class, and Race Relations*. Berkeley: University of California Press, 1994.

Jacobson, Mathew Frye. *Special Sorrows: The Diasporic Imagination of Irish, Polish, and Jewish Immigrants in the United States*. Cambridge, Mass.: Harvard University Press, 1995.

———. *Whiteness of a Different Color: European Immigrants and the Alchemy of Race*. Cambridge, Mass.: Harvard University Press, 1998.

Jeffords, Susan. *The Remasculinization of America: Gender and the Vietnam War*. Bloomington: Indiana University Press, 1989.

Johnson, Barbara. "Thresholds of Difference: Structures of Address in Zora Neale Hurston." In *"Race," Writing, and Difference*, edited by Henry Louis Gates Jr., 317–28. Chicago: University of Chicago Press, 1985.

Johnson, Edward C. *Marine Corps Aviation: The Early Years, 1912–1940*. Edited by Graham A. Cosmas. Washington, D.C.: History and Museums Division, Headquarters, USMC, 1977.

Johnson, Richard. "What Is Cultural Studies Anyway?" In *What Is Cultural Studies? A Reader*, edited by John Storey, 75–114. London: Arnold, 1996.

Johnstone, John H. *A Brief History of the 1st Marines*. Washington, D.C.: Historical Branch, G-3 Division, Headquarters, USMC, 1968.

Jones, G. Williams. *Black Cinema Treasures: Lost and Found*. Denton: University of North Texas Press, 1991.

Jones, Kirkland C. *Renaissance Man from Louisiana: Arna Wendell Bontemps*. New York: Greenwood Press, 1992.

Jones, Robert Kenneth. *The Shudder Pulps: A History of the Weird Menace Magazines of the 1930s*. West Linn, Ore.: FAX Collector's Editions, 1975.

Kane, Robert J. *A Brief History of the 2d Marines*. Washington, D.C.: Historical Division, Headquarters, USMC, 1970.

Kaplan, Amy. "Black and Blue on San Juan Hill." In *Cultures of United States Imperialism*, edited by Amy Kaplan and Donald E. Pease, 219–36. Durham, N.C.: Duke University Press, 1993.

———. "Imperial Triangles: Mark Twain's Foreign Affairs." *Modern Fiction Studies* 43, no. 1 (Spring 1997): 237–48.

———. "Left Alone with America." In *Cultures of United States Imperialism*, edited by Amy Kaplan and Donald E. Pease, 3–21. Durham, N.C.: Duke University Press, 1993.

Kaplan, Amy, and Donald E. Pease, eds. *Cultures of United States Imperialism*. Durham, N.C.: Duke University Press, 1993.

Kelley, Robin D. G. Introduction to *A History of Negro Revolt*, by C. L. R. James. Chicago: Charles H. Kerr, 1995.

Kellogg, Charles Flint. *NAACP: A History of the National Association for the Advancement of Colored People*. Vol. 1, *1909–1920*. Baltimore: Johns Hopkins University Press, 1967.

Kemedjio, Cilas. "Entre le Larousse et le dollar: De l'occupation américaine de 1915 à l'Afrique post-totalitaire." Paper presented at the Haitian Studies Association annual meeting, Port-au-Prince, November 1998.

Kennan, George F. *American Diplomacy, 1900–1950*. Chicago: University of Chicago Press, 1951.

Kennedy, David M. *Over Here: The First World War and American Society*. New York: Oxford University Press, 1980.

Kett, Joseph F. *Rites of Passage: Adolescence in America, 1790 to the Present*. New York: Basic Books, 1977.

Kimmel, Michael S. *Manhood in America: A Cultural History*. New York: Free Press, 1996.

Kirschke, Amy Helene. *Aaron Douglas: Art, Race, and the Harlem Renaissance*. Jackson: University Press of Mississippi. 1995.

Klehr, Harvey, John Earl Haynes, and Kyrill M. Anderson, eds. *The Soviet World of American Communism*. New Haven: Yale University Press, 1998.

Kohli, Wendy. "Raymond Williams, Affective Ideology, and Counter-Hegemonic Practices." In *Views beyond the Border Country*, edited by Dennis L. Dworkin and Leslie G. Roman, 115–32. New York: Routledge, 1993.

Koll, Karla. "Samuel Guy Inman: Venturer in Inter-American Friendship." *Union Seminary Quarterly Review* 42, no. 3 (1988): 45–66.

Kramer, Paul. "Making Concessions: Race and Empire Revisited at the Philippine Exposition, St. Louis, 1901–1905." *Radical History Review* 73 (Winter 1999): 74–114.

———. "The Pragmatic Empire: U.S. Anthropology and Colonial Politics in the U.S.-Occupied Philippines, 1898–1924." Ph.D. dissertation, Princeton University, 1998.

Laguerre, Michel S. *The Complete Haitiana: A Bibliographic Guide to the Scholarly Literature, 1900–1980*. Millwood, N.Y.: Kraus International Publications, 1982.

———. *The Military and Society in Haiti*. Knoxville: University of Tennessee Press, 1993.

———. *Voodoo and Politics in Haiti*. New York: St. Martin's Press, 1989.

Langley, Lester D. *The Banana Wars: An Inner History of American Empire, 1900–1934*. Lexington: University Press of Kentucky, 1983.

———. *The United States and the Caribbean in the Twentieth Century*. 4th ed. Athens: University of Georgia Press, 1989.

LaRossa, Ralph. *The Modernization of Fatherhood: A Social and Political History*. Chicago: University of Chicago Press, 1997.

Lawless, Robert. *Haiti's Bad Press*. Rochester, Vt.: Schenkman Books, 1992.

Lears, T. J. Jackson. *No Place of Grace: Antimodernism and the Transformation of American Culture, 1880–1920*. New York: Pantheon Books, 1981.

Lepore, Jill. *The Name of War: King Phillip's War and the Origins of American Identity*. New York: Alfred A. Knopf, 1998.

Leuchtenburg, William E. "Progressivism and Imperialism: The Progressive Movement and American Foreign Policy, 1898–1916." *Mississippi Valley Historical Review* 39 (December 1952): 483–504.

Levine, Lawrence. "The Folklore of Industrial Society: Popular Culture and Its Audiences." *American Historical Review* 97 (December 1992): 1369–99.

Levy, Eugene. *James Weldon Johnson: Black Leader, Black Voice*. Chicago: University of Chicago Press, 1973.

Lewis, David Levering. *W. E. B. Du Bois: Biography of a Race, 1868–1919*. New York: Henry Holt, 1993.

———. *When Harlem Was in Vogue*. New York: Knopf, 1981.

Lewis, Gordon K. *Main Currents in Caribbean Thought: The Historical Evolution of Caribbean Society in Its Ideological Aspects, 1492–1900*. Baltimore: Johns Hopkins University Press, 1983.

Lindsay, Robert. *This High Name: Public Relations and the U.S. Marine Corps*. Madison: University of Wisconsin Press, 1956.

Link, Arthur S. *The Higher Realism of Woodrow Wilson, and Other Essays*. Nashville, Tenn.: Vanderbilt University Press, 1971.

———. *Wilson: The Struggle for Neutrality, 1914–15*. Vol. 2 of *Wilson*. Princeton, N.J.: Princeton University Press, 1960.

———. *Woodrow Wilson and the Progressive Era, 1910–1917*. New York: Harper and Row, 1954.

Linn, Brian McAllister. *Guardians of Empire: The U.S. Army and the Pacific, 1902–1940*. Chapel Hill: University of North Carolina Press, 1997.

Lipsitz, George. *Time Passages: Collective Memory and American Popular Culture*. Minneapolis: University of Minnesota Press, 1990.

Logan, Rayford W. "James Weldon Johnson and Haiti." *Phylon* 32, no. 4 (Winter 1971): 396–402.

Lott, Eric. *Love and Theft: Blackface Minstrelsy and the American Working Class*. New York: Oxford University Press, 1993.

Lundahl, Mats. *Peasants and Poverty: A Study of Haiti*. New York: St. Martin's Press, 1979.

Lutz, Catherine A., and Jane Collins. *Reading National Geographic*. Chicago: University of Chicago Press, 1993.

Lynd, Staughton, ed. *Nonviolence in America: A Documentary History*. Indianapolis: Bobbs-Merrill, 1966.

Major, Clarence, ed. *Juba to Jive: A Dictionary of African-American Slang*. New York: Penguin Books, 1994.

Manigat, Leslie. "La substitution de la prépondérance américaine à la prépondérance français en Haïti au debut de XXe siècle: La conjoncture de 1910–1911." *Revue d'histoire moderne et contemporaire* 14 (October–December 1967): 321–55.

Marks, Carole. *Farewell—We're Good and Gone: The Great Black Migration*. Bloomington: Indiana University Press, 1989.

Marsden, George M. *Fundamentalism and American Culture: The Shaping of Twentieth-Century Evangelicalism, 1870–1925*. New York: Oxford University Press, 1980.

Marsh, Margaret. "Suburban Men and Masculine Domesticity, 1870–1915." In *Meanings for Manhood: Constructions of Masculinity in Victorian America*, edited by Mark C. Carnes and Clyde Griffen, 111–27. Chicago: University of Chicago Press, 1990.

McAlister, Elizabeth. *Angels in the Mirror: Vodou Music of Haiti*. Compact disc and book. Roslyn, N.Y.: Ellipsis Arts, 1997.

———. " 'Men Moun Yo: Here Are the People': Haitian Rara Festivals and Transnational Popular Culture in Haiti and New York City." Ph.D. dissertation, Yale University, 1995.

———. "New York Lavalas and the Emergence of Rara." Paper presented at the third annual conference of the Haitian Studies Association, Tufts University, Medford, Mass., October 19, 1991.

McCrocklin, James H. *Garde d'Haïti: Twenty Years of Organization and Training by the United States Marine Corps, 1915–1934*. Annapolis, Md.: United States Naval Institute, 1956.

McLaren, Angus. *The Trials of Masculinity: Policing Sexual Boundaries, 1870–1930*. Chicago: University of Chicago Press, 1997.

McLaurin, Melton Alonza. *Paternalism and Protest: Southern Cotton Mill Workers and Organized Labor, 1875–1905*. Westport, Conn.: Greenwood, 1971.

Mcleod, David I. *Building Character in the American Boy: The Boy Scouts, YMCA, and Their Forerunners, 1870–1920*. Madison: University of Wisconsin Press, 1983.

Métraux, Alfred. *Voodoo in Haiti*. 1959. Reprint, New York: Schocken Books, 1972.

Mikell, Gwendolyn. "When Horses Talk: Reflections on Zora Neale Hurston's Haitian Anthropology." *Phylon* 43 (September 1982): 218–30.

Miller, Floyd John. *The Search for a Black Nationality: Black Emigration and Colonization, 1787–1863*. Urbana: University of Illinois Press, 1975.

Miller, Stuart Creighton. *"Benevolent Assimilation": The American Conquest of the Philippines, 1899–1903*. New Haven: Yale University Press, 1982.

Millet, Kethly. "Okipasyon Ameriken ak Abitan Ayisyen." *Sèl* (May 1984): 18.

———. *Les paysans haïtiens et l'occupation américaine, 1915–1930*. La Salle, Quebec: Collectif Paroles, 1978.

Millett, Allan R. *Semper Fidelis: The History of the United States Marine Corps*. New York: Free Press, 1991.

Mintz, Sidney. *Caribbean Transformations*. Baltimore: Johns Hopkins University Press, 1974.

———. "The Employment of Capital by Market Women in Haiti." In *Capital, Savings, and Credit in Peasant Societies*, edited by Raymond Firth and B. S. Yamey. Chicago: Aldine, 1964.

———. "Introduction to the Second English Edition." In *Voodoo in Haiti*, by Alfred Metraux. New York: Schocken Books, 1972.

———. "Slavery and the Rise of Peasantries." *Historical Reflections/Reflexions Historiques* 6, no. 1 (1979): 213–42.

———, ed. *Working Papers in Haitian Society and Culture*. New Haven: Yale University Antilles Research Program, 1975.

Mitchell, Loften. *Black Drama: The Story of the American Negro in the Theatre*. New York: Hawthorn Books, 1967.

Montgomery, David. *The Fall of the House of Labor: The Workplace, the State, and American Labor Activism, 1865–1925*. New York: Cambridge University Press, 1987.

Mooney, Chase C., and Martha E. Lyman. "Some Phases of the Compulsory Military Training Movement, 1914–1920." *Mississippi Valley Historical Review* 38 (1952): 41.

Moral, Paul. *Le paysan haïtien: Étude sur la vie rurale en Haïti*. Paris: Maisonneuve and Larose, 1961.

Morgan, Philip D. *Slave Counterpoint: Black Culture in Eighteenth-Century Chesapeake and Lowcountry*. Chapel Hill: University of North Carolina Press, 1998. Published for the Omohundro Institute of Early American History and Culture, Williamsburg, Va.

Mosse, George. *The Image of Man: The Creation of Modern Masculinity*. New York: Oxford University Press, 1996.

Moya Pons, Frank. "The Land Question in Haiti and Santo Domingo: The Sociopolitical Context of the Transition from Slavery to Free Labor, 1801–1843." In *Between Slavery and Free Labor*, edited by Manuel Moreno Fraginals, Frank Moya Pons, and Stanley Engerman, 181–214. Baltimore: Johns Hopkins University Press, 1985.

Mrozek, David. "The Habit of Victory: The American Military and the Cult of Manliness." In *Manliness and Morality: Middle-Class Masculinity in Britain and America*, edited by J. A. Mangan and James Walvin, 220–41. New York: St. Martin's Press, 1987.

———. *Sport and American Mentality, 1880–1910*. Knoxville: University of Tennessee Press, 1983.

Murphy, Lawrence R. *Perverts by Official Order: The Campaign against Homosexuals by the United States Navy*. New York: Harrington Park Press, 1988.

Murray, Gerald F. "The Evolution of Haitian Peasant Land Tenure: Agrarian Adaptation to Population Growth." 2 vols. Ph.D. dissertation, Columbia University, 1977.

Naison, Mark. *Communists in Harlem during the Depression*. Urbana: University of Illinois Press, 1983.

The National Cyclopedia of American Biography. Vol. 58. Clifton, N.J.: James T. White, 1979.

Nelson, Dana D. *National Manhood: Capitalist Citizenship and the Imagined Fraternity of White Men*. Durham, N.C.: Duke University Press, 1998.

Neverdon-Morton, Cynthia. *Afro-American Women of the South and the Advancement of the Race, 1895–1925*. Knoxville: University of Tennessee Press, 1989.

Nicholls, David. *From Dessalines to Duvalier: Race, Colour and National Independence in Haiti*. New York: Cambridge University Press, 1979.

———. *Haiti in Caribbean Context: Ethnicity, Economy and Revolt*. London: Macmillan, 1985.

———. "Rural Protest and Peasant Revolt." In *Haiti in Caribbean Context: Ethnicity, Economy and Revolt*, 167–85. London: Macmillan, 1985.

Ninkovich, Frank. "Theodore Roosevelt: Civilization as Ideology." *Diplomatic History* 10 (Summer 1986): 221–45.

O'Brien, Thomas F. *The Revolutionary Mission: American Business in Latin America, 1900–1945*. New York: Cambridge University Press, 1996.

O'Connor, John, and Lorraine Brown, eds. *Free, Adult, and Uncensored: The Living History of the Federal Theatre Project*. New York: Simon and Schuster, 1978.

Orlandello, John. *O'Neill on Film*. Rutherford, N.J.: Fairleigh Dickinson University Press, 1982.

Orleck, Annelise. *Common Sense and a Little Fire: Women and Working-Class Politics in the United States, 1900–1965*. Chapel Hill: University of North Carolina Press, 1995.

Painter, Nell Irvin. *Standing at Armageddon: United States, 1877–1919*. New York: W. W. Norton, 1987.

Pells, Richard. *Radical Visions and American Dreams: Culture and Social Thought in the Depression Years*. New York: Harper and Row, 1973.

Perkins, Whitney T. *Constraint of Empire: The United States and Caribbean Interventions*. Westport, Conn.: Greenwood Press, 1981.

Pfister, Joel. *Staging Depth: Eugene O'Neill and the Politics of Psychological Discourse*. Chapel Hill: University of North Carolina Press, 1995.

Pike, Fredrick B. *The United States and Latin America: Myths and Stereotypes of Civilization and Nature*. Austin: University of Texas Press, 1992.

Pleck, Elizabeth Hafkin. *Domestic Tyranny: The Making of a Social Policy against Family Violence from Colonial Times to the Present*. New York: Oxford University Press, 1987.

Pleck, Joseph. "American Fathering in Historical Perspective." In *Changing Men: New Directions in Research on Men and Masculinity*, edited by Michael S. Kimmel, 83–87. Newbury Park, Calif.: Sage Publications, 1987.

Plummer, Brenda Gayle. "The Afro-American Response to the Occupation of Haiti, 1915–1934." *Phylon* 43 (June 1982): 125–43.

———. "Black and White in the Caribbean: Haitian-American Relations, 1902–1934." 2 vols. Ph.D. dissertation, Cornell University, 1981.

———. "The Golden Age of Tourism: U.S. Influence in Haitian Cultural and Economic Affairs, 1934–1971." *Cimarrón* 2 (Winter 1990): 49–63.

———. *Haiti and the Great Powers, 1902–1915*. Baton Rouge: Louisiana State University Press, 1988.

———. *Haiti and the United States: The Psychological Moment*. Athens: University of Georgia Press, 1992.

———. "Race, Nationality and Trade in the Caribbean: The Syrians in Haiti, 1903–1934." *International History Review* 3 (1981): 517–39.

Poovey, Mary. *Uneven Developments: The Ideological Work of Gender in Mid-Victorian England*. Chicago: University of Chicago Press, 1988.

Porter, Bernard. *Critics of Empire: British Radical Attitudes to Colonialism in Africa, 1895–1914*. New York: St. Martin's Press, 1968.

Pratt, Mary Louise. *Imperial Eyes: Travel Writing and Transculturation*. New York: Routledge, 1992.

Price, Michael, and George Turner. "White Zombie: Today's Unlikely Classic." *American Cinematographer* (February 1988): 34–40.

Radway, Janice. "Interpretive Communities and Variable Literacies: The Functions of Romance Reading." In *Rethinking Popular Culture: Contemporary Perspectives and Cultural Studies*, edited by Chandra Mukerji and Michael Schudson, 465–86. Berkeley: University of California Press, 1991.

Rafael, Vicente. "Colonial Domesticity: White Women and United States Rule in the Philippines." *American Literature* 67, no. 4 (December 1995): 639–66.

———. "White Love: Surveillance and Nationalist Resistance in the U.S. Colonization of the Philippines." In *Cultures of United States Imperialism*, edited by Amy Kaplan and Donald E. Pease, 185–218. Durham, N.C.: Duke University Press, 1993.

Rampersad, Arnold. *The Life of Langston Hughes.* Vol. 1, *1902–1941.* New York: Oxford University Press, 1986.

Ramsey, Kate. "Melville J. Herskovits, Katherine Dunham, and the Politics of African Diasporic Dance Anthropology." Paper presented at the American Studies Association annual meeting, Seattle, November 1998.

Randall, Mercedes M. *Improper Bostonian: Emily Greene Balch, Nobel Peace Laureate, 1946.* New York: Twayne Publishers, 1964.

Renda, Mary A. "This American Africa: Cultural Dimensions of U.S. Imperialism in Haiti, 1915–1940." Ph.D. dissertation, Yale University, 1993.

Reynolds, Gary A., and Beryl J. Wright, eds. *Against the Odds: African American Artists and the Harmon Foundation.* Newark, N.J.: Newark Museum, 1989.

Richards, Jeffrey, ed. *Imperialism and Juvenile Literature.* New York: Manchester, 1989.

Roberts, David. *Paternalism in Early Victorian England.* New Brunswick, N.J.: Rutgers University Press, 1979.

Robinson, Cedric. *Black Marxism: The Making of the Black Radical Tradition.* London: Zed Books, 1982.

Rodgers, Daniel T. *Atlantic Crossings: Social Politics in a Progressive Age.* Cambridge, Mass.: Belknap Press of Harvard University Press, 1998.

Roediger, David R. *The Wages of Whiteness: Race and the Making of the American Working Class.* London: Verso, 1991.

Rogin, Michael Paul. *Fathers and Children: Andrew Jackson and the Subjugation of the American Indian.* New York: Knopf, 1975.

Rosaldo, Renato. *Culture and Truth: The Remaking of Social Analysis.* Boston: Beacon Press, 1989.

Rosenberg, Emily. "A Round Table: Explaining the History of American Foreign Relations — Gender." *Journal of American History* 77 (June 1990): 116–24.

———. *Spreading the American Dream: American Economic and Cultural Expansion, 1890–1945.* New York: Hill and Wang, 1982.

Rotundo, E. Anthony. *American Manhood: Transformations in Masculinity from the Revolution to the Modern Era.* New York: Basic Books, 1993.

Rubin, Joan Shelley. *The Making of Middlebrow Culture.* Chapel Hill: University of North Carolina Press, 1992.

Rupp, Leila. *Worlds of Women: The Making of an International Women's Movement.* Princeton, N.J.: Princeton University Press, 1997.

Rydell, Robert. *All the World's a Fair: Visions of Empire at American International Expositions, 1876–1916.* Chicago: University of Chicago Press, 1984.

Sacco, Ellen Fernandez. "Winner Takes All: The Contexts of Conquest and Collecting in the Museums of Pierre Eugene Du Simitiere and Charles Willson Peale, 1779–1796."

Paper presented at the American Studies Association annual meeting, Seattle, November 1998.

Said, Edward W. *Culture and Imperialism*. New York: Alfred A. Knopf, 1993.

———. *Orientalism*. London: Routledge and Kegan Paul, 1978.

Santelli, James S. *A Brief History of the 8th Marines*. Washington, D.C.: History and Museums Division, Headquarters, USMC, 1976.

Schmidt, Hans. *Maverick Marine: General Smedley D. Butler and the Contradictions of American Military History*. Lexington: University Press of Kentucky, 1987.

———. *The United States Occupation of Haiti, 1915–1934*. New Brunswick, N.J.: Rutgers University Press, 1971.

Scott, Joan W. "Deconstructing Equality-versus-Difference: Or, the Uses of Poststructuralist Theory for Feminism." In *Conflicts in Feminism*, edited by Marianne Hirsch and Evelyn Fox Keller, 134–48. New York: Routledge, 1990.

———. " 'Experience.' " In *Feminists Theorize the Political*, edited by Judith Butler and Joan W. Scott, 22–40. New York: Routledge, 1992.

———. "Gender: A Useful Category for Historical Analysis." In *Gender and Politics of History*, 28–50. New York: Columbia University Press, 1988.

Scranton, Philip. "Varieties of Paternalism: Industrial Structures and the Social Relations of Production in American Textiles." *American Quarterly* 36 (Summer 1984): 235–57.

Shacochis, Bob. *The Immaculate Invasion*. New York: Viking, 1999.

Shannon, David A. *The Socialist Party of America*. Chicago: Quadrangle Books, 1967.

Shannon, Magdaline W. *Jean Price-Mars, the Haitian Elite and the American Occupation, 1915–1935*. New York: St. Martin's Press, 1996.

Shapiro, Herbert. *White Violence and Black Response: From Reconstruction to Montgomery*. Amherst: University of Massachusetts Press, 1988.

Sheaffer, Louis. *O'Neill: Son and Artist*. Boston: Little, Brown, 1973.

Showalter, Dennis E. "Evolution of the U.S. Marine Corps as a Military Elite." *Marine Corps Gazette* 63 (November 1979): 44–58.

Silber, Nina. *The Romance of Reunion: Northerners and the South, 1865–1900*. Chapel Hill: University of North Carolina Press, 1993.

Simpson, George Eaton. *Melville J. Herskovits*. New York: Columbia University Press, 1973.

Slotkin, Richard. "Buffalo Bill's 'Wild West' and the Mythologization of American Empire." In *Cultures of United States Imperialism*, edited by Amy Kaplan and Donald E. Pease, 164–81. Durham, N.C.: Duke University Press, 1993.

———. *Gunfighter Nation: The Myth of the Frontier in Twentieth-Century America*. New York: Atheneum, 1992.

Smith, Jennie. "Traditional Peasant Groups, Contemporary Development Agendas and Post-Modernist Strategies for Sustainable Change." Paper presented to the Haitian Studies Association, Port-au-Prince, Haiti, October 29, 1998.

Somerville, Siobhan. *Queering the Color Line: Race and the Invention of Homosexuality in American Culture*. Durham, N.C.: Duke University Press, 2000.

Spector, Robert M. *W. Cameron Forbes and the Hoover Commission to Haiti*. Lanham, Md.: University Press of America, 1985.

Spivak, Gayatri Chakravorty. *In Other Worlds: Essays in Cultural Politics*. New York: Routledge, 1987.

Staudenraus, P. J. *The African Colonization Movement, 1816–1865*. New York: Columbia University Press, 1961.

Stearns, Peter N. "Men, Boys, and Anger in American Society, 1860–1940." In *Manliness and Morality: Middle-Class Masculinity in Britain and America*, edited by J. A. Mangan and James Walvin, 75–91. New York: St. Martin's Press, 1987.

Stearns, Peter N., and Carol Zisowitz Stearns. *Anger: The Struggle for Emotional Control in America's History*. Chicago: University of Chicago Press, 1986.

Steinson, Barbara. *American Women's Activism in World War I*. New York: Garland, 1982.

Stocking, George. "Matthew Arnold, E. B. Tylor, and the Uses of Invention." In *Race, Culture, and Evolution: Essays in the History of Anthropology*, edited by A. L. Kroeber and Clyde Kluckhohn, 69–90. Chicago: University of Chicago Press, 1982.

Stoler, Ann Laura. "Carnal Knowledge and Imperial Power: Gender, Race, and Morality in Colonial Asia." In *Gender at the Crossroads of Knowledge: Feminist Anthropology in the Postmodern Era*, edited by Micaela di Leonardo, 51–101. Berkeley: University of California Press, 1991.

———. *Race and the Education of Desire: Foucault's History of Sexuality and the Colonial Order of Things*. Durham, N.C.: Duke University Press, 1995.

Stowe, Stephen M. *Intimacy and Power in the Old South: Ritual in the Lives of the Planters*. Baltimore: Johns Hopkins University Press, 1987.

Sweetman, Jack. *American Naval History: An Illustrated Chronology of the U.S. Navy and Marine Corps, 1775–Present*. Annapolis, Md.: Naval Institute Press, 1984.

Tebbel, John. *The Golden Age between Two Wars, 1920–1940*. Vol. 3 of *A History of Book Publishing in the United States*. New York: R. R. Bowker, 1978.

Tone, Andrea. *The Business of Benevolence: Industrial Paternalism in Progressive America*. Ithaca, N.Y.: Cornell University Press, 1997.

Torgovnick, Marianna. *Gone Primitive: Savage Intellects, Modern Lives*. Chicago: University of Chicago Press, 1990.

Trouillot, Michel-Rolph. *Haiti, State against Nation: The Origins and Legacy of Duvalierism*. New York: Monthly Review Press, 1990.

———. "The Odd and the Ordinary: Haiti, the Caribbean, and the World." *Cimarrón* 2 (Winter 1990): 3–12.

———. *Silencing the Past: Power and the Production of History*. Boston: Beacon Press, 1995.

Tuttle, William M., Jr. *Race Riot: Chicago in the Red Summer of 1919*. New York: Atheneum, 1970.

Tyack, David. *The One Best System: A History of American Urban Education*. Cambridge, Mass.: Harvard University Press, 1974.

Utley, Robert M. *The Indian Frontier of the American West, 1846–1890*. Albuquerque: University of New Mexico Press, 1984.

Ware, Vron. *Beyond the Pale: White Women, Racism, and History*. London: Verso, 1992.

Weinberg, Robert. *The Weird Tales Story*. West Linn, Ore.: FAX Collector's Editions, 1977.

Weinstein, James. *The Corporate Ideal in the Liberal State, 1900–1918*. Boston: Beacon Press, 1968.

Weiss, Bernard J., ed. *American Education and European Immigrants: 1840–1940*. Urbana: University of Illinois Press, 1982.

Weiss, Nancy J. *Farewell to the Party of Lincoln: Black Politics in the Age of FDR*. Princeton, N.J.: Princeton University Press, 1983.

Wells, Samuel F., Jr. "New Perspectives on Wilsonian Diplomacy: The Secular Evangelism of American Political Economy." *Perspectives in American History* 6 (1972): 395–402.

Weston, Rubin Francis. *Racism in U.S. Imperialism: The Influence of Racial Assumptions on American Foreign Policy, 1893–1946*. Columbia: University of South Carolina Press, 1972.

Wexler, Laura. "No Place like Home: Frances Benjamin Johnston's Photographs aboard

Admiral George Dewey's Flagship Olympia." Paper presented at the American Studies Association annual meeting, Seattle, November 1998.

Wheat, Ellen Harkins. *Jacob Lawrence, American Painter*. Seattle: University of Washington Press, 1986.

Wilentz, Sean. *Chants Democratic: New York City and the Rise of the American Working Class, 1788–1850*. New York: Oxford University Press, 1984.

Williams, Raymond. "Base and Superstructure in Marxist Cultural Theory." In *Rethinking Popular Culture: Contemporary Perspectives and Cultural Studies*, edited by Chandra Mukerji and Michael Schudson, 407–23. Berkeley: University of California Press, 1991.

———. *Keywords: A Vocabulary of Culture and Society*. Rev. ed. New York: Oxford University Press, 1983.

———. *Marxism and Literature*. New York: Oxford University Press, 1978.

———. *What I Came to Say*. London: Hutchinson Radius, 1989.

Williams, Tony. "White Zombie, Haitian Horror." *Jump Cut* 25 (April 28, 1983): 18–20.

Williams, William Appleman. *Empire as a Way of Life: An Essay on the Causes and Character of America's Present Predicament, Along with a Few Thoughts about an Alternative*. New York: Oxford University Press, 1980.

Williamson, Joel. *A Rage for Order: Black/White Relations in the American South since Emancipation*. New York: Oxford University Press, 1986.

Wolff, Leon. *Little Brown Brother: How the United States Purchased and Pacified the Philippine Islands at the Century's Turn*. Garden City, N.Y.: Doubleday, 1961.

Worthington, Marjorie. *The Strange World of Willie Seabrook*. New York: Harcourt, 1966.

Wyatt-Brown, Bertram. *Southern Honor: Ethics and Behavior in the Old South*. New York: Oxford University Press, 1982.

Young, Robert. *Colonial Desire: Hybridity in Theory, Culture and Race*. London: Routledge, 1995.

———. *White Mythologies: Writing History and the West*. London: Routledge, 1990.

Zeiger, Susan. "Finding a Cure for War: Women's Politics and the Peace Movement in the 1920s." *Journal of Social History* 24 (Fall 1990): 69–86.

Zumwalt, Rosemary Lévy. *Wealth and Rebellion: Elsie Clews Parsons, Anthropologist and Folklorist*. Urbana: University of Illinois Press, 1992.

INDEX

Page numbers in italics refer to illustrations.

Acaau, Jean-Jacques, 49

Addams, Jane, 19

Adler, Henry Sloan Coffin, 191

"Advanced Base Forces," 96, 320–21 (n. 84)

Africa: images of, 5; and paternalism, 16; and Haitian culture, 19, 242, 244, 247, 274; and popular culture, 21; roots of Vodou in, 45, 274; colonialism in, 52, 269; associated with Haiti, 125, 236, 237, 243, 250, 254, 262; and travel writing, 255; and African American women, 266

African Americans: and paternalism, 18, 22, 55, 124, 263; and Haitian history, 20, 25, 194, 276–82, 287–88; literature of, 20, 35, 209, 261, 263, 264, 275–84, 288, 305 (*see also* specific authors); and American national identity, 22, 187, 264, 265, 282, 288; and Haiti, 29–30, 49, 187, 196, 265, 291; and Cacos, 33; and racial politics, 35–36, 189, 287, 305; and marines in Haiti, 53; and U.S. South, 54; and citizenship, 55, 110–11, 264; and Ku Klux Klan, 58; and masculinity, 63, 264; Wilson's support from, 109, 110, 332 (n. 102); and Reconstruction, 122; and rape, 163, 257–58; rising militancy of, 186; protest occupation, 188–89, 191; and O'Neill, 209, 210; and racism, 264, 305; national organizations of, 264–65; and World War I, 272; Herskovits on, 274; folklore of, 292. *See also* Harlem Renaissance

Age, and paternalism, 15

Agriculture, 47, 48, 49, 114, 212, 318 (n. 48). *See also* Peasantry; Plantations and plantation system

Alcohol: Daniels attempts to proscribe, 70; and saloon rituals, 72; and moral break-downs, 131, 170; and violence, 162, 163, 164; and illegitimate children, 215; in Port-au-Prince, 216; public condemnation of versus private support for, 292

All-America Anti-Imperialist League, 268–69

Altidor, Capsine, 148–49

"America" (term), xvii, 7–8

American Bible Society, 124

American Communist Party (CP-USA), 268–69, 273, 277, 278, 285

American-Haitian Benevolent Club, 265

American Negro Labor Congress, 269

Americanness. *See* Identity, U.S. national

American Red Cross, 61

American Revolution, 60, 267, 287

Anderson, Benedict, 6

Anderson, Jervis, 210

Annales Capoises, Les, 119

Anthropology, 231; and U.S. occupation, 12; and definition of culture, 23, 27; and Vodou, 45–46, 213; and exoticism, 263, 273–74; and Hurston, 288; and American national identity, 304

Appy, Christian, 76

Arabia, 21

Ardouin, Alexis Beaubrun, 46

Arizona, 7

Arts, visual: and U.S. occupation, 12, 25, 27, 28; Haiti as subject in, 19, 217, 220, 221, 278, 279, 280, 313 (n. 32); in Haiti, 274; and racial identity, 276; and interracial cooperation, 285; and WPA, 285. *See also* specific artists

Asia, 266

Athletics, 5, 11, 64, 212, 234, 256

Atwood, Charlotte, 266

Aux Cayes, Haiti, 130, 147, 148, 229

Aux Cayes Massacre, 34, 221, 269

Azaka, 45

Baber, Zonia, 266
Baheri, William, 324 (n. 141)
Bailly-Blanchard, Arthur, 94
Balch, Emily Greene, 191, 238, 266, 267,
    268
Baldwin, Roger, 268, 269
Balutansky, John, 138, 171
Bankers, 12, 30, 97, 98, 99–100, 330
    (n. 43)
Banque Nationale de la Republic d'Haïti,
    52, 98, 99
Barker, Robert, 55–56
Barnett, George, 89, 160, 165
Bassett, Ebenezer, 30
Batraville, Benoit, 33, 151, 166, 173
Beach, Edward, 30–31, 115, 116
Beard, Daniel Carter, 65
Bederman, Gail, 64
Beebe, William, 239, 313 (n. 32)
Belloni, Heraux, 160
Bertol, Haiti, 142–43
Bethune, Mary McLeod, 191
Beveridge, Albert J., 66, 69
Bible, 229–31. See also Missionaries
Blackface tradition, 198, 227, 343
    (n. 173). See also Cross-dressing: racial
Blaine, Mahlon, 217, 218
Bledsoe, Jules, 211
Boas, Franz, 231
Bobo, Rosalvo, 31, 80–84, 115
Bodies: white male, 16, 24, 64, 69, 71, 72,
    74, 176, 326 (n. 182); black female,
    178, 200, 230, 257; black male, 205,
    207, 208, 210, 217, 256
Bois Caiman, 43, 44, 316 (n. 17)
Bonaparte, Napoleon, 29, 44, 47, 50, 246
Boni and Liveright, 209
Bontemps, Arna, 20, 276, 278, 281–83,
    305
Borno, Louis, 33, 34, 213, 221
Boukman, 43, 52, 273
Boyer, Jean-Pierre, 48–49, 51, 319 (n. 53)
Boyhood, 64–65, 66, 254
Boy Scouts of America, 5, 65
Broadway, 209
Brokaw, Louis A., 159–60, 161, 164
Brooklyn, N.Y., 71, 329 (n. 21)
Brown, Fitzgerald, 162
Brown, Karen McCarthy, 45, 290

Bryan, William Jennings, 91, 94, 96, 97,
    98, 99, 100, 334 (n. 135)
Buenos Aires, Argentina, 196–97
Buffalo Bill's "Wild West," 64
Burks, Arthur J., 18, 165, 173, 175–78,
    216, 217, 223, 225, 275
Burroughs, Edgar Rice, 64
Burroughs, Nannie Helen, 191
Businessmen: and modern corporation,
    11; and U.S. occupation, 12, 99, 120;
    and strikes, 34; and Panama Canal, 93;
    and U.S. government, 97, 99, 109; and
    primitivism, 127, 128. See also United
    States — investments in Haiti of
Butler, Ethel C. P., 91, 107
Butler, Maud Darlington, 90–91
Butler, Noble, 59
Butler, Smedley D.: memoirs of, 4, 71; and
    paternalism, 13, 16, 69, 91, 101–2,
    104–8, 115, 116, 118, 124, 129, 147,
    207, 302, 331 (n. 79); and U.S. Senate
    inquiry, 13, 33, 89, 90, 126, 135, 137;
    and Gendarmerie d'Haïti, 31–32, 90,
    101, 125, 129, 136, 147, 206; and rac-
    ism, 55, 101–2, 104, 105, 124, 136, 331
    (n. 79); as Quaker, 58, 321 (n. 96); fam-
    ily of, 59, 62, 69, 102; roughneck image
    of, 61, 71–72, 101; and homosexuality,
    74; and U.S. Congress, 90, 103; letters
    from Haiti of, 90–91, 101, 103, 104–8,
    116, 125, 129; and Waller, 100, 101–2;
    pre-Haiti military experience of, 101,
    104, 106, 123, 331 (n. 70); and identity,
    103, 206; medals of honor of, 106–7,
    146; and power, 123; anti-imperialism
    of, 321 (n. 96); and militarism, 324
    (n. 141)
Butler, Thomas S., 90, 91, 103, 104–6, 116
Button, William R., 171, 172, 173, 176,
    177

Cacos, 10, 11, 142; and marines in Haiti,
    10, 71–72, 136, 137, 140–45, 151, 165,
    173, 175, 179, 234; and Caperton's
    forces, 30; first phase of U.S. war
    against, 31, 35, 139, 140–46, 147, 149,
    163, 179; second phase of U.S. war
    against, 32–33, 39, 41, 139, 144, 150–
    64, 173; American perceptions of, 41–

42, 144–45, 338 (n. 54); and conches, 43; pre-1915 activities of, 52, 140; and Waller, 100; and S. Butler, 107; and paternalism, 119, 136; and Haitian economy, 120; as plantation workers, 122; defeat of, 130; and discipline, 135, 137, 156, 159, 179; marines kill, 136, 138, 143, 145, 146, 151, 155–56, 158, 160, 161–62, 340 (n. 90), 341 (n. 122); contrasted with peaceful inhabitants, 137–38, 142, 158–59, 179, 236; description of, 140–42, 150–51; and corvée, 150–51; Haitian sympathy for, 151, 340 (n. 87); leaders of, *152, 153*, 155, 161, 162, 166, 173. *See also* Corvée; Péralte, Charlemagne

Campbell, Chandler, 42, 142–43, 145, 146

Canada, 29

Cannibalism: and Haitian elites, 52; Russell's accounts of, 127, 128, 165–66; marines fear, 157, 165, 166, 173, 175, 304, 342 (n. 141); and travel writing, 239

Caperton, William B., 30–33, 80–81, 90, 91, 101, 116, 127, 141–42, 144–46

Cap Haïtien, 43, 91, 105, 140, 213, 216, 233, 239, 240

Capitalism: international, 10, 23; and U.S. occupation, 10, 116; and gunboat diplomacy, 30; and Latin America, 92; and economic development, 94; and Wilson, 97, 113–14; and O'Neill, 205; and Haiti as commodity, 216; and CP-USA, 268

Carby, Hazel, 207

Caribbean: proximity to U.S. South of, 7; U.S. strategic interest in, 10, 96; and U.S. Navy, 30, 95, 96; and American national identity, 62; military interventions in, 94; and U.S. policy, 97, 98, 115; and paternalism, 124; undeclared U.S. war in, 232; missionaries in, 233, 237; and African American women, 266; Inman on, 270; and identity, 294

Carrier, Walter, 124, 180

Casualties, 10, 81, 145, 146, 151. *See also* Killing — by Haitians; Killing — by marines; Violence

Catholicism, 45, 50, 60, 317 (n. 29)

Catholic Welfare Association, 269–70

Cayes Massacre, 34, 221, 269

Central America, 80, 113, 135, 196, 336 (n. 18)

Cercle Bellevue, 194

Chaffin, A. D., 55

Challener, Richard, 95, 96

Chamberlain, Tamerlyn T., 120–21

Chauncey, George, 69–71, 73–74, 204, 325 (n. 161), 326 (n. 182)

Chavannes, 52

Chester, USS, 30

Chicago Defender, 163, 186

Child, metaphor of: Haitians as wards, 13, 16, 89, 108, 191; Haiti as child nation, 13, 67, 102, 115, 118, 119, 179, 243, 249, 299, 303; Haiti as adopted, orphaned, illegitimate, 16, 193, 243, 247, 254, 257; and U.S. occupation, 21, 42; African Americans as wards, 110–11; and Latin America, 113, 333 (n. 123). *See also* Discipline; Paternalism

Children, 16, 67, 127, 128, 166, 266, 297

China, 12, 21, 75, 78, 79, 86, 101, 268

Christophe, Henri: and Haitian Revolution, 46, 52–53, 140, 318 (n. 50); and Haitian economy, 47, 48, 319 (n. 52); and Citadel, 50–51; O'Neill on, 187–88, 197, 203, 211; J. W. Johnson on, 193–94, 196, 203, 207, 263, 276–77; Vandercook's biography of, 216–17, 272, 349 (nn. 157, 158); and tourism, 217, *219*, 237; and film, 226; Inman on, 272; and Hughes, 282; and drama, 285, 286

Churchstone-Lord, S. E., 163, 186

Citadel: and Christophe, 50–51; J. W. Johnson on, 193–94, 196, 203, 207, 263, 276–77; and masculinity, 203, 263, 264, 278; and tourism, 217, 237; marine pamphlet on, 217, 219, 221, 222; in newsreels, 221, 223; and travel writing, 246; and Hughes, 263, 264, 282. *See also* Christophe, Henri; Savage, Augusta

Citadel of Christophe, 217, *219*, 221, 222

Citizenship: imperial, 6–7, 8, 21; U.S., 54–55, 110–11; and African Americans, 55, 110–11, 264; and Puerto Ricans, 61;

and masculinity, 62, 323 (n. 121); and
American women, 63; Haitian, 138
Civilization: industrial, 19; discourses of,
52, 119, 125, 128, 154, 187; in Haiti, 61,
124; and manliness, 64, 66, 194; and
masculinity, 72; and killing by marines,
89; and American women, 133, 234, 236;
and marines in Haiti, 167; and horror
stories, 178; and identity, 187; and black
manhood, 194; and exoticism, 195; and
progress, 206; and O'Neill, 207; in film,
223, 226; in fiction, 223–24; and Great
Depression, 225; and Inman, 232, 233,
270–71, 273; and travel writing, 241,
243, 244, 245, 246, 247, 248, 254;
origins of, 248; Herskovits on, 274
Civil War, U.S., 60
Clark, Maurice, 286, 362 (n. 144)
Class
— in Haiti: and paternalism, 16, 129; and
economy, 114; and U.S. policy, 193; and
Christophe, 194; and primitivism, 195;
Hughes on, 274. *See also* Elites, Haitian;
Peasants
— in United States: and Wirkus, 5; and
paternalism, 15; and culture, 25; and
U.S. occupation, 28, 300; and U.S.
South, 54–55; and race, 58, 180; and
marines, 61, 123; and masculinity, 63,
66–67, 69–74, 194; and homosexuality,
73, 74, 326 (n. 182); and U.S. policy,
95; and rule of law, 115; and Haitian
workers, 215; and Puritanism, 230–31;
and Garvey, 265, 277
Clifford, James, 206
Clothing: military uniforms, 24, 72, 75,
82, 147, 167, 176–77, 207–8, 234, 326
(n. 182); significance of, 55–56, 85,
102, 121, 176; connotations of, 71, 84,
85, 167, 262–63, 356–57 (n. 14); in fiction and drama, 207. *See also* "Undershirt diplomacy"
Coffee plantations, 48, 108, 119, 120
Colombian Line, 217, *219*
Columbia Exposition of 1893, 64
Columbia University, 231, 273
Columbus, Christopher, 246
Commodification, 35, 185–86, 187, 208,
212–23, 216, 217, 246, 305

Communications, 104, 117
Conches, 42, 43–44, 45, 156
Congressional Medal of Honor, 106–7, 146
Connecticut, USS, 79, 85
Constitutions. *See* Haiti — constitutions of;
U.S. Constitution
Cook, Mercer, 19
Coolidge, Calvin, 213, 268
Cooper, Anna Julia, 204–5
Corruption, 51, 160, 194
Corvée: and U.S. occupation, 10; brutality
of, 11, 149; and Gendarmerie d'Haïti,
32–33, 148–49; compared to slavery,
53, 148, 193; and violence, 139, 149,
163; and public works, 148–50, 179;
Russell orders end to, 149–50; Wells
continues, 150, 161; and Cacos, 150–
51; Barnett orders end to, 160; J. W.
Johnson on, 193
Cotton, 121–22, 212, 216
Counterinsurgency, 134, 146, 154, 158,
179
Courlander, Harold, 275
Courrier Haïtien, 49–50, 118–19
Courts martial, 131, 150, 156, 159, 161
Craige, John Houston: *Black Bagdad*, 4,
131, 133, 173, 175; *Cannibal Cousins*, 4,
133; and identity, 56, 82, 169, 170; and
manhood, 65; explains violence, 131–
34, 180–81; and South, 148; and rape,
163; and drums, 167–68, 213, *214*; on
Hanneken and Button, 171, 173; on
Morris, 173, 175; and Haitians as com-
modities, 214–15; on Haitian women,
234
Creole language: and marines in Haiti, 39,
55, 162, 165, 171, 173, 175, 176, 177,
304; and Gendarmerie d'Haïti, 148,
171
Crisis, 19, 188, 193, 210, 262
Croak, Jack, 197, 204
Cross-dressing: gender, 173, 176; racial,
173, 176, 206, 343 (n. 173)
Crumbie, Frank Resler, 213
Cuba, 12, 21, 61, 78, 86, 101, 118, 268,
351 (n. 179)
Cukela, Louis, 161, 164
Cultural conscription, 17–18, 28–29, 66,
123, 301

Cultural relativism, 231, 238, 271

Culture: and imperialism, 4–5, 6, 8; and
U.S. occupation, 9, 12, 15, 17–18, 20,
27, 164, 231, 240, 303, 312 (n. 18); as
process, 20, 23, 25–26; and history,
22–29; defined, 23, 24–26; and meaning, 23, 24–26, 29, 314 (n. 50); and
national identity, 25, 29; and violence,
154, 164, 181
—Haitian: and imperialism, 4, 6, 12, 21,
241; and American national identity,
17; J. W. Johnson on, 19, 228, 241; and
African Americans, 20, 278, 287–88;
and marines in Haiti, 42, 43–46, 84,
171, 173, 179, 212–13, 217, 219, 242,
245, 301, 304; and Haitian Revolution,
43–47; and Haitian elites, 52, 214; as
commodity, 185–86, 187, 208, 212–23,
228; and primitivism, 214; and travel
writing, 241–42, 244, 245, 247, 248,
251, 252; and Hughes, 264; instability
in, 274
—U.S.: and imperialism, 3, 4, 7, 8–9, 12,
21; and mass media, 11; and paternalism, 15; impact of U.S. occupation on,
17, 18–20, 21, 35, 127, 185, 301; popular, 21, 35, 185, 221, 231, 237, 305 (see
also Fiction; Film; Radio; Travel Writing); and exoticism, 22, 208–9, 262;
and race, 25, 35, 54, 180, 181; and
Haiti, 185, 200, 217, 228, 289; politics
of, 185–86; and drama, 198; and
Hughes, 264; and African Americans,
265; destabilization of, 306–7

Dances: Haiti as subject of, 19; and Vodou,
41; Inman on, 233, 270, 272; and tourism, 237; and travel writing, 240, 241–
42, 251, 256; and Hughes, 262; study
of, 278
Daniels, Josephus: and alcohol, 70; and
paternalism, 77–78, 116, 124; and militarism, 96; and Monroe Doctrine, 96;
and S. Butler, 104, 107; and Cacos, 141,
142, 144, 145, 146; and immorality of
marines, 163, 170; and naval inquiry,
191
Dartiguenave, Philippe Sudre, 31, 32, 33,
90, 116, 119, 126, 142, 190

Davis, Beale. See Davis, Robert Beale
Davis, Harold Palmer, 2, 311 (n. 14)
Davis, Robert Beale: as chargé d'affaires,
127; The Goat without Horns, 127, 223–
25, 227, 254; and civilization, 128; and
motherhood, 223–24, 350 (n. 175);
and power, 224, 350 (n. 173); and
Vodou, 275; and sexuality, 305
Debs, Eugene, 197
Debt: and U.S. occupation, 10, 192–
93, 213; French indemnity from, 51,
193
Del Valle, Pedro, 61–62
Democratic Party (U.S.), 109, 110, 187,
191, 285
Desire: for Haiti by Americans, 19, 185,
212, 215, 216, 228; as racial and sexual, 213; in E. Taft, 230, 255, 257; in
B. Niles, 243; in Seabrook, 255. See also
Exoticism
Des Moines, USS, 95
Dessalines, Jean Jacques, 45, 47, 48, 50,
52, 140, 203, 242, 245, 272
Dessez, Lester, 166, 176
Development, economic: and U.S. policy,
10; and Christophe, 47, 48, 319 (n. 52);
and peasantry, 50; and foreign capital,
51; and Wilson, 94, 95, 113, 117–18,
334 (n. 135); of African Americans,
110–11; and paternalism, 116, 136; and
infrastructure, 117; and Haitian elites,
118; and businessmen, 120, 128; and
marines in Haiti, 179; pace of, 212. See
also Economy
Developmentalism, 111, 113, 114, 129;
liberal, 114, 115
Devieux (poet), 243
Dies Committee, 287
Diplomacy: and U.S. occupation, 12, 20,
101; gunboat, 12, 30; and isolation of
Haiti, 29, 50; by Caperton, 31, 90, 101,
141–42; by Van Orden, 81–82; and
Latin America, 92–93; Haitian, 93–94,
147; and Gendarmerie d'Haïti, 103;
"undershirt," 125, 129, 135, 190; by
Russell, 130; and Johnson, 188, 194
Disciples of Christ, 232, 352 (n. 19)
Discipline: and paternalism, 15, 16, 55,
78; metaphors of, 16, 100, 179, 303;

and violence, 55, 135–37, 138, 304; and
boyhood, 64; in USMC, 74–75; in U.S.
Navy, 95; and Cacos, 135, 137, 156, 159,
179; and corvée, 148; and exoticism,
213; Inman on, 237

Discourse: and imperialism, 6–9; on paternalism, 15–17, 22; on Haiti, 17; defined, 23–25, 26; and culture, 26, 27,
314 (n. 53); and U.S. occupation, 28;
psychological, 35, 207, 210, 224, 230,
231, 240, 258, 259, 274, 306, 348
(n. 132); of civilization, 52, 119, 125,
128, 154, 187; of manliness, 66; and violence, 131–34, 158–59, 180–81

Disease, 44, 196, 215. *See also* Insanity

Dize, William, 5, 9

Domesticity: and paternalism, 16, 105–6,
231; and men, 66–67, 69; Protestant,
231; and Toussaint L'Ouverture, 281;
as prescription for women, 302

Dominican Republic, 33, 61, 97, 146, 232,
268, 290

Dorsinville, Roger, 85

Douglas, Aaron, 200

Douglas, Paul H., 191, 266–67, 268

Douglass, Frederick, 30

Drama: Haiti as subject of, 19, 198–
212, 217, 225, 228, 278, 280; and
U.S. occupation, 27, 28; and American national identity, 198, 200, 204,
206, 207, 286, 287, 304; and African
American actors, 198, 210, 276, 278,
280, 285, 287; and racial identity, 276;
and Federal Theatre Project, 285–88,
305

Drums: effect on marines of, 41–42, 131,
133, 156–57, 167, 176; and Haitian history, 43; confiscated by marines, 46,
213; and Craige, 167–68, 213, *214*; and
O'Neill, 197–98, 200, 203; and travel
writing, 240, 241, 257; in Vodou ceremonies, 241; and E. Taft, 259; and
Inman, 271–72

Du Bois, W. E. B., 19, 188, 210, 276, 321
(n. 89), 332 (n. 102)

Dubois, William, 286, 362 (n. 144)

Dudley, Taney, 4

Dunham, Katherine, 20, 213, 278

Duvalier dictatorships, 36

Eaton, W. E., 44

Economy: international capitalist, 10, 23;
and U.S. occupation, 22–23; Haitian,
32, 34, 47, 48–53, 114, 117–20, 144,
215, 260, 319 (n. 52); U.S., 63. *See also*
Development, economic

Education: J. W. Johnson on, 19; under
U.S. occupation, 34, 122, 267; and Haitian elites, 52, 195; and national identity, 60, 68; and Voodoo, 128; and paternalism, 136, 303; and race, 194

Elections: Haitian, 31, 49; U.S. (1920), 33,
89, 187, 198, 227–28; U.S. (1912),
108–9, 110

Eliot, Charles William, 93

Elites, Haitian: and U.S. occupation, 11,
192; and plantation system, 48; and Haitian economy, 49–51, 52, 53; and Haitian workers, 53, 117; and McDonald,
98; and paternalism, 118; and Cacos,
141; J. W. Johnson on, 190, 194–95;
and race, 247; and Hughes, 261, 262;
Inman on, 272; and Guedé, 289

Elliot, George F., 60

Emerson, Haven, 273

Endore, Guy, 273, 275, 285

Enlightenment, 282, 283

Ethiopia, 278

Ethnology, 5, 28, 250, 274, 288, 290

Europe: and Pan-African movement, 52;
and American neutrality, 92; and Caribbean ports, 96; and Latin America, 98;
and developmentalism, 114; compared
to Haiti, 194–95; and Haitian culture,
274

European Americans: and paternalism,
18; and citizenship, 111; and primitivism, 211; and civilization, 223, 246; and
national identity, 305. *See also* Whiteness

Evans, L. Ton, 149, 162, 171, 186, 339
(n. 84), 340 (n. 87)

Exoticism: and paternalism, 19, 208–9,
237, 307; and imperialism, 21, 22, 208;
and U.S. occupation, 21, 187, 209; and
sexuality, 22, 231, 238, 243, 247, 260,
273; in fiction, 127, 225, 237, 288; and
primitivism, 187, 194, 196, 208, 262,
263, 288; critiques of, 194–95, 223,
263, 273, 274, 275, 281; and race, 195,

225, 231; and O'Neill, 210; and Haitian culture, 213, 305; and marines as authors, 216; and Haitian women, 234; in travel writing, 237, 240, 242, 246, 255; in U.S. newspapers, 237–38; and Voodoo, 246, 249; and Inman, 271; and Hurston, 291, 293, 295, 300; and American national identity, 304–5

Expeditionary forces. *See* "Advanced Base Forces"

Family, nuclear: and paternalism, 15–16, 179; as metaphor, 93, 108, 128, 243, 267; and father, 105, 297; and social order, 178, 241; and U.S. rise to power, 192–93, 306; in fiction, 223–25; and Vodou, 275; and African American literature, 281

Farnham, Roger L., 99, 192

Farred, Grant, 278

Fatherhood: and paternalism, 13, 15, 16, 67, 91, 105, 126–27, 128, 129, 145; and marines in Haiti, 13, 123, 136, 169, 254, 303, 304; and paternal authority, 15, 67–69, 104, 324 (n. 146); and masculinity, 66, 69, 107; attitudes toward, 66–67, 106–7; metaphors of, 67, 89–91, 108, 126, 128–29; and U.S. occupation, 128–29, 193–94; Haitian, 193–94

Federal Theatre Project, 285–88, 305

Federal Writers' Project, 285

Federation of British West Indies Negroes, 272

Fellowship of Reconciliation, 267

Femininity, and paternalism, 16, 22

Feminism, 123, 223–25, 256, 302, 305, 335 (n. 155)

Fiction: British, 65; Haitian, 165–66
—U.S.: marines in, 4, 5–6; Voodoo in, 4, 6, 127, 175, 177–78, 224, 236, 288, 292; pulp, 18, 35, 127, 165, 216, 236, 237; Haiti as subject of, 19, 21, 216, 223, 225, 228; and U.S. occupation, 21, 28; adventure, 65; horror, 165, 175–79, 225; historical, 282–84; and national identity, 304; and race and gender hierarchies, 305

Field campaigns, 137, 143, 146, 156, 157–58, 163, 164

Film: and Voodoo, 6, 227, 350 (n. 175); Haiti as subject of, 19, 217, 228; and U.S. occupation, 28; and O'Neill, 209, 280, 347 (n. 105), 348 (n. 124), 360–61 (n. 118); horror, 216, 223, 225–27, 351 (n. 179); exoticism in, 237; and race and gender hierarchies, 305

Fish, Hamilton, Jr., 190

Fisher, Sidney George, 267

Florida, 7, 8, 258

Folk tales, 263, 275, 278, 292, 295, 298, 299, 359 (n. 86)

Fonny, Dwight, 5

Food, 44–45

Forbes, W. Cameron, 34, 350 (n. 167)

Forbes commission, 34, 213, 221, 350 (n. 167)

Foreign Policy Association, 191, 357 (n. 20)

Fort Liberté, 116–17, 142

Fort Rivière, 107

Fort-Whiteman, Lovett, 19, 189, 269

Foucault, Michel, 24, 137, 314 (n. 44)

France: and Haiti's illegitimacy, 16; U.S. relations with, 29; and Haitian Revolution, 43, 44, 46, 47, 52; attempts to retake Haiti, 50–51, 193; and banking, 52; civilization of in Haiti, 61; and Banque Nationale de la Republique d'Haïti, 98, 99, 100; and S. Butler, 106, 108; and Haitian education, 195; and Haitian culture, 242, 243, 250, 254; and Communists, 278; revolution in, 283; in drama, 286

Frank, Benis, 61

Frankfurter, Felix, 191

Franklyn, Irwin, 72–73

Freeman, Joseph, 269

French Revolution, 283

Frontier, images of, 204, 206

Fruit, 120, 212, 216

Galt, Edith Bolling, 100, 112–13, 116

Gannett, Lewis S., 191, 268

Garde d'Haïti, 293. *See also* Gendarmerie d'Haïti

Garvey, Marcus, 189–90, 191, 216, 265, 272, 277, 285

Gede, 289–93, 300

Geffrard, Fabre Nicolas, 29, 49

Geffrard, G. F., 118, 119

Gendarmerie d'Haïti: U.S. Marines in, 5, 10, 86, 102, 103, 104, 125, 131, 133, 147, 180, 190, 244–46; and Wirkus, 5, 155, 158, 168–69; founding of, 31–32, 90, 101; and corvée, 32–33, 148–49; and strikes, 34; and ambiguity of national identification, 102, 103, 107–8, 126, 137, 165, 167, 180, 206; and Haitian government, 102–6, 125–26; and paternalism, 125, 129, 136–37; posts established by, 126, 147; authority of officers of, 137, 147–48, 158, 179; in war against Cacos, 147, 151; and Creole language, 148, 171; and prisoner labor, 150; prisoners killed by, 159, 161, 162; and rape, 163; and U.S. Marine legends, 166; and moral breakdown, 167; and military uniforms, 176; Haitian resistance to, 179, 244; J. W. Johnson on, 190

Gender: and imperialism, 9; and paternalism, 15–16, 22, 129, 188, 301, 303; and Haitian culture, 17, 234, 237, 238, 241, 243, 251, 290; and culture, 25; and U.S. occupation, 28, 29, 36, 137, 300, 301, 306; and race, 28, 36, 306; and U.S. culture, 35; and Vodou, 45; and Haitian economy, 49; and U.S. South, 54; and masculinity, 63; and identity, 66, 248; and clothing, 71, 84, 85, 167, 262–63, 356–57 (n. 14); for men, 73, 74; and U.S. policy, 95; discourses on, 109, 111, 154, 299; and rule of law, 115; and violence, 133; and horror stories, 165; politics of, 185, 187, 198, 223, 225, 226, 228, 302; and Christophe, 194; and O'Neill, 198, 200, 207; and Haitian workers, 215, 241; organization of, 223; ideologies of, 225, 288, 302, 305–6; and Inman, 247, 271; and travel writing, 260, 305; and African Americans, 264, 288, 302; and slavery, 284; and Hurston, 294, 295, 299, 300. See also Fatherhood; Manliness; Masculinity; Motherhood

Germany: and Haitian affairs, 30, 52, 99; merchants from, 51; and German American marines, 60; and railroads, 98; United States enters war against, 106; and rule of law, 114

Gilmore, Glenda, 54

Gilpin, Charles S., 198, 199, 207, 210, 226

Ginzburg, Carlo, 26

"Going native," 169, 170, 171, 181, 295, 297

Goman (insurrection leader), 49

Gomez, Manuel, 268–69

Great Britain, 47, 51, 60, 65, 278

Great Depression, 225, 261, 264, 276, 277, 288

Great Migration, 264

Great Sioux Uprising, 58

Gruening, Ernest, 89, 191

Guam, 7

Guatemala, 97

Guedé, 289–93, 300

Haiti: maps of, 2, 38, 139; U.S. uses of, 4; and U.S. imperialism, 7–8; finances of, 10, 141, 192–93, 213, 259–60, 267; sovereignty of, 11, 31; and popular culture, 21; diplomatic isolation of, 29; and African Americans, 29–30, 49, 187, 196, 265; presidents of, 31, 51–52, 190, 203; as American Africa, 36, 124–30, 232, 303–4; social divisions of, 48; international hostility toward, 50; foreign domination of, 51, 115; writers of, 85, 194, 240, 241, 243; U.S. attitudes toward, 86, 187; civil disorder in, 95; and USMC, 97; nationalism in, 98, 140, 144, 173, 186, 190, 267; associated with Africa, 125, 236, 237, 243, 250, 254, 262; press in, 129; as salable commodity, 185, 187, 212–23, 216, 246, 305; representations of, 206, 207, 211; academic studies of, 231. See also Culture—Haitian; Identity—Haitian national; Women—Haitian; Workers—Haitian
—government of: as democracy, 11; pre-1915, 29–30; and U.S. occupation, 30–31, 106, 116, 119, 125, 134, 140, 349 (n. 152) centralized power of, 36; and Haitian Revolution, 47; corruption in, 51; and McDonald, 98; and U.S. policy, 99; and Gendarmerie d'Haïti, 102–

6, 125–26; U.S. control of, 128–29; and peasants, 140; and Cacos, 142, 144–45; bonds of, 193
— history of: as told by U.S. officials, 11, 13, 15, 21, 135; and Haitain historiography, 11, 17, 46, 52–53, 85; Jordan on, 16; J. W. Johnson on, 19; and African Americans, 20, 25, 194, 276–82, 287–88; and culture, 22–29; and marines in Haiti, 42, 43–46, 79, 86, 316 (n. 22); and travel writing, 241, 242, 243, 245; and Hughes, 264; and Federal Writers' Project, 285–88
— land of: prohibition on foreign ownership of, 32, 47, 51, 52, 191; and peasants, 48, 49, 140, 318 (n. 48); and McDonald, 98; investigation of, 267. See also Haitian Constitution — of 1918; Railroads
— military of. See Gendarmerie d'Haïti
— regions of: and violence, 33; and peasant rebellions, 49; and marines in Haiti, 71, 143; and McDonald, 97; and remapping of Haiti, 139, 139; and Cacos, 140, 145; and corvée, 148, 149–50, 193; and Haitian Revolution, 318 (n. 50)
Haitian American Sugar Company (HASCO), 39, 120, 212, 339 (n. 84)
Haitian-American treaty of 1916, 31, 90, 102, 125, 126, 127, 129, 192
Haitian Congress, 31
Haitian Constitution
— of 1918: and U.S. occupation, 10, 31–32; and FDR, 89; and "undershirt diplomacy," 190
— pre-1918: prohibits foreign land ownership, 32, 47, 51, 52, 191; and monarchy, 48
Haitian Independence Day, 44
Haitian Revolution (1791–1804): American merchants' contributions to, 29; and U.S. culture, 36; and Haitian culture, 43–47; and Christophe, 46, 52–53, 140, 318 (n. 50); and race, 47, 263, 318 (n. 45); and Haitian historiography, 52, 203; and Cacos, 140; and O'Neill, 197, 203; in fiction, 224, 228; E. Taft on, 257; and African American literature, 263, 264, 276–85, 305; antiracist

account of, 269; and visual arts, 278; in drama, 285–87; and African Americans, 288
Haiti–Santo Domingo Independence Society, 191
Hall, G. Stanley, 65, 77, 321 (n. 89), 324 (n. 144)
Halperin, Edward, 226–27
Halperin, Victor, 226–27
Hanneken, Herman, 161–62, 171, 172, 173, 176, 177
Harding, Warren G., 33, 89, 187, 191, 265
Harlem Renaissance, 265, 270, 272, 277, 278, 282, 289, 348 (n. 132)
Harmon Foundation, 261
HASCO, 39, 120, 212, 339 (n. 84)
Haverstock, Gordon, 5
Hawaii, 7, 118
Hazing, 77
Henty, G. A., 65
Herskovits, Melville, 231, 273–74, 275, 288, 359 (n. 86)
Heterosexuality, 66, 69, 74, 227, 230, 231, 255–56. See also Homosexuality; Marriage
Hibben, Paxton, 268
Hinche, Haiti, 142, 150, 159, 162, 175, 338 (n. 42)
Hispaniola, 79
Holly, Theodore, 30
Homosexuality, 72, 73, 74, 326 (nn. 176, 182); and homosociality, 70; and homophobia, 74; female, 290. See also Chauncey, George; Masculinity
Honduras, 101, 196, 205, 206
Hoover, Herbert, 34, 213, 221, 350 (n. 167)
Hoover commission, 34, 213, 221, 350 (n. 167)
Horror: fiction genre of, 165, 175–79, 225; film genre of, 216, 223, 225–27, 351 (n. 179). See also Cannibalism; Zombies
House, Edward Mandel, 94
House Un-American Activities Committee, 287
Howe, Walter Bruce, 126, 135, 137–38
Hughes, Langston: J. W. Johnson influences, 19, 261; Haiti as subject for,

20, 262, 274, 278, 281–83, 286; and
O'Neill, 211; in Haiti, 261–64; and racism, 262, 305; and anti-imperialism,
269; and white publishers, 276; and U.S.
occupation, 291

Hundertmark, C., 78

Hunton, Addie, 191, 266

Hurston, Zora Neale: Haiti as subject for,
20, 278, 288–300; *Tell My Horse*, 36,
264, 288–300, 306, 307; and paternalism, 36, 291, 293, 294–95, 300; and culture and personality, 231; and race relations, 264; and white publishers, 276;
Mules and Men, 292; and racial politics,
306; and individual subjectivities, 307

ICW, 265, 266

Identity: and marines, 3, 75–76, 77, 82,
123, 137, 146, 154–55, 185; and whiteness, 3–4, 22, 53–54, 59, 108, 136, 137,
148, 164, 179, 287, 305, 306–7, 321
(n. 89); and U.S. occupation, 3–4, 29,
74, 86, 126, 164; and subjectivity, 8,
136–37, 155, 165; U.S. regional, 9, 56,
61; and Haitian history, 20; and culture,
23; fragility of, 25, 164, 166–71, 173,
175, 177, 179, 185; ethnic, 58, 59, 62;
and race, 58, 123, 211, 224, 276, 321
(n. 89); racial, 62, 175, 211, 247, 248,
249, 276; and mastery, 66, 123, 148;
and gender, 66, 248; and sexuality, 74,
230, 241, 247; and paternalism, 129,
168–69, 173; and violence, 155, 181;
and O'Neill, 211; and Haitian culture,
215, 242; and dances, 241; and drama,
286–87; Caribbean, 294; and paternity,
297
— Haitian national: and marines in Gendarmerie d'Haïti, 102, 103, 107–8, 126,
137, 165, 167, 180, 206; and patriotism,
242–43; represented as unstable, 250,
274, 295, 297; in fiction, 291–92, 295
— national: and culture, 25, 29; blurring
of, 124, 219, 221; and Hurston, 291–
92, 294, 297–300
— U.S. national: and imperialism, 3, 6, 8,
9, 21–22, 305; and Haitian culture, 17;
and paternalism, 18, 22, 113, 123, 304;
and African Americans, 22, 264, 282,

288; and U.S. occupation, 28, 35, 61,
175, 301, 304, 306; and perceptions of
Haiti, 36; and marines in Haiti, 53–54,
56, 59, 62, 82, 154, 164, 165, 179, 304;
and race, 54, 58; and regional identities,
56, 58, 298–99; and ethnic differences,
59, 60–62; and Gendarmerie d'Haïti,
102, 103, 107–8, 126, 137, 165, 167,
180, 206; ambiguity of, 124, 219, 221,
224, 297, 305; subjective investments in,
165; and military uniform, 176; politics
of, 185, 228; and drama, 198, 200, 204,
206, 207, 286, 287, 304; and Puritanism, 230–31; family as construct of, 243;
and Hughes, 263; instability of, 300;
and exoticism, 304–5

Île de la Gonave, 5, 254–55, 292–93

Illegitimacy: and Haiti as illegitimate,
16, 257; and violence, 158–59, 180; of
Haitian children, 215, 233, 250; and
Hurston, 294, 297

Immigrants
— Haitian: African American, 29–30, 49,
265; Syrian, 297, 298, 299
— U.S.: and paternalism, 15, 122; and
USMC, 54, 59, 164; European, 60; and
fatherhood, 68; and masculinity, 69–70,
71; Haitian, 263, 265

Imperialism: and American national identity, 3, 6, 8, 9, 21–22, 305; violence of,
4, 5, 6–7, 9, 15, 135, 151, 180; and Haitian culture, 4, 6, 12, 21, 241; and culture, 4–5, 6; and citizenship, 6–7, 8, 21;
discourse on, 6–9; and U.S. occupation,
12, 21, 28–29, 36, 267, 301; and exoticism, 21, 22, 208; and paternalism, 21,
129, 136, 208, 231, 303; and travel writing, 35, 259–60; and Spanish-American
War, 54; and masculinity, 64–65; British, 65; and U.S. Navy, 96; and U.S. public opinion, 124, 186; as economic
exploitation, 187; in drama, 188; and
anti-imperialism, 189, 191, 232, 263,
264–70, 301; O'Neill on, 197, 200, 204,
205–6; J. W. Johnson on, 243; and CP-
USA, 268; Inman on, 273; Hughes on,
274; critiques of, 278; extension of, 302;
and subjectivity, 307. *See also* United
States — Haitian occupation by

Ingram, Rex, 287
Inman, Samuel Guy: and missionary
    movement, 232–33, 272, 352 (n. 19);
    Through Santo Domingo and Haiti, 232–
    38; and marines in Haiti, 233, 247; and
    Voodoo, 248, 271; and primitivism, 255,
    270–71; and paternalism, 259; and U.S.
    occupation, 270, 362 (n. 18); *Trailing
    the Conquistadores*, 270–73; and racial
    ideology, 275
Insanity: and marines in Haiti, 86, 132,
    180; as legal defense, 131–33, 160, 164;
    reports of, 148, 166–67; fears of, 164–
    65; in *The Emperor Jones*, 187; and
    Hurston, 297, 299
Intelligence, military, 83, 86, 130, 141,
    173, 315 (n. 70)
Intercollegiate Socialist Society (ISS), 268
International Council of Women (ICW),
    265, 266
International Council of Women of the
    Darker Races, 266
Internationalism, liberal, 113, 117–18,
    129, 302
Investigations, official: of violence, 33;
    Forbes commission, 34, 213, 221, 350
    (n. 167); and Moton, 34; newspaper,
    89; Mayo Court of Inquiry, 119, 129,
    132, 180, 191; of corvée, 150, 160; of
    marines killing prisoners, 161; and J. W.
    Johnson, 187, 190–91; and WILPF, 238,
    266–68. *See also* U.S. Senate — inquiry
    by
Investment. *See* United States —
    investments in Haiti of
ISS, 268
Italy, 278

Jacmel, 149, 229
Jamaica, 189, 272, 288, 289, 294, 300
James, C. L. R., 276, 278, 280–81, 286,
    355 (n. 30)
Jefferson, Thomas, 29, 50
Jérémie, 84, 229
Johnson, Barbara, 292
Johnson, Charles S., 283
Johnson, James Weldon: "Self-
    Determining Haiti," 19, 188–96, 198;
    and paternalism, 19, 191–94, 267; and

Haitian culture, 19, 228, 241; and
    Hughes, 19, 261; and cultural com-
    modification, 35; and U.S. occupation,
    89, 189, 190–91, 291; and interpreta-
    tion of violence, 180; journalism of,
    185, 188; investigative trip to Haiti by,
    187, 190–91; influence of, 187, 276;
    and diplomacy, 188, 194; and NAACP,
    188–89, 276; and marines in Haiti, 190,
    247; and Harding, 191; on Christophe,
    193–94, 196, 203, 207, 263, 276–77;
    and O'Neill, 198, 205; and Burks's fic-
    tion, 216; and masculinity, 223; and
    Haiti as orphan, 243; and U.S. culture,
    264; and Bontemps, 283
Johnson, Walter E., 159–61
Jones Act of 1917, 8
Jordan, Wilhelm F., 16, 118, 124–25, 192,
    232, 303–4
Journalism: and U.S. occupation, 1, 12,
    187, 221; and marines in Haiti, 18, 186;
    and paternalism, 18–19; and marines,
    77; and Wilson, 100; and violence, 134;
    and J. W. Johnson, 185, 188; military
    censorship of, 186; and travel writing,
    246, 247; and national identity, 304. *See
    also* Newspapers; Newsreels

Kelly (Gendarmerie officer), 167, 168
Kelly, Francis Patrick "Pat," 175
Kennan, George, 114–15, 302
Kennedy, Selden, 150
Kenney, Charles E., 162
Killing
— by Haitians: representations of, 79–80,
    127; of prisoners, 80, 81; as savagery,
    138. *See also* Cannibalism; Horror; Prim-
    itivism; Zombies
— by marines: and U.S. invasion of Haiti,
    81, 83; and charges of "indiscriminate
    killing" 89, 156, 158, 159, 160; repre-
    sentations of, 131, 221; of Cacos, 136,
    138, 143, 145, 146, 151, 155–56, 158,
    160, 161–62, 340 (n. 90), 341 (n. 122);
    terminology for, 136, 155, 156, 161,
    337 (n. 21); in military campaigns, 146,
    158; and Gendarmerie d'Haïti, 148; as
    part of corvée, 149, 150; of prisoners,
    159–60, 161, 162, 337 (n. 21), 340

(n. 90); and rape, 163; J. W. Johnson on, 190. *See also* Casualties; Violence; Wars

King, Alexander, 209, 253

Kinsey, Alfred, 73

Kirchwey, Freda, 268, 269

Knapp, H. S., 121–22

Kock, Bernard, 30

Ku Klux Klan, 58

Labor: waged, 66, 68, 108–9, 117, 119, 122, 148, 303; forced (*see* Corvée; Slavery)

—Haitian: resists U.S. occupation, 11, 84, 85; pattern of, 48–49; and U.S. investments, 121–22; prisoner, 150; and violence, 150, 339 (n. 84); female, 233

Laleau, Leon, 85

Langston, John Mercer, 30

Lanoue, Joseph, 49, 119

Lansing, Robert, 31, 100, 116, 186, 334 (n. 135)

Latin America: and diplomatic isolation of Haiti, 50; U.S. relations with, 92–93, 94, 97, 98, 108, 112–13, 115; and U.S. Navy, 95; and child metaphors, 113, 333 (n. 123); and rule of law, 114; and paternalism, 124; compared to Haiti, 194; Inman on, 232, 270, 352 (n. 19); and CP-USA, 268

Law, martial, 31, 119, 129

Lawrence, Jacob, 20, 278, 279

League of Nations, 11

LeClerc, Charles Victor Emmanuel, 47

Lee, Canada, 287

Left, radical, 263, 267–68, 269, 273, 276, 281, 282, 283

Legalism, 114–15, 302

Legba, 259

Lejeune, John A., 100–101, 104–5

Lespinasse, Beauvais, 243

Lewis, David Levering, 210

Lewis, Gordon K., 46

Liberalism, 109–10, 113, 114, 115, 117–18, 129, 302

Liberia, 189

Lincoln, Abraham, 29–30, 58

Link, Arthur S., 113, 151, 333 (n. 123)

Literary Guild, 6, 9, 19, 217, 246

Little, Louis McCarty, 126

Livingston, Lemuel, 97

Lodge, Henry Cabot, 191

Logan, Rayford, 276, 278

London, England, 278, 280

Long, Boaz W., 97, 99

Louisiana, 7

L'Ouverture, Toussaint. *See* Touissant L'Ouverture, François Dominique

Lovett, Robert Morss, 269

Lugosi, Bela, 226–27

Lwa, 45. *See also* Guedé; Legba; Ogou; Vodou

Lynching, 186, 194, 257, 258, 259, 264, 277

Machias, USS, 30

McCormick, Medill, 191

McDonald, James P., 97–98, 118

McDonald contract, 52, 140

McFadden, Bernarr, 64

McGowan, Kenneth, 210

Mackandal, 246, 272

McMillen, Fred, 84, 122

McQuilkin, John J., 159–61

Madiou, Thomas, 46

Mahan, Alfred Thayer, 96

Maine, USS, 60

Malaria, 44, 196

Manhood: and paternalism, 16, 68, 69, 102, 303; changing concept of, 63; challenges to, 64; and marines, 65, 69, 78, 123, 136, 175; assertion of, 66; ideologies of, 67, 69; and homosocial contexts, 70; and sexual violence, 73; and Butler, 106; and violence, 154; and horror stories, 165; J. W. Johnson on, 194; and O'Neill, 200, 207; and Vandercook's Christophe biography, 217, 349 (nn. 157, 158); and lynching, 277; and African American literature, 282; and slavery, 284. *See also* Manliness; Masculinity

Manliness: and citizenship, 62; and civilization, 64, 66, 194; and fatherhood, 67; and sexuality, 73; and sociability, 74; and Wilson, 93, 111; challenges to, 206; and O'Neill, 208; of Haitian men,

233; and marine indoctrination, 327
(n. 200). *See also* Manhood; Masculinity

Mann, James R., 103

Marines. *See* U.S. Marine Corps—
members of; U.S. Marine Corps—
members of in Haiti

Marriage: between Haitian women and
German men, 51; between Haitian
women and marines, 86, 138, 165, 170,
171, 215–16; versus sexual disorder,
192, 233; as value, 223; interracial, 258

"Marronage," 84

Marshall, Harriet Gibbs, 265, 278, 281

Marshall, Napoleon, 265

Masculinity: and paternalism, 16, 22, 302,
306; and militarism, 62, 64, 66, 323
(n. 121); and breadwinning, 63, 66–67,
69; and class, 63, 66–67, 69–74, 194;
and race, 64, 69, 198, 223; cultivation
of, 65; and violence, 66, 69, 107, 154;
and paternal responsibilities, 66–67,
324–25 (nn. 144, 148); rough versus
respectable, 69–74; and hazing, 77; and
marines in Haiti, 123, 137, 234; subjective investments in, 165; and military
uniform, 176; black, 194, 207; and Citadel, 203, 263, 264, 278; and O'Neill,
204, 208, 223; and prostitution, 215;
and J. W. Johnson, 223; of Cacos, 234;
and E. Taft, 256; and Inman, 271–72.
See also Fatherhood; Homosexuality;
Manhood; Manliness; Sexuality

Mason, Charlotte Osgood, 261

Massacre River, 270–71

Mayo, Henry T., 132, 191

Mayo Court of Inquiry, 132, 180, 191

Melling, 129–30, 335–36 (n. 178)

Memory: and identity, 3, 60, 76, 168; in
Haitian culture, 45, 46; in E. Taft, 229,
230, 258–59; in B. Niles, 243–44, 245,
246, 258; in Seabrook, 252, 258, 259

Merman, Ethel, 19

Messenger, 19, 189, 210, 269

Métraux, Alfred, 213

Mexico: and U.S. Southwest, 7; and popular culture, 21; and marines, 78; and
USS *Washington*, 80; and Wilson, 94, 97,
98, 113; and S. Butler, 101, 104; and
Inman, 232; and anti-imperialism, 268

Military campaigns: punitive approach
to, 100, 143, 146, 331 (n. 57), 336
(n. 18); in Haiti, 143, 144, 146, 158,
179. *See also* Field campaigns; War:
against Cacos

Military orders, 135, 143, 146, 148, 151,
158, 159, 179

Military patrols, 143

Miller, Adolph: memoirs of, 4; and German citizens, 60; and moralism, 70;
arrives in Haiti, 79–80, 82–84; observations of, 86; and paternalism, 116–18,
303; and military hierarchy, 123; and
Haitian cooperation, 142; and Gendarmerie d'Haïti, 147, 148, 180; and prostitution, 215

Miller, Helen, 5–6

Miller, Holly, 79

Miller, Ivan, 67, 77, 154

Missionaries: and U.S. occupation, 12, 18,
33, 162, 186, 269; and paternalism, 16,
18, 24, 118, 237; withholding of, 50;
and corvée, 149; and Inman, 232–33,
272, 352 (n. 19); in Caribbean, 233,
237; and images of African exploration,
236; interpretations of, 241

Modernism, 200, 206, 210, 270

Modernization, 10–11, 117, 118, 212,
213, 244

Molas, Nicholas de, 217

Môle Saint Nicholas, 30, 96

Monroe Doctrine, 80, 94, 96, 97

Montana, USS, 30

Montgomery, David, 122

Moralism: and U.S. occupation, 19; and
marines in Haiti, 61, 70–71, 155, 157;
and homosexuality, 74; and USMC
training, 77; and paternalism, 91; and
Wilson, 93–94, 110; and legalism, 114–
15; and Inman, 233–34, 237

Morris, Mike, 173, 175

Motherhood: in Davis, 223–24, 350
(n. 175); in Seabrook, 249, 252, 253,
254; representations of, 253, 294, 300;
and Africa as mother of Haiti, 254

Moton, Robert Roussa, 34

Mrozek, Donald, 77, 326 (n. 182), 327
(n. 200)

Muth, Lawrence, 161, 166, 173, 175

NAACP. *See* National Association for the Advancement of Colored People
NACW, 265, 266
Nation, 19, *89,* 186, 188, 191, 198, 205, 268, 291
National Association for the Advancement of Colored People (NAACP): and U.S. occupation, 19, 33; and J. W. Johnson, 188–89, 276; and U.S. policy, 190; and Patriotic Union, 191; and lynching, 258; and Hughes, 261; and anti-imperialism, 263, 264–65; and Inman, 272; and Great Depression, 277; and Vincent, 291
National Association of Colored Women (NACW), 265, 266
National City Bank of New York, 98, 99, 190, 192–93
Nationalism: in Haiti, 98, 140, 144, 173, 186, 190, 267; black nationalism, 187, 265. *See also* Identity — Haitian national; Identity — national; Identity — U.S. national
National Negro Press Association, 265
Native Americans, 7, 58, 64, 134, 154, 200; reservations for, 15
Neal, Claude, 258
Nearing, Scott, 269
Negro World, 189
Neuhaus, Philip, 167, 168
Neverdon-Morton, Cynthia, 266
New Deal, 277, 278, 285, 287
New England, 68, 229–32
New Mexico, 7
Newspapers
— Haitian: censorship of, 33, 267; and peasants, 49–50; and U.S. occupation, 118–19; and official press, 129; and killing by marines, 131; and Cacos, 143; and Forbes commission, 213
— U.S.: and U.S. occupation, 33, 186; and Spanish-American War, 60; investigations by, *89;* and marines in Haiti, 146, 157, 160; censorship of, 186; and zombies, 225; and exoticism, 237–38; and travel writing, 246; and antiracist activism, 263 (see also *Chicago Defender*; *Crisis*); and anti-imperialism, 269; on Hurston, 293

Newsreels, 221, 223
New York, N.Y., 58, 73, 209, 265, 325 (n. 161)
New York Times, 109
Nicaragua, 12, 61, 78, 97, 101, 188, 331 (n. 70), 336 (n. 18)
Nicholls, David, 140
Niles, Blair Rice: travel writings of, 232, 238–46, 247; *Black Haiti,* 238–46, 270, 275; memory in, 243–44, 245, 246, 258; and France, 250; and race, 255, 275; and paternalism, 259; and unconscious, 260; and peasants, 262; and civilization, 271
Niles, Robert, 239
Noble, Alfred H., 88
Norfolk, Va., 56, 58, 71

Occupation, defined, 20. *See also* United States — Haitian occupation by
Ogé, M., 52
Ogou, 290
Oil, 216
Oklahoma, 7
O'Neill, Eugene: J. W. Johnson influences, 19; as colonial adventurer, 196–97, 346 (n. 67); as socialist, 197, 205; *Hairy Ape, The,* 204, 206–7, 210–11, 226
— *Emperor Jones, The:* and cultural commodification, 35, 217; and appeal of Haiti, 185, 187; writing of, 187, 197–98; and paternalism, 188, 200, 205; Gilpin in, 198, *199,* 207, 210, 226; opening night of, 198, 209; ambiguities in, 198–212; A. Douglas illustrates, 200, *201, 202;* and primitivism, 204, 206–7, 209, 210, 212, 226, 348 (n. 132); and white audiences, 205–6, 208, 209, 210, 211; Robeson in, 207, 209, 278, 280; puppet production of, *208,* 209; as opera, 209; stage productions of, 209; and African American audiences, 209, 211; on film, 209, 280, 347 (n. 105), 348 (n. 124), 360–61 (n. 118); and critics, 210–11, 348 (n. 132); influence of, 225; and racial politics, 306; and individual subjectivity, 307
Open Door, 96
Overley, Homer: memoirs of, 4, 42; as

enlisted man, 39, 41, 123; photographed, *40*, *41*; and U.S. regional identity, 56; and relationship with Haitians, 88; and undeclared war, 136; and violence, 156; and U.S. newspaper reports, 157; and sense of humanity, 164, 171; and Cacos, 236; and militarism, 324 (n. 141)

Owen, Chandler, 189

Padmore, George, 276, 278, 280

Painting. *See* Arts, visual

Pan-African movement, 50, 52, 269, 270, 272, 276, 357 (n. 20)

Panama: and imperialism, 7; Pan-American talks in, 50; and marines, 78; and T. Roosevelt, 94, 97; and S. Butler, 101, 104, 106, 123; and race, 112–13, 124

Panama Canal, 92, 93, 104

Paris, France, 52

Parris Island, S.C., 58, 75

Parsons, Elsie Clews, 231, 359 (n. 86)

Paternalism: and marines in Haiti, 13, *14*, 17, 18, 21, 22, 67, 69, 105, 123, 137, 146, 151, 171, 179, 233, 303, 335 (n. 152); and fatherhood, 13, 15, 16, 67, 91, 105, 126–27, 128, 129, 145; and violence, 13, 15, 19, 35, 55, 111, 135–37, 146, 155, 156, 179–81; and U.S. occupation, 13, 16, 17, 21, 27, 28, 35, 108, 115–24, 125, 135, 137, 139, 145, 146, 156, 165, 175, 179–80, 181, 209, 301, 302–3; of S. Butler, 13, 16, 69, 91, 101–2, 104–8, 115, 116, 118, 124, 129, 147, 207, 302, 331 (n. 79); of USMC, 13, 77; and age, 15; and Native Americans, 15; and racism, 15, 22, 105, 111, 156, 188; defined, 15, 312 (n. 17); as gendered construct, 15–16, 22, 129, 188, 301, 303; and missionaries, 16, 18, 24, 118, 237; and femininity, 16, 22; industrial, 16, 68–69; and domesticity, 16, 105–6, 231; contradictory nature of, 17, 21, 146, 156, 165, 304; and African Americans, 18, 22, 55, 124, 263; and American national identity, 18, 22, 113, 123, 304; and J. W. Johnson, 19, 191–94, 267; and exoticism, 19, 208–9,

237, 307; and imperialism, 21, 129, 136, 208, 231, 303; and Hurston, 36, 291, 293, 294–95, 300; and U.S. South, 54–56; of officers toward enlisted men, 72, 77–78; and political ends, 90; of Wilson, 91, 93, 95, 100, 108–13, 124, 129, 302, 333 (n. 333); and McDonald, 98; Haitian resistance to, 104, 116; and promise of mastery to white men, 105; of T. Roosevelt, 108–9; and primitivism, 116, 124, 126–28; of Jordan, 124–25; and identity, 129, 168–69, 173; and O'Neill, 188, 200, 205, 208; and Inman, 233, 259; cultural superiority underlying, 238; and Haitian culture, 244; and Seabrook, 247, 254, 255, 259; logic of, 249, 254; and E. Taft, 257, 259; and women's movement, 267; and Hughes, 281

Paternity, metaphor of, 16, 193, 249, 294–97, 299

Patriotic Union, 150, 191, 265, 269, 272

Peasantry, 48–49, 190, 318 (n. 49), 319 (n. 54)

Peasants: J. W. Johnson on, 19, 190, 195–96; and corvée, 32, 148, 163; rebellion of, 36, 49, 140; and conches, 43; and Haitian land, 48, 49, 140, 318 (n. 48); and Haitian economy, 49, 53, 119–20, 144; and liberty, 51; and McDonald contract, 52; and marines in Haiti, 55, 62, 120, 303; and McDonald, 98; and subsistence agriculture, 114; and child metaphor, 115; and U.S. occupation, 116–17, 119–20, 192, 193, 291; and public works, 116–17, 150; and paternalism, 122; as Cacos, 140, 150–51; and Gendarmerie d'Haïti, 148; fears of, 165; O'Neill on, 196, 205; and travel writing, 241, 247, 250; and Hughes, 262–63; Inman on, 270, 272. *See also* Class — in Haiti

Penn, William, 59, 112, 113, 124

Péralte, Charlemagne: assassination of, 11, 31, 33, 161, 173, *174*; capture of, 11, 171, 176; and Cacos, 33, 151, 154; and peasants, 49; motto of, 140; and road building, 192

Perkins, J. L., 130

Peru, 97

Peters, Frederick, 227

Pétion, Alexandre, 48, 318–19 (nn. 50, 51, 52)

Pfister, Joel, 197, 207

Philadelphia, Pa., 71

Philippines: and imperialism, 7, 8, 12, 86; and marines, 78; and Waller, 100; and S. Butler, 101; and paternalism, 118; and CP-USA, 268

Phillips, Charles, 268–69

Photography, 120–21, 239–40

Pickens, William, 269

Pifer, Donald, 5

Pignon, 142

Plantations and plantation system: and paternalism, 15; and slave revolution, 43; and Haitian Revolution, 47; and Haitian workers, 48; and Rural Code, 48–49; and McDonald, 98; and peasants, 119–20; and U.S. investments, 122; and anti-imperialism, 269–70. *See also* Agriculture

Plummer, Brenda Gale, 98, 186, 265, 312 (n. 18)

Poisoning, 56

Policy. *See* United States — policy of

Polynesia, 21

Pomerene, Atlee, 149

Popular Government League, 191, 357 (n. 20)

Poritz, Norman, 130

Port-au-Prince: and V. G. Sam's assassination, 19, 127; and Caperton, 30–31; and strike of 1929, 34; and marines in Haiti, 43, 46, 79, 80–82, 85, 105; and Haitian elites, 52; and public works projects, 117; Cacos in, 141; and rape, 163; and J. W. Johnson, 190; European influence in, 194; prostitution in, 215, 216; in newsreels, 221; in fiction, 224; in E. Taft, 229, 256; and tourism, 237–38, 240; Hughes in, 261, 262

Port-de-Paix, 142

Power: and imperialism, 6–7, 11, 187; and paternalism, 15, 24, 54, 69, 104, 108, 124, 127, 129; and marines in Haiti, 17, 123, 137, 212–13; and U.S. occupation, 21, 29, 86, 185, 221, 267; and gender, 22; structures of, 23; and culture, 24, 25; Foucault on, 24, 137, 314 (n. 44); and Toussaint L'Ouverture, 47; and U.S. territorial expansion, 92; and U.S. policy, 95; and U.S. Navy, 96; and fatherhood, 107, 128; and Wilson, 108; and O'Neill, 200; and Haitian culture, 212–13, 216; and R. B. Davis, 224, 350 (n. 173); and zombies, 225; and Herskovits, 274; and slavery, 284; and Guédé, 289; domestic relations of, 302; and U.S. culture, 307

Presidents, Haitian, 31, 51–52, 190, 203

President's Commission for the Study and Review of Conditions in the Republic of Haiti, 34, 213, 221, 350 (n. 167)

Price, Hannibal, 239

Price-Mars, Jean, 53, 250–51, 252, 275

Prichard, Hesketh, 203, 207, 260

Primitivism: and imperialism, 8; and drums, 46; and masculinity, 64–65; and Haitian killing, 80; and S. Butler, 103; and paternalism, 116, 124, 126–28; and peasants, 120; and civilization, 125, 128; and violence, 154; and Craige, 167; and Burks, 178; and exoticism, 187, 194, 196, 208, 262, 263, 288; of J. W. Johnson, 195; and O'Neill, 204, 206–7, 209, 210, 212, 226, 348 (n. 132); modernist, 206, 210; and sexuality, 207; and racism, 211; and Haitian culture, 214; and Vandercook, 217; and R. B. Davis, 223; in fiction, 225; in film, 226, 351 (n. 179); and travel writing, 247, 248–49, 251, 255; and Inman, 255, 270–71; and Hughes, 261; and Van Vechten, 289

Prisoners: under V. G. Sam, 80, 81; under U.S. occupation, 83, 151, *157*, 236; marines kill, 83, 159–60, 161, 162, 337 (n. 21), 340 (n. 90); as workers, 149, 150

Prisons, 149, 151; and torture, 162

Progress, 5, 119, 192, 206, 210

Progressivism, 16, 66, 114

Prosser, Gabriel, 282, 283

Prostitution, 171, 215, 216, 257, 259

Protests: in U.S., 34, 186–87, 191, 212, 228, 263, 265, 268; in Haiti, 34–35, 83–84, 85, 221; of marines in Haiti, 86. *See also* United States — occupation of Haiti by: criticism of

Psychology, 231. *See also* Discourse: psychological

Public works: road building, 10, 11, 117, 148, 149, 150, 179, 192; and paternalism, 13; and Gendarmerie d'Haïti, 104, 147; and A. Miller, 116–17; and corvée, 148–50, 179; prisoner labor on, 150; and marines in Haiti, 212; and travel writing, 247

Publishing, 216, 276

Puerto Rico, 7, 8, 12, 61, 118, 268, 322 (n. 113)

Puller, Louis B. "Chesty," 4, 150, 151, 156, 157, 161, 164, 166

Pumpkins, 44–45

Puritanism, 229–32, 258

Puryear, Bennett, 150

Quakers, 59, 90, 266–67

Race: and imperialism, 9; and riots, 11, 58; and paternalism, 15, 16, 22, 129, 301, 303; and Haitian culture, 17, 228, 243, 245, 247; and U.S. culture, 25, 35, 54, 180, 181; and U.S. occupation, 28, 29, 36, 86, 137, 300, 301; and Haitian Revolution, 47, 263, 318 (n. 45); and U.S. South, 54–55, 320 (n. 69); and marines, 58, 62; and identity, 58, 123, 211, 224, 230, 276, 321 (n. 89); and evolution of racial codes, 58, 321 (n. 89); and masculinity, 69, 198, 223; and U.S. policy, 95; and Wilson, 109; and fatherhood metaphors, 128; and violence, 133, 258, 259; discourses on, 154, 259; and horror, 165; and whitening black race, 170; Darwinian concept of, 180–81; and exoticism, 195, 225, 231; and O'Neill, 198, 200, 207, 209; and Haitian workers, 215; ideology of, 225, 275, 302; and zombies, 227; and Puritanism, 231; essentialism of, 238; Haitian consciousness of, 240; and travel writing, 252, 260; and sexuality, 255; and rape, 257; and African Americans, 264, 302; cultural definitions of, 275, 293; and interracial alliance, 277, 282, 284, 285, 287; pride in, 282

— politics of, Haitian, 194, 223

— politics of, U.S.: and African Americans, 35–36, 189, 287, 305; and paternalism, 122, 302; and Haiti as means of negotiating, 185; changes in, 189–90; and *The Emperor Jones*, 198, 207; and Great Depression, 225; and drama, 226, 287; and Haiti's appeal, 228; and E. Taft, 258; and Bontemps, 276; and U.S. occupation, 293; and gender, 306. *See also* Lynching

Racism: of marines in Haiti, 11, 17, 46, 83, 136, 155–56, 180, 189, 190, 247, 254, 265; paternalism as form of, 15, 22, 105, 111, 156, 188; and U.S. occupation, 29, 188, 190, 288; and Citadel, 51; and S. Butler, 55, 101–2, 104, 105, 124, 136, 331 (n. 79); U.S. regional, 58; and Waller, 100; and Wilson, 109–15, 124, 332 (n. 102); and rule of law, 115; in fiction, 127, 175, 223; and corvée, 148; and U.S. amusement park games, 156; and rape, 163; and O'Neill, 200, 210, 211; and primitivism, 211; and white power, 224, 350 (n. 173); and feminism, 225; and cannibalism, 239; exoticism as form of, 239–40, 293; and travel writing, 256; in Haiti, 258; and Hughes, 262, 305; and antiracist activism, 263; and African Americans, 264, 305; within ICW, 266; and U.S. whites, 270–76; and Inman, 271; and lynching, 277; critiques of, 278; and Haitian culture, 305

Radicals, leftist, 263, 267–68, 269, 273, 276, 281, 282, 283

Radio, 6, 19, 209, 216, 217, 228

Railroads, 30, 52, 97–98, 99, 192

Rampersad, Arnold, 283

Randolph, A. Philip, 189

Rape, 73, 163, 190, 234, 257–58, 264, 283, 284, 326 (n. 174), 355 (n. 130)

Rara, 84

Raymond, Zacharias, 229–30, 259, 352 (n. 7)

Reconstruction, 122

Redfield, Robert, 251

Redman, Paul, 5

Redpath, James, 29

Regions. *See* Haiti—regions of; United States—regions of

Religion. *See* Catholicism; Missionaries; Quakers; Vodou

Remner, Lawrence, 210–11

Republican Party, U.S., 109, 187, 191

Reser, Dr., 294–99

Revolutions: in Haiti, 16, 29, 31, 51, 141; in Latin America, 113; in O'Neill's letters, 197; in fiction, 228, 273, 281, 282. *See also* American Revolution; French Revolution; Haitian Revolution; Russian Revolution

Robeson, Paul, 207, 209, 278, 280

Roosevelt, Franklin D., 89

Roosevelt, Theodore: and national identity, 59; and boyhood, 64, 65; and U.S. policy, 93, 97; and Panama, 94, 97; and paternalism, 108–9; and J. W. Johnson, 187, 190; O'Neill on, 206

Roy, Eugene, 34

Rubber, 216

Rule of law, 100, 113, 114–15, 128, 302

Rural Code, 48–49, 51

Russell, John H.: and U.S. occupation, 20, 33, 119, 127–28, 130; cannibalism accounts of, 127, 128, 165–66; and corvée, 149–50; and "indiscriminate killings," 158–59; and killing of prisoners, 160

Russian Revolution, 189

Said, Edward, 9

Saint Domingue, 43–47, 50, 51, 229, 230, 273, 286. *See also* Haiti

St. John, Spencer, 260

St. Marc, Haiti, 148, 150, 162, 229

St. Michel, Haiti, 121–22, 131–32, 133

Saint Remy, Joseph, 46

Salnave, Sylvain, 49, 140

Salomon, Louis Lysius Félicité, 49, 51–52

Sam, Simon, 52

Sam, Vilburn Guillaume, 19, 80, 81, 127, 197, 204, 211

San Francisco, Calif., 196

Santo Domingo. *See* Dominican Republic

Savage, Augusta, 278, *280*

Schmidt, F. W., 56, 57, 70

Schmidt, Hans, 72, 134, 173, 312 (n. 18), 331 (n. 79), 339 (n. 80)

Schomburg, Arthur, 20, 283

Schuyler, George, 210

Scott, Joan, 23

Scottsboro trial, 283

Seabrook, William B.: *The Magic Island*, 4, 5–6, 8, 19, 196, 246–55, 288, 292; and Wirkus, 4, 5–6, 254–55, 295; travel writing of, 4, 232, 246–55, 259, 260; J. W. Johnson influences, 19, 196, 276; and zombies, 225, 226; and memory, 252, 258, 259; and Hughes, 261; and Inman, 270; and Haitian identity, 274; and Hurston, 288–89, 292, 296–97; and sexual and gender disorder, 305

Seligman, Herbert, 89, 186, 187

Sensationalism: of marines' memoirs, 4; of fiction, 21, 236; and Haitian elites, 52; of R. B. Davis, 223; and zombies, 225; of travel writing, 236; of Seabrook, 247, 250, 252, 289; of E. Taft, 255; challenges to, 274, 281

Servants, 215, 216, 289

Service d'Hygiène, 44, 129

Service Technique de l'Agriculture, 34, 129, 212

Seton, William Thompson, 65

Seward, William H., 30

Sexuality: as trope, 9; and paternalism, 15, 16; and exoticism, 22, 231, 238, 243, 247, 260, 273; and U.S. occupation, 28, 29, 237, 300, 301, 306; and travel writing, 35, 233, 256, 257, 258, 259, 260; and linking of race and promiscuity, 55, 178–79, 237, 238; and masculinity, 69, 70, 71, 73–74; and violence, 73, 154, 163, 255, 257, 284; and identity, 74, 230, 241, 247; and Voodoo, 178; politics of, 185, 228; and primitivism, 207; and Haitian workers, 215; and feminism, 223–25; and psychological discourse, 224, 231; and zombies, 227; and domesticity, 231; and Haitian culture, 241, 242, 243, 252, 274, 281, 306; and unconscious, 249; and Haitian women, 251; and race, 255; interracial, 259; and African Americans, 264, 288. *See also* Heterosexuality; Homosexuality; Marriage; Masculinity

Shannon, Magdaline W., 53

Shepard, Lemuel C., 154
Shipman, Charles, 268–69
Silverthorn, Merwin Hancock, 59, 144, 147, 148, 321 (n. 96), 338 (n. 54)
Simon, Antoine, 52
Simpson, George Eaton, 231
Singer Sewing Machine Company, 197
Sisal, 212
Slavery: U.S., 7, 29, 54–55; Haitian, 43–45, 46, 52, 242, 281; and Vodou, 45; Haitians fear return of, 47, 119, 142, 173; and international relations, 50; corvée seen as, 53, 148, 193; and O'Neill, 210; and zombies, 227; and slave trade, 229–30; and rape, 257; and Inman, 272; in fiction, 282, 283–84; in drama, 287
"Small wars," 133–35
Socialist Party, 268
Socialists, 189, 197, 205, 267
Sociology, 231
Songs: Haiti as subject of, 19; and Haitian protests, 84; popular, 217; Inman on, 233; marines', 233–34, 303; and tourism, 237; and travel writing, 240, 241, 242, 253; and wakes, 262
Soulouque, Faustin, 203
Soup Joumou, 44–45
South, Lieutenant, 131–32, 133, 136, 148, 167
South America, 80, 239
Soviet Union, 278
Spanish-American War, 54, 59–60, 61, 62
Spear, Frederick, 137–38, 154, 160, 166, 176
Speyer and Company, 98
Spingarn, Arthur, 261
Stabler, Jordan H., 97, 98, 147
Statehood, 7
Stoddard, Lothrop, 203
Storey, Moorfield, 189, 191
Strikes: U.S. labor, 11; Haitian student, 34; 1929 general, 34, 221; marines' sit down, 86
"Structures of feeling," 27–28
Subjectivity: and U.S. occupation, 4, 181, 303; and identity, 8, 136–37, 155, 165, 302; and paternalism, 91; marines struggle with, 136, 137, 164, 180, 207–

8; and travel writing, 240–41, 244; and imperialism, 307
Suffrage, woman, 11, 63, 323 (n. 121)
Sugarcane, 48, 120
Swarthmore College, 112
Sweden, 97
Sylvain, Georges, 191
Syrians, 297, 298, 299, 363 (n. 195)

Taft, Edna: A Puritan in Voodoo Land, 19, 231, 255–60, 352 (n. 7); travel writing of, 229–32, 255–60
Taft, William Howard, 93, 94, 98
Tait, Agnes, 19, 229
Talbert, Mary, 266
Tennessee, USS, 15, 80, 84, 85
Terrell, Mary Church, 191, 266
Theatre. See Drama
Thomas, J. Parnell, 287
Thomason, John W., Jr., 76
Topeka, USS, 30
Tourism, 216, 221, 223, 237–38, 240, 262
Toussaint L'Ouverture, François Dominique: and U.S. government, 29; and marines in Haiti, 46; and Haitian Revolution, 47; and Pan-African movement, 52; Price-Mars on, 53; and Garvey, 190; and O'Neill, 197; and Burks, 216; and travel writing, 246; Inman on, 272; and Lawrence, 278, 279; and drama, 278, 286; Marshall on, 281; Bontemps on, 282, 283, 284
Trade, free, 113
Transportation, 11, 117
Travel writing: of Seabrook, 4, 232, 246–55, 259, 260; and U.S. occupation, 18, 28, 238, 247; Haiti as subject of, 19, 225, 229–60; and imperial consciousness, 35, 231–32; of E. Taft, 229–32, 255–60; of B. Niles, 232, 238–46, 247; of Inman, 232–38; exoticism in, 237, 240, 242, 246, 255; and national identity, 304; and racial and gender hierarchies, 305
Tropics: and imperialism, 7; sense of community in, 13; and disease, 44; representations of, 127, 206, 209; beliefs about white men in, 132–33, 206; and undeclared wars, 134

Trotter, William Monroe, 110–11, 124, 332 (n. 102)

Turner, Thomas C., 161

Unconscious, 26, 27, 249, 260. *See also* Discourse: psychological

"Undershirt diplomacy," 125, 129, 135, 190

Unemployment, 70, 273

UNIA, 189–90, 263, 264–65

Uniforms. *See* clothing

Union Patriotique, 150, 191, 265, 269, 272

United Fruit Company, 98

United States: invasion of Haiti by (July 1915), 10, 11, 23, 30, 31, 81–86; acquisitions of, 12, 92; Latin American investments of, 92

— government of: and U.S. occupation, 20, 21, 90; institutional forms of, 22, 94–95; relations with Haiti of, 29, 50, 319 (n. 62); and U.S. investments in Haiti, 30; and businessmen, 109

— investments in Haiti of: and U.S. occupation, 10, 51, 98, 120, 122–23; and infrastructural improvements, 10–11, 117, 179; in late nineteenth century, 30; and economic development, 94, 212; pamphlet promoting, 120–21, *121*; and paternalism, 122–23; and primitivism, 212

— occupation of Haiti by (1915–34): and identity, 3–4, 29, 74, 86, 126, 164; purpose of, 4, 10, 20; and culture, 9, 12, 15, 17–18, 20, 27, 164, 231, 240, 303, 312 (n. 18); and U.S. investments, 10, 51, 98, 120, 122–23; overview of, 10–12, 20, 29–34; attitudes of Haitian elites toward, 11, 192; and paternalism, 13, 16, 17, 21, 27, 28, 35, 108, 115–24, 125, 135, 137, 139, 145, 146, 156, 165, 175, 179–80, 181, 209, 301, 302–3; criticism of, 18, 19, 34, 89–90, 119, 129–30, 160, 186, 227–28, 234, 236, 237, 244, 263, 264–70; and travel writing, 18, 28, 238, 247; U.S. public opinion on, 18–19, 27, 89, 124, 146, 157, 186, 188–89; and race, 28, 29, 36, 86, 137, 300, 301; and gender, 28, 29, 36, 137, 300, 301, 306; and racism, 29, 188, 190, 288; reorganization of, 33, 212; international condemnation of, 34; withdrawal of, 34, 88, 228; process of establishing, 80–88; and J. W. Johnson, 89, 189, 190–91, 291; decision to undertake, 96; and rule of law, 115; and peasants, 116–17, 119–20, 192, 193, 291; and fatherhood metaphors, 128–29, 193–94; Du Bois on, 188–89; and prostitution, 215; and African Americans, 264, 265; and WILPF, 266–67; and Inman, 270, 362 (n. 18); and Hurston, 291–92, 293

— policy of: infrastructure created by, 10–11; marines implement, 12, 82, 302–3; and U.S. culture, 15, 22, 301–2; and culture, 18, 23; and U.S. occupation, 20, 22, 86, 116; and, structures of feeling, 28; and Haiti's transformation, 36; Monroe Doctrine, 80, 94, 96, 97; purposes of, 82; and Caperton, 91; and Latin America, 93; and T. Roosevelt, 93, 97; institutional contexts of, 94–101; and U.S. Navy, 95–96; Open Door, 96; and bankers, 97, 98, 99–100, 330 (n. 43); idealist tradition of, 114; and paternalism, 123–24, 129, 303; Utley on, 134; J. W. Johnson on, 187, 188, 191, 192; and NAACP, 190; and 1920 election, 191; and Haitian family, 192; and Haitian finances, 193; Inman on, 237, 273; and NACW, 266; and national identity, 300; and liberal internationalism, 302

— regions of: Southwest, 7; South, 7, 8, 29, 54–56, 63, 67, 109, 190, 264, 320 (n. 70); North, 7, 8, 56, 63, 109, 263, 264, 265; and identity, 9, 56, 61; and marines in Haiti, 53–54, 180; Midwest, 56

"U.S. American" (term), xvii

U.S. Army, 59, 95, 96, 97, 123, 329–30 (n. 21)

U.S. Congress, 8, 29, 30, 90, 103, 335–36 (n. 178)

U.S. Constitution, 8, 95, 111

U.S. Marine Corps (USMC): training and indoctrination of, 3, 58, 71, 74–80, 82,

303, 327 (n. 200); Gendarmerie d'Haïti modeled after, 10; paternalism of, 13, 77; pre-1915 Haitian landings of, 29, 30, 91; recruitment by, 60, 65, 219; and U.S. Navy, 61, 76, 78, 95, 329–30 (n. 21); roughneck ethos of, 70, 71; and civilian world, 70, 77; as elite fighting force, 75, 76, 82; legends circulated in, 76, 78, 79; and hazing, 77; and U.S. policy, 95, 96–97; institutional history of, 95–97, 329–30 (n. 21); and bankers, 99; and cross-national playacting, 126, 206; counterinsurgency tactics of, 135; public relations efforts by, 217, 219, 221, 222

—members of: memoirs of, 4, 70, 77, 212, 216, 303; and Haiti invasion, 10; racism of, 11; and relations between enlisted men and officers, 12, 39, 41, 72, 73–74, 77–78, 123; enlisted, 12, 60, 70, 72, 123, 147, 163; officer, 12, 60, 72, 123, 147, 163; NCO, 39, 105; ethnic identities of, 53–54, 59, 60; urban and rural backgrounds of, 56, 67–68; U.S. immigrants as, 59, 60–61; in fiction, 224

—members of in Haiti: identity of, 3, 74, 123, 137, 146, 154–55, 185; serving in Gendarmerie d'Haïti, 5, 10, 32, 86, 102, 103, 104, 125, 131, 133, 147, 180, 190, 244–46; and Cacos, 10, 71–72, 136, 137, 140–45, 151, 165, 173, 175, 179, 234; racism of, 11, 17, 46, 83, 136, 155–56, 180, 189, 190, 247, 254, 265; and U.S. policy, 12, 31; and paternalism, 13, *14*, 17, 18, 21, 22, 67, 69, 105, 123, 137, 146, 151, 171, 179, 233, 303, 335 (n. 152); and cultural conscription, 17–18, 123, 301, 303; and Haitian government, 32; and strikes, 34, 86; relationships with Haitians of, 39, 55, 71, 83, 85, 86, 88, 105, 144, 148, 163, 167, 171, 233, 236, 304, 320 (n. 80); initially encounter Haiti, 41–42, 53, 80–83; and Haitian history, 42, 43–46, 79, 86, 316 (n. 22); and Haitian culture, 42, 43–46, 84, 171, 173, 179, 212–13, 217, 219, 242, 245, 301, 304; prior knowledge of Haiti of, 42, 53, 78, 79–80; previous expeditions/tours of duty of, 42, 78,

327 (n. 204); and American national identity, 53–54, 56, 59, 62, 82, 154, 164, 165, 179, 304; and peasants, 55, 62, 120, 303; pacificism among, 66; legends about, 72, 164–79; shipboard instruction of, 78–80; intelligence operations of, 83, 86, 130, 141, 173, 315 (n. 70); as authors, 131–34, 216; fear cannibalism and being skinned alive, 138, 157, 165, 166, 173, 175, 176, 304, 342 (n. 141); and corvée, 149; Haitians blamed for violence of, 151, 154; J. W. Johnson on, 190, 247; and O'Neill, 207; entertainment of, 212; and exoticism, 213; Haitian servants of, 215; and Inman, 233, 247; and tourism, 238; and travel writing, 244–45, 247; and Hughes, 262

U.S. Navy: participates in U.S. occupation, 12, 82, 129; and paternalism, 24, 42; North Atlantic Fleet, 30; and USMC, 61, 76, 78, 95, 329–30 (n. 21); views of officers in, 72; and hazing, 77; and U.S. policy, 95–96; and U.S. South, 320 (n. 70)

U.S. Navy Medical Corps, 10

U.S. Senate: and woman suffrage, 11; and Haitian-American treaty, 102

—inquiry by: and S. Butler, 13, 33, 89, 90, 126, 135, 137; and Caperton, 90; and violence, 132, 137–38, 154, 160–61; and Cacos, 143; and corvée, 148–50; and killing by marines, 160, 161; and marines' fears, 166; and J. W. Johnson, 191; and McCormick, 191; prominent lawyers review, 270

U.S. State Department, 20, 42, 97, 98, 115, 147

United West Indies Corporation, 121–22, 212

Universal Negro Improvement Association (UNIA), 189–90, 263, 264–65

Upshur, William P. "Deacon," 79–80

Utley, Harold, 81–82, 133–34, 338 (n. 52)

Vandegrift, Archer, 54, 65, 335 (n. 152)

Vandercook, John W.: J. W. Johnson's influence on, 19; *Black Majesty*, 196, 216–17, *218*, 246, 270, 272, 276, 283

Vanderlip, Frank A., 98
Van Doren, Carl, 3, 6–8, 21, 62, 260, 305
Van Orden, George, 81–82, 123
Van Vechten, Carl, 289
Vastey, Pompée Valentin, baron de, 46
Venezuela, 188, 194
Versailles, France, 11, 33, 186
Vietnam War, 154
Vieux, Constant, 49, 119
Villa, Pancho, 79
Villard, Oswald Garrison, 186, 332
    (n. 102)
Vincent, Stenio, 34, 291
Violence: of imperialism, 4, 5, 6–7, 9, 15,
    135, 151, 180; and paternalism, 13, 15,
    19, 35, 55, 111, 135–37, 146, 155, 156,
    179–81; of U.S. occupation, 13, 33,
    131, 138, 142–43, 145, 146, 159, 162,
    163, 179, 290, 301; and U.S. culture,
    18; and discipline, 55, 135–37, 138,
    304; and white U.S. boys, 64–65, 107;
    and masculinity, 66, 69, 107, 154; and
    sexuality, 73, 154, 163, 255, 257, 284;
    and hazing, 77; and prisoners, 80, 81,
    159–60, 161, 162, 337 (n. 21), 340
    (n. 90); and "indiscriminate killing,"
    89, 156, 158, 159, 160, 208; and rule of
    law, 114–15, 302; R. B. Davis reports,
    127; defended as insanity, 131–33, 160,
    164; Craige explains, 131–34, 180–81;
    individual, 132, 137, 146; and race,
    133, 258, 259; Utley explains, 133–35;
    and corvée, 139, 149, 163; of Cacos,
    144, 151; and Haitian labor, 150, 339
    (n. 84); routines of, 150–64; marines
    reflect on, 151, 154, 155, 164–65; as
    part of military campaign, 158; le-
    gitimate versus illegitimate, 158–59,
    180; and burning of homes, 160, 341
    (n. 110); and moral breakdown, 167;
    in fiction, 177, 224, 282; and Haitian
    Revolution, 284; in drama, 287. See also
    Corvée; Killing; Rape; Wars
Virgin Islands, 7
Virski, Ivan, 131, 132–33, 136, 167, 170,
    215
Vodou: foreigners' misconceptions and
    stereotypes of, 19, 317 (n. 28); dances
    of, 41; and Haitian history, 43; and con-
ches, 44, 157; African roots of, 45, 274;
    and Catholicism, 45, 317 (n. 29); pro-
    hibited by occupation, 213; and drums,
    241; distinguished from Voodoo, 250–
    51, 317 (n. 28); and Legba, 259; Cour-
    lander on, 275; and Hurston, 289, 295;
    and Guedé, 289–93, 300; and Ogou,
    290
Voodoo: in fiction, 4, 6, 127, 175, 177–78,
    224, 236, 288, 292; in film, 6, 227, 350
    (n. 175); and marines in Haiti, 41, 79,
    170, 212; and Haitian elites, 52, 214,
    292; Russell's account of, 128; and col-
    lections, 213; and maternal role, 224–
    25, 350 (n. 175); in travel writing, 236,
    246–54, 257, 273; exoticist accounts of,
    246, 249; and Inman, 248, 271; distin-
    guished from Vodou, 250–51, 317
    (n. 28)

Waller, Littleton W. T., 31, 32, 33, 100–
    102, 126, 331 (n. 57)
Walling, William English, 58
Waring, Mary F., 266
Wars: "Indian," 7, 134, 154; against Cacos,
    10, 11, 31, 32–33, 35, 39, 41, 138, 139,
    140–46, 147, 149, 150–64, 173, 179;
    Spanish-American, 54, 59–60, 61, 62;
    World War I, 92, 96, 106, 114, 189, 225;
    in Philippines, 100; and rule of law,
    114–15; Utley on, 133–35, 338 (n. 52);
    Vietnam, 154; and civilization, 223
Washington, Booker T., 189
Washington, Margaret M., 266
Washington, D.C., 29
Washington, USS, 15, 80, 81, 127, 224, 291
Watson, Grace, 267
Weed, Helena Hill, 191
Weiss, Nancy J., 277
Welles, Orson, 19, 216, 276, 285
Wells, Clarke H., 150, 161, 162
Wertz, Adam, 8
Westinghouse Electrical Company, 196–
    97
White, Walter, 261
Whiteness: and identity, 3–4, 22, 53–54,
    59, 108, 136, 137, 148, 164, 179, 287,
    305, 306–7, 321 (n. 89); and manhood,
    64; and violence, 154; and horror sto-

ries, 165, 176–78; in fiction, 224–25; and white superiority, 270, 305

Willard, Frances, 265–66

Williams, Alexander S., 125–26, 340 (n. 90)

Williams Lavinia, 278

Williams, Raymond, 27, 314 (n. 50)

Williston, Samuel, 158, 167, 168, 171, 176

WILPF, 215–16, 238, 266–67, 270

Wilson, Woodrow: and League of Nations, 11; and Haitian affairs, 30, 31, 91, 96, 113; and rights of small nations, 33, 114, 129, 186, 198; as Southerner, 54; speeches of, 91, 92, 93, 98, 108, 109, 112, 129; paternalism of, 91, 93, 95, 100, 108–13, 124, 129, 302, 333 (n. 333); and U.S. occupation, 91–92, 99, 116, 139, 221; on concessions versus investments, 92; on U.S. territorial expansion, 92, 93; on trusteeship, 92, 108; on Latin American/U.S. relations, 92–93, 94, 98, 108, 112–13; familial metaphors of, 93; on diplomatic service, 93–94; and moralism, 93–94, 110; and economic development, 94, 95, 113, 117–18, 334 (n. 135); and institutional contexts, 94–100; and USMC, 97; African American support for, 109, 110, 332 (n. 102); and racism, 109–15, 124, 332 (n. 102); and Haitian newspapers, 119; and constitutional government, 128; and Du Bois, 188–89; and J. W. Johnson, 191; legalism of, 302

Wirkus, Faustin: and identity, 3–4, 78; memoirs of, 3–6, 13, 18, 70–71, 76, 78, 155; and Seabrook, 4, 5–6, 254–55, 295; and Gendarmerie d'Haïti, 5, 155, 158, 168–69; citizenship of, 8, 9; and U.S. regional identity, 56; and homosexuality, 74; and indoctrination, 80; reacts to Haiti, 84–85; and withdrawal of occupation, 88; and primitivism, 103; and Cacos, 141, 143–45, 155–56; and violence, 155; and field conditions, 157, 158, 164; and marines in Haiti, 166–67; photographs of, 168, 169; and moral breakdowns, 170–71; and military uniforms, 176; and Hurston, 292–93, 295–96; and Haitian culture, 304

Wise, Frederick May, 70, 71, 72, 84, 160, 274

Withdrawal of U.S. occupation, 34, 88, 228

Wittek, John, 68

Women

—Haitian: and slave resistance, 45; and Haitian Revolution, 46; and Haitian economy, 49; and intermarriage, 51, 86, 165, 170, 171, 215–16; marines' observations and stereotypes of, 80, 175, 234; photographs of, 87, 169, 235; and violence, 132–33, 162, 180; and Cacos, 143; and rape, 163, 234, 257–58; and intercultural contact, 171; in U.S. writings on Voodoo, 177–78, 252–53; in fiction, 189; elite, 195; and primitivism, 195–96; and O'Neill, 200; "illegitimate children of," 215, 233, 250; and race, 230; and E. Taft, 230; manual labor of, 233; and sexuality, 251; and feminism, 256; status of, 266

—U.S.: suffrage for, 11, 63, 323 (n. 121); and paternalism, 22; and citizenship, 63; and boyhood, 64; as wives of marines, 79, 148, 245, 246, 320 (n. 80), 327 (n. 207); civilizing influence of, 133, 234, 236; and feminism, 223–24; and tourism, 238; and desire, 255; and rape, 257, 355 (n. 130); African American, 257–58, 265–66, 302

Women's International League for Peace and Freedom (WILPF), 215–16, 238, 266–67, 270

Women's movement, international, 263, 265–67

Women's Peace Party, 19

Woollcott, Alexander, 210

Workers

—Haitian: resist U.S. occupation, 11, 84, 215; and marines in Haiti, 39, 84, 215; and plantation system, 48; and Haitian economy, 50, 117–18, 215; and Citadel, 51; and Haitian elites, 53; and public works, 117, 150; prisoners as, 150; as servants, 215, 216, 289; and gender, 215, 241

—U.S.: and Boyer, 49; transient, 56, 69–70, 325 (n. 161); and masculinity, 63–64, 69–72; and paternalism, 109

Works Progress Administration, 285
World War I, 92, 96, 106, 114, 189,
    225
Woyshner, Paul, 13, *14*
W. R. Grace Company, 98
Wright, Richard, 283

Young Men's Christian Association
    (YMCA), 163, 352 (n. 18)

Zamor, Oreste, 91
Zombies, 19, 216, 223, 225–27, 254, 288,
    351 (n. 179)

GENDER & AMERICAN CULTURE

Taking Haiti: Military Occupation and the
  Culture of U.S. Imperialism, 1915–1940,
  by Mary A. Renda (2001)
Before Jim Crow: The Politics of Race in
  Postemancipation Virginia, by Jane Dailey
  (2000)
Captain Ahab Had a Wife: New England
  Women and the Whalefishery, 1720–1870,
  by Lisa Norling (2000)
Civilizing Capitalism: The National
  Consumers' League, Women's Activism,
  and Labor Standards in the New Deal Era,
  by Landon R. Y. Storrs (2000)
Rank Ladies: Gender and Cultural Hierarchy
  in American Vaudeville, by M. Alison
  Kibler (1999)
Strangers and Pilgrims: Female Preaching in
  America, 1740–1845, by Catherine A.
  Brekus (1998)
Sex and Citizenship in Antebellum America, by
  Nancy Isenberg (1998)
Yours in Sisterhood: Ms. Magazine and the
  Promise of Popular Feminism, by Amy
  Erdman Farrell (1998)
We Mean to Be Counted: White Women and
  Politics in Antebellum Virginia, by
  Elizabeth R. Varon (1998)
Women Against the Good War: Conscientious
  Objection and Gender on the American
  Home Front, 1941–1947, by Rachel
  Waltner Goossen (1997)
Toward an Intellectual History of Women:
  Essays by Linda K. Kerber (1997)
Gender and Jim Crow: Women and the Politics
  of White Supremacy in North Carolina,
  1896–1920, by Glenda Elizabeth
  Gilmore (1996)
Delinquent Daughters: Protecting and Policing
  Adolescent Female Sexuality in the United

States, 1885–1920, by Mary E. Odem
  (1995)
U.S. History as Women's History: New Feminist
  Essays, edited by Linda K. Kerber, Alice
  Kessler-Harris, and Kathryn Kish Sklar
  (1995)
Common Sense and a Little Fire: Women and
  Working-Class Politics in the United States,
  1900–1965, by Annelise Orleck
  (1995)
How Am I to Be Heard?: Letters of Lillian
  Smith, edited by Margaret Rose
  Gladney (1993)
Entitled to Power: Farm Women and
  Technology, 1913–1963, by Katherine
  Jellison (1993)
Revising Life: Sylvia Plath's Ariel Poems, by
  Susan R. Van Dyne (1993)
Made From This Earth: American Women and
  Nature, by Vera Norwood (1993)
Unruly Women: The Politics of Social and
  Sexual Control in the Old South, by
  Victoria E. Bynum (1992)
The Work of Self-Representation: Lyric Poetry in
  Colonial New England, by Ivy Schweitzer
  (1991)
Labor and Desire: Women's Revolutionary
  Fiction in Depression America, by Paula
  Rabinowitz (1991)
Community of Suffering and Struggle: Women,
  Men, and the Labor Movement in
  Minneapolis, 1915–1945, by Elizabeth
  Faue (1991)
All That Hollywood Allows: Re-reading Gender
  in 1950s Melodrama, by Jackie Byars
  (1991)
Doing Literary Business: American Women
  Writers in the Nineteenth Century, by
  Susan Coultrap-McQuin (1990)

Ladies, Women, and Wenches: Choice and Constraint in Antebellum Charleston and Boston, by Jane H. Pease and William H. Pease (1990)

The Secret Eye: The Journal of Ella Gertrude Clanton Thomas, 1848–1889, edited by Virginia Ingraham Burr, with an introduction by Nell Irvin Painter (1990)

Second Stories: The Politics of Language, Form, and Gender in Early American Fictions, by Cynthia S. Jordan (1989)

Within the Plantation Household: Black and White Women of the Old South, by Elizabeth Fox-Genovese (1988)

The Limits of Sisterhood: The Beecher Sisters on Women's Rights and Woman's Sphere, by Jeanne Boydston, Mary Kelley, and Anne Margolis (1988)